VISUAL NAVIGATION
From Biological Systems to
Unmanned Ground Vehicles

COMPUTER VISION

A Series of Books Edited by Yiannis Aloimonos

VISUAL NAVIGATION
From Biological Systems to Unmanned Ground Vehicles

Edited by
YIANNIS ALOIMONOS
University of Maryland at College Park

Psychology Press
Taylor & Francis Group

New York   London

Reprinted 2009 by Psychology Press

Library of Congress Cataloging-in-Publication Data

Visual navigation : From biological systems to unmanned ground
  vehicles / edited by Yiannis Aloimonos.
       p.   cm. -- (The computer vision series)
    Includes bibliographical references and index.
    ISBN 0-8058-2050-7 (alk. paper)
    1. Robot vision. 2. Computer vision. 3. Visual perception.
  I. Aloimonos, Yiannis. II. Series.
  TJ211.3.V59 1996
  629.8'92637--DC20   96-18717
                                        CIP

10 9 8 7 6 5 4 3 2 1

Contents

CONTRIBUTORS

☐ **Yiannis Aloimonos** Computer Vision Laboratory, Center for Automation Research, Computer Science Department, and Institute for Advanced Computer Studies, University of Maryland, College Park, Maryland 20742

☐ **J. Ross Beveridge** Computer Science Department, University Services Center, 601 South Howes Street, Colorado State University, Fort Collins, Colorado 80523

☐ **Shaoyun Chen** Department of Computer Science, A714 Wells Hall, Michigan State University, East Lansing, Michigan 48824-1027

☐ **David Coombs** Intelligent Systems Division, National Institute of Standards and Technology (NIST), Bldg 220, Room B124, Gaithersburg, Maryland 20899

☐ **Kostas Daniilidis** Computer Science Institute, University of Kiel, Preusserstr. 1-9, D-2300 Kiel, Germany

☐ **Thomas Dean** Department of Computer Science, Brown University, Providence, Rhode Island 02912

☐ **E.D. Dickmanns** Universität der Bundeswehr München, Fakultät für Luft- und Raumfahrttechnik, Institut für Systemdynamik und Flugmechanik, D-85577 Neubiberg, Germany

☐ **Olivier Faugeras** INRIA, 2004 route des Lucioles, B.P. 93, 06902 Sophia-Antipolis, France

☐ **Cornelia Fermüller** Computer Vision Laboratory, Center for Automation Research, Department of Computer Science, and Institute for Advanced Computer Studies, University of Maryland, College Park, Maryland 20742

☐ **Takahashi Hamada** Electrotechnical Laboratory LERC, Nakoji, Amagasaki, Hyogo 661, Japan

☐ **Allen R. Hanson** Department of Computer and Information Sciences, University of Massachusetts, Amherst, Massachusetts 01003

☐ **Martial Hébert** Carnegie Mellon University, 5000 Forbes Avenue, Pittsburgh, Pennsylvania 15213

☐ **Martin Herman** Intelligent Systems Division, National Institute of Standards and Technology (NIST), Bldg 220, Room B124, Gaithersburg, Maryland 20899

☐ **Tsai-Hong Hong** Intelligent Systems Division, National Institute of Standards and Technology (NIST), Bldg 220, Room B124, Gaithersburg, Maryland 20899

☐ **Adrian Horridge** Centre for Visual Sciences, Research School of Biological Sciences, Australian National University, Box 475 P.O., Canberra, A.C.T. 2601, Australia

☐ **Thomas S. Huang** Coordinated Science Laboratory, University of Illinois at Urbana-Champaign, 1101 West Springfield Avenue, Urbana, Illinois 61801-3082

☐ **Rakesh (Teddy) Kumar** David Sarnoff Research Laboratory, Princeton, New Jersey 08540

☐ **Jean-Luc Marion** Department of Computer Science, Brown University, Providence, Rhode Island 02912

☐ **Marilyn Nashman** Intelligent Systems Division, National Institute of Standards and Technology (NIST), Bldg 220, Room B124, Gaithersburg, Maryland 20899

☐ **Randal C. Nelson** Department of Computer Science, University of Rochester, Rochester New York 14627

☐ **Daniel Raviv** Robotics Center and Department of Electrical Engineering, Florida Atlantic University, Boca Raton, Florida 33431

☐ **Edward M. Riseman** Department of Computer and Information Sciences, University of Massachusetts, Amherst, Massachusetts 01003

☐ **Luc Robert** INRIA, 2004 route des Lucioles, B.P. 93, 06902 Sophia-Antipolis, France

☐ **Harpreet Sawhney** David Sarnoff Research Laboratory, Princeton, New Jersey 08540

☐ **Henry Schneiderman** Robotics Institute, Carnegie Mellon University, Pittsburgh, Pennsylvania 15213

☐ **Minas E. Spetsakis** Department of Computer Science, York University, 4700 Keele Street, North York, Ontario, Canada M3J 1P3

☐ **Albert J. Wavering** Intelligent Systems Division, National Institute of Standards and Technology (NIST), Bldg 220, Room B124, Gaithersburg, Maryland 20899

☐ **John J. Weng** Department of Computer Science, A714 Wells Hall, Michigan State University, East Lansing, Michigan 48824-1027

☐ **Gin-Shu Young** Intelligent Systems Division, National Institute of Standards and Technology (NIST), Bldg 220, Room B124, Gaithersburg, Maryland 20899

☐ **Cyril Zeller** INRIA, 2004 route des Lucioles, B.P. 93, 06902 Sophia-Antipolis, France

1   Visual Navigation: Flies, Bees, and UGV's*

Yiannis Aloimonos
University of Maryland

Recent developments in empirical and computational disciplines that study the problem of visual perception have advanced a great deal our understanding of the mechanisms underlying the process of visual navigation. Visual navigation amounts to the control of sensory mediated movement and encompasses a wide range of capabilities, ranging from low-level ones related to kinetic stabilization to high-level ones related to the ability of a system to acquire a memory of a place or location and recognize it (homing). This book consists of articles in several disciplines representing major developments in some area of navigation, and it is divided into three parts. The first part (chapters 2 and 3) describes advances in understanding how biological systems deal with navigation problems, and in particular how insects process images for the purpose of successfully moving around in their world. The second part (chapters 4, 5 and 6) is devoted to recent theoretical developments that will influence the design of autonomous systems and future basic research in the field. The third part (chapters 7 through 12) describes the application of the theoretical developments to the design of autonomous visual navigation systems operating in various environments. This introduction briefly examines the problem of visual navigation from several perspectives, provides a description of basic research questions, and shows how the different chapters relate to different questions and to each other. The treatment is, for the most part, of a computational nature, stressing geometry, statistics, computational techniques, and signal processing.

A system that successfully navigates using its perceptual sensors must have a number of capabilities that we can roughly separate into *local* and *global* ones. Local capabilities enable the system to interact effectively with its immediate surroundings, like understanding its own motion, recognizing obstacles and other moving objects, and obtaining a stable view of the world. Global capabilities enable the

* Unmanned Ground Vehicles. This research on navigation was funded partly by the Office of Naval Research under Grant N00014-96-1-0587, the National Science Foundation under Grant IRI-9057934, and ARPA Order #A422, through grant F49620-93-1-0576 (Integrated Active Vision for UGV RSTA), a project in which the author led a consortium including the Universities of Maryland, Rochester and Pennsylvania, as well as the National Institute of Standards and Technology, in the development of visual competences for an unmanned ground vehicle performing reconnaissance, surveillance, and target acquisition (RSTA on the move).

system to deal with larger spaces, like building a memory of an area and finding particular places in that area (homing). For the computational scientist, the fundamental problem in designing these capabilities lies in understanding and discovering the appropriate spatiotemporal representations that the system should recover from visual information. Having these representations of the outside world and algorithms for obtaining them in real time, efforts can be made to put together a broad range of navigational capabilities or competences [5]. At the same time empirical scientists can form hypotheses on the neural implementation of particular capabilities and design specific experiments for testing them. The combined effort of computational and empirical research can lead to an examination of the nature of the required spatiotemporal representations at various levels of abstraction as well as their extraction with real-time techniques.

A navigating system is in a continuous motion and at the lowest level it should extract a representation of the moving images that it receives. Traditionally this representation has been considered the idealized one of the motion field. As a system moves in some environment, every point in that environment moves with some velocity. The projection of these velocity vectors on the imaging surface constitutes the so-called motion field. This field depends on the 3D motion and the structure of the scene in view. The last fifteen years have seen a very large amount of literature on the interpretation of motion fields as regards the information they contain about the three-dimensional world. The problem is, in general, very difficult and its difficulty is compounded by the fact that the information that can be derived from the sequence of images is not the exact projection of the 3D motion field, but rather only information about the movement of light patterns. The exact movement of every point in the image is termed the optical flow field. In general, accurate values of the optical flow field are not computable; the so-called normal flow, the component perpendicular to the edges, is the only component of the optical flow that is well defined on the basis of local information. This is the well-known aperture problem. In many cases, it is possible to obtain additional flow information for areas (patches) in the image. Thus, the input that a system can use for further motion processing is some partial optical flow information. The question then is, what is the nature of subsequent motion processing?

The conventional wisdom suggests that subsequent motion processing should be directed at estimating the optical flow. It appears that this view is so deeply rooted that even the current views of most neurobiologists regarding the motion pathway in primates suggest that in area V5 or MT the aperture problem is "solved," and from this point specialized "motion processing" areas such as MST and FSP are fed with the appropriate input (see [10] for a review). Recent theoretical and empirical findings suggest that this may not be the case. Although the aperture problem may be resolved in MT, initial local motion measurements far away from an optical flow representation (and thus termed qualitative) may be sufficient to address a number of navigation tasks. The processing may be of such a nature that when it reaches the area MT the system has already at its disposal a vast amount of information about the three-dimensional world [13].

The analysis of Chapter 4, which is basically a statistical and geometrical investigation of motion fields, proves that the problem of interpreting motion fields in order to extract information about the three-dimensional world is ill-posed by investigating the stability of 3D-motion estimation processes. The chances that biological systems or successful real-time visuomotor control systems solve ill-posed problems are very slim. This means that they may possibly use a different input. Chapters 10, 11, and 12 describe the design and construction of real systems working in some environments. Such truly impressive systems demonstrate the power of computational approaches to perception, and reinforce the maturity of the discipline of computer vision, as industrial systems working in specific environments under various assumptions slowly emerge. At the same time, they demonstrate the limitations of current approaches to visual motion analysis, by showing scenarios and situations where the developed systems fail.

This calls for the development of better spatiotemporal representations at several levels of abstraction. Chapter 6 describes an approach to motion analysis based on partial optical flow information. This approach is based on a minimum of knowledge about image motion, namely, the sign of the projection of the optical flow along directions where it can be robustly computed. These measurements along a set of appropriately chosen orientations possess a rich global structure; they give rise to simple patterns in the image, and the location and form of these patterns encode three-dimensional information. This chapter could be considered an implementation of Gibson's transformational invariants [7], and demonstrates that a lot of information can be robustly extracted from a sequence of images before correspondence between the images has been established [3].

Regarding representations of visual space, as Chapters 10, 11, and 12 demonstrate, the overwhelming view has been in favor of Euclidean representations encoding distances between different features in the visible world. As research in the psychophysics of perceptual space advances, researchers in computational vision are examining a variety of space representations less complex than their Euclidean counterparts. Chapter 5 examines the usefulness of projective space representations and other qualitative representations residing between the projective and Euclidean layer, and describes how to use them to achieve a number of tasks. It is expected that the development and extraction of such qualitative representations will continue to be an exciting research area in the future. Visual memories will be studied that can be considered as structures consisting of such spatiotemporal representations [1, 4, 6].

Currently, in the absence of alternative representations, researchers consider memories consisting simply of images and test their limits using digital devices capable of storing large amounts of information and the pattern recognition and statistics technology of the past twenty years. Chapters 7 and 8 describe such an approach, and Chapter 9 examines higher level problems of planning through navigating in large spaces.

Finally, Chapters 2 and 3 describe empirical findings in insects and reinforce the view that activities simplify visual processing. The empirical findings in insects and primates confirm various issues that have been illuminated here from a computational point of view:

1. Visual motion measurements at several stages are of a qualitative nature, i.e., they are not measurements of optical flow but rather measurements of the sign of local motion along various directions [8].

2. Perception resembles a process of pattern matching a great deal. This view, which was popular a number of years ago with the emergence of the discipline of pattern recognition, was abandoned by computational theorists because it was considered extremely difficult to identify patterns encoding properties of the three-dimensional world [12]. For many years the pattern recognition approach, advocated at a philosophical level by Gibson, was severely criticized; however, advances in computational vision now make it possible to design appropriate patterns using geometry and exploiting the physics of light.

3. There is a difference between actual physical space and perceptual space, the representation of physical space in our heads. Euclidean geometry encoding distances between features in space is a good tool to model physical space. However, recent advances indicate that it is too difficult and most probably impossible to exactly match the perceptual and physical spaces, i.e., to extract from images in real-time robust Euclidean reconstructions of physical space. Psychophysics of man has provided rich evidence that humans do not perceive exact metric descriptions of space [9, 11]. What then are these descriptions of space that are robustly extracted in real time? Projective or affine descriptions are candidates having some limitations—projective structures do not carry much information and affine structures only make sense for scenes viewed from far away. The discovery of the large spectrum of such "qualitative" representations represents an exciting research goal for the immediate future [2].

Visual navigation will continue to be a rich source for basic research questions in vision. The potential for applications in autonomous systems operating in real or virtual environments will make the field flourish in the years to come. With regard to virtual environments, research into visual motion and navigational competences will revolutionize the media technology of television by providing the viewer with control of the camera angle. Virtual reality will enable the viewer to see a synthesized scene from any perspective. This can happen realistically only if an adequate model of the scene is automatically extracted. With the hope that readers will find this book useful, I wish to express my thanks to all the contributors, and to Sara Larson for her editorial and graphics skills.

REFERENCES

1. Y. Aloimonos, C. Fermüller, and A. Rosenfeld, "Seeing and understanding: Representing the visual world," *ACM Computing Surveys* **27**(3), 1995, 307–309.

2. O. Faugeras, "Stratification of 3-D vision: Projective, affine, and metric representations," *Journal of the Optical Society of America A* **12**(3), March 1995, 465–484.

3. C. Fermüller and Y. Aloimonos, "Direct perception of three-dimensional motion from patterns of visual motion," *Science* **270**, 1995, 1973–1976.

4. C. Fermüller and Y. Aloimonos, "Representations for active vision," *Proc. Int'l. Joint Conference on Artificial Intelligence*, Montreal, Canada, August 1995.

5. C. Fermüller and Y. Aloimonos, "Vision and action," *Image and Vision Computing* **13**(10), 1995, 725–744.

6. C. Fermüller and Y. Aloimonos, "Ordinal representations of visual space," *Proc. ARPA Image Understanding Workshop*, February 1996.

7. J. Gibson, *The Ecological Approach to Visual Perception*, Houghton Mifflin, Boston, 1979.

8. G.A. Horridge, "What can engineers learn from insect vision," *Proceedings of the Royal Society London B*, August 1992.

9. J.J. Koenderink and A.J. van Doorn, "Relief: Pictorial and otherwise," *Image and Vision Computing* **13**, 1995, 321–334.

10. M. Sereno, *Neural Computation of Pattern Motion*, MIT Press, Cambridge, MA, 1993.

11. J.S. Tittle, J.T. Todd, V.J. Perotti, and J.F. Norman, "Systematic distortion of perceived three-dimensional structure from motion and binocular stereopsis," *Journal of Experimental Psychology: Human Perception and Performance* **21**(3), 1995, 663–678.

12. S. Ullman, "Against direct perception," *Behavioural and Brain Sciences* **3**, 1980.

13. S. Zeki, *A Vision of the Brain*, Blackwell Scientific Publications, Cambridge, MA, 1993.

2 | VISION, ACTION, AND NAVIGATION IN ANIMALS

Takahashi Hamada
Electrotechnical Laboratory LERC

ABSTRACT

With the emergence of active vision [1], most studies [2] concentrated on eye movements; however, such eye movements are very difficult to interpret because volitional controls are added on to them and they often accompany head motions. Concentrating on lower animals, this chapter argues that a fundamental aspect of active vision is, in the spirit of [10], the understanding of self-movement and the separation of rotation and translation. By studying mechanisms used by insects and mammals to stabilize their visual world, we can connect vision and action in two ways: vision for action and action for vision.

1. INTRODUCTION

The visual systems of animals have been separated from action in most psychological, neurophysiological, and theoretical studies. For example, although Marr discussed them in the introduction to his book *Vision* [24] from various perspectives, his theory did not deal with the role of action in vision. In fact, vision in animals is connected with action in two senses: "vision for action" and "action for vision." On the one hand vision is used for controlling action such as hand manipulation and locomotion; on the other hand action such as eye or head movement is used for vision, for example, to estimate depth. The former issue will be described in Section 2 and the latter in Section 3.

2. VISION FOR ACTION

2.1. VISION FOR MANIPULATION

Figure 1 is a model of the human visual system proposed by R. Descartes [9]. An object in the external world has one representation in the brain, which is then seen by the *soul* for producing the awareness of "seeing." Although this model is consistent with our intuition, a clinical phenomenon named "blind sight" [29] shows a complementary aspect of the human visual system. After all the visual cortical areas in one hemisphere have been surgically removed, the patient loses the awareness of "seeing" in the contralateral visual field. However, he can still point his hand toward a target in the "blind" field with significant accuracy. Considering recent evidence [14], we can assume that the visual systems of animals are composed of multiple channels, some of which have action as their outputs, without awareness of "seeing."

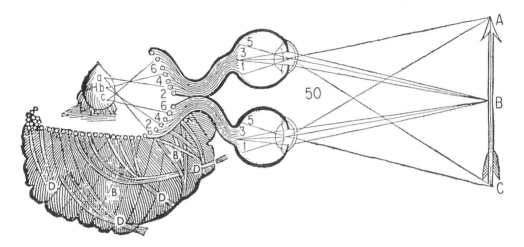

Figure 1. A model of the human visual system by R. Descartes.

A Japanese developmental psychologist Y. Yamada reported that "contemplative" recognition or calm watching, which does not lead to action, begins to develop in infants of nine months old; in contrast, vision for manual action toward a visual target, just as in "blind sight," develops earlier [37]. An important point is that after the age of nine months, vision for action is not replaced by, but "coexists" with, "contemplative" vision.

2.2. VISION FOR EYE MOVEMENT AND LOCOMOTION

About 20 years ago, Hubel and Wiesel studied the visual cortex of the cat and found simple, complex, and hypercomplex cells [20]. Since then, the properties of these cells have been studied in detail. As Marr described in the introduction of his book [24], however, "none of the new studies succeeded in elucidating the function" of these cells. Yet, if the cells have action as their output, we can use the action as a probe for estimating the function of these cells.

When a cat turns its head, the eyes move in the direction opposite to that of the head to stabilize the retinal image. This kind of eye movement is produced vestibularly as well as optokinetically [7].

In a laboratory, the optokinetic eye movement is studied as shown in Figure 2. An animal sees a large screen on which a texture is moved uniformly at a constant velocity. The eyes follow the motion of texture in a slow phase, return quickly, and follow again in another slow phase. This kind of eye movement is named optokinetic nystagmus or simply OKN. We carried out two experiments: a behavioral one and a neurophysiological one.

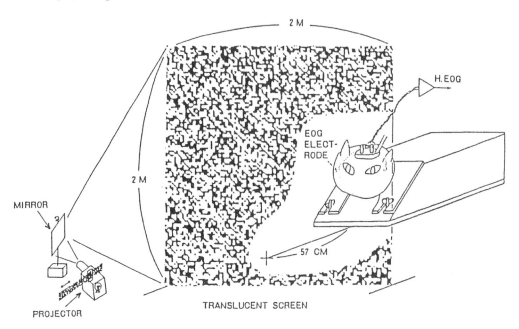

Figure 2. Experiments on OKN in a laboratory.

A behavioral experiment [15]. A texture was moved in the horizontal direction to produce OKN. We used four textures: white noise (N), checkerboard (C), stripes (S), and random stripes (RS) (Figure 3). N and RS are random textures, but C and S are regular; N and C are composed of short contours, but S and RS contain long ones. We asked which texture elicits the strongest OKN. The upper traces in Figure 4 are the eye positions in the OKN and the lower ones are their velocities. When a texture was moved faster than a critical velocity about 10 degrees/second, N and C elicited a stronger OKN than RS or S: the textures composed of short contours were more effective than those of long contours.

A neurophysiological experiment [16]. The optokinetic stimulus is known to be processed in two pathways: cortical and subcortical [30]. The cortical pathway includes an area named PMLS (posteromedial lateral suprasylvian area, Figure 5) [28]. Considering the behavioral study described above, we assumed that neurons in PMLS prefer N to RS. Inserting a microelectrode in PMLS of anesthetized and immobilized cats, we recorded 152 neurons. The motion of texture elicited response in 129 cells, among which 61% preferred N to RS (Figure 6). These neurons had 'hypercomplex' receptive fields with end-inhibitory subregions, which can explain their preference for N over RS (Figure 7).

Presumably, a natural scene is composed of short contours more frequently than long ones (Figure 8). The noise may be a good approximation of the natural scene.

Figure 3. Textures: random noise (N), checkerboard (C), stripes (S), and random stripes (RS).

When a cat turns its head in such a scene, the image of the scene moves on the retina, perhaps stimulating the hypercomplex cells in PMLS, and then produces a strong OKN.

Figure 9 is a distribution of the preferred directions to the motion of texture in the PMLS neurons. All the recordings were carried out from the right hemispheres. To our surprise, although some neurons preferred the horizontal directions, many neurons preferred left-downward directions. Interestingly, the PMLS neurons have receptive fields in the contralateral and lower visual field [39]. Thus, the neurons in the PMLS of the right hemisphere have their receptive fields in the left-lower visual field and prefer left-downward directions of texture motion; similarly, the neurons in the left PMLS should prefer right-downward motions in the right-lower visual field (Figure 10). These motions of textures are exactly the optical flow which an animal experiences during its forward locomotion.

Additionally, it is known that some neurons in area 18 have receptive fields in the middle-lower visual field and prefer downward motion of texture [13], and that both neurons in area 18 and PMLS project to the pontine nucleus in the midbrain and then to the cerebellum, which is an important structure for locomotion.

In summary, we conclude that the PMLS areas process the visual motion of texture for guiding at least two actions: horizontal OKN and forward locomotion. Generally speaking, animals experience two kinds of visual motion: motion of small objects against the stationary background, which is seen by a stationary observer, and global motion or optical flow of the world seen by an active observer. The ethologist von Holst named the former ex-afference, the latter re-afference [17]. Although PMLS has been assumed to play a role for detecting ex-afference, the two functions described above belong to the opposite category. If we ask, "What does the cat's PMLS tell the cat's motor system?" the answer is, "Re-afference!"

3. Action for Vision

3.1. Preliminaries

When Hubel began to study visual properties of neurons in the visual cortex of cats in the late 1950's, he used awake animals with their eyes and heads free to move [19]. Thus, his experiments at the beginning were not far from "active vision." Because this paradigm did not permit precise study of the receptive fields, however, they then immobilized the eyes and the head [20]. This "passive" paradigm has dominated the visual neurophysiology. Neurons in these immobilized animals always responded better to moving than to stationary ON-OFF stimuli, and at least in the simple cells this property is reduced to their spatiotemporally "inseparable" receptive fields [8]. Yet why do they prefer moving stimuli? Does the preference play a role, with the help of "fixational eye movements," for preventing loss of perception of a stationary target? Or are the cells simply devoted to motion perception? As the first step for settling the question, we examine the action for vision in lower animals in the following sections.

3.2. Rotational and translational optical flows

A few animals have one-dimensional retinae, with photoreceptors on a linear band [22]. Slowly scanning their eyes in the direction perpendicular to the line, they presumably expand information from 1D to 2D. For most animals with two-dimensional retinae, however, eye motion seems to have another goal besides effectively expanding the field of view.

In many animals as well as in humans, the eyes rotate against the head, and the head also rotates against the body. Although oculomotor researches have often dealt with eye rotations in the head while the head and the body are artificially immobilized, we should study eye motion with respect to the earth while the head and the body are free to move, if we wish to understand the basic goal of eye motion for vision.

Now consider a human subject who is looking around, walking, etc., in a stationary world, with his eyes and head free to move. The eyes may rotate in a complex way in his forehead and the head itself may also rotate as well as translate. Even if he tries to keep the head stationary, it drifts slightly but continuously [32], because the heavy head is put on his flexible spinal column. We might think then that the eye motion with respect to the earth and motion of the retinal image of the external world resulting from the eye motion was complicated. The situation would be more complex with insects flying in the wind.

However, the motion of the eye with respect to the earth is reduced to a vector sum of only two elements: rotation and translation of the eye. When an eye moves, the stationary visual environment is projected on the retina as an optical flow image. The flows induced by the rotation and translation of the eye are respectively named rotational and translational optical flows [23, 25]. If the eye rotates and translates simultaneously, the optical flow on the retina is a vector sum of the two kinds of optical flow.

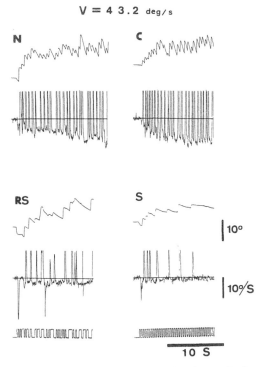

V = 4 3.2 deg/s

Figure 4. OKN to the four textures at stimulus velocity of 43.2 degrees/second. Both eyes are open. The upper traces show horizontal eye positions and the lower their differentiated signals.

Let the rotational angular and translational linear velocities of the eye against the earth be ω and V, respectively. We consider a sphere of projection with the eye at its center and let a point P in the world project on p of the spherical surface. The rotational optical flow consists of velocity vectors, whose directions are tangent to longitude lines, with the poles defined by the axis of rotation. The magnitude of rotational vector of point P is described as

$$\omega_r = \omega \cdot \sin \phi, \tag{1}$$

where ϕ is the angle between the axis of rotation and the vector formed by P and the center of the sphere. Thus the rotational optical flow provides information as to the direction and magnitude of eye rotation, but carries no information regarding the distance of points in the world from the eye. The translational optical flow has the appearance familiar in the studies by J.J. Gibson. It consists of velocity vectors whose directions are parallel to longitude lines, with the poles defined by the direction of translation. The magnitude of translational velocity of point P can be described as

$$\omega_t = V \sin \theta / s, \tag{2}$$

where s is the distance of P and θ is the angle that this point forms with the direction of translation. Thus the angular velocity in the purely translational optical flow is

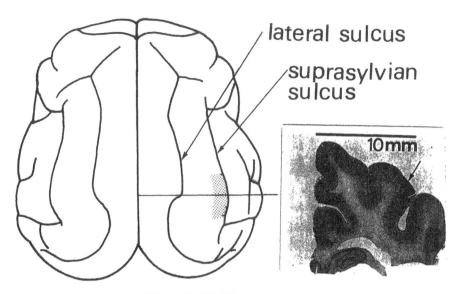

Figure 5. PMLS cortical area.

inversely related to the distance of the corresponding points in the world, carrying information on the 3D structure of the world.

3.3. BEHAVIOR OF THE EYES

In some studies on active computer vision, a camera is translated without any rotations on the stationary platform. The head of a locust is similarly translated while the body is stationary. Interestingly, it keeps the orientation of the head constant against the earth by rotating its neck (Figure 11). Being fixed in the head, the eyes also make pure translations against the earth [5]. A behavioral study proved that by using motion parallax it estimates the absolute depth toward a target before it jumps to it [33].

Most animals suffer from rotational perturbations in their natural living conditions. However, the rotational optical flow on the retina which would be induced by such rotations of their heads does not contain three-dimensional information about the world. Thus, they must keep the orientation of their eye constant somehow.

At first, we will see behavior of the eyes in some animals. Figure 12 shows positions and orientations at intervals of 20 msec of the body of a fly cruising freely in a stationary environment, without pursuing or being pursued by other animals [6]. Because their necks do not rotate during such flights, the orientation also represents the orientations of the eye against the earth. Although the fly may experience perturbations from the wind, the orientations of the eye with respect to the earth are kept constant for a while, quickly changed, and then kept constant again.

Figure 13 is the orientation of a crab's eye during its locomotion [4]. Rotating the eye against the body by its eyestalk (the rod connecting the eye and the body), it again keeps the orientations of the eye against the earth constant for a while, rotates them quickly, and keeps them constant again.

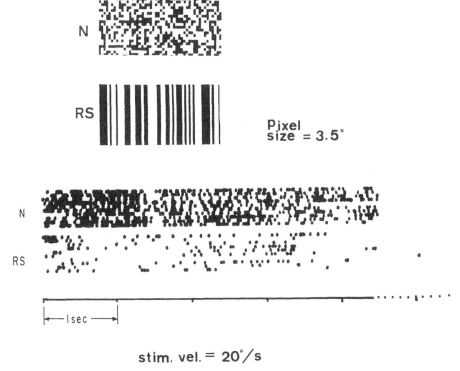

Figure 6. Neural responses to the motion of N and RS at 20 degrees/second.

Figure 14 shows orientations of the eye and the head against the earth in a rabbit [7]. Unfortunately for vision, the head with the eyes in it is often forced to move when the animal eats, sniffs, or coughs, because the head also has a mouth and a nose on it. However, the orientations of the eye are again kept constant against the earth, because the eye rotates in the head in the direction opposite to that of head rotation. When a rabbit tries to gaze backward, it has to rotate its head backward. The problem is that the head cannot rotate rapidly because of its large mass. To speed up the gaze shift, the eyes rotate faster in the same direction of the head. Because the head continues to rotate even after the eyes have finished to rotate toward the target, the eyes then rotate in the direction opposite to that of the head; thus the duration with constant orientation of the eyes against the earth increases. In the fly and the crab, the eyes were translated slowly. In the case of the rabbit, the eyes should also be translated slowly, although the motion is not measured. "Slow translations for a while with constant orientations against the earth + quick rotations at the sacrifice of vision" should be the basic pattern of eye motion.

3.4. SEPARATION OF THE ROTATIONAL COMPONENT FROM THE OPTICAL FLOW

How do animals keep the orientation of their eyes constant with respect to the earth? For detecting rotation of their own eyes, visual feedback should be the most reliable. They must detect the rotational components in the optical flow visually,

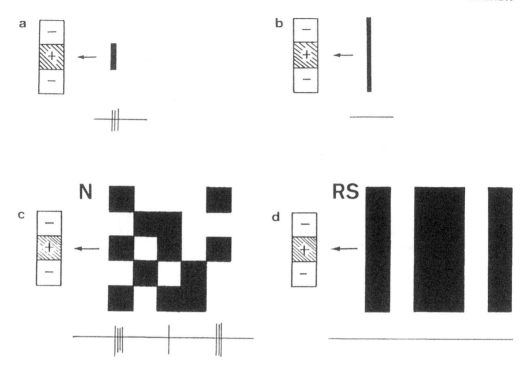

Figure 7. "Hypercomplex" receptive field of a PMLS neuron, which prefers short contours.

Figure 8. Natural scene (small stones on the ground).

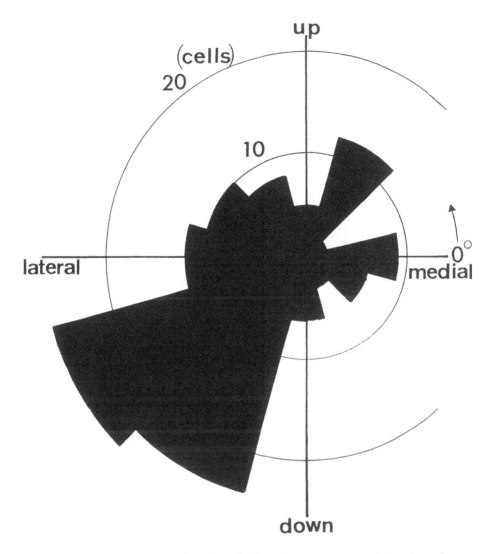

Figure 9. Distribution of preferred direction to textures. Diameter of each sector is proportional to the number of neurons preferring a direction in the sector.

and eliminate the former from the latter by making the eye rotate in the direction opposite to the rotational component.

The basic mechanism for this separation is the optokinetic reflex or OKR (see 2.2), which is present in most animals. The problem is how the animals in their natural habit separate the rotational component from the optical flow. Insects like flies have "complex eyes" with the advantage that they can see almost 360 degrees around themselves. When the eye purely rotates at the angular velocity ω_0, the flow velocities increase by ω_0 in every direction around it. On the other hand, if the eye is purely translated, the directions of the flow are opposite on both sides of the

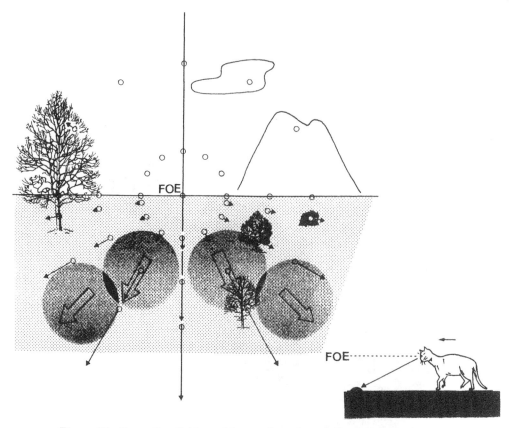

Figure 10. Receptive field position and preferred direction for the neurons in the right PMLS (lower left) and in the left PMLS (lower right).

translation and the two poles without flow velocities are 180 degrees apart. Nelson and Aloimonos proposed a method for separating the rotational component from the optical flow based on these properties (Figure 15) and proved that the method is robust against noise and partial lack of data [27]. It is believed that insects use such kinds of algorithms [18], or algorithms not relying on correspondence [11].

Crabs are divided into two categories: one living in a "flat world" such as a seashore, and the other in a "complex world" such as a cliff. Both kinds of crabs keep the orientation of their eyes constant. It is known that at least the "flat world" crabs use a simple way to separate the rotational component [26]. Although their eyes adapt to see the horizontal directions most precisely, they can also see the upper and the lower visual fields. Now, their optokinetic reflex is sensitive only to the upper field. Because in the "flat world" objects in the upper field are generally far away, the optical flow in the field should be purely rotational in most cases. Thus, the optokinetic reflex sensitive only to the upper visual field can eliminate the rotational components of the flow.

Pigeons can separate the optical flows in a way similar to that of insects, because they have eyes on the sides of their heads. For example, if the right eye sees an upward flow and the left a downward one, the head must be rotating to the right; if both

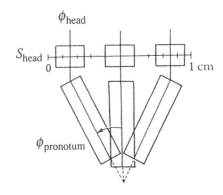

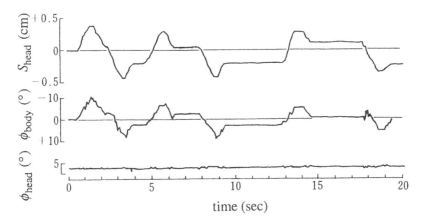

Figure 11. Peering in the locust. Leg movement rotates the body (ϕ pronotum), which results in head translation (S_{head}). Neck rotation nonetheless keeps the head orientation (ϕ_{head}) constant. Redrawn with permission from [5].

eyes see upward flows, the head must be translating downward. In fact, an organ for controlling action named vestibular cerebellum of the pigeons has neurons sensitive to directional combinations of optical flows in both eyes and thus can distinguish between upward and downward translations, rotations of the head around the nose-back axis (roll), and rotations around the top-bottom axis (yaw) [36].

3.5. USE OF THE TRANSLATIONAL OPTICAL FLOW

For bees flying freely in space, it is important to know the three-dimensional structure of the world. Unfortunately they cannot fully use binocular cues, because the eyes are so little separated. Recently Srinivasan *et al.* showed that bees may measure distances by the use of optical flow [34]. Artificial flowers are blooming at various heights (Figure 16). Bees were trained with sugar water as the reward to land on flowers of a specific height. During the training, the flowers with the reward always had the same height, but their sizes and positions were changed randomly from trial to trial. After the trainings, the bees flying over this flow garden for a while finally

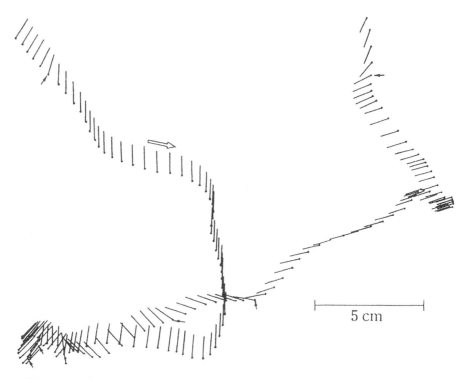

Figure 12. A fly during a cruising flight. Each bar represents position and orientation of the body every 20 ms. The dot on the bar is the head and the dark arrow shows the timing of a saccade. Redrawn with permission from [6].

landed at one of the flowers of the specific height. Interestingly enough, their flight courses before the landing were mostly straight. Because cues of size or position were eliminated, the bees must have used translational optical flow to measure the depth.

N. Franschini *et al.* constructed a moving robot based on the visual mechanism of the fly [12]. The robot has a "complex eye" with a view of 360 degrees. While it is translated for a short straight distance, it estimates the ranges of obstacles using the translational optical flow. If it finds close obstacles, it makes a quick saccade to avoid them. As the complex eye of insects has a high acuity in the center, the retina of the robot also has spatially variant acuities: the separations between two ommatidia are set to be proportional to $\sin \phi$, except the narrow visual fields in front and back of the head, for facilitating later processing (see Formula 1).

3.6. Motion parallax and the role of eye movements in human subjects

Through evolution, the positions of the eyes became closer together. Thus humans, with both eyes looking almost the same direction, cannot use the principle of 360 degrees vision for separating the optical flow. Humans acquired instead binocular

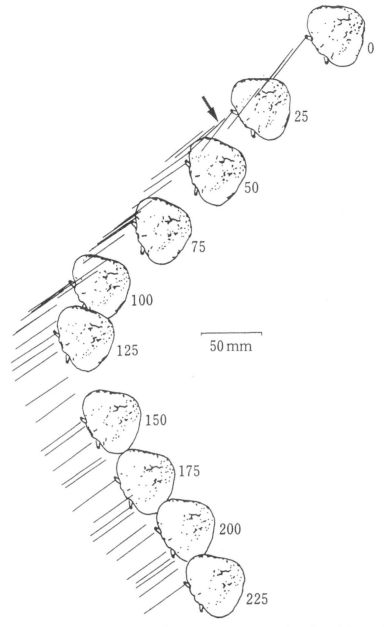

Figure 13. Orientations of the eye every 0.4 second and positions of the body approximately every 2.1 seconds in the crab during walking. The arrow indicates a saccade. Redrawn with permission from [4].

stereopsis. These facts do not necessarily mean, however, that a human does not use translational optical flows for measuring depth.

Rogers and Graham found that differential velocities in the optical flow, namely, motion parallax, produce depth perception [31]. Their subject looks at a CRT screen monocularly while translating his head side by side (Figure 17). If he looks at a real

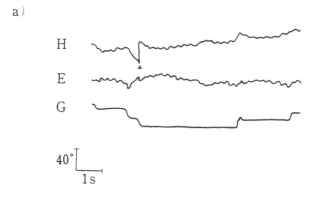

a)

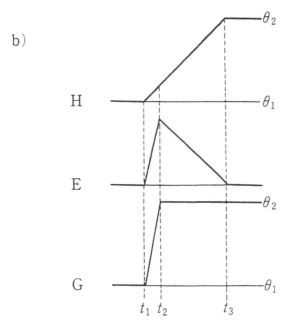

b)

Figure 14. Orientations of the eye (G) and of the head (H) with respect to the earth, and of the eye with respect to the head (E) in the rabbit. $G = H + E$. (a): G is kept constant in spite of H. Redrawn with permission from [7]. (b): G changes from θ_1 to θ_2 rapidly ($t_1 - t_2$) because of the eye rotation against the head (E), in spite of slow head rotation (H).

surface with a depth profile, such as the one on the right of the figure, while translating his head, his retina must see an optical flow with differential velocities corresponding to the profile. In their experiment the head is translated; the translation simulates a differential optical flow, which is then presented on the flat CRT screen. Surprisingly, the subject perceived depth without any ambiguities, without any sensations of motion although the stimulus was moving on the retina. It is known that on one hand binocular stereopsis is rare in insects and develops late in infants; on the other hand the motion parallax could be widely used in insects and develops

a)

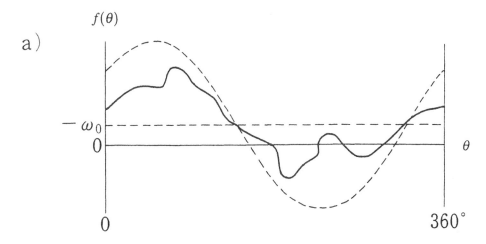

b)

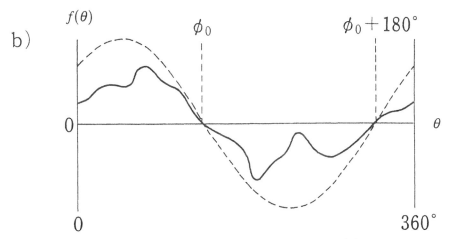

Figure 15. The magnitude of the optical flow velocities $f(\theta)$ at the direction θ in the visual field. The broken sinusoidal line represents the flow velocities when the visual world is at a constant distance from the eye at all the directions. Redrawn with permission from [27]. (a) A rotational flow $(-\omega_0)$ adds to the translational flow. (b) The rotational component is eliminated by shifting the graph of (a) vertically until the two primary zero-crossings are separated by 180 degrees. ϕ_0 is the direction of translation.

just after the birth in infants [38]. This implies that the motion parallax is a depth cue more basic than the binocular disparities.

K. Nakayama found that human acuity for motion parallax is surprisingly high [25]: If the head is translated repeatedly across 1 centimeter at a temporal frequency of 2 hertz and if the stimulus had a spatial frequency less than 0.75 hertz, he can detect the depth of just 0.5 millimeter at 57 centimeters in front of him.

He also found that the acuity is severely degraded if a velocity more than 20 min/second is uniformly added to the motion parallax. In other words, we cannot fully use the motion parallax unless the component of common velocity is reduced less than 20 min/second by eye movements.

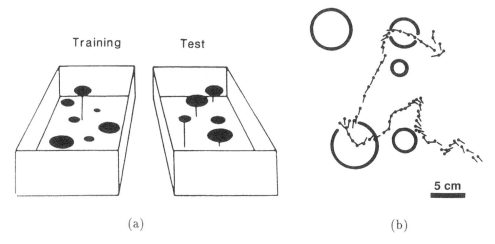

(a)   (b)

Figure 16. (a) An artificial flower garden. (b) Flight course in every 40 ms of a bee over the flowers (shown by circles). Redrawn with permission from [34].

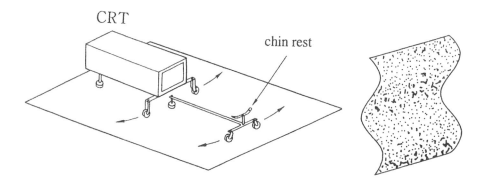

Figure 17. Depth perception by motion parallax. A subject looks at the CRT screen moving his head on the chinrest to the left and right. Redrawn with permission from [31].

When we look at a target at a finite distance without any artificial constraints on head motion, the eye movements required for reducing the common velocity as well as for keeping the target on the central retina are complicated. For instance, if the head is translated, the eyes are also translated at the same velocity. If the head rotates, the eyes not only rotate at the same angular velocity, but also translate because the rotational axis of the head is about 10 centimeters back of the eyes [35]. What kinds of eye movements are required then to spatiotemporally keep the eye on the target? First, against the rotation of the head, the eyes should rotate in the opposite direction at the same velocity of the head. Secondly, against the translational components of the eye, the eye should rotate in the opposite direction and at the angular velocity proportional to the velocity of the translation and inversely proportional to the distance of the target. To achieve these complex eye movements, various kinds of eye movement work in parallel: compensatory eye movements such as vestibulo-ocular reflex, subcortical optokinetic nystagmus, otolish-ocular reflex [3], and cortical optokinetic nystagmus, and also pursuit eye movements.

4. DISCUSSION

Most studies on active computer vision refer to the human saccade while the head is artificially immobilized. These eye movements are difficult to interpret, however, first because volitional controls are often added to them and second because they often accompany head motions, at least in busy situations, with few volitional controls [21]. In rabbits, which are phylogenetically older than humans, saccades always accompany head motion [7].

The most serious shortcoming of immobilizing the head would be that we lose the translational components of the eye with respect to the earth. In Section 3, I showed that lower animals use such translations for acquiring 3D information of the external world by keeping the orientation of their eyes constant. A man also knows 3D structure by translating his head while he keeps the common retinal velocity in the central retina minimum by compensatory eye movements.

Although both visual neurobiology and computer vision traditionally separated vision from action, they have recently connected vision with action [1, 10]. The two areas of research are complementary: the former is analytic and the latter synthetic. Thus I believe they will activate each other under the slogan, "I move, therefore I see" (moveo ergo video).

REFERENCES

1. J. Aloimonos, I. Weiss, and A. Bandopadhay, "Active vision," *International Journal of Computer Vision* **2**, 1988, 333–356.

2. D.H. Ballard, "Animate vision," *Artificial Intelligence* **48**, 1991, 57–86.

3. R.W. Baloh, K. Beyrirch, V. Honrubia, and R.D. Yee, "Eye movements induced by linear acceleration on a parallel swing," *J. Neurophysiol.* **60-6**, 1988, 2000–2013.

4. W.J.P. Barnes, "Sensory basis and functional role of eye movements elicited during locomotion in the land crab *Cardisoma Guanhumi*," *J. Exp. Biol.* **154**, 1990, 99–119.

5. T.S. Collett, "Peering- A locust behaviour pattern for obtaining motion parallax information," *J. Exp. Biol.* **76**, 1978, 237–241.

6. T.S. Collett and M. Land, "Visual control of flight behaviour in the hoverfly *Syritta pipiens L.*," *J. Comp. Physiol.* **A99**, 1975, 1–66.

7. H. Collewijn, *The Oculomotor System of the Rabbit and its Plasticity*, Springer, Berlin, 1981.

8. G.C. DeAngelis, I. Ohzawa, and R.D. Freeman, "Spatiotemporal organization of simple cell receptive field in the cat's striate cortex. 1. General characteristics and postnatal development," *J. Neurophysiol.* **69**, 1993, 1091–1117.

9. R. Descartes, "Traité de l'homme," *Œuvres et lettres*, Bibliotheque de la Pleiade, Gallimard, 1686, 850–857.

10. C. Fermüller and Y. Aloimonos, "Vision and action," *Image and Vision Computing* **13**, 1995, 725–744.

11. C. Fermüller and Y. Aloimonos, "Direct perception of three-dimensional motion from patterns of visual motion," *Science* **270**, 1995, 1973–1976.

12. N. Franchencini, J.M. Pichon, and C. Blanes, "From insect vision to robot vision," *Phil. Trans. Royal Society of London B* **337**, 1992, 283–294.

13. A. Gibson, J. Baker, G. Mower, and M. Glickstein, "Corticopontine cells in area 18 of the cat," *J. Neurophysiol.* **41**, 1978, 484–495.

14. M.A. Goodale and A.D. Miller, "Separate visual pathways for perception and action," *Trends in Neurosci.* **15**(1), 1992, 20–25.

15. T. Hamada, "Binocular and monocular optokinetic nystagmus in cats to textured visual patterns," *Neurosci. Letters* **40**, 1983, 127–131.

16. T. Hamada, "Neural response to the motion of textures in the lateral suprasylvian area of the cat," *Behav. Brain Res.* **25**, 1987, 175–185.

17. E. von Holst and H. Mittelstaedt, "The reafference principle (interaction between the central nervous system and the periphery)," in *The behavioral physiology of animals and man: selected papers of E. von Holst*, Methuen, London, 1973, 139–173.

18. A. Horridge, "Insect vision is active only," *Proceedings of the Third International Congress of Neuroethology*, Montreal, 1992, 56.

19. D.H. Hubel, "Single unit activity in striate cortex of unrestrained cats," *J. Physiol.* **147**, 1959, 226–238.

20. D.H. Hubel and T.N. Wiesel, "Receptive fields, binocular interaction and functional architecture in the cat's visual cortex," *J. Physiol.* **160**, 1962, 106–154.

21. M. Land, "Predictable eye-head coordination during driving," *Nature* **359**, 1992, 318–320.

22. M. Land and R.D. Fernald, "The evolution of eyes," *Annu. Rev. Neurosci.* **15**, 1992, 1–29.

23. H.C. Longuet-Higgins and K. Prazdny, "The interpretation of a moving retinal image," *Proceedings of the Royal Society of London B* **208**, 1980, 385–397.

24. D.C. Marr, *Vision*, W.H. Freeman and Co., San Francisco, 1982.

25. K. Nakayama, "Motion parallax sensitivity and space perception," in A. Hein and M. Jeannerod (Eds.), *Spatially oriented behavior*, Springer, New York, 1983, 223–242.

26. H.-O. Nalbach and G. Nalbach, "Distribution of optokinetic sensitivity over the eyes of crabs: Its relation to habit and possible role in flow-field analysis," *J. Comp. Physiol.* **A160**, 1987, 127–135.

27. R.C. Nelson and J. Aloimonos, "Finding motion parameters from spherical motion fields (or the advantages of having eyes in the back of your head)," *Biological Cybernetics* **58**, 1988, 261–273.

28. L.A. Palmer, A.C. Rosenquist, and R.J. Tusa, "The retinotopic organization of lateral suprasylvian visual areas in the cat," *J. Compl. Neurol.* **177**, 1978, 237–256.

29. M.T. Perenin and M. Jeannerod, "Subcortical vision in man," *Trends Neurosci.*, 1979, 204–207.

30. W. Precht, "Functional organization of optokinetic pathways in mammals," in A.F. Fuchs and W. Becker (Eds.), *Progress in Oculomotor Research*, Elsevier, New York, 1980, 425–433.

31. B. Rogers and M. Graham, "Motion parallax as an independent cue for depth perception," *Perception* **8**, 1979, 125–134.

32. A.A. Skavenski, R.M. Hansen, R.M. Steinman, and B.J. Winterson, "Quality of retinal image stabilization during small natural and artificial body rotation in man," *Vision Res.* **19**, 1979, 675–683.

33. E.C. Sobel, "The locust's use of motion parallax to measure distance," *J. Comp. Physiol.* **A167**, 1990, 579–588.

34. M.V. Srinivasan, M. Lehrer, S.W. Zhang, and G.A. Horridge, "How honeybees measure their distance from objects of unknown size," *J. Comp. Physiol.* **A165**, 1989, 605–613.

35. E. Viire, D. Tweed, K. Milner, and T. Vilis, "A reexamination of the gain of the vestibuloocular reflex," *J. Neurophysiol.* **56-2**, 1986, 439–450.

36. D.R. Wylie and B.J. Frost, "Purkinje cells in the vestilulocerebellum of the pigeon respond best to either translational or rotational wholefield visual motion," *Exp. Brain Res.* **86**, 1991, 229–232.

37. Y. Yamada, *Language before language* (in Japanese), Shinyosha, Tokyo, 1987.

38. A. Yonas and C.E. Granrud, "The development of sensitivity to kinetic, binocular and pictorial depth information in human infants," in D.J. Ingle, M. Jeannerod and D. Lee (Eds.), *Brain mechanisms and spatial vision*, Martinus Nijhoff, Dordrecht, 1985.

39. T.J. Zumbroich, M. von Grunau, C. Poulin, and C. Blakemore, "Differences of visual field representation in the medial and lateral banks of the suprasylvian cortex (PMLS/PLLS) of the cat," *Exp. Brain Res.* **64**, 1986, 77–93.

3 PATTERN AND 3D VISION OF INSECTS

Adrian Horridge
Australian National University

ABSTRACT

Insect vision is predominantly active, depending on egomotion and eye saccades. The two-dimensional (2D) array of retinal receptors in parallel is mapped into a succession of 2D arrays of processing neurons. In different levels of these arrays, the image is operated upon by different kinds of filters, some temporal, some spatial, and some for different kinds of motion. The filters are genetically predetermined groups of neurons, between which there is a strong separation of functions. The filter outputs are coded by groups of neurons with overlapping fields and across-fiber coding, which carry a variety of simultaneous but separate responses to features such as contrast frequency, angular velocity, direction of motion, colour contrast, and edge orientation. Vision is strongly task-oriented. The eye operates with local contrasts in motion and generates a variety of visual responses that control flight speed, lift and turning. This on-line control of flight manoeuvres is mainly colour-blind and is modified by its own adaptive system but is connected only indirectly into the visual memory for landmarks and patterns.

Visual discrimination by bees depends on the nature of the image and on the activity of the bee, so we must distinguish between vision during landing, fixating, hovering, scanning and flying. *Landing* bees are poor at visual discriminations, seeing little more than the temporal frequency caused by their own motion relative to the local pattern. *Fixating* bees can distinguish the rotation of sector patterns to 20°, and they consolidate memories of landmarks while making specialized inspection flights. *Flying* bees are able to distinguish a remarkable number of simple patterns, but they fail to separate edges that cross or the rotation of some patterns by 45°. The results can be modeled with the hypothesis that bees have a family of broadly tuned 2D filters that detect the predominant orientation in each region of the image, and other 2D filters for radial and circular patterns and a vertical axis of bilateral symmetry.

Together with colour and the temporal frequency of flicker, these 2D filters are independent of range. Bees prefer to use landmarks where they can, then global pattern at the largest scale, and lastly the 2D pattern detail around the goal. The invariants of bee visual discrimination of spatial pattern are explained by models based on the overlap of a few broad tuning curves of these input filters, by analogy with the colour triangle in colour discrimination.

1. INTRODUCTION

Insect visual behaviour is incredibly diverse, including the turning of a firefly towards a single flash, and the way that night-flying aquatic insects find ponds by seeing the polarized moonlight reflected from them. All large diurnal insects, in more typical situations, also obviously "see" as judged by their actions. By insects, however, I refer in this chapter to the large day-flying bees, butterflies, dragonflies, flies, and locusts, all of which clearly use vision for manoeuvring in normal flight, escaping enemies, chasing mates or prey, and finding food in an unpredictable cluttered 3D world. Their visual performance is remarkable, considering the small size of their brain, at least in comparison with the computer hardware required to mimic it. How do they do it?

1.1. THE SAMPLING ARRAY

The *retina* of large diurnal insects is a spatiotemporal sampling array of continuously functioning light-absorbing small *receptors in parallel*, upon which an image is continually projected (Figure 1). The receptors, about 2 microns wide, act as light guides, containing rhodopsin pigments that absorb gradually at a rate of about 1% per micron. The principle of dividing the image into a two-dimensional array of receptor fields is the same as in camera-type eyes, but the optics consists of a layer of lenslets (5–15,000 of them in the large diurnal insects), one for each receptor axis. Each receptor projects through the nodal point of its own lens into the outside world, and, unlike single-lens eyes, the fields overlap. The important parameters for the action of the retina are the angles between the adjacent visual axes (usually about 2° in the insects mentioned above) and the angular width of the receptor fields (usually also about 2°) at the 50% contour of sensitivity (Figure 1). The functional advantages of a compound eye is that vision can extend all round the head and receptor fields overlap. The disadvantages of insect eyes are that they are small in absolute terms, so there are relatively few receptors, and the optical apertures are especially small—only about 20–35 microns—so the lens resolution is reduced by diffraction [20], and the receptors are noisy.

Behind the retina lie successive layers of neuron arrays which process the incoming data in parallel (Figure 2). In many of the neurons the excitation is graded, without all-or-none spikes, and the coding of features depends upon combinations of neurons within groups. At each stage, coding involves the relative weighting of the action of each neuron within its group. Initially, as far as the medulla, the image is mapped into the array, but in the deeper layers the neuron fields are larger and more

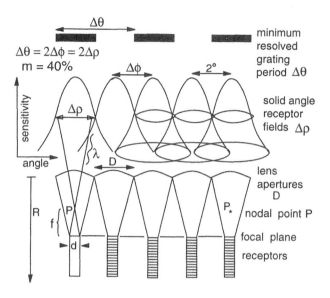

Figure 1. The basic principle of the sampling action by the insect eye, showing the overlap of the fields of sensitivity of the receptor array. Along the top is the minimum period $\Delta\Theta$ of the grating that can be seen by this array. The 2D receptor fields (with sensitivity plotted upwards) are separated by the angle $\Delta\Theta$ and represented as Gaussian curves of width $\Delta\rho$ at the 50% contour of sensitivity. With the typical relations between these angles shown here, the motion of this grating will modulate these receptors by 40%, which is near the middle of the response range. From simple geometry, $D/R = \Delta\phi \approx \Delta\rho$, so $D^2/R = $ constant k for any compound eye, k depending on field overlap. Also we have $d/f \approx \lambda/D$ and $d \approx 0.002$ mm so the F number ≈ 4. Further details in [20].

specific for features. Groups of neurons which descend the ventral cord in groups contribute similarly to coding of task-oriented motor actions.

Insects have no lens accommodation, no controlled convergence of the eyes, and (except within range of the legs and mouth-parts, in a few specialized prey grabbers, such as mantids and dragon-fly larvae), they make little use of the overlapping axes of the two eyes. There is no evidence for binocular visual processing as in man, as defined by a joint projection to groups of neurons with different offsets (called disparities). Instead, the best that insects can do, as illustrated in the praying mantis, is the detection of coincidences in two axes viewing the same target, not necessarily on the midline [41]. In their visual responses most insects behave as if they have a single eye covering a very wide solid angle. Experiments show that flying insects solve the problem of measuring range by assuming their own motion and measuring the induced motion of images that move across the retina (Figure 3).

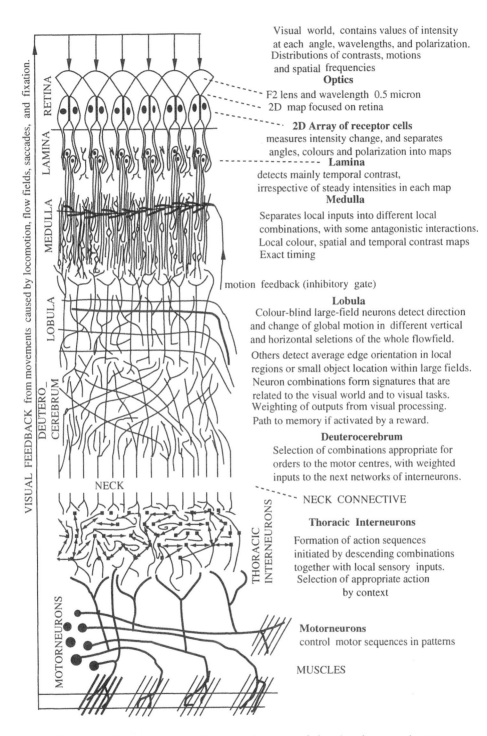

Visual world, contains values of intensity
at each angle, wavelengths, and polarization.
Distributions of contrasts, motions
and spatial frequencies

Optics

F2 lens and wavelength 0.5 micron
2D map focused on retina

2D Array of receptor cells

measures intensity change, and separates
angles, colours and polarization into maps

Lamina

detects mainly temporal contrast,
irrespective of steady intensities in each map

Medulla

Separates local inputs into different local
combinations, with some antagonistic interactions.
Local colour, spatial and temporal contrast maps
Exact timing

motion feedback (inhibitory gate)

Lobula

Colour-blind large-field neurons detect direction
and change of global motion in different vertical
and horizontal seletions of the whole flowfield.

Others detect average edge orientation in local
regions or small object location within large fields.
Neuron combinations form signatures that are
related to the visual world and to visual tasks.
Weighting of outputs from visual processing.
Path to memory if activated by a reward.

Deuterocerebrum

Selection of combinations appropriate for
orders to the motor centres, with weighted
inputs to the next networks of interneurons.

NECK CONNECTIVE

Thoracic Interneurons

Formation of action sequences
initiated by descending combinations
together with local sensory inputs.
Selection of appropriate action
by context

Motorneurons
control motor sequences in patterns

MUSCLES

Figure 2. The succession of neuronal arrays of the visual processing system of a typical large insect, highly schematic, with a summary of functions at each level.

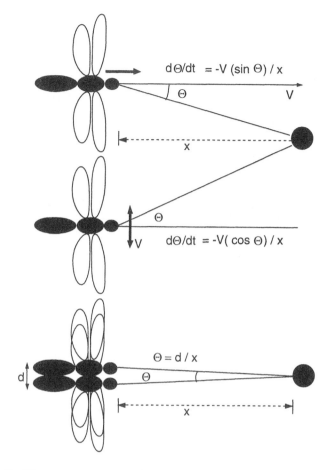

Figure 3. The measurement of range from self-motion. (a). With a known forward velocity V, the angular velocity of the image is given by $d\Theta/dX = -(V\sin\Theta)/X$, where X is the range. (b). With a lateral motion of velocity V, the apparent angular velocity $d\Theta/dX = -(V\cos\Theta)/X$. (c) With a lateral displacement d, the range is given by $\Theta = d/X$.

2. Visual Responses Essential to Locomotion

2.1. Staying Upright

The first requirement is to have predictable reference co-ordinates for using vision in motion, especially when flying or swimming. Insects have a robust *dorsal light response* that helps keep the dorsal side uppermost (or in some cases, like water boatmen, the ventral side uppermost). To mediate or assist with this response, most insects have, at the front of the head, three small supplementary eyes called *ocelli*, which are usually defocused so they detect only very large contrasts [51, 59]. Two mechanisms are known: in one, the sky is kept uppermost, even when the sun is low in the sky; in the other, the eyes are kept horizontal relative to the average horizon, in some cases by reliance upon ultra-violet rays. This is probably how navigation of some insects by the polarized ultra-violet light of the blue of the sky [55] originated in their evolution.

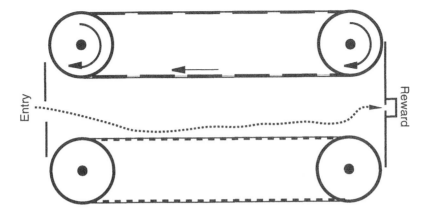

Figure 4. The apparatus in which bees fly down a tunnel with movable patterned walls to obtain a reward. Irrespective of pattern, they equalize the angular velocities on the two sides as seen laterally by the two eyes. Further details in [44, 48].

2.2. THE AVOIDANCE RESPONSE AND THE CENTRING RESPONSE

In the avoidance response, bees will not fly close to a contrast that is moving relative to their eye, at contrast frequencies up to 120 Hz. In the centring response, bees trained to fly along a paper tunnel to obtain a sugar reward (Figure 4), fly along the centre of it, even if there are different patterns on the two walls. If the motion of the walls is controlled experimentally, the bees fly along a line which *equalizes the angular velocity on the two sides*, irrespective of the pattern on the walls or of the direction of the relative motion, even if the latter is up, down, or forwards across the eye [48]. In these responses, the bees do not confuse motion of edges with flicker. They have a non-directional mechanism that can measure the angular velocity of contrasts moving across the eyes. Most of the fast on-line flight control, avoidance of obstacles, and manoeuvering relative to surrounding objects in their apparently amazing flight acrobatics, appears to be controlled by these non-directional mechanisms, which are colour-blind and are connected into the memory of the distance to a food location.

We can model the computation of angular velocity (and range) by several layers of arrays that correspond closely to neuron layers behind the retina (Figure 5). Each receptor is followed by a temporal differentiator at the lamina level (Figure 2) that eliminates the constant background intensities that carry no information, but amplifies intensity changes. This stage has a high gain that saturates all contrasts equally so that the subsequent measurement of angular velocity is not confused by different contrast levels. The next stage is a rectifier that equalizes the effects of increasing or decreasing intensity, i.e., it ignores the polarity of edges. At the next stage, each visual axis inhibits its neighbours, forming an array of centre/surround

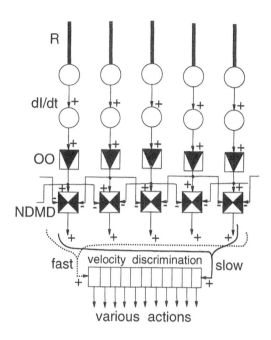

Figure 5. A possible model of the non-directional measurement of the angular velocity of the image. The outputs of the receptor array (R) each yield a temporal derivative which is then rectified. The outputs of these on-off units (OO) inhibit their neighbours so each gives no response to a simultaneous intensity change (flicker), but is sensitive to motion of an edge. The outputs of these non-directional motion detectors (NDMD) are then collected by neurons with medium-sized fields which are sensitive to temporal summation, in either slow or fast velocity ranges. These outputs can then achieve discriminations and initiate different actions for different angular velocities of passing contrasts. Further details in [6, 7].

units that respond to motion of a small contrast or to an edge but not to general intensity changes such as synchronous flicker. Non-directional motion detector neurons like this, with fields of all sizes, are abundant in the medulla columns of the locust optic lobe [36]. In vertebrates, the corresponding neurons are retinal ganglion cells of two types, with on centres and off centres. This array feeds into units with medium-sized fields which are sensitive to summation over time, responding weakly to slow motion across their fields and more strongly as the inputs become more simultaneous, so responding in a graded way to velocity. A disadvantage of this circuit is that in two dimensions it would be sensitive to pattern, in that more edges would cause more input. To get around this difficulty, there can be two types of these medium-field detectors, one temporally low pass, the other high pass, and the ratio between their outputs is then a measure of angular velocity irrespective of pattern. Most steps in this hypothetical model have been observed in neuron recordings. In flies there are fast and slow directional motion detectors which descend the ventral cord from the brain [25], suggesting that the measure of angular velocity is made in the ventral ganglia.

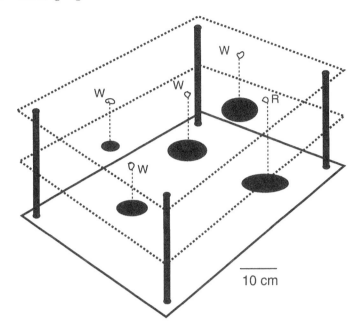

Figure 6. The discrimination of different heights of the target above bench level by flying bees looking downwards. The apparatus consists of three layers of Perspex with 5 cm space between. The targets are discs of black paper of random size and random position. One target at a constant height but of random size and position has a drop of sugar solution as a reward above it on the top sheet, while the other discs have only plain water. The criterion of performance is whether the bees land on the reward drop or on a water drop. In this apparatus, the bees can also learn to discriminate a target of correct angular subtense at the eye, or one of a certain absolute size, irrespective of the other variables [28]. The target appears to be used as a landmark for the reward drop. Further details in [28, 47].

2.3. INSECTS MEASURE PROPERTIES OF RANGE

Flying bees can be trained to visit artificial flowers made of discs of black and white paper on stalks, and select the one of a particular height above the bench level to obtain a reward, when all other aspects of the stimulus such as location, angular size or absolute size are randomized during the training schedule [47]. They learn equally well with plain black discs arranged horizontally on Perspex platforms (Figure 6), or presented vertically [28] at different ranges in the Y-choice chamber (see Figure 11). Other experiments show that bees cannot learn the characteristics of a motion of a target [49], so they must be coding the range into memory as range, not as motion [30]. When bees approach a goal and position themselves to point in the right direction, they use the directions of landmarks and their range, as measured with their own motion. Memory of angular directions of contrasts can use colour vision but those visual responses that are dependent on motion and range are colour-blind, and are mediated by the green class of receptors.

2.4. DYNAMIC STABILITY IN FLIGHT

Known for a century, the *optomotor response* was regarded as an inflexible reflex in which the eyes, head, or whole body of an animal follow the direction of the externally imposed motion of a patterned drum that is rotated around it. Up to the 1980's it was assumed that the optomotor response maintains walking and flight in a straight line and that motion detection can be measured in the turning tendency of the whole animal, but both assumptions are no longer tenable. In the 1950's, Hassenstein and Reichardt [14, 40] pioneered the idea that directional optomotor motion perception is entirely a bottom-up process that can be modeled with one homogeneous class of simple filters. This was one of the influential studies that brought the idea of filters as components into modern theories of vision. A filter is defined as a component that allows a selected part of the signal to pass. Anatomically the filters are neuronal, but their performance is modeled by mathematical operations that are not necessarily related to neurons at all. In these experiments the fly's head was fixed and the responses were averaged (important points, see below). The stimulus consisted of bars or stripes at right angles to the motion. The conclusion was that the averaged insect motion detection can be modeled as the temporal correlation between the intensity changes in adjacent pairs of receptors in the retinal array as contrasts move across the eye. An increment of response is contributed by each edge that passes. A coarse grating moving rapidly, however, gives the same response as a fine grating moving slowly, so that pattern as such cannot be separated from velocity.

With a single set of homogeneous filters, such a system responds well locally to the *directions* (yaw, pitch, and roll) of an unexpected imposed motion, and helps to stabilize the insect dynamically in flight, but confounds everything else, and is not much use for other vision. One set of spatiotemporal filters cannot discriminate different angular velocities, but can detect the average local direction of the flow field very well. The existence of fast and slow motion detectors [25] suggests that there are neurons with a range of optimum velocities (filters with a range of spatiotemporal slopes). The current view is that the optomotor response is to an unexpected change in the flow field, and is always in the background as a phasic directional correction with controlled gain which assists flight stability, while other responses with quite different sensitivities control the flight direction, landing, lift, speed, pursuit of a goal or fixation, and straight flight midway between obstacles.

2.5. THE MECHANISM OF DIRECTIONAL MOTION DETECTION

When an external pattern of contrasts moves from one facet to the next, the correlation between the two intensity sequences at two adjacent facets is ideally 100% for the interval it takes to move from one to the other. So correlation is an optimum which any natural motion detector will evolve to resemble, for the commonest velocity range of the flow field. Also, all models of directional motion detection must include a non-linearity which can be modeled at a first approximation by a second-order effect. Measurements, mainly on flies, show that interactions are between adjacent and sub-adjacent visual axes and that optimum contrast frequencies are in the range 1–10 Hz, which is rather slow compared to other systems. Most of the data on directional motion detection is consistent with a number of models which have a one-way lateral interaction such as inhibition, or non-linear summation [2]. Direct tests, however, have failed to yield positive evidence for pure cross-multiplication, which is the essence of autocorrelation. The dependence of autocorrelation on $(contrast)^2$, however, does provide a test of whether multiplication of the input with itself occurs, but when we checked this in the fly H1 neuron, we [22] found that the response depends on $(contrast)^n$ where n is close to 1, and contrast saturates at low levels. In another critical test, Franceschini [11] showed that motion is detected only when the signal at the two receptors has the same polarity, i.e., an "on" followed by another "on," or an "off" by an "off" at the adjacent receptor, and there is no response at contrast reversal, whereas reversal in the Reichardt model produces a correlation in the opposite direction.

In tests with bars that jump by one inter-receptor spacing and reverse contrast at the same time [23, 24], we could not get a consistent directional effect either way, and concluded that several pathways must be involved in directional sensitivity, as if several neurons respond differently to contrast reversal. Flies respond to the direction of paradoxical motion [39] or non-Fourier motion (for example, a rolling line of contrast reversal in a pattern of 50–50 black/white pixels). This result is difficult to interpret, but suggests that motion perception comes after rectification. These tests, all made in the late 1980's, were not considered in the early systems analysis, where equal amounts of positive and negative gradients were the rule. At present we have no data directly bearing on the neuronal mechanism of directional motion detection, only on its performance. There is no positive evidence for multiplicative autocorrelation in insect vision, and some evidence against it. Almost any non-linear lateral interaction between neurons, followed by a threshold, is an adequate directional model. Moreover, mathematical models based on small local differences are sensitive to noise and in 2D they require long computations to deal with discontinuity at edges. Also, they confound motion direction, the axis of the receptor pair, and edge orientation, so actually they have not been useful in artificial vision.

2.6. SEPARATION OF ROTATION AND TRANSLATION

In their visual responses during flight, insects show that they distinguish very well between the relative motions on the eye caused by their own active rotations (in the three planes, yaw, pitch, and roll) and their quite distinct translations (movement forwards, up-down or sideways). This distinction was ignored until the late 1980's but has recently proved to be the most important aspect of directional motion detection. The overlapping fields and broad tuning curves of neurons descending the ventral cord to the motor centres [34, 38] provide by their overlaps an across-fiber coding mechanism for each distinct large motion in any part of the visual field.

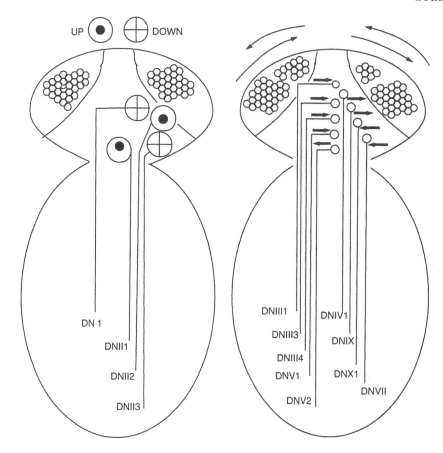

Figure 7. Some of the neurons that descend from the brain of the bee to the motor centres of the thorax and help control the direction of flight, seen from above. On the left are neurons that respond to vertical flow in front of the eyes, upwards ⊙ and downwards ⊕. On the right are neurons that respond to horizontal flow to one eye or the other, or both, in the directions shown by the arrows, with reference to the flow across the eye on the right hand side. This system is apparently not connected to the memory for a food source. After [1].

In the deep optic lobe of all flying insects are many neurons that respond to directional motion but individually they confound pattern and angular velocity. They have long been considered as the pathways of the optomotor response [15]. They converge to other neurons that descend the ventral cord and eventually run to motor centres that turn the neck and steer the wings. At this level, between the brain and the motor centres, there are four sets of them, for upwards, downwards, and horizontal motions to left and to right, sufficient to correct unexpected shifts of the flight path in yaw, pitch, and roll, if the outputs of these four types are active in different combinations in each case [15]. The fields of the optic lobe neurons, plotted in polar co-ordinates about the head, overlap strongly, so that acting in different combinations, they can very well locate local movements, and with good coverage in all directions. By interactions between the two eyes, they can separate translation and rotation [1].

In bees, this separation is apparent in individual neurons descending the cord (Figure 7). In the locust, other neurons respond directionally to the tilt or lift of the horizon and act similarly on the flight control.

Control of flight speed over the ground is also done visually by flying insects, enabling them to set a ground speed and direction irrespective of ground pattern over a range of wind speeds, even though they fly slowly e.g., *Drosophila* at 0.1 m/s [8]. Bees and *Drosophila* fly more slowly through narrower tunnels than they do in the open. Locusts in a swarm fly at the same speed as their neighbours, and the few other insects that have been tested fly with a preferred angular velocity relative to surrounding contrasts [6, 8]. Walking insects tend to ignore even the unexpected optic flow which is not caused by their own motion [6].

2.7. THE FIGURE/GROUND SEPARATION

The analysis of the optomotor response during the 1950's, away from the anecdotal approach towards the mathematical representation of the system, with its influence on the development of artificial vision, was followed in the 1970's by a similar analysis of the fly's response to a patterned vertical stripe moving horizontally on a moving patterned background—the so-called figure/ground stimulus, which was modeled by an additional layer of non-directional non-linear filters [37]. The flies could separate the motions of the object in the foreground and those of the patterned background, but with poorer resolution than in man. Being treated as an extension of the optomotor response in tethered flight with a fixed head, these results were difficult to apply to the wide variety of visual behaviour of insects in flight, and even to the behaviour of freely flying flies. As first demonstrated by Mike Land [29], it turned out that fixing the head to the thorax in all these experiments, and averaging the recordings, had obscured the most important mechanisms in visual flight control, namely, the spontaneous movements of the head, with the result that the flies responded only to contrast frequency irrespective of the pattern. They lack feedback from their own head movements, and the optomoter reflex is the only mechanism left functioning.

A more promising approach appeared when the fixation on small contrasting objects and the pursuit of females or prey were found to be mediated by a system of quite separate optic lobe neurons. Insects in flight respond to the motion of a small spot or patterned object that moves over a similarly patterned background by turning towards or away from it, and in several groups of insects, neurons that respond to this stimulus have been recorded. These object detector neurons [13] function separately but in parallel with those that detect the local motion direction [15], others that detect the non-directional angular velocity of the flow field [44], and yet other neurons that detect the orientations of edges with broad overlapping orientation tuning curves (see below). Almost at the same time as the contemporary shift of interest to parallel computing hardware, models with several separate groups of neurons in parallel replaced the single channel models of 1956–1988.

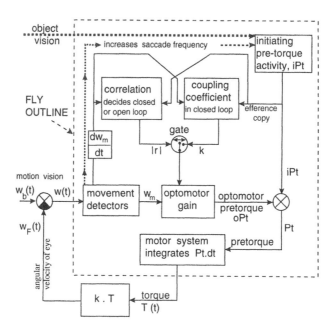

Figure 8. The interactions in the control of flight in the horizontal plane by the fly *Drosophila*. The outline of the fly is represented by the dashed rectangle. The input from the eye to the motion detectors $w(t)$ is the imposed motion $w_b(t)$ less the compensatory feedback $w_F(t)$ from the fly's own motor output. The internal optomotor effect is a pretorque, oPt, which is added to the fly's spontaneous pretorque activity iPt, giving a pretorque which is integrated by the motor system to an angular velocity $w_F(t)$. The temporal derivative of the output of the motion detectors dw_m/dt is correlated internally with the internal copy of the initiating pretorque activity. If there is a correlation, i.e., if the visual input is expected, then the gain in the optomotor pretorque response is switched to zero, but if the rotatory input is unexpected, the optomotor response is switched to a previously learned value k, which is adjusted by the previous relation between pretorque and visual feedback. This diagram amounts to a brief summary that is compatible with the experimental results, not a circuit diagram. After [16].

2.8. FLYING ON A STRAIGHT COURSE

In a new approach in the early 1980's, Martin Heisenberg and Reinhard Wolf [16, 17] working with *Drosophila* in tethered flight, but with its head free to move, showed that the head movements enable it to fixate, to compensate for asymmetry in the wings, and to calibrate its flight on a straight course. High gain recordings show that the fruit fly makes intermittent saccades of the head. *Saccades* are small sudden rotations of the head in the horizontal plane that have several functions. Saccades simultaneously activate all the very sensitive detectors of local contrast across the eye, and they also initiate a controlled turn in an expected direction. The visual feedback so created is the crucial information for calibrating the optomotor response so that the muscles of the two sides are kept in balance (Figure 8). The internal gain of the optomotor feedback loop is continually adjusted between 0 and 100% by the relation between the command to turn and the (non-directional) angular acceleration that is fed back to the eyes. The internal gain factor (the coupling coefficient in Figure 8) depends on the expected feedback and the actual feedback. The command to turn is the pretorque, which represents a neuronal signal. The model takes account of the experimental result that there is no optomotor response to the expected components of motion at the eye, including saccades. Within the nervous system the pretorque is converted to a torque by the motor system, and then to body orientation by integration of the torque over time. Mutant flies (*rol, sol*) with no optomotor response use this remaining control circuit during flight for fixation, which aims them relative to surrounding contrasts. In these experiments the mutants, which have no directional optomotor system, also stabilize themselves visually in straight flight by making fewer saccades when there is less visual feedback, irrespective of the direction of the motion feedback, so they keep going when they are flying straight.

Locusts in tethered flight also fail to align themselves straight ahead against the airstream unless the effects of the locusts own turning and the disastrous effects of asymmetry in the outputs of the wings on the two sides are fed back through the visual flow field [35]. To perform, the locust requires its own complete system.

The *bee-line*, the straight track taken by a flying bee, is governed partly by the pattern of polarisation of the sky and the sun compass [55], and partly by landmarks, but bees apparently avoid the effects of flying in a cross-wind by keeping the optic flow from the ground at a set angle to the sun compass [6] irrespective of the exact direction that they point.

2.9. RESPONSES TO PARALLAX

Insects in active motion do not see the world as flat. Bees, flying towards a raised edge or a twig, respond to the faster relative motion of the foreground over the more distant background by landing at right angles to the approaching edge. They prefer to land on edges where the occlusion of the background contrasts is most apparent, perhaps because it causes most flicker, and they will not land on an edge where there is opening parallax [46]. They therefore land on the near side of raised objects but on the far side of holes (Figure 9).

Locusts, preparing to jump, peer by moving their head sideways and then they jump with a controlled take-off velocity that lands them on their goal. In this measurement of range, they make use of two relative motions. First, they respond to the relative motion caused by their own peering, and this works for objects against the sky with no background. The locust can be fooled by moving the goal while it is making its peering movement. These experiments also show that the extent of the angular motion across the eye, not its direction, is the important detail to which they attend [43]. Secondly, the distance jumped can also be influenced by moving the background closer or further from the goal [7]. This result shows that they make use of the parallax as the foreground moves across a contrasting background as a result

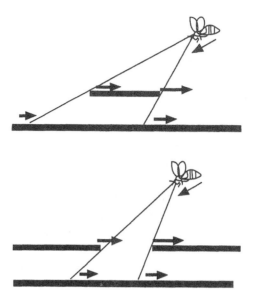

Figure 9. Flying bees that are about to land see the parallax generated by an object in the foreground moving across a patterned background. They prefer to land at right angles to an edge where they see closing parallax and will not land where they see opening parallax. Landing at right angles avoids confusing the orientation with the motion of the edge. Further details in [44].

of their peering. Locusts have a forward-looking fovea that serves this response [20]. No specific neurons have been found to respond to parallax, and once again we must infer that the coding lies in the neuron combinations.

In this behaviour, the significant signal relates to the ranges of surrounding objects, and however much the insect appears to see the objects in its visual field, it may have nothing more in its neurons than a map of contrasts coded in range, not at all in terms of separate objects, as we would have. As the vision is task-oriented, it can be stripped down to the essentials, and a measurement of the range of "something out there" is all that is required.

3. VISUAL INPUTS CAN BE LEARNED

3.1. MODIFYING THE OPTOMOTOR RESPONSE

Late in the summer, we find tattered insects flying about with unequal wings, but they still fly straight, showing that the optomotor reflex adjusts rapidly to damage of one wing. In the experiments with *Drosophila*, referred to above, an additional turning of the drum surrounding the fly can be added to the rotation expected from the output of the wings. The flies then infers itself to be turning more (or less) than expected, and it adjusts the relative outputs of the two wings in relation to the optomotor pretorque, so that it flies again on a straight course (Figure 8). A second mechanism controls the direction and frequency of eye saccades that initiate steering. Even when the visual feedback caused by a self-initiated turn is reversed experimentally, the fly can learn in about half an hour to reverse its optomotor response [16]. Nothing shows better that the measure of the optomotor performance is not a measure of motion detection.

When a locust is flying in a wind-tunnel with visual feedback, the experimenter is able to modify the timing between the wings, and therefore the turning tendency, by imposing a rotation in the visual flow field. The modification persists when the visual feedback is removed [35]. In locusts, the wind-sensitive hairs of the head also supply feedback about the asymmetry of the flight motor during forward flight. The feedback from the self-initiated movement is the essential contribution so that flight in a straight line can be considered as a kind of continually updated flight posture.

Bees flying towards a food source in a large rotating drum quickly learn to head directly towards a single food source, ignoring the drum motion. Inside the rotating drum they cannot discriminate between a black target that is absolutely stationary and one that moves with the drum, but they can distinguish between two targets of different colours and fly directly to the rewarded one [31, 33]. They show that they can switch off their optomotor response and rely on a fixation mechanism to fly on a straight path to a goal. The part played by saccades has not been studied in bees.

4. LEARNING THE LAYOUT OF THE 2D IMAGE

4.1. PATTERN DISCRIMINATION IN BEES

Bees are the outstanding insects for the analysis of two-dimensional pattern vision because they fly freely into all kinds of experimental situations for a reward, they recognize the local landmarks, and they take cues from a pattern around a goal. The more they need water and sugar, the faster they learn and return for more reward. They have "spontaneous" preferences when given a choice; they make discriminations in a learning situation, and finally, having learned to choose between two or more patterns, they reveal preferences and errors when presented with a related but different set of patterns.

4.2. APPARENTLY PECULIAR VISION

In 1875, ignoring the fact that contrasts also move across the retina in camera-type eyes, Exner [9] had proposed that insect vision is dominated by the temporal frequency of the flicker in each facet as the eye moves. The same idea must have influenced the theories of motion detection in insects referred to above [14, 40]. Temporal correlation is now inadequate to explain the 2D visual performance of large diurnal insects [49], but, curiously, has not been disproved in at least one situation, for *landing* bees. Sixty years ago, on the basis of numerous experiments, Mathilde Hertz [18, 19] followed with the same explanation, that reliance upon flicker induced by self-motion is the main factor in the bees' spontaneous preferences and in their frequent failures to learn to discriminate between black and white 2D patterns. The idea has therefore stuck in the literature, although Hertz also showed that other aspects of the pattern related to the form as a whole, and especially flower-like symmetry, are important for visual discriminations.

Progress was limited by the technique, which was to score the bees when they landed upon one of several targets placed on a flat table. This method has several disadvantages. The bees appear to be unable to relate their flight lines to the orientation of edges or contours below them. This would explain why they depend on temporal frequency, why they make many errors with patterns that are similarly disrupted but look quite different to us, and why they favour patterns with rotational symmetry. No wonder the results were puzzling; the activity of the bees influenced the result. Moreover, with landing on the target as the criterion of success, the image of the target expands continually as the bee approaches, so there is no way to estimate what features the bees use, and when finally landing the bees can see only the local detail around them. The experimental set-up limited the conclusions that could be drawn. This stage of data gathering was followed by a long pause before a new experimental design allowed an advance.

Although bees are attracted to flowers mainly by their colours and odours, flowers have different shapes and sizes that might help the bees to discriminate between them visually. Therefore black and white patterns have been used in many studies of bee vision.

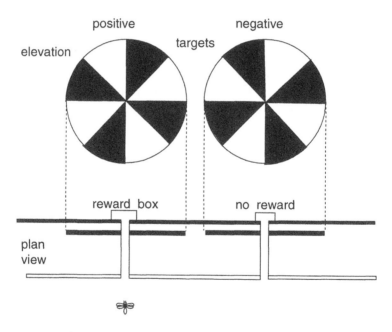

Figure 10. The apparatus used by Wehner to train and test the discrimination of pairs of shapes. The bees enter one of the two tubes to obtain a reward of sugar solution. The targets and the reward are interchanged at regular intervals to make the bees look at them. Before they enter a tube, the bees hover with the pattern subtending an angle of about 130° directly in front of them. They are able to distinguish a rotation of 45° of a single edge or of this sector pattern. Further details in [53, 54].

4.3. DECEPTIVELY NORMAL VISION

In 1967 Rüdiger Wehner [53, 54] introduced the idea of having a tube at a fixed distance in front of each pattern, which was presented on a vertical surface and subtended an angle of 130° at the tube entrance (Figure 10). Note this large angle. The patterns were regularly interchanged during the training and testing to make the bees use their eyes and ignore the location of the reward. This arrangement had the effect of making the bees face the pattern from a hovering position as they entered one of the tubes. They therefore had a vertical reference direction and a controlled visual angle at the decision point. We call these *fixating* bees, and they were able to discriminate between large black and white discs with different numbers of sectors, between two orientations of an edge differing by 45°, and they detected the rotation by 22.5° of a disc with 8 black and 8 white segments. This wave of discoveries suggested that bees have 2D vision of edge orientation rather like our own but with poorer resolution. The angles subtended at the eye were very large, and further tests with this apparatus show that bees rely on the locations of the outer parts of the patterns relative to the head as if they are landmarks (see Figures 13d and e).

4.4. LEARNING LANDMARKS ALONG THE ROUTE

On arrival, bees learn the colour, direction, and apparent size of the landmarks that they will later use to locate a target, and if rewarded they consolidate these cues into memory. On leaving a newly discovered reward, they turn back and look with a characteristic visual examination that combines lateral translation with fixation on the goal. Bees, and especially wasps, turn round and hover, pointing at the goal that they just visited [5]. Then they back away and move sideways, repeating this manoeuvre in a sequence of steps that take them progressively further away, but fixating on the goal from the same directions at different ranges [31]. This special form of active vision only makes sense if they estimate the distance of nearby landmarks in their relative places on the eye. The turn-back-and-look is elaborated in some wasps which fixate alternately on the goal and on the distant background as they back away. This procedure appears to relate local landmarks to more distant landmarks. Then, when the bee subsequently returns and orients itself to put the landmarks in these original positions [4], the flight line will point once again at the goal, whether or not the bee actually recognizes the 2D pattern. There is no suggestion here that bees learn the whole scene or build up an internal map of the landmarks laid out in two dimensions on the ground.

The learning and use of landmarks has been a topic of persistent controversy over the past decade. The present view is that bees recognize landmark colours, shapes, and sizes that they pass on their way to a goal, and that if taken and released at any point familiar to them, they know the correct compass direction to take them home or to the goal relative to the nearest landmarks, and they find the direction using their sky compass for that time of day [56]. If released in an unfamiliar place, they continue on their compass direction until they see a familiar landmark, which might be very large and far away. In addition, many insects, including bees, can integrate their outward path from the nest, however irregular it may be, as they forage for a considerable distance and then fly by the shortest route to home. If they are temporarily deflected away from the direct line as they head towards a goal, they can later adopt a direct track towards it [58]. Their performance shows that they can make some of the necessary dead reckoning calculations by integrating over their track, with a similar result to a knowledge of local geography, but there is little evidence that their knowledge of individual landmarks has been assembled into a comprehensive internal map for consultation later from any point on it [57, 58].

5. VISUAL DISCRIMINATIONS WITH A LIMITED NUMBER OF FILTERS

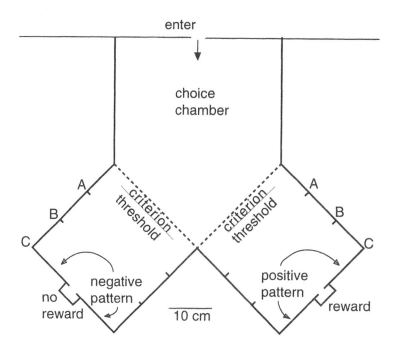

Figure 11. The Y-choice chamber for discrimination tests with flying bees. When the bees enter they see both targets at the same time. The criterion of their choice is counted when they first cross one of the thresholds marked as dashed lines. The targets (with the reward) are regularly interchanged during training and testing, and the criterion range can be varied by placing the targets at A, B or C. The percentage performances with this apparatus appear to represent the effectiveness of the visual discrimination filters.

5.1. ORIENTATION TUNING

In a new apparatus, the Y-choice maze (Figure 11), in which *flying* bees have to choose between two patterns seen at the same time, bees learn to discriminate between two single edges or two gratings of different orientations irrespective of pattern (Figure 12a). So that the bees do not learn the location of the reward, the rewarded

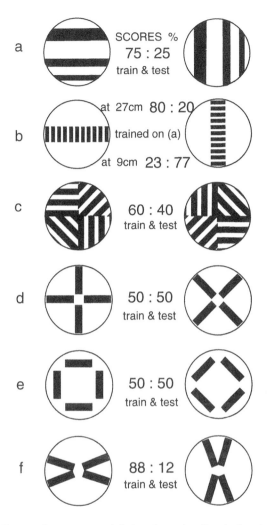

Figure 12. The performances of flying bees in discriminations between pairs of patterns. The rewarded target is on the left, although the two targets were interchanged at intervals during the training and tests. Average scores are taken from a number of publications, see below. (a) An orientation difference of 90° with spatial frequency randomized during the training is discriminated very well. (b) Having been trained on the patterns in (a), bees select the left target with a global view from a criterion distance of 27 cm, but the right target with a local view from 9 cm. (c) With four different orientations in each quadrant, bees can discriminate a rotation of 180°. (d) A + pattern cannot be discriminated from an x, even though the targets subtend 40° at the eye. (e) Four bars in a square cannot be distinguished from themselves rotated by 45°. (f) Discrimination is possible when there is a predominant orientation. Further details of (a) in [45, 50], of (b) in [61], of (c) in [60], of (d) and (f) in [45, 50].

pattern is regularly interchanged with the unrewarded one. The way to reveal the orientation as an invariant was to repeatedly change the spacing between the stripes during the training, but keep the edge orientation constant. This strategy introduced the idea of randomizing those features of a pattern that the bees were not to learn, and rewarding only the feature in question.

Bees are able to learn to discriminate between pairs of gratings or single edges differing in slope by 45°, and then they will generalize the rewarded (positive) orientation when tested on a different pair of patterns that they have not seen before [45, 50]. If presented with two new patterns, they will respond to the orientation as best they can [50, 61]. Orientation is learned irrespective of contrast reversal [45]. They also learn to avoid the unrewarded (negative) pattern, as shown by presenting a neutral pattern as an alternative.

5.2. PRIORITY OF GLOBAL OVER LOCAL FILTERS

Flying bees discriminate the predominant global orientation [61] with higher priority than the local orientation (Figure 12b), as if they have a family of broadly tuned filters with fields of different sizes and different preferred orientations that are modulated by the rotation of a bar or edge. The orientation detectors appear to see the predominant or average orientation and not to separate edges or bars that cross (Figure 12d). At first it was suggested [45, 50] that they simply sum the average orientation over the whole image (Figure 12f). Later work (see below) shows this theory to be untenable. There are signs that the size of the region of attention is under control, with priority given to the global orientation if there is one, rather than a local feature [26, 61]. By dividing the target into quadrants with different orientations of a grating in each (Figure 12c), Zhang and I [60] found that the size of the area over which the orientation is summed must be at least 15–20° and so does not cover the target. The area of attention is reduced from the whole visual field when looking at landmarks, down to about 40° by flying bees with a predominant orientation in the Y-choice apparatus, and then down to about 15° if no global filter is excited.

5.3. TARGETS WITH POLAR SYMMETRY

Discrimination is still possible between patterns that contain no predominant orientation. The cross in Figure 12d is readily discriminated from the square in Figure 12e although both have pairs of bars mutually at right angles. Radial patterns are discriminated from circular ones very well (Figure 13). Therefore orientations are not summed over the broad tuning curves of orientation detectors with fields covering the whole target.

When bees are trained to come to a chequered pattern of randomized unit size and orientation, and are then presented with a variety of other patterns that they had not seen before, they (apparently innately) prefer symmetrical radial patterns of bars and especially sectors, and they select against circular, asymmetrical, and random patterns [32]. They learn to discriminate very well either way round [27], between radial sectors and concentric circles (Figure 13a), and they distinguish either of these

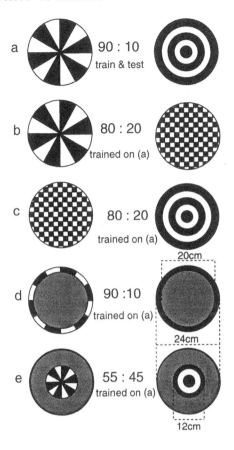

Figure 13. More discriminations in the Y-choice apparatus, all with the criterion distance set at 27 cm, with targets subtending 40° at the bees' eye. (a–c) show that the radial and circular patterns are separately distinguished. (a) Radial and circular patterns are readily discriminated irrespective of contrast reversal or spatial frequency (number of sectors or rings). (b) The rewarded pattern in (a) is preferred to a previously unseen chequered pattern, but (c) the chequered pattern is preferred to the previous negative pattern. (d) Removal of the centre of the target has little effect, but (e) removal of the periphery removes the discrimination.

equally well from a chequered pattern (Figure 13b and c). The training and tests can be done with randomized spatial frequencies. When trained on a sector and a circle pattern, bees can generalize these shapes when tested with similar but not identical patterns, such as the difference between the cross in Figure 12d and the square in Figure 12e, irrespective of rotation.

As there is no predominant orientation in any of these patterns as a whole, the results show that bees do not simply sum orientations, but they must have additional filters. As suggested by the results in Figure 13b and 13c, the minimum number is two types that resemble radial sectors and concentric circles. The model of discrimination also requires that the absence of a pattern can be detected. The high performance (Figure 13a), the innate preferences for flower-like patterns, and the recognition of random patterns [32] show that these filters are not arbitrary choices. All the evidence suggests that numerous local orientation detectors with different field sizes and preferred orientations act in specific combinations for each radially or bilaterally symmetrical pattern.

We have already seen that visual processing filters gain priority when they detect global rather than local features (Figure 12b). The results in Figures 12d, 12e further suggest that the global detectors of polar symmetry inhibit the local orientation detectors, so that bees cannot discriminate between a St. George's cross (+) and a St. Andrew's cross (×), even when they both subtend 40° at the eye. These patterns would strongly excite the global radial filter irrespective of rotation, and the square pattern in Figure 12e would excite the global circular filter irrespective of rotation.

Putting all these new results together, we have evidence that *flying* bees use a group of detectors in parallel for the degree of disruption [18, 19], another group for a signature of the predominant or average global orientation [50], another for a vertical axis of bilateral symmetry, and another for a signature of global polar symmetry (Figures 12 and 13). If these filters are not excited by large targets, then the bees pay attention to more local regions, as if they reduce the area of attention until a detector is excited. Together with filters for a colour signature, these spatial filters are independent of range, and being broadly tuned and overlapping they respond to various intermediate patterns in various combinations and ratios [21]. The form filters would detect a predominant orientation difference on backgrounds of other orientations or random textures, and a flower-like pattern would show symmetry contrast on a background of an irregular texture. Psychophysical observations on man suggest, and single neuron recordings on monkeys demonstrate, that similar neurons with radially symmetrical fields responding to similar patterns in polar co-ordinates, occur in the visual cortex of primates [12]. Bees also discriminate the angle subtended by a target at the eye and even absolute target size [28], so they must be able to measure and remember the angular separation of contrasts on the eye and also the ranges of objects [47] irrespective of pattern or motion, as we know that they do in their use of landmarks [4].

5.4. A WAY TO MODEL 2D DISCRIMINATIONS

Whether or not there are other form detectors feeding into the visual memory of the bee, we can say something about what bees see from their on-line visual control of flight. We can also say that they *see and remember* some features that excited or passed their visual filters in various proportions. Now we need a convenient and economical way of thinking how the outputs of several broad-field filters can act together to yield pattern discriminations. But in vision we already have a simple model which has long been in use, namely, that for colour discrimination in man and bee. In the colour triangle model of colour discrimination (Figure 14), the spectral sensitivities of the bees' three receptor types are arranged at the corners of a triangle. All the colours that they discriminate are then represented by the ratios of the responses of these three at each small area within the triangle. The sizes and therefore the numbers of these small areas depend on the signal/noise level (Figure 15). Each

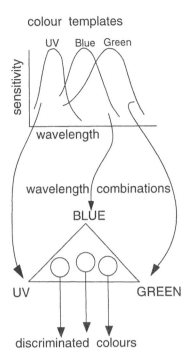

Figure 14. The way that colour discrimination is modeled as a triangle with one broad spectral filter of a receptor type at each corner. The different regions within the triangle then represent different ratios of the responses of the three receptor types. Discriminations are possible between regions of the triangle that have separate outputs.

colour signature is represented in Figure 14 by a circle which has a separate output, representing a different choice. A discrimination between two targets is possible when their signatures differ. As confirmed by discrimination tests, many different mixtures of wavelengths can yield the same colour because the spectral sensitivity curves are broad. Just as green for us can be a pure green or a mixture of blue and yellow, the exact mix of the inputs is not recovered at a discrimination. Colour is discriminated by bees more or less irrespective of brightness, contrast, range, motion, orientation, pattern, or flicker rate.

Similarly, in this method of representation, the *orientation signature* lies in a triangle (Figure 16) which has at its corners the minimum three orientations at 60° to each other which were proposed by Srinivasan et al. [45, 50]. Many different mixtures of orientation can yield the same orientation signature, and the predominant orientation is discriminated irrespective of brightness, contrast, range, colour, motion, or flicker. The tuning curves of the orientation detectors are broad, and separate orientations within their fields are not recoverable, but this cannot be the whole reason why bees fail to discriminate the rotation of a right-angled cross by 45°.

Similarly, the *symmetry signature* lies in a triangle with radial, circular, and random (flicker or disruption) at its corners (Figure 17), and it relates to various

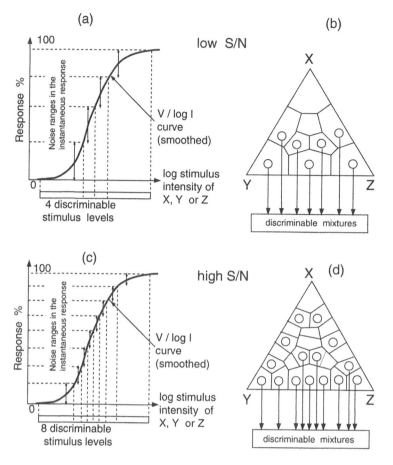

Figure 15. The way that noise limits the number of discriminations in coarse vector processing. (a) In this example, there is so much noise in the instantaneous response that the $V/\log I$ curve can be divided into only four distinguishable levels of the stimulus. (b) The noisy channel in (a) allows only a few discriminations of mixtures of X, Y and Z. (c) With a better signal/noise ratio there are more distinguishable levels of the stimulus. (d) The less noisy channel in (c) allows more mixtures to be discriminated.

ratios of how much of these types of pattern are detected, not to the individual parts of the image. Discriminations are possible when the symmetry signatures differ. Patterns that excite different proportions of radial, circular and random filters will therefore be discriminated irrespective of brightness, contrast, range, colour, motion, or flicker.

On the basis of this model, there is a non-trivial difference between what the bees see and what they can discriminate. They cannot discriminate the patterns in Figures 12d and 12e, from themselves rotated by 45°, but they see them, as shown by their ability to discriminate the patterns in 12d from those in 12e.

A totally different non-directional motion system in parallel measures the range

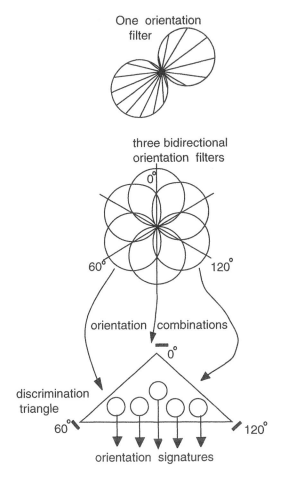

Figure 16. A way to think about orientation discrimination. (a) As in Figure 14, discrimination can be modeled as a triangle, but with orientations 60° apart at each corner. Different points within the triangle represent different ratios of the orientation filter outputs, and register the orientation signatures. These filters could be neurons with oriented fans of dendrites in the hexagonal pattern of columns of neurons of the medulla of the optic lobe.

of the target irrespective of intensity, contrast, orientation, colour, or pattern (Figures 3 and 4). There is also a directional optomotor response, unrelated to discrimination. The basic mechanism of vision is therefore a number of different channels, each composed of a family of neurons at each successive level (Figure 2). Each neuron and family acts as a separate set of filters. This design seems to be adapted to the necessary economy in all visual systems, because combinatorial spatial vision requires an enormous number of reduplicated local units in the early stages, and these are utilized in common by subsequent combinations of more specific detectors. Of course, for lack of detailed neuronal anatomy and experiments at that level, we have no idea how the mechanisms of learning and discrimination actually work in neuronal terms.

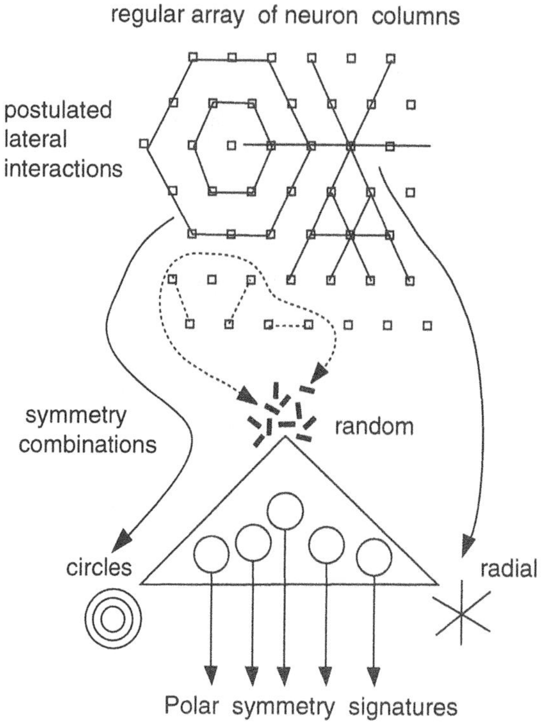

Figure 17. A way to think about discrimination of patterns that are symmetrical about a point and have no predominant orientation. Three filters for radial, circular and disruption (flicker) or random texture patterns originate in hypothetical neurons that arise in the columns of the medulla. As before, three types of feature detectors feed into the corners of a triangle that has numerous discriminations as outputs. These particular filters are the simplest that fit the performance of the bee. This signature would work together with that in Figure 16, so that, if there are no other filters, all of the available form discrimination originally represented in six filters in separate dimensions for each region of the image is digested into a single decision. Recent work replaces the random filter by one for bilateral symmetry about a vertical axis.

5.5. Advantages of global vision

In all the discrimination tests, the patterns subtend a very large angle at the eye of the bee at the moment of decision; in *landing* bees the angle is near 180°, in fixating bees (Figure 10) it was 130°, and in our experiments (Figures 12 and 13) it is about 40°. As in man, the global form has a higher priority than the local features. When we removed the central part of the target in the tests (Figure 13d) we found that the bees could discriminate as well as before, but removal of the outer region of the pattern in the tests spoils the performance (Figure 13e). This unexpected result in fact makes a great deal of sense for a flying bee approaching a goal. There is no need to look at 2D patterns along the route if coarse landmarks will do, no need to look at the actual pattern of the goal if the landmarks lead the way towards it [4, 30], and no need to remember the form of the central region if the outer parts of the target act as landmarks as the bee approaches. By using contrasts on the largest available scale, merely to point in the right direction, the signal/noise ratio is increased [10], and simple geometry shows the advantage of being guided by the largest and most distantly separated parts of the image.

5.6. CONTROL OF VISUAL RESPONSES

At every level, from receptors through the optic lobe to the brain and ventral cord (Figure 2), there is always a group of simultaneously activated neurons. At each stage in the visual processing, the coding of the excitation can be considered as a weighting of the responses within and between the separate groups of neurons. At each synaptic staging post, a different weighting, in some cases incorporating memories, is passed on to another group of neurons at the next level. Similar specific combinations must be available for the pathway that activates memory as well as for recognizing familiar incoming signatures. The assembly of active neurons that descend the ventral cord at each response finally act in concert, with weighting that is appropriate to other activities, upon the groups of interconnected premotor interneurons of the motor centres [42]. Here, in the ganglia of the thorax, the complete and internally self-consistent task-oriented motor acts are initiated or continued for each combination of visual, proprioceptor, and mechanoreceptor inputs [3].

In all of the responses mentioned, the visual performance is closely dependent on the spontaneous activity of the insect at the time. The visual processing depends on whatever image presents itself, but it selects those features that are demanded by the goal-directed behaviour. Vision is therefore adapted to the useful physical properties of the visual world, especially the invariance of certain features such as intensity, contrast, colour, contrast frequency, orientation, and symmetry, irrespective of exact range. The motor output is also an integral part of the seeing process, often generating an essential visual feedback. The control of straight flight illustrates the principles there. The visual processing mechanism is informed internally about the insects activity at every moment, so that non-appropriate processing can be switched off.

6. CONCLUSIONS

6.1. THE BEE'S MINIMAL ROUTE FINDER

Putting ourselves in the place of the bee, we use our sun compass [4] to lead us in the direction of the reward, aided by a few large landmarks [56] and using our obstacle avoidance system [47, 48] on-line all the time (Figures 3 and 4). By placing ourselves relative to the local landmarks in the vicinity of the goal [30], we point ourselves towards the right direction. As we approach it, the target grows in size but we do not look for the goal: we use its outer edges (Figure 13d) like landmarks. We do not necessarily see any objects as such, only their different ranges induced by our own self-motion. The radial and circular filters now respond to symmetrical shapes and centre our track, but there is still little need to look at the goal. In fact, the region dead ahead is not very informative for pattern vision, because it moves little and expands all the time. The orientation detectors provide an orientation signature that is independent of range and is essential for planning the landing.

On the other hand, when attracted to the Y-choice apparatus by a stronger sugar solution, we are forced to pay attention to both of the two-dimensional patterns from a distance of 27 cm because they are continually interchanged (Figure 7). However, we still pay little attention to the region around the goal (Figure 13d) and require only one useful cue. At some point we switch from using landmarks to fixation on a goal. Only at a close approach, we might actually use the two dimensional pattern around the goal, but that fundamental point is not certainly demonstrated, because we might use only one feature of it as a final landmark. The distinction between landmarks and pattern is not a philosophical quibble if we define landmarks as contrasts with direction and range, but pattern vision as essentially requiring filters with two spatial dimensions. Which is used at any one time has to be determined by experiment.

6.2. TASK-ORIENTED VISION

So, summing up, although bees have certain 2D filters, there is no evidence that they put a copy of the image into memory area by area for consultation later, which would be a very inefficient way to digest and retain the mass of mostly irrelevant visual detail. Maps of every pixel are ruled out. A great volume of work on the bee shows that the useful visual cues depend on the activity of the bee [43], the nature of the image at any one time, and the visual feedback that the bee gets from its own activity. While on-line vision for the control of manoeuvres by a variety of visual motor reflexes continues in the background and is not coded into memory, the bees retain a coded version of locations of contrasts at large angles and of selected signatures that are based on colour, orientation of edges, responses of radial and circular filters, angular size, and amount of flicker caused by self-motion. The codes in memory become less temporary when they are rewarded, and they last for days. If we model the six spatial filters that we have inferred and then scan the experimental targets and natural visual scenes with them all simultaneously, we could predict the bees' performance and eventually make an artificial seeing system to perform as well as the bee. The hard fact is, however, that this kind of vision is very task-oriented, and to be useful the filters have to fit the visual task, not only in their shape but also in their tolerances, or widths of their tuning curves. We have seen how bee vision is adapted to visiting flowers. Only some of the tasks for robots, like discriminating between hosepipe and buckets or fruit and leaves, are similar to visual tasks of bees, so how can our findings be useful for engineers? The filters would have to be matched to the tasks in hand, but the valuable principle which emerges is that natural visual systems are built with *broadly-tuned, overlapping fields in parallel* (Figures 14, 16, and 17), and the remarkable invariances and versatility of discrimination vision come from taking ratios with different weightings of their responses within the regions of field overlap. As in colour vision, the taking of signatures which are the ratios of responses of numerous dedicated neurons in parallel eliminates the stimulus variables that influence the input filters equally, and stores the relative differences in an economical code in fewer dimensions [60]. The effectiveness of the whole system depends on the critical interaction between the visual world and the filter properties, which for bees means that flower shapes must have evolved to fit the already well established principles of active insect vision.

ACKNOWLEDGMENTS

Many of the experiments described are part of a series in which several close colleagues including Dr. M. Srinivasan, Dr. S.W. Zhang, and Dr. M. Lehrer (Zürich) have participated in recent years. Ideas about neuronal mechanisms have also come from the patient work of L. Marcelja on the bee. Professor Horridge is a University Fellow and Visiting Fellow of the Centre for Visual Science, Australian National University. Funds for work on object vision in insects came from the Fujitsu Co. of Japan, and we thank them for their support.

REFERENCES

1. N.J. Bidwell and L.J. Goodman, "Possible functions of a population of descending neurons in the honeybee's visuo-motor pathway," *Apidologie* **24**, 1993, 333–354.

2. A. Bouzerdoum, "The elementary movement detection mechanism in insect vision," *Phil. Trans. Royal Society of London B* **339**, 1993, 375–384.

3. M. Burrows, "Local circuits for the control of leg movements in an insect," *Trends in Neurosciences* **15**, 1992, 226–232.

4. T.S. Collett, "Landmark learning and guidance in insects," *Phil. Trans. Royal Society of London B* **337**, 1992, 295–303.

5. T. Collett and M. Lehrer, "Looking and learning: A spatial pattern in the orientation flight of the wasp *Vespa vulgaris*," *Proceedings of the Royal Society of London B* **252**, 1993, 129–134.

6. T. Collett, H.-O. Nalbach, and H. Wagner, "Visual stabilization in arthropods," in F.A. Miles and J. Wallman (Eds.), *Visual Motion and its Role in the Stabilization of Gaze*, Elsevier, Amsterdam, 1993.

7. T.S. Collett and C.J. Patterson, "Relative motion parallax and target localization in the locust," *J. Comp. Physiol.* **A169**, 1991, 615–621.

8. C.T. David, "Mechanisms of directional flight in wind," in T. Payne, M. Birch, and J.S. Kennedy (Eds.), *Mechanisms in Insect Olfaction*, Oxford University Press, Oxford, 1986, 53–69.

9. S. Exner, "Über das Sehen von Bewegungen und die Theorie des zusammengestzten Auges," *Sitzb. Akad. Wiss. Wien, Abt. III* **72**, 1875, 156–170.

10. D.J. Field, "Relations between the statistics of natural images and the response properties of cortical cells," *Journal of the Optical Society of America* **A4**, 1987, 2379–2394.

11. N. Franchencini, A. Riehle, and A. Le Nestour, "Directionally-selective motion detection by insect neurons," in D.G. Stavenga and R.C. Hardie (Eds.), *Facets of Vision*, Springer, Berlin, 1989, 360–390.

12. J.L. Gallant, J. Braun, and D.C. Van Essen, "Selectivity for polar, hyperbolic and Cartesian gratings in macaque visual cortex," *Science* **259**, 1993, 100–103.

13. C. Gilbert and N.J. Strausfeld, "The functional organization of male-specific visual neurons in flies," *J. Comp. Physiol.* **A169**, 1991, 395–411.

14. B. Hassenstein and W. Reichardt, "Systemtheoretische analyse der Zeit-, Reihenfolgen- und Vorzeichenauswertung bei der Bewegungsperzeption des Rüsselkäfers," *Chlorophanus. Zeit. Naturforsch.* **31c**, 1956, 629–633.

15. K. Hausen, "Monocular and binocular computation of motion in the lobula plate of the fly," *Verhandl. Deutsch. Zool. Gesellschaft*, 1981, 49–70.

16. M. Heisenberg and R. Wolf, "Visual control of straight flight in *Drosophila melanogaster*," *J. Comp. Physiol.* **A167**, 1990, 269–283.

17. M. Heisenberg and R. Wolf, "The sensory-motor link in motion-dependent flight control of flies," in F.A. Miles and J. Wallman (Eds.), *Visual Motion and Its Role in the Stabilization of Gaze*, Elsevier Science Publishers, Amsterdam, 1993, 265–283.

18. M. Hertz, "Die Organisation des optischen Feldes bei der Biene," *Z. vergl. Physiol.* **8**, 693–748; ibid. **11**, 107–145; ibid. **14**, 629–674, 1929–1931.

19. M. Hertz, "Die Untersuchungen über den Formensinn der Honigbiene," *Naturwiss.* **23**, 1935, 618–624.

20. G.A. Horridge, "The separation of visual axes in apposition compound eyes," *Phil. Trans. Royal Society of London B* **285**, 1978, 1–59.

21. G.A. Horridge, "Ratios of template responses as the basis for semivision," *Phil. Trans. Royal Society of London B* **331**, 1991, 189–198.

22. G.A. Horridge and L. Marcelja, "Responses of the H1 neuron of the fly to contrast and moving bars," *Phil. Trans. Royal Society of London B* **329**, 1990, 75–80.

23. G.A. Horridge and L. Marcelja, "Responses of the H1 neuron to jumped edges," *Phil. Trans. Royal Society of London B* **329**, 1990, 65–73.

24. G.A. Horridge and L. Marcelja, "A test for multiplication in insect directional motion-detectors," *Phil. Trans. Royal Society of London B* **331**, 1991, 199–204.

25. G.A. Horridge and L. Marcelja, "On the existence of 'fast' and 'slow' directionally sensitive motion detector neurons in insects," *Proceedings of the Royal Society of London B* **248**, 1992, 47–54.

26. G.A. Horridge, "Bee vision of pattern and 3D," *Bioessays* **16**, 1995, 877–884.

27. G.A. Horridge and S.W. Zhang, "Pattern vision in honeybees (*Apis mellifera*): Flower-like patterns with no predominant orientation," *Journal of Insect Physiology* **41**, 1995, 681–688.

28. G.A. Horridge, S.W. Zhang, and M. Lehrer, "Bees can combine range and visual angle to estimate absolute size," *Phil. Trans. Royal Society of London B* **337**, 1992, 49–57.

29. M.F. Land, "Head movements and fly vision," in G.A. Horridge (Ed.), *The Compound Eye and Vision of Insects*, Oxford University Press, Oxford, 1975, 469–489.

30. M. Lehrer, "How bees use peripheral eye regions to localize a frontally positioned target," *J. Comp. Physiol.* **A167**, 1990, 173–185.

31. M. Lehrer, "Spatial vision in the honey bee: the use of different cues in different tasks," *Vision Res.* **34**, 1994, 2363–2385.

32. M. Lehrer, G.A. Horridge, S.W. Zhang, and R. Gadagkar, "Pattern vision in bees: Preference for radial patterns," *Phil. Trans. Royal Society of London B*, 1994 (Submitted).

33. M. Lehrer and M.V. Srinivasan, "Freely flying bees discriminate between stationary and moving objects: Performance and possible mechanisms," *J. Comp. Physiol.* **A171**, 1992, 457–467.

34. U. Lönnendonker and H. Scharstein, "Fixation and optomotor response of walking Colorado beetles: Interaction with spontaneous turning tendencies," *Physiological Entomology* **16**, 1991, 65–76.

35. B. Möhl, "Short-term learning during flight control in *Locusta migratoria*," *J. Comp. Physiol.* **A163**, 1988, 803–812.

36. D. Osorio, "The temporal properties of non-linear transient cells in the locust medulla," *J. Comp. Physiol.* **A161**, 1987, 431–440.

37. T. Poggio and W. Reichardt, "Visual control of orientation in the fly. Part II. Towards the underlying neural interactions," *Quart. Rev. Biophys.* **9**, 1976, 377–438.

38. R. Preiss, "Separation of translation and rotation by means of eye-region specialization in flying gypsy moths (Lepidoptera: Lymantriidae)," *J. Insect Behav.* **4**, 1991, 209–219.

39. T. Quenzer and J.M. Zenker, "Visual detection of paradoxical motion in flies," *J. Comp. Physiol.* **A169**, 1991, 331–340.

40. W. Reichardt, "Autocorrelation: a principle for evaluation of sensory information by the central nervous system," in W.A. Rosenblith (Ed.), *Principles of Sensory Communication*, Wiley, New York, 1961, 303–317.

41. S. Rossel, "Binocular spatial localization in the praying mantis," *J. Exp. Biol.* **120**, 1986, 265–281.

42. C.H.F. Rowell and H. Reichert, "Mesothoracic interneurons involved in flight steering in the locust," *Tissue and Cell* **23**, 1991, 75–139.

43. E.C. Sobel, "The locust's use of motion parallax to measure distance," *J. Comp. Physiol.* **A167**, 1990, 579–588.

44. M.V. Srinivasan, "How insects exploit optic flow: Behavioural experiments and neural models," *Phil. Trans. Royal Society of London B* **337**, 1992, 253–259.

45. M.V. Srinivasan, "Pattern recognition in the honeybee: Recent progress," *J. Insect Physiol.* **40**, 1994, 183–194.

46. M.V. Srinivasan, M. Lehrer, and G.A. Horridge, "Visual figure-ground discrimination in the honeybee: The role of motion parallax at boundaries," *Proceedings of the Royal Society of London B* **238**, 1990, 331–350.

47. M.V. Srinivasan, M. Lehrer, S.W. Zhang, and G.A. Horridge, "How honeybees measure their distance from objects of unknown size," *J. Comp. Physiol.* **A165**, 1989, 605–613.

48. M.V. Srinivasan, S.W. Zhang, and K. Chandrashekara, "Evidence for two distinct movement detecting mechanisms in insect vision," *Naturwissenschaften* **80**, 1993, 38–41.

49. M.V. Srinivasan, S.W. Zhang, and B. Rolfe, "Is pattern vision in insects mediated by 'cortical' processing?" *Nature, London* **362**, 1993, 539–540.

50. M.V. Srinivasan, S.W. Zhang, and K. Witney, "Visual discrimination of pattern orientation by honeybees," *Phil. Trans. Royal Society of London B* **343**, 1994, 199–210.

51. G. Stange, "The ocellar component of flight equilibrium control in dragonflies," *J. Comp. Physiol.*, **141**, 1981, 335–347.

52. R.J. Watt, "Scanning from coarse to fine spatial scales in the human visual system after the onset of a stimulus," *Journal of the Optical Society of America* **A4**, 1987, 2006–2021.

53. R. Wehner, "Pattern recognition in bees," *Nature, London* **215**, 1967, 1244–1248.

54. R. Wehner, "Pattern modulation and pattern detection in the visual systems of Hymenoptera," in R. Wehner (Ed.), *Information Processing in the Visual Systems of Arthropods*, Springer, Berlin, 1972, 183–194.

55. R. Wehner, "'Matched filters'—neural models of the external world," *J. Comp. Physiol.* **A161**, 1987, 511–531.

56. R. Wehner, "The hymenopteran skylight compass: Matched filtering and parallel coding," *J. Exp. Biol.* **146**, 1989, 63–85.

57. R. Wehner, "Do insects have cognitive maps?" *Annu. Rev. Neurosciences* **13**, 1990, 403–414.

58. R. Wehner, S. Bleuler, C. Nievergelt, and D. Shah, "Bees navigate by using vectors and routes rather than maps," *Naturwissenchaften* **77**, 1990, 479–482.

59. M. Wilson, "The functional organisation of locust ocelli," *J. Comp. Physiol.* **124**, 1978, 297–316.

60. S.W. Zhang and G.A. Horridge, "Pattern recognition in bees: Size of regions in spatial lay-out," *Phil. Trans. Royal Society of London B* **337**, 1992, 65–71.

61. S.W. Zhang, M.V. Srinivasan, and G.A. Horridge, "Pattern recognition in honeybees: Local and global analysis," *Proceedings of the Royal Society of London B* **248**, 1992, 55–61.

Understanding Noise Sensitivity in Structure from Motion

Kostas Daniilidis[1] and Minas E. Spetsakis[2]
[1]University of Kiel
[2]York University

Abstract

Solutions to the structure from motion problem have been shown to be very sensitive to measurement noise and the respective motion and geometry configuration. Statistical error analysis has become an invaluable tool in analyzing the sensitivity phenomenon. This paper presents a unifying approach to the problems of statistical bias, correlated noise, choice of error metrics, geometric instabilities, and information fusion, exploring several assumptions commonly used in motion estimation. It reviews several promising techniques for motion estimation. The techniques are based on a small number of principles of statistics and perturbation theory. The analyticity of the approach should enable the design of alternatives for dealing with the observed instabilities.

1. Introduction

The problem of estimating structure and motion from moving sequences of images has been attacked by the research community in three stages. The first stage was to answer the question of existence of a solution. This question was answered in the early eighties with algorithms such as those by Longuet-Higgins [42] and independently by Tsai and Huang [62] for the discrete case, and by Prazdny and Longuet-Higgins [44] and Waxman and Wohn [63] for the differential case. A unique solution was proven to exist and algorithms were developed to find it. The algorithms were practically closed form, simple and easy to implement. Unbeknown to the computer vision community very similar problems had been solved in the context of photogrammetry earlier this century and summarized in standard literature [52].

The second stage was to discover practical algorithms that work under realistic situations where noise is present. The first attempts to solve the problem were frustrated by high sensitivity to noise. Opinions in the research community ranged from the pessimistic (that the problem is unsolvable), to the optimistic (that a few simple heuristics would be sufficient to obtain a general solution). In fact photogrammetrists do have practical algorithms for their needs but these are not directly applicable to most computer vision problems. They depend on extremely high quality cameras, quite often film cameras, and they depend on human intervention to guide the matching process and to take the image sequence. In order for structure from motion to become a general purpose tool, it has to be able to work with general-purpose cameras that have very limited resolution, work quickly on inexpensive computers, and do it with almost no human intervention.

The limited resolution and low quality of the output of ordinary video cameras exaggerates the instabilities in the algorithms for the recovery of structure and motion. Two interrelated problems here are the the possibility of more than one solution (the ambiguity problem) under certain viewing circumstances (e.g., when viewing a plane) and the noise instabilities. By itself the ambiguity problem is not so interesting because such situations are highly improbable (a perfect plane with no visible features outside the plane in the whole scene is rare). But being near an ambiguous configuration in not improbable and the definition of nearness becomes more inclusive when the noise level increases. The result is increased noise sensitivity, especially when the spurious solution is very close to the real one.

Noise sensitivity is usually expressed as a high variance (mean square difference between the ground truth and the estimate) or a bias (mean difference between the ground truth and the estimate). One approach to the problem is to design algorithms to minimize the effects of noise by using a form of constrained minimization [28, 32]; use statistical estimation [55, 60, 64]; analyze the behavior of the error in a wide variety of configurations [2, 16, 17]; analyze the Cramer-Rao lower bound (CRLB) of the estimation [68]; study the effects of bias and devise tools to reduce it [35]; etc. Most of this work has been collected and presented in a recent book by Kanatani [33].

Other approaches include the direct methods [11, 20, 21, 50] that avoid the first step of computing a form of displacement field (flow or correspondence), the subspace methods [25] that provide a solution involving little more than a set of convolutions, and the decoupling methods [61] where the estimation of structure and motion is decoupled using singular value decomposition (SVD).

Yet another approach involves features at a level higher than points. Lines were such a feature that produced a great deal of interest. At first, nonlinear algorithms appeared that could not guarantee unique solutions [41], but later with linearized algorithms it was possible to get unique solutions almost always [59]. The question whether there exists such a linearized algorithm that can use both lines and points was answered positively [54]. When using both points and lines three frames are needed because lines alone provide no constraint for motion with two frames. Even used with points alone this method has the advantage of fewer ambiguous configurations. The reason is that an ambiguous configuration with two frames, let us say the first and second frame, will have spurious solutions that are almost always different from the spurious solutions obtained from the first and third frames. Thus the likelihood of a particular configuration being very close to an ambiguous one is much lower than when dealing with two frames. Unfortunately, while there exist detailed analyses for the ambiguous configurations for two frames there is very little for three frames.

In most approaches the motion estimation involves two steps. The first step uses as input the image sequence itself and produces a displacement field in the form of discrete point (or feature) correspondences or an optical flow field. The flow field has to be accompanied by a representation of the expected error because it is not possible to have reliable dense measurements of the flow over the whole image. Thus a set of discrete correspondences can be considered as a flow field containing data only at places where the certainty of the flow vectors is high or locally maximal. In most literature the flow is considered small, typically a fraction of a pixel and the term discrete displacement field is preferred when the flow is higher than that. The second step consists of the estimation of the motion parameters (rotation and translation) in the form of finite displacements (a vector for the translation and a matrix for the rotation) or infinitesimal displacements (linear and angular velocities). There are algorithms that work either with flow, producing infinitesimal displacements, or with discrete matches, producing finite motion. In terms of noise sensitivity and instability, the two general approaches are qualitatively equivalent and they differ mainly in the clarity with which different ideas can be presented. In this chapter we are going to use the one most appropriate for each case.

The preferred approach in the study of noise sensitivity is to use analytical rather than numerical tools because of the greater freedom they provide. Simple analytical expressions provide direct insight and more complicated ones can be plotted with various parameters.

The third stage is about how to use the output in conjunction with other perceptual information or cognitive processes to achieve intelligent behavior. As mentioned above, the success of the photogrammetric approach is partially due to the intelligent gathering of the data (image sequences) by a skilled operator. An autonomous robotic system has to incorporate techniques that are known as *active vision* [6] to collect data that are more reliable. A great contributor to the mistrust of structure from motion algorithms for real applications comes from the fact that their worst case behavior is very bad. Using some intelligence in the gathering of data, the worst case situations may be avoided. As shown in [6], several ill-posed problems become tractable using this paradigm. A related approach is *purposive vision* [4], where instead of computing the whole structure and motion representation, we compute only the part that is meaningful to the specific purpose of the system in consideration. This paradigm holds great promise for increasing the efficiency of autonomous systems and reducing their complexity [38].

The progress of structure from motion cannot be separated from the progress of establishing one or another form of correspondence. The most impressive progress has come from the area of flow computation. Several novel techniques have been proposed in the past several years, each one with different advantages and shortcomings. Many of these techniques can be combined with often good results. One of the oldest and simplest techniques by Lucas and Kanade [45] was recently found to outperform most other sophisticated ones [9]. Among the techniques that show great promise when combined and which are flexible enough to be combined are: the venerable smoothness constraints [29, 48] that, although they do not provide much stability by themselves, tend to be easy to combine; the hierarchical (or coarse to fine) methods [7], that can help increase the range over which flow can be computed; the statistical techniques proposed by Singh [51] that can relax the Gaussian noise assumption; the affine models of flow that relax the assumption of locally uniform motion [13, 66]; the phase-based methods that work exceptionally well [22] although they are computationally expensive; etc. While flow is usually associated with algorithms having instantaneous linear and angular velocity input, it can be used with any algorithm including the ones that accept as input discrete point correspondences. Using hierarchical techniques, flow can be computed between images that have much more than one pixel displacement [56].

This chapter is divided into two parts. In the first part we study analytically motion and geometry configurations that yield noise sensitive 3D information. We present our results and compare them with recent approaches [25, 31]. In the second part, we try to overcome some of the instabilities of the first part by paying special attention to the statistical terms of bias and variance. Then, we unify our approach by treating both point and line correspondences in the same way. Last, we analyze the case of recovering the motion parameters from statistically correlated displacement fields.

2. ERROR ANALYSIS OF MOTION ESTIMATION

The goal of error analysis is, given the noise level in the measurements, to predict with statistical measures or bounds the error in the motion and depth estimates. These error measures may be computed in closed form or numerically with an algorithm. They express the error in the computed parameters as a function of the true parameters and the measurement noise. Studies like [2, 16, 68, 30, 34] belong to the first category because they contain explicit expressions with respect to the problem parameters. Analyses like those in [10, 40, 64] comprise a second category because they establish bounds or approximations of the estimate error which are computed by sampling the parameter space. Given an expression for the error in the estimate we first study if the error originates in the problem formulation and the algorithm used or if it is inherent in the problem. Since the ultimate goal of error analysis is to find less noise-sensitive solutions, we are particularly interested in explicit error expressions that will allow either correction of the problem formulation or active control of the parameter space. The results of the problem formulation—in particular, the form of the error metric—described below confirm the fact that the only way to avoid such error is to use the statistical analysis of motion estimation described in the statistical part of this chapter. The way to overcome the problem of inherent sensitivities by actively controlling a subset of the parameters is an object of *active vision* we will not describe here.

In this section we will use the instantaneous case because of the easier mathematical treatment due to the linear dependency on the rotational parameters and the presence of measurement noise on the motion field only. In discrete methods the noise can be assumed to corrupt the displacement or each point of the correspondence pair leading to different error measures.

Let an object be moving with translational velocity $V = (V_x, V_y, V_z)^T$ and angular velocity $\boldsymbol{\Omega} = (\Omega_x, \Omega_y, \Omega_z)^T$ relative to the camera. We denote by $\boldsymbol{X}$ the position of a point on the object with respect to the camera coordinate system and by $\boldsymbol{x} = (x, y, 1)^T$ its projection on the image plane $Z = 1$. The direction of the optical axis is given by the unit vector $\hat{\boldsymbol{z}}$. The motion field vector reads (from [50]):

$$\dot{\boldsymbol{x}} = \frac{1}{\hat{\boldsymbol{z}}^T \boldsymbol{X}} \hat{\boldsymbol{z}} \times (\boldsymbol{V} \times \boldsymbol{x}) + \hat{\boldsymbol{z}} \times (\boldsymbol{x} \times (\boldsymbol{x} \times \boldsymbol{\Omega})). \tag{1}$$

In the case of camera egomotion with the above velocities and a stationary environment, the above equation as well as all following equations have to be read with the opposite sign for $\boldsymbol{V}$ and $\boldsymbol{\Omega}$. As can be seen, due to the linear dependency on the angular velocity $\boldsymbol{\Omega}$ in (1) the error estimate in motion and depth does not depend on the rotational parameters. All the results into which we will delve concern the case of a small field of view. In particular, we will describe the following facts—proved by other authors or ourselves—that characterize the instability in the 3D motion estimation from two views:

- A translation can easily be confounded with a rotation in the case of a small field of view, lateral motion, and not sufficient depth variation [2, 17, 30].
- In the case of a small field of view the translation estimate is biased towards the viewing direction if the error metric is not appropriately normalized.
- In the case of a small field of view and an irregular surface the cost function to minimize takes its minima along a line in the space of translation directions that goes through the viewing direction and the true translation direction [30, 46]. If the region of interest is fixated this result implies that the azimuth angle of the translation direction can be estimated much more reliable than the polar angle.
- A relation exists between the critical surfaces causing an ambiguity and the critical surfaces causing an instability. This relation provides geometric hints for error sensitivity—among them the translation-rotation confusion mentioned above.

2.1. THE TRANSLATION-ROTATION CONFUSION

The motion field vector is the sum of two components, a translational component that carries the information about the environment and a rotational one (see also equation (1)). Motions almost parallel to the image plane and in the same direction—like the (V_x, Ω_y) and $(V_y, -\Omega_x)$ pairs—cause a confusion to the observer who cannot disambiguate whether a motion field is induced by translation or rotation (see Figure 1). This confounding becomes dominant if the field of view is small or if there is no depth variation in the environment. However, as already argued by other authors, one may robustly compute the amount of motion represented by the sum $V_x + \Omega_y$ and the difference $V_y - \Omega_x$ since they build the zeroth order terms regarding the motion field as a polynomial with respect to the image coordinates (x, y).

We will first describe the arguments of [30] and then delve into the Cramer-Rao bounds established in [17]. Given the motion field vectors $\dot{\boldsymbol{x}}_{i=1..l}$ in l points we summarize them into an observation vector $\boldsymbol{s}$ of dimension $2l$ and the unknown

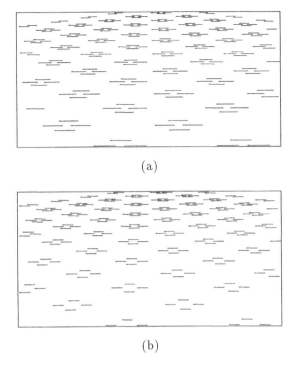

(a)

(b)

Figure 1. Pure translational (a) and pure rotational (b) motion field induced by V_x-translation and Ω_y-rotation, respectively. A large field of view allows the perception of the depth variation through the change of the flow magnitude in (a). A small field of view around the center contains almost identical fields in cases (a) and (b).

depths $Z_{i=1..l}$ into the vector of inverse depths $\boldsymbol{Z}$ of dimension l. We may write the measurement equations (1) for l points as

$$\boldsymbol{s} = C(\boldsymbol{V}) \begin{pmatrix} \boldsymbol{Z} \\ \boldsymbol{\Omega} \end{pmatrix} \qquad \text{with} \qquad C(\boldsymbol{V}) = \begin{pmatrix} A(\boldsymbol{V}) & B \end{pmatrix}, \qquad (2)$$

where

$$A(\boldsymbol{V}) = \begin{pmatrix} V_x - x_1 V_z & \dots & 0 \\ V_y - y_1 V_z & \dots & 0 \\ \vdots & & \vdots \\ 0 & \dots & V_x - x_l V_z \\ 0 & \dots & V_y - y_l V_z \end{pmatrix} \qquad B = \begin{pmatrix} -x_1 y_1 & 1 + x_1^2 & -y_1 \\ -(1 + y_1^2) & x_1 y_1 & x_1 \\ & \vdots & \\ -x_l y_l & 1 + x_l^2 & -y_l \\ -(1 + y_l^2) & x_l y_l & x_l \end{pmatrix}$$

are matrices of dimension $2l \times l$ and $2l \times 3$, respectively. According to [30] the necessary and sufficient condition for an observation vector $\boldsymbol{s}$ to be consistent with a translation $\boldsymbol{V}$ is that

$$\boldsymbol{s} \in \text{range}(C(\boldsymbol{V})). \qquad (3)$$

This condition is equivalent to the requirement that the observation vector $\boldsymbol{s}$ be orthogonal to every vector of the orthogonal complement of range$(C(\boldsymbol{V}))$. Since the orthogonal complement of the range of a matrix is equal to the null-space of the transpose of the matrix, we have

$$s^T \Psi(V) = 0 \qquad \text{for every} \qquad \Psi(V) \in \text{null}(C(V)^T). \qquad (4)$$

The Ψ-vectors are constructed as a linear combination $\sum_{i=1}^{l} c_i(V)\Phi_i(V)$ of l vectors $\Phi_i(V)$ spanning the null-space $\text{null}(A(V)^T)$ of the submatrix $A(V)^T$. The necessary and sufficient condition for $\Psi(V)$ to belong to $\text{null}(C(V)^T)$ is to annihilate the rotational component:

$$B^T \sum_{i=1}^{l} c_i(V)\Phi_i(V) = 0 \qquad \text{or} \qquad E(V) \begin{pmatrix} c_1 & \dots & c_l \end{pmatrix}^T = 0 \qquad (5)$$

with

$$E(V) = B^T \begin{pmatrix} \Phi_1 & \dots & \Phi_l \end{pmatrix}.$$

Hence, the problem is reduced to the computation of the null-space of $E(V)$. The degenerate case of deficient rank of $C(V)$ occurs if the $\Phi_i(V)$ are not independent—this implies that the focus of expansion, FOE, is at one of the points—or if the matrix $E(V)$ has rank less than three. In the latter case, it exists a configuration of depths and rotation $(Z', \Omega')^T$ such that $C(V)(Z', \Omega')^T = 0$. This means that there exists a rotation Ω' that induces a pure translational motion field:

$$B\Omega' = -A(V)Z'.$$

In case of a small field of view it can be proved that the induced depths are planar and the induced translation is perpendicular to the actual one [30].

We next proceed to show the confounding of the space of uncertainty directions as represented by the eigenspace of the Fisher information matrix. In order to reduce the number of the depth unknowns we sacrifice generality and assume that the perceived surface in motion is planar. Let the plane be given by the equation $N^T X = 1$ where $N = (N_x, N_y, N_z)^T$ has the direction of the normal to the plane and a magnitude equal to the inverse of the distance of the origin to the plane. Dividing by the depth we obtain $1/\hat{z}^T X = N^T x$, which we insert in equation (1):

$$\dot{x} = (N^T x)(\hat{z} \times (V \times x)) + \hat{z} \times (x \times (x \times \Omega)). \qquad (6)$$

Let p be the vector of unknown parameters—in our case motion parameters and the normal, but we will define them later—and $\mathcal{Z}$ be the set of all measurements—in our case all motion field vectors. The *Fisher information matrix* is defined as follows (from [53]):

$$F = E[\frac{\partial \ln p(\mathcal{Z}|p)}{\partial p}^T \frac{\partial \ln p(\mathcal{Z}|p)}{\partial p}], \qquad (7)$$

where $p(\mathcal{Z}|p)$ is the conditional probability density function. The uncertainty of an estimator $\hat{p}$ is given by its error covariance $E[(p-\hat{p})(p-\hat{p})^T]$. Following the Cramer-Rao inequality [53], the error covariance of an *unbiased* estimator is bounded from below by the inverse of the Fisher information matrix:

$$E[(p - \hat{p})(p - \hat{p})^T] \geq F^{-1}. \qquad (8)$$

The inequality of matrices means that the difference of the lhs (left-hand sides) minus the rhs (right-hand sides) is a positive semidefinite matrix. Since the diagonal elements of a positive semidefinite matrix are greater or equal to zero we can recover directly the scalar lower bounds for variances of the unknowns. However, the inverse of the Fisher information matrix provides much richer information about the most and least error sensitive directions in the parameter space. In the optimistic case of an efficient estimator, the uncertainty may be illustrated by the following uncertainty ellipsoid:

$$(\boldsymbol{p} - \hat{\boldsymbol{p}})^T F (\boldsymbol{p} - \hat{\boldsymbol{p}}) = c, \tag{9}$$

with the estimate being the center of the ellipsoid. The probability that the true value $\boldsymbol{p}$ lies inside the ellipsoid is given by the constant c, which geometrically expresses the stretching of the ellipsoid. The directions of the axes of symmetry of the ellipsoid are given by the eigenvectors of F. The lengths of the semi-axes are equal to $\sqrt{(c/\lambda)}$ where λ is the corresponding eigenvalue of F. The direction of the lowest uncertainty is given by the eigenvector corresponding to the largest eigenvalue of F—this is not a contradiction, if one recalls that the error covariance lower bound is equal to the inverse of F. This direction allows us to obtain insight into the question of which linear combinations of the unknown parameters (projections of the parameter vector onto subspaces) can be robustly estimated even if each parameter estimate for itself may have a high uncertainty.

The analytic computation of the Fisher information matrix requires a model of the probability density function of the measurements. We assume a Gaussian distribution for all measured motion field vectors, with zero mean and covariance equal to $\sigma^2 I$. Under the above assumptions it can be proved that the Fisher information matrix reads

$$F = \iint_{I_D} \frac{\partial \boldsymbol{h}^T}{\partial \boldsymbol{p}} \frac{\partial \boldsymbol{h}}{\partial \boldsymbol{p}} \, dx \, dy. \tag{10}$$

We assume a dense motion field over the domain D equal to the area of the projection of the environmental part moving relative to the camera, which we call the *effective field of view*. It is equal to the field of view in case of a stationary environment and egomotion of the camera. The measurement function $\boldsymbol{h}(\boldsymbol{p})$ of the motion field (1) is given by

$$\dot{\vec{x}} = D\boldsymbol{q} = \begin{pmatrix} 1 & x & y & 0 & 0 & 0 & x^2 & xy \\ 0 & 0 & 0 & 1 & x & y & xy & y^2 \end{pmatrix} \boldsymbol{q}$$

$$\text{with} \quad \boldsymbol{q} = (V_x N_z + \Omega_y, \; V_x N_x - V_z N_z, \; V_x N_y - \Omega_z,$$
$$V_y N_z - \Omega_x, \; V_y N_x + \Omega_z, \; V_y N_y - V_z N_z,$$
$$\Omega_y - V_z N_x, \; -V_z N_y - \Omega_x)^T.$$

We used a different symbol $\dot{\vec{x}}$ for the motion field vector in $\mathcal{R}^2$ in contrast to $\dot{\boldsymbol{x}}$ in (1), which belongs to $\mathcal{R}^3$ with the third component equal to zero.

The Jacobian $\partial \boldsymbol{q}/\partial \boldsymbol{p}$ is independent of the image coordinates, hence

$$F = \frac{\partial \boldsymbol{q}^T}{\partial \boldsymbol{p}} \left\{ \iint_{I_D} D^T D \, dx \, dy \right\} \frac{\partial \boldsymbol{q}}{\partial \boldsymbol{p}}. \tag{11}$$

We model the integration domain I_D—i.e., the effective field of view—as a rectangle placed in the image center with side lengths equal to α and β. The integral matrix

$$D_{\text{int}} = \iint_{I_D} D^T D \, dx \, dy \tag{12}$$

depends only on the size of the field of view and is a multiple of $\alpha\beta$. Thus, the error covariance is a monotonically decreasing function of the size of the effective field of view. Before we proceed with the computation of the Jacobian $\partial q / \partial p$ we must choose eight independent unknowns among the elements of V, Ω, and N. We assume that $N_z \neq 0$, which implies that the planar surface is not parallel to the optical axis, and we make the following substitutions: $N'_x = N_x / N_z$, $N'_y = N_y / N_z$, $V'_x = V_x / N_z$, $V'_y = V_y / N_z$, and $V'_z = V_z / N_z$. For the sake of simple expressions, we retain the unprimed symbols instead of the primed ones. The vector of independent unknown parameters then reads as follows:

$$p = \left(\begin{array}{cccccccc} V_x & V_y & V_z & \Omega_x & \Omega_y & \Omega_z & N_x & N_y \end{array} \right)^T .$$

Before we recover the inverse of the Fisher information matrix we compute its determinant:

$$\det(F) = \det^2 \left(\frac{\partial q}{\partial p} \right) \det(D_{\text{int}}).$$

After tediously adding and subtracting the rows of the Jacobian $\partial q / \partial p$ we obtain

$$\det \left(\frac{\partial q}{\partial p} \right) = \| N \times V \|^2 \tag{13}$$

which shows as expected that the case of parallel translation and normal causes a high uncertainty as the degenerate case of the merging of the two solutions to one [43]. We carry out the matrix multiplications in (11) and obtain

$$F = \left(\begin{array}{cc} K & L \\ L^T & M \end{array} \right) \tag{14}$$

where K, L, and M are 6×6, 6×2, and 2×2 matrices, respectively. In order to invert the Fisher information matrix computed in the last section we make use of the formula [23]

$$F^{-1} = \left(\begin{array}{cc} E^{-1} & -E^{-1}LM^{-1} \\ -M^{-1}L^T E^{-1} & M^{-1} + M^{-1}L^T E^{-1}LM^{-1} \end{array} \right) \tag{15}$$

$$\text{with} \quad E = \left(K - LM^{-1}L^T \right)$$

and F as in (14). The matrix E obtains the following block-diagonal form:

$$E = \left(\begin{array}{cc} E_{135} & 0 \\ 0 & E_{246} \end{array} \right), \tag{16}$$

if we set $V_y = 0$ and $N_y = 0$. This means that the translational velocity as well as the normal lie on the XZ plane. We introduce the angles ψ and χ between the optical axis and V and N, respectively:

$$V = \begin{pmatrix} V_x & 0 & V_z \end{pmatrix} = \begin{pmatrix} \|V\| \sin\psi & 0 & \|V\| \cos\psi \end{pmatrix}$$

$$N = \begin{pmatrix} N_x & 0 & 1 \end{pmatrix} = \begin{pmatrix} \tan\chi & 0 & 1 \end{pmatrix}.$$

The block matrices E_{135} and E_{246} correspond to the unknown triples (V_x, V_z, Ω_y) and $(V_y, \Omega_x, \Omega_z)$, respectively. We are thus able to invert the matrix E by inverting the two 3×3 block matrices.

$$E^{-1} = \begin{pmatrix} E_{135}^{-1} & 0 \\ 0 & E_{246}^{-1} \end{pmatrix} \tag{17}$$

We used the MAPLE symbolic package to compute the inverses E_{135}^{-1} and E_{246}^{-1}. The uncertainty between the two unknown triples is decoupled. We will study the first triple (V_x, V_z, Ω_y); the study of the second triple can be conducted analogously. We introduce the unit vector $u = (\cos\phi, 0, \sin\phi)^T$. The quadratic form $u^T E_{135}^{-1} u$ represents the uncertainty in direction ϕ. The uncertainty in the (V_x, Ω_y) space can be illustrated geometrically as the intersection of an ellipsoid in $(V_x, , V_z, \Omega_y)$ space with a plane. Let S be the 2×2 submatrix of E_{135} built by the first and third columns and rows of E_{135}. The bounds of the quadratic form $u^T E_{135}^{-1} u$ are given by the smallest and the largest eigenvalue of S [24]:

$$\lambda_{\min}(S) \le u^T E_{135}^{-1} u \le \lambda_{\max}(S). \tag{18}$$

We are interested in the value of the lowest uncertainty which is proportional to $\lambda_{\min}(S)$. The expression for $\lambda_{\min}(S)$ computed by MAPLE is very long. We restrict ourselves to plotting it as a function of ψ and χ. Figure 2 shows that the smallest

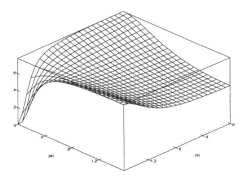

Figure 2. The smallest eigenvalue of S as a function of the angles ψ of translation and χ of the normal with the optical axis for a small field of view: A = 0.1

eigenvalue is not affected by the singularity $\chi = \psi$. However, the error variances of V_x

and Ω_y become infinitely large. This fact substantiates our methodology in exploiting the entire structure of the lower bound covariance matrix. Figure 2 shows that the variance in the direction of the lowest uncertainty is an increasing function of the slant χ if the translation is parallel to the image plane ($\psi = \pi/2$) and a decreasing function of the slant χ if the translation is parallel to the optical axis ($\psi = 0$). We next compute the angle $\phi_{\min}$ that gives the direction of lowest uncertainty with the help of MAPLE. Figure 3 shows that for a small field of view the angle $\phi_{\min}$ takes almost everywhere values close to $\pi/4$. Hence, the direction of lowest uncertainty is $(\cos \pi/4, \sin \pi/4)$, which implies that the sum $V_x + \Omega_y = (1,1)(V_x, \Omega_y)^T$ can be robustly estimated. Values of $\phi_{\min}$ near zero mean that the most robust direction in (V_x, Ω_y)-space is $(1,0)$, implying that the estimate for translational velocity V_x is robust. This happens if the plane is parallel to the optical axis (χ near $\pi/2$) and the translation is parallel to the optical axis (ψ near zero) as well. Planes parallel to the optical axis induce a high variation in the magnitudes of the motion field vectors. Translations parallel to the optical axis induce radially expanding motion fields. In both cases the motion field cannot be confused with a motion field induced by a pure rotation about an axis parallel to the image plane. The effect of a dominant direction in (V_x, Ω_y)-space is weaker if the field of view is large (Figure 3 below). The angle $\phi_{\min}$ may take values greater than $\pi/4$ but is never close to $\pi/2$, which prevents the estimate for Ω_y from having the lowest uncertainty. We have, thus, shown that the

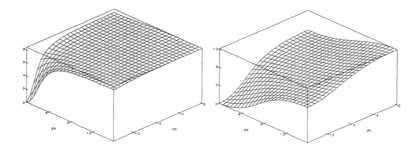

Figure 3. The angle $\phi_{\min}$ of the lowest uncertainty direction as a function of the angles ψ of translation and χ of the normal with the optical axis for two sizes of the field of view: A = 0.1 (a) and A = 1.0 (b). In the case (a) of a small field of view this angle is almost everywhere equal $\pi/4$. Thus the direction of lowest uncertainty is $(1,1)$ and the sum $V_x + \Omega_y$ may be robustly estimated. This effect becomes weaker as the size of the field of view increases.

directions of the lowest uncertainty in the mixed translational-rotational parameter space correspond to the sum and difference of the components of the velocities causing motion parallel to the image plane. The lower bounds for each component individually are higher and this effect is amplified if the size of the field of view and the slant of the plane become smaller. The only way to attenuate this inherent sensitivity is to keep the amount of lateral translation as small as possible by actively fixating on the focus of expansion [18].

2.2. THE BIAS TOWARDS THE VIEWING DIRECTION

In this section we are going to prove the bias in the estimated translation direction towards the viewing direction if the field of view is small. This bias was already observed in [3, 31, 58, 65]. We will show here using the arguments in [16, 34] that this bias can be eliminated if the error metric is derived by the statistical analysis in the first part of the chapter. The bias-affected error metrics are those derived directly from the epipolar constraint in its discrete form

$$\boldsymbol{x}_2{}^T(\boldsymbol{T} \times R\boldsymbol{x}_1) = 0, \tag{19}$$

or its instantaneous form

$$(\boldsymbol{V} \times \boldsymbol{x})^T(\dot{\boldsymbol{x}} - \boldsymbol{\Omega} \times \boldsymbol{x}) = 0, \tag{20}$$

without considering the noise in $(\boldsymbol{x}_1, \boldsymbol{x}_2)$ or $\dot{\boldsymbol{x}}$, respectively. It should be noted that the above equations are valid in both cases of a planar and a spherical image surface. Furthermore, the bias does not affect approaches minimizing

$$\iint_{I_D} \left\| \dot{\boldsymbol{x}} - \frac{1}{\hat{\boldsymbol{z}}^T \boldsymbol{X}} \hat{\boldsymbol{z}} \times (\boldsymbol{V} \times \boldsymbol{x}) - \hat{\boldsymbol{z}} \times (\boldsymbol{x} \times (\boldsymbol{x} \times \boldsymbol{\Omega})) \right\|^2 dx\, dy \tag{21}$$

like [1, 12, 25, 39]   since the error metric obtained after elimination of depth

$$\iint_{I_D} \left\{ \frac{(\boldsymbol{V} \times \boldsymbol{x})^T(\dot{\boldsymbol{x}} - \boldsymbol{\Omega} \times \boldsymbol{x})}{\|\hat{\boldsymbol{z}} \times (\boldsymbol{V} \times \boldsymbol{x})\|} \right\}^2 dx\, dy \tag{22}$$

is correctly normalized. The error-metric (22) is equivalent to the error metrics for the discrete case obtained in the first part of the chapter by statistical arguments. On the contrary, it affects the minimization of the error metric

$$\sum_{n=1}^{N} \left(c_n(\boldsymbol{x} \times \dot{\boldsymbol{x}})^T \boldsymbol{V} \right)^2 \tag{23}$$

used in [31], where the coefficient vector $(c_1 \ldots c_N)$ is chosen to be orthogonal to all quadratic polynomials in (x, y) so that the quadratic rotational component of the motion field will be annihilated. Since the coefficients c_n are independent of the translation $\boldsymbol{V}$, the above error metric is biased in the same way as the metric $(\boldsymbol{x} \times \dot{\boldsymbol{x}})^T \boldsymbol{V}$.

We proceed with introducing essential parameters into the instantaneous epipolar constraint (20), which may be written as

$$\boldsymbol{V}^T(\boldsymbol{x} \times \dot{\boldsymbol{x}}) + \boldsymbol{x}^T \mathcal{K} \boldsymbol{x} = 0 \tag{24}$$

with $\mathcal{K} = \boldsymbol{V}^T \boldsymbol{\Omega} I - \frac{1}{2}(\boldsymbol{V}\boldsymbol{\Omega}^T + \boldsymbol{\Omega}\boldsymbol{V}^T)$. Ignoring the constraints for the decomposability of $\mathcal{K}$ in $\boldsymbol{V}$ and $\boldsymbol{\Omega}$ temporarily, a solution for the minimization of

$$\iint_{I_D} \left(\boldsymbol{V}^T(\boldsymbol{x} \times \dot{\boldsymbol{x}}) + \boldsymbol{x}^T \mathcal{K} \boldsymbol{x} \right)^2 dx\, dy$$

is given by the eigenvector for the smallest eigenvalue of the matrix [34],

$$\mathcal{Y} = \iint_{I_D} (\boldsymbol{x} \times \dot{\boldsymbol{x}})(\boldsymbol{x} \times \dot{\boldsymbol{x}})^T \, dx \, dy - \mathcal{M},$$

where $\mathcal{M}$ depends only on the image coordinates (x, y). Suppose now that the motion field vectors $\dot{\boldsymbol{x}}$ are corrupted by additive noise,

$$\dot{\boldsymbol{x}}' = \dot{\boldsymbol{x}} + \begin{pmatrix} \xi \\ \eta \\ 0 \end{pmatrix}$$

with vanishing expectations and isotropic variances $E[\xi^2] = E[\eta^2] = \sigma^2$ and $E[\xi\eta] = 0$. The expectation of the corrupted matrix $\mathcal{Y}'$ then reads

$$E[\mathcal{Y}'] = \mathcal{Y} + \sigma^2 \begin{pmatrix} \alpha\beta & 0 & 0 \\ 0 & \alpha\beta & 0 \\ 0 & 0 & \alpha\beta\frac{\alpha^2+\beta^2}{12} \end{pmatrix},$$

where α and β are the side lengths of the rectangular domain of integration around the viewing direction assumed to be parallel to the optical axis. The bias in the matrix $\mathcal{Y}$ affects the eigenvector for the smallest eigenvalue and is of the order $\mathcal{O}(\sigma^2)$. It increases with decreasing difference between the two smallest eigenvalues according to the well-known theorem [24] that the perturbed eigenvector $\boldsymbol{x}'_k$ of a perturbed symmetric matrix $A + E$ reads

$$\boldsymbol{x}'_k \approx \boldsymbol{x}_k + \sum_{j \neq k} \frac{\boldsymbol{x}_j^T E \boldsymbol{x}_k}{(\lambda_j - \lambda_k)} \boldsymbol{x}_j, \tag{25}$$

with λ_i, $\boldsymbol{x}_i$ the eigenvalues and eigenvectors of the unperturbed matrix, respectively. Assuming a true motion field arising from a planar surface $N_x X + N_y Y + N_z Z = 1$, it is proved in [16] that:

1. The difference between the two smallest eigenvalues is a monotonically decreasing function of the polar angle θ of the true translational direction

$$|\lambda'_1 - \lambda'_3| = \left(F^2 + G^2 + 2FG\cos 2\theta\right)^{\frac{1}{2}}, \tag{26}$$

where F and G depend on the noise σ^2, the area of the field of view, the slope of the surface, and the ratio of translation to distance.
2. The upper bound on the bias of the eigenvector expressed as the sine of its rotation is a monotonically increasing function of the polar angle of the translation

$$|\sin \delta\varphi| \leq \frac{\sigma^2 \sqrt{\sin^2\theta + (\frac{\alpha^2+\beta^2}{12})^2 \cos^2\theta}}{\lambda_3 + \sigma^2\frac{\alpha^2+\beta^2}{12}}. \tag{27}$$

We conclude that the more lateral the true translation and the smaller the field of view, the more severe are the bias effects.

For the elimination of bias it is proposed by Kanatani [34] to minimize the Rayleigh quotient

$$\frac{V^T \mathcal{Y} V}{V^T \mathcal{B} V}$$

where $\mathcal{B}$ is the bias matrix

$$\begin{pmatrix} \alpha\beta & 0 & 0 \\ 0 & \alpha\beta & 0 \\ 0 & 0 & \alpha\beta\frac{\alpha^2+\beta^2}{12} \end{pmatrix}.$$

This can be reduced to a generalized eigenvalue problem $\mathcal{Y} V = \lambda \mathcal{B} V$. This is equivalent to finding the eigenvector for the smallest eigenvalue of the unbiased matrix $\mathcal{Y} - \lambda \mathcal{B}$ where the unknown λ represents the noise level in the motion field. It can be easily proved that the normalizing denominator is equal:

$$V^T \mathcal{B} V = \iint_{I_D} \|\hat{z} \times (V \times x)\|^2 \, dx \, dy.$$

Thus, the bias can be eliminated if we integrate separately the denominator in (22), which is approximately correct if the field of view is very small.

2.3. THE IMPORTANT LINE

In this section we will describe the results obtained in [30, 46] about the form of the error surface around the minimum in the space of translation directions. We should remark at this point that the curvature of the error surface in the neighborhood of the minimum is a measure of the stability of this minimum. The Fisher information matrix of the last section is nothing but an approximate measure of the flatness of the error surface near the minimum. The error surface used by Jepson and Heeger [30] is the residuum obtained by the pseudoinverse solution of (2):

$$J(V) = \|(I - C(V)C^\dagger(V))s\|^2. \tag{28}$$

For a sufficiently small field of view and an irregular depth variation the residuum $J(V)$ was proved to be proportional to $\sin\theta_o \sin(\phi - \phi_o)$, where

$$V = (\cos\phi \sin\theta, \sin\phi \sin\theta, \cos\theta)^T$$

and (θ_o, ϕ_o) are the polar and azimuth angle of the actual translation. Thus, the residuum varies only in the direction perpendicular to the line connecting the viewing direction and the true translation. We illustrate this fact in the (θ, ϕ) coordinate system of Figure 4.

A similar relationship was derived by Maybank [46, 47] but the residuum after elimination of depths becomes

$$J_m(V) = \sum_{i=1}^{l} \|(V \times x_i)^T(\dot{x}_i - \Omega \times x_i)\|^2. \tag{29}$$

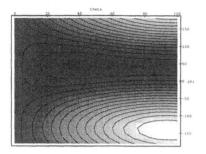
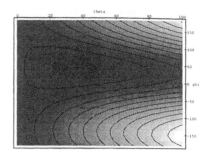

Figure 4. The residuum $J(V)$ as a function of the translation direction
angles (θ, ϕ). The actual translation is $(1/2, 1/2, 1)$, the depth is a step
function, and there is no rotation. The residuum is shown for a small
(0.2×0.2) and a large (1×1) field of view. The valley of minima can be
clearly seen in case of a small field of view (left).

It was proved that under the same assumptions of small field of view and irregular
depth distribution the residuum above is proportional to $\|V^T(V_o \times x_o)\|$ where x_o
is the viewing direction and V_o is the true translation. It is trivial to show that
the triple product has as a factor $\sin(\phi - \phi_o)$. The same valley of minima can be
observed in Figure 5 with a small but expected surprise: Due to the use of the
epipolar constraint as an error metric, the locations of minima are biased towards
the viewing direction $\theta = 0$.

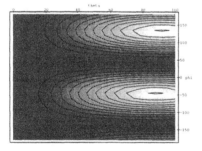
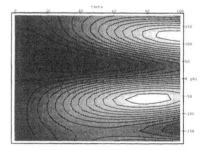

Figure 5. The residuum $J_m(V)$ as a function of the translation direction
angles (θ, ϕ). The actual translation is $(1/2, 1/2, 1)$, the depth is a step
function, and there is no rotation. The residuum is shown for a small
(0.2×0.2) and a large (1×1) field of view. The valley of minima can
be clearly seen in case of a small field of view (left). Furthermore, we
observe the bias towards the viewing direction $(\theta = 0)$ due to the use of
the unnormalized epipolar constraint.

2.4. CRITICAL SURFACES AND INSTABILITY

In this section we switch over again to the discrete case of given point correspondences (x_1, x_2) in order to study the relation between ambiguity and error sensi-

tivity in the structure from motion problem. It has been repeatedly shown in the past that certain configurations of scene points and optical centers—called critical surfaces—cause the existence of two or three solutions given more than five point correspondences (see [47] and the references therein). In the context of error sensitivity we are interested here only in solutions that differ slightly from each other. Given a solution for translation and rotation we study the geometries for which a first order perturbation of the solution yields the same point correspondences. Horn [27] showed that the epipolar constraint remains unaffected by first-order deformations of the motion parameters if the points lie on a quadric with certain properties. The relation of these instability-critical surfaces to the ambiguity-critical surfaces has been an open problem in visual motion.[1] Such a relationship was first established in pure geometric terms by Hofmann [26]. Following [14] we show here that an instability-critical surface arises when the two optical centers take special positions on the ambiguity-critical surface.

Let $(R, \boldsymbol{a})$ and $(S, \boldsymbol{b})$ be two rotation-translation pairs that yield the same point correspondences $(\boldsymbol{x}_1, \boldsymbol{x}_2)$. The pair of the two ambiguity surfaces associated with each of the solutions reads (from [47]):

$$(U\boldsymbol{X} \times \boldsymbol{X})^T\boldsymbol{b} = (U\boldsymbol{a} \times \boldsymbol{X})^T\boldsymbol{b} \tag{30}$$

$$(U^T\boldsymbol{X} \times \boldsymbol{X})^T\boldsymbol{a} = (U^T\boldsymbol{b} \times \boldsymbol{X})^T\boldsymbol{a}, \tag{31}$$

where $U = SR^T$ is the rotation difference and $\boldsymbol{X}$ the scene point with respect to the first coordinate system. The surfaces are quadrics of the form

$$\boldsymbol{X}^T M \boldsymbol{X} + \boldsymbol{l}^T \boldsymbol{X} = 0.$$

We will briefly elucidate the properties of such a quadric by means of the hyperboloid of one sheet which is its nondegenerate shape. The hyperboloid of one sheet (Figure 6) is a doubly ruled surface and has two families of generators. Each family has two main generators passing through the main vertices (the intersections of the ellipse with its major axis) of the smallest ellipse (the ellipse satisfying $x^2/a^2 + y^2/b^2 = 1$ if the hyperboloid has the standard form $x^2/a^2 + y^2/b^2 - z^2/c^2 = 1$). If all the scene points lie on a hyperboloid of one sheet then this hyperboloid is an ambiguity-critical surface [37, 67], iff:

- it is rectangular (every plane perpendicular to the main generator intersects the surface in a circle), and
- the two optical centers $\boldsymbol{o}$ and $\boldsymbol{a}$ lie on generators $g1$ and $g2$ symmetric to the main generator.

Suppose now that the two motion solutions differ only by first-order perturbations $(\delta\boldsymbol{\Omega}, \delta\boldsymbol{a})$:

$$U = I + [\delta\boldsymbol{\Omega}]_\times \qquad \boldsymbol{b} = \boldsymbol{a} + \delta\boldsymbol{a}, \tag{32}$$

---

[1] See [49], *"Because of his [27] particular formulation of the problem, the relationship between his results and those presented here is hard to establish."*

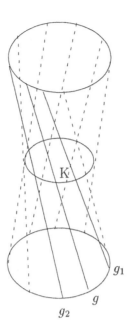

Figure 6. The hyperboloid of one sheet with three lines belonging to the same generator family. The line g through the main vertex of the smallest ellipse is the main generator of the family.

where $[\delta\Omega]_\times$ is the antisymmetric matrix for the vector $\delta\Omega$. We substitute the above terms in (30) and after cancellation of the terms second-order in $(\delta\Omega, \delta a)$ we obtain

$$(\delta\Omega \times X)^T(X \times a) + (a \times (a \times \delta\Omega + \delta a))^T X = 0 \tag{33}$$

which has also the form $X^T M X + l^T X = 0$ where

$$M = \frac{1}{2}(a\delta\Omega^T + \delta\Omega a^T) - a^T\delta\Omega I \tag{34}$$

$$l = a \times (a \times \delta\Omega + \delta a). \tag{35}$$

From the form of the M-matrix it can be easily proved that the quadric is still rectangular.[2] We will prove that the optical centers o and a lie on the main generator of the quadric.

The main generator of the quadric passes through the main vertex of the smallest intersection ellipse. The center of the quadric is given by (from [36])

$$c = -\frac{1}{2}M^{-1}l. \tag{36}$$

The main axis of the considered ellipse is parallel to the second eigenvector of the matrix M

$$u_2 = \frac{a \times \delta\Omega}{\|a \times \delta\Omega\|},$$

---

[2] The algebraic definition for rectangularity of a quadric is that the middle eigenvalue of M is equal to the sum of the other two.

corresponding to the eigenvalue $\lambda_2 = -\boldsymbol{a}^T \delta \boldsymbol{\Omega}$. The length of the semi-axis is

$$\sqrt{c/\lambda_2} \qquad \text{with} \qquad c = \frac{1}{4} \boldsymbol{l}^T M^{-1} \boldsymbol{l}.$$

Hence, the main vertices have position vectors

$$\boldsymbol{c} \pm \sqrt{\frac{c}{\lambda_2}} \boldsymbol{u}_2.$$

After a tedious calculation it can be proved that the line

$$\boldsymbol{c} \pm \sqrt{\frac{c}{\lambda_2}} \boldsymbol{u}_2 + \mu \boldsymbol{a}$$

is the main generator. On the other hand the line $\lambda \boldsymbol{a}$ joining the two optical centers is a generator since $\lambda^2 \boldsymbol{a}^T M \boldsymbol{a} + \lambda \boldsymbol{l}^T \boldsymbol{a} = 0$ for every λ. Because no two lines of a generator family are parallel to each other the line $\lambda \boldsymbol{a}$ is identical to the main generator. Hence, if the two solutions differ by a first-order perturbation the two optical centers lie on the main generator. The instability-critical quadric (33) is identical with the quadric obtained by Horn [27], who studied which scene point configurations left the epipolar constraint $\boldsymbol{x}_1^T (\boldsymbol{a} \times R \boldsymbol{x}_2)$ unaffected by a first-order perturbation $(\delta \boldsymbol{\Omega}, \delta \boldsymbol{a})$. Thus we have made the required link between instability- and ambiguity-critical surfaces.

The degenerate forms of a hyperboloid of one sheet are the hyperbolic paraboloid, the cone, the elliptic cylinder, and the plane pair. We will look at the case of the elliptic cylinder. We obtain a cylinder in the special case of $\boldsymbol{a} \parallel \delta \boldsymbol{\Omega}$. The generators of a cylinder are all parallel to its axis $\boldsymbol{a}$. Thus, we obtain an unstable solution if an observer is moving on a cylinder parallel to the axis and is looking the other side of the cylinder. This is a very realistic situation in the case of a small field of view because a small part of a scene can be often approximated by a quadratic cylinder patch. Since the translation perturbation $\delta \boldsymbol{a}$ is perpendicular to the translation $\boldsymbol{a}$ due to $\|\boldsymbol{a}\| = 1$, we obtain a second slightly different solution including a rotation and a translation around axes $(\delta \boldsymbol{\Omega}, \delta \boldsymbol{a})$ perpendicular to each other. Thus we have given yet another explanation for the confusion between translation and rotation.

3. STATISTICAL BIAS

The goal of estimation is to recover a set of unknown parameters with as little deviation from the ground truth as possible and in practice we need several ways to qualitatively describe the nature of the deviation that we can expect. We concentrate again on two of them, the *bias* and the *variance*. The bias is the difference between the expected value of the estimate and the ground truth, and the variance is the expected value of the squared difference between the estimate and the ground truth. It seems obvious that in most cases reducing the bias will reduce the variance and the opposite; but this is increasingly incorrect as our estimators become better and more complicated, so we move away from straightforward intuition. It is not uncommon to have unbiased solutions with high variance, or for biased solutions to outperform unbiased ones in terms of variance. We could restrict ourselves to linear estimators with Gaussian distribution and preserve the monotone relation between bias and variance but this could be hardly useful for structure estimation using discrete matches where even the so-called *linear solutions* include nonlinear steps.

The bias itself can be a very useful property and worth striving to include among the advantages of an algorithm. It is not without caveats though. Assume that we want to recover the size of a square in three-dimensional space. We use an algorithm to obtain an unbiased estimate of the length of the sides of the square

$$E\{x^*\} = x,$$

where x^* is the estimate and x is the actual length of the side of the square; but using the same algorithm we cannot get an unbiased estimate of the area x^2 by simply squaring the result because

$$E\{x^{2*}\} = x^2 + \sigma^2 \neq x^2,$$

where σ is the standard deviation of x. In other words, the bias is a very fragile property and it might not be always easy to obtain estimators whose bias is exactly zero, although in most cases simple corrections are sufficient.

The estimation of the rotation component of a general motion poses similar problems. If one designs an unbiased estimator of the Euler angles for the motion then the same estimator cannot be simply translated to one that computes the Rodrieguess parameters. Even the translation component poses difficulties depending on whether it is reported as a focus of expansion or a unit vector.

One cannot prove that a certain estimator is unbiased without reference to the exact representation of the required result, because if a certain representation is unbiased we cannot infer that an equivalent one is also unbiased. On the other hand, the bias that appears when we simply change representations is very often too small to be observable by plotting or visualizing the data. If the bias is due to deficiencies in the formulation of the estimator, then in several cases it is very noticeable by simple inspection of the data, which is what happened to the structure from motion problem [55, 60].

Several of the oldest techniques to recover the motion parameters from point matches in two frames involve the minimization of the sum of the squared residuals of the epipolar constraint

$$\boldsymbol{p}_{2i}^T E \boldsymbol{p}_{1i} = 0,$$

where $\boldsymbol{p}_{1i}$ and $\boldsymbol{p}_{2i}$ are the images of the ith point in the first and second image, and the matrix E is

$$E = \begin{pmatrix} 0 & -T_z & T_y \\ T_z & 0 & -T_x \\ -T_y & T_x & 0 \end{pmatrix} R$$

with $\boldsymbol{T} = (T_x, T_y, T_z)^T$. The minimization of

$$\sum_i \left(\boldsymbol{p}_{2i}^T E \boldsymbol{p}_{1i} \right)^2$$

is fairly easy and there are several solutions in the literature [28, 57], but it is heavily biased in the presence of noise. To see intuitively why, we can rewrite the epipolar constraint as

$$\boldsymbol{p}_{2i}{}^T E \boldsymbol{p}_{1i} = \boldsymbol{p}_{2i}{}^T \left(\boldsymbol{T} \times (R\boldsymbol{p}_{1i})\right).$$

It is easy to see that the cross product introduces the sine of the angle between vectors $\boldsymbol{T}$ and $R\boldsymbol{p}_{1i}$ as a factor. This will make the minimization prefer vectors $\boldsymbol{T}$ that are closer to the center of gravity of the bundle of points $R\boldsymbol{p}_{1i}$, so that the sine and hence the residual of the epipolar is smaller [55].

The magnitude of the bias and the suspicious presence of the sine in the form of the epipolar suggest that there is some oversimplification in the way we handled this minimization. We can use the maximum likelihood method from statistics and solve the problem as follows [55]. Assume that every world point $\boldsymbol{P}_{1i}$ is equal to $\boldsymbol{P}_{1i} = Z_i\boldsymbol{p}_{1i}$, where $\boldsymbol{p}_{1i}$ is the image point vector and Z_i is the unknown scalar depth (which is equal to the z component in planar images). If we move the point $\boldsymbol{P}_{1i}$ by a rotation R and a translation $\boldsymbol{T}$ we get:

$$\boldsymbol{P}_{2i} = Z_i R\boldsymbol{p}_{1i} + \boldsymbol{T}.$$

If we project this vector on the second camera we get

$$\boldsymbol{p}_{2i}'' = \frac{\boldsymbol{P}_{2i}}{\hat{z}^T \boldsymbol{P}_{2i}}$$

which in the presence of noise does not coincide with the projection of the same point $\boldsymbol{p}_{2i}$ on the second camera. The noise is the distance between these two vectors $\boldsymbol{n}_i = \boldsymbol{p}_{2i}'' - \boldsymbol{p}_{2i}$. A simple application of the the maximum likelihood method shows that we need to minimize the weighted least squares of the noise for all points

$$\sum_i \boldsymbol{n}_i{}^T \Sigma_i{}^+ \boldsymbol{n}_i \rightarrow \min,$$

where $\Sigma_i{}^+$ is the pseudoinverse of a covariance matrix of suitable form (e.g., for planar images only the top left two by two submatrix is important). We can eliminate Z_i, which is one unknown per pixel, by setting it equal to

$$Z_i = \frac{(\boldsymbol{p}_{2i} \times \boldsymbol{T})^T \Sigma_i (\boldsymbol{T} \times R\boldsymbol{p}_{1i})}{(\boldsymbol{T} \times R\boldsymbol{p}_{1i})^T \Sigma_i (R\boldsymbol{p}_{1i} \times \boldsymbol{p}_{2i})}.$$

After the elimination the expression we have to minimize is

$$\sum_i \boldsymbol{n}_i{}^T \Sigma_i{}^+ \boldsymbol{n}_i = \sum_i \frac{(\boldsymbol{p}_{2i}{}^T E \boldsymbol{p}_{1i})^2}{(E\boldsymbol{p}_{1i})^T \Sigma_i E\boldsymbol{p}_{1i}},$$

which is a much more difficult function to minimize than the simple sum of squared epipolars. One word of caution here: The expression in the denominator is not a weight that increases the importance of the points close to the focus of expansion (for these points the expression is close to zero). It contains the unknowns so it cannot be factored out the way weights are and has to remain part of the minimization. The minimization procedure is more complicated as a result.

As can be seen from the experimental data in [55], the error distribution does not look biased. The question remains though: Is it biased? Just because it does not look biased it does not mean it is not, and in fact it is not unbiased. The failure of such a bias to manifest itself in the experimental data indicates that this is small, and certainly it is smaller than the one we get from minimizing the squared sum of the residuals of the epipolar.

4. USING LINES AND POINTS

Straight-line matching does not suffer from the aperture problem, where one of the two components of the flow field is impossible to estimate if one looks through a sufficiently small aperture; but the aperture problem does not appear everywhere in the image. There are feature points in the image that do not suffer from the aperture problem (e.g., corners and local maxima). If one wants to make use of these feature points then information from the line matching and the point matching should be used at the same time. Such an algorithm needs of course three frames; otherwise the lines do not offer any real constraint.

The idea of using three frames for points without lines has some other advantages of its own. First, fewer points are needed to obtain a finite number of solutions (four instead of five, but for linearized solution we need nine instead of eight). This is because there is the extra constraint that the structure obtained from the first and second frame is the same as the one obtained from the first and third. Second, the ambiguous configurations are fewer. Configurations that are ambiguous in the first pair of frames are either unambiguous in the second pair or the spurious solution is different [54].

Assume that a point P in 3D is projected to points p_1, p_2 and p_3 on the three frames. The motion between frame 1 and frame 2 is R_1 and T_1 for rotation and translation respectively. The motion between frame 1 and 3 is similarly R_2 and T_2. The image points are related by

$$Z_2 p_2 = Z_1 R_1 p_1 + T_1$$
$$Z_3 p_3 = Z_1 R_2 p_1 + T_2,$$

where Z_i is the unknown depth of the points in the corresponding coordinate system of the frame. We eliminate Z_2 and Z_3 by taking the cross-product of the two equations by p_2 and p_3, respectively:

$$0 = Z_1 p_2 \times (R_1 p_1) + p_2 \times T_1$$
$$0 = Z_1 p_3 \times (R_2 p_1) + p_3 \times T_2$$

We can eliminate Z_1 by rearranging the terms so that Z_1 appears in the left-hand side for the one equation and the right-hand side of the other equation

$$Z_1 [p_2]_\times R_1 p_1 = -[p_2]_\times T_1$$
$$[p_3]_\times T_2 = -Z_1 [p_3]_\times R_2 p_1.$$

Taking the outer product we get the following constraint:

$$[\boldsymbol{p}_2]_\times (R_1 \boldsymbol{p}_1 \boldsymbol{T}_2^T)[\boldsymbol{p}_3]_\times = [\boldsymbol{p}_2]_\times \boldsymbol{T}_1 (R_2 \boldsymbol{p}_1)^T \boldsymbol{p}_3,$$

where

$$[\boldsymbol{p}_2]_\times = \begin{pmatrix} 0 & -z_2 & y_2 \\ z_2 & 0 & -x_2 \\ -y_2 & x_2 & 0 \end{pmatrix}$$

with $\boldsymbol{p}_2 = (x_2, y_2, z_2)^T$. If we define

$$K = \boldsymbol{T}_1 (R_2 \hat{\boldsymbol{x}})^T - (R_1 \hat{\boldsymbol{x}}) \boldsymbol{T}_2^T$$
$$L = \boldsymbol{T}_1 (R_2 \hat{\boldsymbol{y}})^T - (R_1 \hat{\boldsymbol{y}}) \boldsymbol{T}_2^T$$
$$M = \boldsymbol{T}_1 (R_2 \hat{\boldsymbol{z}})^T - (R_1 \hat{\boldsymbol{z}}) \boldsymbol{T}_2^T,$$

where $\hat{\boldsymbol{x}}$, $\hat{\boldsymbol{y}}$ and $\hat{\boldsymbol{z}}$ are the unit vectors along the corresponding axes, then the constraint becomes

$$[\boldsymbol{p}_2]_\times (x_1 K + y_1 L + z_1 M)[\boldsymbol{p}_3]_\times = [0]$$

where (x_1, y_1, z_1) are the components of $\boldsymbol{p}_1$. This is a matrix equation that is equivalent to nine scalar equations, but only three of them are independent.

The above equation provides a set of constraints for points. The known data are the points $\boldsymbol{p}_{1i}$ and the unknowns are the rotation and translation parameters, which are hidden in the three matrices K, L, and M. The constraint for the lines is the vector equation

$$\begin{pmatrix} \boldsymbol{\epsilon}_2^T K \boldsymbol{\epsilon}_3 \\ \boldsymbol{\epsilon}_2^T L \boldsymbol{\epsilon}_3 \\ \boldsymbol{\epsilon}_2^T M \boldsymbol{\epsilon}_3 \end{pmatrix} \times \boldsymbol{\epsilon}_1 = \vec{0},$$

where $\boldsymbol{\epsilon}_i$ is the normal vector line representation in frame i. Such a vector passes through the origin and is normal to the image line. Known are the normal line vectors, and the unknowns are again the matrices K, L, and M that contain the motion parameters. The constraints from both points and lines can be included in the same least-squares estimation to take advantage of all the information.

This least-squares problem corresponds to the direct least-squares minimization for the epipolar residual that was shown above to be the reason for the high bias. The question arises whether we can follow the same path and find the maximum likelihood estimator for the points and lines as well. It turns out that we cannot do exactly the same thing because we need to solve a fourth-degree polynomial equation that, although it has a closed form solution, is no more useful than a numerical one due to its complexity.

5. STATISTICALLY CORRELATED NOISE

In the previous paragraphs we dealt mainly with data that were statistically independent. This is a convenient working assumption that is fairly accurate when we deal with point correspondences that are collected either by hand or sparsely enough to make them independent. A computer vision system should not depend on data collected by hand, and sparse data means that we leave a large amount of information unused.

Furthermore, it is possible to extract more information from data corrupted by correlated noise if we know the correlation rather than assuming incorrectly that they are uncorrelated. One example is the motion of a textured patch. While any measurement of the motion of such a patch may be corrupted due to aliasing, the second-order components of the motion (dilation, shear, rotation) may be still recoverable, if we can track the Fourier components in the frequency domain.

There are two distinct problems regarding correlated noise. One is the representation of the variance-covariance matrix. Such a matrix should contain the covariance for every pair of points in the image, which is very large for dense disparity data.

The other problem is that the equations cannot be solved or simplified analytically, because all the image is involved in one set of equations. The equations have to be solved numerically.

The approach to these problems is to solve for the correspondence (or flow) and the motion in one step, by minimizing the match over a region of the intensity subject to the constraint that the correspondences satisfy the epipolar constraint. The Lagrangian equation is:

$$
\mathcal{L} \;=\; \sum_{i_0,j_0} \sum_{\substack{i_0-w\le i\le i_0+w \\ j_0-w\le j\le j_0+w}} \left(\nabla I(i,j)^T \boldsymbol{u}(i_0,j_0) + I_t(i,j)\right)^2 +
$$

$$
\sum_{i_0,j_0} \lambda(i_0,j_0)\left(\boldsymbol{p}_2(i_0,j_0)^T E \boldsymbol{p}_1(i_0,j_0)\right)
$$

where the summation for i, j is over the whole image and i_0 and j_0 are over a small window typically 5 by 5 or 7 by 7,

$$
\boldsymbol{p}_2(i_0,j_0) = \boldsymbol{p}_1(i_0,j_0) + \boldsymbol{u}(i_0,j_0).
$$

$\boldsymbol{u}$ is the disparity with zero as the third element to match the size of $\boldsymbol{p}_2$, I is the intensity, and I_t is the time derivative of the intensity. The first component of $\mathcal{L}$ is the metric used by Lucas and Kanade [45] and seems to produce reasonably accurate results even by itself [9]. Solving this Lagrangian equation for $\boldsymbol{u}$ and E will give a disparity field that is constrained to be one of rigid motion, but the linear equations that come out are hard to solve because the linearized system is not positive definite. Although iterative methods exist for this type of equation, they are slow and unstable. In general it is better to avoid such systems, and although we are not interested in λ, we have to compute it in the process. Adding the constraint that matrix E is decomposable to rotation and translation provides an extra difficulty.

Another formulation of the problem is to use a trade-off parameter λ, which yields a positive definite system

$$
\mathcal{L} \;=\; \sum(\nabla I(i-i_0,j-j_0)^T \boldsymbol{u}(i_0,j_0) + I_t(i-i_0,j-j_0))^2 +
$$

$$
\lambda \sum \frac{(\boldsymbol{p}_2(i_0,j_0)^T E \boldsymbol{p}_1(i_0,j_0))^2}{(E\boldsymbol{p}_1(i_0,j_0))^T \Sigma_i E \boldsymbol{p}_1(i_0,j_0)},
$$

which is a form of regularization; but instead of trading off the problem constraints against a smoothness term, we do so against a rigidity term, which in many cases offers more than stabilization: It can link the disparity estimation to the motion estimation. Unfortunately, if the disparity estimation is severely affected by the aperture problem the whole process is rendered ineffective. Such methods work quite well [8] but the problem of choosing the appropriate λ and Σ_i remains. In general the value of λ has to be as high as possible since it will not have bad side effects like oversmoothing the solution, but too high can be detrimental to the round-off error.

A third approach involves unconstrained minimization by changing unknowns. Instead of having the components of the flow vector field and the motion parameters as unknowns we can use the depth and the motion parameters

$$\mathcal{L} = \sum (\nabla I(i - i_0, j - j_0) \cdot \boldsymbol{u}(i_0, j_0) + I_t(i - i_0, j - j_0))^2$$

where

$$\boldsymbol{u} = \boldsymbol{p}_1 - \frac{ZR\boldsymbol{p}_1 + \boldsymbol{T}}{\hat{\boldsymbol{z}}^T(Z\boldsymbol{p}_1 + \boldsymbol{T})}$$

and Z is the z component of the point before the motion. The flow vectors are simply intermediate variables. A disadvantage of this approach is that it has more difficult nonlinearities to handle, but this can be weighed against the advantage of fewer unknowns and the ability to incorporate information about the depth that comes from another source (previous frames, sonar, known models, etc.). The linearized equations that have to be solved are also positive definite.

All these approaches share something with the ideas behind direct methods [20, 21, 50] and correspondenceless methods [5, 11] for motion recovery that avoids the intermediate step of establishing correspondence or any other kind of disparity field. What they share is the one-step estimation of the motion, but they differ in the kind of input they expect. Direct methods attempt to recover the motion using less information, either constraints that only give the normal component of the motion or the distribution of points without one-to-one correspondence established between them. Methods presented above assume that there is sufficient information in the image to recover deformation; and while it is true that the constraints on the disparity are weak in large areas on the image, using some of the best performing algorithms [9], both components of flow may be approximated in portions of the image containing enough texture and these may be enough to provide some estimate of the motion. The areas that simply do not have enough constraints for both components of flow, do not contribute to the recovery of motion or even to the recovery of depth if no component of flow can be computed reliably.

6. THE FUTURE

The application that has driven the research on structure from motion is autonomous navigation, where scene reconstruction would make the problem simpler, although it has been argued that autonomous navigation could be successful without it. Nevertheless an efficient structure from motion module would be useful for the navigation itself or the other tasks of the autonomous robots. A parallel can be drawn from marine navigation where an accurate map and the exact location of the vessel is not needed in safe waters near the coast, but for offshore navigation or in unsafe waters not only is the exact location on the map required but radar as well.

The recent demand for multimedia, high-quality graphics and virtual reality, has opened new opportunities for applications of structure from motion. One problem that structure from motion can help with is viewpoint interpolation where, given the image of a scene from a set of different viewpoints, one wants the image of the scene from a novel viewpoint. Although with today's technology depth cannot be recovered accurately, it is at least consistent with the gray scale (or color) structure of the scene, so if the novel viewpoint is not very far from the already existing ones one can compute the image from that viewpoint. Another application is interactive video editing where two- or three-dimensional tracking can help map the editing of one frame to the next. There are numerous other applications for scene reconstruction techniques that will emerge sooner or later. The point is that general-purpose scene reconstruction has much broader importance outside what has become traditional in vision research. The presented chapter not only provides us with the reasons for sensitivity but also gives us a unifying treatment by applying solid statistical techniques.

On the other hand, if we follow the paradigm of active or purposive vision the noise sensitivity treatment provides us with guidelines on how to design a purposive algorithm. Given a specific task like the estimation of object translation and the pursuit of the object we may find that an object-centered representation eliminates the translation-rotation confusion—in the case of a small field of view of object tracking—because the direction of least uncertainty in the space of unknowns is now the lateral translation of the object. In the task of ego-translation estimation using fixation we can exploit the results on the important line in the space of translation directions [19]. In particular, it was proved that the use of the polar transformation [15] decouples the azimuth from the polar angle of the translation direction, the former of which was shown already to be insensitive to noise. We hope that this chapter will give further insight towards designing not only computationally inexpensive, but also robust general as well as special-purpose algorithms.

References

1. G. Adiv, "Determining 3-D motion and structure from optical flow generated by several moving objects," *IEEE Transactions on Pattern Analysis and Machine Intelligence* **7**, 1985, 384–401.

2. G. Adiv, "Inherent ambiguities in recovering 3-D motion and structure from a noisy flow field," *IEEE Transactions on Pattern Analysis and Machine Intelligence* **11**, 1989, 477–489.

3. J. Aisbett, "An iterated estimation of the motion parameters of a rigid body from noisy displacement vectors," *IEEE Transactions on Pattern Analysis and Machine Intelligence* **12**, 1990, 1092–1098.

4. J. Aloimonos, "Purposive and qualitative active vision," in *Proc. International Conference on Pattern Recognition*, Atlantic City, NJ, June 17–21, 1990, 346–360.

5. J. Aloimonos and J.-Y. Hervé, "Correspondenceless stereo and motion: Planar surfaces," *IEEE Transactions on Pattern Analysis and Machine Intelligence* **12**, 1990, 504–510.

6. J. Aloimonos, I. Weiss, and A. Bandopadhay, "Active vision," *International Journal of Computer Vision* **2**, 1988, 333–356.

7. P. Anandan, "A computational framework and an algorithm for the measurement of visual motion," *International Journal of Computer Vision* **2**, 1989, 283–310.

8. H. Ando, "Dynamic reconstruction of 3D structure and 3D motion," in *Proc. IEEE Workshop on Visual Motion*, Princeton, NJ, October 7–9, 1991, 101–110.

9. J.L. Barron, D.J. Fleet, and S.S. Beauchemin, "Performance of optical flow techniques," *International Journal of Computer Vision* **12**, 1994, 43–78.

10. J.L. Barron, A.D. Jepson, and J.K. Tsotsos, "The feasibility of motion and structure from noisy time-varying image velocity information," *International Journal of Computer Vision* **5**, 1990, 239–269.

11. A. Basu and J. Aloimonos, "A robust, correspondenceless translation-determining algorithm," *International Journal of Robotics Research* **9**(5), 1990, 35–59.

12. A. Bruss and B.K.P. Horn, "Passive navigation," *Computer Vision, Graphics, and Image Processing* **21**, 1983, 3–20.

13. M. Campani and A. Verri, "Optical flow estimation using discontinuity conforming filters," in *Proc. International Conference on Computer Vision*, Osaka, Japan, December 4–7, 1990, 22–26.

14. K. Daniilidis, *On the error sensitivity in the recovery of object descriptions and relative motions from image sequences*, Doctoral dissertation, Department of Informatics, University of Karlsruhe, Germany, July 1992, in German.

15. K. Daniilidis, "Attentive visual motion processing: Computations in the log-polar plane," *Computing, Archives in Informatics and Numerical Mathematics*, 1995, to appear in the special issue on Theoretical Foundations of Computer Vision.

16. K. Daniilidis and H.-H. Nagel, "Analytical results on error sensitivity of motion estimation from two views," *Image and Vision Computing* **8**, 1990, 297–303.

17. K. Daniilidis and H.-H. Nagel, "The coupling of rotation and translation in motion estimation of planar surfaces," in *Proc. IEEE Conference on Computer Vision and Pattern Recognition 1993*, New York, June 15–17, 1993, 188–193.

18. C. Fermüller, "Navigational preliminaries," in Y. Aloimonos (Ed.), *Active Perception*, Advances in Computer Vision, Lawrence Erlbaum Associates, Hillsdale, NJ, 1993.

19. C. Fermüller and Y. Aloimonos, "The role of fixation in visual motion analysis," *International Journal of Computer Vision* **11**, 1993, 165–186.

20. C. Fermüller and Y. Aloimonos, "Qualitative egomotion," *International Journal of Computer Vision* **15**, 1995, 7–29.

21. C. Fermüller and Y. Aloimonos, "Direct perception of three-dimensional motion from patterns of visual motion," *Science* **270**, 1995, 1973–1976.

22. D.J. Fleet, A.D. Jepson, and M.R.M. Jenkin, "Phase-based disparity measurement," *CVGIP: Image Understanding* **53**(2), 1991, 3.

23. B. Friedland, *Control System Design*, McGraw-Hill, New York, 1986.

24. G.H. Golub and C.F. Van Loan, *Matrix Computations*, Johns Hopkins University Press, Baltimore, MD, 1983.

25. D.J. Heeger and A.D. Jepson, "Subspace methods for recovering rigid motion I: Algorithm and implementation," *International Journal of Computer Vision* **7**, 1992, 95–117.

26. W. Hofmann, *Das Problem der "gefährlichen Flächen" in Theorie und Praxis*, Deutsche Geodätische Kommission bei der Bayerischen Akademie der Wissenschaften, Reihe C, Heft 3, München, 1953.

27. B.K.P. Horn, "Relative orientation," *International Journal of Computer Vision* **4**, 1990, 59–78.

28. B.K.P. Horn, "Relative orientation revisited," *Journal of the Optical Society of America* **A8**, 1991, 1630–1638.

29. B.K.P. Horn and B.G. Schunk. "Determining optical flow," *Artificial Intelligence* **17**, 1981, 185–203.

30. A.D. Jepson and D.J. Heeger, "Subspace methods for recovering rigid motion II: Theory," Technical Report RBCV-TR-90-36, University of Toronto, 1990.

31. A. Jepson and D.J. Heeger, "A fast subspace algorithm for recovering rigid motion," in *Proc. IEEE Workshop on Visual Motion*, Princeton, NJ, October 7–9, 1991, 124–131.

32. C. Jerian and R. Jain, "Polynomial methods for structure from motion," *IEEE Transactions on Pattern Analysis and Machine Intelligence* **12**, 1990, 1150–1165.

33. K. Kanatani, *Geometric Computation for Machine Vision*, Oxford University Press, Oxford, United Kingdom, 1993.

34. K. Kanatani, "3-D interpretation of optical flow by renormalization," *International Journal of Computer Vision* **11**(267-282), 1993.

35. K. Kanatani, "Unbiased estimation and statistical analysis of 3-D rigid motion from two views," *IEEE Transactions on Pattern Analysis and Machine Intelligence* **15**, 1993, 37–50.

36. G.A. Korn and T.M. Korn, *Mathematical Handbook for Scientists and Engineers*, McGraw-Hill, New York, 1968.

37. J. Krames, "Zur Ermittlung eines Objektes aus zwei perspektiven—Ein Beitrag zur Theorie der 'gefährlichen örter,' " *Monatshefte für Mathematik und Physik* **49**, 1940, 327–354.

38. K.N. Kutulakos and C.R. Dyer, "Recovering shape by purposive viewpoint adjustment," *International Journal of Computer Vision* **12**, 1994, 113–136.

39. T. Lawton, "Processing translational motion sequences," *Computer Vision, Graphics, and Image Processing* **22**, 1983, 116–144.

40. C.-H. Lee, "Time-varying images: The effect of finite resolution on uniqueness," *CVGIP: Image Understanding* **54**, 1991, 325–332.

41. Y. Liu and T.S. Huang, "Estimation of rigid body motion using straight line correspondences," *Computer Vision, Graphics, and Image Processing* **43**, 1988, 37–52.

42. H.C. Longuet-Higgins, "A computer algorithm for reconstructing a scene from two projections," *Nature* **293**(11), 1981, 133–135.

43. H.C. Longuet-Higgins, "The visual ambiguity of a moving plane," *Proceedings of the Royal Society of London B* **223**, 1984, 165–175.

44. H.C. Longuet-Higgins and K. Prazdny, "The interpretation of a moving retinal image," *Proceedings of the Royal Society, London B* **208**, 1980, 385–397.

45. B. Lucas and T. Kanade, "An iterative image registration technique with an application to stereo vision," in *DARPA Image Understandig Workshop*, 1981, 121–130.

46. S.J. Maybank, *A theoretical study of optical flow*, Ph.D. thesis, University of London, November 1987.

47. S. Maybank, *Theory of Reconstruction from Image Motion*, Springer-Verlag, Berlin, 1993.

48. H.-H. Nagel, "On the estimation of optical flow: Relations between different approaches and some new results," *Artificial Intelligence* **33**, 1987, 299–324.

49. S. Negahdaripour, "Multiple interpretations of the shape and motion of objects from two perspective images," *IEEE Transactions on Pattern Analysis and Machine Intelligence* **12**, 1990, 1025–1039.

50. S. Negahdaripour and B.K.P. Horn, "Direct passive navigation," *IEEE Transactions on Pattern Analysis and Machine Intelligence* **9**, 1987, 168–176.

51. A. Singh, *Optic Flow Computation*, IEEE Computer Society Press, Los Alamitos, CA, 1991.

52. C.C. Slama, C. Theurer, and S.W. Henriksen, *Manual of Photogrammetry*, American Society of Photogrammetry, Falls Church, VA, 1980.

53. H.W. Sorenson, *Parameter Estimation, Principles and Problems*, Marcel Dekker, New York and Basel, 1980.

54. M.E. Spetsakis, "A linear algorithm for point and line- based structure from motion," *CVGIP: Image Understanding* **56**, 1992, 230–241.

55. M. Spetsakis, "Models of statistical visual motion estimation," *Computer Vision, Graphics, and Image Processing* **60**, 1994, 300–312.

56. M.E. Spetsakis, "Optical flow estimation using discontinuity conforming filters," in *British Machine Vision Conference*, York, United Kingdom, 1994.

57. M.E. Spetsakis and J. Aloimonos, "Optimal computing of structure from motion using point correspondences," in *Proc. International Conference on Computer Vision*, Tampa, FL, December 5–8, 1988, 449–453.

58. M.E. Spetsakis and J. Aloimonos, "Optimal motion estimation," in *Proc. IEEE Workshop on Visual Motion*, Irvine, CA, March 20–22, 1989, 229–237.

59. M. Spetsakis and J. Aloimonos, "Structure from motion using line correspondences," *International Journal of Computer Vision* **4**, 1990, 171–183.

60. M.E. Spetsakis and Y. Aloimonos, "Optimal visual motion estimation: A note," *IEEE Transactions on Pattern Analysis and Machine Intelligence* **14**, 1992, 959–964.

61. C. Tomasi and T. Kanade, "Shape and motion from image streams under orthography: A factorization method," *International Journal of Computer Vision* **8**, 1992, 137–154.

62. R.Y. Tsai and T.S. Huang, "Uniqueness and estimation of three-dimensional motion parameters of rigid objects with curved surfaces," *IEEE Transactions on Pattern Analysis and Machine Intelligence* **6**, 1984, 13–27.

63. A.M. Waxman and K. Wohn, "Contour evolution, neighborhood deformation, and global image flow: Planar surfaces in motion," *International Journal of Robotics Research* **4**(3), 1985, 95–108.

64. J. Weng, N. Ahuja, and T.S. Huang, "Optimal motion and structure estimation," *IEEE Transactions on Pattern Analysis and Machine Intelligence* **15**, 1993, 864–884.

65. J. Weng, T.S. Huang, and N. Ahuja, "Optimal motion and structure estimation," in *Proc. IEEE Conference on Computer Vision and Pattern Recognition*, San Diego, CA, June 4–8, 1989, 144–152.

66. P. Werkhoven and J.J. Koenderink, "Extraction of motion parallax structure," *Biological Cybernetics* **63**, 1990, 185–191.

67. W. Wunderlich, "Zur Eindeutigkeitsfrage der Hauptaufgabe der Photogrammetrie," *Monatshefte für Mathematik und Physik* **50**, 1941, 151–164.

68. G.-S.J. Young and R. Chellappa, "Statistical analysis of inherent ambiguities in recovering 3-D motion from a noisy flow field," *IEEE Transactions on Pattern Analysis and Machine Intelligence* **14**, 1992, 995–1013.

5 APPLICATIONS OF NONMETRIC VISION TO SOME VISUALLY GUIDED ROBOTICS TASKS

Luc Robert,[1] Cyril Zeller,[1] Olivier Faugeras,[1] and Martial Hébert[2]
[1]INRIA
[2]Carnegie Mellon University

ABSTRACT

We usually think of physical space as embedded in a three-dimensional Euclidean space where measurements of lengths and angles make sense. It turns out that for artificial systems, such as robots, this is not a mandatory viewpoint and it is sometimes sufficient to think of the physical space as being embedded in an affine or even projective space. The question then arises of how to relate these geometric models to image measurements and to geometric properties of camera sets.

We first consider that the world is modelled as a projective space and determine how projective invariant information can be recovered from the images and used in applications. Next we consider that the world is an affine space and determine how affine invariant information can be recovered from the images and used in applications. Finally, we do not move to the Euclidean layer because this is the layer where everybody else has been working from the early days on, but rather to an intermediate level between the affine and Euclidean ones. For each of the three layers we explain various calibration procedures, from fully automatic ones to ones that use some a priori information. The calibration increases in difficulty from the projective to the Euclidean layer at the same time as the information that can be recovered from the images becomes more and more specific and detailed. The two main applications we consider are the detection of obstacles and the navigation of a robot vehicle.

1. INTRODUCTION

Many visual tasks require recovering 3D information from sequences of images. This chapter takes the natural point of view that, depending on the task at hand, some geometric information is relevant and some is not. Therefore, the questions of exactly

This work was partially funded by the EEC under Esprit Project 6448 (*VIVA*) and 8878 (*REALISE*).

what kind of information is necessary for a given task, how it can be computed from the data, after which preprocessing steps, are central to our discussion. Since we are dealing with geometric information, a very natural question that arises from the previous ones is the question of the invariance of this information under various transformations. An obvious example is viewpoint invariance, which is of course a direct concern for us.

It turns out that viewpoint invariance can be separated into three components: invariance to changes of internal parameters of the cameras, i.e., to some changes of coordinates in the images, invariance to some transformations of space, and invariance to perspective projection via the imaging process.

Thus, the question of viewpoint invariance is mainly concerned with the invariance of geometric information to certain two- and three-dimensional transformations. It turns out that a neat way to classify geometric transformations is by considering the projective, affine, and Euclidean groups of transformations. These three groups are subgroups of each other, and each one can be thought of as determining an action on geometric configuration. For example, applying a rigid displacement to a camera does not change the distances between points in the scene but in general changes their distances in the images. These actions determine three natural layers, or strata, in the processing of visual information. This has the advantages of: (1) clearly identifying the information that needs to be collected from the images in order to "calibrate" the vision system with respect to each of the three strata; and (2) of identifying the 3D information that can thereafter be recovered from those images.

Point (1) can be considered as the definition of the preprocessing which is necessary in order to be able to recover 3D geometric information which is invariant to transformations of the given subgroup. Point (2) is the study of how such information can effectively be recovered from the images. This viewpoint has been adopted in [4]. In this chapter we follow the same track and enrich it considerably in two ways. From the theoretical viewpoint, the analysis is broadened to include a detailed study of the relations between the images and a number of 3D planes, which are then used in the development of the second viewpoint (absent in [4]), the viewpoint of the applications.

To summarize, we will first consider that the world is modeled as a projective space and determine how projective invariant information can be recovered from the images and used in applications. Next we will consider that the world is an affine space and determine how affine invariant information can be recovered from the images and used in applications. Finally, we will not move to the Euclidean layer because this is the layer where everybody else has been working from the early days on, but rather to an intermediate level between the affine and Euclidean ones. For each of the three layers we explain various calibration procedures, from fully automatic ones to ones that use some a priori information. Clearly, the calibration increases in difficulty from the projective to the Euclidean layer at the same time as the information that can be recovered from the images becomes more and more specific and detailed. The two main applications that we consider are the detection of obstacles and the navigation of a robot vehicle.

Section 2 describes the model used for the camera and its relation to the three-dimensional scene. After deriving from this model a number of relations between two views, we analyze the links between the partial knowledge of the model's parameters and the invariant properties of the reconstructed scene from those two views. Section 3 describes techniques to compute some of the model's parameters without assuming full calibration of the cameras. Section 4 describes the technique of the rectification with respect to a plane. This technique, which does not require full calibration of the cameras, allows us to compute information on the structure of the scene and is at the basis for all the remaining sections. Section 5 shows how to locate 3D points with respect to a plane. Section 6 shows how to compute local surface orientations. Lastly, Section 7 presents several obstacle avoidance and navigation applications based on a partially calibrated stereo rig.

2. STRATIFICATION OF THE RECONSTRUCTION PROCESS

In this section we investigate the relations between the three-dimensional structure of the scene and its images taken by one or several cameras. We define three types of three-dimensional reconstructions that can be obtained from such views. These reconstructions are obtained modulo the action of one of the three groups, Euclidean, affine, and projective, considered as acting on the scene. For example, to say that we have obtained a projective (resp. affine, Euclidean) reconstruction of the scene means that the *real* scene can be obtained from this reconstruction by applying to it an unknown projective (resp. affine, Euclidean) transformation. Therefore the only properties of the scene that can be recovered from this reconstruction are those that are *invariant* under the group of projective (resp. affine, Euclidean) transformations. A detailed analysis of this stratification can be found in [4].

We also relate the possibility of obtaining such reconstructions to the amount of information to be known about the set of cameras in a quantitative manner, through a set of geometric parameters such as the fundamental matrix [5] of a pair of cameras, the collineation of the plane at infinity, and the intrinsic and extrinsic parameters of the cameras.

We first recall some properties of the classic *pinhole* camera model, which we will use in the remainder of the chapter. Then, we analyze the dissimilarity (disparity) between two pinhole images of a scene, and its relation to three-dimensional structure.

2.1. NOTATIONS

We assume that the reader has some familiarity with projective geometry at the level of [3, 21] and with some of its basic applications to computer vision such as the use of the fundamental matrix [5]. We will be using the following notations. Geometric entities such as points, lines, planes, etc., are represented by normal Latin or Greek letters; upper-case letters usually represent 3D objects, lower case letters 2D (image based) objects. When these geometric entities are represented by vectors or matrixes, they appear in boldface. For example, m represents a pixel, $\mathbf{m}$ its coordinate vector, M represents a 3D point, and $\mathbf{M}$ its coordinate vector.

The line going through m and n is represented by $\langle m, n \rangle$. For a three-dimensional vector $\mathbf{x}$, we note $[\mathbf{x}]_\times$ the 3×3 antisymmetric matrix such that $\mathbf{x} \times \mathbf{y} = [\mathbf{x}]_\times \mathbf{y}$ for all vectors $\mathbf{y}$, where $\times$ indicates the cross-product. $\mathbf{I}_3$ represents the 3×3 identity matrix, $\mathbf{0}_3$ the 3×1 null vector.

We will also be using projective, affine, and Euclidean coordinate frames. They are denoted by the letter $\mathcal{F}$, usually indexed by a point such as in $\mathcal{F}_C$. This notation means that the projective frame $\mathcal{F}_C$ is either an affine or a Euclidean frame of origin C. To indicate that the coordinates of a vector $\mathbf{M}$ are expressed in the frame $\mathcal{F}$, we write $\mathbf{M}_{/\mathcal{F}}$. Given two coordinate frames $\mathcal{F}_1$ and $\mathcal{F}_2$, we note $\mathbf{Q}_{\mathcal{F}_1}^{\mathcal{F}_2}$ the matrix of change of coordinates from frame $\mathcal{F}_1$ to frame $\mathcal{F}_2$, i.e., we have $\mathbf{M}_{/\mathcal{F}_2} = \mathbf{Q}_{\mathcal{F}_1}^{\mathcal{F}_2} \mathbf{M}_{/\mathcal{F}_1}$. Note that $\mathbf{Q}_{\mathcal{F}_1}^{\mathcal{F}_2} = (\mathbf{Q}_{\mathcal{F}_2}^{\mathcal{F}_1})^{-1}$.

2.2. THE CAMERA

The camera model that we use is the classic *pinhole* model. Widely used in computer vision, it captures quite accurately the actual geometry of many real imaging devices. It is also very general, and encompasses many camera models used in computer vision, such as perspective, weak-perspective, paraperspective, affine, parallel, or orthographic projection. It can be described mathematically as follows: If the object space is considered to be the three-dimensional Euclidean space $\mathcal{R}^3$ embedded in the usual way in the three-dimensional projective space $\mathcal{P}^3$ and the image space to be the two-dimensional Euclidean space $\mathcal{R}^2$ embedded in the usual way in the two-dimensional projective space $\mathcal{P}^2$, the camera is then described as a *linear projective application* from $\mathcal{P}^3$ to $\mathcal{P}^2$ (see [3]). We can write the projection matrix in any object frame $\mathcal{F}_O$ of $\mathcal{P}^3$:

$$\underbrace{\begin{bmatrix} \alpha_u & \gamma & u_0 \\ 0 & \alpha_v & v_0 \\ 0 & 0 & 1 \end{bmatrix}}_{\mathbf{A}} \underbrace{\begin{bmatrix} 1 & 0 & 0 & 0 \\ 0 & 1 & 0 & 0 \\ 0 & 0 & 1 & 0 \end{bmatrix}}_{\mathbf{K}} \mathbf{Q}_{\mathcal{F}_O}^{\mathcal{F}_C} \tag{1}$$

where $\mathbf{A}$ is the matrix of the *intrinsic parameters*, C the optical center (see Figure 1). The special frame in which the projection matrix of the camera is equal to the matrix $\mathbf{K}$ is called the normalized camera frame.

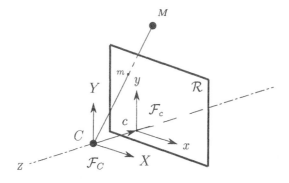

Figure 1. The pinhole model.

In particular, the projection equation, relating a point not in the focal plane $\mathbf{M}_{/\mathcal{F}_C}^T = [X_C, Y_C, Z_C, T_C]^T$, expressed in the normalized camera frame, to its projection $\mathbf{m}_{/\mathcal{F}_c} = [x, y, 1]^T$, expressed in the image frame and written $\mathbf{m}$ for simplicity, is

$$Z_C \mathbf{m} = \mathbf{AKM}_{/\mathcal{F}_C}. \tag{2}$$

2.3. DISPARITY BETWEEN TWO VIEWS

We now consider two views of the scene, obtained from either two cameras or one camera in motion. If the two images have not been acquired simultaneously, we make the further assumption that no object of the scene has moved in the meantime.

The optical centers corresponding to the views are denoted by C for the first and C' for the second, the intrinsic parameters matrixes by $\mathbf{A}$ and $\mathbf{A}'$, respectively, the normalized camera frames respectively by $\mathcal{F}_C$ and $\mathcal{F}_{C'}$. The matrix of change of frame $\mathcal{F}_C$ to frame $\mathcal{F}_{C'}$ is a matrix of displacement defined by a rotation matrix $\mathbf{R}$ and a translation vector $\mathbf{t}$:

$$\mathbf{Q}_{\mathcal{F}_C}^{\mathcal{F}_{C'}} = \begin{bmatrix} \mathbf{R} & \mathbf{t} \\ \mathbf{0}_3^T & 1 \end{bmatrix}. \tag{3}$$

More precisely, given a point M of an object o, we are interested in establishing the disparity equation of M for the two views, that is, the equation relating the projection m' of M in the second view to the projection m of M in the first view.

The general case. Assuming that M is not in either one of the two focal planes corresponding to the first and second views, we have, from equations (2) and (3):

$$Z'_{C'} \mathbf{m}' = \mathbf{A}'\mathbf{KM}_{/\mathcal{F}_{C'}} = \mathbf{A}' \begin{bmatrix} \mathbf{R} & \mathbf{t} \end{bmatrix} \mathbf{M}_{/\mathcal{F}_C} = Z_C \mathbf{A}'\mathbf{R}\mathbf{A}^{-1}\mathbf{m} + T_C \mathbf{A}'\mathbf{t}.$$

This is the general *disparity equation* relating m' to m, which we rewrite as:

$$Z'_{C'} \mathbf{m}' = Z_C \mathbf{H}_\infty \mathbf{m} + T_C \mathbf{e}', \tag{4}$$

where we have introduced the following notations:

$$\mathbf{H}_\infty = \mathbf{A}'\mathbf{R}\mathbf{A}^{-1} \quad \text{and} \quad \mathbf{e}' = \mathbf{A}'\mathbf{t}. \tag{5}$$

$\mathbf{H}_\infty$ represents the *collineation of the plane at infinity*, as it will become clear below in Section 2.3. $\mathbf{e}'$ is a vector representing the *epipole* in the second view, that is, the image of C in the second view. Indeed, this image is

$$\mathbf{A}'\mathbf{KC}_{/\mathcal{F}_{C'}} = \mathbf{A}' \begin{bmatrix} \mathbf{R} & \mathbf{t} \end{bmatrix} \mathbf{C}_{/\mathcal{F}_C} = \mathbf{A}'\mathbf{t}$$

since $\mathbf{C}_{/\mathcal{F}_C} = [0, 0, 0, 1]^T$. Similarly,

$$\mathbf{e} = \mathbf{A}\mathbf{R}^T\mathbf{t} \tag{6}$$

is a vector representing the epipole e in the first view.

Equation (4) means that m' lies on the line going through e' and the point represented by $\mathbf{H}_\infty\mathbf{m}$, which is the *epipolar line* of m. This line is represented by the vector

$$\mathbf{F}\mathbf{m}, \tag{7}$$

where

$$\mathbf{F} = [\mathbf{e}']_\times\mathbf{H}_\infty; \tag{8}$$

or equivalently,[1]

$$\mathbf{F} = \mathbf{A}'^*[\mathbf{t}]_\times\mathbf{R}\mathbf{A}^{-1}. \tag{9}$$

$\mathbf{F}$ is the *fundamental matrix* that describes the correspondence between an image point in the first view and its epipolar line in the second (see [5]).

The case of coplanar points. Let us now consider the special case of points lying in a plane π. The plane is represented in $\mathcal{F}_C$ by the vector $\boldsymbol{\Pi}^T = \begin{bmatrix} \mathbf{n}^T & -d \end{bmatrix}$, where $\mathbf{n}$ is unit normal in $\mathcal{F}_C$ and d, the distance of C to the plane. Its equation is $\boldsymbol{\Pi}^T\mathbf{M}_{/\mathcal{F}_C} = 0$, which can be written, using equation (2),

$$\mathbf{n}^T\mathbf{K}\mathbf{M}_{/\mathcal{F}_C} - T_C d = Z_C\mathbf{n}^T\mathbf{A}^{-1}\mathbf{m} - T_C d = 0. \tag{10}$$

If we first assume that $d \neq 0$, that is, the plane does not go through C, we obtain the new form of the disparity equation[2]:

$$Z'_{C'}\mathbf{m}' = Z_C\mathbf{H}\mathbf{m} \tag{11}$$

where

$$\mathbf{H} = \mathbf{H}_\infty + \mathbf{e}'\frac{\mathbf{n}^T}{d}\mathbf{A}^{-1}. \tag{12}$$

This equation defines the projective linear mapping, represented by $\mathbf{H}$, the *H-matrix* of the plane, relating the images of the points of the plane in the first view to their images in the second. It is at the basis of the idea that consists of segmenting the scene in planar structures given by their respective H-matrices and, using this segmentation, computing motion and structure (see [6] or [27]).

If the plane does not go through either C', its H-matrix represents a collineation $(\det(\mathbf{H}) \neq 0)$ and its inverse is given by

$$\mathbf{H}^{-1} = \mathbf{H}' = \mathbf{H}_\infty^{-1} + \mathbf{e}\frac{\mathbf{n}'^T}{d'}\mathbf{A}'^{-1}, \tag{13}$$

where $\mathbf{n}'$ is the unit normal in $\mathcal{F}_{C'}$ and d', the distance from the plane to C'. If the plane goes through only one of the two points C or C', its H-matrix is still defined by the one of the two equations (12) or (13), which remains valid, but is no longer a collineation; equation (10) shows that the plane then projects in one of the two views in a line represented by the vector

$$\mathbf{A}^*\mathbf{n} \quad \text{or} \quad \mathbf{A}'^*\mathbf{n}'. \tag{14}$$

---

[1] Using the algebraic equation $[\mathbf{A}\mathbf{u}]_\times = \mathbf{A}^*[\mathbf{u}]_\times\mathbf{A}$ (valid if $\det(\mathbf{A}) \neq 0$), where $\mathbf{A}^* = \det(\mathbf{A})\mathbf{A}^{-1T}$ is the adjoint matrix of $\mathbf{A}$.

[2] Using the algebraic equation $(\mathbf{u}^T\mathbf{M}\mathbf{v})\mathbf{w} = (\mathbf{w}\mathbf{u}^T\mathbf{M})\mathbf{v}$.

If the plane is an epipolar plane, i.e., goes through both C and C', its H-matrix is undefined.

Finally, equations (5) and (6) show that e' and e always verify equation (11), as expected, since e' and e are the images of the intersection of the line $< CC' >$ with the plane.

The case of points at infinity. For the points of the plane at infinity, represented by $[0, 0, 0, 1]^T$, thus of equation $T_C = 0$, the disparity equation becomes

$$Z_{C'}'\mathbf{m}' = Z_C \mathbf{H}_\infty \mathbf{m}. \tag{15}$$

Thus, $\mathbf{H}_\infty$ is indeed the H-matrix of the plane at infinity. Equation (15) is also the limit of equation (11), when $d \to \infty$, which is compatible with the fact that the points at infinity correspond to the remote points of the scene.

2.4. RECONSTRUCTION

Reconstruction is the process of computing three-dimensional structure from two-dimensional image measurements. The three-dimensional structure of the scene can be captured only up to a group of transformations in space, related to the degree of knowledge of the imaging parameters. For instance, with a calibrated stereo rig (i.e., one for which intrinsic and extrinsic parameters are known), it is well known that structure can be captured up to a rigid displacement in space. This has been used for a long time in photogrammetry. It has been shown more recently [15] that with noncalibrated affine cameras (i.e., those that perform orthographic projection), structure can be recovered only up to an affine transformation. Then, the case of uncalibrated projective cameras has been addressed [2, 11, 26], and it has been shown that in this case, three-dimensional structure can be recovered only up to a projective transformation.

We will now use the formalism introduced above to describe these three cases in more detail.

Euclidean reconstruction. Here we suppose that we know the intrinsic parameters of the cameras $\mathbf{A}$, $\mathbf{A}'$, and the extrinsic parameters of the rig, $\mathbf{R}$ and $\mathbf{t}$. This is the case when cameras have been calibrated. For clarity we call it the *strong calibration* case. Through equation (5) we can compute $\mathbf{H}_\infty$ and $\mathbf{e}'$. Equation (4) gives us

$$\frac{Z_C}{T_C} = -\frac{(\mathbf{m}' \times \mathbf{e}') \cdot (\mathbf{m}' \times \mathbf{H}_\infty \mathbf{m})}{\|\mathbf{m}' \times \mathbf{H}_\infty \mathbf{m}\|^2}$$

and equation (2)

$$\begin{bmatrix} \frac{X_C}{T_C} \\ \frac{Y_C}{T_C} \\ \frac{Z_C}{T_C} \end{bmatrix} = \frac{Z_C}{T_C} \mathbf{A}^{-1} \begin{bmatrix} x \\ y \end{bmatrix}.$$

Thus, we have computed the coordinates of M with respect to $\mathcal{F}_C$.

The projection matrices for the first and second views, expressed in their respective image frames and in $\mathcal{F}_C$, are then written

$$\mathbf{A} \begin{bmatrix} \mathbf{I}_3 \ \mathbf{0}_3 \end{bmatrix} \quad \text{and} \quad \mathbf{A}' \begin{bmatrix} \mathbf{R} \ \mathbf{t} \end{bmatrix}.$$

These matrices and the coordinates of M are thus known up to an unknown displacement $\mathbf{P}_{\mathcal{F}_O}^{\mathcal{F}_C}$ corresponding to an arbitrary change of the Euclidean reference frame.

Affine reconstruction. We now assume that both the fundamental matrix and the homography of the plane at infinity are known, but the intrinsic parameters of the cameras are unknown.

We show below that by applying an affine transformation of space, i.e., a transformation of $\mathcal{P}^3$ which leaves invariant the plane at infinity, we can compensate for the unknown parameters of the camera system. The guiding idea is to choose the affine transformation in such a way that the projection matrix of the first camera is equal to $\mathbf{K}$ as in [19]. We can then use the same reconstruction equations as in the Euclidean case (strong calibration). Since structure is known up to this unknown affine transformation, we call this case the *affine calibration* case. Let us now describe the operations in detail.

Suppose then that we have estimated H_∞ (see Section 3.4), thus we know $\mathbf{H}_\infty$ up to an unknown scale factor. Let us denote by $\tilde{\mathbf{H}}_\infty$ one of the possible representations of H_∞:

$$\tilde{\mathbf{H}}_\infty = \lambda \mathbf{H}_\infty,$$

where λ is an unknown nonzero scalar. Suppose also that we have estimated the fundamental matrix $\mathbf{F}$ (see Section 3.2) which is of rank 2, i.e., its null-space is of dimension 1. Equation (8) shows that $\mathbf{e}'$ is in the null-space of $\mathbf{F}^T$, hence $\mathbf{e}'$ is known up to a nonzero scalar μ and we write in analogy with the previous case:

$$\tilde{\mathbf{e}}' = \mu \mathbf{e}'. \tag{16}$$

Neither equation (2) nor equation (4) is usable since $\mathbf{A}$, $\mathbf{H}_\infty$, and $\mathbf{e}'$ are unknown. Both equations can be rewritten in another frame $\mathcal{F}_A$ defined by the matrix of change of frame $\mathbf{Q}_{\mathcal{F}_C}^{\mathcal{F}_A}$:

$$\mathbf{Q}_{\mathcal{F}_C}^{\mathcal{F}_A} = \begin{bmatrix} \frac{1}{\lambda}\mathbf{A} & \mathbf{0}_3 \\ \mathbf{0}_3^T & \frac{1}{\mu} \end{bmatrix}.$$

Hence

$$\mathbf{Q}_{\mathcal{F}_A}^{\mathcal{F}_C} = \begin{bmatrix} \lambda \mathbf{A}^{-1} & \mathbf{0}_3 \\ \mathbf{0}_3^T & \mu \end{bmatrix}.$$

Since we have

$$\mathbf{M}_{/\mathcal{F}_{C'}} = \mathbf{Q}_{\mathcal{F}_C}^{\mathcal{F}_{C'}} \mathbf{M}_{/\mathcal{F}_C} = \mathbf{Q}_{\mathcal{F}_C}^{\mathcal{F}_{C'}} \mathbf{Q}_{\mathcal{F}_A}^{\mathcal{F}_C} \mathbf{M}_{/\mathcal{F}_A}$$

this implies

$$\mathbf{M}_{/\mathcal{F}_{C'}} = \begin{bmatrix} \mathbf{R} & \mathbf{t} \\ \mathbf{0}_3^T & 1 \end{bmatrix} \begin{bmatrix} \lambda \mathbf{A}^{-1} & \mathbf{0}_3 \\ \mathbf{0}_3^T & \mu \end{bmatrix} \mathbf{M}_{/\mathcal{F}_A}.$$

If $\mathbf{M}_{/\mathcal{F}_A}^T = [X_A, Y_A, Z_A, T_A]^T$ is a vector representing M in $\mathcal{F}_A$, (4), written in frame $\mathcal{F}_A$, becomes

$$Z_{C'}'\mathbf{m}' = Z_A\tilde{\mathbf{H}}_\infty\mathbf{m} + T_A\tilde{\mathbf{e}}' \tag{17}$$

and equation (2),

$$Z_A\mathbf{m} = \mathbf{K}\mathbf{M}_{/\mathcal{F}_A}. \tag{18}$$

Equation (17) yields

$$\frac{Z_A}{T_A} = -\frac{(\mathbf{m}' \times \tilde{\mathbf{e}}') \cdot (\mathbf{m}' \times \tilde{\mathbf{H}}_\infty\mathbf{m})}{\|\mathbf{m}' \times \tilde{\mathbf{H}}_\infty\mathbf{m}\|^2}$$

and equation (18),

$$\begin{bmatrix} \frac{X_A}{T_A} \\ \frac{Y_A}{T_A} \end{bmatrix} = \frac{Z_A}{T_A}\begin{bmatrix} x \\ y \end{bmatrix}.$$

Thus, we have computed the coordinates of M with respect to $\mathcal{F}_A$.

It is easy to verify that the projection matrices for the first and second views, expressed in their respective image frames and in $\mathcal{F}_A$, are then written

$$\begin{bmatrix} \mathbf{I}_3\ \mathbf{0}_3 \end{bmatrix} = \mathbf{K} \quad \text{and} \quad \begin{bmatrix} \tilde{\mathbf{H}}_\infty\ \tilde{\mathbf{e}}' \end{bmatrix}.$$

They are thus known up to the unknown affine transformation $\mathbf{P}_{\mathcal{F}_O}^{\mathcal{F}_A}$, corresponding to an arbitrary change of the affine reference frame.[3]

Projective reconstruction. We now address the case when only the fundamental matrix $\mathbf{F}$ is known. This is known as the *weak calibration* case. The representation of the epipole $\mathbf{e}'$ is also known up to a nonzero scalar factor, as belonging to the null-space of $\mathbf{F}^T$. Neither equation (2) nor equation (4) is usable since $\mathbf{A}, \mathbf{H}_\infty$ and $\mathbf{e}'$ are unknown. As in the previous paragraph, we eliminate the unknown parameters by applying a projective transformation of space. Here, the plane at infinity is not (necessarily) left invariant by the transformation: It is mapped to an arbitrary plane. Let us now go into more detail:

Let us first assume that we know, up to a nonzero scalar factor λ, the H-matrix of a plane not going through the optical center C of the first camera, as defined in Section 2.3:

$$\mathbf{H} = \lambda(\mathbf{H}_\infty + \mathbf{e}'\frac{\mathbf{n}^T}{d}\mathbf{A}^{-1}) \tag{19}$$

where $\mathbf{n}$ is the unit normal expressed in $\mathcal{F}_C$ of the plane and d, with $d \neq 0$, the distance of C to the plane. We define a frame $\mathcal{F}_P$ by the matrix of change of frame from $\mathcal{F}_C$

$$\mathbf{Q}_{\mathcal{F}_C}^{\mathcal{F}_P} = \begin{bmatrix} \frac{1}{\lambda}\mathbf{A} & \mathbf{0}_3 \\ -\frac{1}{\mu}\frac{\mathbf{n}^T}{d} & \frac{1}{\mu} \end{bmatrix} \tag{20}$$

hence

$$\mathbf{Q}_{\mathcal{F}_P}^{\mathcal{F}_C} = \begin{bmatrix} \lambda\mathbf{A}^{-1} & \mathbf{0}_3 \\ \lambda\frac{\mathbf{n}^T\mathbf{A}^{-1}}{d} & \mu \end{bmatrix}$$

---

[3] It is affine because it does not change the plane at infinity.

so that $\left[\frac{\lambda}{\mu}\frac{\mathbf{n}^T}{d}\mathbf{A}^{-1}\ 1\right]^T$ is the vector representing the plane at infinity in $\mathcal{F}_P$. If $\mathbf{M}^T_{/\mathcal{F}_P} = [X_P, Y_P, Z_P, T_P]^T$ is the vector representing M in $\mathcal{F}_P$, we have then, using equation (2),

$$T_P = -\frac{1}{\mu}\frac{\mathbf{n}^T}{d}\mathbf{K}\mathbf{M}_{/\mathcal{F}_C} + \frac{1}{\mu}T_C = -Z_C\frac{1}{\mu}\frac{\mathbf{n}^T}{d}\mathbf{A}^{-1}\mathbf{m} + \frac{1}{\mu}T_C \qquad (21)$$

and, eliminating T_C from equation (4),

$$Z'_{C'}\mathbf{m}' = Z_C(\mathbf{H}_\infty + \mathbf{e}'\frac{\mathbf{n}^T}{d}\mathbf{A}^{-1})\mathbf{m} + T_P\tilde{\mathbf{e}}'. \qquad (22)$$

Equation (4) is thus written in $\mathcal{F}_P$,

$$Z'_{C'}\mathbf{m}' = Z_P\mathbf{H}\mathbf{m} + T_P\tilde{\mathbf{e}}'. \qquad (23)$$

As for equation (2), it is written in $\mathcal{F}_P$,

$$Z_P\mathbf{m} = \mathbf{K}\mathbf{M}_{/\mathcal{F}_P}. \qquad (24)$$

Equation (23) then gives us

$$\frac{Z_P}{T_P} = -\frac{(\mathbf{m}' \times \tilde{\mathbf{e}}') \cdot (\mathbf{m}' \times \mathbf{H}\mathbf{m})}{\|\mathbf{m}' \times \mathbf{H}\mathbf{m}\|^2}$$

and equation (24),

$$\begin{bmatrix} \frac{X_P}{T_P} \\ \frac{Y_P}{T_P} \end{bmatrix} = \frac{Z_P}{T_P}\begin{bmatrix} x \\ y \end{bmatrix}.$$

Thus, we have computed the coordinates of M with respect to frame $\mathcal{F}_P$.

The projection matrices for the first and second views, expressed in their respective image frames and in $\mathcal{F}_P$, are then written

$$\begin{bmatrix} \mathbf{I}_3\ \mathbf{0}_3 \end{bmatrix} \quad \text{and} \quad \begin{bmatrix} \mathbf{H}\ \tilde{\mathbf{e}}' \end{bmatrix}.$$

Indeed, the projection matrix for the second view is

$$\mathbf{A}'\mathbf{K}\mathbf{P}^{\mathcal{F}_{C'}}_{\mathcal{F}_P} = \begin{bmatrix} \mathbf{A}'\ \mathbf{0}_3 \end{bmatrix} \mathbf{P}^{\mathcal{F}_{C'}}_{\mathcal{F}_C}\mathbf{P}^{\mathcal{F}_C}_{\mathcal{F}_P} = \begin{bmatrix} \mathbf{A}'\mathbf{R}\ \mathbf{e}' \end{bmatrix} \begin{bmatrix} \lambda\mathbf{A}^{-1} & \mathbf{0}_3 \\ \lambda\frac{\mathbf{n}^T}{d}\mathbf{A}^{-1} & \mu \end{bmatrix}$$

and is actually of rank 3 as product of a 3×4 matrix of rank 3 and a 4×4 matrix of rank 4.

Both projection matrices and the coordinates of M are thus known up to the unknown collineation $\mathbf{Q}^{\mathcal{F}_P}_{\mathcal{F}_O}$, corresponding to an arbitrary change of the projective reference frame. This result had already been found in a quite different manner in [2, 11].

The reconstruction described above is possible as soon as the H-matrix of a plane which does not go through C is known. In particular, when $\mathbf{F}$ is known, one is always available as suggested by equations (8) and (22). It is defined by

$$\frac{\mathbf{n}^T}{d} = -\frac{\mathbf{e}'^T}{\|\mathbf{e}'\|^2}\mathbf{H}_\infty\mathbf{A} = -\frac{\mathbf{t}^T\mathbf{A}'^T\mathbf{A}'\mathbf{R}}{\|\mathbf{A}'\mathbf{t}\|^2} \qquad (25)$$

which gives, using (8),[4]

$$\mathbf{H} = [\frac{\mathbf{e}'}{\|\mathbf{e}'\|}]_{\times}\mathbf{F}.$$

The equation, expressed in $\mathcal{F}_{C'}$, of the corresponding plane is $\begin{bmatrix} \mathbf{n}^T & -d \end{bmatrix} \mathbf{P}_{\mathcal{F}_{C'}}^{\mathcal{F}_C} \mathbf{M}_{/\mathcal{F}_{C'}} = 0$, thus, using (25),

$$\mathbf{e}'^T \mathbf{A}' \mathbf{K} \mathbf{M}_{/\mathcal{F}_{C'}} = 0,$$

which shows, using (2), that this plane is the plane going through C', which projects, in the second view, to the line representing by $\mathbf{e}'$, as already noticed in [19].

3. COMPUTING THE GEOMETRIC PARAMETERS

Now that we have established which parameters are necessary to deduce information on the structure of the scene, we describe methods to compute these parameters, from real images.

If no a priori knowledge is assumed, the only source of information is the images themselves and the correspondences established between them.

After showing how accurate and reliable point correspondences can be obtained in general from the images, we describe how they can be used for estimating the fundamental matrix on the one hand, plane collineations on the other hand.

3.1. FINDING CORRESPONDENCES

Matching is done using the image intensity function $I(x, y)$. A criterion, usually depending on the local value of $I(x, y)$ in both images, is chosen to decide whether a point m_1 of the first image and a point m_2 of the second are the images of the same point of the scene. It is generally based on on a physical model of the scene. A classical measure for similarity between the two images within a given area is the cross-correlation coefficient

$$C(m_1, m_2) = \cos(\mathbf{i}_1 - \overline{\mathbf{i}_1}, \mathbf{i}_2 - \overline{\mathbf{i}_2}) = \frac{(\mathbf{i}_1 - \overline{\mathbf{i}_1}).(\mathbf{i}_2 - \overline{\mathbf{i}_2})}{\|\mathbf{i}_1 - \overline{\mathbf{i}_1}\|\|\mathbf{i}_2 - \overline{\mathbf{i}_2}\|}$$

where $\mathbf{i}_j$ is the vector of the image intensity values in a neighborhood around the point m_j and $\overline{\mathbf{i}_j}$ its mean in this neighborhood.

The context in which the views have been taken plays a significant role. Two main cases have to be considered: the case where the views are very similar and the opposite case. The first case usually corresponds to consecutive views of a sequence taken by one camera, the second, to views taken by a stereo rig with a large baseline. In the first case, the distance between the images of a point in two consecutive frames is small. This allows limiting the search space when trying to find point correspondences. Below, we briefly describe a simple point tracker which, relying on this property, provides robust correspondences at a relatively low computational cost. In the second case, corresponding points may have quite different positions in

---
[4] Using the algebraic equation $\mathbf{u}\mathbf{u}^T = \|\mathbf{u}\|^2\mathbf{I}_3 + [\mathbf{u}]_{\times}^2$.

the two images. Thus, point matching requires more sophisticated techniques. This is the price to pay if we want to manipulate pairs of images taken simultaneously from different viewpoints, which allow general reconstruction of the scene without worrying about the motion of the observed objects, as mentioned in Section 2.3.

In both cases, the criterion that we use for estimating the similarity between image points is not computed for all of them, but only for points of interest. These points are usually intensity corners in the image, obtained as the maxima of some operators applied to $I(x, y)$. Indeed, they are the most likely to be invariant to view changes for these operators since they usually correspond to object markings.

The corner detector. The operator that we use is the one presented in [10], which is a slightly modified version of the Plessey corner detector:

$$\det(\hat{\mathbf{C}}) - k(\text{trace}(\hat{\mathbf{C}}))^2$$

where

$$\hat{\mathbf{C}} = \begin{bmatrix} \hat{I}_x^2 & \hat{I_x I_y} \\ \hat{I_x I_y} & \hat{I}_y^2 \end{bmatrix}$$

and $\hat{I}$ denotes a smoothed version of I. Based on experiments, Harris suggests setting $k = 0.04$ for best results. $\hat{\mathbf{C}}$ is computed at each point of the image, and points for which it is larger than a given threshold are retained as corners.

The point tracker. The implementation has been strongly influenced by the corner tracker described in [28].

It works as follows: First, corners are extracted in both images. For a given corner of the first image, the following operation is performed: Its neighborhood is searched for corners of the second image. The criterion C is computed for each pair of the corner of the first image and one of the possible matches in the second image. The pair with the best score is retained as a correspondence if the score is above a fixed threshold.

For each corner of the second image for which a corresponding point in the first image has been found, the preceding operation is applied from the second image to the first. If the corresponding point found by this operation is the same as the previous one, it is then definitely taken as valid.

The stereo point matcher. The method described in the previous section no longer works as soon as the views differ markedly. More precisely, the correlation criterion is not selective enough: There are, for a given point of an image, several points of the other image that lead to a good correlation score, without the best of them being the real correspondent point searched. To achieve correspondence matching, the process must then keep all those potentially good but conflicting correspondences and invokes global techniques to decide between them: A classic relaxation technique is used to converge towards a globally coherent system of point correspondences, given some constraints of uniqueness and continuity (see [29]).

3.2. THE FUNDAMENTAL MATRIX

Once some image point correspondences, represented in the image frame by $(\mathbf{m}'_i, \mathbf{m}_i)$, have been found, the fundamental matrix $\mathbf{F}$ is computed, up to a nonzero scalar factor, as the unique solution of the system of equations, derived from the disparity equations,

$$\mathbf{m}'^T_i \mathbf{F} \mathbf{m}_i = 0. \tag{26}$$

This system can be solved as soon as seven such correspondences are available: Only eight coefficients of $\mathbf{F}$ need to be computed, since $\mathbf{F}$ is defined up to a nonzero scalar factor, while (26) supplies one scalar equation per correspondence and $\det(\mathbf{F}) = 0$, the eighth. If there are more correspondences available, which are not exact, as is the case in practice, the goal of the computation is to find the matrix which best approximates the solution of this system according to a given least-squares criterion.

A study of the computation of the fundamental matrix from image point correspondences can be found in [18]. Here, we mention our particular implementation, which consists, on the one hand, of a direct computation considering that all the correspondences are valid and on the other hand, of a method for rejecting some possible outliers among the correspondences.

The direct computation computes $\mathbf{F}$ which minimizes the following criterion:

$$\sum_i \left(\frac{1}{[\mathbf{F}\mathbf{m}_i]^2_x + [\mathbf{F}\mathbf{m}_i]^2_y} + \frac{1}{[\mathbf{F}^T\mathbf{m}'_i]^2_x + [\mathbf{F}^T\mathbf{m}'_i]^2_y} \right) (\mathbf{m}'^T_i \mathbf{F} \mathbf{m}_i)^2,$$

which is the sum of the squares of the distance of m_i to the epipolar line of m'_i and the distance of m'_i to the epipolar line of m_i. Minimization is performed with the classical Levenberg-Marquardt method (see [24]). In order to take into account both its definition up to a scale factor and the fact that it is of rank 2, a parametrization of $\mathbf{F}$ with seven parameters is used, which parametrizes all the 3×3 matrices strictly of rank less than 3. These parameters are computed from $\mathbf{F}$ the following way: A line l (respectively, a column c) of $\mathbf{F}$ is chosen and written as a linear combination of the other two lines (respectively, columns); the four entries of $\mathbf{F}$ for these two combinations are taken as parameters; among the four coefficients not belonging to l and c, the three smallest in absolute value are divided by the biggest and taken as the last three parameters. l and c are chosen in order to maximize the rank of the derivative of $\mathbf{F}$ with respect to the parameters. Denoting the parameters by p_1, p_2, p_3, p_4, p_5, p_6, and p_7 and assuming, for instance, l and c equal to 1 and the bottom right coefficient being the normalized coefficient, leads to the following matrix:

$$\begin{bmatrix} p_6(p_4p_1 + p_5p_3) + p_7(p_4p_2 + p_5) & p_4p_1 + p_5p_3 & p_4p_2 + p_5 \\ p_6p_1 + p_7p_2 & p_1 & p_2 \\ p_6p_3 + p_7 & p_3 & 1 \end{bmatrix}.$$

During the minimization process, the parametrization of $\mathbf{F}$ can change: the parametrization chosen for the matrix at the beginning of the process is not necessarily the most suitable for the final matrix.

The outliers rejection method used is a classical least median of squares method. It is described in detail in [29].

3.3. THE H-MATRIX OF A PLANE

If we have at our disposal correspondences, represented in the image frames by $(\mathbf{m}'_i, \mathbf{m}_i)$, of points belonging to a plane, the H-matrix $\mathbf{H}$ of this plane is computed, up to a nonzero scalar factor, as the unique solution of the system of equations (11),

$$Z'_{C'}\mathbf{m}'_i = Z_C \mathbf{H}\mathbf{m}_i.$$

This system can be solved as soon as four such correspondences are available; only eight coefficients of $\mathbf{H}$ need to be computed, since $\mathbf{H}$ is defined up to a nonzero scalar factor, while (11) supplies two scalar equation for each correspondence. If there are more correspondences available, which are not exact, as is the case in practice, the goal of the computation is to find the matrix which approximates at best the solution of this system according to a given criterion; a study of the computation of plane H-matrices from image point correspondences can be found in [3].

In general, since e' and e verify equation (11), three point correspondences are sufficient for defining H. In fact, this is true as long as the homography is defined, i.e., when three points are not aligned in either image (a proof can be found in [7]). If the plane is defined by one point and a line L, given by its projections (l, l') so that e does not belong to l and e' does not belong to l', its H-matrix is computable the same way, as soon as we know the fundamental matrix. Indeed, the projections of two other points M and N in the plane are given by choosing two points m and n on l, which amounts to choosing M and N on L. The corresponding points m' and n' are then given by intersecting l' with the epipolar line of m and the epipolar line of n, given by the fundamental matrix.

As an application of this idea, we have a purely image-based way to solve the following problem: Given a point correspondence (m, m') defining a 3D point M, and a line correspondence (l, l') defining a 3D line L, find the H-matrix of the plane going through M and L. In particular, if L is at infinity, it defines a planar direction (all planes going through L are parallel) and we can find the H-matrix of the plane going through M and parallel to that direction. This will be used in Section 6.2.

Given the H-matrix $\mathbf{H}$ of a plane Π and the correspondences (m, m') and (n, n') of two points M and N, it is possible to directly compute the correspondences (i, i') of the intersection I of the line $\langle M, N \rangle$ with Π in the images. Indeed, i' belongs both to $\langle m', n' \rangle$ and the image of $\langle m, n \rangle$ by $\mathbf{H}$, so:

$$\mathbf{i}' = (\mathbf{m}' \times \mathbf{n}') \times (\mathbf{H}\mathbf{m} \times \mathbf{H}\mathbf{n}).$$

(See [25].)

Similarly, given two planes Π_1 and Π_2 represented by their H-matrices $\mathbf{H}_1$ and $\mathbf{H}_2$, it is possible to directly compute in the images the correspondences of the intersection L of Π_1 with Π_2. Indeed, the correspondences of two points of L are computed, for example, as intersections of two lines L_1 and L_2 of Π_1 with Π_2; the correspondences of such lines are obtained by choosing two lines in the first image represented by the vectors $\mathbf{l}_1$ and $\mathbf{l}_2$, their corresponding lines in the second image being given by $\mathbf{H}_1^{-1T}\mathbf{l}_1$ and $\mathbf{H}_1^{-1T}\mathbf{l}_2$.

3.4. THE HOMOGRAPHY OF THE PLANE AT INFINITY

To compute the homography of the plane at infinity $\mathbf{H}_\infty$, we can no longer use the disparity equation (4) with correspondences of points not at infinity, even if we know the fundamental matrix, since $Z'_{C'}$, Z_C, and T_C are not known. We must, therefore, know correspondences of points at infinity $(\mathbf{m}'_i, \mathbf{m}_i)$ and compute $\mathbf{H}_\infty$ like any other plane H-matrices, as described in Section 3.3.

The only way to obtain correspondences of points at infinity is to assume some additional knowledge.

First, we can assume that we have some additional knowledge of the observed scene that allows us to identify some projections in the images of points at infinity, like the vanishing points of parallel lines of the scene, or the images of some points on the horizon, which provide sufficiently good approximations to points at infinity.

Another way to proceed is to assume that we have an additional pair of views. More precisely, if this second pair differs from the first only by a translation of the rig, any pair (M, N) of stationary object points (see Figure 2), seen in the first views as $(\mathbf{m}_1, \mathbf{m}'_1)$ and $(\mathbf{n}_1, \mathbf{n}'_1)$, and in the second as $(\mathbf{m}_2, \mathbf{m}'_2)$ and $(\mathbf{n}_2, \mathbf{n}'_2)$, gives us the images $(\mathbf{i}_1, \mathbf{i}'_1)$ and $(\mathbf{i}_2, \mathbf{i}'_2)$ in the four images of the intersection I of the line $\langle M, N \rangle$ with the plane at infinity. Indeed, on one hand, since I is at infinity and the immobility of M and N implies the immobility of I, we have, from (15) and (4),

$$Z_{C_2}\mathbf{i}_2 = Z_{C_1}\mathbf{H}_{\infty 12}\mathbf{i}_1 \quad \text{and} \quad Z'_{C'_2}\mathbf{i}'_2 = Z'_{C'_1}\mathbf{H}'_{\infty 12}\mathbf{i}'_1$$

where $\mathbf{H}_{\infty 12}$ (respectively, $\mathbf{H}'_{\infty 12}$) is the homography of the plane at infinity between the first (respectively, second) view of the first pair and its corresponding view in the second pair. In the case where the two pairs of views differ only by a translation, $\mathbf{A}_1 = \mathbf{A}_2$, $\mathbf{R}_{12} = \mathbf{I}_3$, $\mathbf{A}'_1 = \mathbf{A}'_2$, $\mathbf{R}'_{12} = \mathbf{I}_3$ and we have, from equation (5),

$$\mathbf{H}_{\infty 12} = \mathbf{I}_3 \quad \text{and} \quad \mathbf{H}'_{\infty 12} = \mathbf{I}_3$$

which implies that $i_1 = i_2 = i$ and $i'_1 = i'_2 = i'$. On the other hand, as I lies on $\langle M, N \rangle$, i_1 lies on $\langle m_1, n_1 \rangle$, i_2 on $\langle m_2, n_2 \rangle$, i'_1 on $\langle m'_1, n'_1 \rangle$ and i'_2 on $\langle m'_2, n'_2 \rangle$. Consequently, i and i' are obtained as the intersections of $\langle m_1, n_1 \rangle$ with $\langle m_2, n_2 \rangle$ and of $\langle m'_1, n'_1 \rangle$ with $\langle m'_2, n'_2 \rangle$, respectively:

$$\mathbf{i} = (\mathbf{m}_1 \times \mathbf{n}_1) \times (\mathbf{m}_2 \times \mathbf{n}_2) \quad \text{and} \quad \mathbf{i}' = (\mathbf{m}'_1 \times \mathbf{n}'_1) \times (\mathbf{m}'_2 \times \mathbf{n}'_2)$$

Once $\mathbf{H}_\infty$ has been obtained, the ratio of the lengths of any two aligned segments of the scene can be computed directly in the images. Indeed, given three points M_1, M_2, and M_3 on a line, as in Figure 3, from their images (m_1, m'_1), (m_2, m'_2), and (m_3, m'_3), we can compute the images (m, m') of the intersection of this line with the plane at infinity, using $\mathbf{H}_\infty$, as explained in Section 3.3. We can compute in each image the cross-ratio of those four points. As a projective invariant, this cross-ratio is then exactly equal to the ratio of M_1, M_2 and M_3. More precisely:

$$\frac{\overline{M_1 M_3}}{\overline{M_2 M_3}} = \frac{\overline{M_1 M_3}}{\overline{M_1 M_\infty}} : \frac{\overline{M_2 M_3}}{\overline{M_2 M_\infty}} = \frac{\overline{m_1 m_3}}{\overline{m_1 m}} : \frac{\overline{m_2 m_3}}{\overline{m_2 m}}$$

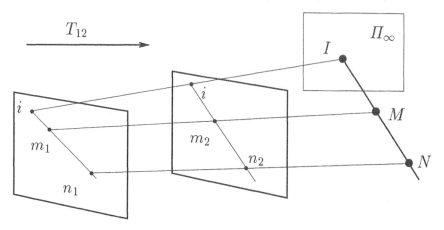

Figure 2. Determining the projections of points at infinity (see Section 3.4).

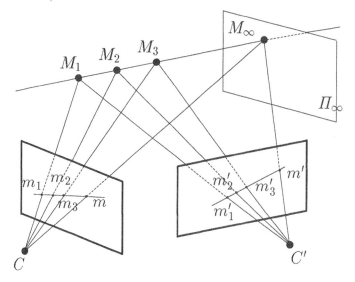

Figure 3. Determining ratios of lengths in affine calibration (see text).

4. RECTIFICATION WITH RESPECT TO A PLANE

In this section, we assume that we know the epipolar geometry. This allows us to *rectify the images with respect to a plane* of the scene. This process, explained below, allows not only computation of a map of image point correspondences, but also assignment of a scalar to each of them that represents a measure of the disparity between the two projections of the correspondence.

4.1. THE PROCESS OF RECTIFICATION

As in Section 2.4, we assume that we know $\mathbf{F}$ up to nonzero scale factors, thus we have $\tilde{\mathbf{e}}'$, given by (16), and the H-matrix $\mathbf{H}$ of a plane Π given by (19). Let us then choose two homographies, represented by the matrices $\hat{\mathbf{H}}'$ and $\hat{\mathbf{H}}$, such that

$$\hat{\mathbf{H}}'\tilde{\mathbf{e}}' = \alpha[1,0,0]^T \qquad (27)$$
$$\hat{\mathbf{H}} = \hat{\mathbf{H}}'\mathbf{H}, \qquad (28)$$

where α is any nonzero scalar. Equation (23) can then be rewritten

$$\hat{z}'Z_{C'}'\hat{\mathbf{m}}' = \hat{z}Z_P\hat{\mathbf{m}} + T_P\alpha[1,0,0]^T, \qquad (29)$$

where $\hat{\mathbf{m}} = [\hat{x}, \hat{y}, 1]^T$, $\hat{\mathbf{m}}' = [\hat{x}', \hat{y}', 1]^T$ and

$$\hat{z}'\hat{\mathbf{m}}' = \hat{\mathbf{H}}'\mathbf{m}' \quad \text{and} \quad \hat{z}\hat{\mathbf{m}} = \hat{\mathbf{H}}\mathbf{m}. \qquad (30)$$

The rectification with respect to a plane consists of applying such matrices, called the *rectification matrices*, $\hat{\mathbf{H}}'$ to the second image and $\hat{\mathbf{H}}$ to the first.

Equation (29) shows that the corresponding point $\hat{m}'$ in the second rectified image of a point $\hat{m}$ of the first rectified image lies on the line parallel to the x-axis and going through $\hat{m}$. Applying a correlation criterion to $\hat{m}$ and each point of this line thus allows us to determine $\hat{m}'$, if the image is not too distorted through the process of rectification. Equations (27) and (28) do not completely determine $\hat{\mathbf{H}}$ and $\hat{\mathbf{H}}'$: This indetermination is used to minimize the distortion of the images, as explained in Section 4.3.

Once $\hat{m}'$ has been determined, a measure of the disparity between $\hat{m}'$ and $\hat{m}$ with respect to this plane is given by $\hat{x}' - \hat{x}$. If M belongs to Π, it is equal to zero since T_P then vanishes as shown by equations (10) and (21); otherwise, its interpretation depends on the information available for the model, as explained in Section 5.

4.2. GEOMETRIC INTERPRETATION OF THE RECTIFICATION

From the QR-decomposition [9] any nonsingular matrix $\mathbf{H}$ decomposed as

$$\mathbf{H} = \mathbf{RU}, \qquad (31)$$

where $\mathbf{R}$ is a rotation matrix and $\mathbf{U}$, a nonsingular upper triangular matrix. Decomposing $\mathbf{H}^{-1}$ like in (31), inverting it, and noticing that the inverse of an upper triangular matrix is also an upper triangular matrix, we see that $\mathbf{H}$ can also be decomposed as

$$\mathbf{H} = \mathbf{U}'\mathbf{R}' \qquad (32)$$

where $\mathbf{R}'$ is a rotation matrix and $\mathbf{U}'$, a nonsingular upper triangular matrix.

To give a geometric interpretation of the rectification, we decompose $\hat{\mathbf{H}}$ and $\hat{\mathbf{H}}'$ the following way: By applying (32) to the nonsingular matrices $\hat{\mathbf{H}}\mathbf{A}$ and $\hat{\mathbf{H}}'\mathbf{A}'$, there exist two scalars $\hat{\lambda}$ and $\hat{\lambda}'$, two rotation matrices $\hat{\mathbf{R}}$ and $\hat{\mathbf{R}}'$, and two upper triangular matrices $\hat{\mathbf{A}}$ and $\hat{\mathbf{A}}'$ of the same form as $\mathbf{A}$ in (1), such that

$$\hat{\mathbf{H}} = \hat{\lambda}\hat{\mathbf{A}}\hat{\mathbf{R}}\mathbf{A}^{-1} \quad \text{and} \quad \hat{\mathbf{H}}' = \hat{\lambda}'\hat{\mathbf{A}}'\hat{\mathbf{R}}'\mathbf{A}'^{-1}. \qquad (33)$$

Then, we study how the constraints on $\hat{\mathbf{H}}'$ and $\hat{\mathbf{H}}$ given by (27) and (28) propagate to $\hat{\lambda}$, $\hat{\lambda}'$, $\hat{\mathbf{R}}$, and $\hat{\mathbf{R}}'$. On one hand, from (27), (33), (5), and (16), we have

$$\hat{\mathbf{R}}'\mathbf{t} = \frac{\alpha}{\mu\hat{\lambda}'}\hat{\mathbf{A}}'^{-1}[1,0,0]^T$$

and we define $\hat{t}_x$ such that

$$\hat{\mathbf{R}}'\mathbf{t} = [\hat{t}_x, 0, 0]^T. \tag{34}$$

On the other hand, from equations (28), (33), (19), (5), and (34), we have

$$\mathbf{I}_3 = \hat{\mathbf{H}}'\mathbf{H}\hat{\mathbf{H}}^{-1}$$
$$\Longleftrightarrow$$
$$\mathbf{I}_3 = \lambda\hat{\lambda}'\hat{\mathbf{A}}'\hat{\mathbf{R}}'\mathbf{A}'^{-1}(\mathbf{A}'\mathbf{R}\mathbf{A}^{-1} + \mathbf{A}'\mathbf{t}\frac{\mathbf{n}^T}{d}\mathbf{A}^{-1})\tfrac{1}{\hat{\lambda}}\mathbf{A}\hat{\mathbf{R}}^T\hat{\mathbf{A}}^{-1}$$
$$\Longleftrightarrow$$
$$\hat{\mathbf{R}}'\mathbf{R}\hat{\mathbf{R}}^T = \tfrac{\lambda}{\lambda\hat{\lambda}'}\hat{\mathbf{A}}'^{-1}\hat{\mathbf{A}} - [\hat{t}_x, 0, 0]^T\frac{\mathbf{n}^T\hat{\mathbf{R}}^T}{d}$$

from which we deduce that $\hat{\mathbf{R}}'\mathbf{R}\hat{\mathbf{R}}^T$ is an upper triangular matrix. Since it is a rotation matrix, this means that

$$\hat{\mathbf{R}}'\mathbf{R}\hat{\mathbf{R}}^T = \mathbf{I}_3. \tag{35}$$

We then also deduce that

$$\lambda\hat{\lambda}' = \hat{\lambda} \tag{36}$$

and

$$\mathbf{I}_3 = \hat{\mathbf{A}}'\hat{\mathbf{A}}^{-1} + \hat{\mathbf{A}}'[\hat{t}_x, 0, 0]^T\frac{\mathbf{n}^T\hat{\mathbf{R}}^T}{d}\hat{\mathbf{A}}^{-1}. \tag{37}$$

We are now able to interpret the equations (30). From equations (27) and (20), we have $\hat{z}'Z'_{C'} = \hat{z}Z_P = \frac{\hat{z}Z_C}{\lambda}$. Using equation (36), we can then define Z_R by

$$Z_R = \frac{\hat{z}'Z'_{C'}}{\hat{\lambda}'} = \frac{\hat{z}Z_C}{\hat{\lambda}} \tag{38}$$

so that the equations (30) are written

$$Z_R\hat{\mathbf{m}} = Z_C\hat{\mathbf{A}}\hat{\mathbf{R}}\hat{\mathbf{A}}^{-1}\mathbf{m} \quad \text{and} \quad Z_R\hat{\mathbf{m}}' = Z'_{C'}\hat{\mathbf{A}}'\hat{\mathbf{R}}'\hat{\mathbf{A}}'^{-1}\mathbf{m}'.$$

They are interpreted as the disparity equations of two pairs of views (see Figure 4): The first pair is composed of the view of optical center C, camera frame $\mathcal{F}_C$, retinal plane $\mathcal{R}$, and intrinsic parameters matrix $\mathbf{A}$ and its rectified view of optical center C, camera frame $\hat{\mathcal{F}}_C$, retinal plane $\hat{\mathcal{R}}$, and intrinsic parameters matrix $\hat{\mathbf{A}}$; similarly, the second pair is composed of the view of optical center C', camera frame $\mathcal{F}_{C'}$, retinal plane $\mathcal{R}'$ and intrinsic parameters matrix $\mathbf{A}'$ and its rectified view of optical center C', camera frame $\hat{\mathcal{F}}_{C'}$, retinal plane $\hat{\mathcal{R}}'$ and intrinsic parameters matrix $\hat{\mathbf{A}}'$. The basis of $\hat{\mathcal{F}}_C$ is the image of the basis of $\mathcal{F}_C$ by the rotation of matrix $\hat{\mathbf{R}}$. Similarly, the basis

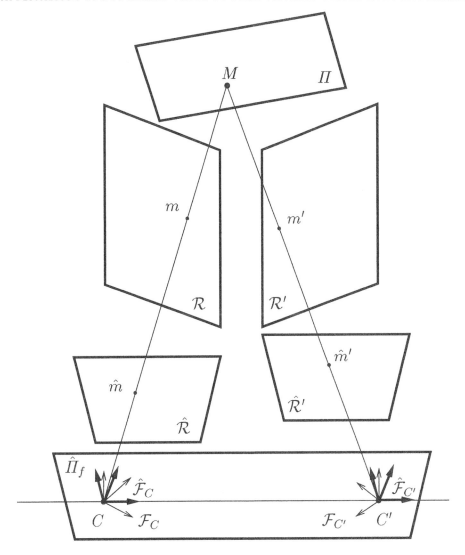

Figure 4. The rectification with respect to a plane Π.

of $\hat{\mathcal{F}}_{C'}$ is the image of the basis of $\mathcal{F}_{C'}$ by the rotation of matrix $\hat{\mathbf{R}}'$. Furthermore, according to equations (35) and (34), we have

$$
\begin{aligned}
\mathbf{Q}_{\hat{\mathcal{F}}_C}^{\hat{\mathcal{F}}_{C'}} &= \mathbf{Q}_{\mathcal{F}_{C'}}^{\hat{\mathcal{F}}_{C'}} \mathbf{Q}_{\mathcal{F}_C}^{\mathcal{F}_{C'}} \mathbf{Q}_{\hat{\mathcal{F}}_C}^{\mathcal{F}_C} \\
&= \begin{bmatrix} \hat{\mathbf{R}}' & \mathbf{0}_3 \\ \mathbf{0}_3^T & 1 \end{bmatrix} \begin{bmatrix} \mathbf{R} & \mathbf{t} \\ \mathbf{0}_3^T & 1 \end{bmatrix} \begin{bmatrix} \hat{\mathbf{R}}^T & \mathbf{0}_3 \\ \mathbf{0}_3^T & 1 \end{bmatrix} \\
&= \begin{bmatrix} 1 & 0 & 0 & \hat{t}_x \\ 0 & 1 & 0 & 0 \\ 0 & 0 & 1 & 0 \\ 0 & 0 & 0 & 1 \end{bmatrix},
\end{aligned}
$$

which shows that $\hat{\mathcal{F}}_C$ and $\hat{\mathcal{F}}_{C'}$ have the same basis $\mathcal{B}_R$ and that the x-axis of this basis is parallel to $\overrightarrow{CC'}$. Lastly, for the two rectified views, the homography of the plane at infinity is $\hat{\mathbf{H}}_\infty = \hat{\mathbf{A}}'\hat{\mathbf{A}}^{-1}$ and the epipole of the second view is $\hat{\mathbf{e}}' = \hat{\mathbf{A}}'[\hat{t}_x, 0, 0]^T$, so that, according to equation (19), the homography of Π is $\mathbf{I}_3$.

In summary, the process of rectification consists of projecting the first image onto a retinal plane $\hat{\mathcal{R}}$ and the second image onto a retinal plane $\hat{\mathcal{R}}'$ such that $\hat{\mathcal{R}}$ and $\hat{\mathcal{R}}'$ are parallel, and choosing the rectified image frames such that the x-axes of the two rectified images are parallel and the homography of Π for the two rectified images is identity.

4.3. MINIMIZING IMAGE DISTORTION

We now examine the distortion caused by $\hat{\mathbf{H}}$ and $\hat{\mathbf{H}}'$ to the images.

How many degrees of freedom are left? $\mathbf{H}$ being known, (28) shows that $\hat{\mathbf{H}}$ is completely determined as soon as $\hat{\mathbf{H}}'$ is. So, all the degrees of freedom left are concentrated in $\hat{\mathbf{H}}'$. Only eight coefficients of $\hat{\mathbf{H}}'$ need to be computed, since $\hat{\mathbf{H}}'$ is defined up to a nonzero scale factor, and (27) supplies two scalar equations: Six degrees of freedom remain, but how many of them are really involved in the distortion?

To answer this question, we propose two approaches: The first one decomposes $\hat{\mathbf{H}}'$ and the second one, $\hat{\mathbf{H}}'^{-1}$. In each case, we propose a method for computing the values of the parameters which minimizes the image distortion.

The decomposition of $\hat{\mathbf{H}}'$. According to (32), there exist two matrices, $\mathbf{U}$ and $\mathbf{R}$, such that

$$\hat{\mathbf{H}}' = \mathbf{U}\mathbf{R}.$$

$\mathbf{U}$ is an upper triangular matrix and $\mathbf{R}$ a rotation matrix. If we decompose $\mathbf{R}$ as a product of three rotations around the x-, y-, and z-axes, we can write:

$$\hat{\mathbf{H}}' = \underbrace{\begin{bmatrix} \mathbf{U}_2 & \mathbf{v} \\ \mathbf{0}_3^T & \lambda \end{bmatrix}}_{\mathbf{U}} \underbrace{\begin{bmatrix} \mathbf{R}_2 & \mathbf{0}_2 \\ \mathbf{0}_3^T & 1 \end{bmatrix}}_{\mathbf{R}_z} \mathbf{R}_y \mathbf{R}_x = \begin{bmatrix} \mathbf{U}_2\mathbf{R}_2 & \mathbf{v} \\ \mathbf{0}_3^T & \lambda \end{bmatrix} \mathbf{R}_y \mathbf{R}_x,$$

where $\mathbf{U}_2$ is a 2×2 upper triangular matrix, $\mathbf{R}_2$, a 2×2 rotation matrix, $\mathbf{v}$ a vector, and λ a scalar. Now, according to equation (31), $\mathbf{U}_2\mathbf{R}_2$ can be rewritten as $\mathbf{R}_2'\mathbf{U}_2'$ where $\mathbf{R}_2'$ is a rotation matrix and $\mathbf{U}_2'$, an upper triangular matrix and we can write:

$$\hat{\mathbf{H}}' = \underbrace{\begin{bmatrix} \mathbf{R}_2' & \mathbf{0}_2 \\ \mathbf{0}_3^T & 1 \end{bmatrix}}_{\mathbf{R}_z'} \underbrace{\begin{bmatrix} \mathbf{U}_2' & \mathbf{R}_2'^T\mathbf{v} \\ \mathbf{0}_3^T & \lambda \end{bmatrix}}_{\mathbf{U}'} \mathbf{R}_y \mathbf{R}_x,$$

where $\mathbf{R}_z'$ is a rotation around the z-axis and $\mathbf{U}'$ an upper triangular matrix. Lastly, if we extract from $\mathbf{U}'$ the translation and scaling components, we have

$$\hat{\mathbf{H}}' = \lambda \mathbf{R}_z' \begin{bmatrix} s_x & 0 & u_0 \\ 0 & s_y & v_0 \\ 0 & 0 & 1 \end{bmatrix} \begin{bmatrix} 1 & s_{xy} & 0 \\ 0 & 1 & 0 \\ 0 & 0 & 1 \end{bmatrix} \mathbf{R}_y \mathbf{R}_x. \tag{39}$$

Based on equation (39), $\mathbf{R}_y$ is chosen so as to cancel out the third coordinate of $\hat{\mathbf{H}}'\tilde{\mathbf{e}}'$, involved in equation (27), (making the epipolar lines parallel), and $\mathbf{R}'_z$ so as to cancel out its second coordinate (making the epipolar lines parallel to the x-axis). The translation terms, u_0 and v_0, are not involved in the distortion; four degrees of freedom are left, given by the two scaling factors, s_x and s_y, the skew s_{xy}, and the rotation angle in $\mathbf{R}_x$.

Minimizing distortion using a criterion based on areas. The criterion to be minimized is the ratio of the area of the rectangle with sides parallel to the x- and y-axes circumscribing the rectified image to the area of the rectified image (see Figure 5).

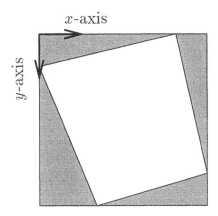

Figure 5. The area-based criterion: minimizing the relative area of the filled region.

This criterion is valid as soon as these areas are not infinite, that is, as soon as the line l (resp. l'), which is mapped by $\hat{\mathbf{H}}$ (resp. $\hat{\mathbf{H}}'$) to the line at infinity, does not go through any point of the first (resp. second) image. If e (resp. e') does not lie in the first (resp. second) image, $\hat{\mathbf{H}}$ (resp. $\hat{\mathbf{H}}'$) can be chosen to verify this constraint, since equation (27) (resp. (28)) shows that l (resp. l'), which is represented by the last row of $\hat{\mathbf{H}}$ (resp. $\hat{\mathbf{H}}'$), is only constrained to go through e (resp. e').

$\hat{\mathbf{H}}'$ is decomposed as explained in the paragraph above so that the criterion is a scalar function of s_x, s_y, s_{xy} and the angle θ_x of $\mathbf{R}_x$. Since the criterion is nonlinear and its derivatives are not easily computable, a direction-set method is used, namely, Powell's method. s_x and s_y are initialized to 1 and s_{xy} and θ_x to 0. At the end of the minimization, s_x, s_y, u_0, and v_0 are adjusted so that the rectified image is of the same size and at the same position in the plane as the initial image.

The decomposition of $\hat{\mathbf{H}}^{-1}$. Here we present another approach in which a particular parametrization of $\hat{\mathbf{H}}^{-1}$ allows us to isolate the parameters responsible for image distortion, and estimate their values so as to minimize distortion.

For simplicity, we express image point coordinates with respect to a normalized coordinate system, in which the image occupies the unit square. Using homogeneous coordinates, we denote by $[e_x, e_y, e_z]$ the coordinates of the epipole e. We now describe a parametrization of $\hat{\mathbf{H}}^{-1}$ that explicitly introduces two free rectification parameters. The other parameters correspond to two scaling factors (one horizontal and one vertical), and one horizontal translation which can be applied to both rectified images. These parameters can be set arbitrarily, and represent the magnification and clipping of the rectified images.

Let us now see how, using the mapping of four particular points, we define a parameterization for $\hat{\mathbf{H}}^{-1}$.

1. $\hat{\mathbf{H}}^{-1}$ maps point $[1, 0, 0]^{\mathrm{T}}$ onto the epipole. This is the condition for the epipolar lines to be horizontal in the rectified images.
2. We impose that the origin of the rectified image be mapped onto the origin of the image. (This sets two translation parameters in the rectified image plane.) In other words, $\hat{\mathbf{H}}^{-1}[0, 0, 1]^{\mathrm{T}} = \lambda[0, 0, 1]^{\mathrm{T}}$.
3. Since $\hat{\mathbf{H}}^{-1}$ maps horizontal lines onto epipolar lines, we impose that the top-right corner of the image be mapped onto point $t_r = [e_x, e_y, e_x]$ of the image, intersection of the epipolar line of the left corner with the right edge of the image[5] (Figure 6). This sets the horizontal scale factor for the rectified image coordinates.
4. Fourth, we impose that the low-left-hand corner of the rectified image be mapped onto the epipolar line of the low-left-hand corner of the image. This sets the vertical scale factor for the rectified image coordinates.

From the first three points, we infer that matrix $\hat{\mathbf{H}}^{-1}$ is of the form:

$$\hat{\mathbf{H}}^{-1} = \begin{bmatrix} e_x & ? & 0 \\ e_y & ? & 0 \\ e_z & ? & e_x - e_z \end{bmatrix}.$$

From the fourth point, we have $(\hat{\mathbf{H}}^{-1}[0, 1, 1]^{\mathrm{T}})^{\mathrm{T}}(\mathbf{e} \times [0, 1, 1]^{\mathrm{T}}) = 0$. In other words, $\hat{\mathbf{H}}^{-1}[0, 1, 1]^{\mathrm{T}}$ is a linear combination of $\mathbf{e}$ and $[0, 1, 1]^{\mathrm{T}}$, so there exist α, β such that

$$\hat{\mathbf{H}}^{-1} = \begin{bmatrix} e_x & \alpha e_x & 0 \\ e_y & \alpha e_y + \beta & 0 \\ e_z & \alpha e_z + \beta + e_z - e_x & e_x - e_z \end{bmatrix}.$$

Assuming that the rectification plane is known (homography H), any choice of α, β defines a rectification matrix for the two images.

Minimizing distortion using orthogonality. We choose α, β so as to introduce as little image distortion as possible. Since there is no absolute measure of global distortion for images, the criterion we use is based on the following observation: In the rectified images, epipolar lines are orthogonal to pixel columns. If the rectification transformation induced no deformation, it would preserve orthogonality, so the image by $\hat{\mathbf{H}}^{-1}$ of lines along pixel columns would be orthogonal to epipolar lines.

---

[5] Since cameras are in a horizontal configuration, this intersection point exists. However, the same method can be easily adapted to other cases.

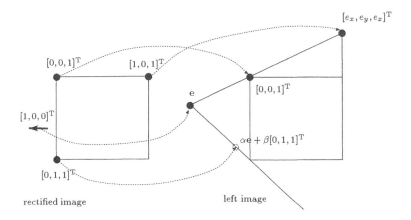

Figure 6. $\hat{\mathbf{H}}^{-1}$ maps three corners of the rectified image onto particular points of the image, and the point at infinity $[1,0,0]^{\mathrm{T}}$ onto the epipole e.

Let us now consider one scanline $\langle d_r \rangle$ of the rectified image, and two points t, b which are respectively the top and bottom points of a vertical line $\langle l \rangle$ of the rectified image. The epipolar line $\langle d_r \rangle$ corresponds to epipolar lines $\langle d_i \rangle, \langle d_i' \rangle$ in the initial images. The two lines d_r and $\langle l \rangle$ are orthogonal. Assuming that the rectification transformation preserves orthogonality, lines $\langle \hat{\mathbf{H}}^{-1}(t), \hat{\mathbf{H}}^{-1}(b) \rangle$ and $\langle d_i \rangle$ should be orthogonal (see Figure 7), as well as lines $\langle \hat{\mathbf{H}}'^{-1}(t), \hat{\mathbf{H}}'^{-1}(b) \rangle$ and $\langle d_i' \rangle$.

For a given value of parameters α, β, we define the residual

$$R(\alpha, \beta) = ((\mathbf{V} \mathbf{d}_i)^T \mathbf{V} (\hat{\mathbf{H}}^{-1} \mathbf{t}) \times (\hat{\mathbf{H}}^{-1} \mathbf{b}))^2$$

with

$$\mathbf{V} = \begin{bmatrix} 1 & 0 & 0 \\ 0 & 1 & 0 \end{bmatrix}.$$

This term is the dot product of the directions of the two lines $\langle \hat{\mathbf{H}}^{-1}(t), \hat{\mathbf{H}}^{-1}(b) \rangle$ and $\langle d_i \rangle$. An analogous term $R'(\alpha, \beta)$ can be defined in the right image, with the rectification transformation $\hat{\mathbf{H}}'^{-1} = \mathbf{H}^{-1} \hat{\mathbf{H}}^{-1}$.

To determine rectification transformations, we compute α, β which minimize the sum $(R(\alpha, \beta) + R'(\alpha, \beta))$ computed for both the left and the right columns of the rectified image, i.e., $\mathbf{t}$ and $\mathbf{b}$ having respective values $[0,0,1]^T$ and $[0,1,1]^T$ on the one hand, $[1,0,1]^T$ and $[1,1,1]^T$ on the other hand. One can see easily that the resulting expression is the square of a linear expression in α, β. It can be minimized very efficiently using standard linear least-squares techniques.

The two epipolar lines $\langle d_i \rangle, \langle d_i' \rangle$ are chosen arbitrarily, so as to represent an "average direction" of the epipolar lines in the images. In practice, the pair of epipolar lines defined by the center of the left image provides satisfactory results.

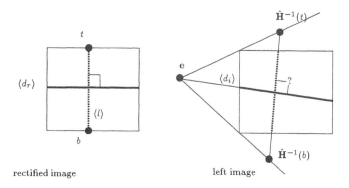

Figure 7. Lines involved in the determination of the rectification transformation (see text).

5. POSITIONING POINTS WITH RESPECT TO A PLANE

Measuring the positions of points with respect to a reference plane is essential for robot navigation. We will show in Sections 6 and 7 several applications which are based on this measurement. In this section we study how to compare distances of points to a reference plane under minimal calibration assumptions.

5.1. COMPARING POINT DISTANCES TO A REFERENCE PLANE

For convenience we will adopt the terminology which corresponds to the particular application of Section 7.3 where the reference plane is the *ground* plane, and the robot needs to estimate the relative *heights* of visible points, i.e., their relative distances to the ground plane.

The distance of a point M to the reference plane is related to the location of M along the direction orthogonal to the plane. This notion can clearly not be captured at the projective level. Let us now see under which calibration assumptions we will be able to compare point heights.

Let us introduce an (arbitrary) reference point O which does not belong to the ground plane. In practice this point is defined by its two image projections o, o', chosen arbitrarily so as to satisfy the above constraints:

- o, o' satisfy the epipolar constraint,
- both o and o' lie outside of the images,
- o and o' do not satisfy the homographic relation of the reference plane.

This guarantees that point O does not lie on the plane, and is different from any observable point.

We now consider the line $\langle D \rangle$ orthogonal to the reference plane and passing through O. Denoting by Q_D the intersection between $\langle D \rangle$ and the ground plane, the height of M is in fact equal to the signed distance $Q_D M_D$, where M_D is obtained by projecting M on $\langle D \rangle$ parallel to the reference plane.

From simple affine geometric properties, ratios of signed distances $Q_D M_D/OQ_D$ and QM/OQ are equal. Thus, if we consider an arbitrary point M_r which we declare to be at height one from the reference plane, the height of M in terms of this unit can be expressed as (see Figure 8)

$$h = \frac{QM/OQ}{Q_r M_r/OQ_r}. \tag{40}$$

Affine projection. In practice, we cannot directly compute distances between 3D points. However, we can compute their projections on the image planes. Ratios of distances are affine invariants, so if we assume that, say, the right camera performs affine projection, we can write

$$h = \frac{q'm'/o'q'}{q'_r m'_r/o'q'_r}.$$

Under affine viewing, this definition of height is exact in the sense that h is proportional to the distance between M and the reference plane. Otherwise, this formula is only an approximation. At any rate, it turns out to be accurate enough for some navigation applications, in which points for which heights have to be compared are at relatively long range from the camera, and within a relatively shallow depth of field (cf. Section 7.3).

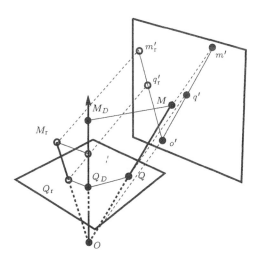

Figure 8. Computation of relative heights with respect to unit point M_r under affine projection (see text).

Perspective projection. If the affine approximation is not valid, we need to compare relative heights to projective invariants. Instead of considering ratios of distances, we consider cross-ratios, which are invariant by projection onto the images.

Let us assume that we know the homography of a plane $\Pi_{//}$ parallel to the ground plane (This is in fact equivalent to knowing the line at infinity of the ground plane). Intersecting line $\langle OM \rangle$ (resp. $\langle OM_r \rangle$) with plane $\Pi_{//}$ defines a point N (resp. N_r) aligned with O, Q, M (resp. O, Q_r, M_r).

The cross-ratio $\{Q, N; M, O\}$ is by definition equal to

$$\frac{QM/OQ}{NM/ON}.$$

Based on simple affine properties, the denominator of the above fraction is also equal to

$$N_D M_D / O N_D$$

where N_D is the projection of N on $\langle D \rangle$ parallel to plane $\Pi_{//}$, i.e., the intersection of $\Pi_{//}$ and $\langle D \rangle$.

Similarly, we have

$$\{O, Q_r; M_r, N_r\} = \frac{Q_r M_r / O Q_r}{N_D M_D / O N_D}.$$

As a consequence, the ratio of cross-ratios $\{Q, N; M, O\}/\{Q_r, N_r; M_r, O\}$ is equal to h (as defined in equation (40)). Using projective invariance, we can then express the height of M with respect to M_r as

$$h = \frac{\{q, n; m, o\}}{\{q_r, n_r; m_r, o\}}.$$

We remark that the ratio of heights with respect to a plane can be captured at a calibration level which is intermediate between projective and affine: Knowing the plane at infinity is not necessary, one only needs to know the line at infinity of the reference plane.

5.2. INTERPRETING DISPARITIES

In this section we assume that images have been rectified with respect to the reference plane, and relate positions ot points relative to the plane to image disparities.

The measure $\mathcal{D}$ of the disparity assigned to a point correspondence after the rectification with respect to a plane and the correlation along the epipolar lines, described in Section 4, is in turn related to the position of the corresponding point of the scene with respect to the plane.

Indeed, with the notations of Section 4,

$$\mathcal{D} = \hat{x}' - \hat{x}.$$

So, according to equations (29) and (38), we have

$$\mathcal{D} = \alpha \frac{T_P}{\hat{z}' Z_{C'}'} = \alpha \hat{\lambda}' \frac{T_P}{Z_R}. \tag{41}$$

In order to interpret $\mathcal{D}$, we introduce the signed distance $d(M, \Pi)$ of a point $M = [X, Y, Z, T]^T$ to a plane Π defined by its unit normal $\mathbf{n}$ and its distance d to the origin:

$$d(M, \Pi) = d - \mathbf{n}^T [\frac{X}{T}, \frac{Y}{T}, \frac{Z}{T}]^T .$$

The sign of $d(M, \Pi)$ is the same for all the points M located at the same side of Π and $|d(M, \Pi)|$ is equal to the distance of M to Π. Similarly, we introduce the signed distance $d(m, l)$ of a point $m = [x, y, z]^T$ to a line l defined by its unit normal $\mathbf{n}$ and its distance d to the origin:

$$d(m, l) = d - \mathbf{n}^T [\frac{x}{z}, \frac{y}{z}]^T .$$

The sign of $d(m, l)$ is the same for all the points m located at the same side of l and $|d(m, l)|$ is equal to the distance of m to l. We have then, according to (21) and (3),

$$T_P = \frac{T_C}{d\mu} d(M, \Pi)$$
$$Z'_{C'} = T_C d(M, \Pi'_f)$$
$$\hat{z}' = \frac{1}{k} d(m', l'_\infty) \quad \text{with} \quad k = \sqrt{h'^2_{31} + h'^2_{32}}$$
$$Z_R = T_C d(M, \hat{\Pi}_f),$$

where Π'_f is the focal plane of the second view, $\hat{\Pi}_f$ the focal plane of the rectified views (see Figure 4), and l'_∞ the line of $\mathcal{R}'$ whose image by $\hat{\mathbf{H}}' = [h'_{ij}]$ is the line at infinity.

Now, using these signed distances, we write $\mathcal{D}$ in three different ways:

$$\hat{z}'\mathcal{D} = \frac{\alpha}{d\mu} \frac{d(M, \Pi)}{d(M, \Pi'_f)} \tag{42}$$

$$\mathcal{D} = \frac{k\alpha}{d\mu} \frac{d(M, \Pi)}{d(m', l'_\infty) d(M, \Pi'_f)} \tag{43}$$

$$\mathcal{D} = \frac{\alpha\hat{\lambda}'}{d\mu} \frac{d(M, \Pi)}{d(M, \hat{\Pi}_f)}. \tag{44}$$

Since α, μ, d, $\hat{\lambda}'$, and k do not depend on M and m, we deduce from these equations the following three interpretations:

- From (42), we deduce that, if M is a visible point, which implies that $d(M, \Pi'_f) > 0$, the sign of $\hat{z}'\mathcal{D}$ gives its position with respect to Π. Furthermore, $|\hat{z}'\mathcal{D}|$ is proportional to the ratio of the distance of M to Π to the distance of M to Π'_f.
- From (43), we deduce that, if M is a visible point, the sign of $\mathcal{D}$ usually gives its position with respect to Π. Indeed, l'_∞ usually does not go through any point of the image so that the sign of $d(m', l'_\infty)$ is usually the same for all the points considered. In fact, l'_∞ is usually far away from the image, so that $d(m', l'_\infty)$ does not really depend on m for the points considered and $|\mathcal{D}|$ is approximately proportional to the ratio of the distance of M to Π to the distance of M to Π'_f.

- From (44), we deduce that the sign of $\mathcal{D}$ gives the position of M with respect to Π and $\hat{\Pi}_f$ and $|\mathcal{D}|$ is proportional to the ratio of the distance of M to Π to the distance of M to $\hat{\Pi}_f$. According to (27), $e' \in l'_\infty$ so that l'_∞ is an epipolar line. l'_∞ is thus the image in the second view of an epipolar plane Π_e. Now, the image in $\hat{\mathcal{R}}'$ of Π_e is the line at infinity, so Π_e is parallel to $\hat{\Pi}_f$. Since $\hat{\Pi}_f$ is an epipolar plane, $\hat{\Pi}_f = \Pi_e$ and l'_∞ is, indeed, the intersection of $\hat{\Pi}_f$ and $\mathcal{R}'$. Consequently, since l'_∞ is usually far away from the image, $\hat{\Pi}_f$ and $\mathcal{R}'$, thus $\hat{\Pi}_f$ and Π'_f, are approximately parallel around the image, so that Π'_f may be approximated by $\hat{\Pi}_f$ for the points considered and we turn again to the preceding interpretation.

When Π is the plane at infinity, according to (21), we have $T_P = T_C$, and, therefore,

$$\hat{z}'\mathcal{D} = \frac{\alpha}{d(M, \Pi'_f)}$$

$$\mathcal{D} = \frac{k\alpha}{d(m', l'_\infty)d(M, \Pi'_f)}$$

$$\mathcal{D} = \frac{\alpha\hat{\lambda}'}{d(M, \hat{\Pi}_f)}.$$

Thus, in that case, $\hat{z}'\mathcal{D}$ is inversely proportional to the distance of M to Π'_f, $\mathcal{D}$ is approximately inversely proportional to the distance of M to Π'_f, and $\mathcal{D}$ is inversely proportional to the distance of M to $\hat{\Pi}_f$.

6. COMPUTING LOCAL TERRAIN ORIENTATIONS USING COLLINEATIONS

Once a point correspondence is obtained through the process of rectification and correlation along the epipolar lines described in Section 4, it is possible to estimate, in addition to a measure of the disparity, a measure of local surface orientations, by using the image intensity function.

The traditional approach to computing such surface properties is first to build a metric model of the observed surfaces from the stereo matches, and then to compute local surface properties using standard tools from Euclidean geometry. This approach has two major drawbacks. First, reconstructing the geometry of the observed surfaces can be expensive because it requires not only applying geometric transformations to the image pixels and their disparity in order to recover three-dimensional coordinates, but also interpolating a sparse 3D map in space to get dense three-dimensional information. Second, reconstructing the metric surface requires having full knowledge of the geometry of the camera system through exact calibration. In addition, surface properties such as slope are particularly sensitive to the calibration parameters, thus putting more demand on the quality of the calibration.

Here, we investigate algorithms for evaluating terrain orientations from pairs of stereo images using limited calibration information. More precisely, we want to obtain an image in which the value of each pixel is a measure of the difference in orientation relative to some reference orientation, e.g., the orientation of the ground plane, assuming that the only accurate calibration information is the epipolar geometry of the cameras.

We investigate two approaches based on these geometrical tools. In the first approach (Section 6.2), we compute the sum of squared differences (SSD) at a pixel for all the possible skewing configurations of the windows. The skewing parameters of the window which produce the minimum of SSD corresponds to the most likely orientation at that point. This approach uses only knowledge of the epipolar geometry but does not allow the full recovery of the slopes. Rather, it permits the comparison of the slope at every pixel with a reference slope, e.g., the orientation of the ground plane for a mobile robot.

The second approach (Section 6.3) involves relating the actual orientations in space with window skewing parameters. Specifically, we parameterize the space of all possible windows at a given pixel by the corresponding directions on the unit sphere. This provides more information than in the previous case but requires additional calibration information, i.e, the knowledge of the approximate intrinsic parameters of one of the cameras and of point correspondences in the plane at infinity.

6.1. THE PRINCIPLE

The guiding principle of this section is the following: The collineation that represents a planar surface is the one that best warps the first image onto the second one.

This principle is used implicitly in all area-based stereo techniques in which the images are rectified and the scene is supposed to be locally fronto-parallel (i.e., parallel to the cameras) at each point [8, 20, 23]. In this case, homographies are simple translations. A rectangular window in image 1 maps onto a similar window in image 2, whose horizontal offset (disparity) characterizes the position of the plane in space. The pixel-to-pixel mapping defined by the homography allows computing a similarity measure on the pixel intensities inside the windows, based on a cross-correlation of the intensity vectors or an SSD of the pixel intensities.

Another example of this concept is the use of windows of varying shapes in area-based stereo by compensating for the effects of foreshortening due to the orientation of the plane with respect to the camera. In the *TELEOS* system [22], for example, several window shapes are used in the computation of the disparity.

We use this principle for choosing, among all homographies that represent planes of various orientations passing through a surface point M, the one that best represents the surface at M. We use a standard window-based correlation algorithm to establish the correspondences between the images (m, m') of M. Since the methods presented above are sensitive to the disparity estimates, we also use a simple subpixel disparity estimator.

6.2. WINDOW-BASED REPRESENTATION

When applying an homography to a rectangular window in image 1, one obtains in general a skewed window in image 2. Since the homographies that we study map m on m', two other pairs of points are sufficient for describing them (see Section 3.3).

This allows us to introduce a description of the plane orientation by two parameters measured directly in the images.

The standard configuration. In order to simplify the presentation, we first describe the relations in the case of cameras in *standard configuration*, i.e., whose optical axes are aligned and so that the axes of the image planes are also aligned. We also assume that the camera's intrinsic parameters are known, and considering metric coordinates in the retinal plane instead of pixel coordinates we end up with $\mathbf{A} = \mathbf{I}$ and $\mathbf{H}_\infty = \mathbf{I}$ (using the same notations as in Section 2). Choosing the frame attached to the first camera as the reference frame, the translation between the cameras is assumed to be $\mathbf{t} = [t_x, 0, 0]^t$. Although we describe the approach in this simplified case, the principle remains the same in the general case, though interpreting the equations is more complicated.

In the current case, equation (12) gives us

$$\mathbf{H} = \mathbf{I} + \frac{\mathbf{t}\mathbf{n}^t}{d} = \begin{bmatrix} 1 + \frac{n_x t_x}{d} & \frac{n_y t_x}{d} & \frac{n_z t_x}{d} \\ 0 & 1 & 0 \\ 0 & 0 & 1 \end{bmatrix}. \tag{45}$$

The distance parameter d can be obtained from the image points as follows: The images m, m' of the three-dimensional point M are known, and related by a horizontal disparity $\mathcal{D}$. From the projection geometry, we have

$$\mathbf{CM} = \frac{t_x f}{d} \mathbf{Cm}. \tag{46}$$

In this equation, $\mathbf{C}$ is the origin of the image coordinate system (a 3D point) and $\mathbf{m}$ is a 2D projective point of the form $[u, v, 1]^t$. Therefore, we have a simple expression of d as a function of the known variables, $\mathbf{m}$ and $\mathcal{D}$:

$$d = \mathbf{n}^t \mathbf{CM} = \frac{t_x f}{\mathcal{D}} \mathbf{n}^t \mathbf{Cm}. \tag{47}$$

Substituting (47) in (45), $\mathbf{H}$ can be expressed as function of $\mathbf{n}$, $\mathcal{D}$, and $\mathbf{m}$:

$$\mathbf{H} = \begin{bmatrix} 1 + \alpha_x & \alpha_y & \alpha_z \\ 0 & 1 & 0 \\ 0 & 0 & 1 \end{bmatrix} \qquad \alpha_x = \frac{\mathcal{D} n_x}{f \mathbf{n}^t \mathbf{Cm}} \qquad \alpha_y = \frac{\mathcal{D} n_y}{f \mathbf{n}^t \mathbf{Cm}}. \tag{48}$$

α_z only has a translational effect through $\mathbf{H}$, so it has no influence on the resulting window shape. The two parameters α_x and α_y fully characterize the effect of $\mathbf{H}$ on the window shape. Geometrically, α_x is the horizontal displacement of the center points of the left and right edges of the correlation window and α_y is the displacement of the centers of the top and bottom edges of the window (see Figure 9b).

The general case. To simplify the equations, this discussion of window skewing is presented in the case in which the cameras are aligned. The property remains essentially the same when the cameras are in a general configuration. In that case, the window shape may still be described by $\alpha = [\alpha_x, \alpha_y]^t$ that represents the displacements of the centers of the window edges along the epipolar lines given by $\mathbf{F}$ instead of along the lines of the image in the case of aligned cameras (see Figure 9c). Also, we have not included the intrinsic parameter matrices in the computations. It can be easily seen that including these matrices does not change the general form of (48); it changes only the relation between α and the orientation of the plane.

We have shown how to parametrize window shape from the corresponding homography. It is important to note that the reasoning can be reversed in that a given arbitrary value of α corresponds to a unique homography at $\mathbf{m}$, which itself corresponds to a unique plane at $\mathbf{M}$.

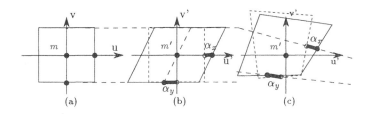

Figure 9. Parametrization of window deformation. (a) Left image. (b) Right image if the cameras are aligned. (c) Right window in general camera configuration.

Slope computation using window shape. The parameterization of window shape as a function of planar orientations suggests a simple algorithm for finding the slope at M. First, choose a set of values for α_x and α_y; then, compute a measure (correlation or SSD) for each possible α, and find the best slope $\alpha^{\min}$ as corresponding to the minimum of the measure. This is very similar to the approach investigated in [1].

If all the parameters of the cameras were known, $\alpha^{\min}$ could be converted to the Euclidean description of the corresponding plane in space.

Otherwise, it is still possible to compare the computed orientation with the orientation of a reference plane Π^o whose line at infinity is known. Indeed, the homography of the plane passing through M and parallel to Π^o can be computed (Section 3.3), and its parameters α^o derived; the distance $D = \|\alpha^{\min} - \alpha^o\|$ is a measure of the difference between the slope of the terrain at M and the reference slope. Figure 10 shows an example in the case of two single pixel correspondences selected in a pair of images. The SSD is computed from the Laplacian of the images rather than from the images themselves in order to eliminate the offset between the intensities of the two images.

In practice, Π^o can be defined by three point correspondences in a pair of training images, two of which lying far enough from the camera to be considered as lying at infinity, thus defining the line at infinity of the plane. Another way to proceed would be to estimate Π^o from any three point correspondences, and to compute its intersection with the plane at infinity Π_∞ estimated with three nonaligned correspondences corresponding to remote points.

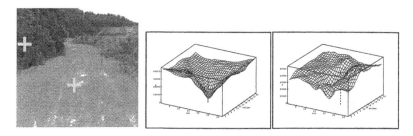

Figure 10. Left: Selected pixels in image 1. Center (resp. right): SSD error as function of $[\alpha_x, \alpha_y]$ at the road (resp. tree) pixel. The reference orientation (α_x^o, α_y^o) is approximately the orientation of the road, and is represented by the vertical dotted lines. Both surfaces have a sharp minimum, but only one (the road point) is located at (α_x^o, α_y^o).

Limitations. There are two problems with the $[\alpha_x, \alpha_y]$ representation of plane directions. First, depending on the position of the point in space, the discretization of the parameters may lead to very different results due to the nonuniform distribution of the plane directions in α-space. In particular, the discrimination between different plane directions becomes poorer as the range to the surface increases. This problem becomes particularly severe when the surfaces are at a relatively long range from the camera and when the variation of range across the image is significant.

The second problem is that it is difficult to interpret consistently the distance D between $\alpha^{\min}$ and α^o across the image. Specifically, a particular value of D corresponds to different angular distances between planes depending on the disparity, but also on the position of the point in the image.

6.3. NORMAL-BASED REPRESENTATION

Based on the limitations identified above, we now develop an alternate parameterization that consists of discretizing the set of all possible orientations in space, and then of evaluating the corresponding homographies. This assumes the intrinsic parameters of the first camera are known as well as the collineation of the plane at infinity.

Slope computation using normal representation. Assuming that we know $\mathbf{H}_\infty$ and $\mathbf{A}$, we can compute the homography $\mathbf{H}$ of a plane Π defined by a given pair of points (m, m') and a normal vector $\mathbf{n}$ in space. Indeed, the plane Π_C that is orthogonal to $\mathbf{n}$ and contains the optical center C projects in the first image onto a line l^∞ and equation (14) tells us that

$$\mathbf{l}_1^\infty = \mathbf{A}^{-T}\mathbf{n}. \qquad (49)$$

This line is the projection in the first image of any line of the plane that does not contain C, so unless C is at infinity, it is the image of the line at infinity of Π_C and thus of Π since both planes are parallel. Given the homography $\mathbf{H}_\infty$ of the plane at infinity, we may compute the corresponding line $\mathbf{l}_2^\infty = \mathbf{H}_\infty^{-1T}\mathbf{l}_1^\infty$ in the second image. Finally, according to Section 3.3, (m, m'), $\mathbf{l}_1^\infty$, $\mathbf{l}_2^\infty$, and the knowledge of the epipolar geometry allow us to compute $\mathbf{H}$.

By sampling the set of possible orientations in a uniform manner, we generate a set of homographies that represent planes of well-distributed orientations at a given point M. Then the algorithm of the previous section is used directly to evaluate each orientation $\mathbf{n}_i$. In the current implementation, we sample the sphere of unit normals into 40 different orientations using a regular subdivision of the icosahedron.

Figure 11 shows the SSD distributions in the case of the two pixels studied in Figure 10. Though correct, the results point out one remaining problem of this approach: The SSD distribution may be flat because of the lack of signal variation in the window. This is a problem with any area-based technique. In Section 6.4, we present a probabilistic framework which enables us to address this problem.

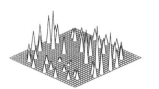 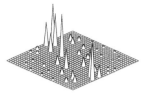

Figure 11. Distribution of SSD at the two selected pixels of figure (left: road; right: trees). The SSD distribution is plotted with respect to (n_x, n_y), i.e., two coordinates of the 3D normal. The reference orientation (close to the road) is represented as a plain surface patch. On the left diagram, the computed SSD values are low in the neighborhood of the reference orientation. On the other one, the low SSD values are further from the reference orientation.

It is important to note that the orientation of the cameras does not need to be known and that the coordinate system in which the orientations are expressed is unimportant. In fact, we express all the orientations in a reference frame attached to the first camera, which is sufficient since all we need is to *compare* orientations, which does not require the use of a specific reference frame. Consequently, it is not necessary to use the complete metric calibration of the cameras.

A priori geometric knowledge. In practice, $\mathbf{H}_\infty$ is estimated as described at the end of the previous section. Since this only gives an approximation, the lines $\mathbf{l}_1^\infty, \mathbf{l}_2^\infty$ that we compute from a given orientation do not really represent a line at infinity. Thus, the planes that correspond to this orientation rotate around a fixed line in space instead of being parallel. For practical purposes, the line is far enough so that this discrepancy does not introduce significant errors.

The matrix $\mathbf{A}$ represents the intrinsic parameters of the first image. Since we are interested in the slopes in the image relative to some reference plane, it is not necessary to know $\mathbf{A}$ precisely. Specifically, an error in $\mathbf{A}$ introduces a consistent error in the computation of the homographies which is the same for the reference plane and for an arbitrary plane, and does not affect the output of the algorithm dramatically.

We finally remark that if $\mathbf{A}$ is modified by changing the scale in the first image, the results remain unchanged. This geometric property, observed by Koenderink [14], implies that only the aspect ratio, the angle of the pixel axes, and the principal point of the first camera need to be known.

6.4. Application to estimation of terrain traversability

Although the accuracy of the slopes computed using the algorithms of the previous section is not sufficient to, for example, reconstruct terrain shape, it provides a valuable indication of the traversability of the terrain. Specifically, we define the traversability at a point as the probability that the angle between a reference vertical direction and the normal to the terrain surface is lower than a given angular threshold. The term traversability comes from mobile robot navigation in which the angular threshold controls the range of slopes that the robot can navigate safely.

Estimating traversability involves converting the distribution of SSD values $S(\boldsymbol{\alpha})$ at a pixel m to a function $f(\boldsymbol{\alpha})$ which can be interpreted as the likelihood that $\boldsymbol{\alpha}$ corresponds to the terrain orientation at m. We then define the traversability measure $T(m)$ as the probability that this orientation is within a neighbourhood R around the direction of the reference plane $\boldsymbol{\alpha}^o$:

$$T(m) = \sum_{\boldsymbol{\alpha} \in R} f(\boldsymbol{\alpha}).$$

We use a formalism similar to the one presented in [20] in order to define f. Assuming that the pixel values in both images are normally distributed with standard deviation σ^2, the distribution of $\boldsymbol{\alpha}$ is given by:

$$f(\boldsymbol{\alpha}) = \frac{1}{K} \exp -\frac{S(\boldsymbol{\alpha})}{\sigma^2}, \tag{50}$$

where K is a normalizing factor.

This definition of T has two advantages. First, it integrates the confidence values computed for all the slope estimates (50) into one traversability measure. In particular, if the distribution of $f(\boldsymbol{\alpha})$ is relatively flat, $T(m)$ has a low value, reflecting the fact that the confidence in the position of the minimum of $S(\boldsymbol{\alpha})$ is low. This situation occurs when there is not enough signal variation in the images or when m is the projection of a scene point that is far from the cameras.

The second advantage of this definition of traversability is that the sensitivity of the algorithm can be adjusted in a natural way. For example, if R is defined as the set of plane orientations which are at an angle less than θ from Π^o, the sensitivity of $T(m)$ increases as θ decreases.

Figure 12 shows the results on two pairs of images of outdoor scenes. The first image of each pair is displayed on the left. The center images show the complete traversability maps, Once again, the influence of the signal is noticeable. In particular, in the top example, a large part of the road has a rather low traversability, because there is little signal in the images. On the contrary, the values corresponding to the highly textured sidewalk are very high.

The right image shows the regions that have a probability greater than the value we would obtain if there were no signal in the images, i.e., the regions that could be considered as traversable. In both cases, the obstacles have low traversability values.

Figure 13 shows the result of evaluating $T(m)$ for three different values of θ. Only the traversable regions are shown. As θ increases, the influence of the signal becomes less noticeable, and the likelihood of a region to be traversable increases.

The measure of traversability can be easily integrated into navigation systems such as the one presented in Section 7.

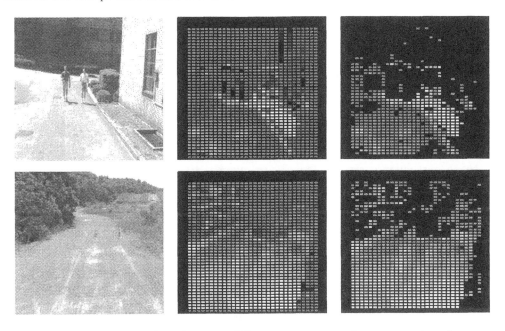

Figure 12. Examples of traversability maps computed on two pairs of images (see text).

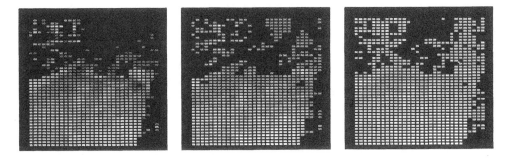

Figure 13. Traversability map from the distribution of slopes on real data. Left: small admissible region $\theta = 20°$. Center: medium admissible region $\theta = 45°$. Right: large admissible region $\theta = 75°$.

7. NAVIGATING

In this section we show three robotic applications of the geometric properties presented in the above sections. In the first one, stereo is used to detect close obstacles.

In the second one, the robot uses affine geometry to follow the middle of a corridor. In the third one, relative heights and orientations with respect to the ground plane are used for trajectory planning.

7.1. DETECTING OBSTACLES

This section describes how to use the previous results to provide a robot with the ability to detect obstacles. The only requirement is that the robot be equipped with a stereo rig which can be very simply calibrated, as explained next.

Let us imagine the following calibration steps:

- as described in Section 3.1, some correspondences between two views taken by the cameras are found;
- these correspondences are used to compute the fundamental matrix, as described in Section 3.2;
- three particular correspondences are given to the system; they correspond to three object points defining a virtual plane Π in front of the robot;
- the H-matrix of Π is computed as described in Section 3.3.

The fundamental matrix, as well as the plane H-matrix, remain the same for any other pair of views taken by the system, as long as the intrinsic parameters of both cameras and the attitude of one camera with respect to the other do not change.

According to Section 5, by repeatedly performing rectifications with respect to Π, the robot knows whether there are points in front between itself and Π by looking at the sign of their disparity and can act in consequence. If the distance d_0 of the robot to Π is known, the robot may, for example, move forward from the distance d_0. Furthermore, if Π and Π'_f intersect sufficiently far away from the cameras, it can detect whether the points are moving away or towards itself. Indeed, Π and the focal plane Π'_f may then be considered as parallel around the images, so that, for the points considered, $d(M, \Pi)$ is proportional to $d(M, \Pi'_f) - d(\Pi, \Pi'_f)$, where $d(\Pi, \Pi'_f) = d(M_\Pi, \Pi'_f)$ for any point $M_\Pi \in \Pi$. According to equation (42), $\hat{z}'\mathcal{D}$ is then approximatively proportional to

$$1 - \frac{d(\Pi, \Pi'_f)}{d(M, \Pi'_f)};$$

thus it is a monotonic function of the distance of M to Π'_f.

At last, since we are only interested in the points near the plane, which have a disparity close to zero, we can limit the search along the epipolar line of the correspondent point $\hat{m}'$ of any point $\hat{m}$ to an interval around $\hat{m}$, which significantly reduces the computation time.

An example is given in Figures 14, 15, 16, and 17. Figure 14 shows as dark square boxes the points used to define a plane and the image of a fist taken by the left camera. Figure 15 shows the left and right images once rectified with respect to this plane. Figure 16 shows the disparity map obtained by correlation. Figure 17 shows the segmentation of the disparity map in two parts. On the left side, points with negative disparities, that is points in front of the reference plane, are shown.

The intensity encodes closeness to the camera. Similarly, the right side of the figure shows the points with positive disparities, that is the points which are beyond the reference plane.

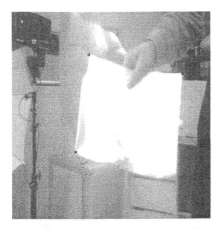
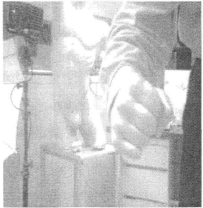

Figure 14. The paper used to define the plane and the left image of the fist taken as an example.

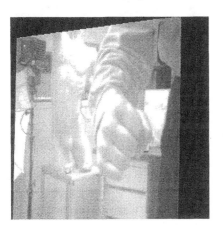
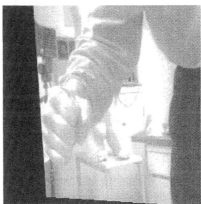

Figure 15. The left and right rectified images of the fist.

7.2. NAVIGATING ALONG THE MIDDLE OF A CORRIDOR

If we add to the computation of the fundamental matrix during the calibration stage, the computation of the homography of the plane at infinity, using the method described in Section 3.4, the robot becomes able to compute ratios of three aligned points, for example, the middle of a corridor, and to do visual servoing.

Indeed, if we represent the projections of the sides S_1 and S_2 of the corridor by s_1 and s_2 in the first image and s_1' and s_2' in the second image (see Figure 18) and choose any point a of s_1 and any point b of s_2, projections in the first image of a point A of S_1 and a point B of S_2, then the corresponding points a' and b' in the second image are computed as the intersections, respectively, of the epipolar line e_a

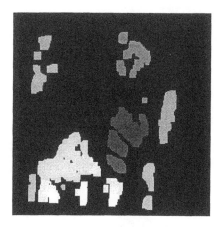

Figure 16. The disparity map obtained from the rectified images of Figure 15.

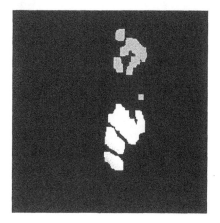
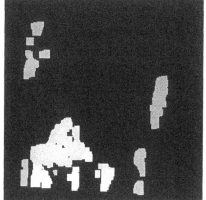

Figure 17. The absolute value of the negative disparities on the left, showing that the fist and a portion of the arm are between the robot and the plane of rectification, and the positive disparities on the right, corresponding to the points located beyond the plane.

of a with s'_1 and the epipolar line e_b of b with s'_2. Having (a, a') and (b, b') allows computing the projections (m, m') of the midpoint M of A and B. If we consider S_1 and S_2 as locally parallel, then M lies on the local middle line of the corridor and computing the projections of another point of this line the same way as M allows us to have the projections of this line in the two images.

Figure 19 shows some real sequences used to perform the affine calibration of a stereoscopic system. Six strong correspondences between the four images have been extracted, from which fifteen correspondences of points at infinity have been computed to finally get the homography of the plane at infinity. Figure 20 shows some midpoints obtained once the system calibrated: The endpoints are represented as black squares and the midpoints as black crosses. Figure 21 shows the midline of a corridor obtained from another affinely calibrated system: The endpoints are

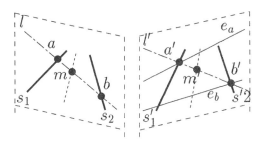

Figure 18. Determining a point at the middle of a corridor (see Section 7.2).

represented as numbered oblique dark crosses, the midpoints as black crosses, and the midline as a black line.

7.3. TRAJECTORY EVALUATION USING RELATIVE ELEVATION

A limitation of the conventional approach to stereo driving is that it relies on precise metric calibration with respect to an external calibration target in order to convert matches to 3D points. From a practical standpoint, this is a serious limitation in scenarios in which the sensing hardware cannot be physically accessed, such as in the case of planetary exploration. In particular, this limitation implies that the vision system must remain perfectly calibrated over the course of an entire mission. Nevertheless, navigation should not require the precise knowledge of the 3D position of points in the scene: What is important is how much a point deviates from the reference ground plane, not its exact position. Based on these observations, we have developed an approach which relies on the measure of relative height with respect to a ground plane (see Section 5.1).

The driving approach. We give only an overview of the approach since a detailed description of the driving system is outside the scope of this book. A detailed description of the stereo driving system can be found in [16]. The autonomous navigation architecture is described in [17] and [12].

In autonomous driving, the problem is to use the data in the stereo images for computing the best steering command for the vehicle, and to update the steering command every time a new image is taken. Our basic approach is to evaluate a set of possible steering directions based on the relative heights computed at a set of points which project onto a regular grid in the image. Specifically, a given steering radius corresponds to an arc which can be projected into a curve in the image. This curve traces the trajectory that the vehicle would follow in the image if it used this steering radius. Given the points of the measurement grid and the set of steering radii, we compute a vote for every arc and every point of the grid which reflects how drivable the arc is. The computed value lies between -1 (high obstacle) and $+1$ (no obstacle) (Figure 22).

For a given steering radius, the votes from all the grid points are aggregated into a single vote by taking the minimum of the votes computed from the individual

Figure 19. The top images correspond to a first pair of views taken by
a stereoscopic system and the bottom images to a second pair taken by
exactly the same system after a translation. Among the 297 detected
corners of the top left image and the 276 of the top right image, 157
points correspondences have been found by stereo points matching (see
Section 3.1), among which 7 outliers have been rejected when computing
the fundamental matrix (see Section 3.2). The top to bottom correspondences matching has been obtained by tracking (see Section 3.1).

grid points. The output is, therefore, a distribution of votes between -1 and $+1$,
-1 being inhibitory, for the set of possible steering arcs. This distribution is then
sent to an external module, which combines the distribution of votes from stereo
with distributions from other modules in order to generate the steering command
corresponding to the highest combined vote. Figure 23 shows examples of vote distributions computed in front of visible obstacles.

Characterization of the reference ground plane. The homography of the reference
ground plane is estimated from a number of point correspondences related to scene
points on this plane. These point correspondences are obtained by selecting points

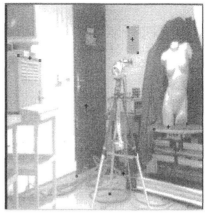

Figure 20. Midpoints obtained after affine calibration (see Section 3.4).

Figure 21. Midline of a corridor obtained after affine calibration (see Section 3.4).

in the first image. Their corresponding points in the second image are computed automatically through the process of rectification and correlation along the epipolar lines, described in Section 4.

Measuring obstacle heights. Let us we consider one point of the grid in the first image, for which a corresponding point in the second image has been found by the stereo process. Based on the results of Section 5.1, we can compute its height with respect to the ground. The unit height is defined by a point of the scene, selected manually in one of the two images at the beginning of the experiment and matched automatically in the other image.

This measurement is not sufficient, since we aim at measuring heights along trajectories which are estimated in the ground plane. So, after determining the elevation of a point selected in one image, we determine the point of the ground plane to which this elevation has to be assigned, by projecting the measured 3D point on the (horizontal) ground plane, along the vertical direction. This means computing the intersection between the ground plane and the vertical line passing through the 3D point. To apply the method of Section 3.3, we need to compute the images of the vertical the line passing through the observed point. For this, we compute the images of the point at infinity in the vertical direction (also called vertical vanishing point) in both images. First, we select manually four points representing two vertical lines in the left image. Matching two of these points we obtain one of the two corresponding lines in the right image. The left vertical vanishing point is obtained by intersecting the two lines in the left image. Computing the intersection of its epipolar line with the line in the right image, we obtain the right vertical vanishing point.

Computing image trajectories. This approach assumes that a transformation is available for projecting the steering arcs onto the image plane. Such a transformation can be computed from features in sequences of images using an approach related to the estimation algorithm described above for computing the homography induced by the ground plane.

We first introduce a system of coordinates in the ground plane, attached to the rover, which we call "rover coordinates." At each time, we know in rover coordinates the trajectory which will be followed by the rover for each potential steering command. Furthermore, for a given motion/steering command sent to the robot, we know from the mechanical design the expected change of rover coordinates from the final position to the initial one. We can even estimate the actual motion using dead reckoning. Since the transformation is a change of coordinates in the plane, it can be represented by a 3×3 matrix $\mathbf{T}^r$ operating on homogeneous coordinates.

The transformation which we compute is the homography $\mathbf{H}^{ir}$ which maps pixel coordinates in the left image onto rover coordinates. The inverse of this matrix then allows us to map potential rover trajectories onto the left image plane.

Computation of $\mathbf{H}^{ir}$ is done by tracking points across the left images taken at various rover positions. Let us consider two images acquired at positions 1 and 2, with a known rover motion $\mathbf{T}^r_{12}$. Given a point correspondence (p_1, p_2) we have the following equation (up to a scale factor):

$$\mathbf{H}^{ir}\mathbf{p}_1 = \mathbf{T}^r_{12}\mathbf{H}^{ir}\mathbf{p}_2$$

where the only unknown is the matrix $\mathbf{H}^{ir}$. This can be also written

$$\mathbf{H}^{ir}\mathbf{p}_1 \times (\mathbf{T}^r_{12}\mathbf{H}^{ir}\mathbf{p}_2) = 0.$$

This yields a system of two independent quadratic equations in the coefficients of $\mathbf{H}^{ir}$. Given a set of displacements and point coordinates, we can write a large system of such equations, which we solve in the least-squares sense using the Levenberg-Marquardt technique.

Using heights to speed up stereo matching. The relative height is also used for limiting the search in the stereo matching. More precisely, we define an interval $[h_{\min}, h_{\max}]$ of heights which we anticipate in a typical terrain. This interval is converted at each pixel to a disparity range $[d_{\min}, d_{\max}]$. This is an effective way of limiting the search by searching only for disparities that are physically meaningful at each pixel.

Experimental results. This algorithm has been successfully used for arc evaluation in initial experiments on the CMU HMMWV [12], a converted truck for autonomous navigation. In this case, a 400-point grid was used. The combination of stereo computation and arc evaluation was done at an average of 0.5 s on a Sparc-10 workstation. New steering directions were issued to the vehicle at that rate. This update rate is comparable to what can be achieved using a laser range finder [17].

An important aspect of the system is that we are able to navigate even though a relatively small number of points is processed in the stereo images. This is in contrast with the more conventional approach in which a dense elevation map is necessary, thus dramatically increasing the computation time. Using such a small number of points is justified because it has been shown that the set of points needed for driving is a small fraction of the entire data set independent of the sensor used [13], and because we have designed our stereo matcher to compute matches at specific points.

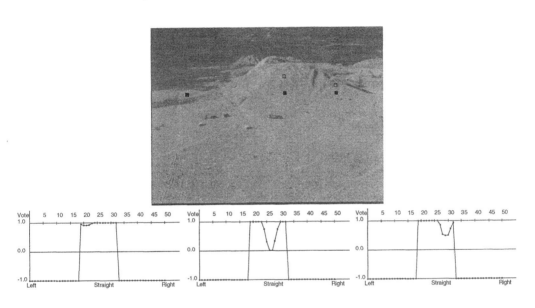

Figure 22. Evaluating steering at individual points. (Top) Three points selected in a stereo pair and their projections. (Bottom) Corresponding votes for all steering directions.

8. CONCLUSION

In this chapter we have pushed a little further the idea that only the information necessary to solve a given visual task needs to be recovered from the images and that this attitude pays off by considerable simplifying of the processing.

Our guiding light has been exploiting the natural mathematical idea of invariance under a group of transformations. This has led us to consider the three usual groups of transformations of 3D space, the projective, affine, and Euclidean groups, which

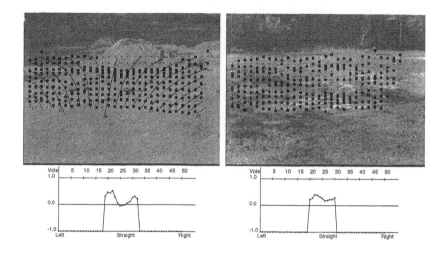

Figure 23. Evaluating steering directions in the case of a large obstacle (left) and a small obstacle (right). (Top) Regular grid of points (dots) and corresponding projections (squares). (Bottom) Distribution of votes (see text).

determine a three-layer stratification of that space in which we found it convenient to think about and solve a number of vision problems related to robotics applications.

We believe that this path offers enough practical advantages to make it worth investigating further. In particular we are convinced that, apart from the robotics applications that have been described in the chapter, the approach can be used in other areas such as the representation and retrieval of images from digital libraries.

REFERENCES

1. F. Devernay and O. Faugeras, "Computing differential properties of 3-D shapes from stereoscopic images without 3-D models," *Proceedings of the International Conference on Computer Vision and Pattern Recognition*, IEEE, Seattle, WA, June 1994, 208–213.

2. O.D. Faugeras, "What can be seen in three dimensions with an uncalibrated stereo rig?" in G. Sandini (Ed.), *Proceedings of the Second European Conference on Computer Vision*, Springer-Verlag, Santa Margherita Ligure, Italy, May 1992, 563–578.

3. O.D. Faugeras, *Three-Dimensional Computer Vision: a Geometric Viewpoint*, MIT Press, Cambridge, MA, 1993.

4. O. Faugeras, "Stratification of 3-D vision: Projective, affine, and metric representations," *Journal of the Optical Society of America A* **12**(3), March 1995, 465–484.

5. O. Faugeras, T. Luong, and S. Maybank, "Camera self-calibration: Theory and experiments," in G. Sandini (Ed.), *Proceedings of the Second European Conference on Com-*

puter Vision, Number 588 in Lecture Notes in Computer Science, Springer-Verlag, Santa-Margherita, Italy, May 1992, 321–334.

6. O.D. Faugeras and F. Lustman, "Let us suppose that the world is piecewise planar," in O.D. Faugeras and G. Giralt (Ed.), *Robotics Research, The Third International Symposium*, MIT Press, Cambridge, MA, 1986, 33–40.

7. O.D. Faugeras and L. Robert, "What can two images tell us about a third one?" in J.-O. Eklundh (Ed.), *Proceedings of the Third European Conference on Computer Vision*, Springer-Verlag, Stockholm, Sweden, May 1994, 485–492.

8. P. Fua, "Combining stereo and monocular information to compute dense depth maps that preserve depth discontinuities," in *Proceedings of the 12th International Joint Conference on Artificial Intelligence*, Sydney, Australia, August 1991.

9. G.H. Golub and C.F. Van Loan, *Matrix computations*, John Hopkins University Press, Baltimore, MD, 1983.

10. C. Harris and M. Stephens, "A Combined Corner and Edge Detector," in *Proceedings Fourth Alvey Conference*, Manchester, August 1988, 147–151.

11. R. Hartley, R. Gupta, and T. Chang, "Stereo from Uncalibrated Cameras," in *Proceedings of the Conference on International Conference on Computer Vision and Pattern Recognition*, IEEE, Urbana-Champaign, IL, June 1992, 761–764.

12. M. Hébert, D. Pomerleau, A. Stentz, and C. Thorpe, "A behavior-based approach to autonomous navigation systems: The CMU UGV project," in *IEEE Expert*, 1994, to appear.

13. A. Kelly, "A partial analysis of the high speed autonomous navigation problem," Technical Report CMU-RI-TR-94-16, The Robotics Institute, Carnegie Mellon University, Pittsburgh, PA, 1994.

14. J.J. Koenderink and A.J. Van Doorn, "Geometry of binocular vision and a model for stereopsis," *Journal of Biological Cybernetics* **21**, 1976, 29–35.

15. J.J. Koenderink and A.J. van Doorn, "Affine structure from motion," *Journal of the Optical Society of America A* **8**, 1991, 377–385.

16. E. Krotkov, M. Hébert, M. Buffa, F.G. Cozman, and L. Robert, "Stereo driving and position estimation for autonomous planetary rovers," *Second International Workshop on Robotics in Space*, Montreal, Quebec, July 1994, 320–328.

17. D. Langer, J. Rosenblatt, and M. Hébert, "A reactive system for autonomous navigation in unstructured environments," in *Proceedings of the International Conference on Robotics and Automation*, San Diego, 1994.

18. Q.-T. Luong, R. Deriche, O.D. Faugeras, and T. Papadopoulo, "On determining the Fundamental matrix: analysis of different methods and experimental results," Technical Report RR-1894, INRIA, 1993.

19. Q.-T. Luong and T. Viéville, "Canonic representations for the geometries of multiple projective views," Technical Report UCB/CSD-93-772, University of California at Berkeley, September 1993.

20. L. Matthies, "Stereo vision for planetary rovers: Stochastic modeling to near real-time implementation," *The International Journal of Computer Vision* **1**(8), July 1992.

21. J.L. Mundy and A. Zisserman (Eds.), *Geometric Invariance in Computer Vision*, MIT Press, Cambridge, MA, 1992.

22. H.K. Nishihara, "RTVS-3: Real-time binocular stereo and optical flow measurement system," Technical report, Teleos, Palo Alto, CA, July 1990, system description manuscript.

23. M. Okutomi and T. Kanade, "A multiple-baseline stereo," in *Proceedings of the Conference on International Conference on Computer Vision and Pattern Recognition*, IEEE, Lahaina, HI, June 1991, 63–69.

24. W.H. Press, B.P. Flannery, S.A. Teukolsky, and W.T. Vetterling, *Numerical Recipes in C*, Cambridge University Press, Cambridge, 1988.

25. L. Robert and O.D. Faugeras, "Relative 3D positioning and 3D convex hull computation from a weakly calibrated stereo pair," *Image and Vision Computing* **13**(3), 1995, 189–197.

26. A. Shashua, "Projective structure from two uncalibrated images: Structure from motion and recognition," Technical Report A.I. Memo No. 1363, MIT, Cambridge, MA, September 1992.

27. T. Viéville, C. Zeller, and L. Robert, "Recovering motion and structure from a set of planar patches in an uncalibrated image sequence," in *Proceedings of ICPR94*, Jerusalem, Israel, October 1994.

28. H. Wang, L.S. Shapiro, and J.M. Brady, "A matching and tracking strategy for independently-moving, non-rigid objects," in *Proceedings of BMVC*, 1992.

29. Z. Zhang, R. Deriche, O. Faugeras, and Q.-T. Luong, "A robust technique for matching two uncalibrated images through the recovery of the unknown epipolar geometry," *Artificial Intelligence Journal* **78**, October 1995, 87–119.

6 DIRECT MOTION PERCEPTION

Cornelia Fermüller and Yiannis Aloimonos
University of Maryland

ABSTRACT

The question of how three-dimensional motion can be understood from visual cues has interested scientists in empirical as well as computational and engineering disciplines for many years. In computational vision most research has been rooted in the view that awareness of the world is indirect. As a consequence motion perception has been treated as an inferential process which involves the estimation of retinal motion fields and their interpretation in the form of optimization procedures. In this chapter it is shown that the perception of motion can also be realized in a direct way by detecting invariant patterns in the two-dimensional spatiotemporal image representation. Thus, this chapter presents a computational theory of some of the ideas set forth by Gibson in the theory of direct perception, in particular the ideas of transformational invariants.

The basis of the theory lies in a global structure inherent in image motion fields due to rigid motion. This structure is independent of the scene in view and manifests itself as geometric entities (areas and contours) whose locations on the image encode 3D motion information. The geometric results presented give rise to constraints that can form the basis for a variety of of algorithms for the recovery of visual information from multiple views. Some of the constraints introduced are based solely on the use of the sign of flow measurements. In order to give theoretical significance to these results, it is also shown that information in the sign of the flow is almost always sufficient to recover 3D motion uniquely.

1. INTRODUCTION

The concept of movement occupies a central position in the efforts of human thought to explain nature. It has persisted as a topic of investigation from the earliest Greek philosophers, who attempted to explain the substance of a constantly changing

---

Supported in part by NSF, ONR and ARPA.

world, e.g., Thales of Miletus and the Ionian philosophers [15]; through the celestial Mechanic theories of Kepler attempting to explain the macrocosm; to the theories of modern Physics engaged in the explanation of the microcosm.

The topic of this chapter is also movement; in particular, movement as it is perceived by a visual system. Systems that exist in space-time and interact with their environment perceive spatiotemporal changes of the 3D world by means of their senses. Thus, perception provides the interface between the system and the 3D world in which it lives.

The study of this interface for visual systems has been a topic of investigation in many disciplines concerned with empirical and theoretical questions about the process of vision. A number of theories have been proposed for studying these questions; among them are Helmholtz's theory of unconscious inference, the Gestaltists' theory, Gibson's theory of direct perception, etc. The study of computational vision, however, has mostly been influenced by one framework—the computational theory of D. Marr.

The psychologist Gibson [13, 14] spent a large part of his work on visual navigation, and he proposed that the understanding of the distal stimulus in the 3D world through the proximal stimulus perceived on the eye is achieved through the recognition of invariants. These invariants can be thought of as higher order properties of stimulation patterns which remain constant during changes associated with the observer, the environment, or both. Commonly, two types of invariants are distinguished: the transformational, which are patterns due to a physical change; and the structural, which are patterns or relationships that remain constant despite the change. Gibson referred to his theory as ecological optics or direct perception, because he explained the process of vision as a direct extraction of the appropriate invariants. His theory was severely criticized by the visionaries advancing the computational theory, although for no particular reason. They thought that local computations must be more efficient [36] than the extraction of invariants and they realized the difficulty of discovering such invariants [22].

The two theories, however, are not necessarily contradictory. The goal of this chapter is to demonstrate that the discovery of physical invariants from the optical array is feasible and the study of invariants can be based on computational considerations. Furthermore, these invariants can be detected "directly," i.e., by means of algorithms that perform pattern recognition in real time. The invariants studied in this chapter relate image measurements to three-dimensional motion, and thus they fall in the category of transformational invariants. It is shown that 3D motion manifests itself in the image displacement field in the form of a certain structure, and detecting this structure leads to direct perception of 3D motion.

The next section provides a discussion of the approaches taken to the problem of 3D motion interpretation in the computational vision literature and discusses the difficulties of the problem. The following section explains briefly the concepts presented in this chapter. To give the reader an intuition about the structures of motion fields studied here, two examples are given and then an outline of the chapter is presented.

2. 3D MOTION INTERPRETATION

In the computational vision literature problems of visual perception that require some 3D motion and shape information have usually been addressed in the context of visual recovery. In its most general form the problem of visual recovery requires the segmentation of the scene in view on the basis of image displacement information and the recovery of the relative motion and the structure of every point in the scene. Thus a number of less complex visual tasks, such as stereo, 3D motion estimation, calibration, obstacle detection, pose recognition, etc., can be regarded as special instances of the general recovery problem [3, 5, 6, 7, 12, 20, 24, 32, 33, 35, 37].

Approaches to various aspects of this problem that have appeared in the literature seek a solution in two computational steps. First, a description that relates local measurements in multiple views is developed; local descriptors include stereo disparity measurements, motion disparity measurements, motion fields, partial disparity fields such as those along the x- and y-axis, or normal motion fields (the projections of motion fields along the gradient direction) [2, 16, 18, 19, 29]. Second, knowledge of the model of the geometric transformation between the multiple views provides constraints on the local descriptors; these constraints are used to relate image measurements to the 3D scene and viewing geometry [8, 17, 20, 23, 25, 30, 31, 34].

It has turned out, however, that the problem of visual recovery is of great difficulty. On the one hand image measurements are very hard to compute accurately. Even if we just compute the normal flow, the projection of the retinal motion on the local image gradients, we need to use infinitesimal computations and have to approximate derivatives by difference quotients, so our computations can only be approximations. Much more difficult is the computation of optical flow or disparity measurements, which requires us to employ some additional assumptions, usually smoothness assumptions, so we run into problems at motion and depth boundaries. On the other hand, even if we had very accurate flow, it is not necessarily the case that a small change in flow implies a small change in three-dimensional motion. Thus, the recovery of 3D motion as it has usually been pursued, in the form of single-feature correspondence or from local flow measurements, has turned out to be a problem of extreme sensitivity.

3. OVERVIEW

This chapter deals with the case where the transformation between the views is described by a rigid motion. The rigid motion model imposes constraints on the local image measurements (disparity measurements, optical flow field, normal flow field), which thus have a certain global structure. The goal of this study is to make explicit aspects of this structure due only to rigid motion. In the remainder of this chapter we will use the terms motion vector and motion field to refer to the 2D image displacements (local descriptors).

The general framework considered for investigating global structures is to study functions of the values of 2D rigid motion fields. This is achieved by defining functions on the vectors of the flow field and studying the location of the level sets of these functions. The functions employed here are simple in nature. In particular, we concentrate on optic flow vectors of constant value on certain directional motion fields, that is, the components of optical flow in particular directions (for example, a normal flow field constitutes a directional motion field), and on certain linear and quadratic functions defined on directional motion vectors. We also show constraints on the sign of directional motion fields, and in order to justify the utilization of these constraints for navigational problems, we study whether there is theoretically enough information in the sign of motion fields to recover 3D motion uniquely.

Before we proceed, in order to provide the reader with an intuitive notion of the forthcoming material, we present in Figure 1 two simple examples. Figure 1a shows a motion field generated by an observer moving rigidly with regard to some surface. The analysis in this paper will show that the rigid motion, independently of the scene in view, constrains the locations of the motion vectors that have certain values. For example, all vectors ($u = 0.5$, $v = 0.5$) lie on the conic section C_1. (This does not mean that all motion vectors on C_1 have value $(0.5, 0.5)$; it only means that if there exists in the image a point with motion vector equal to $(0.5, 0.5)$, this point will lie on the curve C_1.) Similarly, curves C_2 and C_3 contain all points with motion vectors $(0.1, 0.7)$ and $(-0.4, -0.4)$ respectively.

Figure 1b shows a directional motion field resulting from the same rigid motion. Points in the image plane where the directional motion vector can have a particular length and direction are clustered in regions whose boundaries depend on the 3D motion. To illustrate this all directional motion vectors parallel to the y-axis and of length 0.3 are shown to be in the area marked by vertical lines.

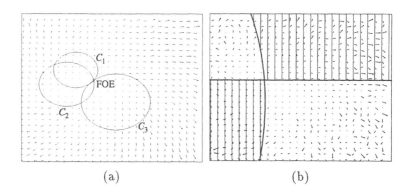

(a)   (b)

Figure 1. (a) The rigid motion constrains the motion vectors to lie on conic sections in the image plane. (b) For a normal motion field all vectors of certain value are constrained to lie within regions. The boundaries of these regions depend on the 3D motion.

The contours and regions shown together with the geometrical relations between them define a global structure on rigid motion fields. This global structure encodes the 3D motion. For example, it will be shown that all contours intersect at one point whose coordinates encode information about the underlying translational motion, i.e., the focus of expansion or FOE, and that the intersection of the boundary regions provides the parameters of the translation as well as the rotation. Thus, uncovering this structure leads to a direct perception of motion.

The concepts and structures described in this chapter could serve as the basis for a variety of perceptual mechanisms underlying visual tasks. Since they are defined globally on the image, they relate motion measurements from different parts of the image to each other, which gives them the potential of being exploited in tasks related to the recovery of the parameters describing the rigid motion configuration. They may be used in algorithms computing the extrinsic as well as the intrinsic parameters of a rigid motion configuration or stereo setting. They also may be exploited to verify that a vector field is only due to rigid motion and to locate areas in the image where this constraint does not hold—for example, in the detection and localization of independently moving objects for a moving observer. In general, they could be utilized whenever navigational problems are addressed that involve estimating aspects of 3D motion, such as image stabilization, servoing, or docking.

The chapter is organized as follows: Section 4 describes the well-known equations relating the image motion field to the 3D motion for the case of a planar retina, and Section 5 explains the structure of the "iso-motion curves" and outlines some relations between different iso-motion curves. An iso-motion curve $C_{\mathbf{u}}$ is a locus of points where the vector field representing the image motion could take on a fixed value defined in terms of $\mathbf{u}$. Analogously, when dealing with directional flow, we encounter the "iso-directional motion regions." Section 6 studies the relationship between such regions and the 3D motion parameters. The concept of selecting vectors of certain lengths and directions is extended to certain vector valued functions. Section 7 discusses how the introduced constraints may be utilized and shows experiments. Section 8 extends the analysis of global motion field structures to spherical images. Section 9 provides a uniqueness analysis investigating the relationship between 3D rigid motion and directional motion fields and Section 10 provides a summary and conclusions.

4. Localization of Motion Measurements

The 2D motion field on an imaging surface is the projection of the 3D motion field of the scene points moving relative to that surface. If this motion is rigid, it is composed of a translation $\mathbf{t}$ and a rotation $\boldsymbol{\omega}$. For the case of a moving camera in a stationary environment each scene point $\mathbf{R} = (X, Y, Z)$ measured with respect to a coordinate system $OXYZ$ fixed to the camera moves relative to the camera with velocity $\dot{\mathbf{R}}$, where

$$\dot{\mathbf{R}} = -\mathbf{t} - \boldsymbol{\omega} \times \mathbf{R}. \tag{1}$$

Projecting the 3D motion vectors on a retina of a given shape gives the image motion field.

If the center of projection is at the origin O and the image is formed on a plane orthogonal to the Z-axis at distance f (focal length) from the nodal point (see Figure 2), the relation between the image point $\mathbf{r} = (x, y, f)$ and the scene point $\mathbf{R}$ under perspective projection is

$$\mathbf{r} = \frac{f}{\mathbf{R} \cdot \hat{\mathbf{z}}} \mathbf{R},$$

where $\hat{\mathbf{z}}$ is a unit vector in the direction of the Z-axis and "·" denotes the inner product of vectors.

If we now differentiate $\mathbf{r}$ with respect to time, and substitute for $\dot{\mathbf{R}}$, we obtain the following equation for $\dot{\mathbf{r}}$:

$$\dot{\mathbf{r}} = \mathbf{v}_{\mathrm{tr}}(\mathbf{r}) + \mathbf{v}_{\mathrm{rot}}(\mathbf{r}) = \frac{1}{\mathbf{R} \cdot \hat{\mathbf{z}}} \left((\mathbf{t} \cdot \hat{\mathbf{z}})\mathbf{r} - f\mathbf{t} \right) - \frac{1}{f}[\mathbf{r}\omega\hat{\mathbf{z}}]\mathbf{r} - \omega \times \mathbf{r}, \tag{2}$$

where $[\mathbf{r}\omega\hat{\mathbf{z}}] = \mathbf{r} \cdot (\omega \times \hat{\mathbf{z}})$ (triple product).

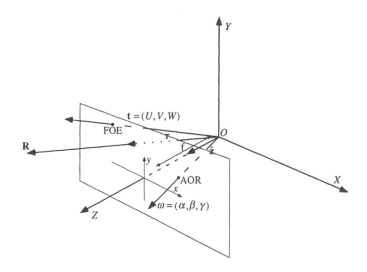

Figure 2. Image formation using perspective projection on a planar retina.

The first term in equation (2), $\mathbf{v}_{\mathrm{tr}}(\mathbf{r})$, denotes the translational motion component, which depends on the depth $Z = \mathbf{R} \cdot \hat{\mathbf{z}}$, while the second term, $\mathbf{v}_{\mathrm{rot}}(\mathbf{r})$, denotes the rotational component, which does not depend on depth, but only on the three rotational parameters. As can be seen from the equations, using perspective projection only the scaled translation $\frac{\mathbf{t}}{Z}$ can be recovered. The points where the axis of translation pierces the retina are called the focus of expansion (FOE) in the case of positive translation along the Z-axis or the focus of contraction (FOC) otherwise, since at these points the translational motion components are zero and all translational motion vectors point away from or towards these points. Similarly, we call the point where ω (the rotation axis) pierces the retina the axis of rotation point (AOR). At this point the rotational motion is zero.

We are concerned with how the rigidity of the motion constrains the image motion vector field. Looking at a single measurement, we see that due to rigidity the motion vector at every point is constrained to lie in a one-dimensional subspace (defined by the rotational component and a translational component of which we know the direction but not the length). Since the distance from the scene to the image is positive, the possible space for the motion vector at every point is further reduced to a half-space.

In order to separate the constraints on the motion field due to shape from those due to motion, we take the approach of studying answers to the following questions: Given a certain value $\mathbf{v}(\mathbf{p})$ for a motion vector at point $\mathbf{p}$ (or a vector valued function), where are the locations $\mathbf{p}$ on the retina, for which the motion vector $\dot{\mathbf{r}}$ at $\mathbf{p}$ (hereafter $\mathbf{r}(\mathbf{p})$) could take the value $\mathbf{v}(\mathbf{p})$? These concepts are explored below.

5. ISO-MOTION CONTOURS IN THE PLANE

5.1. CHARACTERIZATION OF THE FORM OF ISO-MOTION CONTOURS IN THE PLANE

If the scene is projected on a planar retina the image velocity field is given by equation (2). We express this equation in the more common component notation: $\dot{\mathbf{r}} = (r^1, r^2, r^3)$. r^3 is always zero. We denote r^1 by u and r^2 by v, $\mathbf{t} = (U, V, W)$, $\boldsymbol{\omega} = (\alpha, \beta, \gamma)$. If we introduce new coordinates for the direction of translation $(x_0, y_0) = (\frac{Uf}{W}, \frac{Vf}{W})$, we obtain the well-known equations [21]:

$$u = u_{\mathrm{tr}} + u_{\mathrm{rot}} =$$
$$= (-x_0 + x)\frac{W}{Z} + \alpha\frac{xy}{f} - \beta\left(\frac{x^2}{f} + f\right) + \gamma y \tag{3}$$

$$v = v_{\mathrm{tr}} + v_{\mathrm{rot}} =$$
$$= (-y_0 + y)\frac{W}{Z} + \alpha\left(\frac{y^2}{f} + f\right) - \beta\frac{xy}{f} - \gamma x. \tag{4}$$

We are interested in the locus of points with motion vector $\mathbf{u} = (u, v)$. To obtain the locations (x, y) in the image plane for which the motion vector has some constant value (u, v), we bring the rotational components in (3) and (4) to the left side and divide (3) by (4):

$$\frac{u - u_{\mathrm{rot}}}{v - v_{\mathrm{rot}}} = \frac{u_{\mathrm{tr}}}{v_{\mathrm{tr}}}$$

$$\frac{u - \left(\alpha\frac{xy}{f} - \beta\left(\frac{x^2}{f} + f\right) + \gamma y\right)}{v - \left(\alpha\left(\frac{y^2}{f} + f\right) - \beta\frac{xy}{f} - \gamma x\right)} = \frac{x - x_0}{y - y_0}, \tag{5}$$

which results in the equation

$$\phi(x, y, u, v) = y^2\left(\frac{\alpha x_0}{f} + \gamma\right) - xy\left(\frac{\beta x_0}{f} + \frac{\alpha y_0}{f}\right) + x^2\left(\frac{\beta y_0}{f} + \gamma\right) - x\left(\alpha f + \gamma x_0 - v\right)$$
$$- y\left(\beta f + \gamma y_0 + u\right) + x_0\left(\alpha f - v\right) + y_0\left(\beta f + u\right) = 0, \tag{6}$$

describing a second-order curve in the image plane. Hereafter, we will refer to the curves given by (6) as iso-motion contours, in particular as $\mathbf{u}$ iso-motion contours $C_{\mathbf{u}}$ (or (u, v) iso-motion contours $C_{(u,v)}$) when denoting the parameterization by $\mathbf{u}$ $((u, v))$.

Since the values of u and v do not appear in the quadratic terms of (6), but only in the linear and constant terms, the nature of the curve (i.e., whether it is an ellipse, hyperbola, or parabola) is independent of u, v, and thus is the same for all such parametrized curves of a given motion field. The axes of the conics are all parallel to each other with slopes m and $\frac{-1}{m}$, where m is the positive of the two values [27]

$$\frac{(\beta y_0 - \alpha x_0) \mp \sqrt{(\alpha^2 + \beta^2)(x_0^2 + y_0^2)}}{(\beta x_0 + \alpha y_0)}.$$

The nature of the iso-motion contours depends on the values of the translation and rotation. Depending on the value l, where

$$l = \left(\frac{\beta x_0}{f} + \frac{\alpha y_0}{f}\right)^2 - 4\left(\frac{\alpha x_0}{f} + \gamma\right)\left(\frac{\beta y_0}{f} + \gamma\right),$$

the contour is a hyperbola if $l > 0$, an ellipse if $l < 0$, or a parabola if $l = 0$. Figures 3a and b show two classes of iso-motion curves for two different motion fields.

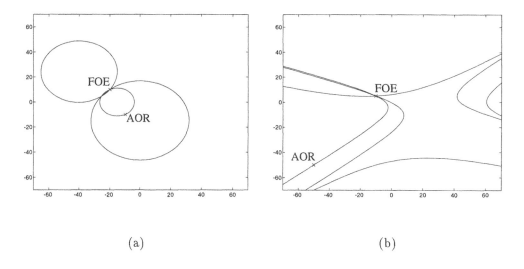

(a)   (b)

Figure 3. (a) Ellipses as iso-motion contours. (b) Hyperbolas as iso-motion contours.

A global structure due to rigid motion manifests itself in the form of the iso-motion contours and especially in the relationship between different contours. A discussion of many such relations can be found in [11]; here to provide an intuition a few properties derivable from simple observations are described and illustrated. From equation (6), it can be seen that all iso-motion contours pass through the FOE. The contours of a family of iso-motion contours corresponding to parallel motion vectors (i.e., the iso-motion contours of values $k(u, v)$ where (u, v) is a unit vector and k a scalar $\in R$) all intersect at two points, one of which is the FOE. The other one is denoted by $\mathbf{P}_{k(u,v)}$ (see Figure 4a). All points on the zero motion contour have motion vectors whose translational and rotational components are parallel to each other and thus also the motion vector itself is parallel to the translation and is oriented in the direction of the FOE (see Figure 4b).

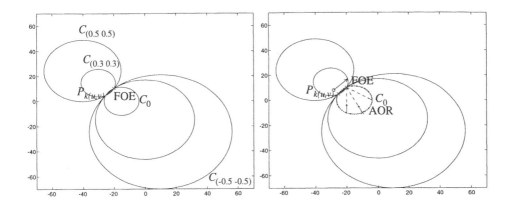

Figure 4. (a) The family $\phi(x, y, u, v, k)$ of iso-motion contours intersect at two points on the zero motion contour: the FOE and $\mathbf{P}_{k(u,v)}$. (b) The motion vector in $\mathbf{P}_{k(u,v)}$ is parallel to (u, v). For every point on the zero motion contour the motion vector lies on a line connecting the point with the FOE.

6. DIRECTIONAL MOTION CONSTRAINTS

In this section we consider directional flow fields, i.e., the components of the flow in certain directions. We investigate the locus of points in the image plane where the directional motion vector can take on a certain value. We first deal with the case of a directional motion vector of constant value, and later generalize to certain vector-valued functions linear and quadratic in the image coordinates. It will be shown that the only constraint for the location of these image points originates from the fact that the depth has to be positive. As a result the possible locations are found to be connected areas in the image plane. The shapes of these areas is defined by the rigid motion.

It should be noted here that if we consider the directional motion field along the spatial gradients, that is, the motion components perpendicular to edges, we obtain the so-called normal motion field [1, 38]. The normal motion field is uniquely defined by local image measurements and can be derived without confronting the aperture problem. Thus, the following constraints, if applied to only the normal flow values, are much easier to compute than if applied to general directional flow vectors.

6.1. ISO-DIRECTIONAL MOTION AREAS

If $\mathbf{u}$ is the motion vector at a point (x, y) and $\mathbf{n} = (n_x, n_y)$ is a unit vector in a certain direction, the directional motion $\mathbf{u_n}$ is

$$\mathbf{u_n} = (\mathbf{u} \cdot \mathbf{n}) \cdot \mathbf{n}.$$

Substituting for the components of **u** from (3) and (4), we obtain u_n for the value of the vector $\mathbf{u_n}$:

$$u_n = u_{\text{rot}} n_x + u_{\text{tr}} n_x + v_{\text{rot}} n_y + v_{\text{tr}} n_y \tag{7}$$

and thus

$$\frac{W}{Z} \left((x - x_0) n_x + (y - y_0) n_y \right)$$
$$= u_n - \left(\alpha \frac{xy}{f} - \beta \left(\frac{x^2}{f} + f \right) + \gamma y \right) n_x - \left(\alpha \left(\frac{y^2}{f} + f \right) - \beta \frac{xy}{f} - \gamma x \right) n_y. \tag{8}$$

We are concerned with the question: Where in the image plane can the directional motion field take on a certain constant value $\mathbf{u_n}$ (i.e., where could directional motion vectors of a certain length u_n and direction (n_x, n_y) be)? The depth has to be positive. If we assume $W > 0$, we obtain the following inequality:

$$\left[u_n - \left(\alpha \frac{xy}{f} - \beta \left(\frac{x^2}{f} + f \right) + \gamma y \right) n_x - \left(\alpha \left(\frac{y^2}{f} + f \right) - \beta \frac{xy}{f} - \gamma x \right) n_y \right] \cdot$$
$$[(x - x_0) n_x + (y - y_0) n_y] > 0$$
$$h(u_n, \alpha, \beta, \gamma, x, y) \cdot g(x_0, y_0, x, y) > 0. \tag{9}$$

$h(u_n, \alpha, \beta, \gamma, x, y) = u_n - (\alpha \frac{xy}{f} - \beta(\frac{x^2}{f} + f) + \gamma y) n_x - (\alpha(\frac{y^2}{f} + f) - \beta \frac{xy}{f} - \gamma x) n_y$ and $g(x_0, y_0, x, y) = (x - x_0) n_x + (y - y_0) n_y$. The equation $h(x, y) = 0$ describes a hyperbola that splits the image plane into an area where $h(x, y) > 0$ and an area where $h(x, y) < 0$. The equation $g(x, y) = 0$ describes a line through the FOE, which is perpendicular to (n_x, n_y), and which separates the plane into an area where $g(x, y)$ is positive and an area where $g(x, y)$ is negative. Thus, through this inequality a region $I_{\mathbf{u_n}}$ consisting of two areas bounded by a hyperbola and a line are defined as the locations where the directional motion could take on a certain value $\mathbf{u_n}$. The two areas meet at one point, the intersection of the hyperbola and the line. This point, which contains information about the whole pattern, will be denoted by $\mathbf{S_{u_n}}$ (see Figure 5).

In the other areas of the image plane the value of the motion vectors in direction (n_x, n_y) is constrained. Where $h(x, y) < 0$ we have $u_n > \mathbf{u_{rot}} \cdot \mathbf{n}$ (i.e., the rotational component of the directional motion is greater than u_n). Where $g(x, y) > 0$ the translational component of the directional motion is greater than zero. In the area where $h(x, y) < 0$ and $g(x, y) > 0$, we can conclude that the directional motion (the sum of its rotational and translational components) is greater than u_n. Similarly, where $h(x, y) > 0$ and $g(x, y) < 0$, the value of the directional motion has to be smaller than u_n (see Figure 6).

To summarize these results, considering for a given motion field due to rigid motion the directional motion vectors along a direction (n_x, n_y), we find that the image plane is split by a hyperbola and a line into four areas. All vectors which are of length u_n are in two opposite areas. One of the two other areas contains only values greater than u_n, and the other only values smaller than u_n.

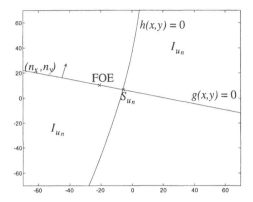

Figure 5. Iso-directional motion regions are bounded by a line ($g(x, y) = 0$) and a hyperbola ($h(x, y) = 0$).

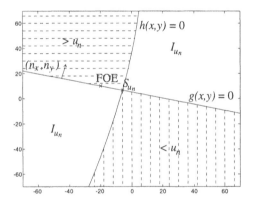

Figure 6. Separation of the image plane into areas by the values of the directional motion vectors in certain directions: In the area marked by horizontal lines all directional motion vectors in direction (n_x, n_y) are greater than u_n. In the area marked by vertical lines all directional motion vectors in direction (n_x, n_y) are smaller than u_n. Vectors of length u_n in direction (n_x, n_y) can only be in the complementary areas (the region $I_{\mathbf{u_n}}$).

The line ($g(x, y) = 0$) is defined by the translational motion; it passes through the FOE and is perpendicular to (n_x, n_y). Therefore, this line is described by only one unknown parameter (its direction is known). Furthermore, the line is independent of u_n, the value of the directional motion vector. For any general $\mathbf{u_n}$ the hyperbola ($h(u_n, x, y)$) is defined by the three rotational parameters. For the case when $u_n = 0$, the number of unknowns reduces to two ($\frac{\alpha}{\gamma}$ and $\frac{\beta}{\gamma}$ expressing the direction of the rotation axis). If we consider parallel directional motion vectors, i.e., directional motion vectors of value $k(u_n, v_n)$, where k is any scalar, we find areas in the image plane which are bounded by a line that is the same for all values and hyperbolas which differ only in their linear terms. (see Figure 7).

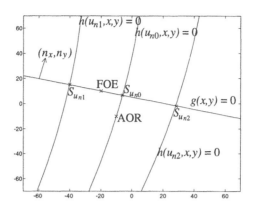

Figure 7. Iso-directional motion regions corresponding to parallel directional motion vectors: The hyperbolas $h(\mathbf{u_{n0}}, x, y)$, $h(\mathbf{u_{n1}}, x, y)$, and
$h(\mathbf{u_{n2}}, x, y)$ correspond to the parallel directional motion vectors $\mathbf{u_{n0}}$,
$\mathbf{u_{n1}}$, and $\mathbf{u_{n2}}$. The length of $\mathbf{u_{n0}}$ is zero, thus $h(\mathbf{u_{n0}}, x, y)$ passes through
the AOR. The line $g(x, y) = 0$ is independent of the length of the direc-
tional motion vector and thus the same for all parallel directional motion
vectors.

6.2. RELATION BETWEEN ISO-DIRECTIONAL MOTION REGIONS AND ISO-MOTION CONTOURS

The intersection point of the line and the hyperbola $\mathbf{S_{un}}$ is a salient point in the
description of the iso-directional motion areas. For points on the line $g(x, y) = 0$ the
translational directional motion vector component in the direction of the gradient
(n_x, n_y) is zero. For points along the hyperbola $h(x, y) = 0$ the rotational directional
motion component in direction (n_x, n_y) is zero. It follows that at the intersection
point $\mathbf{S_{un}}$ the translational motion component is parallel to the rotational motion
component, and thus for all zero iso-normal motion areas $\mathbf{S_{un}}$ lies on the zero iso-
motion contour (see Figure 8a). $\mathbf{S_{un}}$ is also element of every $k(-n_y, n_x)$ iso-motion
contour.

The following can be derived for the intersection point $\mathbf{S_{un}}$ of any general $\mathbf{u_n}$
iso-directional motion area: Since $\mathbf{S_{un}}$ lies on the line $g(x, y) = 0$, the translational
motion component at $\mathbf{S_{un}}$ is parallel to the line and perpendicular to $\mathbf{u_n}$, and the
translational normal motion component along (n_x, n_y) is always zero. Therefore,
through $\mathbf{S_{un}}$ pass all those $\mathbf{u}$ iso-motion contours for which $u_n = \mathbf{u} \cdot \mathbf{n}$ (i.e., all the
motion vectors pass whose projection on $\mathbf{n}$ yield the same directional motion vector)
(see Figure 8b).

6.3. BOUNDED DEPTH MEASUREMENTS

The constraints developed so far are only due to rigid motion. In most practical
applications upper and lower bound estimates of the distance from the image to
the scene, or the scaled distance $\frac{W}{Z}$, are available. If in equation (8) we substitute
$\tau_{\min}$ for the minimum value and $\tau_{\max}$ for the maximum value of $\frac{W}{Z}$, we obtain two
equations of hyperbolas. These equations define the boundaries of the area in which

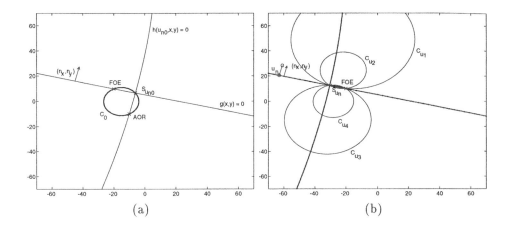

Figure 8. (a) The intersection points $\mathbf{S_{u_n}}$ of the zero normal motion regions lie on the zero motion contour. (b) The iso-motion curves $C_{\mathbf{u_1}}$, $C_{\mathbf{u_2}}$, $C_{\mathbf{u_3}}$, and $C_{\mathbf{u_4}}$, (where $\mathbf{u_1} \cdot \mathbf{n} = u_n$, $\mathbf{u_2} \cdot \mathbf{n} = u_n$, $\mathbf{u_3} \cdot \mathbf{n} = u_n, \mathbf{u_4} \cdot \mathbf{n} = u_n$) intersect on a line through the FOE perpendicular to $\mathbf{n}$.

directional motion vectors of a certain length and direction can be found. We will refer to these areas as directional motion bands; an illustration is given in Figure 9.

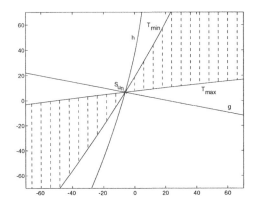

Figure 9. Bounds on the value $\frac{W}{Z}$ constrain the directional motion vectors to an area defined by two hyperbolas, the so-called directional motion band.

If the upper bound for the depth becomes infinity, the corresponding hyperbola approaches the hyperbola of the iso-directional motion area. Such situations often occur in outdoor scenes. If the lower bound for the depth becomes zero, the corresponding hyperbola approaches the line. Clearly, the smaller the possible range for the depth estimates, the smaller the bounded area. In particular, if the motion is only rotational, the measurements are only along the hyperbola of the iso-directional motion area. Considering directional motion vectors of length zero, this hyperbola passes through the AOR. If the motion is purely translational, all directional motion measurements of value zero are on the line. An illustration is given in Figure 10. Figures 10a, c, and d show synthetically created directional motion fields. The fields in Figure 10c and f are due only to translation and rotation, respectively, and the directional motion field in Figure 10a is due to both these motions. Overlaid over the directional motion field in 10a are vectors showing directions n_1 and n_2, for which directional motion vectors of length zero have been selected, and the corresponding boundaries of the directional motion areas. In this and any other implementation shown in this chapter vectors of direction $\mathbf{n}$ and length u_n are selected, if they lie within an interval $[\mathbf{n} + \epsilon_{\mathbf{n}}, \mathbf{n} - \epsilon_{\mathbf{n}}]$ and $[u_n + \epsilon_{u_n}, u_n - \epsilon_{u_n}]$. In Figures 10b, d, and f the areas in the image plane, where directional motion vectors of length zero in direction n_1 and n_2 were found, are marked by black and grey squares.

The following can be concluded about the intersection of general iso-directional motion bands: For different gradient directions $\mathbf{n_j}$ we consider the directional motion vectors of length u_{ni}, where u_{ni} is the projection of the same motion vector $\mathbf{u}$ (i.e., $u_{ni} = \mathbf{u} \cdot \mathbf{n_j}$). Any scaled depth value τ defines a curve as the location of directional motion vectors of value u_{ni}. For one τ the curves corresponding to different gradient directions intersect in one point. This point lies on the $\mathbf{u}$ iso-motion contour. Thus the intersection of all u_{ni} iso-directional motion bands is a curve segment that lies on the $\mathbf{u}$ iso-motion contour. In particular, all iso-directional motion areas of value zero intersect on the zero motion contour (see Figure 11).

6.4. COAXIS AND COPOINT VECTORS

In this section the concept of selection of directional motion vectors of a given length and direction is generalized. Instead of considering vectors of the same value, we examine various classes of vector-valued functions. In particular, we investigate the coaxis and copoint vectors described in [9, 10].

The copoint vectors are defined with respect to a point. The (r, s) copoint vectors are defined as the directional motion vectors which are perpendicular to straight lines passing through the point (r, s). An (r, s) copoint vector at a point (x, y) is parallel to the vector $(s - y, x - r)$ (see Figure 12a).

The coaxis vectors are defined with respect to a direction in space. The (A, B, C) coaxis vectors are defined as follows: A line through the image formation center defined by the directional cosines (A, B, C) defines a family of cones with axis (A, B, C) and apex at the origin. The intersection of these cones with the image plane gives rise to conic sections. The directional motion vectors perpendicular to these conic sections are called (A, B, C) coaxis vectors. At every point (x, y) a coaxis vector is parallel to the vector $(-A(y^2 + f^2) + Bxy + Cx, Axy - B(x^2 + f^2) + Cy)$ (see Figure 12b).

As in the case of the iso-directional motion vectors, we choose vectors of a given length and direction and evaluate the regions with positive depth measurements. We consider the (r, s) copoint vectors and the (A, B, C) coaxis vectors of length $u_n(x, y)$ (with $u_n(x, y)$ a function in x and y). Where $\frac{W}{Z} > 0$ the following inequalities hold:

$$[y(x_0 - r) - x(y_0 - s) - x_0 s + y_0 r] \cdot$$

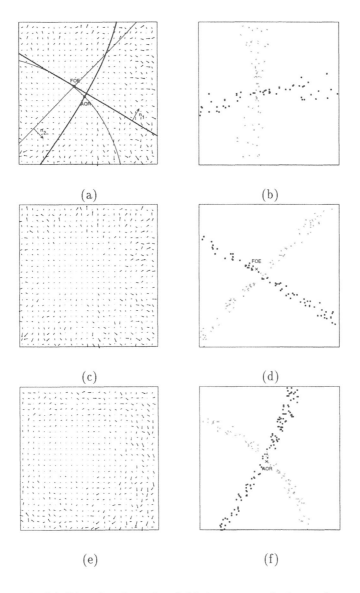

Figure 10. (a) Directional motion field due to translation and rotation (the direction at each point has been chosen randomly). Superimposed on the vector field are the boundaries of the two directional motion areas corresponding to the vectors of length zero in direction n_1 and n_2. (b) The black and grey squares denote locations where in the directional motion field of (a) vectors of length zero in direction n_1 and n_2 were found. (c) and (d) Directional motion field only due to translation and corresponding directional motion vectors of length zero in direction n_1 and n_2. The intersection of areas corresponding to different normal motion vectors of length zero gives the FOE. (e) and (f) Directional motion field only due to rotation and corresponding directional motion vectors of length zero in direction n_1 and n_2. The intersection of areas corresponding to different directional motion vectors of length zero gives the AOR.

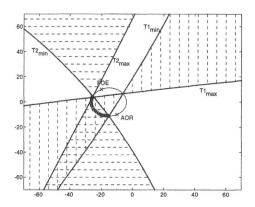

Figure 11. The directional motion bands corresponding to vectors of length zero intersect on the zero motion curve (curve segment marked by circles).

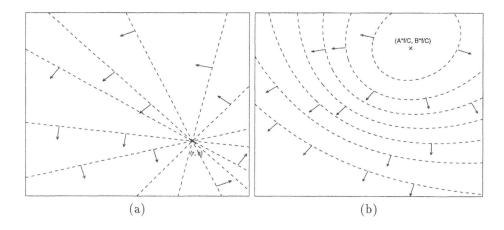

Figure 12. (a) (r, s) copoint vectors. (b) (A, B, C) coaxis vectors.

$$\left[u_n(x, y) - \frac{x^2}{f}(\beta s + \gamma f) - \frac{y^2}{f}(\alpha r + \gamma f) + xy\left(\frac{\alpha s}{f} + \frac{\beta r}{f}\right) \right.$$
$$\left. + y(\gamma s + \beta f) + x(\gamma r + \alpha f) - (\alpha f r + \beta f s) \right] > 0 \qquad (10)$$

$$\left[u_n(x, y) - \right.$$
$$\left(y\left(\frac{C\alpha}{f} - \frac{A\gamma}{f}\right) + x\left(\frac{B\gamma}{f} - \frac{C\beta}{f}\right) + A\beta - B\alpha \right)(x^2 + y^2 + f^2) \right] \cdot$$
$$\left[y^2\left(\frac{Ax_0}{f} + C\right) - xy\left(\frac{Bx_0}{f} + \frac{Ay_0}{f}\right) + x^2\left(\frac{By_0}{f} + C\right) \right]$$

$$-y\left(Bf + Cy_0\right) - x\left(Af + Cx_0\right) + Ax_0f + By_0f\bigg] > 0 \quad (11)$$

For $u_n(x, y) = 0$ we obtain regions defined by a line and a conic section. These structures have been called copoint patterns and coaxis patterns, respectively [9]. In the case of the copoint vectors the line separates the translational components and the conic separates the rotational components of the vectors. The line passes through the FOE and also through the point (r, s), and thus it can be described by only one unknown. The conic is specified by only two unknowns, $\frac{\alpha f}{\gamma}$ and $\frac{\beta f}{\gamma}$. In the case of the coaxis vectors, the line separates the rotational components. It passes through the AOR and through the point (r, s) and thus it is also described by only one unknown. The conic separates the translational components. It is defined by the two coordinates of the FOE, (x_0, y_0). The intersection of the lines and the conics lies on the zero motion curve. One of the two other regions defined by the above described curves contains only vectors of length greater than zero, and the other contains only vectors smaller than zero. An illustration is given in Figure 13, which shows these regions for the class of coaxis vectors displayed on Figure 12b.

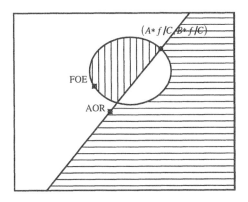

Figure 13. Separation of (A, B, C) coaxis vectors: A line passing through the AOR separates the positive and negative rotational components. A conic through the FOE separates the positive and negative translational components. In the area marked by horizontal lines all (A, B, C) coaxis vectors are greater than zero. In the area marked by vertical lines all (A, B, C) coaxis vectors are smaller than zero. The two other areas contain all the (A, B, C) coaxis vectors of length zero.

It becomes clear that the directional motion vectors of same length and direction can be considered as special cases of the copoint vectors. They represent the copoint vectors, for which r and s both are ∞ and $\frac{r}{s} = \frac{-n_y}{n_x}$. A special class of coaxis vectors, those which correspond to an axis parallel to the XY-plane, is very similar to the iso-directional motion vectors. For all classes of coaxis vectors $(A, B, 0)$ the slope of the line separating the rotational components is $\frac{A}{B}$ and the conics are all hyperbolas.

7. Using the Global Constraints

The global constraints described in this chapter allow us to make explicit aspects of the structure of motion fields which are due to rigid motion. These constraints can be exploited in a variety of ways to address problems of visual navigation. In particular, they could be used to verify the rigidity of a given motion field in order to detect and localize independent motion; to estimate the 3D rigid motion or provide bounds for the motion parameters that in conjunction with other algorithms could lead to accurate estimation; and to address problems in visuomotor control in robotic applications by relating changes in the global structure of motion fields to the system's motor control.

In the remainder of this section we will discuss various issues related to the design of algorithms based on the constraints on directional flow, and we will describe in more detail a number of procedures for 3D motion estimation and present experiments. A discussion on the utilization of the geometric constraints due to the iso-motion contours can be found in [11].

7.1. Applying the constraints to the input available

From the constraints developed in Section 6 we know that directional motion vectors are restricted to areas on the image. These constraints can be applied to image measurements of different kind and different complexity. If a system has the capability to derive optical flow, then the directional flow at every point in every direction is available. In general, accurate value of optical flow are not computable. On the basis of local information, only the directional flow along image gradients is well defined, the so-called normal flow. In many situations some additional information can be computed locally. For example, if an image patch is textured and the texture displays a variety of different directions, the sign of flow may be derived for a large range of directions there. In the simplest case the system only computes the sign of directional flow along one direction at points where strong image gradients are available, for example the sign of normal flow at edge points, or the sign of directional flow as derived with biological models, such as the Reichardt correlator [26].

7.2. 3D motion estimation as a pattern recognition problem

3D motion estimation can be formulated as a problem of localizing the directional motion regions. In particular, we are interested in the boundaries of these regions, whose intersections provide us with the parameters of the 3D motion. The localization of the different regions is a pattern recognition problem which could be solved through template matching.

One way in which we could address the localization is to just simply search through all the possibilities, which means for each possible motion we check whether for the motion measurements available the constraints are satisfied. If we consider the constraints on the sign of directional flow, our search spaces are of dimension three: Each possible constraint defines areas whose boundaries are described by three parameters, and the intersections of different boundaries provide the FOE and the AOR.

In order to evaluate the constraints we might simply count the number of image measurements with correct and incorrect sign. The motion with the highest percentage of correct values will be interpreted as the correct 3D motion. In most cases we will not obtain one unique solution, but we will constrain the possible FOE and AOR to patches on the image.

To improve upon the accuracy of the localization we could give different importance to image measurements in different areas: Let us consider two possible motions and assume that one of them is the correct one. If the other one is estimated incorrectly, there are particular areas in the image that could possibly yield negative depth values (and thus the flow measurements will have the wrong sign). For any two possible motions we can evaluate where these areas are and give more significance to the image measurements there.

Simple search, of course, is very time-consuming, and its complexity is exponential in the number of parameters, even if only linear in the number of constraints. The natural choice to accelerate the search is to employ multiresolution and coarse-to-fine techniques; at the coarse level, where the image is represented through a small number of patches, we consider the dominant sign of directional flow for each patch, and we discretize very coarsely the space of possible motions in which we search; at the finer levels we discretize the image into smaller patches and refine our estimates by searching for the motion parameters at increasingly finer scale till we reach, if necessary, the original image resolution.

By exploiting the particular structure of the positive and negative vectors in every pattern the search can be very much simplified. Let us parametrize every pattern by the location of the point $\mathbf{S_{u_n}}$ (the intersection of the line $g(x,y)$ and the conic section $h(x,y)$) and an additional rotational parameter specifying the exact conic. That is, by specifying $\mathbf{S_{u_n}}$ we also specify the line of the pattern, and there is a one-dimensional family of conics that passes through the same one point $\mathbf{S_{u_n}}$.

The analysis in Section 6.3 showed that $\mathbf{S_{u_n}}$ has to lie in the directional motion band. In the case of patterns defined by positive and negative vectors, the directional motion band is the area where motion vectors of value zero are found, or equivalently, where both positive and negative vectors are found. Thus, we could approximate the directional motion band from these values, and reduce the search for $\mathbf{S_{u_n}}$ to this area. The conics of the one-parameter family passing through $\mathbf{S_{u_n}}$ change in a continuous way, and we can use this fact to prune the search for the additional parameter. In summary, although the parameter spaces for the patterns are three-dimensional, it is sufficient to search only subspaces of the complete parameter spaces.

Another possibility is to search for either the rotational or the translational parameters only and use standard techniques to solve for the other. For example, we might search in the two-dimensional space of rotation axes for the motion vectors that are due to translation only. These are the (A,B,C) coaxis vectors, defined by the actual AOR, that is, $\frac{A}{C} = \frac{\alpha}{\gamma}$ and $\frac{B}{C} = \frac{\beta}{\gamma}$. Their corresponding pattern is solely defined by a two-parameter second-order curve (as given in equation (11)) separating the positive from the negative values. Since the curve is linear in the coordinates of the FOE, the problem of estimating the translation reduces to estimating the linear discriminant function. A number of algorithms from the pattern recognition literature might be used to solve this problem; for example, the Ho-Kashyap algorithm is designed to decide whether data is linearly discriminable and will also find the best discrimination. We might also employ linear programming, which is a much studied subject; the classic simplex algorithm used in implementations is exponential in theory, but there are techniques to make it polynomial in practice. Similarly, we might search in the two-dimensional space of possible FOEs for the copoint vectors which are due to rotation only, the (x_0, y_0) copoint vectors. The values of these vectors are described by a function, which is quadratic in the image coordinates and linear in the rotational parameters. To obtain the rotation we might employ any robust technique for solving linear systems, such as singular value decomposition.

7.3. MORE THAN TWO FLOW FIELDS

If we have more than two images and therefore more than two flow fields, we can study how flow and 3D motion change over time. All the constraints described are independent of the scene in view; thus, if the motion changes as a function of time we may apply the constraints to a number of successive flow fields at a time. If the motion is constant over a number of frames we can simultaneously apply the constraints to all the available flow fields and obtain much more data to use for localizing the directional motion areas. Otherwise the combined use of many flow fields can help us trace the boundaries of the areas, which now become surfaces in space-time.

7.4. MOVING BODY DETECTION

The same constraints may also be used in processes for the detection of independent motion. Since the observer is moving rigidly, an area with a motion field not possibly due to only one rigid motion must contain an independently moving object. The constraints are defined for the whole visual field, but also the motion vectors in every part of the image plane must obey a certain structure. Thus, we can check the constraints for the motion fields within image patches. By considering patches of different sizes and using various resolutions we also can derive information about the independently moving object's motion.

7.5. ESTIMATING BOUNDS OF THE 3D MOTION

If we are not restricted to the sign of directional flow, but also have access to its value, we can employ various additional computations to help us cut down on the amount of searching; for example, we might make use of the motion-parallax constraint to obtain bounds on the FOE's location. In the remainder of this subsection we describe a technique making use of regional flow measurements and a few techniques employing the iso-directional motion areas to obtain bounds on the motion parameters in very simple ways.

Using smoothed flow. Instead of using flow pointwise we might employ regional or smoothed flow [28], that is, we might compute linear expressions of single flow measurements. Let us consider N points $\mathbf{r}_i = (x_i, y_i, f)$ with motion vectors $\dot{\mathbf{r}}$ and at each point a direction $\mathbf{n}_i$ and a weight w_i. Then smoothed flow u_s is derived as

$$u_s = \sum_{i=1}^{N} w_i \dot{\mathbf{r}} \cdot \mathbf{n}_i = \sum_{i=1}^{N} w_i \mathbf{v}_{\text{tr}}(\mathbf{r}_i) \cdot \mathbf{n}_i + \sum_{i=1}^{N} w_i \mathbf{v}_{\text{rot}}(\mathbf{r}_i) \cdot \mathbf{n}_i. \tag{12}$$

According to this definition smoothed flow is a very general concept. For example, it applies to measurements that we can derive with simple filters, such as smoothing kernels if the weights are selected appropriately. Here we want to choose the weights in such a way that we eliminate the rotational component of smoothed flow.

This can be accomplished as follows: Consider the rotational component of smoothed flow, u_{srot}, which becomes

$$u_{\text{srot}} =$$
$$\sum_i w_i \Bigg(\left(\alpha \frac{x_i y_i}{f} - \beta \left(\frac{x_i^2}{f} + f \right) + \gamma y_i \right) n_{x_i}$$
$$- \left(\alpha \left(\frac{y_i^2}{f} + f \right) - \beta \frac{x_i y_i}{f} - \gamma x_i \right) n_{y_i} \Bigg). \tag{13}$$

If we derive the weights by solving the following (overdetermined) system of linear equations

$$\sum_i w_i \left(\frac{x_i y_i}{f} n_{x_i} + \left(\frac{y_i^2}{f} + f \right) n_{y_i} \right) = 0$$
$$\sum_i w_i \left(\left(\frac{x_i^2}{f} + f \right) n_{x_i} + \frac{x_i y_i}{f} n_{y_i} \right) = 0$$
$$\sum_i w_i \left(y_i n_{x_i} - x_i n_{y_i} \right) = 0,$$

the rotational component of the smoothed flow becomes zero. Having available at least four measurements, there exists a solution to the equations above; to be more precise, the solution space is of rank $N - 3$.

The overall smoothed flow, thus, is only due to translation and is given as

$$u_s = \sum_i w_i \frac{1}{Z_i} \left((x_i - x_0) n_{x_i} + (y_i - y_0) n_{y_i} \right). \tag{14}$$

If the weights are chosen appropriately, the sign of the smoothed flow derived in this way contains information about the possible location of the FOE: The left-hand side of equation u_s and the right-hand side must have the same sign. Thus, since Z_i is positive for all i, it is not possible that u_s has one sign and all expressions $(x_i - x_0) n_{x_i} + (y_i - y_0) n_{y_i}$ have the opposite sign. Each inequality $w_i((x_i - x_0) n_{x_i} + (y_i - y_0) n_{y_i}) > 0$ or < 0 defines a halfplane in which the FOE cannot lie. If the intersection of all N halfplanes is nonempty we obtain a constraint for the location of the FOE; it cannot lie in this intersection area. By combining the constraints of different smoothed flow values we find a number of areas where the FOE can possibly lie.

As a final remark, it should be said that the above described technique may be used even if only the sign of projected flow serves as input. If for certain image vectors weights w_i are computed such that all $w_i((x_i - x_0)n_{x_i} + (y_i - y_0)n_{y_i})$ have the same sign, then u_s also has the same sign, and it can be derived without considering any quantitative values.

Using iso-directional motion areas. The location of the FOE can be constrained by using iso-directional motion vectors in different directions. The directional motion vectors of a given value are located within the directional motion bands (see Figure 9). The directional motion bands consist of two areas meeting at the point $\mathbf{S_{un}}$. Through $\mathbf{S_{un}}$ and the FOE passes the boundary line of the iso-directional motion areas, which also separates the translational motion components (Figure 5). The slope of the line is known; it is perpendicular to the directional motion vector. The exact position of the line is defined by the location where the directional motion band is thinnest. It may not be possible to locate one point and thus the exact line, but only a bounded area which contains the line. Since all iso-directional motion areas of different lengths but the same direction define the same line, this bounded area can be located by means of a number of iso-directional motion bands corresponding to parallel motion vectors. The intersection of at least two such bounded areas corresponding to directional motion vectors in different directions gives an area in which the FOE lies. This is demonstrated in Figure 15. Figure 14 shows the synthetic directional flow field, which was used as input data for the localization of the translation axis demonstrated in Figures 15 and 16. The origin of the flow field, the FOE, and the AOR are marked in the image. The flow was created by choosing the depth as well as the direction at every point in a random way.

Figure 14. Synthetic directional motion field used as input data for the localization of the FOE and AOR shown in the next two figures.

Instead of focusing on the thinnest location of the directional motion bands, one could consider various directional motion bands corresponding to different lengths but the same direction. Two such iso-directional motion areas cannot intersect in an area that contains the line. Thus an area for the line passing through the FOE can be located as the region between regions where iso-directional motion areas intersect

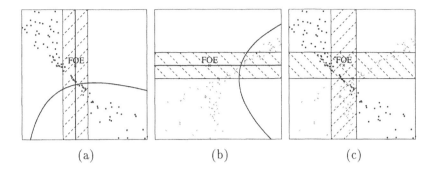

(a)   (b)   (c)

Figure 15. Localization of FOE. (a) Directional motion band due to directional motion vectors of a certain length parallel to the x-axis and
corresponding curves $g(x,y)$ and $h(x,y)$ defining the directional motion
area. By localizing, where this directional motion band is thinnest a
bounded area for the line separating the translational directional motion components is found (marked by diagonal lines). (b) Directional
motion band due to directional motion vectors of a certain length parallel to the y-axis with overlaid curves $g(x,y)$ and $h(x,y)$ defining the
directional motion area and localization of bounded area for the line
separating the translational directional motion components (marked by
diagonal lines). (c) The intersection of these areas gives a bounded area
for the FOE.

(see Figure 16).

Just as a line passing through the FOE bounds the iso-directional motion regions,
a line passing through the point where the rotation axis pierces the image plane
(AOR) bounds regions separating the $(A, B, 0)$ coaxis vectors of length zero. By
finding the locations where the areas separating the $(A, B, 0)$ coaxis patterns are
thinnest and intersecting different such areas, a bounded region for the AOR can be
located.

7.6. EXPERIMENTS

The following two experiments show results obtained with real images using algorithms proposed in this section. In both experiments only normal flow at image
points with strong spatial gradient has been computed as the moving image representation.

The first experiment demonstrates the localization of a bounded area for the
FOE as described in Section 7.5. Figure 17a shows the first image of a calibrated
motion sequence and Figure 17b shows the normal motion field computed between
the first and the second frame. The FOE and AOR are marked with white crosses.
In Figure 18a the points with normal motion vectors parallel to the y-axis of three
different lengths (0.3, 0.1, and -0.1 pixels) are displayed in three shades of grey.
These normal motion vectors constrain the FOE to lie in an area bounded by the two
horizontal lines where there is no intersection of the differently shaded iso-directional

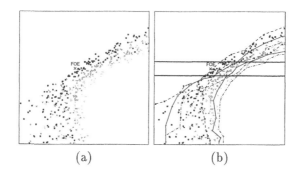

(a)   (b)

Figure 16. Localization of FOE. The FOE cannot lie within the areas where the directional motion bands corresponding to parallel directional motion vectors intersect. (a) Directional motion vectors parallel to the y-axis of three different lengths (displayed in dark, medium, and light grey). (b) Polygonal approximation of the boundaries of directional motion bands and localization of an area in which the FOE can lie.

motion areas, in between the regions of intersection. Similarly, the normal motion vectors parallel to the x-axis (of length -0.3, 0.0, and 0.3) constrain the FOE to lie in an area bounded by two vertical lines as shown in Figure 18b. The intersection of the areas found in 18a and b gives a bounded area for the FOE (see Figure 18c).

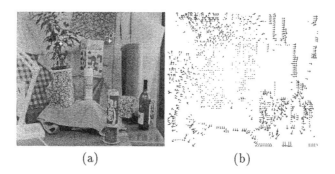

(a)   (b)

Figure 17. (a) First frame of a motion sequence. (b) Normal motion field.

In the second experiment the fitting of positive and negative coaxis vectors using a simple search was tested. An image sequence was captured by a camera mounted on an unmanned ground vehicle, developed by Martin Marietta, as the vehicle moved along rough terrain in the countryside, thus undergoing continuously changing rigid motion. The normal flow has been computed and the coaxis patterns have been fitted in order to estimate the 3D motion. Figures 19a shows one frame of the sequence with the normal flow field overlaid. Figures 19b, d, and f show the positive and negative coaxis vectors corresponding to the x-, y-, and z-axes, and Figures 19c, e, g, and h show the patterns. Figures 19j demonstrates the result of the fitting. Because measurements are not everywhere available (strong spatial gradients appear

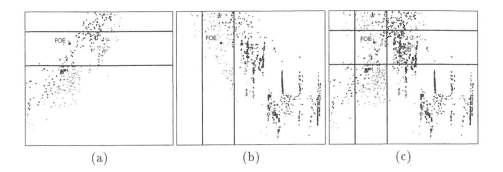

Figure 18. Localization of the FOE from normal flow vectors of same direction and different length. (a) Normal motion vectors parallel to the y-axis of three different lengths (with the corresponding points shown in dark, medium, and light grey) constrain the FOE to lie in an area in between the to horizontal lines. (b) Normal motion vectors parallel to the x-axis of three different lengths constrain the FOE to lie in the area in between the two vertical lines. (c) The intersection of the areas found in (a) and (b) provides a bounded area for the location of the FOE.

sparse) a set of patterns can possibly be fitted resulting in two bounded areas as solutions for the FOE and the AOR. The real intersections of the translation and rotation axes are inside these areas.

8. THE GLOBAL STRUCTURE ON THE SPHERE

The concept of iso-motion contours and iso-directional motion areas can also be defined for other surfaces different from the plane. We will discuss here the spherical image. This is for two reasons. First, for the purpose of analyzing visual motion globally, the sphere is a natural choice because it provides us with a 360° field of view. As is shown in the next two subsections, on the sphere the iso-motion contours, the iso-directional motion areas, as well as the coaxis and copoint patterns take a simple form. Second, we will use some of the spherical constraints in the next section where we analyze the uniqueness of directional motion fields, and this analysis is simpler for the sphere than for the plane, since all directions are equal there, and thus there is no need for a treatment of special cases such as the ones arising from vectors parallel to the plane. We start by reviewing the spherical motion geometry.

On a sphere of radius f (see Figure 20), the image $\mathbf{r}$ of every point $\mathbf{R}$ is

$$\mathbf{r} = \frac{\mathbf{R}f}{|\mathbf{R}|},$$

with $|\mathbf{R}|$ being the norm of the vector $\mathbf{R}$. Recalling from equation (1), if we project the 3D motion on the sphere the motion vector $\dot{\mathbf{r}}$ can be expressed as

$$\dot{\mathbf{r}} = \mathbf{v}_{\mathrm{tr}}\left(\mathbf{r}\right) + \mathbf{v}_{\mathrm{rot}}\left(\mathbf{r}\right) = \frac{1}{|\mathbf{R}|}\left(\frac{1}{f}\left(\mathbf{t}\cdot\mathbf{r}\right)\mathbf{r} - f\mathbf{t}\right) - \boldsymbol{\omega}\times\mathbf{r}. \tag{15}$$

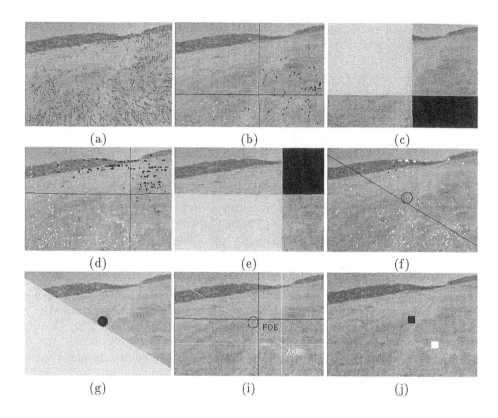

Figure 19. Fitting of coaxis vectors: (a) shows one frame of the image sequence with the normal flow field overlaid. (b), (d), and (f) show the positive (light color) and negative (dark color) vectors of the coaxis patterns corresponding to the x-, y-, and z-axes. (c), (e), and (g) show the corresponding fitted patterns. (i) shows superimposed on the image the boundaries of the patterns whose intersections provide the FOE and the AOR. (j) Result of fitting: two bounded areas have been found as solutions for the FOE (black area) and the AOR (white area).

When employing general imaging surfaces, the motion vectors at a surface point are defined on the local tangent plane. In the discussion of $\mathbf{u}$ iso-motion contours on the plane, we used a simplified notation and did not mention that the vector $\mathbf{u}$ actually results from the projection of a 3D vector on the local tangent plane which happens to be the same everywhere. For the case of a spherical retina, however, we have to be more general and provide definitions in the form of projections of 3D vectors on the local tangent plane. In the following we use the negative projection of a vector, that is, for a 3D motion vector $\mathbf{u}$ we consider for every image point $\mathbf{r}$ the motion vectors $(\mathbf{u} \cdot \mathbf{r})\mathbf{r} - \mathbf{u}$.

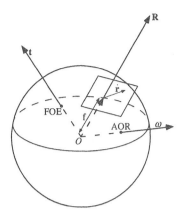

Figure 20. Image formation using perspective projection on a spherical retina.

8.1. SPHERICAL ISO-MOTION CONTOURS

For a rigid motion field on the sphere with radius 1 ($f = 1$), the locus of points $\mathbf{r}$ at which the motion vector could have the value $(\mathbf{u} \cdot \mathbf{r})\mathbf{r} - \mathbf{u}$ is described by a second-order equation that in general gives rise to one or two curves. This curve or group of curves passes through the FOE and the FOC (the points where $\mathbf{t}$ pierces the sphere) and the points $\mathbf{R_u}$ ($\mathbf{R_{u_1}}$ and $\mathbf{R_{u_2}}$) (where the rotational component of the motion is equal to $(\mathbf{u} \cdot \mathbf{r})\mathbf{r} - \mathbf{u}$).

Proof: For the locus of points $\mathbf{r}$ with motion vector $(\mathbf{u} \cdot \mathbf{r})\mathbf{r} - \mathbf{u}$ using (15) we have

$$\frac{1}{|\mathbf{R}|} ((\mathbf{t} \cdot \mathbf{r})\mathbf{r} - \mathbf{t}) - (\boldsymbol{\omega} \times \mathbf{r}) = (\mathbf{u} \cdot \mathbf{r})\mathbf{r} - \mathbf{u}. \tag{16}$$

If $\mathbf{u} = 0$ we obtain

$$((\mathbf{t} \cdot \mathbf{r})\mathbf{r} - \mathbf{t}) \times (\boldsymbol{\omega} \times \mathbf{r}) = 0$$

or $\qquad -(\mathbf{t} \cdot \mathbf{r})(\mathbf{r} \cdot \boldsymbol{\omega})\mathbf{r} + (\mathbf{t} \cdot \boldsymbol{\omega})\mathbf{r} = 0,$

and thus $\qquad \mathbf{t} \cdot \boldsymbol{\omega} - (\mathbf{t} \cdot \mathbf{r})(\mathbf{r} \cdot \boldsymbol{\omega}) = 0 \tag{17}$

or $\qquad (\boldsymbol{\omega} \times \mathbf{r}) \cdot (\mathbf{t} \times \mathbf{r}) = 0. \tag{18}$

Otherwise, projecting both sides of (16) on the vector $(\boldsymbol{\omega} \times \mathbf{r}) \times \mathbf{r}$, provided that $\boldsymbol{\omega} \times \mathbf{r} \neq 0$, and on the vector $\mathbf{u} \times \mathbf{r}$, provided that $\mathbf{u} \times \mathbf{r} \neq 0$, gives

$$\frac{1}{|\mathbf{R}|} (\mathbf{t} \cdot \boldsymbol{\omega} - (\mathbf{t} \cdot \mathbf{r})(\mathbf{r} \cdot \boldsymbol{\omega})) = \mathbf{u} \cdot \boldsymbol{\omega} - (\mathbf{u} \cdot \mathbf{r})(\boldsymbol{\omega} \cdot \mathbf{r}) \tag{19}$$

and $\qquad -\frac{1}{|\mathbf{R}|}\mathbf{t} \cdot (\mathbf{u} \times \mathbf{r}) = \mathbf{u} \cdot \boldsymbol{\omega} - (\mathbf{u} \cdot \mathbf{r})(\boldsymbol{\omega} \cdot \mathbf{r}). \tag{20}$

Equating the left-hand side of (19) with the left-hand side of (20), we derive

$$(\mathbf{r} \cdot \boldsymbol{\omega})(\mathbf{r} \cdot \mathbf{t}) - (\mathbf{t} \cdot \boldsymbol{\omega}) + (\mathbf{u} \times \mathbf{t}) \cdot \mathbf{r} = 0. \tag{21}$$

Each of the equations (18) and (21) describes a second-order curve on the sphere and gives the locus of points, where the motion vector could take the values zero and $(\mathbf{u} \cdot \mathbf{r})\mathbf{r} - \mathbf{u}$, respectively. To show that the points $\mathbf{R_u}$ lie on the curve(s) described by (21) let us denote by $\mathbf{r_1}$ the vector $\vec{OR_u}$. Then

$$- \boldsymbol{\omega} \times \mathbf{r_1} = (\mathbf{u} \cdot \mathbf{r_1})\mathbf{r_1} - \mathbf{u}. \tag{22}$$

From (21) we obtain the following constraint for the points $\mathbf{r_1}$

$$(\mathbf{t} \times (\boldsymbol{\omega} \times \mathbf{r_1})) \cdot \mathbf{r_1} + (\mathbf{u} \times \mathbf{t}) \cdot \mathbf{r_1} = 0. \tag{23}$$

Substituting in (23) for $\boldsymbol{\omega} \times \mathbf{r_1}$ from (22), it can be verified that $\mathbf{r_1}$ is a point on the curves. $\square$

As can be seen from equations (18) and (21), for the case when $\mathbf{u} = 0$ or when $\mathbf{u} \times \mathbf{t} = 0$ (i.e., $\mathbf{u}$ is parallel to $\mathbf{t}$) we always have two curves which pass through the FOE and the AOR. Of special interest are the curves for which $\mathbf{u} = 0$, the zero motion contours. They define the locus of points where the translational flow component $\mathbf{v_{tr}}(\mathbf{r})$ is parallel to the rotational motion component $\mathbf{v_{rot}}(\mathbf{r})$. To give an illustration, in Figure 21 three zero iso-motion contours are displayed, which are defined by the same $\mathbf{t}$ and different vectors $\boldsymbol{\omega}$, where the angle between $\mathbf{t}$ and $\boldsymbol{\omega}$ increases from 21a to 21c: If $(\boldsymbol{\omega} \cdot \mathbf{t}) < 0$, one of the curves contains $\mathbf{t_0} = \frac{\mathbf{t}}{|\mathbf{t}|}$ and $\boldsymbol{\omega}_0 = \frac{\boldsymbol{\omega}}{|\boldsymbol{\omega}|}$, and one contains $-\mathbf{t_0}$ and $-\boldsymbol{\omega}_0$; if $(\boldsymbol{\omega} \cdot \mathbf{t}) = 0$ the two curves become great circles, the one orthogonal to $\mathbf{t}$, the other orthogonal to $\boldsymbol{\omega}$; if $(\boldsymbol{\omega} \cdot \mathbf{t}) > 0$ one of the two curves passes through $\mathbf{t_0}$ and $-\boldsymbol{\omega}_0$ and the other through $-\mathbf{t_0}$ and $\boldsymbol{\omega}_0$.

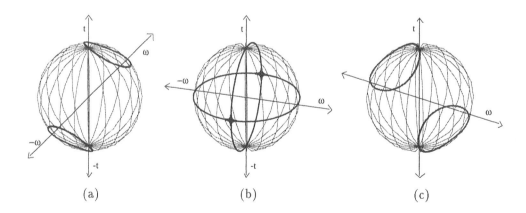

(a)   (b)   (c)

Figure 21. The zero motion contour (the locus of points $\mathbf{r}$ where $\dot{\mathbf{r}}$ could be zero) consists of two closed curves on the sphere which pass through the FOE and the AOR (and FOC and $-$AOR). Three possible configurations are (a) $(\boldsymbol{\omega} \cdot \mathbf{t}) > 0$, (b) $(\boldsymbol{\omega} \cdot \mathbf{t}) = 0$, and (c) $(\boldsymbol{\omega} \cdot \mathbf{t}) < 0$.

General iso-motion contours are displayed in Figure 22. As one can see from equations (21) and (18), if $\mathbf{u} \neq 0$ additional linear terms are introduced, and the locus becomes either one or two curves. As the length of $\mathbf{u}$ becomes large with regard to $\boldsymbol{\omega}$ and $\mathbf{t}$, the curve converges to the great circle $((\mathbf{t} \times \mathbf{u}) \cdot \mathbf{r} = 0)$.

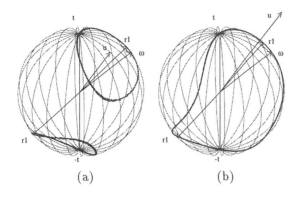

(a)   (b)

Figure 22. General **u** iso-motion contours pass through the FOE, the FOC, and the points $\mathbf{R_u}$—the points where the rotational component of the motion is equal to $(\mathbf{u} \cdot \mathbf{r})\mathbf{r} - \mathbf{u}$. The curves displayed in (a) and (b) are defined by the same **t** and $\boldsymbol{\omega}$ and parallel vectors **u**.

Similar to the planar case, all the iso-motion contours on the sphere pass through the FOE (and the FOC). Furthermore, all $k\mathbf{u}$ iso-motion contours, where $k \in \Re$ and **u** is a motion vector of unit length, intersect in the same points, which lie in a plane. For the general case, if $(\mathbf{u} \times \mathbf{t}) \cdot (\mathbf{t} \times \boldsymbol{\omega}) \neq 0$ these are the FOE, the FOC, and two other points denoted as $\mathbf{P}_{k\mathbf{u}}$ and $-\mathbf{P}_{k\mathbf{u}}$.

8.2. Iso-directional motion areas

To obtain on the sphere an analog to the iso-directional motion areas of the plane, the directions of the directional vectors on the sphere also have to be defined with regard to a 3D vector. Furthermore, the length of the directional motion vector has to be appropriately normalized. We define the directions as follow: If **n** is a unit vector we consider image vectors on the sphere in direction $(\mathbf{n} \cdot \mathbf{r})\mathbf{r} - \mathbf{n}$, that is, vectors along great circles (or longitudes) passing through **n** and $-\mathbf{n}$. Thus, given a 3D vector $\mathbf{u_n}$ (a vector of length u_n and unit vector **n**) we consider the locus of points **r** on the sphere with directional motion vector $\frac{u_n}{\|(\mathbf{n}\cdot\mathbf{r})\mathbf{r}-\mathbf{n}\|^2}((\mathbf{n} \cdot \mathbf{r})\mathbf{r} - \mathbf{n})$ (that is, vectors of length $\frac{u_n}{\|(\mathbf{n}\cdot\mathbf{r})\mathbf{r}-\mathbf{n}\|}$ along the unit vector $\frac{(\mathbf{n}\cdot\mathbf{r})\mathbf{r}-\mathbf{n}}{\|(\mathbf{n}\cdot\mathbf{r})\mathbf{r}-\mathbf{n}\|}$). It can be shown that for a rigid motion field on the sphere this locus consists of areas bounded by a circle and a second-order curve (see Figure 23).

Proof: This can be seen by considering that

$$\left(\frac{1}{|\mathbf{R}|} \left((\mathbf{t} \cdot \mathbf{r})\mathbf{r} - \mathbf{t} \right) - \boldsymbol{\omega} \times \mathbf{r} \right) \cdot \frac{(\mathbf{n} \cdot \mathbf{r})\mathbf{r} - \mathbf{n}}{\|(\mathbf{n} \cdot \mathbf{r})\mathbf{r} - \mathbf{n}\|} = \frac{u_n}{\|(\mathbf{n} \cdot \mathbf{r})\mathbf{r} - \mathbf{n}\|}$$

$$\text{or} \qquad \frac{1}{|\mathbf{R}|} \left((\mathbf{n} \cdot \mathbf{t}) - (\mathbf{t} \cdot \mathbf{r})(\mathbf{r} \cdot \mathbf{n}) \right) = u_n - \mathbf{r} \cdot (\mathbf{n} \times \boldsymbol{\omega}).$$

Since $|\mathbf{R}| > 0$ it follows:

$$(\mathbf{n} \cdot \mathbf{t} - (\mathbf{n} \cdot \mathbf{r})(\mathbf{r} \cdot \mathbf{t}))(u_n - \mathbf{r} \cdot (\mathbf{n} \times \boldsymbol{\omega})) > 0. \tag{24}$$

The right-hand side of the inequality is a product of two terms, which define the boundary of the iso-directional motion area: Equation $\mathbf{n}\cdot\mathbf{t}-(\mathbf{n}\cdot\mathbf{r})(\mathbf{r}\cdot\mathbf{t})=0$ describes a second-order curve passing from the points where $\mathbf{t}$ and $\mathbf{n}$ pierce the sphere similar to the ones of Figure 21. Equation $u_n-\mathbf{r}\cdot(\mathbf{n}\times\boldsymbol{\omega})=0$ describes a circle. When $u_n=0$ this equation represents a great circle passing through the AOR and $-$AOR.$\square$

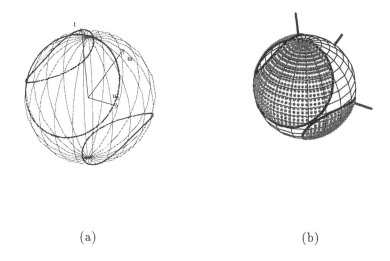

(a)   (b)

Figure 23. Iso-directional motion areas on the sphere are defined by a second order curve and a circle. (a) shows the boundaries of the iso-normal motion regions defined by the vectors $\mathbf{t}$, $\boldsymbol{\omega}$ and $\mathbf{u_n}$ of length 1, 1, and 0.5, where all parts of the sphere (visible and hidden ones) are rendered; (b) shows the corresponding iso-directional areas (filled with grey dots) and the directions of the defining vectors with only the visible parts displayed.

8.3. COAXIS AND COPOINT VECTORS ON THE SPHERE

To obtain an equivalent of the coaxis vectors on the sphere, we intersect the cones defined by an axis $\mathbf{s}=(A,B,C)$ with the sphere, which provides us with circles lying on planes perpendicular to $\mathbf{s}$. The unit vectors perpendicular to the circles lie along the great circles passing through $\mathbf{s}$. Thus the coaxis vectors take the form of vectors along longitudes on the sphere (longitudinal vectors). Similarly, the copoint vectors were obtained as the vectors perpendicular to straight lines passing through a point. The projection of straight lines on the sphere results in great circles, and the unit vectors perpendicular to these circles lie on parallel circles and thus can be considered as the vectors along latitudes defined by an axis $\mathbf{s}$ (latitudinal vectors). As in the case of the plane we obtain a second-order curve (see equation (24)) separating the translational longitudinal components and a first-order curve, that is, a great circle, separating the rotational longitudinal components (see Figure 24). In the case of the latitudinal vectors the rotational components are separated by a second order curve and the translational components are separated by a great circle.

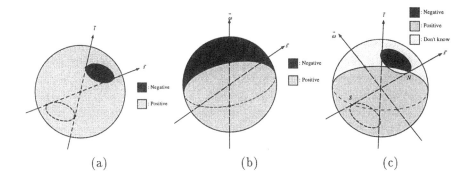

(a)   (b)   (c)

Figure 24. (a) Translational image motion along s-longitudinal vectors. At every point $\mathbf{r}$ consider the translational vector in direction $(\mathbf{s \cdot r})\mathbf{r} - \mathbf{r}$. Curves $(\mathbf{s \cdot t}) - (\mathbf{s \cdot r})(\mathbf{t \cdot r})$ separate the negative and positive values. (b) Rotational image motion along s-longitudinal vectors. A great circle defined by ω and $\mathbf{s}$ separates the negative from the positive values. (c) A general rigid image motion defines a pattern along every s-longitudinal vector field. There is an area of negative values, an area of positive values, and an area of values whose signs are unknown.

9. UNIQUENESS OF DIRECTIONAL FLOW FIELDS

Since exact optical flow is difficult to compute, employing only information about the sign of flow measurements for addressing visual navigation tasks constitutes a promising alternative. The constraints on the sign of directional flow presented in the last sections were derived using only the rigid motion model, with the only constraint on the scene being that the depth in view had to be positive at every point—the so-called "depth-positivity" constraint. In the sequel we are led naturally to the question of what these constraints, or more generally any constraint on the sign flow measurements, can possibly tell us about three-dimensional motion and the structure of the scene in view. Thus we would like to investigate the amount of information in the sign of directional flow. Since knowing the sign of directional motion vectors in all directions is equivalent to knowing the direction of the exact motion vector, our question amounts to studying the relationship between the directions of 2D motion vectors and 3D rigid motion.

The answer to this question is that if the imaging surface is a whole sphere, we have enough information in the direction of motion fields to determine the orientation of the translational component of the rigid motion and also to determine the orientation of the rotational component of motion. Thus we can determine the

FOE and the AOR, but not the magnitude of the rotation. If we restrict the image
to half of a sphere (or an infinitely large image plane) there could be ambiguity.
Two different rigid motions with instantaneous translational and rotational velocities (t_1, ω_1) and (t_2, ω_2) can give rise to motion fields with the same direction if
the plane through t_1 and t_2 is perpendicular to the plane through ω_1 and ω_2 (i.e.,
$(t_1 \times t_2) \cdot (\omega_1 \times \omega_2) = 0$). For this to happen the depth of each corresponding surface
has to be within a certain range, defined by a second- and a third-order surface.

The presentation of the proof is as follows: As imaging surface we consider the
sphere. In Section 9.1 we develop the preliminaries: constraints that will be used
in the uniqueness analysis. Given two rigid motions, we study what the constraints
are on the surfaces in view for the two motion fields to have the same direction at
every point. From these constraints, we investigate for which points on the image
one of the surfaces must have negative depth. The locations where negative depth
occurs are described implicitly in the form of constraints on the sign of functions
depending on the image coordinates and the two three-dimensional motions. The
existence of image points whose corresponding depth is negative ensures that the two
rigid motions cannot produce motion fields with the same direction. In Section 9.3,
which contains the main uniqueness proof, we study conditions under which two
rigid flow fields could have the same direction at every point on a half sphere (i.e.,
conditions under which there are no points of negative depth) and we visualize the
location of negative depth. The constraints developed in Section 9.1 also allow us
to characterize the locations on the image where the motion vectors due to different
motion must have different directions, thus providing significance to the uniqueness
results for a limited field of view.

9.1. CRITICAL SURFACE CONSTRAINTS

If all we have is the direction of the flow we can project the flow $\dot{r}$, as given in equation (15), on any unit vector n_i on the image and obtain an inequality constraint:

$$\dot{r} \cdot n_i = \left(\frac{1}{|R|} ((t \cdot r) r - t) - \omega \times r \right) \cdot n_i > 0 \quad \text{or} \quad < 0.$$

From this inequality we certainly cannot recover the magnitude of translation, since
the optical flow does not allow us to compute it. In addition we are also restricted
in the computation of the rotational parameters. If we multiply ω by a positive
constant, leave t fixed but multiply $\frac{1}{|R|}$ by the same positive constant, the sign of
flow is not affected. Thus from the direction of flow we can at most compute the
axis of rotation.

Let us assume that two different rigid motions yield the same direction of flow
at every point in the image. Let t_1 and ω_1 be translational and rotational velocities
of the first motion, let t_2 and ω_2 be translational and rotational velocities of the
second motion, where all four vectors t_1, t_2, ω_1 and ω_2 are of unit length. Let $Z_1(r)$
and $Z_2(r)$ be the depth maps, the functions mapping points r on the image to the
real numbers, and representing the depth of the surfaces in view corresponding to
the two motions. In this section we investigate the constraints that must be satisfied
by Z_1 and Z_2 in order for the two flow fields to have the same direction.

We assume that the two depths are positive, and allow Z_1 or Z_2 to be infinitely large. Thus we assume $1/Z_1 \geq 0$ and $1/Z_2 \geq 0$.

For brevity reasons throughout the paper we assume $\boldsymbol{\omega}_1 \times \boldsymbol{\omega}_2 \neq 0$ and $\mathbf{t}_1 \times \mathbf{t}_2 \neq 0$. The special cases of $\boldsymbol{\omega}_1 \times \boldsymbol{\omega}_2 = 0$ or $\mathbf{t}_1 \times \mathbf{t}_2 = 0$ do not lead to ambiguous flow fields as has been shown in [4].

We start the proof by defining some notation. We denote

$$
\begin{aligned}
f_\omega(\mathbf{r}) &= [\boldsymbol{\omega}_1 \, \boldsymbol{\omega}_2 \, \mathbf{r}] \\
f_t(\mathbf{r}) &= [\mathbf{t}_1 \, \mathbf{t}_2 \, \mathbf{r}] \\
g_{ij}(\mathbf{r}) &= (\boldsymbol{\omega}_i \times \mathbf{r}) \cdot (\mathbf{t}_j \times \mathbf{r}) \quad \text{for } i, j = 1,2.
\end{aligned}
\tag{25}
$$

These functions have a simple geometrical meaning. Triple product $[\mathbf{a}\,\mathbf{b}\,\mathbf{r}]$ is zero for points lying on a geodesic passing through $\mathbf{a}$ and $\mathbf{b}$. The equation $f_\omega(\mathbf{r}) = 0$ defines the locus of points $\mathbf{r}$ where $\mathbf{v}_{\mathrm{rot}_1}(\mathbf{r})$, the rotational component of the first motion, is parallel to $\mathbf{v}_{\mathrm{rot}_2}(\mathbf{r})$, the rotational component of the second motion and $f_t(\mathbf{r}) = 0$ defines the locus of points $\mathbf{r}$ where $\mathbf{v}_{\mathrm{tr}_1}(\mathbf{r})$, the translational component of the first motion, is parallel to $\mathbf{v}_{\mathrm{tr}_2}(\mathbf{r})$, the translational component of the second motion. The function $g_{ij}(\mathbf{r}) = 0$ defines the zero motion contour of motion $(\mathbf{t}_j, \boldsymbol{\omega}_i)$, as described in Section 8.1, which consists of two closed curves on the sphere. It is at this locus of points that $\mathbf{v}_{\mathrm{rot}_i}(\mathbf{r})$ is parallel to $\mathbf{v}_{\mathrm{tr}_j}(\mathbf{r})$.

To simplify the notation we will usually drop $\mathbf{r}$ and write only f_t and g_{12}. There is a simple relationship between f_i and g_{ij}, as we can show by simple vector manipulation:

$$
g_{11}g_{22} = f_t f_\omega + g_{12}g_{21}.
\tag{26}
$$

At any point, the two flow vectors have the same direction, if there exists $\mu > 0$ such that

$$
-\frac{1}{Z_1}(\mathbf{r} \times (\mathbf{t}_1 \times \mathbf{r})) - \boldsymbol{\omega}_1 \times \mathbf{r} = \mu \left(-\frac{1}{Z_2}(\mathbf{r} \times (\mathbf{t}_2 \times \mathbf{r})) - \boldsymbol{\omega}_2 \times \mathbf{r} \right).
\tag{27}
$$

By projecting (27) on directions $\mathbf{t}_2 \times \mathbf{r}$ and $\mathbf{r} \times (\boldsymbol{\omega}_2 \times \mathbf{r})$ we obtain two scalar equations. Since we also assume that $\mu > 0$, we obtain two constraints for Z_1:

$$
\mathrm{sgn}\left(\frac{1}{Z_1} f_t + g_{12} \right) = \mathrm{sgn}\,(g_{22})
\tag{28}
$$

$$
\mathrm{sgn}\left(\frac{1}{Z_1} g_{21} - f_\omega \right) = \mathrm{sgn}\left(\frac{1}{Z_2} g_{22} \right).
\tag{29}
$$

We define $s_1 = -g_{12}/f_t$ and $s_1' = f_\omega/g_{21}$. At any point, f_i and g_{ij} are constant, so equations (28) and (29) provide simple constraints for $\frac{1}{Z_1}$. We will call them the s_1-constraint and s_1'-constraint, respectively.

Let us now interpret these constraints: $\frac{1}{Z_2}$ is always nonnegative; thus the depth Z_1 must satisfy

$$
\begin{aligned}
&\text{either} \quad \tfrac{1}{Z_1} f_t + g_{12} > 0 \text{ and } \tfrac{1}{Z_1} g_{21} - f_\omega \geq 0 \\
&\text{or} \quad\;\; \tfrac{1}{Z_1} f_t + g_{12} < 0 \text{ and } \tfrac{1}{Z_1} g_{21} - f_\omega \leq 0.
\end{aligned}
$$

We see that the depth Z_1 has a relationship to the surfaces $1/s_1(\mathbf{r})$ and $1/s_1'(\mathbf{r})$. To express the surfaces in scene coordinates $\mathbf{R}$, we substitute in the above equations $Z(\mathbf{r})\mathbf{r} = \mathbf{R}$ and obtain

$$(\mathbf{t}_1 \times \mathbf{t}_2) \cdot \mathbf{R} + (\boldsymbol{\omega}_1 \times \mathbf{R}) \cdot (\mathbf{t}_2 \times \mathbf{R}) = 0 \qquad (30)$$

$$\text{and} \qquad (\boldsymbol{\omega}_2 \times \mathbf{R}) \cdot (\mathbf{t}_1 \times \mathbf{R}) - ((\boldsymbol{\omega}_1 \times \boldsymbol{\omega}_2) \cdot \mathbf{R})\, \mathbf{R}^2 = 0. \qquad (31)$$

Thus Z_1 is constrained by a second-order surface through (30) and by a third-order surface through (31). At some points it has to be inside the first surface and at some points it has to be outside the first surface. In addition, at some points it has to be inside the second surface and at some points it has to be outside the second surface. Figure 25 provides a pictorial description of the two surfaces constraining Z_1.

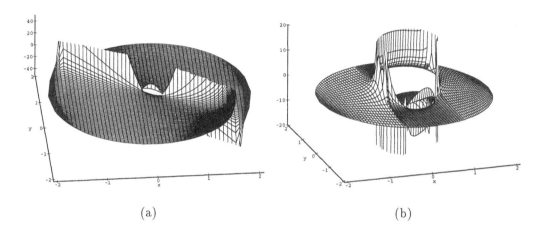

(a)   (b)

Figure 25. Two rigid motions $(\mathbf{t}_1, \boldsymbol{\omega}_1)$, $(\mathbf{t}_2, \boldsymbol{\omega}_2)$ constrain the possible depth Z_1 of the first surface by a second and a third order surface. The particular surfaces shown in the coordinate system of the imaging sphere, projected stereographically, correspond to the motion configuration of Figure 27.

At every point, besides the s_1- and the s_1'-constraint we have in addition the constraint $\frac{1}{Z_1} \geq 0$. If all three constraints can be satisfied simultaneously at a point in the image, then there is an interval (bounded or unbounded) of Z_1 values satisfying them. If the constraints cannot be satisfied, this means that the two flows at this point cannot have the same direction and we say that we have a *contradictory point*.

At a point where $f_i \neq 0$ and $g_{ij} \neq 0$, we can summarize the solutions in a table.

positivity-constraint	s_1-constraint	s_1'-constraint	$\frac{1}{Z_1}$ solution interval	solution exists if
$1/Z_1 > 0$	$1/Z_1 > s_1$	$1/Z_1 \geq s_1'$	$(\max(s_1, s_1', 0), \infty)$	always
$1/Z_1 > 0$	$1/Z_1 > s_1$	$1/Z_1 \leq s_1'$	$(\max(s_1, 0), s_1')$	$s_1' \geq 0$ and $s_1 < s_1'$
$1/Z_1 > 0$	$1/Z_1 < s_1$	$1/Z_1 \geq s_1'$	$(\max(s_1', 0), s_1)$	$s_1 > 0$ and $s_1' < s_1$
$1/Z_1 > 0$	$1/Z_1 < s_1$	$1/Z_1 \leq s_1'$	$(0, \min(s_1, s_1'))$	$s_1 > 0$ and $s_1' \geq 0$

If $f_i = 0$ or $g_{ij} = 0$, we may get constraints that do not depend on Z_1, or equality constraints.

The existence of a solution for Z_1 depends on the signs of f_i and g_{ij}, and also on the sign of $s_1 - s_1'$. Functions $f_i(\mathbf{r})$ and $g_{ij}(\mathbf{r})$ are polynomial functions of $\mathbf{r}$. To find out where they change sign, it is enough to find points where they are zero. The sign of $s_1 - s_1'$ is more complicated, since $s_1(\mathbf{r})$ and $s_1'(\mathbf{r})$ do not have to be continuous; however, their discontinuities occur at points where $f_t(\mathbf{r}) = 0$ or $g_{21}(\mathbf{r}) = 0$. So $\mathrm{sgn}(s_1 - s_1')$ can change at those points, and at points where $s_1 - s_1' = 0$. Using (26), we can write

$$s_1 - s_1' = -\frac{g_{12}}{f_t} - \frac{f_\omega}{g_{21}} = -\frac{1}{f_t g_{21}}\left(f_t f_\omega + g_{12} g_{21}\right) = -\frac{g_{11}\, g_{22}}{f_t\, g_{21}}. \tag{32}$$

So we see that $\mathrm{sgn}(s_1 - s_1')$ can change only at points where at least one of f_i, g_{ij} is zero.

Up to this point, we have been talking about constraints for Z_1. We can repeat the analysis for Z_2 and project equation (27) on vectors $\mathbf{t}_1 \times \mathbf{r}$ and $\mathbf{r} \times (\boldsymbol{\omega}_1 \times \mathbf{r})$ to obtain similar constraints for Z_2:

$$\mathrm{sgn}\,(g_{11}) = \mathrm{sgn}\left(-\frac{1}{Z_2}f_t + g_{21}\right) \tag{33}$$

$$\mathrm{sgn}\left(\frac{1}{Z_1}g_{11}\right) = \mathrm{sgn}\left(\frac{1}{Z_2}g_{12} + f_\omega\right). \tag{34}$$

We define $s_2 = g_{21}/f_t$, $s_2' = -f_\omega/g_{12}$. The functions $1/s_2(\mathbf{r})$ and $1/s_2'(\mathbf{r})$ define two scene surfaces constraining Z_2. At any point, we have the s_2-constraint ($\frac{1}{Z_2} > s_2$, $\frac{1}{Z_2} = s_2$, or $\frac{1}{Z_2} < s_2$), and the s_2'-constraint ($\frac{1}{Z_2} \geq s_2'$, $\frac{1}{Z_2} = s_2'$, or $\frac{1}{Z_2} \leq s_2'$). Again, the type of solution for Z_2 can change only at points where at least one of f_i, g_{ij} is zero.

Now we can summarize the results. The curves $f_i(\mathbf{r}) = 0$ and $g_{ij}(\mathbf{r}) = 0$ separate the sphere into a number of areas. Each of the areas is either contradictory (and contains only contradictory points), or ambiguous (containing ambiguous points). Two different rigid motions can produce ambiguous directions of flow if the image contains only points from ambiguous areas. There are also two scene surfaces constraining depth Z_1 and two surfaces constraining depth Z_2. If the depths do not satisfy the constraints, the two flows are not ambiguous.

9.2. CONTRADICTORY POINTS

In this section we describe combinations of signs of f_i and g_{ij} that yield a contradictory point. We investigate the general case, i.e., $f_i \neq 0$, and $g_{ij} \neq 0$.

There are two simple conditions yielding a contradiction for Z_1, one for the s_1-constraint, one for the s_1'-constraint. There is no solution for Z_1 if $\frac{1}{Z_1} < s_1$ and $s_1 < 0$. From (28) we see that this happens when

$$\mathrm{sgn}\,(f_t) = \mathrm{sgn}\,(g_{12}) = -\mathrm{sgn}\,(g_{22}). \tag{35}$$

Similarly we obtain a contradiction if $\frac{1}{Z_1} \leq s_1'$ and $s_1' < 0$, i.e., when

$$\text{sgn}(f_\omega) = -\text{sgn}(g_{21}) = \text{sgn}(g_{22}). \tag{36}$$

We get similar conditions for Z_2. There is no solution for Z_2, if $\frac{1}{Z_2} < s_2$ and $s_2 < 0$, or if $\frac{1}{Z_2} \leq s_2'$ and $s_2' < 0$. Using (33) and (34), we obtain

$$\text{sgn}(f_t) = -\text{sgn}(g_{21}) = \text{sgn}(g_{11}) \tag{37}$$

or

$$\text{sgn}(f_\omega) = \text{sgn}(g_{12}) = -\text{sgn}(g_{11}). \tag{38}$$

We will call these four constraints CP-conditions.

Let us assume that conditions (35) and (36) are not satisfied at some point, but we still have a contradiction for Z_1. It can be shown that condition (37) holds. Thus if there is no solution for Z_1, at least one of conditions (35), (36), or (37) must hold. Similarly if there is no solution for Z_2, at least one of conditions (35), (37), or (38) must hold. Thus the CP-conditions are necessary and sufficient for proofing ambiguity at a point.

By examining all the possibilities, we can show that at any point, either none of the CP-conditions holds (and the point is ambiguous), or exactly two of the conditions hold (and the point is contradictory).

Let us now look at points $\mathbf{r}$ and $-\mathbf{r}$. We have $f_t(-\mathbf{r}) = -f_t(\mathbf{r})$ and $f_\omega(-\mathbf{r}) = -f_\omega(\mathbf{r})$, but $g_{ij}(-\mathbf{r}) = g_{ij}(\mathbf{r})$. If $\text{sgn}(g_{12}(\mathbf{r})) \neq \text{sgn}(g_{22}(\mathbf{r}))$, then condition (35) holds either at $\mathbf{r}$, or at $-\mathbf{r}$. We get similar results for the remaining three CP-conditions. Thus both points $\mathbf{r}$ and $-\mathbf{r}$ can be ambiguous only if

$$\text{sgn}(g_{11}(\mathbf{r})) = \text{sgn}(g_{12}(\mathbf{r})) = \text{sgn}(g_{21}(\mathbf{r})) = \text{sgn}(g_{22}(\mathbf{r})). \tag{39}$$

9.3. THE GEOMETRY OF THE DEPTH-POSITIVITY CONSTRAINT

In this section we further investigate the CP-constraints; in particular, we would like to know under what conditions two rigid motions cannot be distinguished if our imaging surface is a half sphere or an image plane, and we are interested in studying and visualizing the locations of areas where the CP-conditions are met.

Considering as imaging surface the whole sphere, two different rigid motions cannot produce flow of the same direction everywhere. As shown in Section 9.1, two antipodal points $\mathbf{r}$ and $-\mathbf{r}$ are ambiguous only if (39) holds. Thus for any point on curve $g_{ij} = 0$, since the sign of g_{ij} is positive on one side of the curve and negative on the other, there must exist a neighborhood either around $\mathbf{r}$ or $-\mathbf{r}$ where there is a contradiction.

Using the machinery already developed, we are now ready to study uniqueness properties.

9.4. HALF SPHERE IMAGE: THE GENERAL CASE

Let us assume that the image is a half of the sphere. Let us also assume that

$$(\boldsymbol{\omega}_1 \times \boldsymbol{\omega}_2) \cdot (\mathbf{t}_1 \times \mathbf{t}_2) \neq 0 \tag{40}$$

We show that under this condition the two rigid motions cannot produce motion fields with the same direction everywhere.

Let us consider projections of $\boldsymbol{\omega}_1$ and $\boldsymbol{\omega}_2$ on the geodesic n connecting $\mathbf{t}_1$ and $\mathbf{t}_2$ (see Figure 27). The proof is given in parts A and B.

A: Let us first assume that one of $\boldsymbol{\omega}_1$, $\boldsymbol{\omega}_2$ does not lie on geodesic n. Without loss of generality, let it be $\boldsymbol{\omega}_1$, i.e., let $[\mathbf{t}_1\,\mathbf{t}_2\,\boldsymbol{\omega}_1] \neq 0$.

The projection of $\boldsymbol{\omega}_1$ onto n is

$$\mathbf{r}_1 = \pm\,(\mathbf{t}_1 \times \mathbf{t}_2) \times (\boldsymbol{\omega}_1 \times (\mathbf{t}_1 \times \mathbf{t}_2)) \tag{41}$$

where the sign is chosen so that $\mathbf{r}_1$ is in the image. Then

$$\begin{aligned}
f_\omega\,(\mathbf{r}_1) &= \\
&= \pm\,((\boldsymbol{\omega}_1 \times \boldsymbol{\omega}_2) \times (\mathbf{t}_1 \times \mathbf{t}_2))\,(\boldsymbol{\omega}_1 \times (\mathbf{t}_1 \times \mathbf{t}_2)) \\
&= \mp\,[\mathbf{t}_1\,\mathbf{t}_2\,\boldsymbol{\omega}_1]\,((\boldsymbol{\omega}_1 \times \boldsymbol{\omega}_2) \cdot (\mathbf{t}_1 \times \mathbf{t}_2)) \neq 0
\end{aligned} \tag{42}$$

and $g_{11}(\mathbf{r}_1) = g_{12}(\mathbf{r}_1) = 0$. So the s_2'-constraint is $\mathrm{sgn}(\frac{1}{Z_1}0) = \mathrm{sgn}(\frac{1}{Z_2}0 + f_\omega)$. Clearly, this constraint cannot be satisfied, so $\mathbf{r}_1$ is a contradictory point.

We can also show that at least one of the areas around point $\mathbf{r}_1$ is contradictory. Point $\mathbf{r}_1$ lies on zero motion contours $g_{11}(\mathbf{r}) = 0$ and $g_{12}(\mathbf{r}) = 0$. The two contours cross at this point, and thus we get four areas in the neighborhood of $\mathbf{r}_1$, and all four possible sign combinations of g_{11} and g_{12}. If we look at points close enough to $\mathbf{r}_1$ that f_ω does not change sign, then in one of the areas condition (38) will be satisfied, and that area will be contradictory. For an illustration see Figure 26.

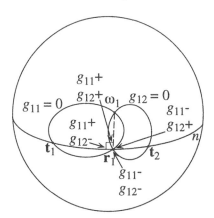

Figure 26. Possible sign combinations of g_{11} and g_{12} in the neighborhood of $\mathbf{r}_1$.

B: If both $\boldsymbol{\omega}_1$ and $\boldsymbol{\omega}_2$ lie on geodesic n, then $f_t(\boldsymbol{\omega}_1) = g_{11}(\boldsymbol{\omega}_1) = g_{12}(\boldsymbol{\omega}_1) = 0$. Also $g_{2i}(\boldsymbol{\omega}_1) = (\boldsymbol{\omega}_2 \times \boldsymbol{\omega}_1) \cdot (\mathbf{t}_i \times \boldsymbol{\omega}_1)$. Since $(\boldsymbol{\omega}_2 \times \boldsymbol{\omega}_1) \| (\mathbf{t}_i \times \boldsymbol{\omega}_1)$, zero motion contour $g_{2i} = 0$ passes through $\boldsymbol{\omega}_1$ only if $(\mathbf{t}_i \times \boldsymbol{\omega}_1)$ is zero; however, we assume that $(\mathbf{t}_1 \times \mathbf{t}_2) \neq 0$, so either g_{21} or g_{22} is nonzero at $\boldsymbol{\omega}_1$.

If $g_{21}(\omega_1) \neq 0$, then condition (33) cannot be satisfied and ω_1 is a contradictory point. The line tangent to g_{11} at ω_1 is perpendicular to n. Since curve $f_t = 0$ is identical to n, curves $g_{11} = 0$ and $f_t = 0$ create four areas around ω_1 with all possible sign combinations. Thus in one of the areas, condition (37) holds and the area is contradictory.

If $g_{22}(\omega_1) \neq 0$, then condition (28) cannot be satisfied at ω_1. Again, at least one area around ω_1 is contradictory, since g_{12} is perpendicular to n at this point.

The rest of this subsection describes properties of the contradictory areas in order to provide a geometric intuition.

Just as we projected ω_1 on geodesic n connecting t_1 and t_2 to obtain r_1, we project ω_2 on n to obtain r_2, and we project t_1 and t_2 on geodesic l, connecting ω_1 and ω_2 to obtain r_3 and r_4 (see Figure 27). By the same argument as before, at each of the points r_i we can choose two of the contours $f_i = 0$ and $g_{ij} = 0$ passing through the point, and we can create four areas of different sign combinations in the corresponding terms f_i and g_{ij} around the point; it then can be shown that one of these areas is contradictory because one of the CP-conditions is met.

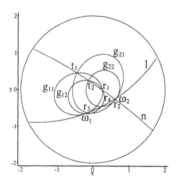

Figure 27. Separation of the sphere through curves $f_i = 0$ and $gij = 0$. Each of t_1, t_2, ω_1, ω_2, r_1, r_2, r_3, and r_4 lies at the intersection of three curves.

The CP-conditions are constraints on the sign of the terms f_i and g_{ij}. Thus the boundaries of the contradictory areas are formed by the curves $f_i = 0$ and $g_{ij} = 0$. As we have shown, the contradictory area and its boundaries must contain the points r_1, r_2, r_3, and r_4. For some motion configurations the boundaries also might contain t_1, t_2, ω_1, and ω_2. Figure 28 shows the contradictory areas for both halves of the sphere for the motion configuration displayed in Figure 27.

Finally, let us consider the boundaries of the contradictory areas. As defined in Section 9.1, we allow the depth of the surfaces in view to take any positive value greater than zero, including infinity. Thus at any point r the motion vector $\dot{r}$ could be in the direction of $v_{rot}(r)$, but not in the direction of $v_{tr}(r)$. This allows us to describe the depth values at possible boundaries of a contradictory area: At points on curve $f_\omega = 0$ both Z_1 and Z_2 can be infinite; thus boundary points on this curve are not elements of the contradictory area. Boundary points on all other curves ($f_t = 0$, or $g_{ij} = 0$) are contradictory, since one of the depths Z_1 or Z_2 would have

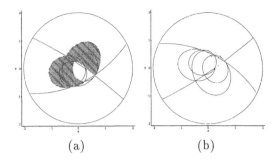

(a)   (b)

Figure 28. Contradictory areas for both halves of the sphere for the two
motions shown in Figure 27.

to be zero.

9.5. HALF SPHERE IMAGE: THE CASE WHEN $(\mathbf{t}_1 \times \mathbf{t}_2)$ IS PERPENDICULAR TO $(\boldsymbol{\omega}_1 \times \boldsymbol{\omega}_2)$

In this section it is shown that there could exist $(\mathbf{t}_1, \boldsymbol{\omega}_1)$ and $(\mathbf{t}_2, \boldsymbol{\omega}_2)$, with $(\mathbf{t}_1 \times \mathbf{t}_2)$ perpendicular to $(\boldsymbol{\omega}_1 \times \boldsymbol{\omega}_2)$, such that there exist no contradictory areas in one hemisphere.

First we investigate possible positions of points $\mathbf{t}_1$, $\mathbf{t}_2$, $\boldsymbol{\omega}_1$, and $\boldsymbol{\omega}_2$ on the hemisphere, bounded by equator q. Then we describe additional conditions on the orientation of vectors $\mathbf{t}_i$ and $\boldsymbol{\omega}_i$ with respect to the hemisphere.

As shown in Section 9.1, two antipodal points $\mathbf{r}$ and $-\mathbf{r}$ can be ambiguous only if (39) holds. Thus, if any curve $g_{ij} = 0$ intersects q at point $\mathbf{p}$, at least one of the areas around $\mathbf{p}$ does not satisfy condition (39). Unless $\mathbf{t}_1$, $\mathbf{t}_2$, $\boldsymbol{\omega}_1$, and $\boldsymbol{\omega}_2$ all are on the boundary of the hemisphere (and then the motions are not ambiguous), there is a contradictory area in the image (either around $\mathbf{p}$ or $-\mathbf{p}$).

Let $\mathbf{n}_0$ be the normal to the plane of q. By intersecting the zero motion contour $g_{ij} = 0$ with the border of the hemisphere, q, we find that real solutions for the intersection point are obtained only if

$$l = [\mathbf{t}\boldsymbol{\omega}\mathbf{n}_0]^2 - 4(\boldsymbol{\omega} \cdot \mathbf{n}_0)(\mathbf{t} \cdot \mathbf{n}_0)(\boldsymbol{\omega} \cdot \mathbf{t}) \geq 0. \tag{43}$$

A half sphere contains for each of the translation vector $\mathbf{t}_i$ and the rotation vectors $\boldsymbol{\omega}_i$, exactly one of the vectors $+\mathbf{t}_i$ or $-\mathbf{t}_i$ and $+\boldsymbol{\omega}_i$ or $-\boldsymbol{\omega}_i$. Let us refer to the vectors in the considered hemisphere as $\tilde{\mathbf{t}}_i$ and $\tilde{\boldsymbol{\omega}}_i$. From equation (43), taking into account that $(\tilde{\mathbf{t}}_i \cdot \mathbf{n}_0) \geq 0$ and $(\tilde{\boldsymbol{\omega}}_i \cdot \mathbf{n}_0) \geq 0$, we see that $l > 0$ either if for any $\tilde{\boldsymbol{\omega}}_i, \tilde{\mathbf{t}}_j, (\tilde{\boldsymbol{\omega}}_i \cdot \tilde{\mathbf{t}}_j) < 0$ (i.e., $\tilde{\boldsymbol{\omega}}_i$ and $\tilde{\mathbf{t}}_j$ form an angle greater than 90°); or if $(\tilde{\boldsymbol{\omega}}_i \cdot \tilde{\mathbf{t}}_j) > 0$ and $\tilde{\boldsymbol{\omega}}_i$ and $\tilde{\mathbf{t}}_j$ are such that $[\mathbf{t}\boldsymbol{\omega}\mathbf{n}_0]^2 > 4(\boldsymbol{\omega} \cdot \mathbf{n}_0)(\mathbf{t} \cdot \mathbf{n}_0)(\boldsymbol{\omega} \cdot \mathbf{t})$, which means that $\tilde{\boldsymbol{\omega}}_i$ and $\tilde{\mathbf{t}}_i$ must be close to the border.

When $f_t = 0$ is perpendicular to $f_\omega = 0$, the projections of $\boldsymbol{\omega}_1$ and $\boldsymbol{\omega}_2$ on $f_t = 0$ and the projections of $\mathbf{t}_1$ and $\mathbf{t}_2$ on $f_\omega = 0$ coincide in one point $\mathbf{r}_1$, i.e., $\mathbf{r}_1 = \mathbf{r}_2 = \mathbf{r}_3 = \mathbf{r}_4$. Point $\mathbf{r}_1$ lies at the intersection of all six curves $f_i = 0$ and $g_{ij} = 0$.

Any three curves $f_i = 0$, $g_{ii} = 0$, and $g_{kl} = 0$, with $k \neq l$ intersect only in $\mathbf{r}_1$ and one of the points $\tilde{\mathbf{t}}_1$, $\tilde{\mathbf{t}}_2$, $\tilde{\boldsymbol{\omega}}_1$, or $\tilde{\boldsymbol{\omega}}_2$. Furthermore, since all the zero motion contours have to be closed curves on the hemisphere, we conclude that if there exists a contradictory area, it also has to be in a neighborhood of $\mathbf{r}_1$. By considering all possible sign combinations of terms f_i and g_{ij} around $\mathbf{r}_1$ it can be verified that the motions are contradictory unless the two translations have the same sign and the two rotations have the same sign, that is, unless

$$\text{sgn}\,(\mathbf{t}_1 \cdot \mathbf{n}_0) = \text{sgn}\,(\mathbf{t}_2 \cdot \mathbf{n}_0) \tag{44}$$

$$\text{sgn}\,(\boldsymbol{\omega}_1 \cdot \mathbf{n}_0) = \text{sgn}\,(\boldsymbol{\omega}_2 \cdot \mathbf{n}_0)\,. \tag{45}$$

Furthermore, the relative positions of $\mathbf{t}_1$, $\mathbf{t}_2$, $\boldsymbol{\omega}_1$ and $\boldsymbol{\omega}_2$ have to be such that

$$\text{sgn}\,(((\boldsymbol{\omega}_1 \times \boldsymbol{\omega}_2) \times (\mathbf{t}_1 \times \mathbf{t}_2)) \cdot \mathbf{n}_0) = \text{sgn}\,(\mathbf{t}_1 \cdot \mathbf{n}_0)\,\text{sgn}\,(\boldsymbol{\omega}_1 \cdot \mathbf{n}_0)\,.$$

Intuitively this means, when rotating $f_\omega = 0$ in the orientation given by the rotations in order to make $f_\omega = 0$ and $f_t = 0$ parallel, that the order of points $\mathbf{t}_1$ and $\mathbf{t}_2$ on $f_t = 0$ is opposite to the order of points $\tilde{\boldsymbol{\omega}}_1$ and $\tilde{\boldsymbol{\omega}}_2$ on $f_\omega = 0$ (moving along the same direction along $f_\omega = 0$ and $f_t = 0$), if $\text{sgn}(\mathbf{t}_1 \cdot \mathbf{n}_0) = 1$. Otherwise, if $\text{sgn}(\mathbf{t}_1 \cdot \mathbf{n}_0) = -1$, the order of points $-\mathbf{t}_1$ and $-\mathbf{t}_2$ on $f_t = 0$ must be the same as the order of points $\tilde{\boldsymbol{\omega}}_1$ and $\tilde{\boldsymbol{\omega}}_2$ on $f_\omega = 0$.

In summary, we have shown that two rigid motions could be ambiguous on one hemisphere if $(\mathbf{t}_1 \times \mathbf{t}_2)$ is perpendicular to $(\boldsymbol{\omega}_1 \times \boldsymbol{\omega}_2)$, but only if certain sign and certain distance conditions on $\mathbf{t}_1$, $\mathbf{t}_2$, $\boldsymbol{\omega}_1$, and $\boldsymbol{\omega}_2$ are met. In addition, as shown in Section 9.1, the two surfaces in view are constrained by a second- and a third-order surface. Figure 29 gives an example of such a configuration.

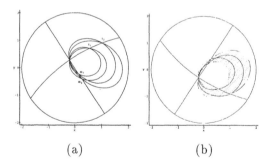

(a)   (b)

Figure 29. Both halves of the sphere showing two rigid motions for which
there do not exist contradictory areas in one hemisphere.

In [4] the analysis has been extended to multiple 3D motions, and it has been shown that three or more rigid motions $(\mathbf{t}_i, \boldsymbol{\omega}_i)$ could give rise to the same direction of the motion field only if all $\mathbf{t}_i$ lie on one geodesic and all $\boldsymbol{\omega}_i$ lie on another geodesic (perpendicular to the first) and all the zero motion contours $g_i i = 0$ intersect at the same points. Thus directions of motion fields are hardly ever ambiguous.

10. SUMMARY AND CONCLUSION

The motion field or the displacement field due to rigid motion on a system's retina possesses a global structure that is independent of the scene in view and depends only on the parameters of the underlying 3D motion. In this chapter, in order to make explicit aspects of this structure, we analyzed the locus of points on the image where motion vectors and directional motion vectors can take on certain values. We found constraints in the form of equalities and inequalities which showed that motion vectors of certain length lie on contours in the image and directional motion vectors of certain values or sign lie within bounded regions. In order to provide significance to the latter constraints we also presented an analysis proving theoretically that there is almost always enough information in the direction of motion fields to recover 3D motion uniquely.

The theory described here proves that there is valuable information encoded globally in motion fields, that has not yet been utilized in computational studies of visual navigation. The geometric analysis presented shows that global information can be made explicit through constraints, allowing us to formulate problems of visual navigation as simple pattern recognition problems that potentially can be solved in real time, thus leading to direct perception. The analysis also points to new ways of studying problems of visual motion. For example, to extend the framework one can study additional 2D image representations such as measurements obtained with differentiation and integration operators. Furthermore, we have only considered constraints manifested in one flow field, but there is information in the evolution of flow fields over time that arises from the constant scene structure which we need to unravel in order to account for the intrinsically dynamic nature of motion perception.

REFERENCES

1. J. Y. Aloimonos, "Purposive and qualitative active vision," in *Proc. Image Understanding Workshop*, 1990, 816–828.

2. P. Anandan and R. Weiss, "Introducing a smoothness constraint in a matching approach for the computation of optical flow fields," in *Proc. 3rd Workshop on Computer Vision: Representation and Control*, 1985, 186–194.

3. F. Bergholm, "Motion from flow along contours: A note on robustness and ambiguous cases," *International Journal of Computer Vision* **3**, 1988, 395–415.

4. T. Brodsky, C. Fermüller, and Y. Aloimonos, "Directions of motion fields are hardly ever ambiguous," Technical Report CAR-TR-780, Center for Automation Research, University of Maryland, 1995.

5. K. Daniilidis, *On the error sensitivity in the recovery of object descriptions and relative motions from image sequences*, Doctoral dissertation, Department of Informatics, University of Karlsruhe, Germany, July, 1992, in German.

6. K. Daniilidis and H.-H. Nagel, "Analytical results on error sensitivity of motion estimation from two views," *Image and Vision Computing* **8**, 1990, 297–303.

7. O.D. Faugeras, *Three-Dimensional Computer Vision: a Geometric Viewpoint*, MIT Press, Cambridge, MA, 1993.

8. O. Faugeras and S. Maybank, "Motion from point matches: Multiplicity of solutions," *International Journal of Computer Vision* 4, 1990, 225–246.

9. C. Fermüller, "Passive navigation as a pattern recognition problem," *International Journal of Computer Vision* 14, 1995, 147–158.

10. C. Fermüller and Y. Aloimonos, "Qualitative egomotion," *International Journal of Computer Vision* 15, 1995, 7–29.

11. C. Fermüller and Y. Aloimonos, "On the geometry of visual correspondence," *International Journal of Computer Vision*, 1995, to appear.

12. J. Gårding, J. Porrill, J. Mayhew, and J. P. Frisby, "Binocular stereopsis, vertical disparity and relief transformations," Technical Report TRITA-NA-P9334, CVAP, Royal Institute of Technology, Stockholm, Sweden, 1993.

13. J. Gibson, *The Perception of the Visual World*, Houghton Mifflin, Boston, MA, 1950.

14. J. Gibson, *The Ecological Approach to Visual Perception*, Houghton Mifflin, Boston, MA, 1979.

15. W.K.C. Guthrie, *The Greek Philosophers: From Thales to Aristotle*. Harper & Row, New York, 1950.

16. E. Hildreth, "Computations underlying the measurement of visual motion," *Artificial Intelligence* 23, 1984, 309–354.

17. B.K.P. Horn, "Relative orientation," *International Journal of Computer Vision* 4, 1990, 59–78.

18. B.K.P. Horn and B.G. Schunck, "Determining optical flow," *Artificial Intelligence* 17, 1981, 185–203.

19. J. Koenderink, "Optic flow," *Vision Research* 26, 1986, 161–180.

20. J.J. Koenderink and A.J. van Doorn, "Affine structure from motion," *Journal of the Optical Society of America* 8, 1991, 377–385.

21. H.C. Longuet-Higgins and K. Prazdny, "The interpretation of a moving retinal image," *Proceedings of the Royal Society of London B* 208, 1980, 385–397.

22. D.C. Marr, *Vision*, W.H. Freeman and Co., San Francisco, 1982.

23. S. Maybank, *Theory of Reconstruction from Image Motion*. Springer-Verlag, Berlin, 1993.

24. R.C. Nelson and J. Aloimonos, "Finding motion parameters from spherical motion fields (or the advantages of having eyes in the back of your head)," *Biological Cybernetics* 58, 1988, 261–273.

25. K. Prazdny, "Egomotion and relative depth map from optical flow," *Biological Cybernetics* 36, 1980, 87–102.

26. W. Reichardt and T. Poggio, "Figure-ground discrimination by relative movement in the visual system of the fly," *Biological Cybernetics* **35**, 1979, 81–100.

27. S. Selby, editor, *Standard Mathematical Tables*, Chemical Rubber Co., Cleveland, OH, 1972.

28. D. Shulman, "Qualitative vision," in *Proc. OEGAI Workshop on Vision Milestones*, Vorau, Austria, 1995.

29. D. Shulman and J.-Y. Hervé, "Regularization of discontinuous flow fields," in *Proc. IEEE Workshop on Visual Motion*, 1989, 81–86.

30. M.E. Spetsakis and J. Aloimonos, "Optimal computing of structure from motion using point correspondences," in *Proc. International Conference on Computer Vision*, Tampa, FL, December 5–8, 1988, 449–453.

31. M. Spetsakis and J. Aloimonos, "Structure from motion using line correspondences," *International Journal of Computer Vision* **4**, 1990, 171–183.

32. M. Spetsakis and J. Aloimonos, "A multiframe approach to visual motion perception," *International Journal of Computer Vision* **6**, 1991, 245–255.

33. M. Tistarelli and G. Sandini, "Dynamic aspects in active vision," *CVGIP: Image Understanding*, Special Issue on Purposive, Qualitative, Active Vision, Y. Aloimonos (Ed.), **56**, 1992, 108–129.

34. R.Y. Tsai and T.S. Huang, "Uniqueness and estimation of three-dimensional motion parameters of rigid objects with curved surfaces," *IEEE Transactions on Pattern Analysis and Machine Intelligence* **6**, 1984, 13–27.

35. S. Ullman, *The Interpretation of Visual Motion*, MIT Press, Cambridge, MA, 1979.

36. S. Ullman, "Against direct perception," *Behavioural and Brain Sciences* **3**, 1980.

37. S. Ullman and R. Basri, "Recognition by linear combinations of models," *IEEE Transactions on Pattern Analysis and Machine Intelligence* **13**, 1991, 992–1006.

38. A. Verri and T. Poggio, "Motion field and optical flow: Qualitative properties," *IEEE Transactions on Pattern Analysis and Machine Intelligence* **11**, 1989, 490–498.

Visual Navigation
Using Fast Content-Based Retrieval

John J. Weng,[1] Shaoyun Chen,[1] and Thomas S. Huang[2]
[1]Michigan State University
[2]University of Illinois

Abstract

This chapter presents a recently developed approach to vision-guided autonomous navigation. The system recalls information about scenes and navigational experience using content-based retrieval from a visual data base. To achieve high applicability and adaptability to various road types, we do not impose a priori scene features, such as road edges, that the system must use, but rather the system automatically selects features from images during supervised learning. To accomplish this, the system uses multiclass, multidimensional discriminant analysis to automatically select the most discriminating features (MDF) for scene classification. These features best classify the population of the scenes and approximate complex decision regions using piecewise linear boundaries up to a desired accuracy. A crucial problem that must be solved is the efficiency, due to the real-time requirement and the large size of the data base. A new self-organizing scheme called a recursive partition tree (RPT) is used for automatic construction of a vision-and-control data base, which quickly prunes the data set in the content-based search and results in a low time complexity of $\log(n)$ for retrieval from a data base of size n. The system has been tested on a mobile robot, Rome, in an unknown indoor environment to learn scenes and the associated navigation experience. In the performance phase, Rome navigates autonomously in similar environments, while allowing presence of scene perturbations such as the presence of passersby.

1. Introduction

A central part of an autonomous vision-guided navigation system is the navigator. It accepts an input image $\mathbf{X}$ as well as an intention signal $\mathbf{P}$ which indicates which path to take. The navigator outputs the control signal vector $\mathbf{C}$ which controls the

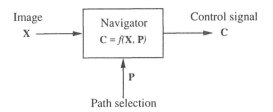

Figure 1. Navigator as a mapping from the image and path selection space to the control signal space.

vehicle. Figure 1 gives a schematic illustration of such a view. Thus, the navigator can be denoted by a function f that maps elements in the space of $(\mathbf{X}, \mathbf{P})$ to elements in the space of $\mathbf{C}$. The space of $\mathbf{X}$ includes all the images that the navigator can see and $\mathbf{P}$ is typically a vector in a low dimensional space, e.g., a one-dimensional signal with three discrete values $1, 0, -1$ to indicate the intention to take the left, straight-ahead, and right path, respectively, in a cross intersection. A challenging task of autonomous navigation is to construct an automatic system which approximates (i.e., learns) the complicated function $f(\mathbf{X}, \mathbf{P})$ and computes quickly in real time given $\mathbf{X}$ and $\mathbf{P}$. This functionality is needed in applications such as road following in various outdoor environments, hallway following in various indoor environments, making turns, navigation in irregular settings such as in a warehouse or on a factory floor, etc. In this chapter, we concentrate on this challenging task.

1.1. EXISTING SYSTEMS

The function f is extremely complex, because of the high dimension of the image space of $\mathbf{X}$. One common way to address this problem is to design some rules based on a particular type of image collection and then a system is developed to implement these rules. For example, some outdoor road followers use human-designed rules to follow road edges (e.g., Wallace *et al.* [34], Dickmanns and Zapp [7], Thorpe *et al.* [31], Hébert [11]). Indoor hallway followers mainly rely on floor or ceiling edges (e.g., Meng and Kak [22], Lebesgue and Aggarwal [19]). In the past, autonomous navigation systems that use only intensity images relied very much on a type of predefined feature, such as a road edge, lane mark, floor edge, etc.

The amount of road condition variation is a crucial factor in determining the applicability of a system. To handle a variety of environment conditions, several experimental navigation systems have employed certain adaptation mechanisms to various degrees. For navigation on paved driveways, when lane marks are well illuminated and easily traceable, a simple technique such as adaptive color thresholding [18] can be used. In situations with unstructured roads with unmarked lanes and sudden changes in illumination (e.g, the sun is occluded by clouds, or shadows cast from nearby buildings), the design of a reliable autonomous navigation system becomes a great challenge. Investigation around the Navlab developed different adaptation mechanisms for different outdoor driving environments. SCARF [5, 32] was designed to handle various roads with adaptive color classification. YARF [15, 32] deals with different structured roads by explicitly modeling different available constraints and features, since a single technique for road detection may fail on different structured roads.

For indoor navigation, Meng and Kak [22] presented a mobile robot that couples low-level, neural network-based modules with high-level semantically based planning. The Hough transform was used to detect edges from intensity images. The result was then fed into neural networks to produce a qualitative output. The method of Lebesgue and Aggarwal [19] tracked major edges in an indoor scene to guide navigation. Some other studies used stereo to extract depth maps for indoor navigation [1, 17].

Many existing systems predefine the type of features that the system will use. For greater adaptability, some systems do not specify which specific features to use. With ALVINN [27, 32], an artificial neural network trained by a back-propagation training algorithm, maps input images to output steering signals for autonomous navigation. ALVINN does not explicitly impose the type of image geometric features which the system is based upon. The neural network approach is computationally simple with a relatively low system development cost. ALVINN has been successfully tested in a variety of road situations.

1.2. SOME MAJOR DIFFICULTIES IN AUTONOMOUS NAVIGATION

As we discussed above, significant advances have been made toward autonomous navigation. However, we face some major difficulties.

The first major difficulty is in dealing with different road types. Existing approaches to autonomous navigation typically impose restrictions on the environment, such as good pavement conditions, clear marks, absence of shadow, continuous road edges, etc. Unfortunately, although such conditions may often be met, they are typically not always met. Thus, it seems desirable to seek a method that is maximally general—applicable to *virtually any* scene that may be encountered in real-world driving conditions. With this objective in mind, it is not totally unreasonable to consider that a real-world navigation system may have to possess a general scene recognition capability, not restricted to using a fixed set of features.

Another major difficulty lies in the lack of efficiency. The above generality requirement means that the system must learn a huge number of scenes, e.g., a few hundreds to a few millions. Almost all the existing autonomous navigation systems have significant limitations on the type of applicable scenes, with one exception: ALVINN, which virtually does not impose any restriction on the scene type and thus, is capable of learning any scene. However, it has several problems. A major one is a lack of capability to handle a large number of scene types. Other major ones include the local minima problem, the slow learning problem, and the high space complexity problem.

1.3. RESTRICTED LEARNING VERSUS COMPREHENSIVE LEARNING

It is natural to consider a navigator as an edge follower and edge following is all that one needs for a navigator in a well-controlled environment. However, edge following is not always possible or reliable in realistic environments. For example, there is no reliable single edge one can follow in a warehouse or on a factory floor. If a floor edge is occluded by several boxes of various sizes placed against the wall, an edge follower will fail. Therefore, it appears that restricting a navigation system to a predefined shape feature (such as road or floor edges) may seriously hamper the applicability and reliability of the system. A wide variation of road conditions may occur in both indoor and outdoor environments, which implies that a reliable navigation system for the real world environments must have a high level of adaptability.

The concept of *comprehensive visual learning* introduced by Weng in 1994 [35] is twofold: (1) learning must comprehensively cover the entire visual world; (2) learning must comprehensively cover the entire vision system. The first point means that the learning mechanism must be applicable to virtually any scene; and the second point means that hand-crafted shape rules should be avoided as much as possible, because (a) they are not always applicable and (b) there is no effective method to automatically verify their applicability given any input image. The concept of comprehensive visual learning calls for open-ended learning systems, very much like human beings. Such systems make good use of abundant real-working-environment images that are available in day-to-day operation so as to learn under a wide variety of situations. Such a system is open-ended because it never stops learning and it corrects as soon as it makes a mistake. On the other hand, for efficiency, it spends resources to learn new things only when necessary and avoids overlearning and wasting resources. For example, if the performance is good enough, the resources (e.g., memory and time) should not be further spent to over sample the learning space; but when a mistake occurs or the performance is not up to the standard, further learning continues.

1.4. THE MOTIVATION

The work presented here is a navigational part of the SHOSLIF [35], which is a unified framework for a variety of vision and control problems. The navigation system SHOSLIF-N [3, 36] described here was motivated by the following considerations.

The new framework avoids imposing any restriction on the type of the scene the system will handle. Therefore, the method is potentially applicable to a wide variety of conditions, both indoor and outdoor. Instead of relying on a particular scene feature, it uses an entire scene for decision making, and thus is relatively insensitive to local and small scene changes, such as road edges being occluded by objects or frequent presence of passing-by pedestrians.

The approach uses a comprehensive *self-organizing* mechanism for systemwise extensive learning, which is responsible from intensity image all the way to generating vehicle control signals.

To avoid the "opaque box" problem with the neural network approach, the new framework automatically selects the most expressive features (MEF) and the most discriminating features (MDF), which maximize representation and classification powers, respectively, from information available in the input data.

To address the complexity issue in learning a large number of scenes, a recursive space-partition tree is introduced, which has a logarithmic retrieval complexity. Due to this low complexity, the experimental system Rome is capable of real-time navigation while performing, on a SUN SPARC-1, content-based searching in a data base that has stored knowledge about 363 learning images.

1.5. SCOPE OF THE CHAPTER

The scope of the work presented in the chapter is limited in the following aspects.

1. The current system does not make any high-level inference. The primary objective for the current experimental system is to navigate according to the system's experience with a navigation path that has been learned, allowing some disturbance such as pedestrians passing by.
2. The current system does not perform general recognition in that it does not generalize for size, position, or orientation. In fact, in navigation applications, the actual values of scene size, position, and orientation are themselves useful for navigation in judging the heading direction, self-position, etc.
3. The current system is still sensitive to drastic change in lighting, because intensity images are used directly. For the current system to work in various lighting conditions, it needs to learn these conditions separately. The future research will use edge information in addition to intensity information.
4. The current system does not have a path-planning part. What it does is repeat the path which it has learned. Intention commands will be incorporated into future systems so that different navigation paths can be chosen at each intersection.

Although it has these limitations, the current system is directly useful in certain repeated navigation applications where a fixed path is all that is required. The strength of this approach is its passive nature (using only a single video camera), potential applicability to a wide variety of scenes, and easy training for the system to adapt to each environment.

The remainder of this chapter is organized as follows. Section 2 introduces basic concepts and establishes related results. Section 3 discusses tools for automatically extracting linear features from learning samples. Section 4 explains the self-organizing method which automatically constructs a tree. Some experimental results are reported in Section 6, and Section 7 provides some concluding remarks.

2. LEARNING AS EFFICIENT FUNCTION APPROXIMATION

2.1. IMAGE SPACE

A digital image with r pixel rows and c pixel columns can be denoted by a vector in (rc)-dimensional space. For example, the set of image pixels $\{f(i,j) \mid 0 \leq i < r, 0 \leq j < c\}$ can be written as a vector $\mathbf{X} = (x_1, x_2, \ldots, x_d)^t$ where $x_{ri+j} = f(i,j)$ and $d = rc$. The actual mapping from the 2D position of every pixel to a component in the d-dimensional vector $\mathbf{X}$ is not essential but is fixed once it is selected. Since the pixels of all the practical images can only take values in a finite range, we define $\mathbf{X}$ as a point in a *domain* S of a finite size, where

$$S = \{\mathbf{X} \mid \mathbf{X} = (x_1, x_2, \ldots, x_d)^t, |x_i| \leq M/2, i = 1, 2, \ldots d\} \tag{1}$$

which can be called a d-dimensional hyper cube. Without loss of generality, we consider S as a hyper cube for donational convenience, since it can always be large enough to include any practical finite domain. In order to deal with an astronomical number of images that can be present in an application, we may consider observed input image vectors $\mathbf{X}$ as random samples from S. The second-order statistics between pixels is represented by the corresponding covariance matrix Σ_x of the random vector $\mathbf{X}$, as we will see later. For example, if two pixels $f(i,j)$ and $f(i',j')$ are neighbors in the original image, their corresponding cross-covariance stored in the corresponding element at $(ir+j, i'r+j')$ of the matrix Σ_x typically has a large absolute value. Therefore, treating a two-dimensional image as a one-dimensional vector $\mathbf{X}$ is for notational convenience and the representation itself does not necessarily lose any two-dimensional information.

2.2. FUNCTIONS IN THE IMAGE SPACE

The navigator shown in Figure 1 is a function f defined in a huge space of $(\mathbf{X}, \mathbf{P})$. For notational simplicity, we drop the input $\mathbf{P}$ in notation and simply denote $f(\mathbf{X}, \mathbf{P})$ as $f(\mathbf{X})$, regarding $\mathbf{P}$ as a part of $\mathbf{X}$.

In fact, many sensor-based understanding and control problems can be modeled as a function $\mathbf{C} = f(\mathbf{X})$, where $\mathbf{X}$ is the input vector and the output vector $\mathbf{C}$ can be real-valued. In a control problem, $\mathbf{C}$ is a real-valued vector. In an autonomous navigation problem, the vector can be, e.g., $\mathbf{C} = (c_1, c_2, c_3)$ where c_1 is the heading direction, c_2 the speed, and c_3 the next step size. In classification problems, $\mathbf{C}$ can be a scalar $y \in \{1, 2, 3, \ldots, k\}$ indicating a class label of the input $\mathbf{X}$. However, in practice, such a classification output is often not sufficient without a confidence measure. More generally, the nominal output for n classes can be n dimensional, with the ith component indicating the confidence (or some probability measure) for the input $\mathbf{X}$ to arise from the ith class. Therefore, the categorical output can be considered as a special case of real-valued output.

From the discussion, we can see that many problems in sensor-based classification and control can be represented by a partial function f that maps elements in a domain S to an element in a codomain C:

$$f : S \mapsto C, \tag{2}$$

where S is defined in (1) and C is an n-dimensional space $C = R^n$. We regard f as a partial function because it is not necessarily defined on the entire set of S. For example, S may denote all the possible images but the images we see in our life are only a subset of S.

2.3. LEARNING AS AN APPROXIMATION PROCESS

Our objective of constructing a navigator is equivalent to approximating function $f : S \mapsto C$ by another function $\hat{f} : S \mapsto C$. The error of approximation can be indicated by certain measure of the error $\hat{f} - f$. One such measure is the mean square error

$$E(\hat{f} - f)^2 = \int_{\mathbf{X} \in S} (\hat{f}(\mathbf{X}) - f(\mathbf{X}))^2 dF(\mathbf{X}),$$

where $F(\mathbf{X})$ is the probability distribution function of $\mathbf{X}$ in S. In other words, $\hat{f}$ can defer a lot from f in parts where $\mathbf{X}$ never occurs, without affecting the error measure. Another measure is the pointwise absolute error $\|\hat{f}(\mathbf{X}) - f(\mathbf{X})\|$ for any point $\mathbf{X}$ in S', where $S' \subset S$ is a subset of S that is of interest to a certain problem. In navigation, S' may consist of all the inputs that may arise.

Of course, f is typically high-dimensional and highly complex. For navigation, it maps from a high-dimensional input vector $\mathbf{X}$, which represents a meaningful image and the current intention, to the correct control parameter vector.

A powerful method of constructing $\hat{f}$ is using learning. Specifically, a series of cases is acquired as the learning data set:

$$L = \{(\mathbf{X}_i, f(\mathbf{X}_i)) \mid i = 1, 2, \ldots, n\}. \tag{3}$$

Then, construct $\hat{f}$ based on L. For notational convenience, the sample points in L are denoted by $X(L)$:

$$X(L) = \{\mathbf{X}_i \mid i = 1, 2, \ldots, n\}.$$

$X(L)$ should be drawn from the real situation so that the underlying distribution of $X(L)$ is as close to the real distribution as possible.

2.4. CASE-BASED LEARNING FOR FUNCTION APPROXIMATION

Superficially, the function approximation problem we are dealing with here looks very much like a typical regression problem in statistics or pattern recognition, i.e., predicting y from a given feature vector $\mathbf{X}$. They are in fact very different due to the underlying assumption. In statistics, features are preselected so that a simple relationship between y and $\mathbf{X}$ exists. Therefore, the linear regression tree and the k-d tree (also called the tree classifier) are popular in statistics [2, 9] and pattern recognition [4, 8]. However, those methods do not work well here because of the very complex nature of the function f: It is highly nonlinear, high-dimensional (both in domain and codomain), and the number of samples can be even smaller than the dimension of the domain. For example, such a function cannot be reasonably approximated by any parameter set, let alone the linear regression parameter vector used in linear regression. The k-d tree does not work either because no threshold on any component of $\mathbf{X}$ can give a meaningful intermediate classification. The challenging problem of learning a highly nonlinear and high-dimensional function from real-world cases is fundamental to intelligence but has not received much attention in the past. In the following, we introduce some concepts for this task and establish related results.

A learning set L as in (3) consists of a sequence of cases. We need to investigate its relation with the space S.

Definition 1 *A partition $P = \{P_1, P_2, \ldots, P_n\}$ of S (i.e., $P_i \cap P_j = \emptyset$ when $i \neq j$ and $\bigcup_{i=1}^{n} P_i = S$) is consistent with a learning set L if $\mathbf{X}_i \in P_i$, $i = 1, 2, \ldots, n$.*

A partition P consistent with L can be considered as a result of partitioning S based on the learning set L. Given an L, infinitely many consistent partitions are possible.

The Dirichlet tessellation, also well known as the Voronoi diagram [13], is a special partition consistent with L in which each P_i consists of those points of S that are closer to $\mathbf{X}_i$ than to any other $\mathbf{X}_j$ in $X(L)$ with $i \neq j$.

Definition 2 *Given a learning set L, a nearest-neighbor (NN) approximator $\hat{f}$ of f associated with L is defined as follows. For any $\mathbf{X} \in P$,*

$$\hat{f}(\mathbf{X}) = f(\mathbf{X}_i)$$

where $\mathbf{X}_i$ is the nearest neighbor of $\mathbf{X}$ in $X(L)$. That is, $\mathbf{X}_i \in X(L)$ and $\|\mathbf{X} - \mathbf{X}_i\| < \|\mathbf{X} - \mathbf{X}_j\|$ for any $\mathbf{X}_j \in X(L)$ with $i \neq j$.

An NN approximator $\hat{f}$ of f is a piecewise constant function, constant in every P_i of the Dirichlet tessellation $P = \{P_1, P_2, \ldots, P_n\}$ which is consistent with L. The NN approximator is not unique, given an L, because the value at the boundary of the Dirichlet tessellation is arbitrary. In practice, its value along the boundary can take the value of either side of the boundary, whichever is convenient.

Definition 3 *Given a learning set L, a k-nearest-neighbor distance-based (KNDB) approximator $\hat{f}$ of f associated with L is defined as follows. For any $\mathbf{X} \in P$,*

$$\hat{f}(\mathbf{X}) = \frac{1}{\sum_{i=1}^{k} w_i} \sum_{i=1}^{k} w_i f(\mathbf{X}_{n_i})$$

where $\mathbf{X}_{n_i} \in X(L)$ is the i-th nearest neighbor of $\mathbf{X}$ and $w_i = w(\mathbf{X}, \mathbf{X}_{n_1}, \mathbf{X}_{n_i})$ is the value of a scalar weighting function.

The KNDB approximator uses more neighbors than the NN version and thus is more immune to noise in the learning set L. When the top $s \leq k$ nearest neighbors have the same distance to $\mathbf{X}$, the value of $\hat{f}(\mathbf{X})$ takes roughly the average of these top s neighbors. As an example, the weighting function $w(\mathbf{X})$ can take the form

$$w(\mathbf{X}, \mathbf{X}_{n_1}, \mathbf{X}_{n_i}) = \alpha^{-\|\mathbf{X} - \mathbf{X}_{n_i}\|^2 / (\epsilon + \|\mathbf{X} - \mathbf{X}_{n_1}\|^2)}$$

where ϵ is a small positive number to avoid the denominator becoming zero. The value of α determines how fast the weight will decrease for other runners up. A point $\mathbf{X}_{n_i}$ at twice the distance compared to that of the nearest neighbor $\mathbf{X}_{n_1}$ will have its weight decreased by a factor of $1/(\alpha^4)$ from that of the nearest neighbor. For example, $\alpha = 2$ is a reasonable choice for α. When α approaches infinity, the KNDB degenerates into the NN approximator.

Other interpolation schemes that may be used here include generalized multi-quadratics [30, 35] or radial basis functions [10, 25, 26].

2.5. GENERALITY OF THE APPROXIMATOR

An important issue to study here is how well the above approximators can approximate a function f. Its answer is closely related to the way samples are generated for the learning set L. Due to a high complexity and undetermined nature of the way in which a learning set L is drawn from the real world, it is effective to consider that $X(L)$, the set of samples in S, is generated randomly. We know that a fixed L is a special case of random L in that the probability distribution is concentrated at the single location.

Thus, we consider $\mathbf{X}$ in $X(L)$ as a random sample from S. The learning set L is generated by acquiring samples from S with a d-dimensional probability distribution function $F(\mathbf{X})$.

Definition 4 *A point $\mathbf{X_0} \in S$ is positively supported if for any $\delta > 0$ we have $P\{\|\mathbf{X} - \mathbf{X_0}\| \leq \delta\} > 0$, where $P\{e\}$ denotes the probability of the event e.*

If S consists of a finite number of discrete points, a point $\mathbf{X}$ in P is positively supported means that the probability of selecting $\mathbf{X}$ as a sample is not a zero-probability event. If S consists of infinitely many points, a point $\mathbf{X}$ in P is positively supported means that in any small neighborhood centered at $\mathbf{X}$, the probability of selecting any point in the neighborhood is not a zero-probability event. In practice, we are not interested in cases that almost never appear in a real-world application, i.e., those cases that do not have a positive support. An approximate function $\hat{f}$ can assume any value in subregions of S that will never be used in the application, without hurting the real performance of the system. Thus, we just need to investigate how well the approximation can approximate f at points $\mathbf{X}$ that are positively supported.

Theorem 1 *Suppose $\mathbf{X}$ is a positively supported point in a bounded S as in (1), and f is a differentiable function $f : S \mapsto C$ with a bounded Jacobian in S. Given any small positive number $\delta > 0$, consider the event $\|\hat{f}(\mathbf{X}) - f(\mathbf{X})\|^2 > \delta$. Given any small $\epsilon > 0$, there is a positive number $k_0 > 0$, so that as long as we independently draw $k > k_0$ learning sets $L_1, L_2, \ldots, L_k$, the resulting NN approximate $\hat{f}$ has the following property:*

$$P\{\|\hat{f}(\mathbf{X}) - f(\mathbf{X})\|^2 > \delta\} < \epsilon$$

for any Dirichlet partition P of S that is consistent with the combined learning set $L = \{L_1, L_2, \ldots, L_k\}$.

The proof is presented in Appendix A. The requirement for a bounded Jacobian is not very restrictive. In a practical control system, a small change in input should not result in unbounded change in the output. Otherwise, the controller is not a stable one, as defined in control theory. In a classification case, although f might be discontinuous along class boundaries, we can let f be continuous when it crosses each decision boundary because near-boundary input does not allow a perfectly confident decision in practice. In fact, as we discussed earlier, it is more reasonable to define the ith component of f as the confidence for $\mathbf{X}$ to arise from the ith class. Therefore, it is reasonable to assume a smooth differentiable extension of f.

In Theorem 1, L is a collection of sample batches L_i. In other words, all the points in each L_i do not have to be independently drawn. This allows the data for each L_i to be collected in the sequence of real operation, in which cases may sequentially dependent. The condition of the theorem requires that different sample batches are independent. This is satisfiable since one can independently collect a batch at a time.

Theorem 1 means that the NN approximator approaches f *pointwise* in probability: $P\{\|\hat{f}(\mathbf{X}) - f(\mathbf{X})\| > \delta\} \to 0$, as the size of learning set L increases. Pointwise convergence in probability does not directly implies that the entire function $\hat{f}$ converges to f. Whether such a convergence is true depends on the uniformity in which the positively supported points converge to f.

Definition 5 *Let S' be the subset of S consisting of all the positively supported points in S. The points in S' uniformly converge to f in probability if, given any $\delta > 0$ and $\epsilon > 0$, there is a sufficiently large k_0, so that when $k \geq k_0$,*

$$P\{\|\hat{f}(\mathbf{X}) - f(\mathbf{X})\| > \delta\} < \epsilon$$

holds true for all the points in S'.

The uniformity excludes the cases where samples are collected in such a severely biased way that a neighborhood around some positively supported events gets sampled much more slowly than other areas. As long as the samples are collected in a real situation so that each likely event will get a proportional number of sample points collected, the uniform convergence in probability is typically satisfied.

Theorem 2 *If the positively supported points in $S' \in S$ uniformly converge to f in probability, then the NN approximator $\hat{f}$ of f satisfies*

$$\int_{\mathbf{X} \in S'} (\hat{f}(\mathbf{X}) - f(\mathbf{X}))^2 dF(\mathbf{X}) \to 0 \qquad (4)$$

when k in the learning set $L = \{L_1, L_2, \ldots, L_k\}$ increases without bound.

The proof is relegated to Appendix B.

The major difference between Theorem 1 and Theorem 2 is that with the former, some regions of S' can get well approximated more quickly than other regions of S'; but in the latter, the entire approximator $\hat{f}$ approaches f in the sense of L_2 norm in the Hilbert space with a probability measure [14, 21].

The problem of function learning based on random learning samples is very different from conventional theory of function fitting where samples in S are selected systematically in a predefined structure (e.g., on a predefined grid). In our problem here, the function is unknown, and so is the distribution of the samples in the domain S. We do not intend to approximate the entire function f, but rather, only the useful part of it, defined by S'. All we need to do is draw learning samples from the real application (i.e., satisfy the uniformity condition) or, in other words, let the system learn in the real situation. The above established results mean that the learned behavior of the system will approach what is desired as indicated case by case in the learning set.

The result about the generality of the NN approximator is important. The generality allows a high degree of adaptability. The approximator does not impose any restrictive model that might be applicable for a particular problem. A method that uses a particular model is restricted inherently by the applicability of the model. Due to the extremely complex nature of vision problems and the associated control problem in a natural environment, imposing a particular model results in an algorithm that cannot deal with all variations in the sensed environment.

2.6. Hierarchical partition and the RPT

An immediate issue that arises here is that a large number of samples is required in the learning phase to approximate a high-dimensional function f. In the performance phase, given an input $\mathbf{X}$, the NN approximator needs to find the nearest neighbor from a large number n of recorded items. A linear search in this data base will require $O(n)$ time, which is not acceptable for real-time navigation with a large n, e.g., $n = 1,000,000,000$. The following hierarchical space partition scheme leads to a $\log(n)$ retrieval complexity (e.g., $\log_{10}(1,000,000,000) = 9$)!

Definition 6 *A hierarchical partition P of S is a partition set $P = \{P_0, P_1, \ldots, P_m\}$, where every P_i, $i = 0, 1, \ldots, m$ is a partition of S. P_{i+1} is a finer partition of P_i. Suppose $P_i = \{P_{i,j+1}, P_{i,j+2}, \ldots, P_{i,j+l}\}$. For each $P_{i,j} \in P_i$, P_{i+1} contains either $P_{i,j}$ itself or $P_{i+1,k+1}, P_{i+1,k+2}, \ldots, P_{i+1,k+b}$ so that*

$$P_{i,j} = \bigcup_{i=1}^{b} P_{i+1,k+i}.$$

A recursive partition tree (RPT) is a tree which represents a hierarchical partition P. $P_0 = S$ at level 0 is the root, representing the entire space S. A node $P_{i,j}$ at level i has b children if $P_{i,j}$ is further partitioned at level $i + 1$ by b cells $P_{i+1,k+1}, P_{i+1,k+2}, \ldots, P_{i+1,k+b}$. A node $P_{i,j}$ is a leaf node if it is not further partitioned by more cells in P_{i+1}. If $P_{i,j}$ appears at several levels, $P_{i,j}$ is represented by a leaf at the lowest level at which it appears.

A hierarchical Dirichlet tessellation (or hierarchical Voronoi diagram) is a hierarchical partition that satisfies an additional condition: Every cell is further partitioned at a deeper level, if it does, only by a Dirichlet tessellation. As shown in Figure 2, although further partition of each cell is a Dirichlet partition, the entire partition P_m which corresponds to all the leaf nodes in the RPT tree is not necessarily a Dirichlet partition.

The entire space S is typically huge. The hierarchical partition covers the space using cells of different sizes. In areas where samples are very sparse, only large cells are created to cover them. In areas where samples are very dense, many small cells are created to cover them. As we will see, the size of the cells is directly related to the accuracy of approximation. In other words, regions in which f is not defined or of low probability are approximated very roughly by a few coarse cells, but regions of high density are approximated in detail by many small cells.

2.7. Approximation using the RPT

We defer our discussion about the construction of the RPT to Section 4. In this section, we study how to use the RPT for function approximation.

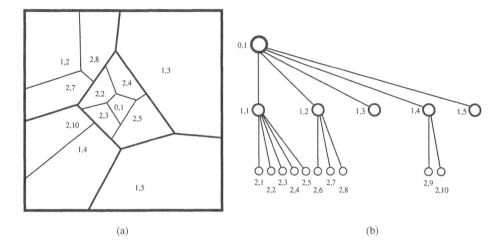

(a)   (b)

Figure 2. A 2D illustration of a hierarchical Dirichlet partition and the corresponding recursive partition tree (RPT). (a) The partition, where the label indicates the center of a cell. The label of the child to which its parent's center belongs is not shown due to lack of space. (b) The recursive partition tree.

The use of hierarchical partition structure drastically reduces the complexity to find the cell in P_m to which a given $\mathbf{X}$ belong.

RPT Search Algorithm: Given $\mathbf{X}$, find a leaf node c so that $\mathbf{X} \in c$.

```
node = root;
for each child c of node {
    if (X ∈ c) {
        if (c is not a leaf)
            node = c;
        else return(c);
    }
}
```

Suppose L is a complete tree in which every internal node has b children. A tree of level $l+1$ has $n = b^l$ leaf nodes. At each level, the algorithm needs to visit b children. The number of nodes visited by the above search algorithm is $bl = b \log_b(n)$. The tree is built in a way so that b is bounded above by a constant for a fixed dimension of input $\mathbf{X}$. Therefore, with a complete tree, the search complexity is logarithmic $O(\log_b(n))$ in the number of leaf nodes. We will analyze the complexity in detail in Section 5.

Although a hierarchical partition allows a very fast retrieval algorithm, the final partition P_m in a hierarchical partition P is not a Dirichlet partition in general, as indicated in the example shown in Figure 2. This is because the boundary of a coarse cell at level l is defined according to the cells at level l. Such a coarse-level boundary is present at the finest partition P_m and is typically inconsistent with that of the Dirichlet tessellation defined on all the given samples. Therefore, the NN approximator cannot be directly defined on a hierarchical partition.

Our way of dealing with this problem is to explore k competitive paths down the RPT and use the technique of the KNDB approximator at the k leaf nodes that are reached.

Definition 7 *Given an RPT that corresponds to a hierarchical partition $P = \{P_1, P_2, \ldots, P_m\}$ and an integer constant $k > 0$, the k competitive leaves of an input $\mathbf{X}$ are defined recursively as follows:*

1. *At level 1, the k children of the root whose centers are the k nearest neighbors of $\mathbf{X}$, among all nodes at level 1, are competitors at level 1.*
2. *At level l, let C contain all the children of the k competitors at level $l - 1$ plus those competitors at level $l - 1$ which are already leaves at a level $\leq l - 1$. The k elements in C whose centers are the k nearest neighbors of $\mathbf{X}$, among all other elements in C, are the k competitors at level l.*

The k competitive leaves of $\mathbf{X}$ are the k competitors at the last level m.

Note that the k competitive leaves of an RPT are not necessarily the k nearest neighbors of $\mathbf{X}$, although they could be. In particular, the nearest neighbor of $\mathbf{X}$ is included in the k competitive leaves only if every node along the path from the root to the nearest-neighbor leaf is included in the k competitors at the corresponding level. The larger k is, the more likely it is that that will occur.

Definition 8 *A k-competitive-leaves distance-based (KCDB) approximator $\hat{f}$ of f associated with the given learning set L and the associated RPT is the same at the KNDB, except that the k nearest neighbors are replaced by the k competitive leaves obtained from the RPT.*

As long as the nearest neighbor is included in the k competitors, the value of interpolation from k competitive leaves is typically very close to that of the KNDB approximator, because it is the nearest neighbor of $\mathbf{X}$ that plays a major role in the interpolation. If the nearest neighbor is missing from the k competitive leaves, the result of interpolation should still be reasonably good if the k competitive leaves are not all too far from $\mathbf{X}$. The resilience of the KCDB approximator is due to the use of interpolation instead of using a single nearest neighbor from the k competitive leaves.

The next important issue is how to select features to determine the shape and size of the cells in partition so that each cell will cover a large region in which the function f is nearly constant or does not change much. This is very important since it not only reduces the number of leaves in the RPT for efficiency, but also allows the RPT to generalize effectively from a relatively small number of learning samples. This and other related issues are discussed in the following section. In a feature space, the distance measure discussed in this section can also be applied, and thus, our distance concept is no longer restricted to the original space S.

3. AUTOMATIC FEATURE EXTRACTION

If we cannot restrict the type of scenes that a vehicle can come across, it is then improper to predefine features that the system can use. For example, if we define long straight edges to use for indoor navigation, the system will fail in curved hallways or places where no long straight edges are available. If we define smooth curved edges for use in outdoor navigation, the system will fail when road conditions are so poor that no clearly definable edges are present. Even when road edges are clear, an edge tracker may fail in the presence of passersby who occlude road edges. Therefore, we must let the system automatically extract features by itself, depending on the type of environment in which the system learns and operates.

3.1. MEANINGFUL IMAGES IN THE IMAGE SPACE

We know that the dimension of an image space is typically very large. For a moderate 128×128-pixel image, the dimension is $d = rc = 128 \times 128 = 16,384$! Suppose that the absolute intensity value of all image pixels is bounded by a number M, and the space of all the *possible* images is given by S in (1). Now, consider randomly picking a point in this space (hypercube). With a probability nearly 1, the picked point corresponds to a random-noise image. This is true because the images we see are from the real world, in which objects have a congruence property. For example, a uniform surface of a single object projects to an image region with a uniform intensity. A textured surface is projected to an image region whose intensity is spatially repetitive. Therefore, all the images a robot can see in its operational environment must distribute within a very small subset S' of this huge space S, although the region shape of S' can be very complex. In other words, the function $\hat{f}$ needs only to approximate f within a much smaller space S'. An objective of learning is to find a representation to describe the subspace S' well enough for approximation of f in it. The actual value of f in $S - S'$ is not of major concern.

The Karhunen-Loeve projection [6] is a very efficient way to represent a small subspace in a high-dimensional space. It reduces the dimension of representation from d in S to a much lower dimension for S' while still keeping most of the information in the data. However, the Karhunen-Loeve projection is not effective for discriminating different scenes, for which we will use the discriminant analysis to select best features. For a general discussion of dimension reduction using projection pursuit, the reader is referred to a good survey by Huber [12].

3.2. THE MOST EXPRESSIVE FEATURES

As we discussed above, images of objects in a category can be regarded as samples represented by a d-dimensional random vector $\mathbf{X}$ in S, which can be represented by a linear combination of d orthonormal basis vectors, $\mathbf{v}_1, \mathbf{v}_2, \ldots, \mathbf{v}_d$, so that

$$\mathbf{X} = \sum_{i=1}^{d} y_i \mathbf{v}_i = V\mathbf{Y}$$

where V is an orthogonal $d \times d$ matrix consisting of orthonormal column vectors $\mathbf{v}_i, i = 1, 2, \ldots, d$. Without loss of generality, we can assume that the mean of the random vector $\mathbf{X}$ is a zero vector, since we can always redefine $\mathbf{X} - E\mathbf{X}$ as the feature vector.

To represent vectors in S', we can predict that it might be enough to use a relatively small number of expansion terms to characterize the object scene with some degree of precision. Suppose we use m basis vectors, each of which is a column vector of V, and the covariance matrix of $\mathbf{X}$ is $\Sigma_x = E[(\mathbf{X} - E\mathbf{X})(\mathbf{X} - E\mathbf{X})^t]$. The approximate representation of $\mathbf{X}$ is $\hat{\mathbf{X}}(m) = \sum_{i=1}^m y_i \mathbf{v}_i$. It has been proved [20] that the optimal $\mathbf{v}_1 \mathbf{v}_2 \cdots \mathbf{v}_m$ that minimize mean square error

$$\epsilon^2(m) = E\|\mathbf{X} - \hat{\mathbf{X}}(m)\|^2 = \|\mathbf{X} - \sum_{i=1}^m y_i \mathbf{v}_i\|^2$$

are the m unit eigenvectors of the covariance matrix Σ_x associated with the m largest eigenvalues. After the computation of $\mathbf{v}_i$'s, the m components, y_i, of the projected vector of $\mathbf{X}$ can be computed by

$$y_i = \mathbf{v}_i^t(\mathbf{X} - E\mathbf{X}) \quad i = 1, 2, \ldots, m \tag{5}$$

or $\mathbf{Y} = V^t\mathbf{X}$, where $V = [\mathbf{v}_1 \ \mathbf{v}_2 \ \ldots \ \mathbf{v}_m]$. This is known as the Karhunen-Loeve projection [20]. Since the m features, $\mathbf{v}_i$'s in (5), give the minimum mean-square error, we can call them the *most expressive features* (MEF) in that they best describe the sample population in the sense of a linear transformation.

We can choose m so that the ratio of the mean square error over the total variance satisfies

$$\frac{\sum_{i=m+1}^d \lambda_i}{\sum_{i=1}^d \lambda_i} \leq \tau \tag{6}$$

(e.g., $\tau = 5\%$).

In practice, we are given a set of n learning images, $\mathbf{X}_1, \mathbf{X}_2, \ldots, \mathbf{X}_n$, and Σ_X is approximated by the scatter matrix

$$S = \sum_{i=1}^n \frac{1}{n}(\mathbf{X}_i - \mathbf{m})(\mathbf{X}_i - \mathbf{m})^t = UU^t \tag{7}$$

where $U = [\mathbf{U}_1 \ \mathbf{U}_2 \ \ldots \ \mathbf{U}_n]$ with $\mathbf{U}_i = \mathbf{X}_i - \mathbf{m}$, $\mathbf{m} = (1/n)\sum_{i=1}^n \mathbf{X}_i$. If the number of learning images n is smaller than dimension d, instead of computing the eigenvalues and eigenvectors of the a very large $d \times d$ matrix UU^t directly, we can find the eigenvector and eigenvalues of a smaller $n \times n$ matrix U^tU, which in fact has the same nonzero eigenvalues as $S = UU^t$. If $\mathbf{w}_i$ is an eigenvector of U^tU associated with the eigenvalue λ_i, then $\mathbf{v}_i = U\mathbf{w}_i$ is the eigenvector of $S = UU^t$ associated with the same eigenvalue.

The Karhunen-Loeve projection reduces the image dimension from d to m, which is typically a lot smaller than d. Figure 3 illustrates the meaning of the MEFs. The regions within which the sample points distribute has a much lower dimension than the original space. The first two eigenvectors $\mathbf{v}_1$ and $\mathbf{v}_2$ tell the most significant directions of sample variation. The MEFs are useful to reduce the dimension of representation. They are the best linear features to maximally preserve the Euclidean norm among the samples. For some works on using MEF for recognition-related problems, the reader is referred to [24, 33].

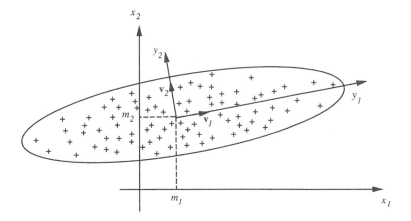

Figure 3. A 2D illustration of the most expressive features (MEF). The MEFs are $\mathbf{v}_1$ and $\mathbf{v}_2$ and the MEF values are the projected values onto y_1 and y_2 axes.

3.3. THE MOST DISCRIMINATING FEATURES

During navigation, the system needs to distinguish a variety of road types. Is it a cross intersection, a Y-shaped branching, a T-junction or a straight way? The road types will be used, coupled with the intention $\mathbf{P}$, to decide the next navigation action. Furthermore, given the same type of scene, different current heading directions (assuming that the camera is fixed on the vehicle), result in different scene appearances. For example, the next heading direction should depend on the way in which the road extends as seen from the current heading direction, left, straight, or right. All these require the navigator to classify scenes according to what it sees.

In the MEF space, a nearest-neighbor type of criterion is not well suited for scene classification, since the Euclidean distance in MEF space does not necessarily indicate a perceptual distance. Due to the effects of many unrelated factors, such as lighting, the Euclidean distance between two views of the same scene at different times may be much larger than those between two different scenes. In other words, the pixel-to-pixel distance, whether in the original image space or MEF space, cannot well characterize why two scenes are considered different.

When the category labels of the sample data are known, the discriminant analysis explained below can be used to automatically extract features that best characterize different categories.

Suppose samples, $\mathbf{Y}$'s, are m-dimensional random vectors from K classes. The ith class has a probability p_i, a mean vector $\mathbf{m}_i$, and a scatter matrix Σ_i. The *within-class scatter matrix* is defined by

$$S_w = \sum_{i=1}^{K} p_i E\{(\mathbf{Y} - \mathbf{m}_i)(\mathbf{Y} - \mathbf{m}_i)^t \mid \omega_i\} = \sum_{i=1}^{K} p_i \Sigma_i. \tag{8}$$

The *between-class scatter matrix* is $S_b = \sum_{i=1}^{K} p_i(\mathbf{m}_i - \mathbf{m})(\mathbf{m}_i - \mathbf{m})^t$ where $\mathbf{m}$ is defined as $\mathbf{m} = E\mathbf{Y} = \sum_{i=1}^{K} p_i M_i$. The *mixture scatter matrix* is defined by $S_m =$

$E\{(\mathbf{Y} - \mathbf{m})(\mathbf{Y} - \mathbf{m})^t\} = S_w + S_b$. We want to maximize the between-class scatter with respect to the within-class scatter. In the discriminant analysis [37], an objective function we wish to maximize is

$$\text{trace}\{S_w^{-1} S_b\}. \tag{9}$$

In other words, we want to find features in which the scatter between classes is large but the scatter within every class is small. Suppose we use k-dimensional linear features $\mathbf{Z} = W^t \mathbf{Y}$ where W is an $m \times k$ rectangular matrix whose column vectors are linearly independent. The above mapping represents a linear projection from m-dimensional space to k dimensional space. The objective is to determine an $m \times k$ matrix W so that in the new space, the objective function in (9) $f_Z(m) = \text{trace}\{S_{Zw}^{-1} S_{Zb}\}$ is minimized. Alternatively, we can also consider another objective function. $\det\{S_{Zb}\}$ and $\det\{S_{Zb}\}$ measure the hyperellipsoidal scattering volume of S_{Zw} and S_{Zb}, respectively. We may maximize their ratio,

$$\frac{\det\{S_{Zb}\}}{\det\{S_{Zw}\}} = \frac{\det\{W^t S_{Yb} W\}}{\det\{W^t S_{Yw} W\}}. \tag{10}$$

It has been proved that both objective functions (9) and (10) lead to the same projection matrix W whose column vectors are the eigenvectors of $S_{Yw}^{-1} S_{Yb}$ associated with the first k largest eigenvalues. The column vectors of W are called *the most discriminating features* (MDF). They are the best linear features that maximize the ratio in (10). Since the rank of S_{Yb} is at most $K - 1$, we know that only at most $K - 1$ features are needed, and others do not contribute to the maximum of the objective functions.

Figure 4 illustrates the meaning of MDF. Without class labels, all the samples

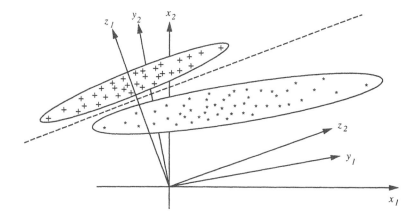

Figure 4. A 2D illustration of the most discriminating features (MDF). The MDF is the projection along z_1. The MEF along y_1 cannot separate the two subclasses.

are used to compute MEFs. In the figure, the first MEF along y_1 cannot separate the two subclasses. The direction along the difference of the two means cannot either.

Although the variation along the first MDF z_1 is not large, it catches the major feature that is crucial for classifying two subclasses.

In practice, we are given images from K categories. Let the number of samples belonging to the ith class be n_i, the jth sample in ith class be $\mathbf{Y}_j^{(i)}$ and the mean vector of the ith class be $\mathbf{m}^{(i)}$. The grand mean vector for all samples is replaced by the grand sample mean

$$\mathbf{m} = \frac{1}{n} \sum_{i=1}^{K} n_i \mathbf{m}^{(i)} \quad \text{where } n = \sum_{i=1}^{K} n_i.$$

The mixture scatter matrix is replaced by the sample scatter matrix:

$$S_m = \sum_{i=1}^{K} \sum_{j=1}^{n_i} (\mathbf{Y}_j^{(i)} - \mathbf{m})(\mathbf{Y}_j^{(i)} - \mathbf{m})^t.$$

Define the sample scatter matrix for the ith class as

$$S^{(i)} = \sum_{j=1}^{n_i} (\mathbf{Y}_j^{(i)} - \mathbf{m}^{(i)})(\mathbf{Y}_j^{(i)} - \mathbf{m}^{(i)})^t.$$

The within-class scatter matrix is replaced by

$$S_w = \sum_{i=1}^{K} S^{(i)},$$

and the between-class scatter matrix is replaced by

$$S_b = \sum_{i=1}^{K} n_i (\mathbf{m}^{(i)} - \mathbf{m})(\mathbf{m}^{(i)} - \mathbf{m})^t.$$

The relation $S_m = S_w + S_b$ still holds for the sample scatter matrices.

$S_{Yw}^{-1} S_{Yb}$ is generally not a symmetric matrix, and direct computation of its eigenvectors and eigenvalues is sometimes not as stable as the following method, which uses diagonalization of two symmetric matrices. Suppose the diagonalization of S_w is given by

$$S_w = H \Sigma H^t,$$

where H is an orthogonal matrix and Λ is a diagonal matrix. Then, obtain the diagonalization of the matrix $\Lambda^{-\frac{1}{2}} H^t B H \Lambda^{-\frac{1}{2}}$,

$$\Lambda^{-\frac{1}{2}} H^t B H \Lambda^{-\frac{1}{2}} = U \Sigma U^t$$

where H is orthogonal and Σ is diagonal. The MDFs are the normalized columns of $M = H \Lambda^{-\frac{1}{2}} U$, since we have

$$S_w^{-1} S_b = M \Sigma M^{-1}.$$

In fact, M diagonalizes S_w and S_b simultaneously, which is a known technique in linear algebra.

3.4. THE DKL PROJECTION

The discriminant analysis procedure breaks down when the within-class scatter matrix S_w becomes degenerate, which is true when the dimension of the input image is larger than the number of learning samples.

In fact, the discriminant analysis can be performed in the space of the Karhunen-Loeve projection (i.e., MEF space), where the degeneracy typically does not occur. Thus, the new overall discriminant projection is decomposed into two projections, the Karhunen-Loeve projection followed by the discriminant projection. To do this, we first project the d-dimensional $\mathbf{X}$-space onto m-dimensional MEF space ($\mathbf{Y}$-space) using the Karhunen-Loeve projection. Then, we project $\mathbf{Y}$-space on to the k-dimensional MDF space ($\mathbf{Z}$-space). Mathematically, we define the new *DKL projection* (short for discriminant Karhunen-Loeve projection) from the d-dimensional space of $\mathbf{X}$ to the k-dimensional space of $\mathbf{Z}$ as $\mathbf{Z} = W^t V^t \mathbf{X}$.

We must determine the dimension m of $\mathbf{Y}$ so that S_w is not degenerate. Given s samples from K classes, the maximum rank of S_w is $s - K$. Therefore, in order to make S_w nondegenerate, the input space of MDF projection m (i.e., the size of S_w) cannot be larger than $s - K$. That is, $m \leq s - K$. This means that, in the MEF projection, we need to discard the $(s - K + 1)$th up to the $(s - 1)$th largest eigenvalues of Σ_X. As we can expect, these eigenvalues are typically extremely small, because the $(s - 1)$th eigenvalue is the smallest among all the nonzero eigenvalues. In practice, we would like to discard more because it is very unlikely that they are important for classification either. On the other hand, m cannot be smaller than the number of classes K. Therefore we have $k < K \leq m \leq s - K$. Typically, s is much larger than K and thus, m can be chosen as an integer value in $[K, s - K]$ which also satisfies the variation criterion in (6).

3.5. SEPARABILITY

All the features we discussed here are linear features since only linear projections are considered for extracting features. These linear features possess the optimal properties as we discussed above and they allow a fast computation. However, an important question is the separability, that is, whether linear features can separate regions of arbitrary shapes in the space S.

Geometrically, we have seen in Section 2.7 that the final partition in a hierarchical partition P is the finest partition P_m. Other intermediate partitions are used mainly to speed up the search. The use of linear features here implies that cells in the partition P_m are bounded by hyperplanes. Geometrically, we can see from Figure 2 that piecewise linear hyperplanes can approximate virtually any region to a desired accuracy.

Mathematically, Section 2.5 has proved that the NN approximator is a general approximator, although the nearest neighbor means that the boundaries of decision regions are piecewise linear. Therefore, using our coarse to fine hierarchical partition scheme where the tessellation is based on the finest cells, linear features are sufficient to solve virtually any smooth nonlinear problem.

4. SELF-ORGANIZING RPT GENERATION THROUGH LEARNING

4.1. DATA ORGANIZATION

First, consider how to automatically organize visual data. We might first find clusters in the sample data and search for the best clusters to be assigned to each child. Then, cells are defined, each corresponding to a child. Recursively, a hierarchical clustering structure in the data may be explored so that a hierarchical tree can be constructed. However, algorithms for clustering analysis are very time-consuming due to their iterative nature, and their complexity is not suited for learning a huge number of samples.

Our objective is to approach a learning complexity that is close to $O(n)$ for a learning set of size n. We cannot hope for any lower complexity since each item needs to be examined for learning.

With this goal, we can recursively partition samples into smaller and smaller sets, without worrying about whether each cell corresponds to a cluster or not. Because we are interested in finding the best matching sample for an input, clusters are not a major concern.

Our partition tree is different from the existing ones in that features are recursively defined (extracted) depending on the actual samples each node receives in the learning phase. In other words, nodes at the same level or different levels all use different sets of features, and each is best for the task of each node.

4.2. BINARY RECURSIVE PARTITION TREE

For real-time navigation, the speed of a tree search is a central issue. To project a d-dimensional input onto a k-dimensional space, k inner products need to be computed, each for a d dimensional vector. Since d is large, ranging from 300 to 4800 with a reduced-resolution image in our experiment, we chose to adopt $k = 1$ for the advantage of a minimum computation. In other words, each node uses only a single feature.

Since only one feature is used at each internal node, we use the sample feature mean as the threshold to break the samples into two groups, one for the left child and one for the right. Thus, the result is a binary tree, as shown in Figure 5.

In the context of organizing samples into a decision tree, various ways have been used to select the feature at each node to assign samples to child nodes. Mui and Fu [23] used an iterative method to classify nucleated blood cells. Sethi and Sarvarayudu [29] maximized the amount of average mutual information gain at each partition step. Chou [4] employed the criterion of information divergence. In our case, we use the Karhunen-Loeve projection or DKL projection, respectively, to automatically extract linear features that are best at each node. In applications where no sample label is available, the MEF feature is used. When a class label is available, the MDF is used.

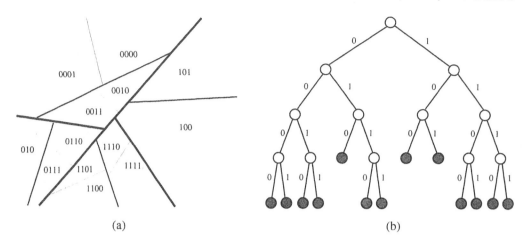

(a)   (b)

Figure 5. Geometrical illustration of the binary RPT. (a) The geometric cells. Thicker lines indicate the boundary of coarser-level cells. The thinner lines and dashed lines indicate the boundary of finer-level cells. (b) The corresponding RPT.

4.3. Constructing MEF RPT

Given a set of learning samples

$$L = \{(\mathbf{X}_i, f(\mathbf{X}_i)) \mid i = 1, 2, \ldots, n\}, \tag{11}$$

the objective is to automatically construct an MEF RPT. The root of the tree accepts the entire set L for learning. At each node, the samples that go to this node are used to compute the first MEF feature vector. All the samples that have a negative MEF value go to the left child and the remaining ones go to the right. Such a process is performed recursively from the root down to each node's children. The recursive subdivision is terminated at a node when it has only one sample.

When the number of learning samples is very large, the computation of MEF features becomes time-consuming. The time complexity of MEF computation is $O(n^3)$ with n learning images (supposing $n \leq d$, the number of samples is smaller than the dimension of input samples). Coarse-level nodes correspond to large cells and thus they have more samples than finer level nodes. However, at a coarse level we do not need to use all the samples to compute the exact MEF, because the partition at a coarse level is rough anyway. Thus, we adopt a constant q as the maximum number of samples used to compute MEF at every level. Whenever the number of samples available at a node exceeds q, a subset of q samples are randomly selected to be used for MEF computation. Of course, we will not waste the other samples. All the samples of a node will be assigned to the corresponding children using the MEF which is probably computed from a reduce set. At fine levels, the number of samples assigned to each node becomes small. As soon as the number of samples of a node is not larger than q, all the samples are used for its MEF computation. The following is a pseudo code of the algorithm.

MEF RPT Construction Algorithm: Given L, construct the MEF RPT.

```
call construct(root, L);
construct(node, L) {
    If (||L|| = 1) { node = L; return; }
    else if (||L|| > q}) L' = pick-q-samples(L);
    else L' = L;
    compute MEF1 from L';
    mean = average of MEF1-projections of all s in L';
    left-set = right-set = ∅;
    for each s in L {
        if (MEF1-projection(s) - mean < 0)
        left-set = left-set∪{s};
        else right-set = right-set∪{s};
    }
    construct(node→leftchild, left-set);
    construct(node→rightchild, right-set);
}
```

4.4. CONSTRUCTING MDF RPT

The MDF RPT uses MDF's and thus class labels are required for each sample in the learning set. Two types of labels can be used, single-level labels or hierarchical labels. A hierarchical label is of the form $X_1.X_2.\ldots.X_t$, where each X_i is a class label for level i. The hierarchical label is intended to direct the RPT to group the samples in the way desired by the hierarchical label. For example, a coarse-level label X_1 can have two classes, hallway and corner, so that the tree will try to group samples into hallway images and corner images before further subdividing samples into finer classes. A single-level label is a special case of the hierarchical label in that $t = 1$.

The construction algorithm of MDF RPT is similar to that of the MEF RPT. The major difference is the computation of MDF instead of MEF, and the use of a label. Given a set of labeled learning samples

$$L = \{(\mathbf{X}_i, f(\mathbf{X}_i), b_i) \mid i = 1, 2, \ldots, n\}, \tag{12}$$

where b_i is the label of sample $\mathbf{X}_i$. If the labels are hierarchical, $b = X_1.X_2.\ldots.X_t$, where the label X_i is intended to be used at level i. For any node at a level number larger than t, the deepest level label, X_t, is used. The recursive subdivision of the samples is terminated at a node if the node has only samples of a single label X_t. A form of pseudo code of the algorithm is given bellow.

MDF RPT Construction Algorithm: Given a labeled L, construct the MDF RPT.

```
call construct(root, L, 0);
construct(node, L, level) {
    If (samples in ||L|| have the same deepest label X_t) { node = L; return; }
    else if (||L|| > q}) L' = pick-q-samples(L);
```

```
        else L' = L;
        compute MDF1 from L' using labels in L';
        mean = average of MDF1-projections of all s in L';
        left-set = right-set = ∅;
        for each s in L {
            if (MDF1-projection(s) - mean < 0)
            left-set = left-set∪{s};
            else right-set = right-set∪{s};
        }
        construct(node→leftchild, left-set, level+1);
        construct(node→rightchild, right-set, level+1);
    }
```

Of course, instead of using the mean only for assigning the left and right sets, the mean and variance of the samples in each class can be used to select a better threshold so that the boundary will not cut through a single-class cluster. Again, as we know, the boundary does not have to be a perfect classification due to the coarse-to-fine nature of the RPT partition. A fast algorithm is more important when the number of sample images is very large.

4.5. Learning phase and performance phase

The result of the learning phase is an RPT, as illustrated in Figure 6. At each leaf node, the corresponding control signal vector f is attached.

In the performance phase, the KCDB approximator will use more than one leaf node if $k > 1$. However, which k leaves will be used depends on query input $\mathbf{X}$. Therefore, the connection from k leaves to the interpolation part is neither a part of a tree nor stored. It is generated in run-time. The RPT can be regarded as a visual information data base. Since the entire input $\mathbf{X}$ is used for query instead of using a key word or a feature vector, the retrieval from this data base is content-based.

5. Complexity

We analyze the complexity of the navigation system in learning and navigation phases, respectively. Detailed complexity analysis of the scheme using MEF RPT is given. The analysis for MDF RPT is similar, except that at each nonleaf node MEF and MDF projections (i.e., DKL) are both employed.

5.1. Complexity in the learning phase

Time complexity. Given a set of N learning images with a dimension d_0, the time complexity of the learning algorithm can be analyzed by the following steps:

First consider C_1, the complexity for the root-node MEF analysis. The complexity C_1 is $O((\min(d_0, q))^3) + O(qd_0^2)$. As mentioned in Section 3.2, in solving the eigensystem of Σ_x, when the number of learning images is less than the dimension of image, we can solve the eigenvalues and eigenvectors of $U^t U$, which is $q \times q$.

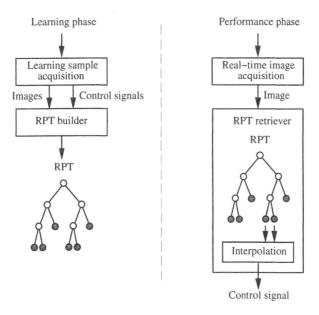

Figure 6. The learning and navigation phases.

Thus, the dimension of the matrix for eigensystem computation is $\min(d_0, q)$. The complexity of using the Jacobian method to compute the eigenvalues and eigenvectors of a symmetric $m \times m$ matrix is $O(m^3)$ [28]. The complexity of computing the $m \times m$ covariance matrix of q samples is $O(qm^2)$. Therefore, The complexity C_1 is $O((\min(d_0, q))^3) + O(qd_0^2)$.

Next, consider C_2, the complexity for the root-node MDF analysis. The root-node MEF's are fed directly to the MDF analysis. The order of MEF's is denoted by M which is typically within 100 in our experiment. Both S_w^{-1} and S_b are $M \times M$ symmetric matrix. The eigenvalues and eigenvectors of $S_w^{-1}S_b$ can be solved by calculating only eigensystems of symmetric matrices. The complexity C_2 is $O(M^3) + O(qM^2)$.

The remaining one is C_3, the complexity for subsequent RPT subtrees. Assume that the reduced dimension sequences corresponding to every node of the tree is

$$(d_{1,0}, d_{1,1}), (d_{2,0}, d_{2,1}, d_{2,2}, d_{2,3}), \ldots, (d_{n,0}, \ldots, d_{n,2^n-1})$$

where $d_{i,j}$ is the dimension of MEF subspace of jth node at i level and n is the height of the tree. Define d_i to be the maximal number of MEF's at level i of the, which is given by

$$d_i = \max_{0 \leq j \leq 2^i - 1} d_{i,j} \quad i = 1, 2, \ldots, n.$$

The time complexity is

$$\sum_{l=1}^{n} \sum_{i=1}^{2^l} \left[O((d_{l,i-1})^3) + O\left(N_{l,i-1} d_{l,i-1}^2\right) \right]$$

where $N_{l,i}$ is the number of learning images coming to the ith node at level l. We know that $\sum_{i=1}^{2^l} N_{l,i-1} \leq N$. The total number of nodes of a binary tree with l leaf nodes is $2l - 1$ [16], because the number of internal nodes of a l-leaf binary tree is equal to $l - 1$. In our case $l \leq N$. Thus, traversal of the tree takes $O(N)$ amount of time. Let ρ denote the maximal number of MEF features in the tree,

$$\rho = \max_{1 \leq l \leq n, 0 \leq i \leq 2^l - 1} (d_{l,i})$$

which is typically less than 100 in our experiment. Therefore,

$$C_3 \leq O(N\rho^3) + O(Nq\rho^2)$$

where the second term is the time complexity for computing scatter matrices for $2N - 1$ nodes.

Based on the above analysis, the time complexity $C_1 + C_2 + C_3$ is

$$O\left(\min(q, d_0)^3\right) + O(qd_0^2) + O(\rho^3) + O(q\rho^2) + O(N\rho^3) + O(Nq\rho^2).$$

Typically a low resolution (30×40) for images is sufficient for navigation, and we use a large set of learning images. Therefore, $N > d_0$. The complexity is then

$$O(d_0^3) + O(qd_0^2) + O(q\rho^2) + O(N\rho^3) + O(Nq\rho^2) = O(\rho^3 N). \qquad (13)$$

The time complexity is $O(\rho^3 N)$, where ρ is the maximum dimension of the MEF used and N is the number of learning samples. If ρ is considered as a constant, the complexity is $O(N)$.

This low learning complexity is reached because the method avoids time-consuming iterative analysis of input samples, which makes it possible to extend to incremental learning. In incremental learning, the time of concern is not the entire time spent, but rather the time required for learning a single sample at a time. This may allow real-time incremental learning, and the entire learning process can cover a relatively long period (as with human learning). In incremental learning, MEF and MDF features can be computed only periodically in a batch fashion. Between the batch processing, samples are collected one at a time and are fed into the tree right away. Each sample item takes $O(\log N)$ time, if ρ is regarded as a constant.

Space complexity. The number of nodes in the binary RPT tree is no more than $2N - 1$ and the number of leaves in the RPT is no more than N. Each child node needs only to store the MEF projection of its parent node, which is proportional to ρ. Thus, we have

The space complexity of learning phase is $O(\rho N)$. If ρ is considered as a constant, the space complexity of learning phase is then $O(N)$.

5.2. COMPLEXITY IN THE PERFORMANCE PHASE

Time complexity. The average leaf-node depth of an N-leaf binary tree is $O(\log N)$. Using the same notation as the previous analysis for learning, the complexity of retrieving the best match for a new image is

$$O(d_0 d_1) + O((\log N)\rho^2) \leq O\left((\log N)\rho^2\right) + O(d_0 \rho)$$

where $d_l = \max_{0 \leq i \leq 2^l - 1} d_{l,i}$. Using the $KCDB$ approximator, the constant k does not affect the order of complexity.

The average time complexity of retrieving for a new input image is

$$O\left((\log N)\rho^2\right) + O(d_0\rho)$$

where d_0 is the dimension of input image. If ρ and d_0 are regarded as constants, the complexity is then $\log(N)$.

d_0 is typically constant and ρ is the maximal number of MEF features, which is typically a small number. When the number of leaf nodes N is large, ρ tends to be constant. Thus, the complexity is $O(\log N)$, which is a logarithmic complexity.

Space complexity. For each internal node of the learning tree, we need to maintain the projection matrix of either MEF or MDF analysis. Denoting the number of nodes at level l as p_l, with $\sum_{l=1}^{n} p_l \leq 2N$, the space complexity is

$$O(d_0 d_1) + O\left(\sum_{l=1}^{n} p_l(d_{i-1} d_i)\right)$$
$$\leq O(d_0\rho) + O(N\rho^2) = O(d_0\rho) + O(N\rho^2).$$

The space complexity of the performance phase is $O(d_0\rho) + O(N\rho^2)$. When d_0 and ρ are treated as constants, the space complexity is $O(N)$.

In a usual case, $N > d_0$. The dominant term is $O(N\rho^2)$.

6. EXPERIMENTAL RESULTS

The experiments include performance evaluation and real runs with a mobile robot at MSU, Rome, which is built on a Labmate platform from TRC.

6.1. IMAGE ACQUISITION

The test site for our navigation experiments was the Engineering Building at MSU. The experimental area consists of several hallways with various turns. Rome was controlled manually to take pictures at different positions for learning. At each position, a set of five images with different heading directions was obtained: two left headings (5 and 10 degrees), two right headings (5 and 10 degrees), and the straight-ahead direction. The corresponding corrected heading directions were also recorded. For straight hallways, each set of pictures was taken at roughly every 2 to 3 meters. At turns, learning images were taken during sample drives controlled manually using a joystick. The corresponding corrected heading directions were obtained using consecutive heading increments. The pictures at turns were grabbed in shorter steps, less than 0.5 meter per step, since more frequent heading updates are needed during a turn. Some of the sample learning images are shown in Figure 7.

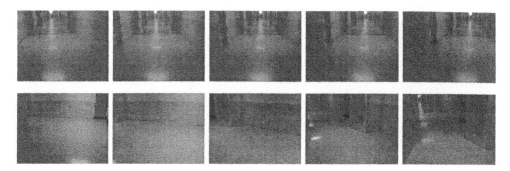

Figure 7. Some sample learning images in straight hallways and turns. The upper row is a straight hallway. The lower one is a left turn.

6.2. CLUSTERING EFFECTS OF MEF'S AND MDF'S

We show some experimental results to indicate quantitatively how the MEF and the MDF may perform very differently in classifying scenes. To do that, we compute MEF's and MDF's, respectively, using 210 images along a straight hallway and 108 images at a corner into 6 classes. The first five classes are straight hallways classified corresponding to the desired next heading direction needed to recover the correct heading. That is, class 0 for 10°; class 1 for 5°; class 2 for 0°; class 3 for −5°; and class 4 for −10°. Class 5 consists of 108 images at the corner. Figure 8a shows the learning samples in the subspace spanned by the first 2 MEF's and Figure 8b shows them in the subspace spanned by the first 2 MDF's. As clearly shown, in the MEF subspace,

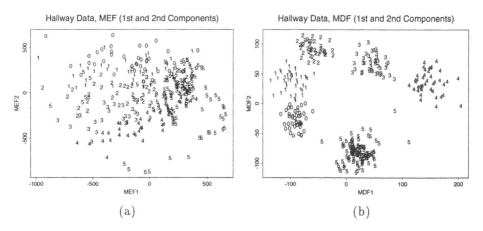

Figure 8. The difference between MEF and MDF in representing learning samples from a straight hallway and a turn. (a) Learning samples represented in the subspace spanned by the first two MEF's. (b) Learning samples represented in the subspace spanned by the first two MDF's. The numbers in the plot space are the class labels of the learning samples.

samples from a single class spread out widely and samples of different classes are not far apart. In fact, some samples from different classes mingle together. However, in the MDF subspace, samples of each class are clustered more tightly and samples from different classes are farther apart. From Figure 8, we can see that given an unknown image from the same environment, the MEF values are not as reliable as the MDF values in classification of the image.

To observe how the first two MEF's and MDF's, respectively, perform when they are used to represent images that have not been included in the learning sample set, we plot a set of 227 new images, of which 170 are from a straight hallway, 34 from the trained corner, and 33 from a untrained corner as shown in Figure 9. In Figure 9b

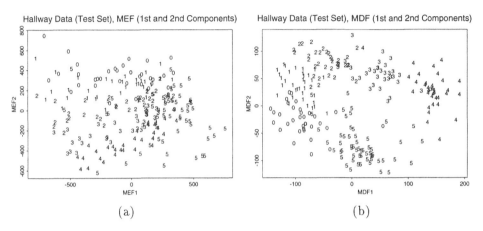

(a)   (b)

Figure 9. Test images in the subspace spanned by the first two MEF's and MDF's, respectively, all of which are not included in the learning set. (a) The MEF subspace. (b) The MDF subspace.

the structure of each cluster is still visible in the MDF subspace, though not as clearly as the case with the learning set.

6.3. EFFECT OF FEWER CLASSES IN LEARNING

In the RPT, the children of a node divide the sample images handled by the parent node into smaller groups and each group has a smaller number of classes, in general. To see how fewer classes will allow the MDF to cluster classes more effectively, we computed MDF's separately, one set from straight hallway images and another set from corner images.

Using the first two MDF computed from the corresponding images, the straight hallway learning images are shown in Figure 10 for the corresponding MEF and MDF subspaces, respectively. Comparing Figure 10b with Figure 8b, we see that each class in Figure 10b groups tighter and between-class distance is larger. In Figure 11 straight hallway images not in the learning set are plotted in the subspaces of MEF and MDF, respectively, that used only hallway images as the learning set. As we can predict, the test images now group more tightly than that in Figure 9.

In Figure 12, the MEF's and MDF's are computed from a set of 108 corner images in which there are 10 classes labeled from 0 to 9, for heading direction $15°$, $10°$, $5°$, $0°$, $-5°$, $-10°$, $-15°$, $-20°$, $-25°$, and $-30°$, respectively.

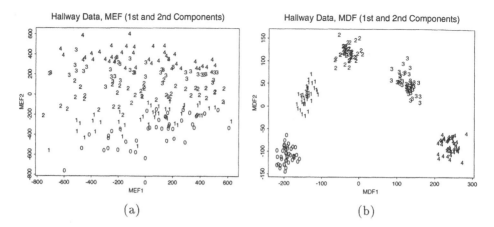

Figure 10. Fewer classes in the learning set: using only straight hallway images for training. (a) Learning samples represented in the subspace spanned by the first two MEF's. (b) Learning samples represented in the subspace spanned by the first two MDF's. The numbers in the plot space are the class labels of the learning samples.

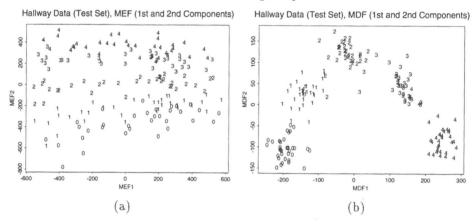

Figure 11. Test images represented in the subspaces learned from a learning set with 170 hallway images only (without corner images). (a) The MEF subspace. (b) The MDF subspace.

6.4. EFFECTS ON TREE SIZE

For the purpose of comparison, two types of tree are experimented with, *MEF RPT* and *MDF RPT*. The former uses MEF features and the latter uses MDF features. However, since a pure MEF RPT does not perform well, as shown in the previous examples, we used MDF for the root level of the MEF RPT to classify coarse scene types, hallway and corner, before using MEF's for further classification.

Table 1 shows the distribution of nodes over the levels in the MDF tree and MEF tree, respectively. Both the trees used the same 318 learning images, 210 from the straight hallway and 108 from the corner. The MDF tree has only a total of 69 nodes, with only 35 leaf nodes, while the MEF tree has a total of 635 nodes, with

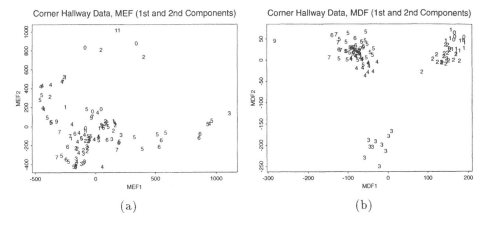

Figure 12. Learning images represented in the subspaces spanned by the first two MEF's and MDF's, respectively. (a) The MEF subspace. (b) The MDF subspace.

318 leaf nodes.

Table 1. The sizes of MDF tree and MEF tree, trained with the set of 318 images.

MDF Tree		MEF Tree	
Level	Number of nodes	Level	Number of nodes
0	1	0	1
1	2	1	2
2	4	2	4
3	8	3	8
4	10	4	16
5	14	5	32
6	22	6	64
7	8	7	128
		8	208
		9	138
		10	34
Total	69	Total	635

6.5. RPT RETRIEVAL

Since we have taken a large number of test images that are not in the learning set, we conducted some "virtual runs." The retrieval method for the data shown here explores only one path from the root to the leaf. In other words, the approximated function is a KCDB approximator with $k = 1$. Figure 14 shows the error distribution of retrieving the set of 227 test images, when the trees are trained using the set of 318 images, with straight hallway and corner. Comparing Figure 14a and Figure 14b, we can see that the errors in retrieving MDF tree are relatively smaller, especially for

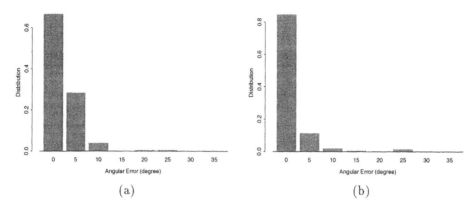

Figure 13. Distribution of absolute angular error (degree) of retrieved heading directions. These two plots are based on queries using a test set of 204 images, of which 170 are from a straight hallway and 34 from the learned corner. (a) Using an MEF RPT. (b) Using an MDF RPT.

the bin of 5-degree error, which implies a more stable performance. However, there is a small number of cases where the retrieved corrected heading has a large absolute error, mostly in the corner. Figure 13 is the same as Figure 14 except that the test image set includes 33 images taken from a corner that has not been learned.

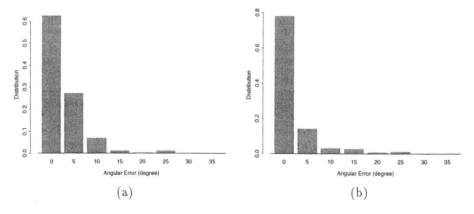

Figure 14. Distribution of absolute angular error (degree) of retrieved heading directions. These two plots are based on queries using the test set of 227 images, including those used in that shown Figure 13 plus 33 images from a corner that has not been learned. (a) Using an MEF RPT. (b) Using an MDF RPT.

As shown, a few images resulted in large angular errors. When a query image is far away from the correct cluster, it may go to a wrong subtree. Once that happens, the angular error will be large. It is expected that when k is increased to two for the KCDB approximator, such cases could be corrected to some degree. In real drives, sudden changes in heading corrections are rejected, because we assume a smooth navigation trajectory. Since the error rate of incorrect retrieval is very low, such a rejection based on smooth trajectory worked very well. Nevertheless, the failure rate of navigation in the untrained corner is high. Only when Rome was trained with this untrained corner did it give stable performance at this corner.

To give some intuition about what kind of images are retrieved using the RPT, some retrieval results are shown in Figure 15. Examples are shown for both successful and unsuccessful retrieval cases.

6.6. REAL RUNS

For the real runs, the chosen control signal has three components: corrected heading direction, speed, and step size. Whenever a new input image comes, the retrieval program searches down the RPT for the matching leaf node, and uses the corresponding stored control signal to control the robot. For the learning, τ in (6) is set to 5%. We trained Rome through three learning drives in which 363 learning images were taken, 280 of which from two straight hallways and 83 from a turn.

The image size for the root-node MEF and MDF projections is 15×20. In the subtree, once the number of images belonging to a internal node becomes less than 300, the node uses a higher image resolution (30×40). This way saves some computation time for the learning phase since the root node uses a large number of images to compute the eigenvalues and eigenvectors.

The total computer time for a learning phase ranged from 17 to 30 minutes, as shown in Table 2, depending on the SUN workstation model. With $\tau = 5\%$ in (6), the number of MEF's at the root level is shown in Table 3, for different image sizes, although only the first MEF was used for the RPT at the first level and further MEF analysis was done at deeper tree levels. The numbers of MEF's, corresponding to $\tau = 5\%$, in the tree are shown in Figure 16. Leaf nodes were typically at level 8.

Table 2. The total learning time for a set of 363 images.

Workstation	Time (minutes)
SPARC-20	17
SPARC-10	30

Table 3. The numbers of root-level MEF's, corresponding to different choices of image sizes. The same set of 363 learning images was used.

Image Size	Number of root level MEF
15×20	37
30×40	68
60×80	121

We let the Rome, which had learned using the MEF-RPT, navigate autonomously over 30 times along three straight hallways and two turns (including one hallway

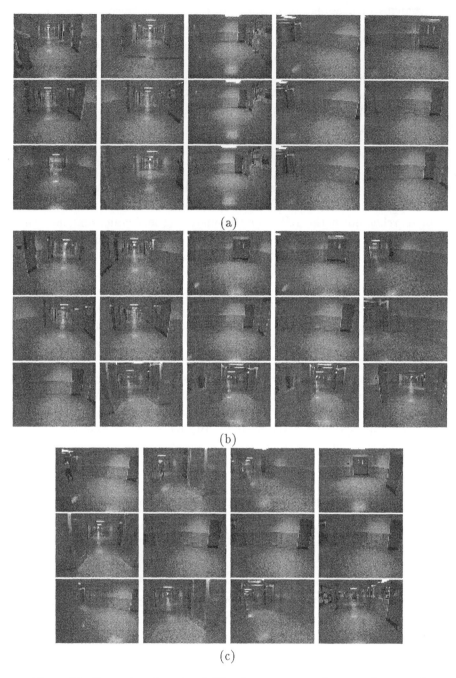

Figure 15. Examples of retrieval. The first row: query images; the second row: retrieved using MDF RPT; the third row: retrieved from MEF RPT. (a) Both MEF and MDF RPT's give good results. (b) The MDF RPT gives good results while MEF RPT does not. (c) The MDF RPT gives bad results, whereas in the first three columns the MEF RPT turns out fine, and in the fourth column neither gives a good image.

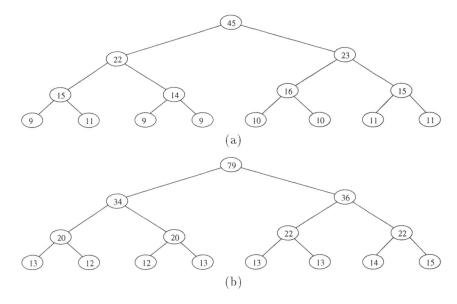

Figure 16. The number of MEF features (shown in circles) in the first four levels 1, 2, 3, 4 in MEF-RPT using the set of 280 straight hallway learning images. The root is at level 0. (a) The image size is 15×20. (b) The image size is 30×40.

Table 4. Time for retrieving from the trained RPT, given a new input.

Workstation	Average time per retrieval	Total time for 363 retrievals
SPARC-10	49.3 ms	17.9 s
SPARC-2	77.7 ms	28.2 s
SPARC-1	128.1 ms	46.5 s

that was not learned). All these over 30 drives were successful as reported in [3]. In spring 1995, the MDF RPT version had been implemented and it has been used for Rome testing and demonstrations since then. The MDF version exhibited more consistent direction history than the MEF version. During various tests and demonstrations, there were people walking along the hallways, but Rome was not bothered because it recognized the entire scene instead of a particular type of landmark (e.g., road edges).

Table 4 shows the time used for retrieval from the trained MEF RPT. Clearly, a SPARC-1 is fast enough for real-time navigation in this experiment. The MDF RPT is even faster.

Figure 17 shows a trajectory of a sample navigation, and Figure 18 shows some images to illustrate the environment.

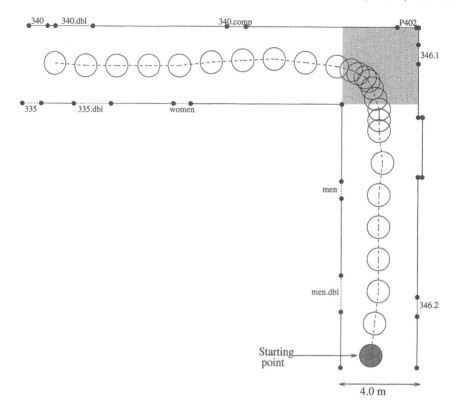

Figure 17. A sample of autonomous navigation in the trained hallway: two straight hallways and one turn. The circles indicate the locations where images are taken.

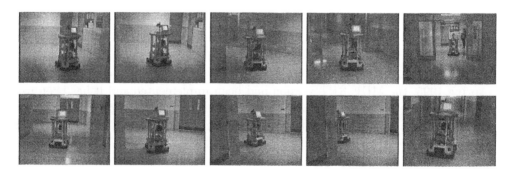

Figure 18. Rome navigates automatically at two turns: the first turn in the 1st row and the second turn in the 2nd row.

7. CONCLUSIONS AND FUTURE WORK

The framework presented here is general. It does not restrict the scene type and thus is potentially applicable to both indoor and outdoor environments. The MDF version of the RPT seems better than the MEF version due to its relatively tighter class clusters and a smaller tree size. With a consideration of the wide availability of inexpensive hard disks (e.g., several GBytes for a typical navigation application) and the fast logarithmic retrieval that is made possible by the RPT, it seems that the requirement of a large number of learning images is not unreasonable. The method presented seems particularly attractable for situations where consistent floor edges are not available or with the frequent presence of passersby. Future work includes edge information more explicitly by using certain types of edge image as a part of input, and experiments with a wide variety of driving environments, indoor and outdoor. Since this approach requires a large number of images for learning, real-time incremental learning is a future direction of its development.

Acknowledgments

This work was supported in part by NSF grant No. IRI 9410741. As a part of the SHOSLIF endeavor, Yuntao Cui and Dan Swets have shared parts of their programs with this project. Many thanks also go to those who have contributed to the construction of MSU's mobile robot Rome, which has been extensively used by the project as a testbed.

Appendix A

Proof of Theorem 1. Let the norm of the Jacobian matrix of f in S be bounded by a number B. That is $\left\| \frac{\partial f(\mathbf{X})}{\partial \mathbf{X}} \right\| \leq B$ for all $\mathbf{X} \in S$. Let η be a positive number $\eta = \delta/(B+1)$. We use D_k to denote the event that the nearest neighbor of $\mathbf{X}$ in the *union* $\bigcup_{i=1}^{k} X(L_i)$ has a distance larger than η while E_i denotes the event that the nearest neighbor of $\mathbf{X}$ in the *single* $X(L_i)$ has a distance larger than η. Since each L_i is independently and identically drawn, we have

$$P\{D_k\} = \prod_{i=1}^{k} P\{E_i\}.$$

On the other hand, $\mathbf{X}$ is positively supported, which means that $1 - P\{E_i\} > 0$. Say, $1 - P\{E_i\} = \beta > 0$. Then, $P\{E_i\} = 1 - \beta < 1$. Thus,

$$P\{D_k\} = (1 - \beta)^k$$

which approaches zero when $k \to \infty$. In fact, given any $\epsilon > 0$, let $k_0 = \lceil \log_{1-\beta}(\epsilon) \rceil$. If $k > k_0$, we have

$$P\{D_k\} \leq (1 - \beta)^{\lceil \log_{1-\beta}(\epsilon) \rceil} < \epsilon. \tag{14}$$

Suppose $\overline{D_k}$, the negative event of D_k, is true. That is, there is a nearest neighbor $\mathbf{X}'$ of $\mathbf{X}$ in $\bigcup_{i=1}^{k} X(L_i)$ so that $\|\mathbf{X}' - \mathbf{X}\| \leq \eta$. Then, $\hat{f}(\mathbf{X}) = f(\mathbf{X}')$ according to the NN approximator $\hat{f}$. Taylor's theorem for multivariate function gives

$$f(\mathbf{X}) = f(\mathbf{X}') + \frac{\partial f(\mathbf{X}')}{\partial \mathbf{X}}(\mathbf{X} - \mathbf{X}') + o(\|\mathbf{X} - \mathbf{X}'\|).$$

We know that $\left\|\frac{\partial f(\mathbf{X})}{\partial \mathbf{X}}\right\| \leq B$. For a sufficiently small η, we have $o(\|\mathbf{X} - \mathbf{X}'\|)/\|\mathbf{X} - \mathbf{X}'\| \leq 1$. It follows that

$$\|f(\mathbf{X}) - f(\mathbf{X}')\| \leq \left\|\frac{\partial f(\mathbf{X}')}{\partial \mathbf{X}}\right\| \|(\mathbf{X} - \mathbf{X}')\| + \frac{o(\|\mathbf{X} - \mathbf{X}'\|)}{\|\mathbf{X} - \mathbf{X}'\|} \|(\mathbf{X} - \mathbf{X}')\|$$

$$\leq (B+1)\|\mathbf{X} - \mathbf{X}'\| \leq (B+1)\eta = \delta.$$

In other words, $P\{\overline{D_k}\} \leq P\{\|f(\mathbf{X}) - f(\mathbf{X}')\| \leq \delta\}$. Thus, from (14)

$$P\{\|f(\mathbf{X}') - f(\mathbf{X})\| > \delta\} = P\{\|f(\mathbf{X}) - f(\mathbf{X}')\| > \delta\} \leq P\{D_k\} < \epsilon.$$

APPENDIX B

Proof of Theorem 2. Consider a particular partition P of $[0, \infty)$ with $0 = \alpha_0 < \alpha_1 < \cdots < \alpha_m$. P partitions $[0, \infty)$ into disjoint measurable sets:

$$D_i = \{\mathbf{X} \mid \alpha_i \leq (\hat{f}(\mathbf{X}) - f(\mathbf{X}))^2 < \alpha_{i+1}\}$$

for $i = 0, 1, \ldots, m - 1$ and $D_m = \{\mathbf{X} \mid \alpha_m \leq (\hat{f}(\mathbf{X}) - f(\mathbf{X}))^2\}$. The integral in (4) is a Lebesgue-Stieltjes integral with a probability measure. In other words,

$$\int_{\mathbf{X} \in S'} (\hat{f}(\mathbf{X}) - f(\mathbf{X}))^2 dF(\mathbf{X}) = \sup_P \sum_{i=0}^m \alpha_i P\{D_i\} \tag{15}$$

where $\sup_P$ denotes the least upper bound of all such P's and $P\{D_i\}$ is the probability measure of D_i in S'. Given any $\epsilon > 0$, we want to prove

$$\sum_{i=0}^m \alpha_i P\{D_i\} < \epsilon$$

for any partion P, as long as a sufficiently large learning set is used. To do that, we need to use the given condition of uniform convergence in probability. For any such a partition P, let $\delta = \epsilon/2$ and $\eta = \epsilon/(2\alpha_m)$, and there is a sufficiently large k_0, so that when $k \geq k_0$,

$$P\{\|\hat{f}(\mathbf{X}) - f(\mathbf{X})\| > \delta\} < \eta.$$

Suppose δ is between α_k and α_{k+1}, $\alpha_k \leq \delta < \alpha_{k+1}$. Then, the summation in (15) can be written in two parts:

$$\sum_{i=0}^m \alpha_i P\{D_i\} = \sum_{i=0}^k \alpha_i P\{D_i\} + \sum_{i=k+1}^m \alpha_i P\{D_i\}$$

$$\leq \delta \sum_{i=0}^k P\{D_i\} + \alpha_m \sum_{i=k+1}^m P\{D_i\}$$

$$< \delta + \alpha_m \eta = \epsilon/2 + \alpha_m \frac{\epsilon}{2\alpha_m} = \epsilon. \tag{16}$$

For the remaining case $\delta \geq \alpha_m$, we have

$$\sum_{i=0}^{m} \alpha_i P\{D_i\} \leq \delta \sum_{i=0}^{k} P\{D_i\} < \delta = \epsilon/2 < \epsilon.$$

The above means that

$$\sup_{P} \sum_{i=0}^{m} \alpha_i P\{D_i\} \leq \epsilon$$

or

$$\int_{\mathbf{X} \in S'} (\hat{f}(\mathbf{X}) - f(\mathbf{X}))^2 dF(\mathbf{X}) \to 0$$

as the size of k in $L = \{L_1, L_2, \ldots, L_k\}$ approaches infinity.

REFERENCES

1. N. Ayache and O.D. Faugeras, "Maintaining representations of the environment of a mobile robot," *IEEE Transactions on Robotics and Automation* **5**(6), 1989, 804–819.

2. L. Breiman, J.H. Friedman, R.A. Olshen, and C.J. Stone, *Classification and Regression Trees*, Chapman & Hall, New York, 1993.

3. S. Chen and J. Weng, "SHOSLIF-N: SHOSLIF for autonomous navigation (Phase I)," Technical Report CPS-94-62, Department of Computer Science, Michigan State University, East Lansing, MI, December 1994.

4. P.A. Chou, "Optimal partitioning for classification and regression trees," *IEEE Transactions on Pattern Analysis and Machine Intelligence* **13**(4), 1991, 340–354.

5. J. Crisman and C. Thorpe, "Color vision for road following," in C. Thorpe (Ed.), *Vision and Navigation: The Carnegie Mellon Navlab*, Kluwer, Norwell, MA, 1990, 9–23.

6. P.A. Devijver and J. Kittler, *Pattern Recognition*, Prentice Hall, Englewood Cliffs, NJ, 1982.

7. E.D. Dickmanns and A. Zapp, "A curvature-based scheme for improving road vehicle guidance by computer vision," in *Proc. SPIE Mobile Robot Conf.*, Cambridge, MA, October 1986, 161–168.

8. K. Fukunaga, *Introduction to Statistical Pattern Recognition*, 2nd Edition, Academic Press, San Diego, 1990.

9. D.J. Hand, *Discrimination and Classification*, Wiley, Chichester, 1981.

10. S. Haykin, *Neural Networks: A Comprehensive Foundation*, Macmillan, NY, 1994.

11. M. Hébert, "Building and navigating maps of road scenes using an active sensor," in *Proc. IEEE International Conference on Robotics and Automation*, Philadelphia, April 1988, 1136–1142.

12. P.J. Huber, "Projection pursuit," *Annals of Statistics* **13**(2), 1985, 435–475.

13. A.K. Jain and R.C. Dubes, *Algorithms for Clustering Data*, Prentice Hall, Englewood Cliffs, NJ, 1988.

14. L.V. Kantorovich and G.P. Akilov, *Functional Analysis in Normed Spaces*, Pergamon, Oxford, 1964.

15. K. Kluge and C. Thorpe, "Explicit models for robot road following," in C. Thorpe (Ed.), *Vision and Navigation: The Carnegie Mellon Navlab*, Kluwer, Norwell, MA, 1990, 25–38.

16. D.E. Knuth, *The Art of Computer Programming: Sorting and Searching*, Addison-Wesley, Reading, MA, 1973.

17. D.J. Kriegmaan, E. Triendl, and T.O. Binford, "Stereo vision and navigation in buildings for mobile robots," *IEEE Transactions on Robotics and Automation* **5**(6), 1989, 792–803.

18. D. Kuan, G. Philips, and A. Hsueh, "Autonomous land vehicle road following," in *Proc. International Conference on Computer Vision*, IEEE, Piscataway, NJ, 1987.

19. X. Lebesgue and J.K. Aggarwal, "Significant line segments for an indoor mobile robot," *IEEE Transactions on Robotics and Automation* **9**(6), 1993, 801–816.

20. M.M. Loeve, *Probability Theory*, Van Nostrand, New York, 1955.

21. D.G. Luenberger, *Optimization by Vector Space Methods*, John Wiley, New York, 1969.

22. M. Meng and A.C. Kak, "Mobile robot navigation using neural networks and non-metrical environment models," *IEEE Control Systems*, August 1993, 31–42.

23. J.K. Mui, and K.S. Fu, "Automated classification of nucleated blood cells using a binary tree classifier," *IEEE Transactions on Pattern Analysis and Machine Intelligence* **2**(5), 1980, 429–443.

24. H. Murase and S.K. Nayar, "Illumination planning for object recognition in structured environments," in *Proc. IEEE Conference on Computer Vision and Pattern Recognition*, Seattle, WA, June 1994, 31–38.

25. T. Poggio, "A theory of how the brain might work," *Cold Spring Harbor Symposium on Qualitative Biology* **LV**, 1990, 899–910.

26. T. Poggio and F. Girosi, "Networks for approximation and learning," *Proceedings of the IEEE* **78**(9), 1990, 1481–1497.

27. D.A. Pomerleau, "Efficient training of artificial neural networks for autonomous navigation," *Neural Computation* **3**(1), 1991, 88–97.

28. W.H. Press, S.A. Teukolsky, W.T. Vetterling, and B.P. Flannery, *Numerical Recipes in C* (2nd Edition), Cambridge University Press, Cambridge, 1992.

29. I.K. Sethi and G.P.R. Savarayudu, "Hierarchical classifier design using mutual information," *IEEE Transactions on Pattern Analysis and Machine Intelligence* **4**(4), 1982, 441–445.

30. S.E. Stead, *Smooth multistage multivariate approximation*, Ph.D. thesis, Department of Mathematics, Brown University, 1983.

31. C. Thorpe, M.H. Hébert, T. Kanade, and S. Shafer, "Vision and navigation for the Carnegie-Mellon Navlab," *IEEE Transactions on Pattern Analysis and Machine Intelligence* **10**(3), May 1988, 362–373.

32. C. Thorpe, M. Hébert, T. Kanade, and S. Shafer, "Toward autonomous driving: The CMU Navlab," *IEEE Expert*, August 1991, 31–42.

33. M. Turk and A. Pentland, "Eigenfaces for recognition," *Journal of Cognitive Neuroscience* **3**(1), 1991, 71–86.

34. R. Wallace, K. Matsuzaki, J. Crisman, Y. Goto, J. Webb, and T. Kanade, "Progress in robot road-following," in *Proc. IEEE International Conference on Robotics and Automation*, San Francisco, CA, April 1986, 1426–1432.

35. J. Weng, "On comprehensive visual learning," *Proc. NSF/ARPA Workshop on Performance vs. Methodology in Computer Vision*, Seattle, WA, June 24–25, 1994, 152–166.

36. J.J. Weng and S. Chen, "SHOSLIF convergence properties and MDF version of SHOSLIF-N," Technical Report CPS-95-22, Department of Computer Science, Michigan State University, East Lansing, MI, May 1995.

37. S.S. Wilks, *Mathematical Statistics*, Wiley, New York, 1963.

8 | FROM VISUAL HOMING TO OBJECT RECOGNITION

Randal C. Nelson
University of Rochester

ABSTRACT

Navigation is a group of fundamental behaviors by which an agent, biological or mechanical, guides itself through the world on the basis of sensory information. Such fundamental behaviors are interesting, because in the behavioral paradigm for intelligence they form the foundation upon which more sophisticated abilities are developed. This chapter begins by describing, analyzing, and demonstrating an associative memory based method for homing and for navigating along a prescribed path on the basis of visual landmarks. We then show how the basic associative mechanisms used to implement the simple navigation behavior may be modified to form the basis for a general method for three-dimensional object recognition. An implementation of such a system is described, and its performance on a data base of three-dimensional objects is illustrated.

1. INTRODUCTION

We start this chapter with an investigation of visual homing. Homing is an elementary navigation process by which an autonomous system guides itself to a particular location on the basis of sensory input. The term was originally used to describe animal behavior, but has since acquired an analogous meaning in the context of automation. Visual homing, therefore, refers to a process which utilizes images as the primary sensory input. The definition can apply to motion in a variety of spaces, for instance, movement in the joint space of a robot arm. However, we focus here on controlling the motion of a compact sensor in a real-world environment. In particular, the motion is presumed to be in three-dimensional space, possibly with some constraints on the degrees of freedom, and the goal is a specified position and orientation along with associated tolerances.

Visual homing is an interesting basic problem for several reasons. To begin with, it is relatively well-defined for arbitrary environments, and thus potentially valuable as a general purpose component for autonomous navigation systems in which it would operate in conjunction with lower-level systems, providing, for example, stabilization and obstacle avoidance (see [36, 37], also [20, 41, 47, 49]). This is in contrast to many navigational problems which must ultimately be defined with respect to a specific environment (for example, road-following vehicles [50]). There are also a large number of potential practical uses for a visual homing system, including docking maneuvers, tool positioning, and grasp operations, as well as the obvious vehicle guidance applications.

More generally, however, the problem is interesting because it appears to be one of the simplest visual operations performed by biological systems that involves substantial amounts of learned information. (For instance, certain bees and wasps are able to home visually in the immediate vicinity of their nests.) The problem thus has implications in the foundations of machine learning and knowledge representation. Because the mechanisms performing more complicated biological operations presumably developed from preexisting simpler ones, it seems plausible that a general mechanism for performing visual homing might provide a foundation for implementing more complex abilities. In the second part of this chapter, we demonstrate how this idea bears fruit and show how the basic associative machinery developed for visual homing can be modified to produce a more general object recognition system.

2. VISUAL HOMING

2.1. OVERVIEW

Because of its practical importance, homing has received a fair amount of attention. The most successful current systems have been nonvisual. Methods based on internal coordinates, inertial guidance, and radio beacons are widely used in robots, missiles, and autopilots, but these techniques are unsuited for many applications, especially ones involving autonomous operation in loosely constrained environments. There also exist several experimental systems which attempt to navigate on the basis of range images, e.g., [12, 19] or by recognizing specific landmarks, e.g., [27]. In general, these methods involve maintaining a geometric representation of the environment. The problem with this approach is that such geometric models tend both to contain a lot of irrelevant information, and to exclude cues that may be visually significant.

We describe here a method of visual homing based on direct association between visual patterns and motor control. The basic idea is to store a large set of reference patterns, each of which represents a concise description of the environment as seen from the neighborhood of a particular position. Enough patterns are stored to cover the domain of competence. Associated with each reference pattern is information specifying an action to be taken (for instance, a direction of movement). Homing is accomplished by comparing an index pattern computed for the currently visible scene against the reference patterns and determining the best match. If the match is good enough, the scene is considered to be recognized and the associated action is executed. The basic technique is somewhat similar to the "memory bases reasoning" employed by [45] in the domain of English word pronunciation.

A significant characteristic of this technique when employed for navigation is that it does not utilize an explicit model of the world; rather, the relevant characteristics of the environment are implicitly encoded in what might be viewed as the stimulus-response behavior of the system. Pomerleau [40] describes a road-following method using a neural net trained by backpropagation to associate steering actions with visual patterns. This is related to the work described here in that it characterizes a navigational in terms of stimulus response association. The network works fairly well for some classes of roads, and can thus be considered to have learned a general concept. The back-prop algorithm does not, however, lend itself to analysis that would indicate under what situations a similar technique could be applied, or when it would be expected to fail. A major aim of this paper is to identify and analyze the criteria that the transformation mapping images to patterns must satisfy in order to implement robust homing in a particular environment.

2.2. Basic definitions and operations

Two elements central to associative homing are the notion of a pattern, and a definition of similarity between patterns which allows novel patterns to be compared to reference patterns in memory and to be recognized on the basis of a partial match. The definitions we use are fairly classical, and were chosen to be as elementary as possible in order to facilitate analysis of the system. Nevertheless, these simple definitions can be used in conjunction with experimentally verifiable assumptions about the structure of the visual environment to implement a robust system of visual homing.

A *pattern* is defined to be a tuple $(a_1, a_2, \ldots, a_m)$ which is an element of a *pattern space* $A_1 \times A_2 \times \cdots \times A_m$ where $A_1, \ldots, A_m$ represent finite sets referred to as *features*. The idea behind this definition is the description of a scene in terms of discrete primitives. The features can be high-level or low-level, binary or multiply valued, depending on the desired characteristics of the pattern space. For example, a high-level binary feature might be the presence or absence of a blob having a particular parameterization in the scene; a low-level multiply-valued feature might be the dominant edge direction in a particular receptive field.

The *similarity* $s(p_1, p_2)$ of two patterns which are elements of the same pattern space is defined to be the fraction of positions in the tuple at which the values are identical. Thus, for example, if the pattern space is chosen to be strings of length 3 over the English alphabet, then $s(CAT, RAT) = 2/3$ since the strings match in the last two positions, while $s(ARM, MAR) = 0$ since the strings match in no position, despite the fact that they contain the same characters. The similarity is related to a distance metric d_p, which is equal to the number of locations where the tuples differ, by the formula $s = (1 - d_p)/m$ where m is the length of the tuples. In the binary case, this metric is the well-known Hamming distance.

The above definitions form the basis for a nearest neighbor strategy that can be used to classify patterns on the basis of a set of training samples. First, store in memory all the sample patterns and their classifications. These constitute the set of *reference patterns*. When the system is presented with an unknown *index pattern*, it compares it against all the reference patterns, and extracts the one having the highest similarity. If this similarity is above a certain *recognition threshold t*, then the associated classification of the reference pattern is returned; otherwise, the system returns a "don't know" response. This can be considered to be a primitive associative memory, since classification is, in a sense, an associated pattern (see e.g., [23, 24]).

A memory constructed as above has an effective limit on the number of patterns that can be stored. Specifically, it is undesirable to store so many different patterns that an arbitrary "random" index pattern has a significant probability of yielding a response above the recognition threshold. This would lead not only to false recognition, but to mistakes in classification as well, since if a random pattern is likely to be recognized, it is also likely that the best match will be due to a chance coincidence and not the result of a meaningful similarity. The simplest way of avoiding such classification errors is to make the pattern space much larger than is necessary to span the desired domain of competence, and rely on statistical expectations to distribute the reference patterns across this space so that they do not interfere unexpectedly with each other. This idea is developed and made precise in the analysis section of this paper where it is used to derive measurements from which the performance of the system can be predicted.

2.3. DESIGN PRINCIPLES

The method of pattern classification described above can be adapted to the homing problem as follows. First, design an appropriate mapping Φ from images to a pattern space, and select an appropriate recognition threshold t. Then, at each of an appropriately chosen set **R** of reference points in the motion space, store in memory the corresponding pattern, and associate with that pattern either a direction of motion which will ultimately bring the observer closer to the goal, or information specifying that the goal has been reached. The set of patterns so stored constitutes a set **P** of reference patterns, and the associated information can be viewed as the classification. Once the system has been trained by storing the set of reference patterns, homing is accomplished by applying Φ to the currently visible image to obtain an index pattern, and searching the memory to find the reference pattern that best matches. Assuming that a good match is found, the associated action is executed. This system operates without the use of an explicit global model of the world, utilizing only locally available information. Such a system is potentially extremely robust and, moreover, is more easily analyzable than one based on a global model, since all the interactions are local in nature.

The performance of the system depends on the mapping, the recognition threshold, and the reference points. If the system is to home reliably, two basic conditions must be met. First, the parameters must be selected so that every point in the space of competence **C** of the observer generates an index pattern which matches one of the reference patterns, i.e.,

$$(\forall x \in \mathbf{C})(\exists y \in \mathbf{R})s(P_x, P_y) \geq t \qquad (1)$$

where s is the similarity previously defined, and P_x and P_y are the patterns corresponding to points x and y, respectively. Two points whose corresponding patterns have a similarity greater than or equal to the recognition threshold are said to be *similar*. For any point y in the reference set, the *recognition neighborhood* of y is defined as the largest connected set of points similar to y that contains y. Thus this condition simply states that the recognition neighborhoods of the set of reference points cover the desired domain of competence. Second, the index pattern for a point x should match a reference pattern with antecedent point y only if x and y are near each other in the motion space. More formally, there must exist a function $r(x)$, sufficiently small for all points, such that

$$(\forall x)(\forall y)s(P_x, P_y) \geq t \rightarrow d(x, y) < r(x), \tag{2}$$

where d is a distance measure on the motion space. r can be thought of as representing the desired accuracy of the system. This condition prevents misclassification of points. The underlying assumption is that the variety of features present in complex scenes will, in general, be sufficient to allow a particular scene to be uniquely identified. In practice, what will be shown is that the probability of misclassification is sufficiently small.

If these two conditions hold, and the appropriate actions are associated with the reference patterns, then the homing system is guaranteed to work in a static environment. If the probability of misclassification is nonzero but small, as will generally be the case in practice, then the system will work with high probability. In this case, the probability of error is bounded by the probability of making a misclassification on the path from the starting point to the goal. The situation is, in fact, significantly better since the locality of reference implies that the system can generally recover from the effects of an occasional misclassification.

The two equations given above and the nature of the homing problem impose specific constraints that can be used to guide the design of the pattern space. First, the patterns produced for viewpoints that are close to each other in terms of observer movement should be similar, since similar motions will probably be required. This ensures that the reference points generate meaningful recognition neighborhoods. Second, and conversely, the patterns produced at widely separated locations should be dissimilar since dissimilar motions will probably be necessary. Third, the pattern space must be large enough to hold the required number of viewpoints without impairing its "don't know" capacity. Fourth, the patterns should be relatively small in terms of the information required to describe them, since many will be stored. Thus, for example, storing the gray-level representation for the entire image would not be a good strategy. Finally, since the system is desired to work in real-world environments, the visual features chosen should be relatively insensitive to changes in lighting and to small perturbations in the physical environment.

A simple idea that satisfies these constraints fairly well, and that we used in our experiments, is to utilize patterns representing the dominant edge orientation in an array of receptive fields. The image is divided into a set of receptive fields (for example, a 5×5 grid of squares). Edges in the image are identified and classified into one of n (say 8) directions by an operator scaled so that, for well textured images, only a few edges run through each of the fields. The pattern consists of the vector representing the dominant edge orientation for each field.

Such patterns are concise, and edges are relatively stable features under changes in lighting. Since the dominant orientation is determined by a few edges in each receptive field, it takes a substantial change in observer position to move all of the edges out of their original fields. Thus the patterns change slowly under observer motion. The size of the pattern space also seems to be adequate. For example, if the patterns are vectors of length 25 with 8 possible values, and the recognition threshold is 50%, then the probability that two patterns chosen randomly from a uniform distribution will have a similarity $> t = 50\%$ is about 1.5×10^{-5}. For patterns of length 49 (corresponding to a 7×7 array of receptive fields) the value is about 5.5×10^{-10}. (These values can be computed from the cumulative binomial distribution.) Of course there is no guarantee that the patterns arising from real images will be uniformly distributed through this space. In fact, the existence of large-scale structure in the world would suggest otherwise; however, the scale of the probabilities suggests that there is enough room in the pattern space to deal with practical problems. The question of the actual distribution and the error probability in patterns taken from the real world is taken up in Section 2.4.

The method described here essentially depends on a comprehensive catalog. Though we believe that the most important aspect of the problem is the design of invariant mappings and concise patterns, there are a number of techniques that can (sometimes dramatically) reduce the problems involved in dealing with a large number of patterns. Physical search, multiresolution strategies, and dynamically activated, topological partitioned memory are all effective means of reducing the search space and the storage required. These should be used where appropriate.

2.4. ANALYSIS OF THE ASSOCIATIVE MEMORY

In the previous section, two equations were presented that established conditions under which the homing method could be expected to work. Informally stated, these conditions were first, that it be possible to store patterns corresponding to a set of reference points whose recognition neighborhoods cover the desired domain of competence, and second, that the probability of an index pattern being misclassified be sufficiently low. For a given pattern space and environment, there are two pieces of information that are critical to determining whether the conditions can be satisfied. The first is the size of the recognition neighborhoods. This will determine how many patterns must be stored to cover the desired domain of competence. The second is the probability p_f that two patterns corresponding to mutually distant points will match (i.e., have similarity $\geq t$). From these, the probability p_s of misclassification can be determined.

Recall that the recognition neighborhood of a reference point is the largest connected set of similar points containing it. In order to effectively design a training set, some estimate of the size and shape of the recognition neighborhoods (which may depend on position) must be obtained. One approach would be to determine average neighborhood size empirically, by comparing patterns at a large number of positions around each of a large number of reference points. However, for spaces of more than two dimensions, this is a lot of work. An alternative procedure would be to determine, either empirically or on the basis of knowledge about the features composing the patterns, the one-dimensional extent of the recognition neighborhood along each degree of freedom, and estimate the volume of the full neighborhood on the basis of these values. The naive formula would be to take the volume of the resulting n-dimensional rectangle, which corresponds to an n-ball in the motion space under a scaled max-length or chessboard metric. However, this ignores the cumulative effect of motion along different degrees of freedom, and produces an overly optimistic estimate of the volume. Use of a different metric can take this into account. It is shown below that, under reasonable assumptions, the recognition neighborhood will contain, in the worst case, an n-ball under an appropriately scaled sum or city-block metric, which corresponds to the n-dimensional analog of the octahedron.

To compute the volume of the recognition neighborhood, change in the motion space must be related to change in the pattern space. If the patterns are produced by a fixed resolution process, then the motion space can be ultimately decomposed into a finite (though large) number of connected cells within which the same pattern is produced. These will be referred to as *identity neighborhoods*. Consider a path l connecting points x and y in the motion space. If both the path l and the boundaries of the identity neighborhoods are piecewise differentiable, then l crosses a finite number of cell boundaries and, at each boundary, a finite number of features in the corresponding pattern change. Let $f_c(l)$ be the total number of feature changes that occur as the observer moves from x to y along l. The function f_c is valuable because it bounds the distance between the patterns corresponding to x and y. In particular, for all piecewise differentiable paths connecting x and y,

$$d_p(P_x, P_y) <= f_c(l) \tag{3}$$

where d_p is the number of locations at which the patterns differ.

Now assume that the effect of movement in each degree of freedom x_i can be characterized, at least locally, by a parameter c_i that specifies the expected number of feature changes per unit distance. Two points separated by $\Delta x = (\Delta x_1, \ldots, \Delta x_n)$ can be connected by a piecewise linear path $l_1, \ldots, l_n$ that changes one coordinate at a time. Because the parameters c_i are locally constant, the number of features that change in the pattern during movement is bounded, in the worst case, by the sum of f_c along each piece of the path, which by equation (3) also bounds the distance between the patterns. Thus the expected distance between patterns is bounded by the relation

$$E[d_p(P_x, P_{x+\Delta x})] <= \sum_{i=1}^{n} |\Delta x_i| c_i. \tag{4}$$

The recognition neighborhood is thus expected to contain an n-ball under an appropriately scaled city-block distance measure. In practice, the neighborhoods tend to lie somewhere between the worst-case city-block n-ball and the Euclidean n-ball.

As an example, consider an observer translating in two dimensions parallel to a flat patterned surface, and using the edge orientation pattern described previously. In this mapping, feature values tend to be dominated by a single strong edge, and will change when that edge moves out of the field. The diameter of the recognition neighborhood can thus be estimated by determining the motion that would, on the average, cause a fraction $1 - t$ of a randomly distributed set of points to move from their original fields. For translational motion, the decrease should be fairly linear; thus for a recognition threshold of 0.5, the recognition radius along each coordinate should correspond to a movement that causes the image to translate about halfway across the local receptive field.

The above situation can be easily simulated by windowing in a single large image. A series of tests was run using the four images shown in Figure 1. The pattern space utilized a 5×5 array of nonoverlapping receptive fields each 9×9 pixels with a recognition threshold of 0.5. For each image, results for 100 different positions were combined to obtain an idea of the typical behavior in the neighborhood of a reference point. The arrays shown in Figure 2 depict, for each image, the average recognition neighborhoods in the two-dimensional motion space. Unit distance corresponds to a motion that would cause an apparent motion in the image of one pixel. The symbol "□" indicates the location of the reference point and "+" indicates locations where the scene was recognized. Note that the shapes of the recognition neighborhoods fall between a diamond (city-block metric) and a circle (Euclidean metric). Also note that the radii, as predicted, are approximately the distance required to move the image halfway across the receptive field (here 4–5 units since a unit corresponds to a motion of one pixel).

Figure 1. Images used in statistical tests. (a) "Stone," (b) "Tree," (c) "Orchard," (d) "Storm."

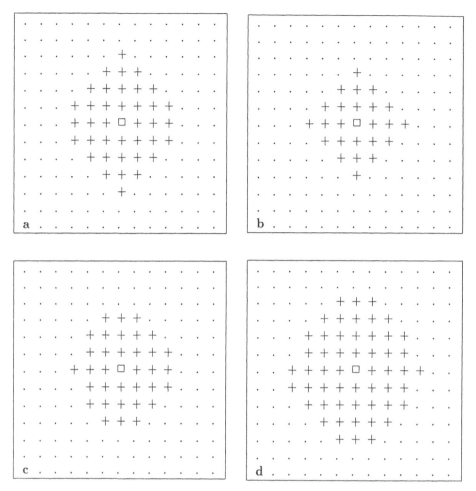

Figure 2. Average recognition neighborhoods for images of Figure 1. **a:** "Stone," **b:**"Tree," **c:**"Orchard," **d:** "Storm."

The shape of the recognition neighborhood becomes increasingly significant as the dimensionality of the motion space increases. Table 1 compares the volumes of the n-dimensional analogs to the octahedron, the sphere, and the cube, which correspond to n-balls in the city-block, Euclidean, and chessboard metrics. In two dimensions, a factor of two separates the worst-case city-block volume from the from the naive cubical volume; in six dimensions, it is approximately 700. The combination this effect with the exponential explosion of the space with increasing dimensionality implies that the required number of reference points becomes unmanageable very quickly for dimensions above three or four. Fortunately, three dimensions is sufficient to address many interesting navigational problems, and, as noted previously, there are techniques that can be used to reduce the effective dimensionality of the motion space.

The second problem is showing that the classification errors are unlikely. In particular, we want to show that if two points produce similar patterns, then, with

Table 1. Volume of n-balls of radius 1.

Dimension	city-block	Euclidean	chessboard
1	2	2	2
2	2	π	4
3	4/3	$4\pi/3$	8
4	2/3	$\pi^2/2$	16
5	4/15	$8\pi^2/15$	32
6	4/45	$\pi^3/6$	64

high probability, they are close together in motion space. Two patterns are said to match if they have a similarity greater than the recognition threshold t. Now consider a scalar function $r(x)$ on the motion space, which can be viewed as the desired accuracy of the system with respect to some distance metric d. If index pattern P_x and reference point P_y with antecedent points x and y match, i.e., $s(P_x, P_y) > t$), but $d(x, y) > r(x)$, then the match is said to be spurious. In such a case, the similarity is presumably due to chance rather than physical proximity of the antecedent points.

Using the function r, we can define precisely the probability of misclassification. Let x and y be an index point and a reference point respectively, and let P_x and P_y represent the corresponding patterns. Now let p_s represent the conditional probability that $d(x, y) \geq r(x)$ given that $s(P_x, P_y) > t$, where d is an appropriate metric, and s is the pattern similarity. In other words, p_s represents the probability that a given match is spurious. If it can be shown for a given r that

$$p_s < \mu \tag{5}$$

for some sufficiently small value μ, then a bound can be placed on the probability of the system making a navigational error due to misclassification of a pattern. The best possible result would be to show that the relation holds for values of r that are just slightly greater than the radius of the recognition neighborhood.

One way to show that (5) holds is to compute the "spurious match" probability p_s directly for a given r, and show that it is sufficiently low. Two values are needed to do this: a "near match" probability p_n, which is the probability that the patterns with antecedent points x and y will match given that $d(x, y) < r(x)$, and a "far match" probability p_f, which is the probability that the patterns will match given that $d(x, y) \geq r(x)$. In general, p_n is expected to be fairly large, and p_f very small. These values depend both on the structure of the pattern space and on the nature of the environment, and thus represent a real-world component in the analysis.

Consider an index-reference point pair (x, y) drawn from some distribution $\mathbf{D}$, with corresponding patterns P_x and P_y. Let $p_{d \geq r}$ be the unconditional probability that $d(x, y) \geq r(x)$) and $p_{d < r}$ be similarly defined. The spurious match probability p_s is just the conditional probability $p_{d \geq r}$ given that P_x and P_y match. Hence from Bayes' rule we have

$$p_s = \frac{p_f p_{d \geq r}}{p_f p_{d \geq r} + p_n p_{d < r}} = \frac{p_f (1 - p_{d < r})}{p_f (1 - p_{d < r}) + p_n p_{d < r}}. \tag{6}$$

In general, the region from which the points are drawn will extend over distances much larger than r. If $\mathbf{D}$ is at all close to a uniform distribution, then $p_{d<r}$ is small compared to 1. Thus p_s can be approximated by

$$p_s \approx \frac{p_f}{p_f + p_n p_{d<r}}. \tag{7}$$

Furthermore, in the anticipated event that p_s is small, p_f must be small with respect to $p_n p_{d \leq r}$. Thus the further approximation

$$p_s \approx \frac{p_f}{p_n p_{d<r}} \tag{8}$$

can be made.

The value of $p_{d<r}$ is given, in general, by an integral depending on $\mathbf{D}$ and the function r. Under the assumption of uniform $\mathbf{D}$, this is the ratio $\overline{v_r}/v_{\text{tot}}$, where $\overline{v_r}$ is the expected volume of a ball of radius r, and v_{tot} is the total volume of the region of interest. The near match probability in this case is the expected value of the ratio v_{rn}/v_r where v_{rn} is the volume of the recognition neighborhood about y. In general, r can be selected so that this ratio is approximately constant, in which case $p_n \approx \overline{v_{\text{rn}}}/\overline{v_r}$. Hence

$$p_s \approx \frac{p_f v_{\text{tot}}}{\overline{v_{\text{rn}}}}. \tag{9}$$

One interpretation of this is that the probability of misclassification by the system is approximately the minimum number of recognition neighborhoods required to cover the region of interest, times the probability of two patterns matching accidentally. This is more or less what would be expected intuitively.

It remains to determine a value for the "far probability" p_f which represents likelihood that the patterns for two points separated by a distance greater than r will match. The simplest approach is to assume that patterns for such points are both independent and uniformly distributed. In this case, p_f can be computed directly from the characteristics of the pattern space. The independence assumption is reasonable, since a pattern space that works well for the homing application tends to have this property. For example, in the edge-based pattern space discussed previously the long-range correlation of edges, at least in messy natural images, is fairly low. The assumption of uniform distribution is questionable, since it implies that there is also no short-range correlation of the features making up the pattern. It is certainly suspect for the edge-based space, since short-range correlation of edges will be found in almost any image. However, the value for p_f computed under the assumption of uniform distribution has value as a best-case screening test since p_f can not possibly be any smaller.

A uniform distribution of the edge-based pattern spaces we considered can be represented by vectors of n independent features, each of which can take on m values with equal probability. The probability that two patterns selected independently from such an ensemble will match in k or more positions is just the value of the cumulative binomial

$$\sum_{i=k}^{n} \binom{n}{i} (1/m)^i (1 - 1/m)^{n-i}. \tag{10}$$

Table 2 lists the value of this expression with $m = 8$ for a number of pattern lengths (n) and several similarity coefficients (k/n).

Table 2. Probability of $100k/n$ percent match between two random strings of length n over alphabet of size 8.

$100k/n$	Length of String				
	10	20	30	40	50
10%	7.4×10^{-1}	7.3×10^{-1}	7.4×10^{-1}	7.5×10^{-1}	7.6×10^{-1}
20%	3.6×10^{-1}	2.3×10^{-1}	1.6×10^{-1}	1.2×10^{-1}	8.8×10^{-2}
30%	1.2×10^{-1}	3.1×10^{-2}	9.0×10^{-3}	2.7×10^{-3}	8.6×10^{-4}
40%	2.7×10^{-2}	1.8×10^{-3}	1.4×10^{-4}	1.1×10^{-5}	9.3×10^{-7}
50%	4.4×10^{-3}	5.2×10^{-5}	6.8×10^{-7}	9.6×10^{-9}	1.4×10^{-10}
60%	5.1×10^{-4}	6.9×10^{-7}	1.1×10^{-9}	1.7×10^{-12}	2.9×10^{-15}
70%	4.0×10^{-5}	4.2×10^{-9}	4.9×10^{-13}	6.2×10^{-17}	8.0×10^{-21}
80%	2.1×10^{-6}	1.0×10^{-11}	5.8×10^{-17}	3.4×10^{-22}	2.1×10^{-27}
90%	6.6×10^{-8}	8.2×10^{-15}	1.1×10^{-21}	1.7×10^{-28}	2.5×10^{-3}

The table indicates that a great deal of space is available for modest-sized patterns and reasonable (e.g., 50%) recognition thresholds. Moreover, the match probability at a given recognition threshold decreases exponentially with increasing pattern size. Hence as long as additional features with some degree of independence can be added, there should be little trouble devising a pattern space of sufficient size for any particular problem, assuming that the features used are adequate in other respects.

As was mentioned above, the ensemble of patterns generated from a real environment is unlikely to be uniformly distributed, and consequently p_f tends to be higher than would be predicted from the above formula. Empirical estimates of p_f were obtained for edge-based pattern spaces by comparing large numbers of pattern generated from non-overlapping sets of image points. Tests were run on patterns consisting of 5×5, 6×6, and 7×7 arrays of local receptive fields for the tree, orchard, storm, and stone images used previously. Regions without visible features, such as uniform sky, were excluded from the analysis. The estimates are compared with each other and with the best-case uniform distribution probabilities in Table 3.

As expected, the match probabilities are higher than would be predicted from a uniform distribution, with the magnitude of the difference varying according to the image used. In general, the match probabilities are still low enough to be useful. For example, an edge-based pattern space utilizing a 7×7 array of receptive fields (49 features) would permit on the order of 10^4 reference patterns to be stored with only a small (1%) chance of misclassification. The table also illustrates the dramatic effect of a modest increase in the size of the pattern. Going from a 5×5 array to a 6×6 increases the storage requirements by less than 50%, but results in a

Table 3. Match probability for "unrelated" patterns.

Source	Size of Array		
	5×5	6×6	7×7
Uniform	1.5×10^{-5}	5.2×10^{-8}	5.5×10^{-10}
Stone	6.5×10^{-5}	3.6×10^{-6}	$< 10^{-6}$
Tree	5.2×10^{-5}	6.3×10^{-6}	3.3×10^{-6}
Orchard	2.8×10^{-5}	1.7×10^{-7}	$< 10^{-7}$
Storm	1.1×10^{-4}	$4.0 \times 10-6$	9.1×10^{-7}

10-fold or greater increase in the number of patterns that can be stored at a given misclassification probability.

As an example of how this information might be used, suppose that the motion space corresponds to two-dimensional translation at constant altitude with a downward looking observer over an environment where the vertical relief is relatively small compared to the altitude of the system. In order to make the results meaningful, suppose that the motion space is scaled so that one unit corresponds to a movement that will cause an image shift the diameter of the visual field. One unit of area in the motion space thus corresponds to a "camerafull." If the image contains 7×7 visual fields, the recognition neighborhood would be expected to have a diameter of about $1/7$ unit, and an area (if the worst-case city-block metric is assumed) of about $1/2 \times 1/7 \times 1/7 \approx 1/100$ square units. 10^4 reference points will thus permit a domain of competence corresponding to about 100 camerasfull. This is fairly sizable in a local sense. In concrete terms, it corresponds to learning about 4 square miles from an altitude of 1000 feet with a $60° \times 60°$ field of view. This may not seem like much, but we note that a homing system does not need to know about the whole environment in such detail. If the same information were used in a multiresolution mode or used to cover key regions in conjunction with a mechanism for selective attention, a considerably greater area could be covered.

2.5. Implementation and testing

The ideas presented here were tested experimentally using a mobile platform implemented by attaching a small CCD camera to a robot arm. The pattern association system utilizes edge-based patterns composed of 25 features, corresponding to the dominant edge direction in a 5×5 array of nonoverlapping receptive fields. The feature values specify either one of eight possible directions, or a "don't know" condition indicating insufficient information. The recognition threshold is set at 12 matches, i.e., approximately 0.5. The results of Section 2.4 indicate that this pattern space would be expected to have a p_f somewhere between 10^{-5} and 10^{-4}, which would permit on the order of 100 patterns to be stored with less than a 1% chance of spurious identification. This capacity was sufficient to permit the initial experiments to be successfully carried out. The array was scaled to cover the $35° \times 48°$ field of view, and thus is useful for homing at rather coarse resolution. If better ultimate resolution were required, a smaller subfield could be used for fine-tuning the position near the goal.

A system memory is created by moving the camera to each of a number of preselected reference points, taking a picture, and associating the corresponding pattern with the appropriate direction of motion or termination condition. Homing is accomplished by computing the pattern for the currently available scene, and comparing it against all those in memory to find the best above threshold match. If a directional code is associated with the winning reference pattern, an incremental move is made in the specified direction. If two successive goal-reached codes are encountered along an established direction of movement, the system halts. If no above-threshold match is found for the index pattern, an additional move is made in the previous direction in the hope of skipping over the "blind spot"; otherwise the system enters a random search.

As a test of the system, a model environment fancifully christened "Tinytown" was constructed using HO-scale scenery: trees, bushes, buildings, etc. (Figure 3). The robot was configured so that the camera pointed towards the "ground" and was constrained to move in a two-dimensional motion space parallel to the this ground plane. The resulting images thus simulate low-altitude aerial photographs. Figure 4 shows one such image and the results of various stages of processing. Figure 4a shows the original image, 4b a reduced resolution version, 4c the results of edge extraction, and 4d the 5×5 pattern of dominant edge directions.

Figure 3. Tinytown.

The model environment consists of about four camerasfull at the selected elevation. In order to exercise the ability of the system to deal with occasional unclassifiable patterns, a slightly coarse sampling grid was chosen for training. Approximately 120 reference points were needed to cover the two-dimensional motion space. A goal position was selected in which the camera was approximately centered over the model and the patterns corresponding to the 3×3 block of reference points

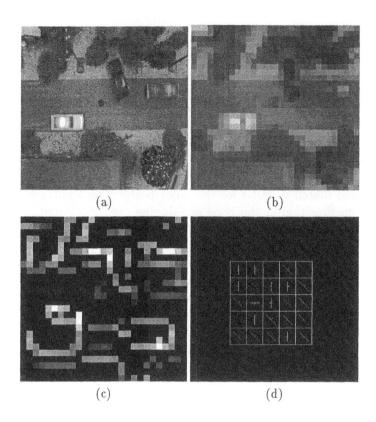

Figure 4. Processing steps in reducing image to pattern. (a) Original image, (b) reduced resolution image, (c) edge image, (d) pattern.

surrounding this positions were assigned goal-reached action codes. The rest of the reference patterns were assigned one of eight directional codes corresponding to the straight-line direction to the goal.

Figure 5 shows the results of testing the system on a grid with twice the sampling rate of the reference grid in a region surrounding the goal. The figure indicates the value of the action code determined for each point, or whether the pattern was unclassifiable. As expected, because of the coarse spacing of the reference points, a fair number of the points (about 25%) yield unclassifiable patterns. However, of the points where an action code was returned, only one has a value that would misdirect the system. This is consistent with the estimate mentioned at the beginning of this section, that the pattern space could result in a 1% spurious classification rate for 100 stored patterns. However, information provided by the memory, even with the coarse reference sample, is sufficient to permit the system to home reliably. Figure 6 shows a typical path taken by the system in returning from the periphery of the domain of competence to the goal. In this case, the step size was set to 0.7 times the sample spacing to prevent a misleading positive result. Note that the goal zone represents a fairly extensive region. If a more accurate final position is required, the above procedure would represent only the first step of a multiresolution process.

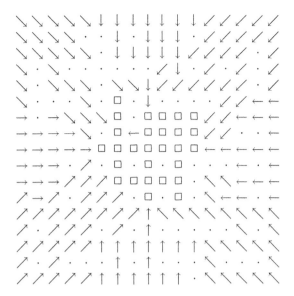

Figure 5. Results of testing associative memory for homing in Tinytown. The sampling interval is 1/2 inch, which subsamples the 1-inch grid of reference points. Arrows indicate direction of associated motion, squares a "goal reached" condition, and dots a "don't know" condition.

The above results support the position that an associative memory based on the principles presented can be used to implement visual homing, at least in domains where the movement of the observer is somewhat restricted. The results of the analysis and empirical experiments involving the storage of thousands of reference patterns described above are persuasive evidence that the system could be made to work in a more extensive environment. The only change necessary would be to use a slightly larger pattern, say one based on a 7×7 array of receptive fields, in order to provide more capacity in the pattern space.

Dealing with situations where the system can move with more than three degrees of freedom is a more difficult problem due to the combinatorial explosion of configurations. As noted previously, there are situations where a considerable amount can be accomplished without dealing with a high dimensional configuration space, but the question remains as to whether a more general strategy can be devised along the same lines. Of particular interest is the question of whether the technique can be adapted to handle situations involving large-scale rotational and scale changes. These same issues are also fundamental to the problem of 3D object recognition. As it turns out, attempting to adapt our technique to the more general situation leads directly to a method of 3D object recognition. This is described in the next section.

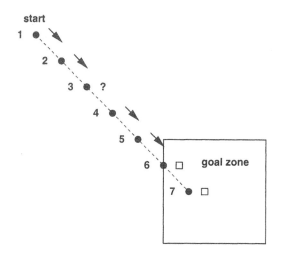

Figure 6. Typical path followed by robot. Numbers indicate the sequence of positions. The symbols indicate the action code recovered from the associative memory at each position. Arrows indicate a direction of movement, boxes a "goal reached" condition, and question marks a "don't know" condition.

3. Adaptation to Object Recognition

3.1. The visual recognition problem

Object recognition is probably the single most studied problem in machine vision. It is also one of the most ill defined. The standard intuitive definition typically involves establishing a correspondence between some internal model of an object, and 2D patterns of light produced by an imaging system. Attempts to formalize this notion, however, generally lead to problem statements that are either unsolvable, or so restrictive as to be practically useless. For example, a statement such as "the ability to determine which members of an arbitrary set of objects contributed to the formation of a particular image, with no restrictions on environment, viewpoint, or lighting" is easily shown to represent an impossible task. Highly restricted versions such as "the ability to distinguish single images of an arbitrary group of ten polyhedral shapes with fewer than 100 faces and differing from each other by at least distance x in shape metric Z taken from an arbitrary viewpoint given Lambertian reflectance, point illumination, isolated presentation, and at least N pixels on target" tend to be unsatisfying, and even these generally contain unresolvable instances that are not easy to characterize.

There remains a pervasive intuition, stemming from human subjective visual experience, that visual recognition works, and that the bad cases, even in the general statement, are somehow pathological. This leads to a belief that a problem statement of the sort "the ability to recognize an image of an arbitrary normal object from any natural viewpoint in any reasonable environment most of the time" is sensible. The difficulty, of course, is making scientific sense of words such as "normal," "natural," and "reasonable."

The operative word in the above paragraph is "works," because it leads to the question, "Works for what?" There is considerable evidence, from thirty years of research, that "what" is not arbitrary establishment of correspondences between abstract object models and images. One idea is to interpret "works" in the context of a particular problem or problem area. The subjective terms in the previous paragraph can then be given meaning. A natural viewpoint is thus one that is expected to occur in the context of the application, a normal object is one whose identification is important, and a reasonable environment is one in which the application must be carried out. We have called this a behavioral approach [33]. In this context, recognition appears less as a process of solving a geometric/optical puzzle and more as a matter of using sensory information to get at a stored state that permits the system to successfully interact with the environment, however success is defined. In other words, recognition is the evocation of memory.

Recognition as memory access. In this section, we take the position that the phenomenon of recognition, rather than representing the establishment of a correspondence between an object in the world and some abstract model, should be viewed as sensory keyed access to a memory that is part of a behaving system. The navigation system described in the last section is an example of just such a system. In this view, memory is any stored information that the system uses in order to interact competently with the world. Such information can be procedural, analogical, or declarative, and at any level of abstraction. Thus we view evoking a particular activity on the same level as accessing a stored picture of an object or producing a sentence describing a visual scene. All three examples use sensory data to evoke stored information that is behaviorally relevant to the situation.

Viewing recognition as a process of memory access has several advantages. First, it frees us from what might be called the tyranny of the model. What we are referring to are situations in which a predetermined notion about the representation drives the development of the system and its applications rather than the other way around. For example, observing that object boundaries in an image often occur as long, straight structures and noting the similarity to the mathematical concept of a line segment may be useful as far as it goes, but it does not imply that the next structuring element to try should be quadratic curves or ellipses. This is a prime example of false generalization from mathematics. A memory-based view does not, of course exclude the use of model correspondence, but neither does it restrict us to such a formalism if the application does not require it.

Second, taking a memory-based view can allow us to recognize and profit by relationships with other visual processes not generally thought of as recognition, for example, visual stabilization, and homing [34]. More generally, it provides a functional definition of recognition that ties in well with the behavioral notion of intelligence that has been gaining currency recently. It also provides a direct connection to learning and experience. Learning has traditionally been considered as orthogonal to recognition, which allowed the question of model acquisition to be finessed. If recognition is viewed as memory access, then the question of how the information in the memory was acquired and organized is substantially more immediate, forcing system designers to deal with it up front.

Finally, taking a memory-access approach forces us to develop a usable sensory-keyed memory architecture and access tools for it. The power and implications of such tools are not alway apparent at the outset. For example, during the development of the system described here, we needed an associative memory that could be keyed by different types of sensory input—the original idea being to make use of multiple feature types. It is widely believed that raw sensory input (e.g., individual pixels) is not likely to be an effective memory key, and hence the system we developed allowed for preprocessing of the sensory data. It was only after implementing the system that we realized that passing sense data through the associative memory was effectively preprocessing it, and the result could be fed back in as a key. This observation was the basis for the second-stage use of the associative memory as an evidence accumulator that we describe below, but the process is general. The idea of recurrent association is, in fact, well known both in psychology and classical AI, but we had not considered using it in this context until we had the tool in our hands.

Active vision. Addressing vision from the standpoint of behavior and memory is not a new idea. In fact, prior to the development of electronic computers, behavioral description was the only avenue available for investigating the phenomenon of vision. This precomputational work culminated in a series of books by Gibson [13, 14, 15], who advanced the central postulate that vision was essentially a modality that allowed biological systems to react to invariants in the structure of the world. What Gibson overlooked, however, was the complexity of computing the visual invariants used as primitives. The first influential theory of computational vision, due to [29], essentially defined vision as the problem of determining what is where, and focussed almost entirely on the computational and representational aspects of the problem. Marr's theory of vision essentially described a staged computational architecture leading from image, to primal sketch, to 2-1/2 D sketch, to invariant object centered descriptions. The processing hierarchy however, was static, and provided no structure for incorporating behavioral constraints. Moreover, the final, critical step, from 2-1/2 D image to object-centered representation, proved problematical, suggesting that something important was missing.

What distinguishes the recent interest in behavioral vision from the historical efforts is the commitment to establish it within a computational framework. The resurgence of interest in the behavioral aspects of intelligence is perhaps most clearly illustrated by the subsumption architecture proposed by Brooks [8, 9]. This paradigm is rather rigorously Gibsonian in that it explicitly disavows the notion of internal representation, relying instead on purely reactive strategies. The architecture works quite well for implementing low-level behaviors such as walking using simple sensors; however it now seems clear that higher level behaviors and more sophisticated sensory modalities such as vision, require some form of representation.

Recent work on active vision [2, 4, 5, 11] has focussed on how directed control of the sensor characteristics (e.g., eyes or tactile receptors) can simplify the process of obtaining the desired information. Most work to date has focussed on the effect of the ability to move the sensor [38, 51] or dynamically change an internal focus of attention [43]. Work on purposive or behavioral vision [1, 25, 32, 33] attempts to take the context of the task explicitly into account.

Approaches and problems. The most successful work to date in object recognition has been using model-based systems. Notable recent examples are [16, 21, 26, 28]. The 3D geometric models on which these systems are based are both their strength and their weakness. [17, 18]. On the one hand, explicit models provide a framework that allows powerful geometric constraints to be utilized to good effect. On the other, model schemas are generally severely limited in the sort of objects that they can represent, and obtaining the models is typically a difficult and time-consuming process. There has been a fair amount of work on automatic acquisition of geometric models, mostly with range sensors, e.g., [6, 22, 44], but also visually, for various representations [3, 7, 46, 48]. However, these techniques are limited to a particular geometric schema, and even within their domain, especially with visual techniques, their performance is often unsatisfactory.

Memory-based object recognition methods have been proposed in order to make recognition systems more general, and more easily trainable from visual data. Most of them essentially operate by comparing an image representation of object appearance against many prototype representations stored in a memory, and finding the closest match. They have the advantage of being fairly general, and often easily trainable. In recent work, Poggio has recognized wire objects and faces [10, 39]. Rao and Ballard [42] describe an approach based on the memorization of the responses of a set of steerable filters. Mel [30] takes a somewhat similar approach using a data base of stored feature vectors representing multiple low-level cues. Murase and Nayar [31] find the major principal components of an image dataset, and use the projections of unknown images onto these as indices into a recognition memory.

In general, memory-based methods have previously proven to be a useful technique; however, because matches are generally made to representations of complete objects, these methods tend to be more sensitive to clutter and occlusion than is desirable, and require good global segmentation for success. Hough transform methods (and other voting techniques), on the other hand, allow evidence from disconnected parts to be effectively combined, but the size of the voting space increases exponentially with the number of degrees of visual freedom. Difficulties deriving from the size of this space make it difficult to apply such techniques directly when more than about 3 DOF are involved, thus limiting the use of the technique for 3D object recognition, which generally involves at least 6 DOF.

3.2. THE METHOD

Overview. The method described here, by combining an associative memory with a Hough-like evidence combination technique, resolves both the clutter and occlusion sensitivity of traditional memory-based methods, and the space problems of voting methods for high DOF problems. The method is based on the two-stage use of a general purpose associative memory. This stores both semi-invariant, local objects called *keys* associated with object hypothesis, and object configuration hypotheses associated with evidence. What we describe here is the application of the technique to principle views recognition of rigid 3D objects, but the underlying principles are not dependent on rigid geometry.

In order to adapt the primitive recognition system used above for navigation to the more general recognition problem, we needed to make two basic modifications. The first is to make use of some form of segmentation or grouping procedure to obtain higher-level structures (though not whole objects, which is generally not feasible bottom up, in the presence of any significant clutter or occlusion). Such structures provide a handle to manage the combinatorial explosion of possible views as freedoms increase. We will call such structures *keys*. The second is to provide a method of evidence combination since individual matches at the level of extractable structures may no longer provide sufficient evidence for unambiguous identification. This is accomplished by making dual use of the associative memory.

To elaborate, we define a key to be any semi-invariant, robustly extractable, part or feature that has sufficient information content to specify a configuration of an associated object plus enough additional parameters to provide efficient indexing and meaningful verification. Configuration is a general term for descriptors that provide information about where in appearance space an image of an object is situated. For rigid objects, configuration generally implies location and orientation, but more general interpretations can be used for other object types. Semi-invariant means that over all configurations in which the object of interest will be encountered, a matchable form of the feature will be present a significant proportion of the time. Robustly extractable means that in any scene of interest containing the object, the feature will be in the N best features found a significant proportion of the time.

The basic idea is to utilize an associative memory organized so that access via a key feature evokes associated hypotheses for the identity and configuration of all objects that could have produced it. These hypothesis are fed into a second-stage associative memory, keyed by the configuration, which maintains a probabilistic estimate of the likelihood of each hypothesis based on statistics about the occurrence of the keys in the primary data base. The idea is similar to a multidimensional Hough transform without the space problems. In our case, since 3D objects are represented by a set of views, the configurations represent two-dimensional transforms.

The approach has several advantages. First, because it is based on a merged percept of local features rather than global properties, the method is robust to occlusion and background clutter, and does not require prior segmentation. This is an advantage over systems based on principal components template analysis, which are sensitive to occlusion and clutter. Second, entry of objects into the memory is an active, automatic procedure. Essentially, the system explores the object visually from different viewpoints, accumulating 2D views, until it has seen enough not to mix it up with any other object it knows about. Third, the method lends itself naturally to multimodal recognition. Because there is no single, global structure for the model, evidence from different kinds of keys can be combined as easily as evidence from multiple keys of the same type. The only requirement is that the configuration descriptions evoked by the different keys have enough common structure to allow evidence combination procedures to be used. This is an advantage over conventional alignment techniques, which typically require a prior 3D model of the object. Finally, the probabilistic nature of the evidence combination scheme, coupled with the formal definitions for semi-invariance and robustness, allows quantitative predictions of the reliability of the system to be made.

General associative memory. Our approach is based on an efficient associative memory. The basic operation we need is partial match association over heterogeneous keys. More specifically, we want a structure in which we can store and access (key, association) pairs where the key and association objects may be any of a number of disparate types. Associated with each object type employed as a key is a distance metric. The ideal query operation takes a reference key and returns all stored (key, association) pairs where the key is of the correct type and within a specified distance of the reference key in the appropriate metric. In practice, this ideal may have to be modified somewhat for efficiency reasons. In particular, highly similar association pairs may be merged in storage, and we may place a bound on the number of associations that are returned for any given query, or on the maximum separation that can be handled.

In the current implementation, the memory is just a large array of buckets each of which can hold a variable number of (key, association) pairs. This allows a number of different access schemes to coexist. In particular, hashing, array indexing, and tree search can all be implemented efficiently. Associated with each key type are functions defining a distance metric and a search procedure for locating keys in the memory. Thus if a certain key type has an efficient indexing method, it can be implemented for this type, rather than using a uniform but less efficient policy. This allows a large amount of flexibility in the system, and also permits new key types to be added efficiently in a modular fashion.

Key features. The recognition technique is based on the the assumption that robustly extractable, semi-invariant keys can be efficiently recovered from image data. More specifically, the keys must posses the following characteristics. First, they must be complex enough not only to specify the configuration the object, but to have parameters left over that can be used for indexing. Second, the keys must have a substantial probability of detection if the object containing them occupies the region of interest (robustness). Third, the index parameters must change relatively slowly as the object configuration changes (semi-invariance). Many classical features do not satisfy these criteria. Line segments are not sufficiently complex, full object contours are not robustly extractable, and simple templates are not semi-invariant.

A basic conflict that must be resolved is that between feature complexity and robust detectability. In order to reduce multiple matches, key features must be fairly complex. However, if we consider complex features as arbitrary combinations of simpler ones, then the number of potential high-level features undergoes a combinatorial increase as the complexity increases. This is clearly undesirable from the standpoint of robust detectability, as we do not wish to consider or store exponentially many possibilities. The solution is not to use arbitrary combinations, but to base the higher-level feature groups on structural heuristics such as adjacency and good con-

tinuation. Such *perceptual grouping* processes have been extensively researched in
the last few years.

The use of semi-invariance represents another necessary compromise. From a
computational standpoint, true invariance is desirable, and a lot of research has
gone into looking for invariant features. Unfortunately, such features seem to be
hard to design, especially for 2D projections of general 3D objects. We settle for
semi-invariance and compensate by a combination of two strategies. First, we take
advantage of the statistical unlikelihood of close matches for complex patterns (another advantage of relatively complex keys). Second, the memory-based recognition
strategy provides what amounts to multiple representations of an object in that the
same physical attribute of the object may evoke several different associations as the
object appears in different configurations. The semi-invariance prevents this number
from being too large. Possible keys for recognition of rigid 3D objects include robust contour fragments, feature normalized templates, keyed color histograms, and
normalized texture vectors.

The current system has been trained to recognize a set of 3D polyhedral objects
on the basis of their shape, using a set of 2D views as the underlying representation.
We have also trained the system in an essentially 2D recognition task involving more
curved objects. This particular context derives from a robot assembly system we are
implementing that servos off shape and geometric relationships between parts.

We tried two different key feature types for this application. The first is based
on chains of line segments, variously referred to in the literature as polylines or
supersegments. In particular, we first run a line segment finder on the image, and
then extract perceptual groups of three segments whose properties are consistent
with the hypothesis that they form a section of a 3D boundary. We call such groups
3-chains. The base segment of a 3-chain provides enough information to determine
the 2D configuration of any view of which it might be a part. In addition, associated
with each 3-chain are two angles and two length ratios, which are absolute invariants
for rigid 2D transformations, and semi-invariant for 3D rigid transformation of the
projected object.

The second key feature type is quite similar to the directional templates used
in the navigation application, and consisted of curve orientation templates normalized by robust curve fragments. We call these features *curve patches*. Specifically, a
curve-finding algorithm is run on an image, producing a set of segmented contour
fragments broken at points of high curvature. The strongest curves are selected as
normalizing base curves, and a fixed-size template constructed with the endpoints
of the base curve occupying canonical points in the template. All image curves that
intersect the normalized template are mapped into it with a code specifying their orientation relative to the base curve. Matching of a candidate template involves taking
the model key curve points and verifying that a curve point with similar orientation
lies nearby in the candidate template. (Essentially this amounts to directional correlation.) Note that these features are not limited to representing polyhedral objects,
although we have not yet compiled a data base of curved objects on which to test
the system.

3.3. RECOGNITION ALGORITHMS

The basic recognition procedure consists of four steps. First, potential key features are extracted from the image using low- and intermediate-level visual routines. In the second step, these keys are used to access the associative memory and retrieve information about what objects could have produced them, and in what relative configuration. The third step uses this information, in conjunction with geometric parameters factored out of the key features such as position, orientation, and scale, to produce hypotheses about the identity and configuration of potential objects. Finally, these hypotheses are themselves used as keys into a second-stage associative memory, which is used to accumulate evidence for the various hypotheses.

In the final step, an important issue is the method of combining evidence. The simplest technique is to use an elementary voting scheme—each piece of evidence contributes equally to the total. This is clearly not well founded, as a feature that occurs in many different situations is not as good an indicator of the presence of an object as one that is unique to it. An evidence scheme that takes this into account would probably display improved performance. The question is how to evaluate the quality of various pieces of evidence. An obvious approach in our case is to use statistics computed over the information contained in the associative memory to evaluate the quality of a piece of information. Having said this, it is clear that the optimal quality measure, which would rely on the full joint probability distribution over keys, objects and configurations is infeasible to compute, and we must use some approximation.

A simple example would be to use the first-order feature frequency distribution over the entire data base, and this is what we do. The actual algorithm is to accumulate evidence proportional to $\log(1 + 1/(kx))$ where x is the probability of making the particular matching observation as approximated from data base statistics, and k is a proportionality constant that attempts to estimate the actual geometric probability associated with the prediction of a pose from a key. The underlying model is that the evidence represents the log of the reciprocal of the probability that the particular combination of features is due to chance. The procedure used makes an independence assumption which is unwarranted in the real world, with the result that the evidence values actually obtained are serious overestimates if interpreted as actually probabilities. However, the rank ordering of the values is fairly robust to distortion due to this independence assumption. Since only the rank ordering enters into the decisions made by the system, we are more comfortable with the scheme than might be expected.

In the above discussion we have assumed that the associative memory already existed in the requisite form. However, one of the primary attractions of a memory-based recognition system is that it can be trained efficiently from image data. The basic process of model acquisition is simply a matter of providing images of the object to the system, running the key detection procedures on these images, and storing the resulting (key, association) pairs. The number of images needed may vary from one, for simple 2D applications, to several tens for rigid object recognition, and possibly more for complicated nonrigid objects. The process is efficient, and essentially runs in time proportional to the number of pairs stored in memory. This is in contrast to many learning algorithms that scale poorly with the the number of stored items. (Actually, indexed memory building process are apt to scale as $N \log(N)$, for very large numbers of items. However, since the processing for all data bases run so far is dominated by the key-feature extraction image processing, the complexity has essentially been linear.)

3.4. EXPERIMENTS

Using the principles described above, we implemented a memory-based recognition system for polyhedral objects using first 3-chains, and then curve patches as the basic keys. Component segments were extracted using a stick-growing method developed recently at Rochester [35], and organized into chains. A modified version of the same algorithm allowed us to extract curves as well. For objects entered into the data base, the best 10 key features were selected to represent the object. For the curve representation, the key curves were generally pretty straight, but the patch template representation still applies. The threshold on the distance metric between features was adjusted so that it would tolerate approximately 15-20 degrees deviation in the appearance of a frontal plane (less for oblique ones). The practical considerations leading to this selection were to allow the system to discriminate pentagons from hexagons without requiring more than about 50 views for an object.

We performed experiments using a set of 7 polyhedral objects from a child's toy. These are shown in Figure 7, and, from the top appear as a triangle, a square, a trapezoid, a pentagon, a hexagon, a star, and a cross. Note, however, that the objects are not simple prisms, but have an H-shaped cross section. This produces interesting edges and shadow effects when the objects are viewed from any angle other than straight down.

We obtained a training data base of approximately 150 views of these objects from different directions ranging from 12 for the hexagon, to 60 for the trapezoid, and covering all viewing angles except straight on from the side, since from that point of view a number of the objects are indistinguishable without measurements accurate to a few percent. The variation in the number of views needed is due to varying degrees of symmetry in the objects. All training images were acquired under normal room illumination, with the objects in isolation against a dark background. The training data base was used to compile a segment-based associative memory for recognition of the objects.

We then subjected the recognition system to a series of increasingly stringent tests. Recall that the geometric design of the geometric indexing system ensures invariance to 2D translation, rotation, and scale down to the point where there are insufficient pixels to provide a good estimate of segment attributes. Invariance to out-of-plane rotations is provided by the combination of slightly flexible match criteria for the key features coupled with multiple views. Robustness against clutter and occlusion is provided by the representation in terms of multiple features. The experiments were designed to test various aspects of this design.

A basic assumption made during these tests is that some other process has isolated a region of the image where a recognizable object may occur. We do not assume prior segmentation, but we do assume that only one or at most a few objects

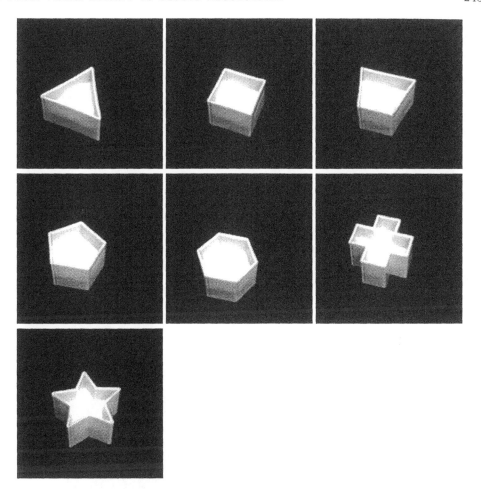

Figure 7. The polyhedral objects used in the test set.

of interest (as opposed to tens or hundreds) will occur in a window handed to the system. The system has a certain capability to state that it recognizes nothing in a window (don't know), and, in fact, tended to do this when given windows in which none of the known objects appeared. However, we have not statistically grounded this ability and hence the results reported here should be considered to be essentially forced-choice experiments.

The first test was simply to identify top down views of the objects, in various positions, scales, and rotations. This was essentially a test of the 2D invariance built into the geometry. The system was tested first with a reduced data base generated from 7 top down views (one for each object), and then with the full 3D data base, to ensure that the additional information stored did not produce enough cross-talk to interfere with the recognition. Object presentations were under ordinary room lighting, with the objects isolated against a dark background. The system performed as expected in both cases, with no mistakes.

For the second test, we acquired 14 additional views of the objects, two of each, again isolated against a dark background, and taken from viewpoints intermediate between the ones in the data base. The idea here is to test the 3D rotation invariance. No errors were made in the 14 test cases, even between similar objects such as the square and the trapezoid, or the pentagon and the hexagon, despite the fact that we had anticipated some confusion in these cases. These results alone allow us to say that the system is probably at least 90 percent accurate in situations of this type. Results from other tests lead us to believe that the actual performance is, in fact, somewhat better.

In the third test we took a number of images containing multiple objects viewed from modest angles (45 degrees or less from overhead) under normal lighting against a dark background. An example is shown in Figure 8. We then supplied the system with windows containing one object and parts of others. Since the system performs no explicit segmentation of its own, the intent of this experiment is to test robustness against minor clutter. Examples of the sort of windows passed to the system are shown in Figure 9. In twenty plus tests, we observed no errors due to clutter. We did have one failure, but it was due to an object in the image being too small for the segment finder to find good boundary sets. We also tried examples with two objects in the window. In this case, the system typically identified one of the objects, and when asked what else was there identified the second as well.

Figure 8. View of a group of objects.

The fourth experiment was a more severe clutter test. Here we took pictures of different objects held in a robot hand at various angles. Examples are shown in Figure 10. This was a harder problem for our system, and we obtained recognition rates on the order of 75 to 90 percent, with better performance being obtained with the curve patch keys. These experiments produced a significant number of failures. On analysis, we found that the primary reason for failure was not cross-talk in the memory caused by clutter, but poor performance of the low-level feature identification process caused by the added complexity in the image. Thus the memory index

Figure 9. A set of windows containing objects and minor clutter. The central object was correctly identified in all these cases.

has nothing to work on. Potential solutions involve improving the segment finder, which at present is strictly bottom up, and does no local grouping of its own, or using other features.

We also tested the system on a small data base containing objects with a mixture of curved and straight boundaries. These objects are shown in Figure 11. The objects themselves are three-dimensional, but the test problem was essentially two-dimensional as we did not develop a complete 3D data base. The chain-based keys failed completely in this case, giving results at the chance level. The presence of curved edges and rounded corners makes the segmentation into line segments sufficiently ill defined that stable chains are not robustly extractble in different views. The curve patch keys worked much better, giving results somewhere above 90%.

In the various tests, the curve patch keys generally performed as well as or better than the segment chains. This is as expected, since the the curve patches can represent all the features representable by segment chains, and some others as well. Also, since only a single segmented boundary fragment is needed to key a curve patch, features are less likely to be missed due to failure in the low-level segmentation. On a typical window containing one object plus clutter, the indexing process in the full database took a couple of seconds on a SPARC-1 for chains. The low-level processing could take a few tens of seconds, depending on the complexity of the image. The matching look longer for the patches, since it is more complex, but since the processing was generally dominated by feature extraction, the overall difference was not large.

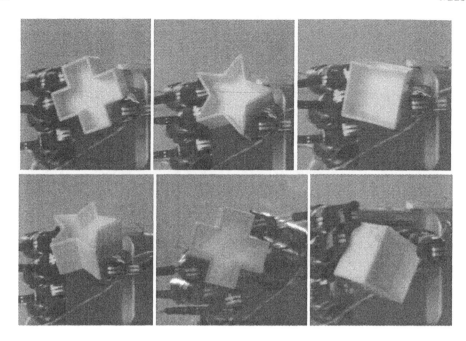

Figure 10. A set of windows containing objects held by a robot hand representing moderate clutter. The system successfully identified the object in all cases except the example in the lower right.

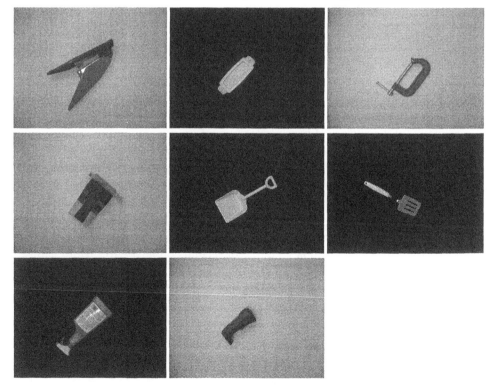

Figure 11. Set of objects containing curved boundaries.

4. CONCLUSIONS AND FUTURE DIRECTIONS

This paper began by describing an approach to the problem of visual homing based on the direct association of visual patterns with observer motions. The method relies on the existence of mappings that take images into a concise pattern space in such a way that the patterns corresponding to images from close pairs of points are similar, and the patterns corresponding to images from distant pairs are unlikely to be similar. It was shown that both the required number of reference points and the probability of error can estimated on the basis of the structure of the pattern space and measurable properties of the environment. A group of edge-based patterns was considered in detail. On the basis of empirical tests and theoretical analyses, it was concluded that a homing system using an edge-based pattern space is practical for performing accurate navigation in "fat" one- or two-dimensional spaces. Problems such as city street navigation and terminal docking can be put in this form. As a practical demonstration, the method was implemented using a camera mounted on a robot arm to navigate in a model environment.

Coarse orientation in several dimensions requires a modified strategy, and investigation of methods needed to achieve this led to a general strategy for memory-based object recognition. Two essential modifications were needed in order to accomplish this: the use of grouping or segmentation processes to provide normalization, and multistage use of the associative memory in order to combine evidence. We illustrated the concept by implementing a memory-based recognition system for 3D polyhedral objects using chains of line segments and curve patches as memory keys. The system actually performs quite well for a small data base of 3D shapes, and exhibits a certain amount of robustness against clutter and occlusion. When the algorithm fails, it is not due to cross-talk in the memory, but to failure of the low-level processes to extract robust features. We are currently engaged in embedding the system into a robotic manipulation system that we will use for assembly tasks.

Future directions include more extensive testing of the keys based on boundary curves to identify non-polyhedral objects. This involves assembling and testing on a large database of distinct curved objects. We also plan to incorporate multimodal features into the data base, including color and texture as well as shape information. We anticipate that this will give us a capability to recognize less well structured objects such as leaves or clothing in addition to objects having a strictly defined shape.

REFERENCES

1. J. Y. Aloimonos, "Purposive and qualitative active vision," in *Proc. Image Understanding Workshop*, 1990, 816–828.

2. J. Aloimonos, I. Weiss, and A. Bandopadhay, "Active vision," *International Journal of Computer Vision* **2**, 1988, 333–356.

3. N. Ayache and O. Faugeras, "Hyper: A new approach for the recognition and positioning of two-dimensional objects," *IEEE Transactions on Pattern Analysis and Machine Intelligence* **8**(1), January 1986, 44–54.

4. D.H. Ballard, "Reference frames for animate vision," in *Proceedings of the International Joint Conference on Artificial Intelligence*, August 1989, 1635–1641.

5. D.H. Ballard and C.M. Brown, "Principles of animate vision," *CVGIP: Image Understanding*, Special Issue on Purposive, Qualitative, Active Vision, Y. Aloimonos (Ed.), **56**, 1992, 3–21.

6. A.F. Bobick and R.C. Bolles, "Representation space: An approach to the integration of visual information," in *Proceedings of the IEEE Computer Society Conference on Computer Vision and Pattern Recognition*, San Diego, CA, June 1989, 492–499.

7. R.C. Bolles and R.A. Cain, "Recognizing and localizing partially visible objects: The local-features-focus method," *International Journal of Robotics Research* **1**(3), Fall 1982, 57–82.

8. R.A. Brooks, "Achieving artificial intelligence though building robots," Technical Report TR 899, MIT, 1986.

9. R.A. Brooks, "A robust layered control system for a mobile robot," *IEEE Journal of Robotics and Automation* **2**, April 1986, 14–23.

10. R. Brunelli and T. Poggio, "Face recognition: Features versus templates," *IEEE Transactions on Pattern Analysis and Machine Intelligence* **15**(10), 1993, 1042–1062.

11. P.J. Burt, "Smart sensing within a pyramid vision machine," *IEEE Procedings* **76**(8), 1988, 1006–1015.

12. M. Daily, J.G. Harris, and K. Reiser, "An operational perception system for cross-country navigation," in *Proceedings of the DARPA Image Understanding Workshop*, Cambridge, MA, April 1988, 568–575.

13. J.J. Gibson, *The Perception of the Visual World*, Houghton Mifflin, Boston, 1950.

14. J.J.Gibson, *The Senses Considered as Perceptual Systems*, Houghton Mifflin, Boston, 1966.

15. J.J.Gibson, *The Ecological Approach to Visual Perception*, Houghton Mifflin, Boston, 1979.

16. W.E.L. Grimson, *Object Recognition by Computer: The Role of Geometric Constraints*, MIT Press, Cambridge, MA, 1990.

17. W.E.L. Grimson and D.P. Huttenlocher, "On the sensitivity of geometric hashing," in *Third International Conference on Computer Vision*, 1990, 334–338.

18. W.E.L. Grimson and D.P. Huttenlocher, "On the sensitivity of the Hough transform for object recognition," *IEEE Transactions on Pattern Analysis and Machine Intelligence* **12**(3), 1990, 255–274.

19. M. Hébert and T. Kanade, "3-D vision for outdoor navigation by an autonomous vehicle," in *Proceedings of the DARPA Image Understanding Workshop*, Cambridge, MA, April 1988, 593–601.

20. E.C. Hildreth, *The Measurement of Visual Motion*, MIT Press, Cambridge, MA, 1983.

21. D.P. Huttenlocher and S. Ullman, "Recognizing solid objects by alignment with an image," *International Journal of Computer Vision* **5**(2), 1990, 195–212.

22. R. Kjeldsen, R.M. Bolle, and D. Sabbah, "Primitive shape extraction from range data," in *Proceedings of the IEEE Workshop on Computer Vision*, Miami, FL, November-December 1989, 324–326.

23. T. Kohonen, *Associative Memory—A System Theoretic Approach*, Springer, New York, 1977.

24. T. Kohonen, *Content-Addressable Memories*, Springer, New York, 1980.

25. K.N. Kutulakos and C.R. Dyer, "Recovering shape by purposive viewpoint adjustment," in *Proceedings of the IEEE Computer Society Conference on Computer Vision and Pattern Recognition*, Champaign, IL, June 1992, 16–28.

26. Y. Lamdan and H.J. Wolfson, "Geometric hashing: A general and efficient model-based recognition scheme," in *Proceedings of the International Conference on Computer Vision*, Tampa, FL, December 1988, 238–249.

27. S. Levitt, D.T. Lawton, D.M. Chelberg, K.V. Koitzsch, and J.W. Dye, "Qualitative navigation II," in *Proceedings of the DARPA Image Understanding Workshop*, Cambridge, MA, April 1988, 319–326.

28. D.G. Lowe, "Three-dimensional object recognition from single two-dimensional images," *Artificial Intelligence* **31**, 1987, 355–395.

29. D.C. Marr, *Vision*, W.H. Freeman and Co., San Francisco, 1982.

30. B. Mel, "Object classification with high-dimensional vectors," in *Proceedings of the Telluride Workshop on Neuromorphic Engineering*, Telluride, CO, July 1994.

31. H. Murase and S.K. Nayar, "Learning and recognition of 3D objects from appearance," in *Proceedings of the IEEE Workshop on Qualitative Vision*, 1993, 39–50.

32. R.C. Nelson, "Qualitative detection of motion by a moving observer," *International Journal of Computer Vision* **7**(1), November 1991, 33–46.

33. R.C. Nelson, "Vision as intelligent behavior: Research in machine vision at the University of Rochester," *International Journal of Computer Vision* **7**(1), November 1991, 5–9.

34. R.C. Nelson, "Visual homing using an associative memory," *Biological Cybernetics* **65**, 1991, 281–291.

35. R.C. Nelson, "Finding line segments by stick growing," *IEEE Transactions on Pattern Analysis and Machine Intelligence* **16**(5), May 1994, 519–523.

36. R.C. Nelson and J. Aloimonos, "Finding motion parameters from spherical motion fields (or the advantages of having eyes in the back of your head)," *Biological Cybernetics* **58**, 1988, 261–273.

37. R.C. Nelson and J. Aloimonos, "Using flow field divergence for obstacle avoidance in visual navigation," in *Proceedings of the DARPA Image Understanding Workshop*, Cambridge, MA, April 1988, 548–567.

38. T.J. Olson, D.J. Coombs, and C.M. Brown, "Gaze control and segmentation," in *Proceedings of the AAAI Qualitative Vision Workshop*, Boston, August 1990.

39. T. Poggio and S. Edelman, "A network that learns to recognize three-dimensional objects," *Nature* **343**, 1990, 263–266.

40. D. Pomerleau, "Neural network based autonomous navigation," in C.E. Thorpe (Ed.), *The Carnegie-Mellon Navlab*, Kluwer, Dordrecht, 1990.

41. K. Prazdny, "Determining the instantaneous direction of motion from optical flow generated by a curvilinear moving observer," *Computer Vision and Graphical Image Processing Journal* **22**, 1981, 238–248.

42. R.P.N. Rao, "Top-down gaze targeting for space-variant active vision," in *Proceedings of the ARPA Image Understanding Workshop*, Monterey, CA, November 1994, 1049–1058.

43. R.D. Rimey and C.M. Brown, "Where to look next using a bayes net: Incorporating geometric relations," in *Proceedings of the Second European Conference on Computer Vision*, May 1992, 542–550.

44. F. Solina and R. Bajcsy, "Recovery of parameteric models from range images," *IEEE Transactions on Pattern Analysis and Machine Intelligence* **12**, February 1990, 131–147.

45. C. Stanfill and D. Waltz, "Towards memory-bases reasoning," *Communications of the ACM* **29**, 1986, 1213–1228.

46. F. Stein and G. Medioni, "Efficient 2-dimensional object recgnition," in *Proceedings of the International Conference on Pattern Recognition*, Atlantic City, NJ, June 1990, 13–17.

47. S. Ullman, *The Interpretation of Visual Motion*, MIT Press, Cambridge, MA, 1979.

48. S. Ullman and R. Basri, "Recognition by linear combinations of models," *IEEE Transactions on Pattern Analysis and Machine Intelligence* **13**, 1991, 992–1006.

49. A. Waxman, "Image flow theory: A framework for 3-D inference from time varying imagery," in C.M. Brown (Ed.), *Advances in Computer Vision*, Lawrence Erlbaum Associates, Hillsdale, NJ, 1987.

50. A. Waxman, J. LeMoigne, L. Davis, E. Liang, and T. Siddalingaiah, "A visual navigation system for autonomous land vehicles," *IEEE Journal of Robotics and Automation*, 1987.

51. D. Wilkes and J. Tsotsos, "Active object recognition," in *Proceedings of the IEEE Computer Society Conference on Computer Vision and Pattern Recognition*, Champaign, IL, June 1992, 136–141.

PLANNING AND NAVIGATION IN STOCHASTIC ENVIRONMENTS

Thomas Dean and Jean-Luc Marion
Brown University

ABSTRACT

This chapter is concerned with modeling robot navigation problems involving uncertainty as discrete-time and -state dynamical systems represented by stochastic automata. Solving navigation problems is reduced to computing policies for Markov decision processes. Classical methods for solving Markov decision processes cannot cope with the size of the state spaces for typical navigation problems. As an alternative, we investigate methods that decompose large global navigation problems into a number of smaller local problems, solve the local problems separately, and use solutions to local problems in order to construct solutions to global problems. The methods described in this chapter efficiently generate competitive solutions to problems without the use of procedures that require repeated quantification over the entire state space.

1. INTRODUCTION

In general, planning of any sort and path planning for navigation in particular benefit from a global perspective. In order to find a good solution you have to stand far enough back to anticipate problems that are not obvious when the problem is considered from a more local perspective. At the same time, you cannot ignore the details that are apparent from taking a closer look. Keeping track of all the details at once, however, can make planning computationally complex.

In planning a long trek through the mountains you have to use a global perspective to pick out a convenient pass through a range of steep peaks while at the same time using a local perspective to anticipate the consequences of traversing difficult terrain. In this chapter, we consider methods for representing planning problems at different levels of abstraction to support both global and local perspectives.

We represent the continuous world in terms of discrete states and actions that move an agent from one state to another. We introduce a model that enables us to estimate the costs and benefits of various courses of action accounting for uncertainty in their outcomes. During the past two decades, the problem of robot navigation has been studied extensively; however, most of the research has focused on the motion planning of a perfect robot in a perfect environment.

In navigation problems there are two important sources of uncertainty. First, there is uncertainty in sensing; for example, when you make an observation of a nearby mountain peak and mistake it for another peak some distance away. Second, there is uncertainty in control. Actions do not always have their intended effects; for example, you may try to traverse a given rock face only to discover it impassable, forcing you to take a lower path on the mountain. We focus almost exclusively on uncertainty in control in this chapter. This would be the case for a robot with a global positioning device and a detailed map.

Figure 1. Modeling produces a dynamical model useful for prediction. Evaluation produces a performance criterion. Planning produces a policy for action. Execution produces a particular behavior.

By way of example, suppose that we are interested in air travel planning as illustrated in Figure 1. We divide the process of decision making into four stages, *modeling*, *evaluating*, *planning*, and *executing*. Modeling is the process of generating a *dynamical model* of the environment including descriptions of actions, states and their associated uncertainties. This model is used to predict the outcomes of various courses of action.

In the case of air travel planning, a model might be generated from airline flight schedules and statistics regarding actual flight arrival and departure times. In navigation problems, spatial considerations are important, but there are generally other considerations that affect performance. In air travel planning, the weather, time of day, and day of the week significantly affect travel time.

Evaluation is the process of establishing the value of outcomes. The result of evaluation is a *performance criterion*. For example, we might wish to travel to Boston and Chicago starting in Los Angeles, minimizing the overall travel time. Planning is the process of choosing among various courses of action. The result of planning is called a *policy*. In Figure 1, a policy is represented as a book in which the decision making agent can look up the appropriate action to take depending on its current state. Finally, executing a policy results in a particular *behavior*.

Figure 2. Abstract (aggregate) states and abstract actions corresponding to local policies.

To simplify planning with a dynamical model involving a large number of states, we might partition the model into smaller regions and for each of the smaller regions plan routes and consider the potential hazards of traversing those regions. The regions are called abstract or *aggregate* states and the abstract actions for moving between aggregate states correspond to local policies. Figure 2 illustrates the case in which the map of the United States is partitioned into aggregate states corresponding to geographical states (e.g., Oregon, Washington, Kansas). For each geographical state there is a separate policy, indicating which action (flight) to take when in a particular city trying to get to some other city.

Given two or more abstract actions for each aggregate state, abstract decision making amounts to choosing from among the alternative abstract actions. For instance, there might be several policies for moving about in Boston as illustrated in Figure 3, each policy indicating a concrete action to take depending on the circumstances that the decision making agent finds itself in.

We can apply this process of abstraction recursively to obtain a hierarchy of abstractions as shown in Figure 4. A policy for a given level of abstraction provides a mapping from abstract states (at the given level of abstraction) to abstract actions (at the same level of abstraction). Each abstract action (recursively) maps abstract states at the next (more concrete) level of abstraction to abstract actions at that level of abstraction, until finally we arrive at the most concrete level of description

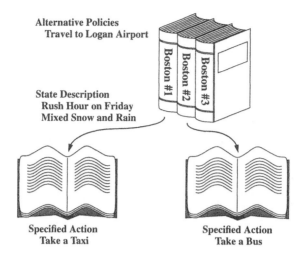

Figure 3. Choosing among alternative abstract actions corresponding to local policies.

and the recursion bottoms out.

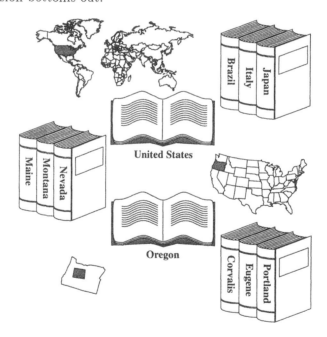

Figure 4. A schematic example of a hierarchical partition involving countries, states, and counties.

In this chapter, we consider a very general method for constructing abstractions to aid in planning. We proceed using a state-space approach and casting the problem in terms of control. We motivate the use of discrete state representations for navigation problems. We address the uncertainty in control through the use of Markov decision processes. Finally, we investigate a particular method for decomposing dynamical models with very large state spaces that appears promising for navigation problems.

2. DISCRETE DYNAMICAL SYSTEMS

A *dynamical system* is a mathematical model of how one entity called *controller* interacts with a second entity called *plant* or *environment*. A description of the controller and its environment at a particular instant of time is referred to as the *state* of the system and the set of all possible such states is called the *state space* of the dynamical system. Dynamical systems are used to predict the behavior of controllers or to design new controllers to exhibit a particular, desired behavior.

The state is only as detailed as is required for modeling purposes. Robots with rigid components connected by rotating and sliding joints are often modeled using a state space determined by the freedom of their joints to move about without hitting obstacles in the surrounding environment. This state space is called *configuration space* because it corresponds to the possible configurations of the robot in terms of the positions and relative angles of its constituent parts [20].

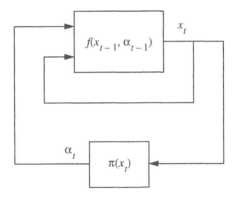

Figure 5. A dynamical system modeling a controller embedded in a dynamic environment in the fully observable case.

Let Ω_X denote the state space of the dynamical system and Ω_A the space of actions available to the controller. Let $f : \Omega_X \times \Omega_A \to \Omega_X$ represent the state transition function and $\pi : \Omega_X \to \Omega_A$ the operation of the controller. Figure 5 illustrates the relationship between the controller and the environment in which it is embedded. Figure 5 depicts the case in which the controller can directly observe the state of the environment. This is referred to as the *fully observable* case and the resulting decision problem is called a fully observable problem (or process).

In many navigation problems, the controller will not be able to directly observe the complete state of environment. This is referred to as the *partially observable* case and the resulting decision problem is called a partially observable problem (or process). Let Ω_Y denote the set of possible observations and $h : \Omega_X \to \Omega_Y$ a function that determines what the controller can observe in a given state. We add another component to the controller called an *observer* whose task it is to try to recover the actual state (or at least those aspects useful for navigation purposes) from observation. Let $\sigma : \Omega_Y \to \Omega_X$ represent the observer.

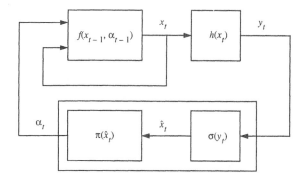

Figure 6. A dynamical system modeling a controller embedded in a dynamic environment in the partially observable case.

Figure 6 illustrates the relationships involving f, h, σ, and π. The observer outputs its best guess for the current state, $\hat{x}$, which is input to the controller as if it were the actual state, and the controller outputs an action accordingly.

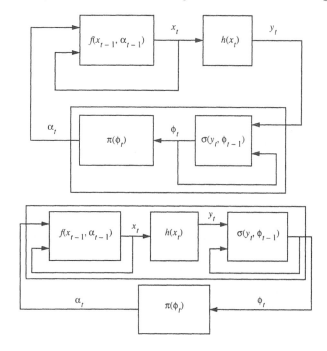

Figure 7. A dynamical system illustrating the role of informational states (top) and the system repackaged as a fully observable process (bottom).

In some cases, the best guess regarding the current state is not sufficient for the controller to generate an appropriate action. We can modify σ and π so that σ takes the current observation and returns a distribution over Ω_X that summarizes its information regarding the state of the dynamical system. The set of all such distributions over Ω_X is called an *informational* state space and denoted Ω_Φ. It is straightforward to construct an optimal observer that can compute a sufficiently detailed summary of its informational state given the current observation and the last informational state. Using this optimal observer, we can transform the original partially observable problem involving the original state space into a fully observable problem involving the informational state space [19, 21, 25]. The top diagram in Figure 7 shows a partially observable process with an embedded optimal observer. The bottom diagram in Figure 7 repackages the components of the top diagram to construct a new transition function composed from f, h, and σ, that results in a fully observable process.

The transformation from state space to informational space might not appear to be advantageous. In general, if we begin with a finite state space, then we end up with a continuous informational space that has dimensionality the same as the size of the original state space. In some cases, however, we can considerably simplify the resulting informational space.

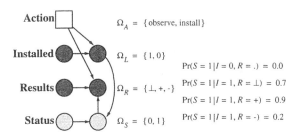

Figure 8. A simple partially observable planning problem.

Figure 8 graphically depicts the decision problem faced by an embedded controller on each tick of the clock. At time t, the controller can observe whether a particular device is installed or not. The controller can also observe the results, $\perp$, $+$, or $-$, of a particular test it is able to perform. The controller cannot observe the status, 0 or 1, of the device and so the problem is only partially observable. If the device has not been installed, then it doesn't matter what the test results are, the probability that the status is 1 is zero. If the device has been installed and results are $\perp$, indicating that the test has not yet been performed on the installed device, then the probability that the status is 1 corresponds to a prior probability, 0.7. If the test returns $+$ then the posterior probability is 0.9, and if the test returns $-$ then the posterior probability is 0.2. The test is deterministic and so it does no good to repeat the test.

Figure 9 shows the decision problem that results from converting the partially observable variable corresponding to the device's status, into the fully observable informational state variable corresponding to the probability that the status of the device is 1. Note that the resulting decision problem is fully observable and that the resulting informational state space is finite, and not a great deal larger than the original state space. We use this method of transformation as a (somewhat) weak excuse for ignoring issues of observability in the remainder of this paper. At the same

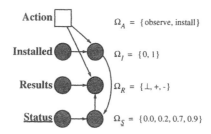

Figure 9. A fully observable planning problem obtained by transforming the original state space into an informational state space.

time, we admit that in some cases such transformations can considerably increase the size of the state space, thus wreaking computational havoc.

The state space for a simple mobile robot interacting with a structured environment such as office building might be modeled as a continuous, three-dimensional, Euclidean space. However, this same environment might also be modeled as a finite number of discrete locations. If the robot can execute commands such as "traverse the corridor" or "turn left at the next junction," then the discrete representation may be entirely appropriate for designing a navigation system for a robot that delivers mail or empties trash. In this chapter, we focus exclusively on such discrete dynamical systems. We also concentrate on *clocked* systems in which the state of the system changes on a fixed, regular interval of time. This last requirement can be relaxed, but the assumption of a clocked system considerably simplifies the discussion.

The purpose of a navigation system for a robot is to issue a sequence of commands to the robot hardware in order to achieve a goal such as moving the robot from some initial location to some final location. In some cases, commands are issued in an *open loop* with the navigation system issuing a command on each tick of the clock without observing the current state of the system. In the cases we consider, however, commands are issued in a *closed loop* with the navigation system issuing a command on each tick based on current state of the system.

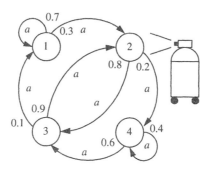

Figure 10. State transition diagram for a simple Markov process.

The deterministic variant of a discrete dynamical system can be represented as a graph called a *state transition diagram* in which the vertices are locations or possible configurations of the robot embedded in its environment. The edges of the state transition diagram are simple local motion strategies that allow the robot to move from one cell to an other. In order to model uncertainty in control, we use a stochastic variant of a finite state automaton called a *Markov process*. The state transition diagram for a simple Markov process is shown in Figure 10; arcs are labeled with the action taken and the probability that the action will take the robot to the state that the arc points to.

In the following sections, we define the underlying mathematical objects more carefully, but for the time being suffice it to say that the next state in a Markov process is governed by a probability distribution that depends only on the current state. In terms of a robot maneuvering in an office environment, 90% percent of the time when the navigation system issues a command to turn left at the next intersection, the robot executes the command as requested, but 10% of the time it misses the turn and ends up going straight ahead. In the following sections, we consider how to formulate the general problem of generating closed-loop control laws for discrete dynamical systems modeled as Markov processes, but first we consider the notion of abstraction a little more carefully.

3. ABSTRACTION AND DECOMPOSITION

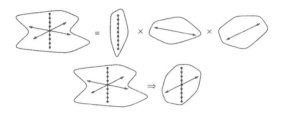

Figure 11. Three-dimensional state space for a robot navigation problem (top) and a two-dimensional abstraction of that space (bottom).

Abstraction amounts to ignoring distinctions. For instance, we might abstract a three-dimensional space by projecting it onto two dimensions, thereby ignoring the third dimension. Consider a mobile robot navigation problem modeled using three dimensions, location L, battery level B, and illumination I. L might take on one of a finite number of discrete locations, while B and I might be real-valued. In the top graphic in Figure 11, the resulting state space is shown as a product of possible values for L, B, and I. For a robot that uses sonar, illumination may be irrelevant for navigation purposes and so the abstract two-dimensional space shown on the bottom in Figure 11 and obtained by projecting out illumination may be just as effective as the three-dimensional space for planning purposes.

Decomposition involves dividing up a space into subspaces. Figure 12 graphically distinguishes between abstraction and decomposition. We assume that all of the dimensions are relevant in at least some portion of the state space and so the dimensionality of the problem cannot be reduced without suffering some loss in performance. However, it is very likely that not all dimensions are relevant in all portions of the state space. For a robot that uses infrared sensors, strong sunlight can be a problem, but for a delivery robot in an office building, only those areas with large south-facing windows may pose a real hazard.

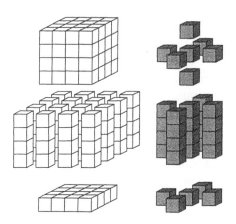

Figure 12. Original detailed model (top), decomposed model (middle), and abstracted model (bottom).

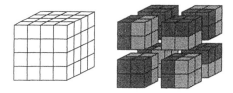

Figure 13. Three-dimensional space represented in terms of two-dimensional subspaces (shaded darker).

In the best of all worlds, we might partition the state space into regions such that in each region only a small number of dimensions are relevant in any given region. Figure 13 illustrates how a three-dimensional state space might be represented as the union of two-dimensional abstract subspaces. Even if such region-by-region dimensionality reduction is not possible, decomposition can still be an effective strategy for coping with complexity. By partitioning the state space into regions, we may be able to construct a policy in each region independent of all but a few neighboring regions.

4. MARKOV DECISION PROCESSES

Let $M = (\Omega_X, \Omega_A, p, c)$ be a Markov decision process with finite state space Ω_X, actions Ω_A, state transition matrix p, and cost matrix c. Let $\Omega_X = \{1, 2, \ldots, N\}$. X_t (A_t) is a variable indicating the state (action) at time t.

$$p_{ij}(a) = \Pr(X_t = j | X_{t-1} = i, A_{t-1} = a)\, i, j \in \Omega_X\ a \in \Omega_A$$
$$c_{ij}(a) = \mathrm{C}(X_t = j | X_{t-1} = i, A_{t-1} = a)\, i, j \in \Omega_X\ a \in \Omega_A$$

where $\Pr(.|.)$ is a conditional probability distribution and $\mathrm{C}(.|.)$ is a real-valued cost function. A *policy* π is a function mapping states to actions $\pi : \Omega_X \to \Omega_A$.

To completely define a Markov decision process we also need a performance criterion. Two criteria that we consider are *expected discounted cumulative cost* and *expected cost to reach a specified goal.* In the former, the task is to find a policy minimizing the expected cumulative cost function,

$$E_\pi(\Sigma_\gamma|i) = \sum_{j \in \Omega_X} p_{ij}(\pi(i)) [c_{ij}(\pi(i)) + \gamma E_\pi(\Sigma_\gamma|j)]$$

for all $i \in \Omega_X$ where $0 < \gamma < 1$ is the *discount rate*, Σ_γ represents the discounted cumulative cost, and $E_\pi(.|.)$ denotes an expectation with respect to the policy π. For the criterion of expected cost to reach a specified goal, a subset of Ω_X is designated as a target and performance is measured as the expected cost until arriving in some target state. Informally, we can model each target state as a sink (all transitions out have probability zero, $p_{ij \neq i}(a) = 0$) and proceed as in the case of expected discounted cumulative cost but with $\gamma = 1$.

We mention two standard methods for solving Markov decision processes. Bellman's value iteration method [2] iterates by computing the optimal expected cumulative cost function accounting for n steps of lookahead using the optimal expected cumulative cost function accounting for $n - 1$ steps of lookahead. Value iteration is guaranteed to converge in the limit to the optimal expected cumulative cost function accounting for an infinite lookahead. Howard's policy iteration [11] iterates by first computing the expected cumulative cost function for the current policy and then improving the policy by using this cost function. Policy iteration is guaranteed to converge to the optimal policy in a finite number of iterations. Puterman [23] provides an up-to-date overview of algorithms for solving Markov decision processes.

5. DECOMPOSING MARKOV DECISION PROCESSES

In this section, we describe a general method of decomposing a Markov decision process defined on a large state space into smaller Markov decision processes defined on local regions. Based on this regional decomposition framework, we develop two approaches in the following two sections that combine the solutions to the smaller Markov decision processes into a solution to the original Markov decision process.

Let P be any partition of Ω_X, $P = \{R_1, \ldots, R_m\}$ such that $\Omega_X = \bigcup_{i=1}^{m} R_i$ and $R_i \cap R_j = \emptyset$ for all $i \neq j$. We refer to a region $R \in P$ as an *aggregate* state. We refer to a state in Ω_X as a *base-level* state.

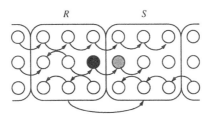

Figure 14. Aggregate state R is adjacent to aggregate state S ($R \leadsto S$).

The *periphery* of an aggregate state R (denoted Periphery(R)) is the set of all base-level states not in R but reachable in a single transition from a base-level state in R, $\{j | j \notin R \wedge \exists i \in R, a \in \Omega_A, p_{ij}(a) > 0\}$. We say that aggregate state R in P is *adjacent* to aggregate state S in P (denoted $R \rightsquigarrow S$) just in case Periphery$(R) \cap S \neq \emptyset$. Figure 14 shows a pair of adjacent aggregate states.

The *boundary* of an aggregate state R (denoted Boundary(R)) is the set of all base-level states in R from which you can reach a base-level state not in R in a single transition, $\{i \mid i \in R \wedge \exists j \notin R, a \in \Omega_A, p_{ij}(a) > 0\}$.

Next, we introduce a set of parameters that we will use to model interactions among regions. Let $U = \bigcup_{R \in P}$ Periphery(R), and λ_i for each $i \in U$ denote a real-valued parameter. Let $\bar{\lambda} \in \mathbf{R}^{|U|}$ denote a vector of all such λ_i parameters, and $\bar{\lambda}|_R$ denote a subvector of $\bar{\lambda}$ composed of λ_i where i is in Periphery(R). U is the medium for interregional interactions; a region R can only communicate with the other regions through the states in U. Parameter λ_i serves as a measure of the expected cumulative cost of starting from a periphery state, and $\bar{\lambda}|_R$ provides an abstract summary of how the other regions affect R.

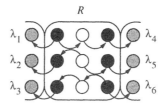

Figure 15. Lambda parameters for states on the periphery of R.

Given a particular $\bar{\lambda}$, the original Markov decision process can be decomposed into smaller Markov decision processes, each of which determines a local policy on a local region. Figure 15 shows the lambda parameters associated with a given aggregate region. For a region R and the subvector $\bar{\lambda}|_R$ of $\bar{\lambda}$, we define a Markov decision process $M_{\bar{\lambda}|_R} = (R \cup \text{Periphery}(R), \Omega_A, q, k)$ and the corresponding local policy $\pi_{\bar{\lambda}|_R}$ as follows.

1. $R \cup \text{Periphery}(R)$ is the (local) state space for $M_{\bar{\lambda}|_R}$.
2. q_{ij} is the (local) state transition matrix for $M_{\bar{\lambda}|_R}$, where
   - $q_{ij} = p_{ij}$ for $i \in R$
   - $q_{ii} = 1$ for $i \in \text{Periphery}(R)$
3. k_{ij} is the (local) cost matrix for $M_{\bar{\lambda}|_R}$, where
   - $k_{ij} = c_{ij}$ for $i, j \in R$
   - $k_{ij} = \lambda_j + c_{ij}$ for $i \in R$ and $j \in \text{Periphery}(R)$
   - $k_{ii} = 0$ for $i \in \text{Periphery}(R)$
4. $\pi_{\bar{\lambda}|_R}$ corresponds to the local policy that is optimal for $M_{\bar{\lambda}|_R}$ with performance criterion expected cost to goal and target set Periphery(R).

$M_{\bar{\lambda}|_R}$ is the subproblem we associate with region R given $\bar{\lambda}|_R$ as an abstract summary of R's interaction with the other regions. $\pi_{\bar{\lambda}|_R}$ is the solution to the subproblem $M_{\bar{\lambda}|_R}$. A particular $\bar{\lambda}$ determines a set of local policies (abstract actions) which in turn determines a policy on the entire state space. Let π^* denote an optimal policy for M. If $\lambda_i = \mathrm{E}_{\pi^*}(\Sigma_\gamma | i)$, then the resulting local policies as defined above define an optimal policy on the entire state space. The algorithms considered in the following sections offer various methods for either guessing or successively approximating $E_{\pi^*}(\Sigma_\gamma|i)$ for all $i \in U$.

6. HIERARCHICAL POLICY CONSTRUCTION

In this section, we first describe a general method for constructing an abstract decision process from a base-level process given a fixed partition of the state space. We then present a hierarchical policy construction method for using an abstract decision process to construct policies for the base-level process.

6.1. ABSTRACT DECISION PROCESSES

Let $P = \{R_1, \ldots, R_m\}$ be any partition of Ω_X. Each region $R \in P$ is considered as an *abstract state*. A particular local policy $\pi_{\bar{\lambda}|R}$ on region R is considered as an *abstract action* on R, which reflects our bias toward different periphery states described by $\bar{\lambda}|_R$. Abstract actions for stochastic domains are the rough equivalent of macro operators for deterministic domains. The abstract action $\pi_{\bar{\lambda}|R}$ indicates how to act optimally in region R if the interactions with the other regions are captured in $\bar{\lambda}$. For example, a large value for λ_j naturally discourages us from entering the periphery state j since it induces a large cost in k_{ij}. The family of all abstract actions is denoted $\mathcal{F} = \{\pi_{\bar{\lambda}|R}|R \in P, \bar{\lambda} \in \mathbf{R}^{|U|}\}$.

The probability of ending up in S starting in R and following an abstraction $\pi_{\bar{\lambda}|R}$ is defined by

$$p'_{RS}(\pi_{\bar{\lambda}|R}) = \frac{1}{|\text{Boundary}(R)|} \left[\sum_{i \in \text{Boundary}(R)} \varphi_i \right]$$

$$\varphi_i = \left[\sum_{j \in S \cup \text{Periphery}(R)} p_{ij} \right] + \sum_{j \in R} p_{ij} \varphi_j$$

where $p_{ij} = p_{ij}(\pi_{\bar{\lambda}|R}(i))$. Note that we assume here that there is an equal probability of starting in any state in the boundary of R.

The cost of ending up in S starting in R and following $\pi_{\bar{\lambda}|R}$ is defined by

$$c'_{RS}(\pi_{\bar{\lambda}|R}) = \frac{1}{|\text{Boundary}(R)|} \left[\sum_{i \in \text{Boundary}(R)} \vartheta_i \right]$$

$$\vartheta_i = \left[\sum_{j \in S \cup \text{Periphery}(R)} p_{ij} \right] + \sum_{j \in R} p_{ij}[1 + \vartheta_j]$$

where $c_{ij} = c_{ij}(\pi_{\bar{\lambda}|R}(i))$.

The resulting abstract decision process is then defined by $M_{\bar{\lambda}} = (P, \mathcal{F}, p', c')$. It is important to note that $M_{\bar{\lambda}}$ need not be Markov; in some cases, we may simply accept this as one of the inevitable consequences of abstraction and proceed as if the process is Markov; in other cases, we may attempt to ameliorate this condition (at some increase in computational cost) by using one of several standard techniques.

6.2. Hierarchical policy construction

In the following algorithm, called *hierarchical policy construction*, we restrict our attention to a finite subset of $\mathcal{F}$. For each R and each S adjacent to R, we construct a local policy $\pi_{R \to S}$ by setting $\lambda_i = 0$ for $i \in S \cap \mathrm{Periphery}(R)$ and setting $\lambda_i = \kappa$ for $i \in \mathrm{Periphery}(R) - S$, where κ is some fixed constant. If the performance criterion for the base-level process is expected cost to goal, then for each R containing one or more target states, we add an additional action in which all the peripheral states get $\lambda_i = \kappa$ and all of the target states are made into sinks with $k_{ii} = 0$. The abstract decision process is $(P, \mathcal{F}_{\rightsquigarrow}, p', c')$ where $\mathcal{F}_{\rightsquigarrow} = \{\pi_{R \to S} | R, S \in P \wedge R \rightsquigarrow S\}$ and the performance criterion is expected discounted cumulative reward for a discount rate γ.

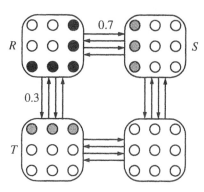

Figure 16. Four-state abstract decision process with three aggregate states labeled R, S, and T.

The local policies have the interpretation that $\pi_{R \to S}$ is the policy to take starting in R if you want to get to S. The larger κ is, the more incentive there is to get to S and avoid the rest of the periphery of R. Figure 16 illustrates an example in which $p'_{RS}(\pi_{\bar{\lambda}|R}) = 0.7$ and $p'_{RT}(\pi_{\bar{\lambda}|R}) = 0.3$. The abstract policy has the interpretation of providing a global perspective and indicating for each region the best local policy to use. Generally, it is best to set γ very close to one or use an alternative performance criterion such as average expected cost per step [10].

The following is an algorithm to construct a global policy using the abstract decision process $(P, \mathcal{F}_{\rightsquigarrow}, p', c')$.

1. Set κ and compute $\pi_{R \to S}$ for $R \rightsquigarrow S \in P$.
2. Calculate the abstract transition probabilities p' and abstract costs c'.
3. Set γ and solve the abstract decision process to obtain an abstract policy $\Pi : P \to \mathcal{F}_{\rightsquigarrow}$.
4. To determine the action to take in base-level state i, determine $R \in P$ such that $i \in R$ and take action $\Pi(R)(i)$.

The above algorithm for constructing and solving abstract processes can be applied recursively and hence applies to hierarchical partitions.

Hierarchical policy construction produces an optimal policy only in special cases; however, it does so relatively efficiently and has an intuitive interpretation that makes it particularly suitable for robot navigation domains. For a simple partition of the state space with no aggregation within regions, standard algorithms [23] on the base-level state space would be dominated by a factor quadratic in the size of the state space ($|\Omega_X|$), while hierarchical policy construction would be dominated by the number of regions in the partition ($|P|$) times the maximum number of neighbors for any region ($\max_{R \in P} |\{S | S \in P \wedge R \rightsquigarrow S\}|$) times the square of the size of the largest region ($\max_{R \in P} |R|$).

7. APPLICATION TO NAVIGATION PROBLEMS

The previous sections considered the problem of navigation in a large domain given an abstract representation of the dynamics. In the example of the travel planning in the United States, we used the country's geographical division into states to aggregate locations. However, a preexisting partition is not always available or suitable for a given navigation problem. Furthermore, it is not computationally reasonable to explore all of the possible partitions; it is also difficult to devise a criterion for comparing these partitions.

In this section, we present a simple method for computing a partition for navigation problems. The method is based on random sampling the state space, and is similar in motivation to a method used by Kavraki and Latombe [13] for path planning problems in which no uncertainty is involved. We first introduce our method using the example of the travel planning in the United States where the performance criterion is to optimize the expected time to reach a target city from another city.

From a Markov decision process $M = (\Omega_X, \Omega_A, p, c)$, we construct an abstract decision process $M' = (\mathcal{S}, \mathcal{F}, p', C)$, where $\mathcal{S}$ is the set of abstract states (the partition of our state space into regions) and $\mathcal{F}$ is a set of local policies. For the sake of simplicity and computational efficiency, the abstract process M' shall be completely deterministic (we do not compute the probability distribution p'). We justify this simplification in Section 7.3.

7.1. ABSTRACTION AND DECOMPOSITION

Starting with an atlas of all of the cities in the United States (the *base-level* states of our Markov decision process) and all possible means of transportation between them (the transitions of our process), the first step is to randomly select a small subset of cities that will represent our abstract states. An abstract state then consists of the *neighborhood* of its representative city.

The first natural way to define the neighborhood is to use a distance criterion when it is available, as in our travel planning problem. If we group each city with its closest geographical representative, there results a similar partition as the individual states which currently constitute the United States. However, this partition is not necessarily compatible with the real means of transportation available; although two cities separated by a river are geographically close, our atlas (the set of possible transition between two base-level states) does not indicate any roads between them. We must also take into account the cost associated with navigation in the base-level space. From a given city it might be faster to reach a sampled city at some greater distance than the physically closest sampled city.

In order to define our abstract states, we iteratively choose some cities in the list of all the cities in the United States. Since we select them randomly, we do not take into account the possible transitions in and out of these cities we select. For instance, we may choose a small city like Cambridge, Massachusetts, instead of Boston, not considering such factors as the international airport or the train stations which intuitively would make Boston a better choice. However, for computational reasons, we use random selection.

Having chosen a city like Cambridge, we then suppress its neighboring cities. For instance, if our criterion is to minimize the expected time between two cities, then in our example we remove from our list of cities all those that can be reached from Cambridge in less than an hour. In practice, we use a breadth-first search, assuming some symmetry in the navigation problem. We continue this iterative process of selection until there are no more cities on our list. In this first part, we have built a random set of cities more or less evenly spread across the country. We then define the aggregate states by using local search from each sampled state.[1]

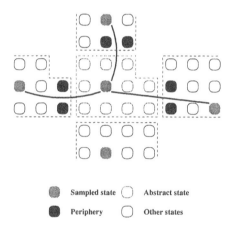

Figure 17. An abstract state S and its adjacent states.

In the following, if R is an aggregate state then $j = \text{Focus}(R)$ is the sampled state associated with R. If i is any base-level state then $R = \text{Region}(i)$ is the aggregate state containing i.

7.2. ABSTRACT DECISION PROCESS

The next step is to compute the costs associated with the transitions in the abstract representation. In the experimental results we present later, we define the cost of a transition as being the expected time needed to navigate from one sampled state to another adjacent sampled state. We construct a *partial Markov decision process* as defined in [7]. The solution of the process is a *partial policy* π_{XY} which is the abstract action for traveling between two states $X, Y \in \mathcal{F}$.

[1] In practice, see Section 7.4, we define our partition by associating each city with the sampled city which minimizes the expected travel time, though it is more expensive computationally.

The next step is to define the interactions between abstract states. If S and T are two adjacent abstract states in $\mathcal{S}$, we define an abstract action $\pi_{ST} \in \mathcal{F}$. π_{ST} is a defined over the two abstract states S and T and their periphery (see Figure 17).

Notice the slight difference with Section 5 in which π_{ST} was defined over $S \cup$ Periphery(S). In Section 7.3, we present an algorithm that decomposes the policy π optimal over the entire state spaces as the sum of the *local policies* $\pi_X, \forall X \in \mathcal{S}$, which are defined exactly as in Section 5. If π is optimal, then its local restriction π_X is also optimal over X. The vector λ_X is then defined by

$$\forall i \in \text{Periphery}(X), \lambda_X(i) = V_\pi(i),$$

where $V_\pi(i)$ is the expected cost in state i while executing the policy π. In our planning example, this cost is the expected time needed to reach the goal-city. This λ_X is dependent upon the goal of the global policy. Therefore, we do not know its value when we compute the abstract representation which is independent of any goal.

An abstract action π_{ST} is also defined by such a vector λ_{ST} which summarizes the interaction of $S \cup T$ with the peripheral states. Note that neither π_{ST} nor $\lambda_{ST}(i)$ are known at that time and they are both dependent on each other.

We first build a restricted Markov decision process $M_{\lambda_{ST}}$ as defined in Section 5 over $S \cup T \cup \text{Periphery}(S) \cup \text{Periphery}(T)$. The peripheral states are goals in this process. The local problem we have to solve is a small planning problem on this restriction: the starting state is $s = \text{Focus}(S)$ and the target state (or goal) is $t = \text{Focus}(T)$ with reward 0. Then the abstract action π_{ST} is the optimal policy $\pi_{s \rightsquigarrow t}$ on this restricted process. Its cost C_{ST} is the value of s for this policy and for our example, this cost represents the expected time for traveling from one (sampled) city to another (sampled) city. The problem is that the policy π_{ST} depends on λ_{ST}, and therefore the cost C_{ST}; if for a peripheral state i, the cost $\lambda_{ST}(i)$ is low, then all the states near i in $S \cup T$ will tend to reach i instead of t. If this value is too high, it will incur a large penalty for falling out into state i and the cost C_{ST} will be affected.

In order to deal with this difficulty, we proceed iteratively taking into account the following consideration. If in the abstract state S we decide to apply the abstract action π_{ST}, this is because, intuitively, we expect a lower cost going through T (see Figure 18):

$$V(V) + C_{SV} \geq V(T) + C_{ST}$$

where $V(X)$ is the value in X of the optimal policy, i.e., the expected cost to reach the global goal.

When computing $\pi_{ST} = \pi_{s \rightsquigarrow t}$, T is the goal and its value is 0. The previous condition becomes

$$V(V) \geq C_{ST} - C_{SV}. \tag{1}$$

For each peripheral state i, if $V = \text{Region}(i)$, then we approximate $\lambda_{ST}(i)$ with $\lambda(V) = C_{ST} - C_{SV}$. At first, none of the terms in equation (1) are known so we initialize $\lambda(V)$ with a large value and we compute the optimal policy based on this value. There results from this initialization phase a first estimation of the cost of the

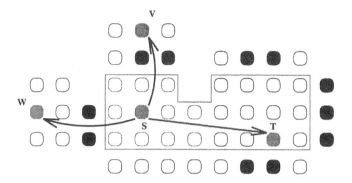

Figure 18. To compute an abstract action π_{ST}, we compute a partial policy $\pi_{s \leadsto t}$ defined over S, T and their peripheral states (shown in black), where s is the starting state, t is the local goal, and the sampled states are shown in grey.

transition C_{SX} where X is one of the neighbors of S, and therefore an estimation of $\lambda(V)$. We iterate this process, each time obtaining a more accurate value of the cost of the transition.

The cost C_{ST} is the value of the base-level sampled state s executing $\pi_{s \leadsto t}$ after the last iteration. At this point, if we are not satisfied with a deterministic abstract representation, we can also compute the distribution p' where $p'_{SV}(\pi_{ST})$ is the probability of falling out of S in a peripheral state in V, while executing π_{ST}.

7.3. THE PLANNING ALGORITHM

Once the preprocessing has been done, a planning problem can be stated as: What is the fastest route from s (San Francisco) to t (Boston)? We first solve this problem in the higher-level representation, using the approximate values in the abstract process. This provides estimated values for all the sampled states. We then use these estimated values to optimize locally at the base level in order to obtain a base-level policy Π defined on the entire space. This global policy Π is defined as the union of partial policies $\pi_X, X \in \Omega_X$ by

$$\forall i \in \Omega_X, \Pi(i) = \pi_{\text{Region}(i)}(i).$$

The high-level optimization. If t is the goal of the Markov decision process M, then $T = \text{Region}(t)$ is the goal of the abstract Markov decision process M' and t is set as a goal with cost 0 for the local process M_T. λ_T is arbitrarily set to a high value to avoid falling out of the neighborhood of t. π_T is an optimal policy for M_T, and the cost $C_{TT}(T)$ is initialized with $V_{\pi_T}(t')$, the value of the sampled state $t' = \text{Focus}(T)$ for the policy π_T.

Now we can optimize the abstract process M', which is a shortest path problem in this case since our abstract representation is purely deterministic. For each abstract state X, we obtain an estimated cost $V(X)$ which represents the expected time needed to reach t from $x = \text{Focus}(X)$.

In the case of multiple goals, we repeat this procedure, optimizing for each goal t_i the restricted process $M_{\text{Region}(t_i)}$. In practice, to obtain the initial value $V(T = \text{Region}(t))$ for a goal t, we consider a larger restricted process whose state space consists not only of T, but also of the adjacent neighbors of T. This provides us with a better estimate of T and limits the effect of the peripheral states.

Initialization of the global policy Π. For each abstract state X, we build a restricted Markov decision process M_X over the state space $X \cup \text{Periphery}(X)$ as defined in Section 5. M_X depends on the vector λ_X which is defined for all $i \in \text{Periphery}(X)$ with $Y = \text{Region}(i)$ by:

- $\lambda_X(i) = V_\Pi(i) = V_{\pi_Y}(i)$ if π_Y has been previously been computed,
- otherwise, $\lambda_X(i) = \max(V(X), V(Y))$ (we use the approximate value computed in the abstract representation).

Given λ_X, we compute the optimal (partial) policy π_X for M_X. Thereafter, it becomes the restriction of Π on X.

For efficiency, we start this process around the abstract goal since we already have optimized π_T. We can then compute the local policy for each adjacent state of T. We further continue the process, back-propagating the the values.

Π is then defined for every base-level state but it is not yet optimal. We need to iterate the optimization of the local policies π_X, each time using more accurate values for the peripheral states:

$$\forall i \in \text{Periphery}(X), \text{ with } Y = \text{Region}(i), \lambda_X(i) = V_{\pi_Y}(i).$$

Ultimately this *local policy iteration* algorithm converges to the optimal policy. Note that local policy iteration can be performed in parallel, one processor in charge of one local decision process.

7.4. EXPERIMENTAL RESULTS

The basic example domain is the same domain as in Dean *et al.* [7] and Kirman [14]. This domain involves a high-level mobile-robot path planning problem. The smallest domain that we use in our experiments is divided into 158 locations representing the layout of the fourth floor of the Brown Computer Science Department. Four directional states, $\mathcal{D} = \{N, S, E, O\}$, corresponding to the direction the robot is facing, are associated with each location. The resulting domain then has 632 states (see Figure 19).

The robot is given the task of navigating from a given starting location to a target location. The available actions are $\Omega_A = \{$Stay, Go, Turn-Right, Turn-Left, Turn-About$\}$. Larger domains are obtained by juxtaposing and connecting multiple copies of the original area so that the size of the experimental domain expands to 10112 states. Different levels of uncertainty (the transition probabilities) were tested for each domain, as described in [14]. Finally, some states were made *semi-sinks* where the probability of staying in a semi-sink for any action is higher than 95% to 99%; the proportion of sinks varies from 0% up to 40%. Overall 100 different domains were tested.

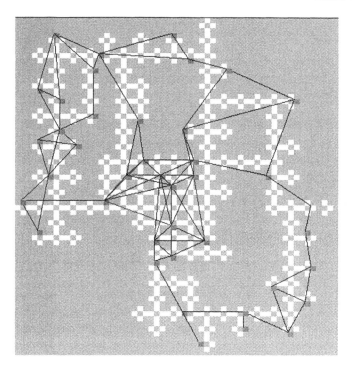

Figure 19. Plan of the Brown Computer Science Department used for the mobile-robot domain. Each square is a state which corresponds to a location and one out of four orientations of the robot. Sampled states are darkened. The segments between those states represent the possible transitions in the abstract model.

Abstract model. An abstract decision process has been constructed for each domain in the previous section. The result can be represented as the graph on Figure 19. In order to define the partition, we construct a decision process on the whole domain. The set of goals for this process is the set of sampled states. The optimal policy for this process, which is computed using policy iteration, induces a partition of the state space Ω_X, by associating each base-level state with the *closest* (in expected time) sampled state.

Our method was tested against policy iteration, and the following results are based on 2000 experiments (20 for each domain). The measure we use is the CPU time taken on a single-processor SUN SPARCstation 10.

We perform the construction of the abstract decision process only once for each domain. Experiments show that this process, obtained by a random sampling of the state space, results in the optimal policy for domains that we explored. Since this part is considered as a preprocessing, further work should be done in order to test and improve the abstract representation, as is done in [13]. For now, we ensure the optimality by applying policy iteration to the solution of our methods. In more than 60% of the experiments, the solution was already optimal and the average distance to the optimal[2] is less than 0.01.

Figures 20, 21, and 22 compare the CPU time for policy iteration (PI) and local iteration (LI) (the extra time due to the final policy iteration is included even if the policy was already optimal) for the different parameters (size, uncertainty, and regularity).

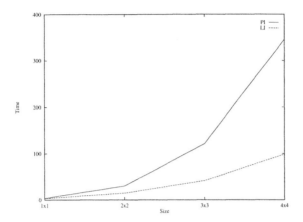

Figure 20. Comparing CPU time versus domain size.

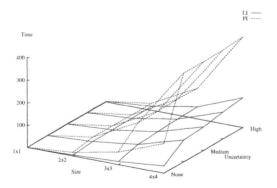

Figure 21. Comparing CPU time versus size and uncertainty.

Figure 23 shows the speed of convergence for a representative experiment on a domain of 5688 states.

8. RELATED WORK

The combined fields of motion planning and stochastic processes are vast. We refer the interested reader to Latombe [18] for a survey of motion planning problems and algorithms. Bertsekas [3] and Puterman [23] provide good overviews of Markov decision processes. For more on viewing planning problems in terms of control see [9]. For

---

[2] The measure of a policy is the average value of its states.

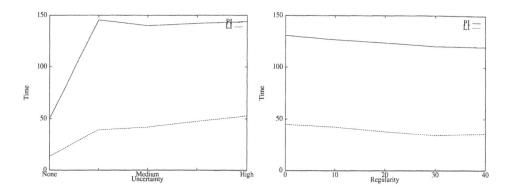

Figure 22. Comparing CPU time versus determinism and regularity.

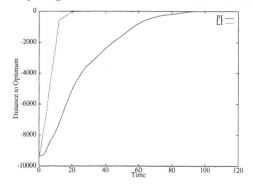

Figure 23. Convergence to optimal as a function of CPU time.

one approach to using Markov decision processes to solve robot navigation problems see [1].

The related work on abstraction and decomposition is extensive. In the area planning and search assuming deterministic action models, there is the work on macro operators [16] and hierarchies of state-space operators [15, 24]. Closely related is the work on decomposing discrete event systems modeled as (deterministic) finite-state machines [5, 26].

Methods for using abstraction and decomposition to solve Markov decision processes with large state spaces include [4, 7, 8, 17]. Cassandra *et al.* [6] provide an improved method for an interesting perspective on solving partially observable Markov decision processes.

In the area of reinforcement learning with applications to navigation and path planning, there is work on deterministic action models and continuous state spaces [22] and stochastic models and discrete state spaces [12].

9. CONCLUSION

In this chapter, we explored the idea of representing navigation problems involving uncertainty in terms of finite-state and finite-time Markov decision processes. We assume for this representation that navigation in continuous time and space can be described using high-level commands such as "turn left at the next corridor junction" and discrete regions of three-dimensional space. The stochastic system that is used to represent the underlying dynamics allows us to summarize over regions of continuous space and time. The resulting discrete representation allows us to apply standard methods from operations research and combinatorial optimization. However, the resulting state spaces are often so large that the standard methods are impractical.

We consider methods of abstraction and decomposition that allow us to generate optimal or near-optimal solutions to very large problems by exploiting the structure in the base-level state space. In particular, we consider methods for partitioning the state space to generate an abstract or aggregate state space. We then formulate an abstract decision process using this aggregate state space. This abstract reformulation enables us to solve large-scale navigation problems in a hierarchical manner, introducing as many levels of abstraction as is necessary.

The framework for building abstract decision processes described here is quite general and applies to a wide variety of decision problems. We consider an instance of the general framework developed specifically for navigation problems and demonstrate its effectiveness empirically. It is our contention that, as navigation techniques are extended to handle additional factors (e.g., fuel costs, hazards) resulting in state spaces of high dimensionality, methods such as the ones described in this paper will become increasingly important. Fortuitously, there is a wealth of techniques from operations research, combinatorial optimization, and management science that can be brought to bear on such difficult navigation problems.

REFERENCES

1. K. Basye, T. Dean, J. Kirman, and M. Lejter, "A decision-theoretic approach to planning, perception, and control," *IEEE Expert* **7**(4), 1992, 58–65.

2. R. Bellman, *Dynamic Programming*, Princeton University Press, Princeton, NJ, 1957.

3. D.P. Bertsekas, *Dynamic Programming: Deterministic and Stochastic Models*, Prentice Hall, Englewood Cliffs, NJ, 1987.

4. C. Boutilier and R. Dearden, "Using abstractions for decision theoretic planning with time constraints," in *Proc. AAAI-94*, AAAI, Seattle, WA, 1994.

5. P.E. Caines and S. Wang, "COCOLOG: A conditional observer and controller logic for finite machines," in *Proc. 29th IEEE Conference on Decision and Control*, Hawaii, 1990.

6. A.R. Cassandra, L. Kaelbling, and M. Littman, "Acting optimally in partially observable stochastic domains," in *Proc. AAAI-94*, AAAI, Seattle, WA, 1994, 1023–1028.

7. T. Dean, L. Kaelbling, J. Kirman, and A. Nicholson, "Planning with deadlines in stochastic domains," in *Proc. AAAI-93*, AAAI, Washington, DC, 1993, 574–579.

8. T. Dean and S.-H. Lin, "Decomposition techniques for planning in stochastic domains," in *Proc. International Joint Conference on Artificial Intelligence 14*, IJCAII, Montreal, Canada, 1995.

9. T. Dean and M. Wellman, *Planning and Control*, Morgan Kaufmann, San Mateo, CA, 1991.

10. C. Derman, *Finite State Markovian Decision Processes*, Cambridge University Press, New York, 1970.

11. R.A. Howard, *Dynamic Programming and Markov Processes*, MIT Press, Cambridge, MA, 1960.

12. L.P. Kaelbling, "Hierarchical learning in stochastic domains: A preliminary report," in *Proc. Tenth International Conference on Machine Learning*, 1993.

13. L. Kavraki and J.-C. Latombe, "Randomized preprocessing of configuration space for fast path planning," in *Proc. IEEE International Conference on Robotics and Automation*, San Diego, CA, 1994, 2138–2145.

14. J. Kirman, *Predicting Real-Time Planner Performance by Domain Characterization*, Ph.D. thesis, Department of Computer Science, Brown University, Providence, RI, 1994.

15. C.A. Knoblock, "Search reduction in hierarchical problem solving," in *Proc. AAAI-91*, AAAI, Anaheim, CA, 1991, 686–691.

16. R. Korf, "Macro-operators: A weak method for learning," *Artificial Intelligence* **26**, 1985, 35–77.

17. H.J. Kushner and C.-H. Chen, "Decomposition of systems governed by Markov chains," Technical Report, Brown University, Department of Applied Mathematics, Providence, RI, 1974.

18. J.-C. Latombe, *Robot Motion Planning*, Kluwer, Boston, 1990.

19. W.S. Lovejoy, "A survey of algorithmic methods for partially observed Markov decision processes," *Annals of Operations Research* **28**, 1991, 47–66.

20. T. Lozano-Pérez, "Spatial planning: A configuration space approach," *IEEE Transactions on Computers* **32**, 1983, 108–120.

21. G.E. Monahan, "A survey of partially observable markov decision processes: Theory, models, and algorithms," *Management Science* **28**(1), 1982, 1–16.

22. A.W. Moore and C.G. Atkeson, "The parti-game algorithm for variable resolution reinforcement learning in multidimensional state spaces," to appear in *Machine Learning*, 1995.

23. M.L. Puterman, *Markov Decision Processes*, John Wiley & Sons, New York, 1994.

24. E. Sacerdoti, "Planning in a hierarchy of abstraction spaces," *Artificial Intelligence* **7**, 1974, 231–272.

25. R.D. Smallwood and E.J. Sondik, "The optimal control of partially observable markov processes over a finite horizon," *Operations Research* **21**, 1973, 1071–1088.

26. H. Zhong and W.M. Wonham, "On the consistency of hierarchical supervision in discrete-event systems," *IEEE Transactions on Automatic Control* **35**(10), 1990, 1125–1134.

10 | Minimalist Vision for Navigation

Martin Herman,[1] Marilyn Nashman,[1] Tsai-Hong Hong,[1]
Henry Schneiderman,[3] David Coombs,[1] Gin-Shu Young,[1]
Daniel Raviv,[2] and Albert J. Wavering[1]

[1]National Institute of Standards and Technology
[2]Florida Atlantic University
[3]Carnegie Mellon University

Abstract

The minimalist approach to vision involves performing a minimum of vision processing to recover the information critical to achieving the desired task or behavior [2]. In general, the richness and complexity of the information recovered will depend on what is required to achieve the task or behavior efficiently and effectively. This chapter describes an approach to vision for navigation which is minimalist in two respects. First, only task-specific information is extracted from the imagery. Second, for many visual servoing tasks, all information may be represented in the 2D image coordinate system; no 3D reconstructions need be performed. The advantages of this approach include simplicity, speed, and in many cases robustness. This chapter provides a discussion of these ideas and how they can be embedded in a general perception/control system (such as the NIST multilevel control system) using mechanisms related to focus of attention. Five specific examples of work done at NIST that demonstrate this approach in the area of navigation for both indoor and outdoor robots are presented. The specific navigation behaviors described include road following, car following, and obstacle avoidance with centering (or lateral clearance). Results are described for complex indoor and outdoor environments.

This chapter was derived from several independent research projects performed by the various co-authors. The different sections were authored as follows: Section 3 was authored by Martin Herman and Daniel Raviv; Section 4 by Henry Schneiderman and Marilyn Nashman; Section 5 by Henry Schneiderman, Marilyn Nashman, and Albert J. Wavering; Section 6 by Marilyn Nashman, Tsai-Hong Hong, Martin Herman, and David Coombs; and Section 7 by Gin-Shu Young, Tsai-Hong Hong, and Martin Herman.

1. Introduction

The classical approach to autonomous navigation, as well as intelligent robotic control in general, is to use vision and other sensing to recover a 3D geometric model of the environment—often a reasonably complete model—and then generate plans and motion commands from this model. The 3D model is represented either iconically (e.g., a grid of points representing terrain elevation), as state variables (e.g., a 4D spatiotemporal representation of important environmental points), symbolically (e.g., 3D line, surface, or object descriptions), or some combination of these. Information from multiple sensors is often fused to obtain this single model. Examples of navigation systems that take these approaches are [11, 12, 30, 38, 39, 42]. Many of these systems convert the information extracted from images into a 3D, vehicle-centered cartesian coordinate system, often aligned with the ground plane. Steering, acceleration, and braking decisions are then determined in this coordinate system. A 3D reconstruction is therefore performed before control decisions are made.

In this chapter, we describe an alternative approach which takes a minimalist approach to vision processing and environmental modelling. In this approach, vision processing is heavily driven by the requirements of the task that the system is performing. Using focus-of-attention mechanisms, the minimum environmental description critical to performing the task efficiently and effectively is recovered. This also means that a minimum of vision processing is performed. Plans and motion commands are then generated from information in this minimal model.

Since this is a task-driven approach, the richness and complexity of the information in the environmental model depend on what is required for achieving the task. For some tasks, a rich, complex description with both high-level and low-level descriptions of small portions of the environment (the objects upon which attention is being focused) is required. For other tasks, the environmental model need not be rich since only a few features of the environment may be critical. In either case, the minimalist approach attempts to move away from complete environmental models to models that contain only that which is important for the task at hand.

The minimalist approach is minimalist in two respects. First, as just described, only task-relevant information is extracted from the imagery and represented in the model. The information is relevant to achieving a desired task or desired behavior. Second, a minimum of vision processing is performed to extract this information. In fact, for many situations, such as those involving visual servoing, this information may be in the form of visual cues represented in the 2D image coordinate system. In such cases, no 3D reconstruction is performed. Such a 2D approach is particularly useful in closing control loops with vision at lower levels of a multilevel control system [1]. The minimalist approach results in a reduced and focused environmental model which can be continuously and rapidly updated from image data. Motion commands are then generated from information in this model.

In order to achieve this minimalist approach, two things are required: (1) a well-defined set of behaviors, together with environmental features that need to be extracted or monitored to achieve each of these behaviors, and (2) the ability to provide context so that the appropriate behaviors can be invoked. Examples of behaviors to be detailed later in this chapter include road following, car following, obstacle avoidance, and centering. Other behaviors relevant to navigation include boundary following, terrain following, motion relative to objects in the environment, and approaching an object without collision. If context can be used to determine the appropriate behavior and the type of environment expected, then navigation can be achieved using the minimalist approach.

There are several advantages to this 2D-based, minimalist approach.

1. *Conceptually simple.* Fewer hypotheses, sensor measurements, and calibrations need to be performed for control when using 2D image information rather than visually reconstructed 3D information. The reason is that the problem of converting 2D image information to 3D world information requires either hypotheses about the scene to be made (e.g., smoothness hypotheses, lighting hypotheses, object hypotheses), calibrations to be made (e.g., camera calibrations, stereo calibrations, inertial navigation system calibrations), or many sensor measurements to be made (e.g., inertial navigation system measurements). This approach is therefore simpler.

2. *Fewer errors.* In many cases, this approach results in fewer errors. The process mentioned in (1) above involves converting from the 2D image coordinate system to a 3D coordinate system using object and scene hypotheses, calibrations, and/or additional sensor measurements. These three methods introduce errors. Therefore the transformation of image information to a 3D coordinate system always results in the accumulation of errors: the errors in the original image acquisition and processing as well as the errors in these methods. By staying in the original image coordinate system, the sources of errors are reduced. Of course, if one of the sensors involved were to measure properties of surfaces in the environment, e.g., a laser range finder, then it could serve to reduce errors, not increase them.

3. *Task-dependent.* The approach is task-dependent; therefore only relevant information has to be extracted from the images. For example, road-following behavior may only require information dealing with road boundary points. Other information about the road may not be necessary as inputs to the steering control algorithm. Each navigation behavior will, in general, need different *relevant* information. Such relevant information may be a set of spatial or temporal features. Using only a small set of information from a sequence of images implies simpler and less computationally expensive processes.

4. *Computationally efficient.* Control algorithms directly use observable image information represented in the 2D image sequence. This requires less computation than 3D reconstruction. Such an approach is therefore simpler and faster.

5. *Exploits context.* Our working model of the overall control system architecture is one in which control loops are closed at multiple levels, all running in parallel (e.g., NIST real-time control (RCS) system [1]). Tasks at a higher level are used to provide context at a lower level in the form of the appropriate behavior and type of environment expected. These expectations can be used to predict which features are visible in the image, and where in the image they appear. Such predictions are very powerful for analyzing and interpreting imagery, and lead to

fast, robust solutions.

The approach taken here derives from several approaches in the literature, including "purposive and active vision" [3, 4], "animate vision" [5, 6], and "direct perception" [16]. The approach results in a tight perception-action loop [33].

In this chapter, we describe five specific examples of work done at NIST that demonstrate visual servoing behaviors that directly use 2D image cues, without performing explicit 3D reconstructions. Three of the examples involve real-time visual servoing demonstrations on indoor or outdoor robots (including the NIST high mobility multipurpose wheeled vehicle (HMMWV), Figure 1), while two of the examples involve non-real-time studies. The first two examples deal with road following. In the first example, it is shown that the image position and image velocity of road edge points can be used directly to generate action commands. In the second example, it is shown how lane markers can be tracked using 2D road models without 3D reconstruction.

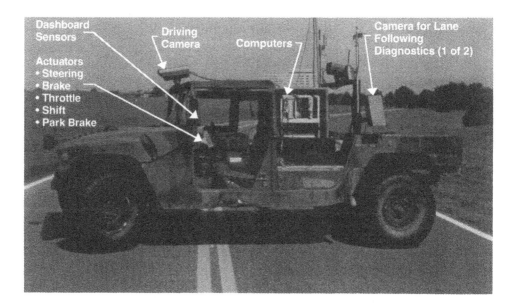

Figure 1. NIST HMMWV, used for autonomous driving experiments.

The next example deals with car following, in which a vehicle is guided by following the path of another vehicle. It is shown that the lead vehicle can be tracked in the 2D image plane using a 2D model.

The final two examples deal with obstacle avoidance. In the first example, it is shown that image flow and flow divergence can be used directly to steer the robot. In the second example, it is shown that image flow normal to arbitrary image lines can be used to detect obstacles above or below the ground, without performing 3D reconstruction. Other examples showing how obstacle avoidance behavior can be achieved using the 2D-based minimalist approach can be found in [19, 21, 22].

2. FOCUS OF ATTENTION

The minimalist approach depends heavily on the ability to focus attention on those environmental objects and features that are relevant to the task at hand. This section expands on the role of focus of attention in the approach.

Suppose that the task to be achieved by a robot is to "go to point A," where point A is some description of a goal location for the robot. This task is a command from a higher level of the control system. There are many different behaviors that can be used to achieve this task, depending on the environment in which the task is to be performed. If the robot is on a road, then a "road-following" behavior might be followed. A robot at a road intersection might follow a "go through intersection" behavior. If the robot is inside an office building, a "corridor-following" behavior might be followed. All of these behaviors would have "obstacle-avoidance" behaviors associated with them.

Tasks and behaviors are closely related concepts. A task is a piece of work to be done or an activity to be performed. Let us define a behavior-plan as a way of accomplishing a task. A behavior is the resulting sequence of actions that take place when the behavior-plan is executed.

A plan is a particular sequence of activities for carrying out the task. Plans may be either predetermined or computed in real time. Predetermined plans are called behavior-plans, i.e., a behavior-plan is a stored sequence of actions that accomplishes a task in a particular manner. They may be represented as (say) state graphs [9].

One way in which a task can be represented is by means of a task frame [1], which has slots for various behavior-plans and other information associated with the task. Figure 2 shows a GO-TO task frame. Behavior-plans can be represented as "behavior-plan frames." In Figure 2, the GO-TO frame has a pointer to the ROAD-FOLLOWING behavior-plan frame. This frame would have links to either a procedural representation of the behavior (e.g., a program to be executed) or a declarative representation (e.g., a state graph [9]).

For each behavior-plan, there are one or more world situations that must hold in order for that behavior-plan to be followed. For example, if a road-following behavior-plan is to be followed, then the world situation must be such that the robot is on a road. If the robot drives off the road, then "road following" no longer makes sense, and some other behavior-plan must be invoked. The world situations might be represented as frames [26], schemas [14], or entities [1]. These world situations provide the context discussed above. The association between a particular behavior-plan and the possible world situations that must hold in order for the behavior-plan to be followed can be explicitly indicated in the task frame. Unless the particular world situation is in effect, the corresponding behavior-plan should not be invoked. This implies that recognition mechanisms need to be in place that can determine which of the world situations in the task frame currently holds (unless it is already known beforehand).

Note that in the behavior-plan frame, the world situation that must be in effect during the execution of the behavior-plan is explicitly indicated. This world situation must be continuously monitored (through verification mechanisms). If the world

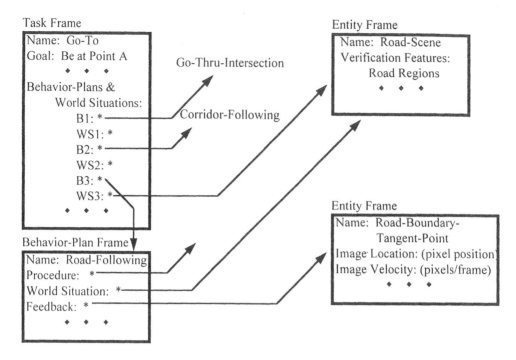

Figure 2. Focus of attention mechanisms.

situation changes, then the behavior-plan currently executing is terminated. Then, in order to complete the task specified by the task frame currently in effect, other world situations in the task frame are examined. Once a new world situation is recognized, its associated behavior-plan can be invoked.

Figure 2 shows a GO-TO task frame with pointers to the ROAD-FOLLOWING behavior-plan frame and its associated world situation—the ROAD-SCENE entity frame. The ROAD-FOLLOWING behavior-plan frame also has a world situation pointer to the ROAD-SCENE entity frame.

As a particular behavior-plan is being executed, certain sensor-derived features of the world will need to be identified. For example, the road-following behavior will need to identify road boundary points, the go-through-intersection behavior will need to identify the roads that meet at an intersection, and the obstacle avoidance behavior will need to identify nearby obstacles. These features represent feedback to the behavior-plan as it is being executed, and these features are ones upon which sensory attention must be focused. These features can be explicitly represented in the behavior-plan frame. In Figure 2, the FEEDBACK slot of the ROAD-FOLLOWING behavior-plan frame has a pointer to the ROAD-BOUNDARY-TANGENT-POINT entity frame. As will be described below, one of our example road-following behaviors uses only the image location and image velocity of the road boundary tanget point to servo the vehicle. These needed features are indicated in the FEEDBACK slot for this particular behavior-plan and are also used to define the current environmental model in Figure 3. As long as the world situation associated with the particular behavior-plan holds, the behavior can be achieved by generating and updating a reduced and highly focused environmental model consisting only of these features. Such a model can be easily and rapidly updated so that servoing can be accomplished. We claim in this chapter that for many visual servoing behaviors, visual features that are part of this model can be represented in the 2D image plane, without 3D reconstruction being performed.

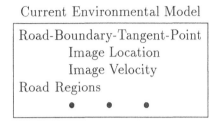

Figure 3. Example of current environmental model.

If the current world situation changes (e.g., the robot travels off the road), then the ROAD-SCENE frame in Figure 2 will no longer be in effect. In that case, the ROAD-FOLLOWING behavior-plan frame will terminate execution since its required world situation no longer holds. At this point, the GO-TO task frame will attempt to instantiate a different world situation in order to initiate a different behavior-plan.

This implies that the world situation must continuously be monitored to determine whether it still holds. This can be accomplished by continuously performing a process of verification perception, i.e., verifying that the world situation still holds. In Figure 2, the entity frame ROAD-SCENE contains a slot for verification features which, in this case, are road regions. These features are continuously monitored to determine whether the current world situation still holds. The features are therefore included as part of the environmental model (Figure 3), since they must be continuously extracted and monitored.

If the current world situation does not hold, then the robot needs to identify the new world situation that currently holds. This requires recovering a more elaborate environmental model. Through the process of recognition, the robot attempts to match this recovered environmental model with internally stored world-situation models.

Note that the process of identifying the new world situation that currently holds (a recognition process) is more elaborate than verification perception, since (a) the latter involves only a single world situation model, while the former involves multiple world situation models that need to be considered and (b) the latter has the advantage of temporal and spatial continuity to drastically limit the number and complexity of expectations.

If none of the world situations in the GO-TO task frame hold, then a plan to accomplish the task must be computed in real time, using methods such as state-space search, random plan generation, etc. Since state-space search typically requires an elaborate world model description, sensory focus of attention will not be as useful in limiting the amount of sensory processing required.

Notice in Figure 3 that under normal operation, the current environmental model is used to focus sensory attention. Only the objects and features in this model are relevant to the current behavior, and therefore these are the only ones extracted from the imagery. This creates a reduced, sometimes sparse, model which is easier and faster to update than traditional models.

The next several sections provide specific examples of work done at NIST showing how the minimalist approach has been used for visual servoing applications in navigation. In all of these examples, vision processing is used to generate only reduced, focused, task-specific information, and only visual cues represented in the 2D image domain are used; no 3D reconstructions are performed.

3. Visual Road Following Using the Tangent Point

This section approaches the road following problem by building on the recently developed theory of zero flow circles [34]. This theory provides quantitative relationships between a stationary 3D environment and a moving camera. The theory involves precomputing the expected instantaneous optical flow values in the camera imagery arising from every point in 3D space.

In this section, we show that for many road following situations, a sufficient road feature that can be used to generate motion commands (for curved, convex roads) is the tangent point on the road edge (i.e., the point on the road edge lying on an imaginary line tangent to the road edge and passing through the camera) and its optical flow. We then show that fast, computationally inexpensive, and simple control algorithms can be used. These algorithms require as visual input only the location of the tangent point (in the image) and its optical flow. The steering commands are directly related to the change of the tangent point location. There are several advantages to using this visual cue: (1) It is extracted directly from the image, i.e., there is no need to reconstruct the scene; (2) it can be used in a tight perception-action loop to directly generate action commands; (3) for many road following situations this visual cue is sufficient; and (4) the related computations are relatively simple and thus suitable for real-time applications.

3.1. Coordinate System and Two-Wheeled Vehicle

The equations for this approach are defined in a coordinate system (Figure 4) which is fixed with respect to the camera on board the vehicle. This coordinate system is used to measure angles to points in space and to measure optical flow at these points, using spherical coordinates (R-θ-ϕ). In this system, angular velocities ($\dot{\theta}$ and $\dot{\phi}$) of any point in space, say P, are identical to the optical flow values at P' in the image domain.

For our analysis, we use a theoretical two-wheeled vehicle (Figure 5). A rigid frame of length 2 m holds both wheels. A steering wheel angle is applied to both wheels simultaneously, i.e., if one wheel is rotated by an angle β relative to the frame, the other wheel will rotate by the same angle. The camera is mounted such

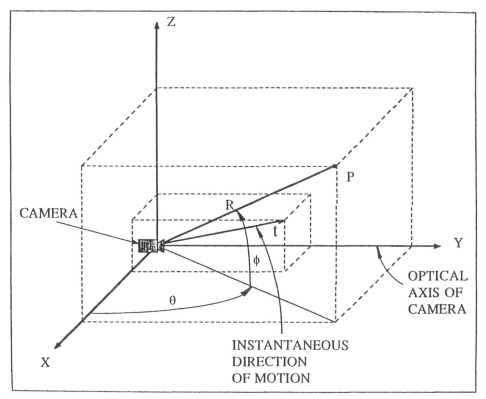

Figure 4. Coordinate system fixed to camera.

that its pinhole point is located above the front wheel center, and it rotates with the front wheel. The optical axis of the camera coincides with the instantaneous translation vector (heading) of the front wheel.

3.2. EQUATIONS OF MOTION AND OPTICAL FLOW

We have recently developed a new theory that relates six-degree-of-freedom camera motion to optical flow for a stationary environment [34]. This section reviews this theory as it relates to the road following problem.

Let the instantaneous coordinates of a 3D point P (Figure 4) be $\mathbf{R} = (X, Y, Z)^T$ (where the superscript T denotes transpose), the instantaneous translational velocity of the camera be $\mathbf{t} = (U, V, W)^T$, and the instantaneous angular velocity of the camera be $\omega = (A, B, C)^T$. Now consider a specific motion in the instantaneous $XY(\phi = O)$ plane of the camera coordinate system defined by:

$$\mathbf{t} = (U, V, 0)^T, \tag{1}$$

$$\omega = (0, 0, C)^T. \tag{2}$$

This means that the translation vector may lie anywhere in the instantanous

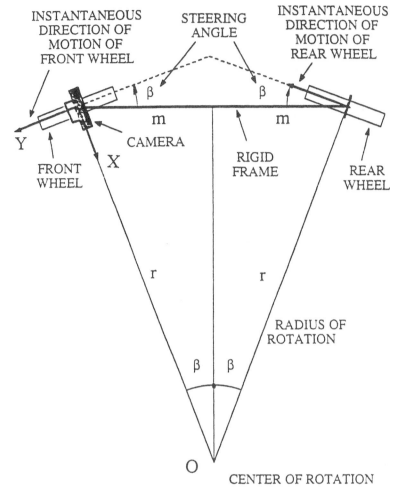

Figure 5. Two wheel vehicle with camera.

XY plane while the rotation is about the Z-axis. It can be shown [34] that

$$\begin{bmatrix} \dot{\theta} \\ \dot{\phi} \end{bmatrix} = \begin{bmatrix} \frac{-Y}{X^2+Y^2} & \frac{X}{X^2+Y^2} & 0 \\ \frac{-XZ}{\sqrt{X^2+Y^2}(X^2+Y^2+Z^2)} & \frac{-YZ}{\sqrt{X^2+Y^2}(X^2+Y^2+Z^2)} & \frac{\sqrt{X^2+Y^2}}{X^2+Y^2+Z^2} \end{bmatrix} \begin{bmatrix} -U + CY \\ -V - CX \\ 0 \end{bmatrix}. \quad (3)$$

As mentioned earlier, $\dot{\theta}$ and $\dot{\phi}$ of a point in space (i.e., the angular velocities in the camera coordinate system) are the *same* as the optical flow components $\dot{\theta}$ and $\dot{\phi}$.

Consider the case where the optical flow value of $\dot{\theta}$ is constant. From equation set (4), the points in space that result from constant $\dot{\theta}$ (regardless of the value of $\dot{\phi}$) form a cylinder of infinite height whose equation is

$$\left(X + \frac{V}{2(C + \dot{\theta})}\right)^2 + \left(Y - \frac{U}{2(C + \dot{\theta})}\right)^2 = \left(\frac{V}{2(C + \dot{\theta})}\right)^2 + \left(\frac{U}{2(C + \dot{\theta})}\right)^2. \quad (4)$$

The meaning of equation (5) is the following: All points in 3D space that lie on the cylinder described by equation (5) and which are visible (i.e., unoccluded and in the field of view of the camera) produce the same instantaneous horizontal optical flow $\dot{\theta}$. We call the cylinder on which equal flow points lie the *equal flow cylinder*.

One of the equal flow cylinders corresponds to points in 3D space that produce zero horizontal flow. We call this cylinder a *zero flow cylinder*. The equation that describes the zero flow cylinder can be obtained by setting $\dot{\theta} = 0$ in equation (5), i.e.,

$$\left(X + \frac{V}{2C}\right)^2 + \left(Y - \frac{U}{2C}\right)^2 = \left(\frac{V}{2C}\right)^2 + \left(\frac{U}{2C}\right)^2. \tag{5}$$

3.3. Road following

In this section, we consider following along a circular road by gazing at the inner road edge. Given visual cues, a goal of the control system is to find the steering angle. If the vehicle is already on a path that follows the road, then only *changes* in steering angle are necessary. Figure 6 shows a vehicle moving around a circular road of radius l. The path traversed by the vehicle is a circle of radius r. Let the unit vector $\hat{t}$ indicate the direction of the *tangent line*, a line that contains the camera pinhole point and is tangent to the inner road edge.

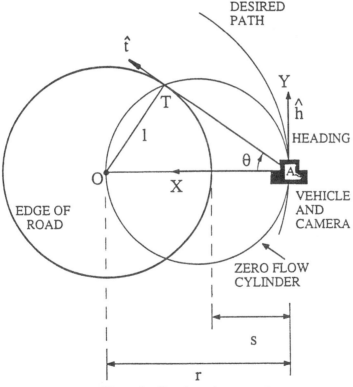

Figure 6. Circular edge: top view.

We have proved in [32] that the tangent point T lies on the instantaneous zero flow cylinder if the camera orientation is fixed relative to the vehicle. This proof holds no matter what the diameter of the circular road edge. This means that no matter how far the vehicle is from the inner road edge (Figure 7), the tangent point lies on the zero flow cylinder. Thus the horizontal component of optical flow of the tangent point is always zero.

Figure 7. Road tangent points.

From Figure 6, the following expression can be derived [32, 34]:

$$\dot{\beta} = \dot{\theta} \tan \beta \cot \theta. \tag{6}$$

Equation (6) suggests a partial control scheme whose inputs are the current steering angle β, the current angle θ of the tangent line relative to the X-axis, and the optical flow $\dot{\theta}$ of the tangent point. All of these inputs can be measured. The variable being computed is the rate of change of the steering angle, $\dot{\beta}$.

This expression holds only for the vehicle depicted in Figure 5. Vehicles with other wheel and steering configurations will result in different expressions relating steering angle to the radius of curvature of motion. In all such expressions, however, there should be a one-to-one relationship between β and r. These expressions can then be used to derive the relevant control signals.

If the rate of change of the steering angle, $\dot{\beta}$, is the only variable being controlled (as indicated in equation (6)), then in practice the vehicle may not maintain a constant distance from the edge of the road; however, the following expression can be derived [32, 34]:

$$\beta = \arcsin\left[\frac{m}{s}(1 - \sin\theta)\right]. \tag{7}$$

Equation (7) suggests a partial control scheme whose inputs are the measured angle θ of the tangent line relative to the X-axis, the desired distance s of the vehicle from the inner road edge, and the distance 2 m between the front and rear wheels. The variable being computed is the steering angle β.

The main significance of this approach is that (1) it shows that the tangent point and its optical flow are important visual control signals for road following, and that potentially they are sufficient to achieve road following; (2) a tight perception-action loop is possible for road following which is simple and therefore computationally inexpensive; (3) image information can potentially be used *directly* as input into a control algorithm; (4) only a few measurements may be needed to control the vehicle; (5) the approach is independent of the speed of the vehicle; (6) the approach is independent of the camera height above the road; and (7) only a very small portion of the image—the portion around the tangent point—may need to be analyzed, in principle.

In order to embed this road-following algorithm in a larger system, the behavior-plan frame for this behavior would require pointers to one or more entity frames that represent necessary world situations, such as the vehicle being on a road with curved boundaries. Then the mechanisms outlined in Figures 2 and 3 can take effect.

4. A LANE MARKER TRACKER FOR VISION-BASED AUTONOMOUS DRIVING

Accurate and reliable interpretation of the road is necessary for autonomous driving. An inaccurate interpretation of the road can lead to catastrophic results. In this section, we describe a method for lane marker tracking that addresses the needs of robustness and real-time performance.

In the area of reliability, our method is strongly motivated by statistical reasoning. It is recognized that low-level image segmentation is error prone. Shadows on the roadway and cracks in the pavement may be mistaken for lane markings. These failures are typically localized in space and time. To reduce the influence of these local failures, our method strives to combine observations over space and time to achieve the best possible global estimate of lane marker shape and position.

The estimate of the lane markers is further strengthened by explicitly modelling and compensating for uncertainty. We address two forms of uncertainty. The first is the uncertainty about how quickly the road changes as a function of time (assuming a nominally constant vehicle speed). The second is uncertainty in the visibility of the lane markers in each individual image.

To address the real-time constraints of autonomous driving, we use streamlined models of the lane markers consisting of second-order polynomials in the image plane. 3D reconstruction of the scene is not performed.

This method has been used for autonomously driving the NIST HMMWV (Figure 1). In our testing, autonomous driving has been demonstrated on both local roads and highways at speeds up to 100 km/h. The algorithm performs well in the presence of nonideal road conditions including small gaps in the lane markers and momentary loss in visibility of lane markers. Reliable performance has also been achieved in the presence of sharp curves, shadows, cracks in the pavement, wet roads, rain, dusk, and nighttime driving.

In the approach presented here, the road is represented by a 2D model in the image plane as opposed to a full 3D model. With this representation, the model is directly estimated from the image without any intervening geometric transformations. Many approaches transform the detected features from 2D to 3D and update a 3D road model. The 3D road model is then backprojected into 2D and used to search for features in the next image. The problem with these approaches is that these transformations are never exact. They produce errors because they depend on camera calibration and approximations (the small angle approximation, the flat road assumption, linearization of nonlinear models). By representing the model in 2D, these sources of error are avoided.

The 2D representation also simplifies the geometric road model update computation. This representation allows both spatial and temporal information to be combined in one simple recursive estimation formulation instead of separate estimates of spatial and temporal model parameters.

Further advantages of the approach are that (1) no terrain model is required, (2) no camera calibration is required, (3) knowledge of camera motion (i.e., translation and rotation parameters) are not required, and (4) the method is simple, fast, and robust. Further details about this approach are presented in [35].

4.1. LANE MARKER TRACKING ALGORITHM

This algorithm requires that lane markings be present and attempts to track the lane markings on each of two lane boundaries in the lane of travel. There are three successive stages of vision computation (Figure 8):

1. *Edge detection.* Extracting edge point position and orientation.
2. *Data association.* Determining likely groupings of edge points to each lane marker.
3. *Model updates.* Updating the lane marker models.

A single CCD camera, mounted above the cab of the HMMWV, provides video images to stage 1 at the rate of 15 hertz. Stages 2 and 3 interact with geometric models of each lane marker. Stage 2 attempts to group the extracted edge points obtained from stage 1 with each lane marker by comparing each edge point against the current models. Stage 3 then updates the models using those edge points that have been grouped to each lane marker. Stage 4, the steering and servo control of the vehicle, is described in [27, 37].

Representation of the lane markers. All representations are maintained in 2D with respect to the image plane throughout all computations in this algorithm. Both the left and right lane markings in the lane of travel are modelled. These markings correspond to the white or yellow lines painted on the road.

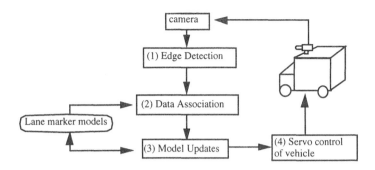

Figure 8. Processing overview.

Each of these lane boundaries is modelled by a second-order polynomial in the image plane:

$$x_L = a_{L1} + a_{L2}y + a_{L3}y^2 \qquad x_R = a_{R1} + a_{R2}y + a_{R3}y^2. \tag{8}$$

The parameters, a_1, a_2, a_3, govern the shape and position of each lane marker model. The endpoints of each lane marker model are given by the intersection of the model equation with the boundary of the window of interest (see below). A second-order model was chosen because it provides an adequate representation of shape within the constraints of real-time performance required for autonomous driving.

Initial conditions. The algorithm requires an initially approximate model of the lane markers before tracking can begin. This initial correspondence between the road markings and the models of the road markings is established by a teleoperator. The teleoperator manually positions the models on the video monitor to align them with the appearance of the lane markers in the image.

Edge extraction. In the first processing step, edge extraction is performed on each image (stage (1) in Figure 8). For every point in the image, edge magnitude and edge orientation are computed using the directional 3×3 Sobel gradient operators. A binary edge image is produced by thresholding the edge points in magnitude. Figure 9 shows a typical image of a road viewed from the camera mounted on the vehicle. The thresholded edges in this image are shown in Figure 10.

Data association. The raw edges in each image are produced by various visual entities including lane markers, shadows, potholes, cracks, and other vehicles. A data association algorithm (stage (2) in Figure 8) is used to determine which of these raw edge points are likely to be associated with each lane marker and to discard those edges that do not seem to be associated with either lane marker.

The algorithm compares each edge pixel to the current model of each lane marker. An edge pixel must satisfy two criteria to be associated with a lane marker. The first criterion is two-dimensional spatial proximity of the edge point to the model.

The second criterion is similarity of direction of the edge point with the angular orientation of the model.

In each image, many edges can be discarded immediately on the basis of the spatial proximity criterion. This is done by eliminating all edges that fall outside a window of interest. This eliminates many, but not all edges that violate the spatial proximity criterion. Figure 11 represents the results of masking the thresholded edge image with the window of interest.

For all edge points falling within the window of interest, the two data association criteria are applied on a point by point basis. First, the edge direction of each candidate edge point is compared with the angular direction of the model. When this angular criterion is satisfied, the distance is computed between the edge point and the model. If this distance is less than a pre-specified threshold, the edge point is associated with that lane marker. Figure 12 shows the thresholded edges extracted from the original image that are grouped to the right lane marker. (In Figure 12, edges forming the right lane marker do not appear as continuous as they do in Figure 10. This is due to sampling of the edge image.)

Figure 9. Original image.

Figure 10. Thresholded edge image.

Figure 11. Edges within window of interest.

Figure 12. Edges grouped to right lane marker.

Figure 13. Computed lane markers graphically superimposed on image.

Lane marker model update. Using the associated edge points, each of the two polynomial lane marker models is updated independently. Several principles are followed to obtain robust lane marker updates. First we describe below how an estimate improves with more data. Also, in updating the lane marker models, two types of uncertainty are addressed. There is uncertainty in how quickly the road changes as a function of time and there is uncertainty in the visibility of the lane markers in each image. These factors are formulated into a criterion of optimality for the lane marker estimate. This criterion of optimality is satisfied by a weighted recursive least squares (WRLS) with exponential decay estimator.

In general, an estimate can be improved by using more data. It can be shown that if a measurement consists of a sum of a stationary signal and unbiased noise, the estimate of the signal will improve—the variance in the estimate will decrease—as more measurements are averaged [18, 20, 31].

To obtain the best possible estimate from each image, it is important to make use of all visible portions of the lane markers. Valuable information is wasted if visible portions of the lane markers are partially masked out.

An estimate can be further improved by using data from multiple images in a sequence. This is particularly important for lane marker sensing where the edge data from any one image may be too weak or contaminated by incorrect data associations.

However, as mentioned above, in order to improve an estimate by using more data, measurement noise must be unbiased. In lane marker tracking this assumption is fairly viable due to a combination of two phenomena. First, the immediate surroundings of the lane markers (as viewed in the image) are constantly changing because of the motion of the vehicle. Secondly, any surrounding spurious edge points, e.g., shadows and cracks in the pavement, are not inherently biased to either side of the lane markers.

The lane markers are not strictly stationary signals across successive images; however, they change relatively slowly assuming a nominal vehicle speed. Therefore, a compromise must be mediated between robustness of the estimate—by using data over a large temporal span—and responsiveness to actual changes in the lane markers—by using data over a smaller temporal span. This compromise is achieved by the relative weighting of new data with respect to older data.

This relative weighting between new data and old data may be simply governed by an exponential decay factor where the weight contributed by the exponential decay, λ, for each edge point is:

$$\lambda^{t-t_o} \tag{9}$$

where $0.0 < \lambda \leq 1.0$, t is the current time, and t_o is the time the image was sampled.

For example, if $\lambda = 0.5$, all edge points in the current image, $t_o = t$, have a weight of 1.0. All edge points in the image read at time $t_o = t - 1$ have a weight of 0.5, etc. Values of λ anywhere in the range $0.5 < \lambda < 0.75$ produced acceptable tracking.

In each image, lane marker visibility is measured by the number of edge points matched to the lane marker model. If a lane marker is clearly visible, many edge points will be matched to the model. Conversely, if a lane marker is obscured fewer edge points will be matched to the model. This measure of visibility acts as an additional weight when edge data are combined temporally in an estimate.

In updating a lane marker model, the two contributions of uncertainty are directly formulated into a criterion of optimality, J_R:

$$J_R = \sum_{j=0}^{t} \left(\lambda^{t-j} \sum_{i=1}^{N_j} \left[x_{j,i} - \left(a_1 + a_2 y_{j,i} + a_3 y_{j,i}^2 \right) \right]^2 \right) \qquad (10)$$

where t is current time and N_j is number of matched edge points in image j.

This represents the residual least-squares error as weighted by the uncertainty measures. By computing a_1, a_2, a_3 such that J_R is minimized, these uncertainties are minimized in the least-squares sense in the estimate.

Expanding the outer summation in equation (10) in reverse order gives:

$$J_R = \sum_{i=1}^{N_t} \left[x_{t,i} - \left(a_1 + a_2 y_{t,i} + a_3 y_{t,i}^2 \right) \right]^2$$

$$+ \lambda \sum_{i=1}^{N_{t-1}} \left[x_{t-1,i} - \left(a_1 + a_2 y_{t-1,i} + a_3 y_{t-1,i}^2 \right) \right]^2 + \cdots \qquad (11)$$

Each summation in (11) represents the edge points from one image grouped to the lane marker. The weight measuring image visibility is implicitly included; that is, each summation is over the number of edge points matched to the lane marker for that image, N_t points. An image in which many edge points are matched will therefore contribute more terms to the residual and thereby carry more influence in the determination of a_1, a_2, a_3. The exponential decay is achieved by multiplying each summation by a power of λ where older images are multiplied by increasing powers of λ.

For each new image, a_1, a_2, a_3 must be recomputed for each lane marker model such that J_R is minimized. Excepting pathological cases, a unique solution for a_1, a_2, a_3 exists. This solution is recursively formulated using weighted recursive least squares with exponential decay [17] and is implemented using the square root information filter [8].

4.2. EVALUATION OF ALGORITHM

Autonomous driving experiments using the NIST HMMWV have been performed on several roads including the NIST campus, Great Seneca Highway in Gaithersburg, Maryland, and Montgomery County Police Test Track in Rockville, Maryland. These roads contained standard lane markings such as double yellow lines, single white lines, and dashed white lines. On all these roads the algorithm performed quite successfully and reliably. The only failure occurred on one portion of road where the pavement abruptly changed from dark asphalt to light cement for an overpass. The lane markings did not provide enough contrast to be detected on the cement pavement. Otherwise, the vehicle maintained centering in the lane of travel. It was able to successfully traverse sections in which there were significant gaps of 6–7 m in the lane marking for small intersections and through an underpass. The roads were moderately shadowed by surrounding trees and varied from mild curvature and hills to severe rises and drops and sharp curves on the Montgomery County Police Test Track. Pavement quality varied significantly, including stretches of old pavement with many cracks and discolorations. Top speeds of 100 km/h were also demonstrated. On all roads the vehicle was able to travel at the legal speed limit. Testing also included a wide variety of conditions including rain (wet roads), nighttime driving with headlights, and driving at dusk into the sunlight.

The algorithm has also been widely tested using videotaped road scenes. Tracking was maintained on video tapes of roads with sharp curves, hills, and moderate shadows. However, on one portion of videotaped road, tracking was temporarily lost when the vehicle travelled through a sharply curved hilly portion of road that was shadowed by a heavily wooded area. Tracking was maintained in typical traffic situations: oncoming traffic, passing vehicles, and traveling behind other vehicles.

5. A Target Tracker for Vision-Based Autonomous Convoy Driving

In autonomous convoy driving, a vehicle is guided by following the path of another vehicle. Figure 14 describes the scenario in which a 2D target is mounted on the back of the lead vehicle. The target is used to determine the position of the lead vehicle with respect to the autonomous following vehicle. The latter vehicle uses the model position feedback to define its steering commands and to maintain reasonable following distances. In this section, we describe a system for visual target tracking for a convoy driving application.

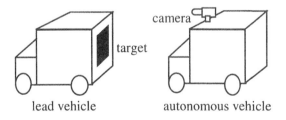

Figure 14. Autonomous convoy driving.

The method used for target tracking follows many of the principles of the lane marker tracker described in the previous section (also see [35]). In particular, uncertainty measurements enter into all computations to account for the varying degrees of confidence in the feature measurements and in entities derived from the feature measurements. However, the known geometry of the target allows for several enhancements that were not feasible for the lane marker tracking:

- Clutter rejection
- Global feature consistency constraints
- Modelling and prediction of target motion

The target is modelled in the 2D image plane and tracking occurs in the image plane. The depth of the target need not be recovered, and therefore the true dimensions of the target need not be known. Initially, the image position and dimensions of the target at some arbitrary depth are measured. The subsequent changes in the appearance of the target are assumed to arise only from x-y translation in the image plane and scale changes (arising from depth changes). Orientation of the target relative to the camera is assumed to be fixed. Therefore, initially the target scale parameter is assigned the value of 1. A recursive estimation formulation is then used to update the image position of the target center, as well as the target scale parameter.

The method requires no camera calibration. Relative motion of the target is assumed to consist of three degrees of positional freedom—arbitrary x, y image translations and depth. Although a target model is required, the model may be obtained initially from an image; true target dimensions need not be known. The method is simple, fast, and robust.

In actual testing, autonomous convoy driving has been demonstrated using the NIST HMMWV. In one experiment, a continuous autonomous run of over 20 miles was successful at speeds averaging between 50 and 75 km/h. In addition, in a laboratory setting, this algorithm has achieved very promising performance at tracking targets moving at significant speed and in the presence of partial occlusion, shadows, and cluttered background scenery. Further details about the system are presented in [36].

5.1. THE MODEL-BASED TRACKING ALGORITHM

An overview of the processing scheme is shown schematically in Figure 15. A single CCD camera, mounted above the cab of the HMMWV, provides video images to the system at the rate of 30 hertz. Image data flows through the diagram as indicated by the arrows. There are several successive stages of computation:

1. *Edge detection.* Extract position and orientation for all edge points.
2. *Data association.* Determine likely groupings of edge points to each model feature.
3. *Feature measurement.* Use grouped edge points to determine location of each feature.
4. *Feature aggregation.* Determine the overall location of the target by fitting the target model to the conglomerate of computed feature locations.
5. *Update motion model.* Use computed object location to update parameters (e.g., velocity, acceleration) that describe how the target moves as a function of time.
6. (a) *Predict target location in next image.* Extrapolate motion model to predict target location in next image. Use predicted target location to determine corresponding predicted feature locations.
   (b) *Predict target location at next servo cycle.* Predict target location at next steering trajectory point.
7. *Steering and servo control of vehicle.* [27, 37].

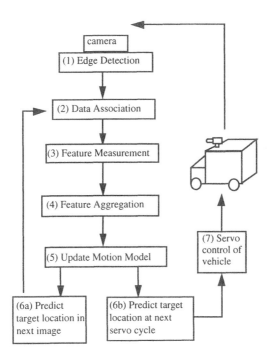

Figure 15. Processing overview.

Geometric model of target. Geometrically, the target is modelled in terms of its edge features, i.e., light-to-dark transitions. Each of these edges is modelled by a straight line segment. One such model is shown in Figure 16 for the target shown in Figure 17. The corner features of the object, derived from the intersection of these line segments, are used for determining overall target location.

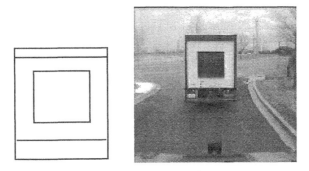

Figure 16. Model   Figure 17. Target.
of target.

Initialization of tracking. Registration between the model and the target is initially established by a teleoperator. Using a graphic representation of the model superimposed on the live video image, the teleoperator positions and scales the model such that it graphically aligns with the image of the target.

Edge extraction and data association. These processing steps are very similar to those described for lane marker tracking [35]. However, for target tracking the edge points are grouped to straight-line features instead of polynomials.

Feature measurement. After edge pixels have been grouped to each model line feature, the slope and intercept parameters (m, b) of each of these lines are determined such that they give the best least-squares fit to each group of edge pixels:

$$
\begin{bmatrix} y_1 \\ y_2 \\ \cdots \\ y_n \end{bmatrix} = \begin{bmatrix} x_1 & 1 \\ x_2 & 1 \\ \cdots & \cdots \\ x_n & 1 \end{bmatrix} \begin{bmatrix} m \\ b \end{bmatrix} \tag{12}
$$
$$
b \quad = \quad A \quad \quad x
$$

where (x_i, y_i) are the coordinates of the ith edge point and n is the total number of edge points.

There are many least-squares methods that exist for solving this set of equations. One such solution is

$$
\hat{x} = \left(A^T A \right)^{-1} A^T b. \tag{13}
$$

Feature confidence. Some computed feature locations are more accurate and reliable than others. The differences in feature reliability are consequences of the fallibility of the data association algorithm. Since edge pixels are only discriminated on the basis of spatial and angular proximity, it is unlikely that all spurious edges will be discarded.

It is valuable to know how much trust can be placed in each of these computed feature locations. One way this can be measured is in the empirical variance in feature location as given by

$$
\sigma_{\hat{x}}^2 = \frac{1}{n} \left(b - A\hat{x} \right)^T \left(b - A\hat{x} \right). \tag{14}
$$

A large variance corresponds to a scattered distribution of edge points about the computed feature location. Such a scattering of edge points may indicate the presence of clutter. This will happen when edge pixels from two visual entities—the desired target edge and undesired background edge—are grouped to a model feature. If this happens, the variance in this line segment's location will be larger than for other line segments. This feature will then carry less weight when the features are aggregated to determine the overall target location.

Corner features. The location of each corner feature, $v = (v_x, v_y)$, is computed by the intersection of the appropriate pairs of line features:

$$\begin{aligned}\begin{bmatrix} -b_1 \\ -b_2 \end{bmatrix} &= \begin{bmatrix} m_1 & -1 \\ m_2 & -1 \end{bmatrix} \begin{bmatrix} v_x \\ v_y \end{bmatrix}. \\ w &= \quad F \quad\quad v \end{aligned} \tag{15}$$

Since corner position is a linear function of the line parameters, the covariance in v is then given by [18, 31]

$$C_v = F^{-1} \Sigma F^{-T} \qquad \Sigma = \begin{bmatrix} \sigma_{\hat{x}1}^2 & 0 \\ 0 & \sigma_{\hat{x}2}^2 \end{bmatrix}. \tag{16}$$

Feature aggregation. In this stage of processing, the overall target location is computed that gives the best fit of the target model to the conglomerate of computed corner feature locations. The target is assumed to be moving with only three degrees of positional freedom (2D translation and depth) with respect to the camera (orientation of the target is assumed fixed with respect to the camera). More specifically, the target location is determined by finding $(c_x, c_y, 1/c_z)$ such that this weighted least-squares residual is minimized:

$$J_l = \sum_{i=1}^{n} \frac{1}{C_{vi}(1,1)} \left(c_x + \frac{1}{c_z} p_x u_{xi} - v_{xi} \right)^2 + \sum_{i=1}^{n} \frac{1}{C_{vi}(2,2)} \left(c_y + \frac{1}{c_z} p_y u_{yi} - v_{yi} \right)^2 \tag{17}$$

where n is the number of corner features, u_{xi} and u_{yi} are the model coordinates of the ith corner when the object is viewed from a nominal range, and v_{xi} and v_{yi} are computed coordinates for the ith corner. For the purpose of illustration, it is assumed that the C_{vi} are diagonal. p_x and p_y account for camera calibration and the nominal range of the object.

The first summation corresponds to horizontal positioning of the object and the second summation corresponds to vertical positioning of the object. The range to the object c_z enters into both summations. For example, the term $(1/c_z)p_x$ can be thought of as a scale factor that is a function of range. Thus in each summation, the center of the object and the inverse of range are determined such that the computed feature locations are brought into correspondence with the object model. The object model consists of feature locations given at a nominal range. The weighting by the inverse of variance in feature location will then give the best linear unbiased estimate (BLUE) [20] in the object's position.

To solve for the coordinates of the object position, (17) can be rewritten in matrix form:

$$J_l = \left(b_f - A_f x_f\right)^T C_f^{-1} \left(b_f - A_f x_f\right) b_f = \begin{bmatrix} v_{x1} \\ v_{y1} \\ . \\ . \\ . \\ v_{xn} \\ v_{yn} \end{bmatrix} \quad A_f = \begin{bmatrix} 1 & 0 & p_x u_{x1} \\ 0 & 1 & p_y U_{y1} \\ . & . & . \\ . & . & . \\ . & . & . \\ 1 & 0 & p_x u_{xn} \\ 0 & 1 & p_y u_{yn} \end{bmatrix} \tag{18}$$

$$C_f = \begin{bmatrix} C_{v1} & 0 & 0 & 0 & 0 \\ 0 & . & 0 & 0 & 0 \\ 0 & 0 & . & 0 & 0 \\ 0 & 0 & 0 & . & 0 \\ 0 & 0 & 0 & 0 & C_{vn} \end{bmatrix} \quad x_f = \begin{bmatrix} c_x \\ c_y \\ \frac{1}{c_z} \end{bmatrix}.$$

The solution for x_f that minimizes J can be expressed by

$$\hat{x}_f = L b_f \qquad L = \left(A_f^T C_f^{-1} A_f\right)^{-1} A_f^T C_f^{-1}. \tag{19}$$

Confidence in object location. The reliability of the computed target location will vary from image to image. Reliability will depend on how well the object's features are discriminated. Since object location is a linear function of feature location, covariance in object location could be propagated as in (16) by

$$C_l = L C_f L^T. \tag{20}$$

However, C_f is derived from an empirical estimate of the variance based on the spread of edge points around each feature. It is not the true statistical variance in each measured feature location. Moreover, it is based strictly on image data in the local neighborhood of the feature. It does not account for how much each feature contributes to the overall least squares error in the object location (i.e., b_f is completely absent from the formulation).

A better expression for the variance in feature location can be determined by accounting for the global consistency of all computed feature locations. The global consistency of the features can be measured by the normalized least-squares error in the target's location:

$$e = \frac{\left(C_f^{-1/2}\right)(b - A\hat{x})}{\text{trace}\left(C^{-1/2}\right)}. \tag{21}$$

This is a measure of the overall accuracy in fitting the target model to the conglomerate of feature locations. Each component of e, e_j, measures the consistency of the jth feature measurement to the overall object location as computed by $\hat{x}_f$. Using this information, the covariance in the target's location can be approximated by

$$C_l = L C_{fe} L^T \qquad C_{fe} = \begin{bmatrix} e_1^2 & 0 & \cdots & 0 \\ 0 & e_2^2 & \cdots & 0 \\ \cdots & \cdots & \cdots & \cdots \\ 0 & 0 & \cdots & e_n^2 \end{bmatrix}. \tag{22}$$

Update of motion model and prediction. Using the computed target location, parametric models for the target motion are updated. Target motion is represented by separate second order models along each coordinate direction. For example, motion along the x coordinate is represented by

$$c_x[t] = a_{cx0} + a_{cx1}t + a_{cx2}t^2 \tag{23}$$

where $t =$ time, a_{cx0} represents position, a_{cx1} represents velocity, and a_{cx2} represents $0.5 *$ acceleration.

After each measurement of target location, the computed x coordinate, c_x, is used to update the parameters of the model, $a_{cx0}, a_{cx1}, a_{cx2}$. These parameters are updated by fitting the model to the time history of c_x. A weighted least-squares fit with exponential decay is used. Each observation is weighted by the inverse of its covariance. In addition, the exponential decay gives increasingly less weight to older data. More specifically, the parameters $(a_{cx0}, a_{cx1}, a_{cx2})$ are determined by minimizing

$$\sum_{n=0}^{t} \frac{1}{C_l(1,1)} \left(c_x[n] - \left(a_{cx0} + a_{cx1}n + a_{cx2}n^2\right)\right)^2 \lambda^{t-n} \tag{24}$$

where λ is the exponential decay factor: $0 < \lambda < 1$.

To solve for the model parameters in (24), a recursive algorithm called the square root information filter algorithm is used. The procedure for updating the other two models corresponding to c_y and c_z is identical to that described for c_x.

The computed model parameters are then used to predict the location of the target in the next image and at the time of the next servo cycle (in Figure 15 this is represented by the arrows coming out of (6a) and (6b), respectively). For instance, the predicted x coordinate in the next image is

$$\bar{c}_x[t+1] = a_{cx0} + a_{cx1}(t+1) + a_{cx2}(t+1)^2. \tag{25}$$

Using the prediction of object location, it is a straightforward computation to determine where the features of the object will fall on the image plane. These predicted feature locations are then used by the data association algorithm (processing stage (2) in Figure 15).

5.2. EXPERIMENTAL RESULTS

This algorithm has been used to autonomously steer the NIST HMMWV [3, 30] while pursuing the truck shown in Figure 17. Testing has been performed on the grounds of NIST and nearby roads. Robust performance was demonstrated in the presence of various lighting conditions including shadowing, other traffic, turns at intersections, curves, and hills. A continuous autonomous run of over 20 miles was successful, at speeds averaging between 50 and 75 km/h and following distances ranging between 5 and 20 m. At following distances of greater than 20 m the target became too small in the image to be reliably tracked. The algorithm also became susceptible to failure if the vehicle drove directly into the sun causing saturation of the image.

The algorithm has also been extensively tested in the laboratory using TRI-CLOPS [15, 40], a high-performance camera pointing system developed at NIST. In these tests the system was able to track and servo on the target as it moved at velocities of up to 1 m/s at a distance of 0.85 m. The equivalent angular velocity for this tracking speed is about 1.2 rad/s (69 deg/s). The algorithm has demonstrated promising results in tracking the target in the presence of partial occlusion; it was not confused by any of the background scenery it encountered. The algorithm is also fairly robust to deviations from the assumed fixed orientation of the target; it begins to fail when there are errors greater than 15 degrees in orientation. It will also fail if the target is moved with very sudden motions.

Further details regarding the performance specifications of TRICLOPS and the implementation of its motion control system, as well as additional discussion of predictive filter characteristics, may be found in [40, 41].

6. Real-Time Obstacle Avoidance Using Central Flow Divergence and Peripheral Flow

The system described in this section uses time-to-contact (T_c) estimates derived from flow divergence to detect imminent head-on collision [29]. Flow divergence is the sum of optical flow derivatives in two directions perpendicular to one another. In the direction of the camera's heading, divergence is inversely related to time-to-contact. This is combined with a centering behavior that compares left and right peripheral flows to steer the robot down a conceptual corridor [10]. When the corridor-following behavior drives the robot into a "dead end" in the "corridor," the central time-to-contact predictions warn the robot of the impending collision. The robot stops, turns, and resumes wandering, following a new "corridor." These integrated behaviors have driven the robot around the lab at 30 cm/s for as long as 20 minutes without collision. A more complete description of the system is presented in [9].

In our system, video images are obtained from two on-board cameras. One of the cameras is above the other, and both are mounted on a single-pan motor. Neither camera is calibrated. Central/peripheral visual sensing is achieved with narrow and wide lenses. The narrow central camera has a 40° field of view. It is tilted downward so that its visual axis intersects the floor 2 or 3 meters in front of the robot. The wide camera, mounted slightly below the narrow one, has a 115° field of view. The robot's view from these cameras is shown in Figure 18. The images from the two cameras are processed independently, and they are independently used to control behavior.

Our system consists of five processing modules. The first process computes normal flow, the component of motion perpendicular to edges in the images of the two cameras. The magnitude and quantized direction of the normal flow are presented to the second processing module, which computes divergence and time-to-contact in three overlapping windows of the central image. In the wide image, the process estimates maximum flow in two peripheral visual fields (left and right). Accuracy is sacrificed to achieve real-time performance. The resulting errors in normal flow estimates produce errors in divergence and time-to-contact measurements as well. The

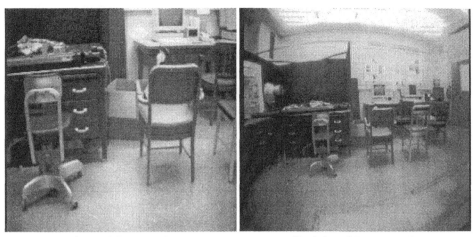

Central Lens: 40°   Peripheral Lens: 115°

Figure 18. Robot's view of the scene.

third process temporally filters maximum flow and T_c to reduce errors. Recursive estimation is used to update current flow and T_c estimates and to predict flow and T_c at the next sample time.

The fourth process uses flow to steer the robot down the conceptual corridor estimated by comparing peripheral flows in the wide camera. Using active gaze control, the cameras are rotationally stabilized so that their motion is approximately a translation. If the flow is larger on one peripheral side than the other, then objects in the scene are closer on that side, and the robot steers away. When the camera points too far away from the heading, a saccade is made toward the heading. When T_c predictions in the central camera indicate imminent collision in a "dead end" in the conceptual corridor, the robot stops, turns away, and resumes wandering. The inputs to the body and gaze controllers consist of driving, steering, and gaze velocities.

Flow and flow divergence are 2D image quantities; no explicit 3D reconstructions are performed. The difference between the magnitudes of optical flow in the two peripheral fields is computed and used directly to control the robot's steering. Therefore, decisions on how to steer the robot depend directly on the difference between these two image quantities. The determination of whether or not to stop and turn is made directly from the 2D flow divergence values in the image. The method requires no camera calibration, and the only knowledge needed about the camera's translational motion is the approximate heading direction. The camera's rotation in the 2D plane of the robot's motion is compensated through active gaze control.

6.1. MAXIMUM FLOW IN THE VISUAL PERIPHERY

The system estimates the maximum flows in the left and right peripheral visual fields of the wide-angle camera. The cameras are rotationally stabilized using active gaze control so that their motion is approximately a translation. For comparing clearance to obstacles on each side of the path, the maximum flow value in each peripheral receptive field is a function of the distance to the nearest object in that field [10]. The optical flow processing in each field is implemented in two parts: First, dense normal flow is estimated as described above; then the maximum magnitude flow in each receptive field is identified by examining the histogram of flows in each field.

It should be noted that this implementation does not attempt to compute true range for objects in the image. To do so would require calibrating the focal length, the wide-angle lens distortion, and the vehicle velocity (both direction and magnitude).

6.2. DIVERGENCE AND TIME-TO-CONTACT

The system computes flow divergence in the central camera. The equations for the x and y components of optical flow (O_x, O_y) due to general camera motion (arbitrary translation and rotation) in a stationary environment are

$$O_x = \left(\frac{1}{Z}\right)(-T_x + xT_z) + \left(xy\omega_x - \left(1 + x^2\right)\omega_y + y\omega_z\right) \tag{26}$$

$$O_y = \left(\frac{1}{Z}\right)(-T_y + yT_z) + \left(\left(1 + y^2\right)\omega_x - xy\omega_y - x\omega_z\right) \tag{27}$$

where Z is the depth of the object in the environment relative to the camera; (T_x, T_y, T_z) and $(\omega_x, \omega_y, \omega_z)$ are the translational and rotational motion of the environment relative to the camera [8]. The divergence of an optical flow field is defined as

$$\nabla^\circ (O_x, O_y) = \frac{\partial O_x}{\partial x} + \frac{\partial O_y}{\partial y}. \tag{28}$$

Note that

$$\frac{\partial O_x}{\partial x} + \frac{\partial \rho}{\partial x}(-T_x + xT_z) + \rho T_z + y\omega_x - 2x\omega_y \tag{29}$$

$$\frac{\partial O_y}{\partial y} = \frac{\partial \rho}{\partial y}(-T_y + yT_z) + \rho T_z + 2y\omega_x - x\omega_y \tag{30}$$

where $\rho = 1/Z$. From (28) through (30), at $(x, y) = (0, 0)$:

$$\nabla^\circ (O_x, O_y) = \frac{\partial \rho}{\partial x}(-T_x) + 2\rho T_z + \frac{\partial \rho}{\partial y}(-T_y). \tag{31}$$

From (31),

$$\nabla^\circ (O_x, O_y) = 2\rho T_z \tag{32}$$

whenever the imaged surface is a mostly perpendicular surface *or* the gradient of the imaged surface is perpendicular to the transverse velocity (T_x, T_y). Time-to-contact (T_c), or nearness in time, can be estimated directly from divergence (32):

$$T_c = \frac{Z}{T_z} = 2/\nabla^\circ (O_x, O_y). \tag{33}$$

This measurement is particularly useful for obstacle avoidance during visual navigation because divergence is invariant under the rotational motion of the sensor that is inevitable due to imperfect stabilization.

Equation (33) suggests that T_c has only time as its dimension. The values of T_c over any significant area in the image represent the time needed to reach an object at distance Z with velocity T_z in the z direction. A family of simple fixed flow divergence templates can be applied to any image sequence to estimate divergence [23]. Each template is symmetrically divided into positive and negative halves (Figure 19). Flow divergence is calculated by convolving the template with a window in the flow image and computing the sum of the image flow derivatives in perpendicular directions. Only normal flow values in the direction of the particular mask are considered for each mask. Since there are few accurate flow values in the implementation, a large window is needed to accumulate multiple samples. (The flow estimates are inaccurate particularly because their directions are quantized.) Each time-to-contact value has an associated confidence, which is the number of points in the window that have measurable flow values. In order to improve the consistency of the estimation of T_c, we apply a recursive least-squares update procedure.

Figure 19. Flow divergence templates.

6.3. RECURSIVE LEAST-SQUARES ESTIMATION

A temporal model is used to estimate and predict T_c values. A linear model is maintained for the time-to-contact in each of the three windows:

$$T_c = a_1 + a_2 t \qquad (34)$$

where $t = 0, -1, -2, \ldots$. For each measurement of time-to-contact, model parameters a_1 and a_2 are updated by a weighted recursive least squares computation with exponential decay [8, 17, 23, 35]. This involves determining a_1 and a_2 such that the residual J is minimized:

$$J = \sum_{t=0}^{-n} \lambda^t w_t \left[T_c - (a_1 + a_2 t) \right]^2 \qquad (35)$$

where $t = 0, -1, -2, \ldots, -n$; $t = 0$ is the present; λ is the forgetting factor; and w_t is the confidence of the tth T_c measurement (the number of flow data points in the window).

Since the camera is approximately aligned with the robot's heading, the objects viewed in the estimation windows change as the robot steers away from obstacles. The windows' sample data therefore change constantly when the vehicle is turning, i.e., old obstacles disappear from view and new obstacles become visible. The forgetting factor, λ, adjusts for this behavior by controlling the relative weighting of new and old data. λ is changed dynamically as a function of the control system's commanded angular velocity. In this way, the weight of past events is reduced when the robot turns faster and a new scene becomes visible. Similarly, past observations weigh more heavily when the robot moves straight ahead.

Figure 23 plots a history of time-to-contact predictions for straight line motion of the robot. The last entries in the plot are decreasing and approaching zero. However, although the general trend is downward, the progression is nonmonotonic. No single time-to-contact datum provides sufficient confidence to conclude that collision is likely. There appears to be a correlation between collision, the time-to-contact value (a_1 in equation (34)), the slope of the predicted line (a_2), and the confidence (w_0) which represents the number of normal flow pixels contributing to the current divergence estimate. A combination of short predicted time-to-contact ($a_1 < 0.07$), negative slope of T_c predictions ($a_2 < 0$), and at least a moderate number of current data ($w_0 > 20$) seem to reliably indicate imminent collision.

6.4. Driving control

The robot's behavioral goal is simply to drive forward, steering away from obstacles, and to stop and turn when it senses that collision is imminent. This is implemented with a finite-state automaton, with a command associated with each state (Figure 20). Some state transitions are triggered by sensed events, and others merely provide command sequencing.

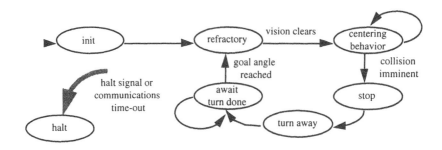

Figure 20. Body control automaton.

The robot steers smoothly to a new desired heading with saturated negative visual feedback controls [13]. The desired heading, θ_v, is chosen to attempt to balance the peripheral flows and is represented in retinotopic (visual) coordinates:

$$\theta_v = k_h \left(O_{\nabla I}^L - O_{\nabla I}^L \right). \tag{36}$$

$O_{\nabla I}^L$ and $O_{\nabla I}^L$ are the left and right maximal normal flows in the peripheral visual fields. The gain k_h is chosen empirically to produce a sensible desired heading in the visual space. Desired change in heading, $\Delta\theta$, is then calculated, accounting for the current gaze angle, θ_g, with respect to heading:

$$\Delta\theta = \theta_v + \theta_g \tag{37}$$

The steering control policy is simply a saturated steering velocity proportional to the desired heading:

$$\dot{\theta} = \text{Saturate}\left(k_s \cdot \Delta\theta \cdot \frac{1}{T_b}, s\right). \tag{38}$$

The gain k_s (usually < 1) determines how quickly the steering is servoed to the desired heading. Time is normalized to seconds by dividing by the body control cycle time, T_b. Thus, angular velocity is expressed in degrees/s rather than degrees/cycle. The angular velocity is saturated at $\pm s$ deg/s to limit the peak rotation rate to reasonable levels.

6.5. GAZE CONTROL

In order for the centering behavior to work properly, the cameras should be translating approximately along the heading. In this way, the relationship between flow and range in the two peripheral fields will be the same. Therefore, the behavior and motor control systems must minimize rotation of the cameras. This is accomplished by stabilizing the cameras with active motor commands and by limiting rotation of the body so the gaze stabilization is not overstressed.

The nonlinear gaze control is a *nystagmus*, a repetitive eye motion of slow-phase rotations punctuated by quick-phase rapid returns. It is also implemented as a finite-state automaton (Figure 21). The camera is rotated at velocity $\dot{\phi} = -\dot{\theta}$ to counter the body rotation and stabilize the camera images. The gaze control also checks the deviation of the gaze angle, θ_g, from the robot's heading and snaps the camera back to the heading if the limit is exceeded.

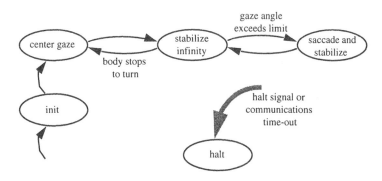

Figure 21. Gaze control automaton.

6.6. EXPERIMENTS AND RESULTS

Experiments with the obstacle avoidance system were conducted in a laboratory containing office furniture and robot and computing equipment. Furniture and equipment lined the walls and there was free space roughly 5 m by 3 m in the center of the lab. Office chairs provided obstacles.

In typical experiments, the robot began the trial at one end of the lab. Obstacles were placed in the cameras's views. The robot drove forward at 30 cm/s. As images were processed, time-to-contact was estimated. Figure 22 shows a sequence of images taken with the 40° field-of-view camera as the robot approached a stack of chairs. Figure 23 plots the T_c recorded during such a trial against time, represented by sampling numbers. The time-to-contact dimension is not calibrated.

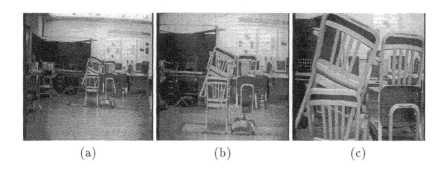

(a)   (b)   (c)

Figure 22. Sequence of images as robot approaches obstacles.

A typical trace of the robot's path using obstacle avoidance and wandering behaviors is plotted in Figure 24. Variability in steering and stopping depends in part on the textures visible from a particular approach. Stopping distances may vary just because the angle of approach varies. As time-to-contact and peripheral flows are computed, the robot moves forward toward open areas while centering itself in the open space. Upon detection of an imminent collision, it turns to avoid the obstacle and continues its wandering behavior. The system has run successfully for up to 20 min.

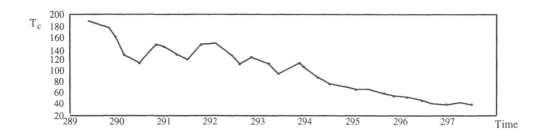

Figure 23. Time-to-contact versus time.

7. TERRAIN NAVIGATION USING VISUAL INVARIANTS

To achieve terrain navigation safely for autonomous vehicles, obstacles must be discriminated from terrain before any path planning and obstacle avoidance activity is undertaken. Obstacles are defined as any regions in space where a vehicle should not

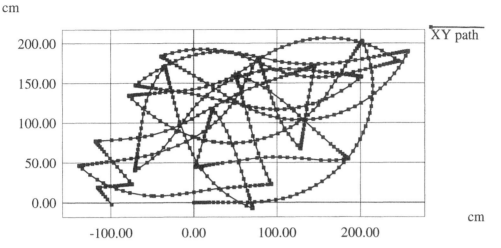

Figure 24. Robot's path.

or cannot traverse, such as protrusions (objects lying on top of the terrain), depressions (potholes, ruts, gullies in the terrain), or steep terrain. This section describes a simple, fast, and general method for obstacle detection under general vehicle motion while navigating through man-made roadways or natural outdoor terrain. The method finds obstacles in the 2D image space, as opposed to 3D reconstructed space, using optical flow. The advantages of this 2D-based approach include greater simplicity and speed because fewer hypotheses, sensor measurements, and calibrations, as well as fewer computations, need to be performed. The theory for our method uses new visual invariants based on optical flow.

Our method specifically assumes that both nonobstacle terrain regions as well as regions with obstacles will be visible in the imagery. Therefore, our goal is to discriminate between terrain regions with obstacles and terrain regions without obstacles. The visual invariants we develop involve the mapping of points that lie on any straight line segment in 3D space into an image-based space, i.e., a space whose coordinate axes represent parameter values extracted from the image domain. There are certain image-based spaces such that straight line segments in these spaces are mapped only from straight line segments in 3D space. Such a mapping is described as invariant for linear relationships, or simply linearly invariant, since linear relationships are always preserved.

Our approach to obstacle detection is different from previous approaches in that it uses optical flow to discriminate between obstacles and terrain without 3D reconstruction, for arbitrary camera motion, and without knowledge of the pose of the camera relative to the ground, camera motion or terrain models; it requires relatively little calibration and a priori knowledge.

7.1. VISUAL INVARIANTS THEORY AND DERIVATION

The equations for optical flow due to general camera motion (arbitrary translation and rotation) in a stationary environment are

$$\dot{x} = \frac{1}{Z_c}\left(-T_x + xT_z\right) + xy\omega_x - \left(1 + x^2\right)\omega_y + y\omega_z \tag{39}$$

$$\dot{y} = \frac{1}{Z_c}\left(-T_y + yT_z\right) + \left(1 + y^2\right)\omega_x + \left(-xy\omega_y\right) - x\omega_z \tag{40}$$

$$F = \left(\dot{x}^2 + \dot{y}^2\right)^{\frac{1}{2}} \tag{41}$$

where Z_c is the depth of the object in the environment relative to the camera, (T_x, T_y, T_z) and $(\omega_x, \omega_y, \omega_z)$ are the translational and rotational motion of the environment coordinate system relative to the camera, and F is the magnitude of optical flow. We have shown in [43, 44] that for all points on the image line $\overline{ab}$ (i.e., $y = $ constant) in Figure 25 that arise from points in the scene lying on line $\overline{AB}$,

$$\dot{x} = b_1 + b_2 x + b_3 x^2 \tag{42}$$

where b_1, b_2, and b_3 are constants. This equation represents a quadratic curve in the $\dot{x}$ vs. x image-based space corresponding to a line in 3D space. However, for the same line in 3D space, the $\dot{y}$ vs. x image-based space has the following linear relationship:

$$\dot{y} = a_1 + a_2 x \tag{43}$$

where a_1 and a_2 are constants for all points on line $\overline{AB}$. This equation represents a line in the $\dot{y}$ vs. x image-based space corresponding to a line in 3D space. This is a visual linear invariant.

7.2. OBSTACLE DETECTION: PROTRUSIONS AND DEPRESSIONS

In this section, we show how to detect protrusions and depressions using a purposive and direct approach (i.e., directly from optical flow without 3D reconstruction). The method employs the properties of visual linear invariants. Although the discussion thus far has been concerned only with single lines, many lines in the image plane can be processed in parallel to detect obstacles on the full terrain ahead of the vehicle.

As described above, mappings are linearly invariant only for certain image-based spaces. It is shown in [43, 44] that only these invariant mappings are useful for obstacle detection.

Algorithm. To apply the property of linear invariance to obstacle detection, four steps are involved.

Step 1: Selection of an arbitrary straight line in the image.
    This line should intersect an image feature of interest, e.g., a potential obstacle. The chosen image line need not correspond to a linear feature in the scene or in the image. In principle, many image lines can be processed in parallel.

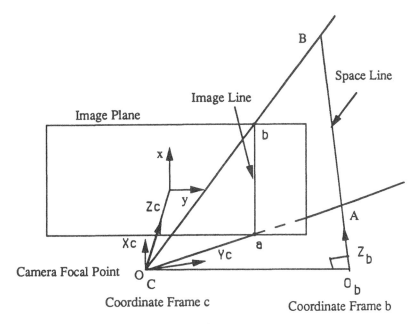

Figure 25. Definition of two coordinates frames.

Step 2: Estimation of the reference flow line for the image line.

The reference flow line in the image-based space, say $\dot{y}$ vs. x for an image line y, corresponds to a reference space line in 3D space. The latter reference line and the camera focal point define a plane in space (Figure 25). The intersection of this plane with objects and terrain in the environment defines a set of curves lying in the plane which are visible in the camera. Deviations between these curves and the 3D reference line are represented in the image-based space. The 3D reference line can be arbitrarily chosen but it should probably arise from a surface in the environment such that deviations from this surface represent protrusions and depressions. On a road, for example, the 3D reference line should probably lie on the road surface.

Step 3: Computation of the deviation.

The deviation between the reference line obtained in step 2 and the measured flow at all image positions lying on that image line (i.e., component of flow normal to the image line) is computed.

Step 4: Segmentation of obstacle regions.

The computed deviation in step 3 is used to detect obstacles. Points on the image line with deviation larger than some threshold value represent obstacles.

In this method, only one component of the optical flow is needed. Information such as specific knowledge of vehicle (or camera) motion, or knowledge of the coordinate transformation between the camera and the ground, is not required. Therefore, the method reduces error sources to a minimum since it employs minimum information. The approach is simple because obstacles are detected directly in the image-based space, without performing 3D reconstruction. Without any assumption of a terrain model, this method can be used for ground vehicles navigating in man-made roadways or natural outdoor terrain.

7.3. Experimental results

In this section, we present the results of several experiments demonstrating the simplicity and usefulness of visual linear invariants applied to obstacle detection. Both synthetic and real indoor and outdoor scenes are considered. Only the components of optical flow normal to the selected image lines are used.

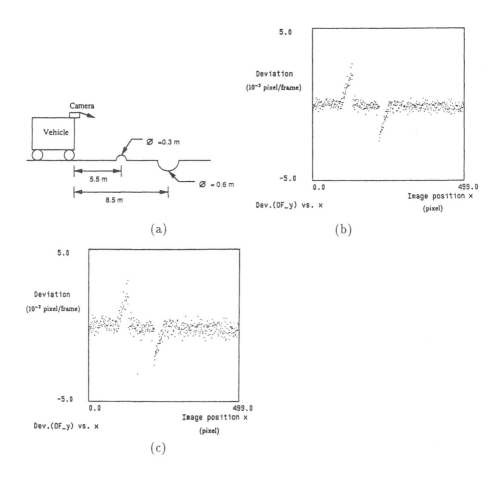

Figure 26. (a) Side view of terrain with a bump and a pothole. (b) $\Delta \dot{y}$ vs. x in experiment 1 (10% noise). (c) $\Delta \dot{y}$ vs. x in experiment 1 (15% noise).

Experiment 1. This experiment simulates a ground vehicle moving over terrain with a bump and a pothole, as shown in Figure 26a. The experiment uses synthetic data with three different levels of noise, 5%, 10%, and 15%. The noise is generated randomly using a Gaussian distribution and is added to the optical flow obtained through simulation. This noise represents the uncertainty value of the measured flow.

Only one image line is used in this experiment. The bump is a semicircle which is 5.5 m ahead of the camera, with a height of 0.3 m above the flat terrain. The pothole is a semicircle which is 8.5 m ahead of the camera, with a depth of 0.6 m below the terrain. The camera is mounted on top of the vehicle (2 m above the ground) and moves under general motion with $(T_x = -927, T_y = -4, T_z = 2853$ mm/s) and $(\omega_x = 0.05, \omega_y = 0.05, \omega_z = 0.05$ rad/s). Points that lie above the horizontal straight line result from protrusions on the terrain, while points below the horizontal line result from depressions. Two obstacles, a protrusion and a depression, can easily be detected in Figures 26b and 26c.

Experiment 2. This experiment involves detecting a stationary car on a roadway in a real outdoor scene (Figure 27a). A camera is mounted on the NIST HMMWV, which is on a road and approaching a stationary car. The vehicle (or camera) motion is unknown. Flow perpendicular to the scan line is analyzed using the linear invariance method. Optical flow was obtained using a 3D hermite polynomials method [24]. The component of flow in the y direction is shown in Figure 27b. To reduce the effects of highly noisy data, a spatiotemporal median filter is applied to the optical flow imagery. Figure 27c shows the result for scan line 118 using the measured $\dot{y}$ as inputs. Scan line 118 is labelled in Figure 27a. All the scan lines in the middle portion of the image were processed, and obstacle points were extracted at each scan line. Figure 27d shows all the obstacle points superimposed on the image in Figure 27a. The white region denotes the detected obstacle.

Experiment 3. This experiment involves detecting multiple obstacles in a real outdoor parking lot scene (Figure 28a). A camera is held by a passenger in a moving vehicle, approaching several parked cars on the right side. The vehicle (or camera) motion is unknown. Optical flow was obtained using the method of Lucas and Kanade [25] implemented by Barron et al. [7]. Here, we only consider scan lines 130 and 133 labelled in Figure 28a. The results for these scan lines are shown in Figures 28b and 28c, respectively. The protrusions denoting parked cars on the right side are easily detected. Note that the right-most image positions show the largest deviations. This is because the parked cars in the right-most image positions are closest to the observer.

7.4. Discussion

The main features of the approach described in this section are that (1) 2D visual information (i.e., optical flow) is directly used to detect obstacles; no range, 3D motion, or 3D scene geometry is recovered; (2) knowledge about the camera-to-ground coordinate transformation is not required, reducing the amount of camera calibration required; (3) knowledge about the vehicle (or camera) motion is not required, eliminating the need for motion sensors and calibration of the camera relative to these sensors; (4) no terrain model is required, making the method useful for unknown environments; (5) arbitrary camera motion (both translation and rotation) is allowed, making the method completely general; and (6) the error sources involved are reduced to a minimum, since the only information required is one component

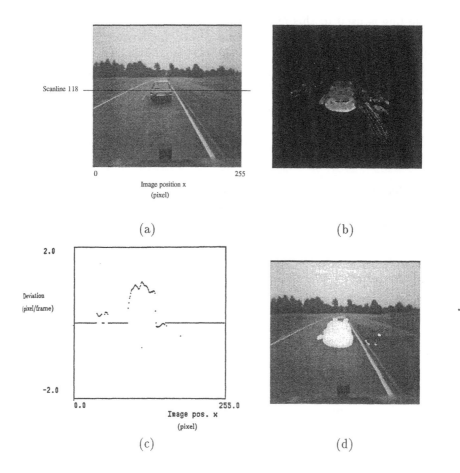

Figure 27. (a) One image frame of a sequence in experiment 2. (b) The y component of the measured flow in experiment 2. (c) Obstacles detected at row no. 118 in experiment 2. (d) Obstacles detected for the full image in experiment 2.

of optical flow. The method is therefore a general method which requires relatively little calibration and a priori knowledge.

8. CONCLUSION

This chapter presents a minimalist approach to visual servoing for navigation in which (1) only task-relevant information is extracted from the imagery, and (2) all information is represented in the 2D image coordinate system (no 3D reconstructions are performed). The approach is demonstrated using five specific examples in the area of navigation for both indoor and outdoor robots.

Although the examples in this chapter focus on visual servoing for navigation, we believe that the lessons can be carried over into sensory servoing using acoustic, laser range, touch and other methods of sensing. The main lesson is that sensory processing should be focussed so that only task-relevant sensory information is extracted.

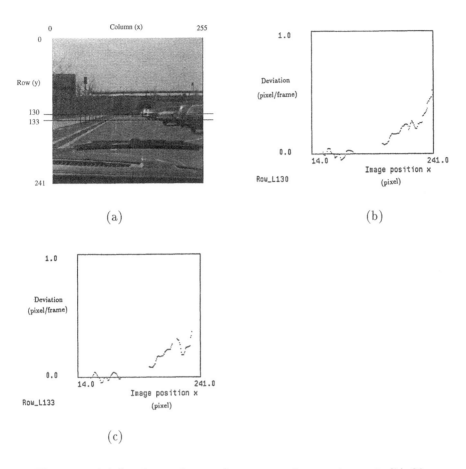

Figure 28. (a) One image frame of a sequence in experiment 3. (b) Obstacles detected at scan line 130 in experiment 3. (c) Obstacles detected at scan line 133 in experiment 3.

Once extracted, the sensory information should be represented only in the coordinate system of the sensor (e.g., in the 2D image coordinate system for a camera) or in a coordinate system which is easy to calibrate relative to the original coordinate system. This sensory information can then be used to directly control the motion of a robot [2]. For example, this approach has been used to perform visual servoing of a touch probe for inspection tasks [28].

REFERENCES

1. J.S. Albus, "Outline for a theory of intelligence," *IEEE Transactions on Systems, Man, and Cybernetics* **21**(3), 1991, 473–509.

2. J. Y. Aloimonos, "Purposive and qualitative active vision," in *Proc. Image Understanding Workshop*, Pittsburgh, PA, 1990, 816–828.

3. J. Aloimonos, I. Weiss, and A. Bandopadhay, "Active vision," *International Journal of Computer Vision* **2**, 1988, 333–356.

4. R. Bajcsy, "Active perception," *Proceedings of the IEEE* **76**(8), August 1988.

5. D.H. Ballard, "Animate vision," *Artificial Intelligence* **48**, 1991, 57–86.

6. D.H. Ballard and C. Brown, "Principles of animate vision," *CVGIP: Image Understanding* **56**(1), 1992, 3–21.

7. J. Barron, D. Fleet, and S. Beauchemin, "Performance of optical flow techniques," *International Journal of Computer Vision* **12**(1), 1994.

8. G. Bierman, *Factorization Methods for Discrete Sequential Estimation*, Academic Press, New York, 1977.

9. D. Coombs, M. Herman, T.-H. Hong, and M. Nashman, "Real-time obstacle avoidance using central flow divergence and peripheral flow," *Proc. 5th International Conference on Computer Vision*, Cambridge, MA, June 1995.

10. D. Coombs and K. Roberts, "Centering behavior using peripheral vision," in *Proc. of CVPR 1993, the IEEE Conference on Computer Vision and Pattern Recognition*, New York, June 15–17, 1993.

11. E. Dickmans and V. Graefe, "Applications of dynamic monocular machine vision," *Machine Vision and Applications* **1**, 1988.

12. E. Dickmans and V. Graefe, "Dynamic monocular machine vision," *Machine Vision and Applications* **1**, 1988.

13. R. Dorf, *Modern Control Systems*, Addison-Wesley, Reading, MA, 1980.

14. B.A. Draper, R.T. Collins, J. Brolio, A.R. Hanson, and E.M. Riseman, "The schema system," *International Journal of Computer Vision* **2**(3), 1989, 209–250.

15. J.C. Fiala, R. Lumia, K.J. Roberts, and A.J. Wavering, "TRICLOPS: A tool for studying active vision," *International Journal of Computer Vision* **12**(2/3), 1994.

16. J.J. Gibson, *The Ecological Approach to Visual Perception*, Lawrence Erlbaum Associates, Hillsdale, NJ, 1986.

17. G. Goodwin and K. Sin, *Adaptive Filtering, Prediction and Control*, Prentice Hall, Englewood Cliffs, NJ, 1984.

18. C. Helstrom, *Probability and Stochastic Processes for Engineers*, Macmillan, New York, 1984.

19. K. Joarder and D. Raviv, "A new method to calculate looming for autonomous obstacle avoidance," Internal Report NISTIR 5512, National Institute of Standards and Technology, Gaithersburg, MD, November 1994.

20. S.M. Kay, *Fundamentals of Statistical Signal Processing: Estimation Theory*, Prentice Hall, Englewood Cliffs, NJ, 1993.

21. S.R. Kundur and D. Raviv, "An image-based texture-independent visual motion cue for autonomous navigation," Internal Report NISTIR 5567, National Institute of Standards and Technology, Gaithersburg, MD, January 1995.

22. S.R. Kundur and D. Raviv, "Texture-independent vision-based closed-loop fuzzy controllers for navigation tasks," Internal Report NISTIR 5637, National Institute of Standards and Technology, Gaithersburg, MD, April 1995.

23. C. Lawson and R. Hanson, *Solving Least Squares Problems*, Prentice Hall, Englewood Cliffs, NJ, 1974.

24. H. Liu, T.-H. Hong, M. Herman, and R. Chellappa, "A general motion model and spatio-temporal filters for computing optical flow," NIST-IR 5539, National Institute of Standards and Technology, Gaithersburg, MD, January 1995; to appear in *International Journal of Computer Vision*, 1996.

25. B. Lucas and T. Kanade, "An iterative image registration technique with an application to stereo vision," *Proc. DARPA Image Understanding Workshop*, Washington, DC, 1981, 121–130.

26. M. Minsky, "A framework for representing knowledge," in *The Psychology of Computer Vision*, P. Winston (Ed.), McGraw-Hill, New York, 1975, 211–277.

27. K. Murphy, "Navigation and retro-traverse on a remotely operated vehicle," *Proceedings of the IEEE Conference on Intelligent Control and Instrumentation*, Singapore, February 1992.

28. M. Nashman, W. Rippey, T.-H. Hong, and M. Herman, "An integrated vision touch-probe system for dimensional inspection tasks," Internal Report NISTIR 5678, National Institute of Standards and Technology, Gaithersburg, MD, June 1995.

29. R. Nelson and Y. Aloimonos, "Obstacle avoidance using flow field divergence," *IEEE Transactions on Pattern Analysis and Machine Intelligence* 11(10), 1989, 1102–1106.

30. D.N. Oskard, T.-H. Hong, and C.A. Shaffer, "Real-time algorithms and data structures for underwater mapping," *IEEE Trans. on Systems, Man, and Cybernetics* 20(6), 1990.

31. A. Papoulis, *Probability, Random Variables, and Stochastic Processes*, 2nd Edition, McGraw-Hill, New York, 1984.

32. D. Raviv and M. Herman, "A new approach to vision and control for road following," *IEEE Workshop on Visual Motion*, Princeton, NJ, October 1991.

33. D. Raviv and M. Herman, "Visual servoing from 2-D image cues," in *Active Perception*, Y. Aloimonos (Ed.), Lawrence Erlbaum Associates, Hillsdale, NJ, 1993, 191–226.

34. D. Raviv and M. Herman, "A unified approach to camera fixation and vision-based road following," *IEEE Transactions on Systems, Man, and Cybernetics* 24(8), August 1994.

35. H. Schneiderman and M. Nashman, "A discriminating feature based tracker for vision-based autonomous driving," *IEEE Transactions on Robotics and Automation* 10(6), December 1994.

36. H. Schneiderman, M. Nashman, and R. Lumia, "Model-based vision for car following," *SPIE's International Symposium on Optical Tools for Manufacturing and Advanced Automation* **2059**, 1993.

37. S. Szabo, H. Scott, K. Murphy, S. Legowik, and R. Bostelman, "High-level mobility controller for a remotely operated land vehicle," *Journal of Intelligent and Robotic Systems* **5**, 1992, 63–77.

38. C. Thorpe, M. Hébert, T. Kanade, and S. Shafer, "Vision and navigation for the Carnegie-Mellon navlab," *IEEE Trans. on Pattern Analysis and Machine Intelligence* **10**(3), 1988.

39. M. Turk, D. Morgenthaler, K. Gremban, and M. Marra, "VITS—A vision system for autonomous land vehicle navigation," *IEEE Trans. on Pattern Analysis and Machine Intelligence*, May 1988.

40. A.J. Wavering, J.C. Fiala, K.J. Roberts, and R. Lumia, "TRICLOPS: A high-performance trinocular active vision system," in *Proc. IEEE Conference on Robotics and Automation* **3**, Atlanta, GA, 1993, 310–317.

41. A.J. Wavering and R. Lumia, "Predictive visual tracking," in *Proc. Intelligent Robots and Computer Vision XII: Active Vision and 3D Methods* **2056**, Boston, MA, September 8–9, 1993, 86–97.

42. A. Waxman, J. LeMoigne, L. Davis, and T. Siddalingalah, "A visual navigation system for autonomous land vehicle," *IEEE Journal Robotics and Automation* **3**, April 1987, 124–141.

43. G.-S. Young, "Safe navigation and active vision for autonomous vehicles: A purposive and direct solution," University of Maryland, Ph.D. dissertation, May 1993.

44. G.S. Young, T.H. Hong, M. Herman, and J.C.S. Yang, "New visual invariants for obstacle detection using optical flow induced from general motion," *Proc. IEEE Workshop on Applications of Computer Vision*, Palm Springs, CA, November 30–December 2, 1992, 100–109.

11 Landmark-Based Navigation and the Acquisition of Environmental Models

Edward M. Riseman,[1] Allen R. Hanson,[1] J. Ross Beveridge,[2]
Rakesh (Teddy) Kumar,[3] and Harpreet Sawhney[3]
[1]University of Massachusetts, Amherst
[2]Colorado State University
[3]David Sarnoff Research Laboratory

Abstract

Navigation in large-scale space, and the execution of a coherent set of actions in this space, requires the use of some knowledge of the environment. A long-range research program in computer vision at UMass has had as one of its primary goals the integration of a diverse set of research efforts into a knowledge-based system that ultimately achieves robust, real-time navigation. The focus of this paper is on robust landmark-based navigation in the UMass mobile robot navigation project, including issues of how to acquire, utilize, extend, and modify three-dimensional models of the domain that is being navigated. Much of this chapter discusses mechanisms and algorithms that can be utilized for navigation assuming a partial geometric model is available, but the general concepts can be applied more widely and are fundamental to applications such as object recognition and three-dimensional (3D) reconstruction.

1. Navigation in the World

1.1. Knowledge is required

Mobile robots that are to move through the world in a goal-oriented manner must have a variety of perceptual capabilities. Some of these are "low-level" in the sense that they are focused primarily on the immediate local results of perceptual processing, often for safety (e.g., emergency stops and obstacle avoidance), and might have only secondary importance for achieving the actual global goal. For example, stereo processing might be used during navigation for obstacle avoidance and have priority in the control of the vehicle whenever obstacles are in the chosen path.

This work was supported in part by the Advanced Research Projects Agency under contract DAAE07-91-C-R035 and by the National Science Foundation under grant number CDA-8922572.

Others are "high-level" in the sense that they are focussed primarily on establishing and maintaining the 'goals' of the vehicle. Often these have a lower priority compared to those concerned with the safety of the robot. This has led many to the development of reactive and hierarchical "behaviors" as a control methodology for mobile robots, and some relatively simple systems have been constructed using this paradigm [8, 9, 29, 30, 101, 102, 108]. However, we believe that there is an obvious upper limit on the complexity of tasks which can be achieved without use of more general world knowledge and higher-level reasoning mechanisms [132, 133]. For a system to achieve goal-oriented navigation in complex large-scale domains (e.g., to move beyond the immediately visible world) relying solely on action-oriented and reactive behaviors is problematic.

At the foundation of our work is the premise that higher-level vision beyond the first stages of sensory processing, and other cognitive abilities such as planning, will greatly benefit from, and in many cases require, the use of knowledge and models of objects and the environment. It is unlikely that humans can navigate large-scale space without some form of prior knowledge, even if it is embedded in the goal specification. For example, the goal statement "travel east on Route 9 until you come to the town of Amherst" involves access to a large amount of stored knowledge that one often is not conscious of. This includes an a priori map relative to one's location (to navigate on roads), a visual model for recognizing the general class of roads, a visual model for the general class of road signs (in order to determine the road sign instance of "Route 9"), knowledge for navigation on roads such as the standard driving conventions involving lane markers, traffic signs and lights, pedestrians, other vehicles, etc., and finally the class of towns (to recognize the town instance "Amherst").

This chapter does not attempt to deal with many of the topics implied by the previous discussion. For example, neither the artificial intelligence (AI) issues associated with applying general knowledge of traffic conventions [109, 110] nor the recognition of general classes of objects in outdoor scenes [20, 23, 33, 34, 41, 42, 51, 55, 63, 64, 65, 66, 92, 93, 96, 97, 98, 99, 112, 125] is considered here. Rather, it is an attempt to address a smaller set of well-defined problems whose solution will provide a scientific and engineering foundation upon which to build flexible and general navigation systems of the future. Our research is intended to complement the work of others.

Landmark recognition, and the ability to reason spatially within the environment, provide fundamental capabilities that support large-scale autonomous navigation. Recognizing landmark instances within a 3D model of the local environment and deriving its 3D position in the world allow an autonomous system to link a sequence of such local contexts indefinitely, always determining approximately where it is in a global coordinate system. A hierarchical planning system would then be able to reason about landmarks at the proper level of spatial resolution to navigate effectively in the world, as well as communicate with humans. An example prototype of such a system was developed at UMass using a "locale" data structure for 3D space, implemented as frames with slots that organize the topological, geometrical, and physical properties of the objects and environment they represent [52].

While the Global Positioning System (GPS) is an alternative mechanism for determining the general location of a mobile robot, there are many reasons why such a system cannot (or should not) completely replace visual landmark recognition during intelligent navigation. An important one is the ability to reason about navigation goals in terms of distinctive features of the local visible environment.

1.2. WHERE DOES THE KNOWLEDGE BASE COME FROM?

Before discussing our approach to landmark-based navigation, we should address the question of where the initial knowledge base comes from. How would a system acquire the landmark models? In some closed-world domains, a 3D model might be provided by the user. However, in the complex domain of natural scenes, the infinite variety of detail of shapes, colors, and textures that typically appear in the world will be absolutely impossible to capture by any means short of divine intervention [111]. Nevertheless, specification of landmarks may be possible in terms of general classes of objects—trees, mountains, cars, houses, signs, etc., and their spatial relationships—but even the construction of sparse partial models in terms of general classes would be extremely difficult to construct manually with any level of spatial accuracy for a given set of landmarks.

The daunting complexity issues that must be dealt with may be a major reason why there are very few model-based mobile robot systems that function in outdoor environments. Generally, current vision-based robot projects have a very specific focus, such as lane tracking for on-road driving, or obstacle avoidance for stable off-road navigation on irregular terrain. Consequently, model-based vision is employed far more often for object recognition (a task that is usually much more constrained than navigation) or in indoor robotic domains that are much more controlled.

In contrast, the UMass mobile robot project had a long-range research strategy of building systems that use and acquire models autonomously via direct experience in the world. Initial models were originally intended to be acquired via stereo or motion analysis, and then a sparse 3D model would be extended using the techniques of landmark-based navigation presented here. The ultimate goal was to be an autonomous mobile vehicle capable of exploring an unknown environment while acquiring an environmental model that would be used to support further model-directed navigation in a robust and efficient manner. While this ambitious goal has not yet been achieved, we believe the work presented here is a step in that direction.

1.3. LANDMARK RECOGNITION DIFFERS FROM GENERAL OBJECT RECOGNITION

The problem of landmark recognition differs from other common recognition problems in several important aspects, and these are reflected in our approach to the problem. In many other situations object recognition systems are applied in constrained domains under controlled conditions, often in indoor contexts. These differences lead to a change in assumptions and focus of the research in landmark-based navigation.

The first difference serves to somewhat simplify the problem. In landmark-based navigation, it is common to have a rough idea of what landmarks to look for and some initial guess as to their placement relative to the sensor. This means the general problems of object indexing into a large set of stored object classes and the requirement for complete viewpoint invariance are somewhat less important. Consequently, these problems are not addressed in the work presented here.

A second difference, however, serves to make landmark recognition more difficult than many other commonly studied object recognition problems.[1] In most scene domains, even the best feature extraction algorithms are imperfect, but complex outdoor environments are typically characterized by uncontrolled lighting, cluttered backgrounds, and imprecise control over viewing angles and positions: The extracted features (here, line segments) are always noisy, fragmented, and incomplete. Thus, the matching algorithms face a cluttered set of data lines that exhibit significant amounts of fragmentation, missing elements, and overgrouped line segments. In general, the landmark data to be matched represents a very challenging problem.

The third major difference is perhaps the most significant. The nature of landmark-based navigation is that a vehicle will be moving freely through the environment, and therefore the spatial relationship of the sensor to the landmarks changes continuously. Typically, only an approximate value of the pose is known. In an environment containing a significant amount of depth variation, errors in the pose can lead directly to perspective distortion of the model relative to the sensed environment. Thus, 3D model matching algorithms must deal with problems involving significant variations in model appearance arising out of 3D perspective and changes in viewpoint induced by the error. Most object recognition algorithms do not deal with full 3D perspective in a flexible manner.

1.4. OVERVIEW OF THE PAPER

This paper is concerned primarily with landmark-based navigation. For navigation in unmodeled or sparsely modeled environments, our general scenario involves the initial acquisition of prominent visual features that can serve as landmarks. This initial phase of partial model acquisition is necessary because there are few situations where a model of a complex environment will be available a priori. Given a partial geometric model, the vehicle pose (i.e., position and orientation) in a vehicle-centered coordinate system can be recovered by recognizing landmarks (i.e., objects in the environment) by matching them to the model. Our approach involves matching a set of 3D model features to the sensed 2D data by optimizing an error function which contains terms for the degree of spatial misalignment of the model with the data and the degree of model omission. From the set of model-data correspondences, a nonlinear iterative optimization procedure determines the best 3D pose estimate.

Misalignment is measured with respect to 2D variations in landmark appearance, that is, in the image plane. However, as pose is recovered during matching, a variety of alternative control strategies can be defined in which the 3D model is reprojected into the image plane for more accurate matching. This leads to a family of 2D and

---

[1] The problem of general object recognition suffers from the same problems mentioned here; however, most object recognition systems are developed and tested under much more highly controlled situations. Very few have been tested in noisy, cluttered domains.

3D model matching strategies which utilize a variety of constraints. Some of these strategies are quite effective in the face of perspective effects that occur when the view of the target model contains significant depth variations. This chapter examines trade-offs between robustness and computation, culminating in an effective hybrid algorithm that is robust in perspective-sensitive situations, while requiring little additional computation relative to the simpler 2D model matching strategies.

In addition to providing the geometric constraints necessary for determining the vehicle pose, the partial model can be extended into a more complete environmental model using the same geometric constraints used for building the initial model. New unmodeled features (points and/or lines) can be tracked over time, simultaneously with tracking landmarks in the current partial model. Then, recovery of the camera pose over the sequence allows triangulation of the new features and the incorporation of their 3D geometry into the 3D model. As navigation experience in the domain is accumulated, model extension and refinement should be an ongoing process that continually improves the geometric accuracy, visual detail, and spatial extent of the 3D model, accumulating the navigational experience in the domain into a usable form.

In the next section, the problems of matching known landmarks to image features and recovering the vehicle pose are discussed. The underlying assumption in this section is that the 3D world model already exists in a form amenable to the matching process. Section 3 discusses the problem of bottom-up acquisition of the initial partial model. In Section 4, the initial model is extended and refined by acquiring and tracking new feature points over multiple frames, determining their 3D structure by triangulation, and incorporating them into the 3D model. During this process, existing 3D model structure is refined by the same mechanism. Section 5 briefly describes a control system for an autonomous vehicle built on the idea of a programmable finite-state machine model and demonstrates how the landmark and pose algorithms can be embedded in a general system.

All of the key concepts and algorithms described in this paper have been tested on real data in several application domains, including vehicle navigation in outdoor and indoor real-world environments, aerial photo-interpretation, and robotics manufacturing.

1.5. NOTATION

In mathematical equations, scalars (s) are in italics, bold characters represent matrices ($\mathbf{R}$), and bold italic characters denote vectors ($\boldsymbol{p}$), except as otherwise defined. All other notation should be self-explanatory.

2. RECOVERING THE SENSOR/VEHICLE POSE BY LANDMARK MATCHING/RECOGNITION

2.1. INTRODUCTION

The approach developed in this and succeeding sections for determining sensor position and orientation involves first matching landmark (object) models to an image to establish image-model correspondences. These corresponding features are then used to recover the pose of the sensor relative to the model (and hence the world). The subtasks of model matching and pose recovery/refinement are mutually dependent, since an object model's pose relative to the camera in 3D space cannot be recovered without determining a correspondence between image features and model features. At the same time, evaluating a correspondence in order to determine the best one requires knowledge of the pose of the sensor with respect to the model.

Our experience suggests that there are many situations where the effects of perspective projection seriously distorts the image appearance of 3D landmarks. This is particularly true as the depth variation in an object or set of objects becomes large compared to the distance from the sensor to the object(s). Matching in the image domain under these circumstances is far more effective if the matching/recognition algorithm modifies the 3D pose during matching. This approach is fundamental in our work, but is lacking from most prior work on model-based object recognition (however, see [88]). The problem that arises is due to the fact that the combinatorics of establishing correspondences between extracted image features and object model features dominate the recognition process. This results in serious computational problems, since for every correspondence tested in the search of correspondence space, some form of either 3D or 2D geometric constraint must be applied and evaluated in order to establish the 'best' fit between model and image data. Consequently, it is computationally advantageous to solve as much of the problem as possible in the geometrically simpler 2D image space.

An effective "hybrid" solution is embodied in our approach to this problem, whereby the benefits of 3D matching are obtained at only a slightly greater computational expense than the simpler 2D matching. Local search is used to explore the combinatorial search space of object model-to-image data features. These local search algorithms find the best match with high probability. While searching through spaces with 2^{50} to 2^{100} possible matches, 2D computations are used to rank alternative moves through the search space, and 3D pose is only computed when moving from a current state to a better match.

2.2. RELATED APPROACHES

Previous work on model-based object recognition can be broadly categorized into three groups: (1) key-feature algorithms, (2) generalized Hough transform and pose clustering algorithms, and (3) tree search. Key-feature algorithms search for distinctive local features to find an expected object. Bolles and Cain [25] provided early motivation for this approach, which was further developed by Lowe [87, 89, 90] and later by a number of others [7, 10, 59, 69, 74].

Generalized Hough transform [16, 36, 37, 71] and pose clustering [123] algorithms shift search from correspondence space into pose space. Explicit representations of pose space make the use of high-dimensional spaces impractical and most algorithms match 2D rigid objects, introduce viewpoint restrictions [122], utilize subspace projections [131], or use clustering techniques [70, 123].

Early work on tree search includes [12, 56], but Grimson [60, 61, 62] further developed the technique and has shown that it has polynomial complexity for 2D-rigid matching using an assumed threshold on the minimum quality of a match. Breuel [27] and Cass [32] improve this somewhat using pose equivalence analysis, which for scaled 2D models has complexity $O(k^4 m^4 d^4)$ for m model features, d data features and k-sided polygonal uncertainty regions about each feature.

Our approach will be shown to readily generalize to 3D problems involving significant amounts of perspective distortion. In contrast, little evidence has appeared to suggest that these other approaches similarly generalize. Past work is characterized by reliance either solely upon 2D models or scaled-orthographic projection. One notable exception is the work by Lowe on 3D object tracking [88].

2.3. THE UMASS APPROACH TO LANDMARK NAVIGATION

The focus of this section is on matching models to images and using the correspondences to recover more accurate pose. The general discussion in Section 1.3 pointed out a number of problems which must be dealt with by a matching/pose recovery system. These are briefly discussed here in the context of the specific approaches adopted in succeeding sections. Sections 2.4 and 2.5 develop the basic techniques underlying model matching and pose recovery. With respect to these basic techniques, we assume knowledge of a set of 3D models and an approximately known sensor pose. The following sections then generalize the basic techniques into a combined system.

When matching models to noisy, fragmented, overgrouped, and incomplete image features (in this case extracted line segments), the system developed here differs from previous systems in two important respects. While virtually all previous object recognition work has considered only one-to-one or at best one-to-many mappings between model and image features, we support *many-to-many mappings* between features. This allows the basic matching algorithms to perform well in the face of both fragmented and merged data line segments by matching subsets of model lines to subsets of data lines. During the optimizing search, cluttered and incomplete data are dealt with robustly without using any customized techniques for the different kinds of feature extraction errors.

A third major difference between the system developed here and other object recognition approaches is the ability to recover from incorrect pose estimates by integrating pose algorithms with model matching. As new 3D poses are computed, model matching can be repeated to produce better model-data matches. Since our own work initially developed using 2D models, we will use this simpler class of problem to introduce the essential elements of model matching. The generalization to 3D matching is delayed until after the 3D pose algorithm is described in Section 2.5.

2.4. 2D MODEL MATCHING

At the heart of our approach to geometric matching of a 3D landmark model to an image is the repeated application of 2D model matching. Solutions to this simpler problem utilize projections of the 3D landmark model from an estimated viewpoint to produce a set of 2D model features (straight line segments) that are matched to extracted 2D image features.

The problem of 2D model matching becomes one of minimizing a match error by solving *two subsidiary optimization problems*:

1. the *correspondence problem*—determine the correspondence set between model elements (from a particular projected 3D pose) and data line segments (extracted from an image) that minimizes the match error; and

2. the *spatial fitting problem*—for each correspondence, determine the best four parameter affine transform of 2D position, 2D rotation, and scale so that the spatial fit error of the model lines to data lines is minimized.

Structuring the problem as one of optimization sets up a goal of a "best" match to be found, even under adverse circumstances arising out of incomplete world knowledge and imperfect data. An objective function for *match error* will be defined over the correspondence space of matches. The error function measures *spatial fit error*—penalizing matches to the degree that the model and data cannot be made to spatially coincide—and it measures *omission error*—penalizing matches which leave portions of the model uncovered. The combinatorial correspondence space and the match error formulation are developed in the next two sections.

The combinatorial space of possible correspondences. All models and image features are represented in terms of straight line segments. Model line segments represent the linear structure of landmark objects, while a line algorithm (in our case Burns [31] or Boldt [24]) extracts straight lines from images. Clearly, this choice of representation affects the structure of the matching algorithm. Line extraction is by its very nature an imperfect process. To make matters worse, error-prone piecewise linear approximations arise in situations involving objects with curves. As stated earlier, these factors require that correspondence mappings between model and image line segments must allow the possibility of many-to-many mappings; that is, one or more model lines will be matched to one or more data lines. This allows both fragmentation and overgrouping of image line segments without compromising the effectiveness of a match. It also allows effective matching of piecewise linear approximations to curves without being overly concerned with the possible choices of breakpoints in either model or data lines.

Let $\mathbf{M}$ be the set of model line segments, $\mathbf{D}$ the set of image line segments, and $\mathbf{S}$ be a subset of all possible pairs of model and image line segments $\mathbf{M} \times \mathbf{D}$. If there are no constraints available to restrict which model lines might match which image lines, all pairings are possible and $\mathbf{S} = \mathbf{M} \times \mathbf{D}$ is the correspondence space. However, there are usually reasonable domain constraints which preclude some correspondences. For example, in robot navigation the sensor is often constrained to be approximately stable with respect to gravity (i.e., vertical), and therefore relative line orientation constrains possible model-data line associations. In our examples both orientation and approximate relative translational position (i.e., sensor pose) are used to limit the candidate pairings.

Hence, more generally $\mathbf{S} \subseteq \mathbf{M} \times \mathbf{D}$ is called the *set of candidate pairs*. A match is a correspondence mapping $\mathbf{c}$ belonging to the space of possible correspondences

C, the powerset of all candidate pairs:

$$\mathbf{C} = 2^{\mathbf{S}}$$

An example landmark matching problem will be used to illustrate these ideas. Figure 1a shows a 512×512 intensity image taken from a small mobile robot looking down a walkway. The landmark is the telephone pole. The pole consists of distinctive image features and might not be considered a difficult recognition problem. However, the practical issues that arise in real-world object recognition can make this a very challenging problem, including noisy feature extraction, obscuration, and multiple symmetric lines as candidate data features in the image.

The close-up in Figure 1b better indicates the sometimes poor quality of image features. The cross bar at the top of the telephone pole is no more than two pixels wide (vertically), and aliasing along this structure is pronounced. Figures 2a–d illustrate the matching process. Figure 2a shows the three line segments making up the telephone pole model. Figure 2b shows the image line segments extracted in the vicinity of the telephone pole. The lines in black are those actually found to match the model. Figure 2c shows the model in black drawn in proper registration to the data as determined by the fitting procedure described in the following section.

Figure 2d is a table which indicates various aspects of the combinatorial search space. Rows are indexed by model line segments and columns by image line segments; cells in the table indicate the status of a specific pairing of model and image segments. For example, the first cell for model segment A and image segment 0 (that is, the pair $(A, 0)$), is gray. This indicates $(A, 0)$ is not considered a possible match. Cells that are white or black indicate candidate pairs in the correspondence space, white meaning no match and black denoting a match. Thus, the adjacent cell, pair $(A, 1)$, is an unfilled white square indicating the pair is a possible correspondence but is not part of this match, while $(A, 2)$, indicates the pair belongs to this match.

For this example, $|\mathbf{S}| = 30$, so there are 2^{30} possible matches in the correspondence space $\mathbf{C}$. This is a relatively simple problem in terms of the size of $\mathbf{C}$, since $|\mathbf{S}|$ can easily grow into the hundreds as the complexity of the scene increases and as the number of extracted data lines increases. The best match (shown in Figure 2c) is indicated by the black squares in Figure 2d; the manner in which it is found is discussed below. However, first the issue of how alternative matches are evaluated and ranked will be examined.

Fitting models to data and measuring match quality. The first step in evaluating the quality of a hypothesized correspondence $\mathbf{c}$ between model and image features is to find the unique "best-fit" spatial registration associated with this correspondence. The second step, that of assessing the degree to which the corresponding data completely accounts for the model, can only be evaluated after the first fitting step has been carried out.

Spatial fit is accomplished by minimizing a sum-of-squares error criterion. Care is taken to define a fitting criterion which is insensitive to corruption of the image data. The specific fit criterion used here is the sum of the integrated squared perpendicular

(a)   (b)

Figure 1. Outdoor scene looking down walkway. (a) Full 512 by 512 image; (b) section of image containing telephone pole and street lamp.

distance between image line segments and infinitely extended model lines. This measure is selected because it is invariant with respect to fragmentation in the image line segments. To be more specific, this measure does not change the best spatial fit of the match when any of the image segments are fragmented into multiple adjoining segments; the measure (and hence the best spatial fit) will change only when the union of these data lines changes its length or position. This criterion also supports our goal of proper fitting given a many-to-many correspondence mapping.

To fit the model to the data, the unique 2D similarity transformation (rotation, translation and scale) which minimizes error summed over all corresponding features in **c** must be determined. As has been reported elsewhere [21] and fully derived in [17], this may be done efficiently by solving a single closed-form quadratic equation.

This closed-form solution to the fitting problem holds for essentially all possible correspondence mappings between possible sets of model and image features. The only exception is that some matches involving too few lines will not possess sufficient geometric constraints to yield a unique best fit. For example, corners and "T" junctions do not have enough lines to completely specify the four-parameter affine transformation; for example, scale cannot be determined. To reduce this problem, an additional regularizing term is added to the fitting criterion which minimizes midpoint to midpoint distances between corresponding line segments. The overall weight given this term is very small, so there is no observed effect for those matches not requiring regularization. However, it does produce unique best fits for simple configurations such as corners and "T'" junctions.

The residual error from the least-squares fit is one measure of match quality.

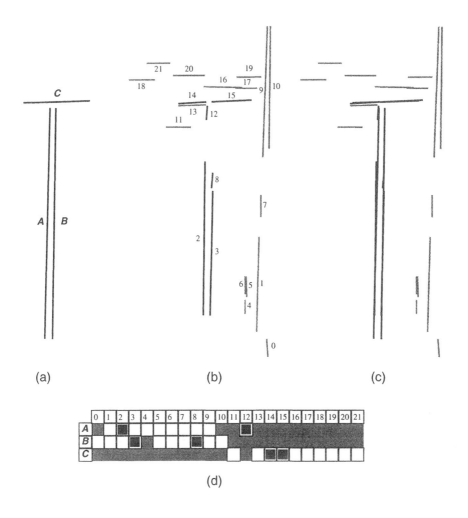

Figure 2. Telephone pole match example. (a) Model segments labeled with letters; (b) image segments labeled and those matched to model indicated in black; (c) the model fit to the data for the best match; (d) table indicating correspondence space and the best match (pairs denoted by black squares).

However, it alone is not an adequate guide to match quality. A very small portion of a model might be matched almost perfectly producing little or no fit error. In this case it is nearly always possible to reduce this error function by removing pairs from a correspondence mapping **c**. Thus, the other factor which must be taken into account is *omission*. There must be a penalty for failing to find image segments that cover portions of the model.

A general and meaningful match error measure may be defined by extending the error function with an omission error computed after the model is in the best-fit spatial configuration:

$$\mathbf{E\_match(c)} = 1/\sigma^2 \mathbf{E\_fit(c)} + \mathbf{E\_om(c)}.$$

The weighting coefficient σ controls the relative importance of these factors and modulates the allowable maximum distance between matched segments. It may be loosely thought of as the standard deviation of an image segment error process. However, a formal connection to a process error model has not been made rigorous.

A variety of additional terms may be added to the match error depending upon the form of matches to be favored within a given problem domain. For example, an additional term may be added which penalizes model-to-image matches in which an image segment protrudes significantly beyond its corresponding model segment. These variations, as well as details associated with parameterizing and normalizing the match error, are presented in [17].

Local search as an optimization strategy. The problem of finding the best match of a landmark to image features reduces to that of solving the following combinatorial optimization problem:

$$\text{find } \mathbf{c}^* \text{ such that } \quad \mathbf{E\_match(c^*)} \leq \mathbf{E\_match(c)} \quad \forall \mathbf{c} \subset \mathbf{C}$$

As already suggested, the combinatorics of this problem are daunting, with 2^n possible correspondences for n potentially paired line segments. Our approach to solving these problems has been to adapt the general concepts of local search to the matching problem.

Local search is recognized as one of the most effective means of solving many difficult combinatorial optimization problems, and it traces its roots to early work on the traveling salesman problem by Kernighan and Lin [73, 85, 86]. Given its demonstrated success on other complex problems, it is surprising how seldom it is used within the computer vision community. A general textbook introduction to local search can be found in [100].

The heart of local search is remarkably simple. First, a neighborhood of tractable size is defined relative to all elements in the search space; computational tractability, of course, is problem dependent. The neighborhood is the set of states that will be examined from the current state. For our problem, the search space consists of all correspondence mappings in $\mathbf{C}$. Starting from any correspondence $\mathbf{c}$, the quality of neighboring solutions is tested, and if a better neighbor is found, this neighbor becomes the current element. Search proceeds until a locally optimal element is found, where local optimality means $\mathbf{E\_match(c)}$ is less than or equal to that of all its immediate neighbors.

The first and most basic neighborhood defined for local search matching is the Hamming-distance-1 neighborhood. To understand this neighborhood, observe that all elements $\mathbf{c} \subset \mathbf{C}$ have a unique bit string encoding of length $\mathbf{n}$, where $\mathbf{n} = |\mathbf{S}|$. Thus, in the bitstring encoding for the problem illustrated in Figure 2, the first bit represents the pair $(A, 1)$, and has value 0 in the optimal match, The second bit represents the pair $(A, 2)$, and has value 1 in the optimal match, and so on for the

30 bits needed to represent all possible matches for this problem. The Hamming-distance-1 neighborhood of a correspondence **c** consists of all correspondences whose bitstring representation differs from that of **c** by 1 bit.

Early work [21] considered only the Hamming-distance-1 and Hamming-distance-2 neighborhoods. However, we found that a more sophisticated neighborhood definition greatly improved the overall performance of the search algorithm. This new technique, called *subset-convergent* local search (first introduced in [22]), is based upon restarting local search from partial matches which are subsets of a Hamming-distance-1 locally optimal match. Subset-convergent local search has been demonstrated to find the best match on a single trial much more reliably than does local search using only the Hamming-distance-1 neighborhood [17].

Thus far, little has been said about the starting point for local search. Since a single trial will rarely arrive at the global minima, it is fairly common to use multiple trials of local search initiated from randomly selected starting states; this technique is used throughout our work on matching. Random start local search, as this technique is called, has the property that even if local search is unlikely to find the best match on a single independent trial, the probability of missing the best in a series of trials can be made arbitrarily small by increasing the number of trials. Better still, the number of trials needed typically does not grow unreasonably. For example, if the probability of seeing the best match on a single trial is 0.5, then 5 trials are sufficient to obtain the best match with probability 0.95. If the probability of seeing the best on a single trial drops to 0.1, then the number of trials must be increased to 29.

The power of running multiple trials of local search can be illustrated with the following example. The goal is to match a straight-line approximation of a horizon curve to line segments extracted from an image. The underlying assumption is that the image is taken at the same spot for which the horizon model has been built, but the sensor pointing angle is uncertain. This problem is important in situations in which an autonomous vehicle, which may have Global Positioning Satellite (GPS) and inertial sensors, moves to a known point on a terrain map and attempts to relate the terrain map to its estimated position and orientation (an example of such a vehicle is the ARPA Unmanned Ground Vehicle, or UGV [94]). Typically, orientation will be known to within several degrees, but this generates 100 to 200 pixel uncertainties in the registration of imagery to the terrain map. The solution is to resolve the uncertainty in the sensor pointing angle by matching a horizon silhouette model derived from a 3D terrain map with the actual horizon visible to the vehicle. These line segment models approximate curves and, as we have pointed out, it is crucial for the matching algorithm in this domain to embody many-to-many mappings between features.

Since small uncertainties in pointing angle manifest themselves essentially as 2D translations and rotations of image features, the 2D matching system can easily account for this variability by producing a 2D projection from an approximate sensor pose and the given terrain map. Figure 3 shows four matches found by the geometric matching system. The horizon model is shown in black. Image segments found not to match are gray, and image segments found to match the model are white. However, these are difficult to see since they are mostly covered by the model segments. The images shown are captured screen images generated by the matching system. Below the images are the number of potentially matching pairs, 766 in this case, and the match error. Three other values are shown: the first is always 1 and has no meaning in this particular test, the second indicates the total number of matches tested to arrive at this match, and the third indicates the number of states through which search moved from the initial randomly selected match until it arrived at the locally optimal match indicated.

Figure 3 shows three suboptimal matches along with the best match. The best match is shown in the lower right. The suboptimal matches hint at the multitude of possible solutions a system can find, often causing significant confusion when working with such imperfect models and data. While these and many other local optima are found by the 2D geometric model matcher, the key empirical result is that the optimal match is found on any given trial with probability 0.1. Thus, because the probability of failing to see this best match one or more times in t trials drops exponentially, only 29 trials are required to find this match with probability 0.95. Running this many trials on a SPARC 10 requires approximately 14 minutes. Reducing the number of potentially matching pairs by assuming the true position is known to within 75, rather than 150, pixels drops the run time to under 5 minutes. Of course, running multiple trials simultaneously on a multiprocessor involves simple conceptual modifications to the basic algorithm, and can easily cut down the response time.

2.5. 3D POSE DETERMINATION

Given a set of correspondences between the 3D landmark features and 2D image features, as obtained from the model matching system described in the previous section, now the goal is to find the sensor (or robot) 3D rotation $\mathbf{R}$ and translation T which maps the world coordinate system to the camera coordinate system (or vice versa) under perspective projection. Due to the well-known difficulties encountered in trying to establish accurate endpoints for image lines [76, 90, 135], our algorithm is based on correspondences between lines instead of points (although an equivalent formulation based on points can be easily derived [75]). In addition, intrinsic camera parameters, such as focal length, field of view, and the image center are assumed to be known [67, 76, 84]. A perspective projection model is also assumed.

Kumar [75, 76] has developed a series of least-squares techniques to solve the pose determination problem, each of which performs better than the previous ones. The least-squares techniques minimize nonlinear functions, are iterative in nature, and require an initial estimate. However, experiments show that there is rapid convergence even with significant errors in the initial estimates. For those cases in which an initial estimate of rotation and translation is not available, techniques based on sampling the rotation space to provide multiple initial starting points have been developed [68]. Mathematical and empirical analyses of the uncertainty in the pose parameters, given noise in both the image and the three-dimensional model, have also been performed [75, 79].

Figure 3. Example of 2D matching to find horizon lines. Model is in black, matched image segments in white, and other image segments in gray. The figure shows three suboptimal matches along with the best match (shown in the lower right).

Least-squares methods are known to be sensitive to gross errors or outliers in the data. Two different robust statistical techniques for handling outliers have been explored: M-estimation and least median squares. M-estimation techniques seem to be susceptible to initial estimates and are not able to handle a large number of outliers (a limit of approximately 20% contamination). Their advantage is that efficient computational methods exist for minimizing the associated error functions. In contrast, LMS (least median square) methods handle a larger degree of contamination by outliers (up to 50%) and are less sensitive to the initial estimates. Their disadvantage is that they are computationally much slower than the M-estimation methods. However, in our application, the total computational cost is dominated by the earlier model matching process to determine correspondences and therefore LMS techniques were used.

Pose constraints for lines. Given a correspondence between a set of model lines and a set of image lines, the goal is to find the rotation matrix $\mathbf{R}$ and the translation vector $\boldsymbol{T}$ which map the world coordinate system to the camera coordinate system. Therefore, the constraint equations must relate the rotation and translation parameters to the 3D model line coordinates and the corresponding 2D image line coordinates. These constraints can then be used to develop objective functions which, when minimized, will result in an optimum set of pose parameters given noisy input data.

Let $\boldsymbol{p}$ be a point in 3D model space and $\boldsymbol{p}_c$ be a point in 2D image space. Lines in 3D space are represented by their endpoints $\boldsymbol{p}_1$ and $\boldsymbol{p}_2$, respectively. The rigid body transformation mapping point $\boldsymbol{p}$ onto point $\boldsymbol{p}_c$ can be written as

$$\boldsymbol{p}_c = \mathbf{R}(\boldsymbol{p}) + \boldsymbol{T}. \tag{1}$$

In the ideal case with no noise, the basic constraint can be stated rather easily: Any point on the 3D model line must lie on the projection plane formed by the optical center of the sensor and the infinite image line. Conversely, any point on the 2D image line must lie on the projection plane formed by the optical center and the infinite 3D model line. Pose determination algorithms have been developed from both of these constraints; here we concentrate on the infinite model line version, since the resulting algorithm has been shown to be superior [75]. The infinite model line constraint can be expressed algebraically as

$$(1/M)\mathbf{R}^T \boldsymbol{B} \cdot (\boldsymbol{p}_2 - \boldsymbol{T}\boldsymbol{w}) \times (\boldsymbol{p}_1 - \boldsymbol{T}\boldsymbol{w}) = 0 \tag{2}$$

where $\boldsymbol{B}$ is the vector corresponding to the projection ray from the optical center to an image point $\boldsymbol{I}$, M is a scalar, and $\boldsymbol{T}\boldsymbol{w}$ is the location of the origin of the camera coordinate system in world coordinates. The resulting objective function is the sum of squares of the perpendicular distances of the endpoints of the image lines to the projected (infinite) model line.

The geometric interpretation of constraint (2) and the alignment error for one line pair is shown in Figure 4. Algebraically, the objective function is expressed as

$$E_3 = \sum_{i=1}^{n} \sum_{j=1}^{2} \frac{w_i}{M_i^2} \left(\mathbf{R}^T \boldsymbol{B}_{ji} \cdot (\boldsymbol{p}_{2i} - \boldsymbol{T}_w) \times (\boldsymbol{p}_{1i} - \boldsymbol{T}_w) \right)^2. \tag{3}$$

Minimizing the objective function: Least squares. Ideally, with no noise, the minimal set of constraint equations for three sets of line correspondences could be used to solve for the unknown pose parameters. The resulting pose would then cause perfect alignment between the projected models and the image measurements. In practice, however, measurements are always noisy and perfect alignment cannot be realized. Therefore, an objective function is minimized to find the pose parameters. Since all

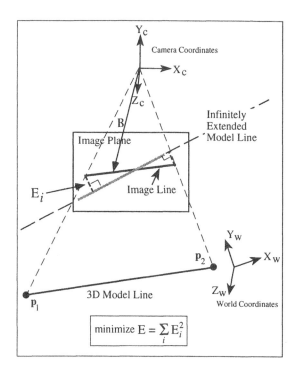

Figure 4. Error function based on the infinite model line constraint (2).

of the objective functions used for pose computations are nonlinear, crucial factors in their selection include the ability to construct suitable minimization algorithms. Suitability includes issues of speed of minimization, convergence from an appropriately large distribution of initial estimates, and numerical stability of the algorithms with respect to noise, finite length calculations, etc.

To optimally estimate the pose parameters, the error for each model feature must be appropriately weighted based on the assumed noise model of the measurement process. Developing proper noise models is a crucial factor in specifying the optimization algorithm and is discussed in some detail in [75]. Generally, the algorithms take into account errors in both the image measurements and the model.

To minimize E_3, an iterative technique formulated by Horn [68] for solving the problem of relative orientation is modified and adapted to the pose estimation problem. An initial estimate of $\mathbf{R}$ and $\mathbf{T}$ is required. The technique linearizes the error terms about the current estimate for $\mathbf{R}$ and $\mathbf{T}$. At each iteration, the linearized error function is minimized to determine adjustment vectors for the rotation and translation terms. The iterative adjustments are made to the rotation and translation terms until the objective function converges to a minimum. Note that the algorithm, like all such descent algorithms, does not guarantee a global minimum. Complete details of the minimization procedure are found in [75, 92].

The complexity of the algorithm is $O(kn)$ where n lines and k iterations are needed to converge to the optimal solution. At the last iteration, the covariance matrix is computed. It is worth noting that the minimization process contains a mechanism for determining whether or not the process is degenerate, that is, whether or not the incremental adjustments to the current pose estimate can be computed.

For the near singular cases where the technique might diverge, a simple solution is based on the Levenberg-Marquardt method for minimizing non-linear functions; its application to pose estimation was first noted in [87]. The technique combines first and second-order methods. The Levenberg-Marquardt method attempts to combine the best of both methods by moving along directions close to the gradient only if moving in the direction computed by the second order method causes divergence. Note that moving along the gradient guarantees descent and hence convergence, but gradient-descent algorithms are often slow to converge. At any given iteration, the increments are first calculated by second-order methods. If the new estimate causes the objective function to increase, then the increment is reestimated by adding a component of the gradient to the old estimate of the increment.

Algorithm performance. The nonlinear algorithm described in the previous section requires an initial estimate for rotation and translation. How close the initial estimate must be to the final values, in order to ensure convergence, depends on the particular data set. In numerous trials with both real and synthetic data, convergence from estimates that differ considerably from the correct solution has been observed. For some data sets, the convergence is virtually independent of the starting point; for others, the initial rotation estimate must be within 40° of the correct solution for all three Euler angles representing the rotation.

Figure 5a shows a model projected onto an image using rotation and translation estimates that were off by 15° and over 100 feet, respectively. Figure 5b shows the reprojection of the model using the pose parameters determined after three iterations of the least-squares algorithm. Note that in this figure, additional model lines have been projected to demonstrate the accuracy of the projection, but only the lines shown in 5a were used during the pose computation.

For problems which contain lines distributed in depth and which do not contain outliers (see paragraph 5 of this section), the least-squares pose estimation algorithms have shown excellent performance and convergence. In numerous tests on both synthetic and real image data, the estimated pose parameters result in a model projection with very small errors when compared to ground truth data.

Algorithm analysis. Based on a model of image noise and the assumption that the 3D model data is accurate, closed form expressions for the uncertainty in the pose refinement results (rotation and translation) have been derived. It can be shown analytically that the error in the output parameters (i.e., the pose parameters) is linearly related to the noise in the input data. If multiple images are available, it is possible to use a Kalman filtering approach to good advantage.

For all of the pose recovery methods, the intrinsic camera parameters, such as focal length, field of view, center of the image, size of image, etc., are assumed to be known. However, the effect of errors in estimates of the image center and focal

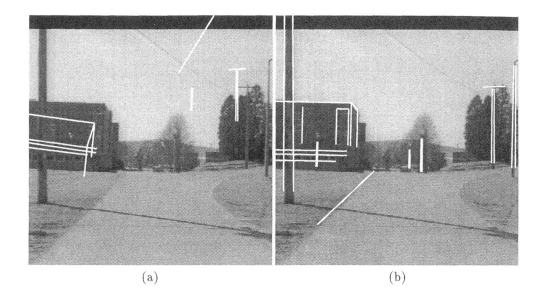

(a)   (b)

Figure 5. Algorithm performance for an errorful initial pose estimate. (a) Initial model projection with a 15° error in rotation and over 100 feet in translation. (b) Reprojection of model after three iterations of the pose optimization algorithm.

length on the pose results returned by these algorithms has been extensively studied [77]. We have shown analytically that incorrect values of the camera center do not significantly affect the computed 3D location of the sensor, although the rotation component is affected. Incorrect estimates of the camera focal length significantly affects only the z-component (depth) of the computed pose.

Least median squares techniques. It is well known that least-squares techniques are extremely sensitive to outliers in the data, although they are optimum and reliable when the noise in the data is gaussian. In the pose estimation problem, outliers may occur due to incorrect discrete image-to-world correspondences or if parts of the 3D model are incorrect. A single correspondence error can have a disastrous effect on the computed pose when least-squares techniques are used—hence, we look for methods that are robust with respect to outliers.

Two robust algorithms were developed [75], one based on M-estimation techniques using the Tukey weighting function [95] and the other based on the minimization of the median of the squares [116] of the residual errors (LMS: least median of squares). We consider only the latter method in this section. The LMS method is able to handle data sets which contain up to 50% outliers. However, since the median is not a differentiable function, it has to be minimized by a combinatorial method and is therefore slower than comparable M-estimation methods.

The LMS method is based on minimizing the median of the square of the error function over all data elements:

$$\text{minimize } \underline{\text{Median}}_i e_i^2.$$

The objective function corresponding to (3) is now

$$E_{m3} = \underline{\text{median}}_i \frac{1.0}{M_i^2} \left(\left(\mathbf{R}^T \left(\boldsymbol{B}_{i1} \right) \cdot \boldsymbol{C}_i \right)^2 + \left(\mathbf{R}^T \left(\boldsymbol{B}_{i2} \right) \cdot \boldsymbol{C}_i \right)^2 \right), \tag{4}$$

where

$$\boldsymbol{C}_i = \left(\boldsymbol{p}_{2i} - \boldsymbol{T}_w \right) \times \left(\boldsymbol{p}_{1i} - \boldsymbol{T}_w \right).$$

The algorithm for minimizing (4) is a combinatorial one, in which candidate poses are generated by using the least-squares algorithm developed earlier on subsets of the data elements. The pose which gives the minimum median error across all data elements is chosen as the optimal median pose. In this algorithm, the goal is to find at least one subset which does not contain outliers; this should give the minimum median error. The algorithm is:

Step 1: Select k random subsets of size m from the input data (see note 1).

Step 2: For each subset, determine the pose by minimizing (3) and estimate the residual error for all n lines given this pose. Find the median square error.

Step 3: Select the pose which gives the minimum median error and compute the "scale" s (see note 2).

Step 4: Filter away as outliers those lines whose squared residual error for that pose is greater than $(a \times s)^2$, where a is an algorithm parameter.

Step 5: Minimize the error function given in (3) on the remaining lines using the least-squares algorithm and return the estimated translation and rotation as the final output.

Algorithm Notes

1. To speed up computation, only k random subsets from all possible size m subsets are used. k can be related to the probability that the correct answer will be found by the median algorithm.
2. The notion of scale is inherent in robust methods (not to be confused with the affine scale parameter discussed earlier) and is defined as the standard deviation of the residual errors of the non-outlier data. Various methods exist for estimating the scale if it is not known a priori; see [75] for a discussion.

Since the pose algorithm requires a minimum of three input lines, subsets of size $m \geq 3$ should be chosen. In practice, the choice of m is important. The larger m is, the greater the probability that subsets of this size contain an outlier. However, choosing $m = 3$ often leads to local minima. In general, we have obtained good results with $m = 6$ or more.

Performance of least median squares algorithm. Comprehensive experimental performance tests of the LMS pose algorithm show that the robust algorithms perform comparably to the least-squares algorithms when no outliers are present, and (as to be expected) performs significantly better when outliers are present. Figure 6 compares the results of the two algorithms in the presence of outliers. The images were part of an experiment on indoor robotic navigation [54, 78]. Figure 6a shows the input set of image lines (19 lines) for one of the indoor frames in a sequence of images. The correspondence set for this frame has eight outliers. Approximately 40% of the data is contaminated, with only the 11 correct correspondences involving lines close to the left wall. Figure 6b shows the reprojection of the 3D model using the output of the least-squares algorithm developed in paragraph 15 of this section; as expected, the result is highly skewed due to the presence of the outliers. The computed position of the robotic sensor is more than 5 feet off its ground truth location, with a high rotation error. In contrast, Figure 6c shows the reprojection of the model using the pose parameters returned by the LMS algorithm. In this case, the position of the sensor is within 0.05 feet of the true position, with very small rotation error.

It is worth noting that the output of the pose refinement process depends heavily on the quality of the input data provided to it. The best constraints are derived from model lines having different orientations and extents in depth. If only a small fraction of the lines have large depth variations, then these should have a significant amount of weight assigned to them—that is, the pose is determined primarily by this small number of lines. Such lines are called "high leverage" lines. Consider the case of a correspondence set in which all of the lines but one are at approximately the same depth. A consensus-based algorithm tries to find the pose which best explains a significant proportion of the set of lines. Because only one line is in depth, it is possible that this line is classified as an outlier by the algorithm, since doing so would allow the remaining lines to be "explained" very well; but the remaining lines do not constrain the pose as effectively, possibly resulting in an inaccurate pose estimate. In general, a consequence (and inherent danger) of the incorrect removal

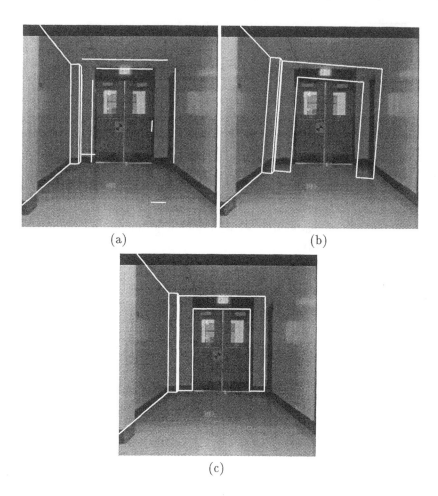

(a)   (b)

(c)

Figure 6. Performance of the LMS pose estimation algorithm. (a) Input set of image lines; this set of 19 lines results in 8 outliers in the initial correspondence set. (b) Reprojection of hallway model using final estimate of least-squares algorithm showing the expected skewing of the results. (c) Reprojection of model using pose estimate from LMS pose estimation algorithm.

of the high-leverage lines as outliers from an impoverished data set is that the output covariance matrix of the computed pose parameters will be much higher than what is optimally obtainable for that data set. The consensus-based algorithms will work best when there are no observations with high leverage, but rather the data set is well rounded, with a sufficient number of input data lines in all directions that are well distributed in depth with respect to the camera.

2.6. Integrating pose determination and 3D model matching

The 2D model matching and 3D pose estimation algorithms were developed in the previous sections as isolated modules. The question now arises as to how they might be effectively integrated to provide landmark-based navigation capabilities. Once again in this discussion we assume there are a priori models of visually significant objects in the environment represented in terms of straight lines.

The basic 2D model matcher followed by 3D pose determination. Let us review what has been developed to this point. The first strategy discussed is the simple one that produced the results presented earlier, in which the model matcher and pose determination modules are connected in a strictly feedforward manner. This system is called the 2D model matcher because the 2D model lines are generated only once by projecting the 3D model from an estimated pose (the data lines extracted from the image are always 2D). Various search strategies can be employed to find a match that optimizes an error function that includes components of spatial fit error and model omission. The set of model-image line correspondences produced by the matcher is then used as the input to the nonlinear iterative pose recovery algorithm that aligns the local sensor coordinate system with the world coordinate system.

The key point of this simple control strategy is that it is sequential, with no attempt at feedback from the pose recovery algorithm to improve the model matching process. Note that the generation of the 2D model is done once and for all, limiting the potential quality of matches to transformations with a weak perspective model of translation, rotation, and scaling in the image plane (i.e., four-parameter affine). This strategy works quite well when there are no significant perspective effects in the environment and the initial pose estimate is reasonably accurate.

The situation changes dramatically when the initial estimate of sensor pose is largely erroneous and/or the environment contains significant perspective effects. As a brief aside, consider the extreme case when the pose is completely unknown, for example when the vehicle has become lost. In this case, both position and orientation are unconstrained. In general, the system would not even know which landmarks were in the field of view (if any) and would not be able to predict their appearance in the image. This is essentially the problem of unconstrained object recognition and additional mechanisms are needed for indexing into the set of possible landmark models and poses, such as aspect graphs [26]. Such algorithms must allow a system to rapidly and efficiently infer an approximate viewpoint from a few key features extracted from an image. They can be generally organized as lookup tables for indexing into the viewing sphere. The topic of viewpoint indexing has not been a focus of our work, and we do not discuss it further here.

Recovering from incorrect perspective projection. As discussed previously, the pose estimation algorithm can be expected to work most effectively in those environments which contain lines in depth with a wide distribution of orientations. In Figure 5, for example, the line along the sidewalk is called a high-leverage line [75] since it has considerable extent in depth and from certain nominal sensor positions its image position changes dramatically with small changes in the pose parameters. In this case, the error surface in pose parameter space is quite sharp and pose can be accurately determined. Similarly, the lines along the baseboard and ceiling/wall boundary in Figure 6 are high-leverage lines. Contrast this to the situation in Figure 3 in which the environment contains lines at approximately the same depth (the horizon) and whose depth range is small compared to the distance to the sensor (see the discussion on "shallow structures" in Section 3). Here, the sensitivity of image position to changes in the pose parameters is quite small; that is, there are some fairly large changes in the pose parameters that can result in relatively small changes in the projected image lines. The error surface in pose parameter space is very broad (with $\mathbf{R}$ and $\mathbf{T}$ being able to compensate for each other), and therefore the pose estimate may have significant error.

From the point of view of the model matcher, the situation is exactly the reverse. Under the assumption that the pose is approximately known, the ideal situation for the model matcher occurs when the projected appearance of the landmark model does not change dramatically under changes in the pose parameters. Since 2D affine transforms exactly describe the projection in the case of a planar (2D) world, that is, for strictly 2D-to-2D projections under weak perspective/scaled orthography, the 2D model matching system is capable of describing the changes in the model caused by changes in the pose parameters and is able to effectively align the model with the data. When the environment contains lines in depth, perspective effects dominate the projection, and the affine transformation is no longer a valid approximation. In this case, the optimal spatial fit to ideal data with no model omission still has large error, and therefore it may not be possible to determine the correct correspondences unless adjustments for perspective effects can be made during matching.

The next sections will modify the matching control strategy to deal with this issue in different ways: (a) a 3D matcher that extends the 3D pose algorithm by using local search to update the 3D pose at every node in the search space, and (b) a hybrid 3D-to-2D algorithm that allows feedback of 3D pose updating to the 2D matcher.

The full-perspective 3D matching algorithm (3D pose with local search). The 2D matching algorithm uses a closed form solution to a quadratic equation in order to determine the parameters of an affine transformation which results in the best fit between the model-data pairs in a particular correspondence set. It is this step which must be replaced with a transformation that supports full 3D perspective projection—but of course this is precisely what the pose estimation algorithm provides. Therefore, the first, and perhaps most obvious, approach to integrating the two algorithms is to embed the pose estimation at each state in the local neighborhood of the search space of the model matcher where a correspondence set is being evaluated. This means that a new 3D pose is computed using the nonlinear iterative pose algorithm at every Hamming-distance-1 state of the local neighborhood. While this modification is reasonably simple, it comes at the price of a great increase in computational expense. Note that in this case, the robust version of the pose estimation is not required, since the correspondence pairs being evaluated are hypothesized at each node to be the correct set; hence, the nonrobust version is used. This algorithm is referred to as the "full-perspective 3D matching algorithm."

The essential idea is quite simple. The set of candidate pairs $\mathbf{S}$ defined above now contains pairs of 3D landmark and 2D image segments. The fit error component of the match error $\mathbf{E\_fit}(\mathbf{c})$ is redefined as a function of the residual least-squares error between 3D and 2D features after application of the pose determination algorithm. The iterative least-squares pose is computed using $\mathbf{E\_fit}(\mathbf{c})$ and then the omission error $\mathbf{E\_om}(\mathbf{c})$ is computed as before using the 2D projection of the 3D landmark via this pose. Otherwise, the construction of the set of candidate pairs $\mathbf{S}$ and the local search matching algorithm remains largely unchanged.

With these changes, it has been shown that the new 3D matching algorithm is capable of solving matching problems involving considerable perspective distortion. To clarify what is meant by problems involving perspective, consider the following practical scenario. A robot moving down a hallway is intended to update its position and orientation based upon recognizing modeled 3D features. Figure 7 shows how a partial wireframe model of the hallway changes 2D appearance based upon small changes in robot position. Note the change in projected relative 2D orientation of the landmark features associated with the 2-foot displacements of the robot to the right and to the left of the true position. These deformations are significant, and prevent the 2D model matcher from achieving accurate landmark recognition and subsequent pose determination starting from the projection of an incorrect initial pose.

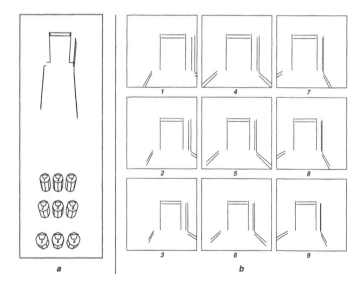

Figure 7. Changes in appearance in a landmark model due to changes in the vehicle pose. (a) Nine vehicle poses in relation to the hallway model; each pose differs from its neighbors by a 2-foot displacement. (b) Views of the model from the nine positions shown in (a).

The full perspective local search algorithm performs reliably by finding the same correct and optimal match from each of the 9 pose estimates shown in Figure 7. In particular, for each of the nine positions, no more than 100 trials are required to find the optimal match with better than 95% confidence; usually far fewer trials are required. Reiterating, full perspective matching recovers the correct pose in all the cases tested.

Figure 8 shows four of the matches found for this problem, including the best (Figure 8d). The actual hallway image is shown as it appears to the robot from pose estimate 5 as labeled in Figure 7. The model is drawn in black, the matched image segments in white, and the unmatched image segments in grey. Three of the matches (Figures 8a–c) are locally optimal matches. In each of the nonoptimal matches, the model-to-data correspondences produce poses that are incorrect and, as in Figure 8a, sometimes wildly incorrect.

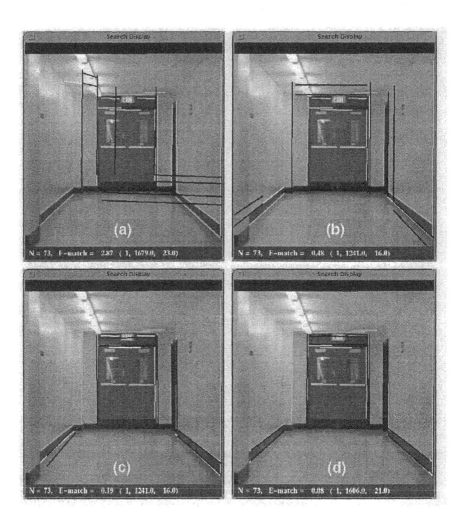

Figure 8. Sample results from 3D perspective matching algorithm. (a–c) Locally optimal matches found during the multiple trial search for the optimal match (shown in (d)).

The hybrid 2D-3D system. The straightforward extension of the local search matching algorithm to directly compute 3D pose is quite effective in solving perspective-sensitive problems. However, it is also computationally expensive compared to the simple 2D algorithm, primarily due to the cost of computing a 3D fit between a 3D model and 2D data using Kumar's nonlinear iterative pose recovery algorithm. In practice, 3D fitting using the pose algorithm has been found to take ten times the computation required to apply the closed form 2D fitting, and of course this must be done at every node considered in the local neighborhoods that are examined during search.

The combinatorics of establishing correspondences between extracted image features and object model features dominates computation in the recognition of 3D landmarks. Since the geometric computations that are fundamental to this process are simpler in 2D than in 3D, there are significant computational advantages for solving as much of the recognition problem as possible in 2D image space. At the same time, the algorithm must be capable of recovering from perspective distortion in the appearance of the projected landmark model(s) due to initially incorrect poses. By modifying the control structure, while using the same component algorithms, a very effective "hybrid" solution to this problem can be obtained, whereby the benefits of 3D matching are obtained at only slightly more computational cost than simple 2D matching.

The hybrid 2D-3D system uses the less costly 2D fitting procedure—with associated 2D fit error and resulting match error—to rank alternative matches in the Hamming-distance-1 neighborhood. However, once a match is selected as the best of the n choices in the local neighborhood, Kumar's algorithm is used to recompute the 3D pose based upon the new correspondence. This new pose is then used to reproject the 3D model into the 2D image plane. Thus, when the neighborhood of this new match is tested, it is tested using the updated 2D projection of the 3D landmark. The change in strategy involves reducing the number of 3D pose updates to 1 of n states in the local search neighborhood at each update.

This algorithm can occasionally find itself in the position where a match which appeared better based upon the 2D ranking is worse after application of the 3D pose algorithm and recomputation of the match error. To maintain the advantage of the efficiency of 2D spatial fitting process in finding and investigating potential promising paths in the search space, yet not ultimately result in worse matches, the local search strategy is modified slightly in this version. Under the new rules, search is allowed to continue some number of steps even if the error is increasing. In practice, up to 10 such steps are permitted. This is an example of a modification to local search typically called *tabu search* [58], and it has proven to be a minor but important modification.

The hybrid algorithm has been compared to the full-perspective algorithm where 3D pose determination and reprojection occurs at every node in the search process. The comparison has taken place on over 20 distinct matching problems arising in the hallway domain illustrated above. The value for n in these problems varied between 36 and 112. The results show that the full-perspective algorithm consistently finds the best and correct match much more reliably on a single trial of local search.

However, each trial takes roughly one order of magnitude longer than does a trial using the hybrid algorithm.

The comparatively long time required for a single trial of full-perspective search negates any advantage it might have had due to its higher probability of finding the best match on a given trial. Thus the hybrid is clearly the faster algorithm and maintains robustness through multiple trials. Recovering correct matches and pose on the problems illustrated in Figures 7 and 8, the hybrid finds the best match with confidence better than 95% in under 5 seconds on a SPARC 10. This timing for the hallway matching problems assumes sign-of-contrast is known for the image line segments, a constraint that is available for this problem, and may exist in well-modeled domains. Without the benefit of this constraint the number of potentially matching pairs roughly doubles, and the size of the search space increases from 2^n to 2^{2n}. Despite the extreme growth in the search space, these harder problems are still solved in roughly 1 minute.

3. Bottom-up Acquisition of the Initial Partial Model

The previous sections have shown that once environmental models exist they can be used effectively for landmark-based navigation. However, for these techniques to be widely applicable, automatic methods have to be developed to build new 3D models and enhance the existing models. Ideally, a robot would continuously build and update its world model as it explores the environment, or continues its routine function. Shortly, we will show that pose recovery can be performed while tracking unmodeled features, and this technique naturally supports a process of dynamic model extension via triangulation. Thus, we return to the original problem of constructing initial landmark models.

Numerous methods have been proposed in the vision literature for the acquisition of 3D information in a bottom-up manner, including processing of stereo, monocular motion, shape-from-X, and a variety of active range sensors. Our interests at UMass have focused entirely on passive recovery of depth from a sequence of images, and primarily on sequences of monocular images [1, 2, 4, 5, 6, 47, 48, 50, 81, 82, 117, 119, 120, 121, 129, 130, 126, 127, 128], although some interesting work has been carried out on binocular motion processing in our lab [13, 14, 15]. However, the subject of motion and stereo involves an enormous research literature, and we will not be able to discuss these issues in any level of detail here. Rather, we will present the motion techniques developed by Sawhney, which have been combined with the 3D pose recovery algorithm. Their integration has empirically demonstrated successful acquisition of initial 3D models using no a priori information; these models have then been used as the basis for model extension.

3.1. Tracking and correspondence

An important problem to be solved either before or in the process of 3D motion and structure computation is that of identifying corresponding features—points, lines, regions, or other features—over image sequences. Optical flow or displacement fields are a low-level representation of pixel correspondences over two frames. Anandan [6] developed an algorithm for computing dense displacement fields with vector confidence measures using minimization of a sum-of-squared-difference error measure defined over filtered multiresolution representations of images. The algorithm computes displacements of many pixels by a coarse-to-fine projection and incremental integration of the motion estimates over a number of levels of a Gaussian or Laplacian pyramidal representation.

Displacement fields, however, are local measurements of the underlying motion field. They correspond well to the motion field only in high gradient regions where reliable gradient estimates exist in at least two significantly different directions, for instance, corner-like structures or textured regions. In order to be able to compute reliable 3D motion and structure parameters, good estimates of the underlying motion field need to be derived. We address this problem by translating the displacement fields into correspondences of line segments. The rationale here is that lines describe significant brightness boundaries that may, in general, correspond to significant scene brightness and structural discontinuities. Therefore, they will remain fairly stable over image sequences. Williams and Hanson [135] presented a solution to the problem of tracking lines over multiple frames. Displacement fields computed between pairs of frames are used to predict the position of lines. Predictions of sets of lines are matched against candidate sets within the scope of prediction neighborhoods while enforcing certain coverage constraints over the resulting bipartite graphs. Earlier work of Burns et al. [31] and Boldt et al. [24] is used to group local gradient measurements into significant linear structures.

One problem with the above work on line correspondences, and with almost all contemporary line trackers (e.g., [35, 38]), is that no 3D motion and/or structure constraints are utilized in the process of tracking and correspondence (however, see [40]). This has been the focus of the work of Sawhney and Hanson [120].

3.2. AFFINE TRACKABILITY FOR OBSTACLE DETECTION AND MODEL ACQUISITION

Sawhney's approach [120] employs 2D affine constraints to compute descriptions of aggregate structures in the imaged scene. This is a significant difference from the tracking algorithms developed by Crowley et al. [35] and Deriche and Faugeras [38] who employ only partially valid heuristics involving 2D motion. An advantage of the approach is that 3D structure information is derived reliably without the intermediate step of explicitly computing the 3D motion parameters. The well-known inherent ambiguities [3, 49, 134] in the process of decomposing the image motion into a 3D rotation and a translation can lead to large errors in the 3D structure estimation.

The goal is to discover and reconstruct aggregate structures in the imaged scene which can be characterized as *shallow structures*. Shallow structures are 3D structures with the property that the difference in depth within the whole structure is small compared to its distance from the camera. Figure 9 shows an image of a hallway. This scene consists of compact structures like the cones and the trash can, and extended structures like the walls, the floor, and the ceiling. When viewed from distances at which it might be desirable for a mobile robot to represent these internally, the variation in depth within the compact structures is small compared to their average distances from the camera. That is, the structures can be characterized as shallow at distances where the path planner for the robot might need an internal representation of the structures (e.g., for obstacle avoidance). In such scenarios, which are typical of many man-made environments, it might be sufficient to derive a 3D representation of structures at different depths directly in front of a robot's path instead of trying to attempt a complete reconstruction of the environment. Sawhney's work demonstrates that automatic robust detection, tracking, and 3D reconstruction of shallow structures is feasible.

Shallow structures are *affine describable* over time. Given a set of 3D points whose extent in depth δZ about a nominal point Z_0 is small compared to Z_0, and assuming that the rotations between two image frames are small, then the transformation of the projections of the point sets at the two time instants can be accurately approximated by a four-parameter affine transformation. This can be easily seen. Choose a camera-centered coordinate system in which the X- and Y-axes are in the image plane and the Z-axis points into the scene along the optical axis of the camera. The origin is the center of projection and lies on the optical axis with the image plane a focal length away from it along the positive Z-axis. Let $\boldsymbol{P}$ represent the 3D vector of an image point at time t and let $\boldsymbol{p}$ be its projection in the image plane; $\boldsymbol{P}'$ and $\boldsymbol{p}'$ represent the same points at time $t+1$. The relationship between the projections of the point sets at time t and $t+1$ can then be written as:

$$\frac{1}{f}\boldsymbol{p}' \approx \frac{1}{f}s\mathbf{R}_Z\boldsymbol{p} + s\Omega + \frac{1}{Z'_0}\mathbf{T}_{2D}$$

where s is the scale factor defined as Z_0/Z'_0, $\mathbf{R}_Z$ is the 2×2 rotation matrix for rotations around the Z-axis, Ω is the 2D vector $(-\omega_y, \omega_x)$, $\boldsymbol{T}_{2D}$ is the vector $[T_x, T_y]$, and the subscript i for the ith point has been dropped for simplicity. The transformation is a four-parameter affine transformation (also called a similarity transformation): scale change, rotation around the optical axis, and translation in the plane [131].

We emphasize that these assumptions are easily satified in most visual motion scenarios using commonly available CCD cameras. For instance, rotations up to 0.1 radians (about 5 degrees), FOVs of up to 25 degrees (maximum X/f of about 0.2), and translations in the X and Y directions of up to 1 unit for objects as close as 10 units satisfy these assumptions. Similarly, structures possessing a $\delta Z/Z_0$ ratio of 0.1 or less can be reasonably characterized as shallow and are therefore affine describable over time. A model of measurement errors for 2D line tokens has been developed for computing the affine parameters and their covariances. These parameters with their associated covariances represent the 2D dynamic parameters of a hypothesized shallow structure; complete details can be found in [117, 120].

Shallow structures are represented as collections of line tokens. Many triplets of nearby lines using 2D distance of endpoints as a grouping constraint are used to hypothesize aggregate structures as shallow. The concept of affine *trackability* can be applied dynamically to each of these clusters of image features across a sequence of images to verify that they are shallow structures and in effect provide a segmentation. Those hypothesized aggregates that don't behave as a shallow structure

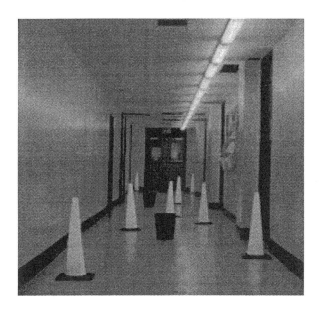

Figure 9. An image of a hallway scene which contains shallow structures.

(i.e., do not follow the prediction of remaining as a coherent planar structure at the approximately correct depth) are removed.

Two important insights have been developed within an estimation theoretic framework (Kalman filtering and data association) for the problem of robust shallow structure tracking. First, note that matching an aggregate structure as a whole is generally unambiguous in comparison to independent matching of features within the structure. Representation of a structure as a state vector along with the associated covariance matrix (which allows for uncertainties in modeling and measurements) provides a natural representation for the aggregate structure as a *whole* that is suitable for model matching. Second, in order to circumvent the high dimensionality of this representation in matching using the Mahalanobis distance [39, 91], it is shown that the structure parameters can be decoupled, leading to a matching problem of lower complexity.

Experimental results on image sequences demonstrate the robustness of aggregate structure tracking and 3D reconstruction. Errors in line extraction, problems of occlusions, and motion discontinuity are handled within the same uncertainty modeling framework. In addition, the algorithm can also be applied to independently moving objects if they satisfy the shallow structure constraint.

In summary, affine trackability can be used to segment shallow structures in a scene and locate them in the 3D environment. Instead of representation of the depth of individual primitive tokens such as points and lines, the entire aggregate structure is directly represented in terms of its 3D location and dynamics. The derived description of the scene can be viewed as a set of fronto-parallel planes (cardboard cut-out surfaces) of constant depth, one for each shallow object in the scene. The result of applying this algorithm on a test sequence are shown in the next section; additional experiments and results are described in [80, 120].

4. Model Extension and Refinement

In this section we present techniques for extending and refining an initial partial model (possibly noisy) by viewing the scene over a sequence of frames. This capability is directly achieved via tracking and pose recovery. The partial model is derived from the reconstruction of shallow structures as described in the previous section. The partial model is used to compute the pose that relates the model coordinate system and the camera coordinate system of the image frames in the sequence. The unmodeled 3D features (those not recovered by the shallow structure reconstruction) are tracked over the image sequence using a line tracking algorithm [6, 135]. Using the correspondence of image features derived from the tracking step, and the poses computed from model-to-image feature correspondences for a sequence of image frames, new 3D points are located by triangulation (see Figure 10). The estimation of the new 3D points is done using both batch and quasi-batch or sequential methods. Triangulation requires at least two frames and therefore the minimum batch size is two. Results from batch to batch are integrated by the standard Kalman filter covariance update equations. The triangulation process is also used to make new 3D measurements of the initial model points, which are then fused with the previous estimates to refine the set of initial model points.

The approach adopted in the model extension and refinement step is basically *induced stereo*. Tracking image features over a large sequence often leads to a large baseline for stereo and improves the robustness of the 3D reconstruction. Note that this approach does not require any models of inter-frame motion. Due to the availability of the partial model, new points are located in a stable world coordinate system. The pose computed for each frame is independent of the other frames, so each frame provides an independent measurement to the whole process.[2] This does not lead to the cascading problems of noise and error which most of the sequential multiframe "structure from motion" techniques suffer from because, in the latter, the noisy prior estimates of motion in the previous frame are used to propagate the structure estimates to the next frame which are then integrated with the new estimates in the current frame. While relative orientation between consecutive image frames is not explicitly computed, it can be inferred from the respective pose estimates. The pose computation is somewhat less error-prone than traditional relative orientation techniques [1, 68, 118].

Results will be presented for two image sequences where new 3D points are located with average errors less than 1.75%. These results are far superior to those obtained by the traditional structure-from-motion techniques employed in computer vision. In the first experiment the initial model was built manually, and in the second experiment the initial model was derived from the shallow structure reconstruction algorithm.

---

[2] Note that this would not be true if there was significant noise in the initial partial model.

The errors in the initial partial model (for the model extension and refinement step) are assumed to be either gross errors or gaussian noise. If gross errors are present in the 3D model, these would be detected and filtered as outliers by the LMS pose recovery algorithm, and would not be used by the Kalman filter triangulation process. Note that outliers can also arise due to incorrect correspondences. However, if a modeled landmark appears as an outlier over a large number of frames, then it probably is due to a gross error in the 3D model and it could eventually be removed from the 3D model database. Thus, for the remainder of this paper, the noise in the input 3D model is modeled as gaussian.

4.1. POSE DETERMINATION FROM A NOISY 3D MODEL

Using the depths of the shallow structures recovered by the affine-based algorithm, a partial model of the environment can be built. This model has the same coordinate system as that of the first frame's coordinate system. Given correspondences between model and image tokens in subsequent image frames, the pose parameters (rotation and translation) that relate the subsequent frames' coordinate systems to the model coordinate system can be computed. The least-squares pose determination algorithm is optimal with respect to gaussian noise in the input image measurements [75], and here the least-squares techniques are extended to handle gaussian noise in the 3D model. The techniques presented in this section assume point correspondences, but are easily modified for line correspondences.

The rigid body transformation from the world coordinate system to the camera coordinate system can be represented as a rotation ($\mathbf{R}$) followed by a translation ($\mathbf{T}$). A point $\boldsymbol{p}$ in world coordinates gets mapped to the point $\boldsymbol{p}_c$ in camera coordinates using equation 1; assuming perspective projection, the pose constraint equations for the ith point $\boldsymbol{p}_i$ in a set of "m" points can be written as follows:

$$\frac{1}{\boldsymbol{p}_{czi}} \boldsymbol{C}_{xi} \cdot (\mathbf{R}\boldsymbol{p}_i + \boldsymbol{T}) = 0$$
$$\frac{1}{\boldsymbol{p}_{czi}} \boldsymbol{C}_{yi} \cdot (\mathbf{R}\boldsymbol{p}_i + \boldsymbol{T}) = 0 \tag{5}$$

where

$$\boldsymbol{C}_{xi} = (s_x, 0, -I_{xi})$$
$$\boldsymbol{C}_{yi} = (0, s_y, -I_{yi})$$
$$\boldsymbol{p}_{czi} = (\mathbf{R}\boldsymbol{p}_i + \boldsymbol{T})_Z .$$

(I_{xi}, I_{yi}) is the image projection of the point and (s_x, s_y) is the focal length in pixels along each axis.

Since both the image measurements and the 3D model locations are assumed to be noisy, it will not be possible to satisfy the above constraint equations exactly. Let the measurement error in pixels of image point locations be given by $(\Delta X, \Delta Y)$ and the error in the 3D model points be given by $\Delta\boldsymbol{p}$. Given the current estimate $\mathbf{R}$ and $\boldsymbol{T}$, the constraint equations (5) are linearized about the estimate:

$$\frac{1}{\boldsymbol{p}_{czi}} (\boldsymbol{C}_{xi} \cdot \Delta\boldsymbol{T} + \delta\omega \cdot \boldsymbol{b}_{xi}) = \frac{-1}{\boldsymbol{p}_{czi}} \boldsymbol{C}_{xi} \cdot \boldsymbol{p}_{ci} + \eta_x$$
$$\frac{1}{\boldsymbol{p}_{czi}} (\boldsymbol{C}_{yi} \cdot \Delta\boldsymbol{T} + \delta\omega \cdot \boldsymbol{b}_{yi}) = \frac{-1}{\boldsymbol{p}_{czi}} \boldsymbol{C}_{yi} \cdot \boldsymbol{p}_{ci} + \eta_y \tag{6}$$

where
$$\boldsymbol{b}_{xi} = \mathbf{R}\boldsymbol{p} \times \boldsymbol{C}_{xi}$$
$$\boldsymbol{b}_{yi} = \mathbf{R}\boldsymbol{p} \times \boldsymbol{C}_{yi}.$$

The noise terms in the two equations, η_x and η_y are functions of both the model noise $\Delta\boldsymbol{p}$ and the image noise $(\Delta X, \Delta Y)$:

$$\eta_x = \Delta X + \frac{1}{\boldsymbol{p}_{czi}}\boldsymbol{C}_{xi} \cdot (\mathbf{R}(\Delta\boldsymbol{p}_i))$$
$$\eta_y = \Delta Y + \frac{1}{\boldsymbol{p}_{czi}}\boldsymbol{C}_{yi} \cdot (\mathbf{R}(\Delta\boldsymbol{p}_i)). \tag{7}$$

Therefore for the ith point, two such equations (5) can be written and for a set of m points, a total of $2m$ equations are obtained. This linear system of equations relates the pose increments $\delta\omega$ (rotation) and $\Delta\boldsymbol{T}$ (translation) to the computed measurement errors using the current pose estimate. At each iteration in the minimization process, the linear system of equations is solved to find the best increment vector. This increment is added to the current pose estimate and the process repeated until there is convergence.

In the above system of equations, η_x and η_y represents the measurement noise. If the correct estimate of pose were known, η_x and η_y would be equal to the sum of the measurement error of the image point location and the projection of the error in the model point along the image x-axis and y-axis, respectively. The measurement of the image point location is assumed to be corrupted with zero-mean independent gaussian noise. In our case, for lack of any other knowledge, it is assumed that the noise in the measurements is independent across all points and is also identically distributed. The 3D model points are also assumed to be corrupted by zero-mean independent gaussian noise. Therefore in the $2m$ system of linear equations, the noise in the two equations for each point is correlated. Thus the covariance matrix $\mathbf{V}$ corresponding to the noise is a band matrix in which the nonzero entries are 2×2 matrices about the diagonal. The linear equations are solved for the best linear unbiased estimate for the pose parameters [106, 124]. The output covariance matrix for the pose rotation and translation parameters is also evaluated at the computed pose estimate.

4.2. MODEL-BASED MULTIFRAME TRACKING AND TRIANGULATION

In this section, we present techniques for computing 3D estimates of new points in the world coordinate system from their tracked image locations over a multiframe sequence. The mathematics for both extending the model and refining the initial modeled points is presented. Computed with the estimate of each new model point is an estimate of the covariance of its error. These covariances are functions of the input image measurement covariances and the initial 3D model point covariances.

Image features (both new features and modeled features appearing in the images) are tracked over a sequence of frames using the computed optic flow between pairs of successive frames [135]. Typically corners (defined by the intersection of two image lines) are tracked, although any image feature which can be reliably tracked may be used. The initial match of image features to the partial model for the first frame is done using either shallow structure tracking or the 2D-3D hybrid algorithm

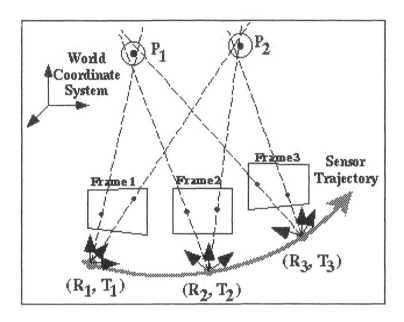

Figure 10. The geometry of model extension by triangulation over a sequence of images.

presented earlier [17, 20]. Combining the results of the initial matching and the feature tracking, correspondences between image features and the partial model for each frame are established. Using these correspondences, pose estimation is done for each frame using the method presented in the previous section.

The image projection ray for an image point in a particular frame is defined as the ray originating from that frame's optic center and passing through the image point. Given the pose estimates for each frame, the vectors corresponding to these projection rays in the world coordinate system can be obtained. The 3D estimate of the point is the pseudo-intersection of all the image projection rays for a tracked image point. In order to combine 3D measurements from a sequence of frames, a stable coordinate frame should be used; a nice property of the system described here is that the pose estimation process provides the world coordinate frame as this stable coordinate frame. Independent measurements can be made that relate the coordinate system of each frame in the sequence to the world coordinate frame.

Points are located by the pseudo-intersection process in two steps. In the first step, a 3D error function is minimized to find an initial estimate of the point's location. This step, however, does not yield the optimal estimate since the various error terms are not weighted by the input covariances. In the second step, an image-based error function is optimized in which the error terms are inversely weighted by a combination of the input covariances of the pose estimate and the image measurements.

Let r_i be the unit vector corresponding to the image projection ray for an image point in the ith frame. The pose estimation for this frame is given by the rotation R_i and translation T_i (see (1)). Since the image projection rays do not intersect at a unique point due to noise both in image measurements and pose estimates, the 3D pseudo-intersection point p is obtained by minimizing an error function E:

$$E = \sum_{i=1}^{n} \|(\mathbf{R}_i p + T_i) \times \mathbf{r}_i\|^2, \tag{8}$$

which is the sum of squares of the perpendicular distances from the pseudo-intersection point p to the image projection rays. Differentiating E with respect to the unknown variable p leads to a set of linear equations, which are then solved to give the initial estimate for p.

In the second step, the pose constraint equations (5) are used to formulate image-based error equations for the X and Y projections of the model points:

$$\begin{aligned}
\frac{1}{p_{cz}} C_{xi} \cdot \mathbf{R}_i(p) &= \frac{-1}{p_{cz}} C_{xi} \cdot T_i + \zeta_x \\
\frac{1}{p_{cz}} C_{yi} \cdot \mathbf{R}_i(p) &= \frac{-1}{p_{cz}} C_{yi} \cdot T_i + \zeta_y
\end{aligned} \tag{9}$$

where ζ_x and ζ_y are the noise terms in the two equations. ζ_x and ζ_y are functions of both noise in pose ΔT_i and $\delta\omega_i$ and image noise $(\Delta X, \Delta Y)$:

$$\begin{aligned}
\zeta_x &= \Delta X + \frac{1}{p_{cz}} C_{xi} \cdot \Delta T_i + \frac{1}{p_{cz}} \delta\omega_i \cdot b_i \\
\zeta_y &= \Delta X + \frac{1}{p_{cz}} C_{yi} \cdot \Delta T_i + \frac{1}{p_{cz}} \delta\omega_i \cdot b_i.
\end{aligned} \tag{10}$$

In this case the 3D model point p is the unknown variable. The denominator p_{cz} in (9) corresponds to the depth of the point and is a function of the unknown variable p. Therefore, for each frame over which the point is tracked, two nonlinear constraint equations (9) are obtained.[3]

An iterative procedure is employed to solve the system of nonlinear equations; details can be found in [75]. In practice, we have found one iteration is sufficient for robust results. In the batch solution method, information from all frames is used simultaneously to estimate the 3D locations of tracked image points. However, it may be desired to sequentially update the location of new points after every pair (or a larger subset) of frames. In this sequential or quasi-batch mode, (9) is again used to estimate the 3D location of image points tracked over the current set of frames. However, these new estimates must be fused with the previous estimates to obtain the current optimal estimate. Associated with each estimate is a covariance matrix representing the uncertainty in the estimate. These covariance matrices are used to fuse the two estimates and provide a new uncertainty matrix using the standard Kalman filtering equations.

Let the estimate of the point's 3D location and its covariance at frame t_1 be $p(t_1)$ and $\Lambda p(t_1)$, respectively. A new 3D location measurement Q with uncertainty (covariance matrix Λ_Q) is computed from a batch of n image frames. The fused location estimate $p(t_n)$ and updated covariance matrix $\Lambda p(t_n)$ at frame t_n are given by

$$\begin{aligned}
p(t_n) &= \Lambda p(t_n) \left[\Lambda p(t_n)^{-1} p(t_1) + \Lambda_Q^{-1} Q \right] \\
\Lambda p(t_n) &= \left[\Lambda p(t_1) + \Lambda_Q^{-1} \right]^{-1}
\end{aligned} \tag{11}$$

---

[3] A minimum of two frames is needed to solve the system of equations.

This same method is used for model refinement. Initial model points also have associated input covariance matrices. When the model is tracked over a new batch of frames, 3D measurements can also be made for the model points by the above pseudo-intersection procedure. These new measurements are fused with the old estimate using the above equations.

Model Extension and Refinement Algorithm. The algorithm for model extension and refinement using a current batch size of n ($n \geq 2$) frames can be summarized as follows:

Step 1: Given a partial 3D model and an image, establish correspondences between model points and image points using matching techniques such as those discussed earlier.

Step 2: Track image points corresponding to the model points, as well as an additional set of unknown points, over the batch of n frames.

Step 3: Using the correspondences established above between model points and image points, compute the pose for each image frame.

Step 4: Estimate the 3D location of all tracked image points (both new points and original model points in world coordinates) using the two-step approach developed in Section 4.2.

Step 5: Fuse initial estimates of both the new points and the model points with any previous estimates using (11).

4.3. EXPERIMENTAL RESULTS AND DISCUSSION

In this section, we present results for two multiframe sequences. The first sequence (PUMA) also demonstrates the model extension and refinement algorithm described in the previous section.

Figure 11 shows an example image from the PUMA sequence. The initial model for this sequence was built manually. Synthetic noise was added to the initial model and the results for both model extension and refinement are described in the first two subsections of this section. The images in the sequence were digitized to 256×242 pixels using an effective FOV of 40 degrees.

The second sequence is called the A211 sequence, and experimental results for both shallow structure recovery and model extension are shown. Using the computed depths of a few points on the recovered shallow structures, an initial model was selected as input for the model extension and refinement algorithm. Figure 13a shows an example image from the A211 sequence. The image sequence was digitized to 256×242 pixels with an effective FOV of 24 degrees.

In both experiments the image center was assumed to be at the center of the image frame and the effective focal length was calculated from the manufacturers specification sheets. Since we have shown in [77] that errors in the image center do not significantly affect the location of new points in a world coordinate system (for a small field of view imaging system), calibration for the image center was not carried out.

PUMA sequence. The sequence of thirty frames was generated by fixing a camera to a PUMA arm and rotating the arm in 4° increments for a total angular displacement of 116°. The field of view of the imaging system was 40 degrees. Figure 11 shows the 14th frame of this sequence. The plane of rotation of the camera is approximately parallel to the image plane. The (off-centered) axis of rotation intersects the image plane somewhere between points 8 and 18 in Figure 11. The radius of rotation is approximately 2 feet. The maximum displacement of the camera in these thirty frames is approximately 2 feet along the world y-axis (vertical direction) and 1 foot along the world x-axis (parallel to the x-axis of the image in Figure 11. This corresponds to the longest baseline over these 30 frames. The location of 32 points (marked in Figure 11 by circles and crosses) in a world coordinate system was measured to an accuracy of approximately 0.2 feet along each axis. The depth of the points (in the first frame's coordinate system) used in our experiment varied from 13 feet to 33 feet. Most of the 32 points were tracked over the entire set of 30 frames.

Figure 11. PUMA image. The points marked by crosses (without numbers) were used to compute the 3D pose for each frame. Using these pose estimates, the 3D location of the numbered points marked by circles was computed.

The twelve points marked by crosses in Figure 11 were chosen as the 3D model points (the measured values were used as the 3D locations of these points) and were used to do pose estimation for each frame. For this experiment, no noise was added to the initial twelve model points. Table 1 shows the errors in computing the 3D locations of the remaining 20 points (marked by numbered circles in Figure 11). The results shown in Table 1 are the output of the algorithm when run in a batch mode using all 30 frames.

The point numbers in Table 1 correspond to the numbered circled points in Figure 11. The depth of each point from the first camera coordinate frame is also shown.[4] The average error for the twenty points was 0.27 feet. The maximum error was 0.731 feet and the minimum error was 0.019 feet; this should be compared to the 13–33 foot distance of the points from the sensor. The average percentage error was 1.22%. The reader should note that there are points in the sequence for which the error is relatively large. Points 1–4 in Table 1 have larger errors because they were not localized accurately; in this case, the line extraction algorithm that determines corners via junctions was not able to find correctly the borders of the lights. Points 17–20 have fairly large errors because they are close to the point where the rotation axis pierces the image plane. These points therefore do not have large disparities. Finally, as noted above, the imaging system has not been calibrated.

Table 1. Absolute and percentage 3D location errors for new points in PUMA sequence determined by model-based triangulation.

Point Number	Depth (feet)	Absolute Error (feet)	Percentage Error (%)
1	24.59	0.616	2.50
2	26.02	0.355	1.36
3	28.32	0.373	1.32
4	22.06	0.440	1.99
5	30.20	0.217	0.72
6	28.62	0.281	0.98
7	31.56	0.472	1.50
8	32.61	0.038	0.12
9	14.33	0.125	0.87
10	15.34	0.279	1.82
11	14.46	0.019	0.13
12	13.50	0.081	0.60
13	21.75	0.054	0.25
14	18.81	0.022	0.12
15	21.73	0.036	0.17
16	20.28	0.104	0.51
17	21.26	0.402	1.89
18	20.28	0.731	3.60
19	21.55	0.234	1.09
20	20.42	0.594	2.91
Average Error		0.274	1.22

---

[4] Since the plane of motion was roughly parallel to the image plane, these depths are approximately constant for the entire sequence.

Figure 12 is a graph of the same experiment when run in a sequential mode using a batch size of 2 frames to generate 3D locations. The y-axis in Figure 12 is the average error in locating the 20 new points and the x-axis is the frame number. Again, the average error is reduced from about 1.5 feet after the first pair of frames to about 0.3 feet at the end of 30 frames.

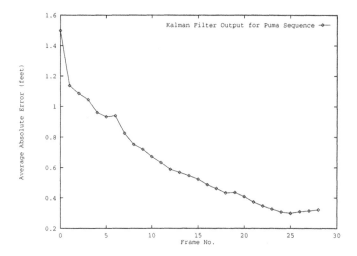

Figure 12. PUMA sequence. Plot of average absolute error over the frame sequence for the new points (model extension).

A211 sequence. The A211 sequence was generated by taking images from a camera mounted on a mobile robot. The robot was translated 0.38 feet between consecutive frames, roughly along the optical axis of the camera; a total of 10 image frames were captured. Thus the total translation of the camera was 3.42 feet. Figure 13a shows the first frame in the image sequence. Objects in the scene ranged from 8 feet to 20 feet away in the first image frame. The depth of some salient structures was measured with a tape measure. In each frame lines are extracted using Boldt's [24] line grouping system.

The tracking algorithm was applied to the image sequence to identify the shallow structures in the scene. Line triples were automatically selected to hypothesize aggregate structures. Each of these was tested for affine trackability, resulting in its labeling as a shallow or a non-shallow structure. Figure 13b shows in bold lines (either black or white) the structures identified as shallow by the shallow structure algorithm, all of which have been correctly identified.

For a model extension experiment, seven points lying on the recovered shallow structures (the points marked by crosses in Figure 13a) were used as the initial

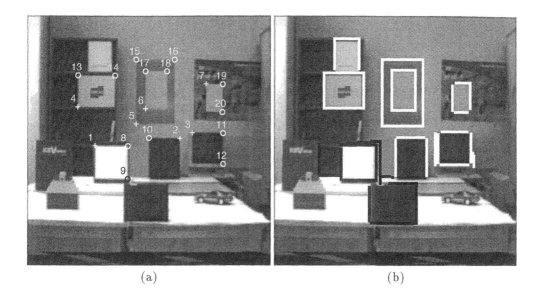

(a)   (b)

Figure 13. Model extension using the A211 sequence. (a) The first frame
in the sequence. The seven points marked by crosses were used to compute the 3D pose for each frame. Using these poses, the 3D location of the
thirteen numbered points marked by circles was computed. (b) Shallow
structures identified in the A211 sequence.

model points. These points are defined by corners formed by some of the pairs
of lines belonging to shallow structures. The 3D model locations were constructed
by extending the image projection rays in the first image's coordinate frame of
these seven points to the depth computed by the model extension and refinement
algorithm described in Section 4.2. Thus, the model coordinate frame remains as
the first image's coordinate frame.

The model extension and refinement algorithm was run in a sequential mode.
Table 2 shows the result of locating the 13 new points (circled and numbered from
8 to 20 in Figure 13a) and refining the 7 initial model points. The ground truth
available for the experiment was only the depths (as opposed to 3D location) of
the points in the first image's coordinate frame. Thus the results shown in Table 2
compare the measured depth value (ground truth) with the recovered depth value.
Column 2 in the table shows the measured depth of the point in the first image
coordinate frame. Columns 3 and 4 show the output error and percentage error
in depth, respectively, for the seven model points as recovered by the affine-based
tracking algorithm. Columns 5 and 6 show the output error and percentage error in
depth (after model refinement), respectively. For points numbered 8 to 20, it was
assumed that no initial model was available, therefore columns 3 and 4 are blank.
Note that these points also belong to the reconstructed shallow structures. However,
their reconstructed locations were not used as a part of the initial partial model.
Instead, these points were used to demonstrate model extension because the ground

Table 2. Absolute and percentage 3D location errors for points in A211 sequence (see Figure 13a).

Pt. No.	Depth	INPUT		OUTPUT	
		Abs. Err.	% Err.	Abs. Err.	% Err.
	ft.	ft.		ft.	
Initial Points					
1	13.4	0.24	1.80	0.24	1.78
2	14.6	0.19	1.31	0.20	1.34
3	19.0	0.74	3.88	0.66	3.46
4	19.0	0.16	0.86	0.11	0.60
5	20.4	0.13	0.62	0.17	0.86
6	20.4	0.39	1.90	0.32	1.60
7	20.4	0.49	2.38	0.46	2.25
Average Error		0.33	1.82	0.31	1.7
New Points					
8	13.4	-	-	0.11	0.79
9	13.4	-	-	0.00	0.01
10	14.6	-	-	0.53	3.65
11	19.0	-	-	0.73	3.86
12	19.0	-	-	0.54	2.82
13	19.0	-	-	0.11	0.59
14	19.0	-	-	0.07	0.34
15	20.4	-	-	0.23	1.13
16	20.4	-	-	0.27	1.32
17	20.4	-	-	0.12	0.57
18	20.4	-	-	0.34	1.65
19	20.4	-	-	0.62	3.02
20	20.4	-	-	0.59	2.92
Average Error				0.33	1.74

truth was available only for these structures. Columns 5 and 6 show the output error and percentage error in depth after the model extension process. In the table, the percentage error in depth is computed with respect to the depth in the first image's coordinate frame.

The average input error in depths of the seven initial model points (as recovered by the affine-based tracking algorithm) was 0.4 feet (1.85% error). At the end of the ten frames, the average error of the 7 initial points was 0.37 feet (1.76%). The thirteen new points were located to an average accuracy of 0.4 feet (1.63%). Thus, in this experiment there was only slight improvement in the initial model as a result of the model refinement process because points 1 and 3 actually increased in error. The model extension process was, however, fairly accurate in locating new points. If the initial model given to the model extension process is noise free, then the average error in recovering the thirteen new points is 0.2 feet (0.94%).

5. CONTROL OF VISUAL MODULES DURING NAVIGATION

One application of the model-matching/pose estimation system described in previous sections is in a navigation system for on/off road driving. The task of autonomous navigation can be decomposed into specific subtasks such as road following, obstacle avoidance, landmark recognition, and pose recovery. In the outdoor autonomous navigation application (part of the ARPA/DOD Unmanned Ground Vehicle program), the matching and pose system was used to recognize visual landmarks, such as buildings, in order to update the pose of the vehicle [43, 45, 114, 115]. The system was also applied to the problem of indoor navigation using a Denning robotic vehicle; model matching/pose estimation was used with a hallway model (doors, walls, floor/wall boundaries, etc.) to accurately position an indoor robot to within a few inches over distances on the order of 60–80 feet [18, 19, 53, 54, 78].

Figure 14. The Mobile Perception Laboratory contains on-board sensors, computing facilities, and driving controls.

Once algorithmic solutions to the specific subtasks have been developed, they must be integrated into a coherent system in such a way that the system is capable of flexibly reacting to events in the environment and taking the appropriate action. To achieve the desired flexibility, a control/integration system based on the idea of a "programmable" finite-state machine (FSM) was developed for the Mobile Perception Laboratory (MPL; see Figure 14) [43, 45, 114, 115]. In this approach, the states represent the different modes of operation of the vehicle and the state transitions correspond to the system's reactions to events (either external or internal). The composition of the states and the transitions is not fixed, so the FSM can be tailored to the particular task the system is trying to achieve.

5.1. BEHAVIOR-BASED CONTROL

The term behavior has generally been used in the literature to describe processes that connect perception to action, i.e., a behavior senses the environment and takes an appropriate action based on what was perceived. We have chosen to think of a behavior as a mode of operation [101, 102], in which several perception-action processes [43, 45] are executed concurrently. Each process converts sensory data into some kind of action (either physical or cognitive), and at any time may generate an event—a signal to let the system know that "something" significant and discretely discernible has occurred. This general view is related to a set of approaches, including Brooks' subsumption architecture [29], the Distributed Architecture for Mobile Navigation system (DAMN) [101, 102], and DEDS [108, 107].

5.2. A FINITE-STATE MACHINE REPRESENTATION FOR BEHAVIORS

An autonomous system must react to events by changing its behavior; hence the sequence of behaviors actually executed depends upon the sequence of events. Since the latter is unpredictable, so is the former. To program such a system, one must specify which processes constitute a behavior and for each possible event describe the system's reaction. In order to specify such a system, a finite-state machine (FSM) formalism has been chosen, in which the states represent behaviors and the transitions are reactions to events.

As an illustrative example, the following set of statements describe a system that was successfully tested on the MPL at a test site on the UMass campus:

1. Drive on the road, while avoiding obstacles, for x meters.
2. Estimate vehicle position using landmarks.
3. Drive on the road, while avoiding obstacles, for y meters.
4. Estimate vehicle position using landmarks.
5. Turn left. (This command is a transition to off-road navigation.)
6. Drive off road (by servoing on a compass heading), while avoiding obstacles, for z meters.

These statements correspond to the FSM in Figure 15; note that a state represents a behavior or mode of operation, i.e., a set of concurrent perception-action processes.

This example can be implemented with a subset of the following perception-action processes:

{pe} Vehicle pose estimation based on landmark model matching [17, 43, 44, 45, 46, 75, 79, 80]
{rf} Neural-network road following (ALVINN) [103, 104, 105].
{se} Servo-based steering [52, 54].
{od} Obstacle detection via stereo [11].
{oa} Reflexive obstacle avoidance [11].
{dm} Monitor distance traveled.
{dt} Turning via dead reckoning.
{vs} Vehicle stop.

Listed below the state name in the figure are the perception-action processes that should be run and killed (marked with a $\sim$) in that state. The FSM also shows a potential link to a high-level planning system (not implemented) which is activated (in this example) by failure of the pose estimation state to localize the vehicle. In this case, the vehicle is considered to be lost—it then stops and initiates planning

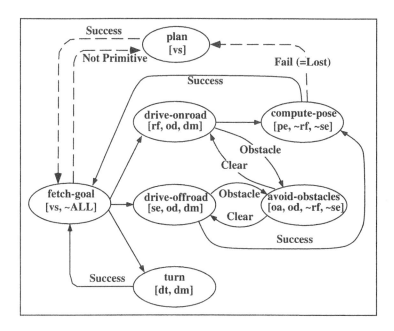

Figure 15. An augmented finite state machine (FSM) for on/off road navigation.

to resolve its location. Note that planning may result in modifications to the goal stack.

Based on the notion of behaviors represented as states of a finite-state machine, a Behavior Description Language (BDL) was designed and implemented. Behaviors are described as two sets of perception-action processes, and a transition table. The run set specifies the minimum set of processes that form the behavior; the kill set specifies those processes that should not be running for the correct execution of the behavior, and often will be specified as part of the state transition. The choice of two sets implies that processes that were running when the behavior started will continue to run unless explicitly killed. The transition table specifies what to do for each of the valid events (those events not specified in the state description are not considered valid). The representation of this example expressed in the BDL is shown in Figure 16. First, the perception-action processes available are listed. Then the set of states (or behaviors) and the set of events are declared. Finally, a description of each state is provided; parameters required for the perception-action processes associated with each state are fetched from the blackboard prior to their initiation.

5.3. THE SCRIPT MONITOR

The script monitor is in charge of "high-level" control[5]: reading, interpreting, and executing BDL scripts. Essentially, the script monitor is a *plan execution system* [57]

---

[5] In this context, "high-level" control is used to differentiate the control of processes from the control of the "low-level" vehicle actuators.

similar to PRS [72, 83] in some aspects. The monitor does not perform any direct action on the vehicle controller by itself; rather, it controls the set of running processes which *do* take direct action.

The script monitor consists of two modules, an *interpreter* and an *execution system.* The interpreter takes a BDL script S and builds the transition (δ), kill (κ), and run (ρ) tables. After this, the subgoals in the S' plan are stacked into the *execution stack G.* The system starts in the *fetch-goal* state where it reads goals (in terms of behaviors) from the execution stack.

All interprocess communication is achieved through a global blackboard, which is a section of shared memory accessible to all processes. The blackboard is built on top of the ISR3 which provides a very efficient memory management mechanism (built on top of UNIX) and a set of primitives necessary for inter- and intraprocess communication using shared memory [28, 44, 46]. When a goal is retrieved, the script monitor writes relevant blackboard messages into the blackboard before creating the perception-action processes associated with the state. Once a perception process is running, it looks for its parameters on the blackboard.

The *fetch-goal* state differs from all other states in two ways: (1) Transitions out of the state are unlabeled since the next state is explicitly specified in the goal retrieved from the script; (2) unless the plan is empty, the kill and run sets are ignored. Complete details of the system are found in [43, 113, 115]. The extremely sketchy discussion here only provides motivation for the range of complexities that are involved in building real navigation control systems that must robustly select and execute many different fundamental tasks.

Successful execution of both drive-onroad and drive-offroad behaviors triggers the compute-pose process (which is essentially the 3D model matching system described in earlier sections). Figure 17 shows the results of executing this behavior during one leg of the MPL navigation experiment. Figure 17a shows the wireframe model of two of the buildings used as landmarks. Figure 17b shows the initial projection of the two buildings from the assumed (though erroneous) position of the vehicle when the behavior was initiated. Figure 17c shows the projection resulting after execution of the compute-pose behavior.

6. CONCLUSION AND SUMMARY

This chapter developed a set of related techniques for landmark-based robot navigation. During a navigation scenario, sensor position and orientation errors frequently accumulate due to mechanical properties of the vehicle, the nature of the environment, and inaccuracies in the vehicle sensors. Consequently, at intermittent moments during navigation, it is necessary to update the pose of the vehicles using visual cues.

When this occurs, the current estimate of the vehicle pose is used to obtain an image which is expected to contain one or more landmarks. Straight line segments are extracted from the image, and the approximate sensor pose is used to project the 3D landmark into the image in order to produce a set of expected 2D model line segments. This data forms the input to the 2D model matcher. Any available geometric constraints are applied to constrain the correspondence space of model-data

```
PROCS = {
        pe          "PoseEstimate"
        rf          "RoadFollow"                    WHILE turn (dir, dist) {
        od          "ObstacleDetect"                        SET direction = dir;
        oa          "Obstacle Avoid"                        SET distance = dist;
        se          "Servo"                                 RUN dt, dm;
        dm          "DistanceMonitor"                       EVENT success GOTO fetch;}
        dt          "DeadReckoningTurn"
        vs          "VehicleStop"}                  WHILE avoid-obstacles ( ) {
                                                            KILL rf, se;
STATES = {drive-onroad, drive-offroad,                      RUN oa, od;
        turn, compute-pose,                                 EVENT clear GOTO BACK;}
        avoid-obstacles}
                                                    WHILE compute-pose ( ) {
EVENTS = {success, obstacles, clear}                        KILL rf, se;
                                                            RUN pe;
WHILE drive-onroad (dist) {                                 EVENT success GOTO fetch;}
        SET distance = dist;
        RUN rf, od, dm;                             GOALS {
        EVENT success GOTO                                  drive-onroad (100);
         compute-pose;                                      drive-onroad (150);
        EVENT obstacle GOTO                                 turn (left, 10);
         avoid-obstacles;}                                  drive-offroad (50);}

WHILE drive-offroad (dist) {
        SET distance = dist;
        RUN se, od, dm;
        EVENT success GOTO
         compute-pose;
        EVENT obstacle GOTO
         avoid-obstacles;}
```

Figure 16. BDL script for the navigation example with $x = 100$, $y = 150$, and $z = 50$.

line pairs for the local search algorithm. Various search strategies can be employed to find a match that optimizes an error function that includes components of spatial fit error and model omission.

The correspondences from the optimal match are fed to the 3D pose determination module, and since these subsystems are interdependent various control strategies were examined for updating pose and determining new matches. The best system was a hybrid 2D-3D system that performs robustly and efficiently even when significant perspective effects exist in the input data. The pose estimate is updated intermittently during the search so that the hybrid 2D-3D system uses only modestly more computation than the 2D affine-based model matcher.

The use of prior models in navigation is a very effective mechanism for localizing the vehicle in the world and determining the orientation of the sensor. However, the strategy assumes that a world model exists and the question naturally arises as to how this model is acquired. It is well known that manual construction of complex

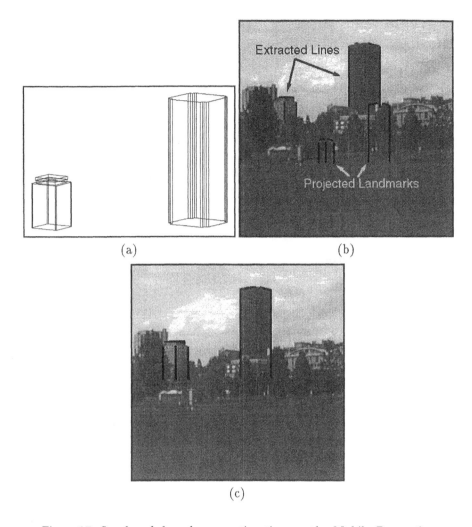

Figure 17. Landmark based pose estimation on the Mobile Perception Laboratory. (a) Building models; (b) initial projection of model from assumed vehicle pose and the extracted image lines; (c) projected model after model-matching and pose update.

models is an extremely tedious, expensive, time-consuming, and error-prone process. Consequently, it is highly desirable that the navigation system have the ability to acquire the initial 3D structure automatically, perhaps during an exploratory phase or from multiple images obtained in some other manner (e.g., aerial reconnaissance). In this chapter, results of a monocular tracking system using the concept of affine trackability were presented to demonstrate the feasibility of model acquisition and model extension. There are many other approaches which could also be applied to the problem of initial 3D model construction, including stereo analysis, two frame and multiframe motion, stereo motion, and active sensors. However, model extension from an initial partial model using 3D model matching, pose recovery, feature tracking, and model-based triangulation of new points is a plausible and, we be-lieve, highly effective process. It can be applied at any time during any exploratory or goal-oriented navigation experience.

Although the primary emphasis of the discussion throughout this chapter has been on robotic navigation, the algorithms themselves have broader applicability in the areas of object recognition, robotic assembly and inspection, and general image understanding. Navigation scenarios provide a very rich set of vision problems with the added constraint of maximizing execution performance (although this was not a focus of our paper here). The algorithms discussed in this chapter were developed more generally than the specific area of vehicle navigation, but were integrated into a functioning system under the ARPA Unmanned Ground Vehicle program.

The UMass robot navigation project was a large-scale group effort that took place over a period of approximately a decade, partially integrating a diverse set of theses of a number of graduate students. During such an extended period there were the expected and natural changes in research goals that take place in an evolving field . Our navigation effort began as an indoor robot navigation project supported by the ARPA Image Understanding (IU) program. Both indoor and outdoor data sets were collected for meaningful experiments using a Denning mobile robot as an experimental base. The next phase involved a transition to the national coalition of ARPA UGV contractors that committed to a large scale integration effort through the prime contractor Martin-Marietta Corporation. At this point our effort involved the construction of the Mobile Perception Laboratory from an Army HMMWV ambulance. There was a very strong emphasis on working demonstrations, and the need for significant systems level support of a very complex working environment. The fundamental algorithms that developed from this effort form a foundation for general landmark-based navigation systems.

REFERENCES

1. G. Adiv, "Determining 3-D Motion and structure from optical flow generated by several moving objects," *IEEE Transactions on Pattern Analysis and Machine Intelligence* **7**, 1985, 384–401.

2. G. Adiv, *Interpreting optical flow*, Ph.D. Thesis, Computer Science Department, University of Massachusetts, Amherst, MA, 1985. Available as Technical Report 85-35.

3. G. Adiv, "Inherent ambiguities in recovering 3-D motion and structure from a noisy flow field," *IEEE Transactions on Pattern Analysis and Machine Intelligence* **11**, 1989, 477–489.

4. P. Anandan, *Measuring visual motion from image sequences*, Ph.D. Thesis, Computer Science Department, University of Massachusetts, Amherst, MA, 1987. Available as Technical Report 87-21.

5. P. Anandan, "A unified perspective on computational techniques for the measurement of visual motion," *Proc. of DARPA Image Understanding Workshop*, Los Angeles, CA, 1987, 719–732.

6. P. Anandan, "A computational framework and an algorithm for the measurement of visual motion," *International Journal of Computer Vision* **2**, 1989, 283–310.

7. N. Ansari and E.J. Delp, "Partial shape recognition: A landmark-based approach," *IEEE Transactions on Pattern Analysis and Machine Intelligence* **12**(5), 1990, 470–483.

8. R.C. Arkin, "Reactive/reflexive navigation for an autonomous vehicle," *Proc. of American Institute of Aeronautics and Astronautics—Computers in Aerospace*, Wakefield, MA, 1987, 298–306.

9. R. Arkin, E. Riseman, and A. Hanson, "AuRA: An architecture for vision-based robot navigation," TR 88-07, Computer Science Department, University of Massachusetts, Amherst, MA, 1988.

10. N. Ayache and O.D. Faugeras, "HYPER: A new approach for the recognition and positioning of 2-D objects," *IEEE Transactions on Pattern Analysis and Machine Intelligence* **8**(1), 1986, 44–54.

11. S. Badal, S. Ravela, B. Draper, and A.R. Hanson, "A practical obstacle detection and avoidance system," *Proc. of IEEE Workshop on Applications of Computer Vision*, Sarasota, FL, 1994.

12. H.S. Baird, *Model-Based Image Matching Using Location*, MIT Press, Cambridge, MA, 1985.

13. P. Balasubramanyam, *A model for binocular motion processing*, Ph.D. Thesis, Computer Science Department, University of Massachusetts, Amherst, MA, 1993.

14. P. Balasubramanyam and M.A. Snyder, "The P- field: A computational model for binocular motion processing," *Proc. of IEEE Conference on Computer Vision and Pattern Recognition*, Maui, HI, 1991, 115–120.

15. P. Balasubramanyam and M.A. Snyder, "A computational model for binocular motion processing," *Proc. of DARPA Image Understanding Workshop*, San Diego, CA, 1992, 515–519.

16. D.H. Ballard, "Generalizing the Hough transform to detect arbitrary shapes," *Pattern Recognition* **13**(2), 1981, 111–122.

17. J.R. Beveridge, *Local search algorithms for geometric object recognition: Optimal correspondence and pose*, Ph.D. Thesis, Computer Science Department, University of Massachusetts, Amherst, MA, 1993. Available as Technical Report 93-71.

18. J. Beveridge and E.M. Riseman, "Hallway navigation in perspective," *Proc. of AAAI Fall Symposium: Sensory Aspects of Robotic Intelligence*, Asilomar, CA, 1991, 125–132.

19. J.R. Beveridge and E. M. Riseman, "Can too much perspective spoil the view? A case study in 2D affine and 3D perspective model matching," *Proc. of DARPA Image Understanding Workshop*, San Diego, CA, 1992.

20. J.R. Beveridge and E.M. Riseman, "Optimal geometric model matching under full 3D perspective," *CVGIP: Image Understanding* **61**(3), 1995, 351–364.

21. J.R. Beveridge, R. Weiss, and E.M. Riseman, "Combinatorial optimization applied to variable scale 2D model matching," *Proc. of IEEE International Conference on Pattern Recognition*, Atlantic City, NJ, 1990, 18–23.

22. J.R. Beveridge, R. Weiss, and E.M. Riseman, "Optimization of 2-dimensional model matching" in N. Hatem (Ed.), *Selected Papers on Automatic Object Recognition*, SPIE, Bellingham, WA, 1991.

23. T.O. Binford, "Survey of model-based image analysis," *IJRR* **1**(1), 1982, 18–64.

24. M. Boldt, R. Weiss, and E.M. Riseman, "Token-based extraction of straight lines," *IEEE Transactions on SMC* **19**(6), 1989, 1581–1594.

25. R.C. Bolles and R.A. Cain, "Recognizing and locating partially visible objects: The local-feature-focus method," *IJRR* **1**(3), 1982, 57–82.

26. K.W. Bowyer and C.R. Dyer, "Aspect graphs: An introduction and survey of recent results," *International Journal of Imaging Systems and Technology* **2**, 1990, 315–328.

27. T.M. Breuel, "An efficient correspondence based algorithm for 2D and 3D model based recognition," A.I. Memo 1259, MIT, Cambridge, MA, 1990.

28. J. Brolio, B. Draper, J.R. Beveridge, and A.R. Hanson, "The ISR: A database for symbolic processing in computer vision," *IEEE Computer Magazine Special Issue on Image Database Management* **22**(12), 1989, 22–30.

29. R.A. Brooks, "A robust layered control system for a mobile robot," *IEEE JR&A* **2**(1), 1986, 14–25.

30. R.A. Brooks, "Intelligence without representation," TR, MIT Artificial Intelligence Laboratory, Cambridge, MA, 1988.

31. J.B. Burns, A.R. Hanson, and E.M. Riseman, "Extracting straight lines," *IEEE Transactions on Pattern Analysis and Machine Intelligence* **8**(4), 1986, 425–455.

32. T.A. Cass, "Polynomial-time object recognition in the presence of clutter, occlusion, and uncertainty," *Proc. of Image Understanding Workshop*, Los Altos, CA, 1992, 693–704.

33. C.H. Chen and A.C. Kak, "A robot vision system for recognizing 3D objects in low order polynomial time," *IEEE T-SMC* **19**(6), 1989, 1535–1563.

34. Y. Cheng, R. Collins, C. Jaynes, A. Hanson, E. Riseman, H. Schultz, F. Stolle, and X. Wang, "Collected University of Massachusetts RADIUS papers," TR 95-43, Computer Science Department, University of Massachusetts, Amherst, MA, 1995.

35. J.L. Crowley, P. Stelmaszyk, and C. Discours, "Measuring image flow by tracking edge-lines," *Proc. of Second International Conference on Computer Vision*, Tampa, FL, 1988, 658–664.

36. L.S. Davis, "Hierarchical generalized Hough transforms and line-segment based generalized Hough transforms," *Pattern Recognition* **15**(4), 1982, 277–285.

37. L.S. Davis and R. Yam, "A generalized Hough-like ransformation for shape recognition," TR 134, University of Texas, Computer Science, Austin, TX, 1980.

38. R. Deriche and O. Faugeras, "Tracking line segments," *Proc. of First European Conference on Computer Vision*, France, 1990, 259–268.

39. R. Deriche, R. Vaillant, and O.D. Faugeras, "From noisy edge points to 3D reconstruction of a scene: A robust approach and its uncertainty analysis," *Proc. of 7th Scandinavian Conference on Image Analysis*, Aalborg, Denmark, 1991.

40. E.D. Dickmanns and B.D. Mysliwetz, "Recursive 3d road and relative ego-state recognition," *IEEE Transactions on Pattern Analysis and Machine Intelligence* **14**(2), 1992, 199–213.

41. B.A. Draper, *Learning object recognition strategies*, Ph.D. Thesis, Computer Science Department, University of Massachusetts, Amherst, MA, 1993. Available as Technical Report 93-50.

42. B.A. Draper, R.T. Collins, J. Brolio, A.R. Hanson, and E.M. Riseman, "The schema system," *International Journal of Computer Vision* **2**(3), 1989, 209–250.

43. B. Draper, C. Fennema, B. Rochwerger, E.M. Riseman, and A.R. Hanson, "Integration for navigation on the UMass mobile perception lab," *Proc. of AIAA/NASA Conference on Intelligent Robots in Field, Factory, Service, and Space* (CIRFFSS), Houston, TX, 1994.

44. B. Draper, A.R. Hanson, and E.M. Riseman, "ISR3: A token database for integration of visual modules," *Proc. of DARPA Image Understanding Workshop*, Washington, DC, 1993, 1155–1161.

45. B. Draper, A.R. Hanson, and E.M. Riseman, "Integrating visual procedures for mobile perception" in H. Christensen and J. Crowley (Eds.), *Experimental Environments*, World Scientific Press, Singapore, 1994, 183-193.

46. B. Draper, G. Kutlu, A.R. Hanson, and E.M. Riseman, "ISR3: Communication and data storage for an unmanned ground vehicle," *Proc. of International Conference on Pattern Recognition*, Jerusalem, Israel, 1994.

47. R. Dutta, *Depth from motion and stereo: parallel and sequential algorithms*, Ph.D. Thesis, Computer Science Department, University of Massachusetts, Amherst, 1994.

48. R. Dutta, R. Manmatha, L. Williams, and E.M. Riseman, "A data set for quantitative motion analysis," *Proc. of International Conference on Computer Vision and Pattern Recognition*, San Diego, CA, 1989.

49. R. Dutta and M. Snyder, "Robustness of correspondence-based structure from motion," *Proc. of CVPR*, Osaka, Japan, 1990, 106–110.

50. R. Dutta, and M.A. Snyder, "Robustness of structure from binocular known motion," *Proc. of IEEE Workshop on Visual Motion*, Princeton, NJ, 1991, 81–86.

51. O.D. Faugeras and M. Hébert, "The representation, recognition, and locating of 3D objects," *IJRR* **5**(3), 1986, 27–51.

52. C. Fennema, *Interweaving reason, action, and perception*, Ph.D. Thesis, Computer Science Department, University of Massachusetts, Amherst, MA, 1991. Available as Technical Report 91-56.

53. C. Fennema and A.R. Hanson, "Experiments in autonomous navigation," *Proc. of CVPR*, Atlantic City, NJ, 1990, 24-31.

54. C. Fennema, A.R. Hanson, E.M. Riseman, R. Beveridge, and R. Kumar, "Towards autonomous mobile robot navigation," *IEEE Transactions on SMC*, Special Issue on Unmanned Systems and Vehicles, **20**(6), 1990, 1352-1369.

55. M.A. Fischler and T.M. Strat, "Recognizing objects in a natural environment: A contextual vision system (CVS)," *Proc. of DARPA Image Understanding Workshop*, Palo Alto, CA, 1989, 774-796.

56. P.C. Gaston and T. Lozano-Perez, "Tactile recognition and localization using object models: The case of polyhedra on a plane," *IEEE Transacations on Pattern Analysis and Machine Intelligence* **6**, 1984, 721-741.

57. M.P. Georgeff, "Planning" in *Readings In Planning*, Morgan-Kaufmann, San Francisco, CA, 1990, 5-25.

58. F. Glover, "Tabu search-Part I," *ORSA Journal on Computing* **1**(3), 1989, 190-206.

59. P.G. Gottschalk, J.L. Turney, and T.N. Mudge, "Efficient recognition of partially visible objects using a logarithmic complexity matching technique," *IJRR* **8**(6), 1989, 110-131.

60. W.E.L. Grimson, "The combinatorics of object recognition in cluttered environments using constrained search," *AIJ* **44**(1), 1990, 121-165.

61. W.E.L. Grimson, "The effect of indexing on the complexity of object recognition," *Proc. of Third International Conference on Computer Vision*, Osaka, Japan, 1990, 644-651.

62. W.E.L. Grimson, *Object Recognition by Computer: The Role of Geometric Constraints*, MIT Press, Cambridge, MA, 1990.

63. A.R. Hanson and E.M. Riseman, "VISIONS: A computer system for interpreting scenes" in A.R. Hanson and E.M. Riseman (Eds.), *Computer Vision Systems*, Academic Press, New York, 1978, 303-333.

64. A.R. Hanson and E.M. Riseman, "The VISIONS image understanding system" in C. Brown (Ed.), *Advances in Computer Vision*, Lawrence Erlbaum Associates, Hillsdale, NJ, 1987, 57-87.

65. M. Hébert and T. Kanade, "Outdoor scene analysis using range data," *Proc. of IEEE International Conference on Robotics and Automation*, 1986.

66. M. Herman and T. Kanade, "Incremental reconstruction of 3D scenes from multiple, complex images," *AI* **30**(3), 1986, 289-341.

67. B.K.P. Horn, *Robot Vision*, MIT Press, Cambridge, MA, 1986.

68. B.K.P. Horn, "Relative orientation," *International Journal of Computer Vision* 4, 1990, 59–78.

69. D.P. Huttenlocher and S. Ullman, "Recognizing solid objects by alignment with an image," *International Journal of Computer Vision* 5(2), 1990, 195–212.

70. V.S.S. Hwang, "Recognizing and locating partially occluded 2-D objects: Symbolic clustering method," *SMC* **19**(6), 1989, 1644–1656.

71. J. Illingworth and J. Kittler, "A survey of the Hough transform," *Computer Vision, Graphics, and Image Processing* 44, 1988, 87–116.

72. F.F. Ingrand, M.P. Georgeff, and A.S. Rao, "An architecture for real-time reasoning and system control," *IEEE Expert*, 1992.

73. B.W. Kernighan and S. Lin, "An efficient heuristic procedure for partitioning graphs," *Bell Systems Tech. Journal* **49**, 1972, 291–307.

74. T.F. Knoll and R.C. Jain, "Recognizing partially visible objects using feature indexed hypotheses," *IJR&A* **2**, 1986, 3–13.

75. R. Kumar, *Model dependent inference of 3D information from a sequence of 2D images*, Ph.D. Thesis, Computer Science Department, University of Massachusetts, Amherst, MA, 1992. Available as Technical Report 92-04.

76. R. Kumar and A.R. Hanson, "Robust estimation of camera location and orientation from noisy data having outliers," *Proc. of IEEE Workshop on Interpretation of 3D Scenes*, Austin, TX, 1989, 52–60.

77. R. Kumar and A.R. Hanson, "Sensitivity of the pose refinement problem to accurate estimation of camera parameters," *Proc. of IEEE Third International Conference on Computer Vision*, Osaka, Japan, 1990, 365–369.

78. R. Kumar and A.R. Hanson, "Model extension and refinement using pose recovery techniques," *Proc. of IEEE Special Workshop on Passive Ranging*, Princeton, NJ, 1991.

79. R. Kumar and A.R. Hanson, "Robust methods For estimating pose and a sensitivity analysis," *CVGIP: Image Understanding* **60**(3), 1994, 313–342.

80. R. Kumar, H.S. Sawhney, and A.R. Hanson, "3D model acquisition from monocular image sequences," *Proc. of IEEE Computer Vision and Pattern Recognition*, Champaign, IL, 1992, 209–215.

81. D. Lawton, "Processing restricted sensor motion," *Proc. of DARPA Image Understanding Workhsop*, Arlington, VA, 1983, 266–281.

82. D. Lawton, *Processing dynamic image sequences from a moving sensor*, Ph.D. Thesis, Computer Science Department, University of Massachusetts, Amherst, MA, 1984. Available as Technical Report 84-05.

83. J. Lee, M.J. Huber, E.H. Durfee, and P.G. Kenny, "UM-PRS: An implementation of the procedural reasoning system," TR, Artificial Intelligence Laboratory, University of Michigan, Ann Arbor, MI, 1993.

84. R.K. Lenz and R.Y. Tsai, "Techniques for calibration of the scale factor and image center for high accuracy 3-D machine vision metrology," *IEEE Transactions on Pattern Analysis and Machine Intelligence* **10**(5), 1988, 713–719.

85. S. Lin, "Computer solutions of the traveling salesman problem," *Bell Syst. Comput. J.* **44**, 1965, 2245–2269.

86. S. Lin and B. Kernighan, "An effective heuristic algorithm for the traveling salesman problem," *Operations Research* **21**, 1973, 498–516.

87. D.G. Lowe, "Solving for the parameters of object models from image descriptions," *Proc. of DARPA Image Understading Workshop*, 1980, 121–127.

88. D.G. Lowe, "Fitting parameterized three-dimensional models to images," *IEEE Transactions on Pattern Analysis and Machine Intelligence* **13**(5), 1991, 441–450.

89. D.G. Lowe and T.O. Binford, "The perceptual ORGANIZATION of visual images: Segmentation as a basis for recognition," *Proc. of DARPA Image Understanding Workshop*, Stanford, CA, 1983, 203–209.

90. D.G. Lowe and T.O. Binford, "The recovery of three-dimensional structure from image curves," *IEEE Transactions on Pattern Analysis and Machine Intelligence* **7**(3), 1985, 320–325.

91. P.C. Mahalanobis, "On the generalized distance in statistics," *Proc. of National Institute of Science*, Delhi, India, 1936, 49–55.

92. T. Matsuyama, "Expert systems for image processing: Knowledge-based composition of image analysis processes," *Computer Vision, Graphics, and Image Processing* **48**, 1989, 22–49.

93. D. McKeown, W.A. Harvey, and J. McDermott, "Rule based interpretation of aerial imagery," *IEEE Transactions on Pattern Analysis and Machine Intelligence* **7**(5), 1985, 570–585.

94. E.G. Mettala, "The OSD tactical unmanned ground vehicle program," *Proc. of ARPA Image Understanding Workshop*, San Diego, CA, 1992, 159–171.

95. F. Mosteller and J.W. Tukey, *Data Analysis and Regression*, Addison-Wesley, Reading, MA, 1977.

96. M. Nagao and T. Matsuyama, *A Structural Analysis of Complex Aerial Photographs*, Plenum Press, New York, 1980.

97. A.M. Nazif, *A rule-based expert system for image segmentation*, Ph.D. Thesis, Electrical Engineering Department, McGill University, Montreal, 1983.

98. R. Nevatia and K.E. Price, "Locating structures in aerial images," *IEEE Transactions on Pattern Analysis and Machine Intelligence* **4**(5), 1982, 476–484.

99. Y. Ohta, *Region-oriented image-analysis system by computer*, Ph.D. Thesis, Information Science Department, Kyoto University, Kyoto, 1980.

100. C.H. Papadimitriou and K. Steiglitz, *Combinatorial Optimization: Algorithms and Complexity*, Prentice Hall, Englewood Cliffs, NJ, 1982.

101. D.W. Payton, "An architecture for reflexive autonomous vehicle control," *Proc. of IEEE Robotics and Automation Conference*, San Francisco, CA, 1986, 1838–1845.

102. D.W. Payton, K. Rosenblatt, and D.M. Keirsey, "Plan guided reaction," *IEEE Transactions on SMC*, 1990, 1370–1382.

103. D.A. Pomerleau, "Neural network based autonomous navigation," in C.E. Thorpe (Ed.), *Vision and Navigation: The Carnegie Mellon Navlab*, Kluwer Academic Publishers, London, 1990.

104. D. Pomerleau, "Neural network vision for robot driving" in M. Arbib (Ed.), *The Handbook of Brain Theory and Neural Networks*, The MIT Press, Cambridge, MA, 1995, 1008–1009.

105. D.A. Pomerleau, J. Gowdy, and C.E. Thorpe "Combining artificial neural networks and symbolic processing for autonomous robot guidance," *Proc. of DARPA Image Understanding Workshop*, San Diego, CA, 1992, 961–967.

106. W.H. Press, B.P. Flannery, S.A. Teukolsky, and W.T. Vetterling, *Numerical Recipes*, Cambridge University Press, Cambridge, MA, 1988.

107. P.J. Ramadge and W.M. Wonham, "The control of discrete event systems," *P-IEEE* **77**(1), 1989, 81–98.

108. P. Ramadge and W. Wonham, "Supervisory control of a class of discrete event processes," *SIAM J. Contr. Optimization* **25**(1), 1989, 206–230.

109. D.A. Reece, *Selective perception for robot driving*, Ph.D. Thesis, Computer Science Department, Carnegie Mellon, Pittsburgh, PA, 1992. Available as Technical Report CMU-CS-TR-92-139.

110. D.A. Reece and S.A. Shafer, "Planning for perception in robot driving," *Proc. of DARPA Image Understanding Workshop*, San Diego, CA, 1992, 953–960.

111. E.M. Riseman and A.R. Hanson, "Divine inheritance vs. experience in the world: Where does the knowledge base come from?," *Proc. of AAAI Fall Symposium Series on Sensory Aspects of Robotic Intelligence*, Asilomar, CA, 1991, 57–61.

112. E.M. Riseman and A.R. Hanson, "A methodology for the development of general knowledge-based vision systems," in C. Torras (Ed.), *Computer Vision: Theory and Industrial Applications*, Springer-Verlag, New York, 1992, 293–336.

113. B. Rochwerger, C. Fennema, B. Draper, A.R. Hanson, and E.M. Riseman, "An architecture for reactive behavior," *Proc. of International Conference on Pattern Recognition*, Jerusalem, Israel, 1994, 305–309.

114. B. Rochwerger, C. Fennema, B. Draper, A. Hanson, and E. Riseman, "Executing reactive behavior for autonomous navigation," TR 94-05, Computer Science Department, University of Massachusetts, Amherst, MA, 1994.

115. B. Rochwerger, C. Fennema, B. Draper, A.R. Hanson, and E.M. Riseman, "Executing reactive behavior for autonomous navigation," *Proc. of Computer Vision and Pattern Recognition*, Seattle, WA, 1994, 838–841.

116. P.J. Rousseeuw and A.M. Leroy, *Robust Regression and Outlier Detection*, John Wiley & Sons, New York, 1987.

117. H. Sawhney, *Spatial and temporal grouping in the interpretation of image motion*, Ph.D. Thesis, Computer Science Department, University of Massachusetts, Amherst, MA, 1992. Available as Technical Report 92-05.

118. H. Sawhney and A.R. Hanson, "Comparative results of some motion algorithms on real image sequences," *Proc. of DARPA Image Understanding Workshop*, Pittsburgh, PA, 1990, 307–313.

119. H. Sawhney and A.R. Hanson, "Identification and 3D description of shallow environmental structure in a sequence of images," *Proc. of IEEE Computer Vision and Pattern Recognition*, Lahaina, Maui, HI, 1991 179–185.

120. H. Sawhney and A.R. Hanson, "Trackability as a cue for potential obstacle identification and 3D description," *International Journal of Computer Vision* **11**(3), 1993 237–265.

121. H. Sawhney, J. Oliensis, and A.R. Hanson, "Image description and 3D reconstruction from image trajectories of rotational motion," *IEEE Transactions on Pattern Analysis and Machine Intelligence* **15**(9), 1993, 885–898.

122. T.M. Silberberg, D. Harwood, and L.S. Davis, "Object recognition using oriented model points," *Computer Vision, Graphics, and Image Processing* **35**, 1986, 47–71.

123. G. Stockman, "Object recognition and localization via pose clustering," *Computer Vision, Graphics, and Image Processing* **40**, 1987, 361–387.

124. G. Strang, *Introduction to Applied Mathematics*, Wellesley-Cambridge Press, Wellesley, MA, 1986.

125. T.M. Strat, *Natural object recognition*, Ph.D. Thesis, Computer Science Department, Stanford University, Stanford, CA, 1991.

126. I.J. Thomas, "Obtaining the robot path using automatically acquired models," *Proc. of International Conference on Intelligent Autonomous Systems* (IAS), Pittsburgh, PA, 1993, 489–497.

127. I.J. Thomas, *Reducing Noise in 3D Models Recovered From a Sequence of 2D Images*, Ph.D. Thesis, Computer Science Department, University of Massachusetts, Amherst, MA, 1994. Available as Technical Report 93-74.

128. I.J. Thomas, A.R. Hanson, and J. Oliensis, "Understanding noise: The crucial role of motion error in scene reconstruction," *Proc. of International Conference on Computer Vision*, Berlin, Germany, 1993, 325–329.

129. I.J. Thomas, A.R. Hanson, and J. Oliensis, "Refining 3D reconstructions: A theoretical and experimental study of the effect of cross-correlations," *CVGIP: Image Understanding* **60**, 1994, 350–370.

130. I.J. Thomas and J. Oliensis, "Automatic position estimation of a mobile robot," *Proc. of Ninth IEEE Conference on AI Applications*, Orlando, FL, 1993, 438–444.

131. D.W. Thompson and J. Mundy, "Three-dimensional model matching from an unconstrained viewpoint," *Proc. of IEEE International Conference on Robotics and Automation*, Sacramento, CA, 1987, 208–220.

132. J.K. Tsotsos, "How does human vision beat the computational complexity of visual perception?" in Z.W. Pylyshyn (Ed.), *Computational Processes in Human Vision: An Interdisciplinary Perspective*, Ablex, Norwood, NJ, 1990, 286–338.

133. J.K. Tsotsos, "On the relative complexity of active vs. passive visual search," *International Journal of Computer Vision* **7**(2), 1992, 127–141.

134. J. Weng, T.S. Huang, and N. Ahuja, "Motion and structure from two perspective views: Algorithms, error analysis, and error estimation," *IEEE Transactions on Pattern Analysis and Machine Intelligence* **11**(5), 1989, 451–476.

135. L.R. Williams and A.R. Hanson, "Translating optical flow into token matches and depth from looming," *Proc. of IEEE International Conference on Computer Vision*, Tarpon Springs, FL, 1988, 441–448.

E.D.Dickmanns
Universität der Bundeswehr München

ABSTRACT

The introduction of bifocal vision systems with active viewing direction control according to road curvature and objects of interest in combination with increased computing power has enabled autonomous vehicles to drive at higher speeds in normal traffic on roads with pronounced curvatures and to negotiate turn-offs onto crossroads with small radii of curvature. This development and the resulting mission performance capabilities are discussed with the example of the autonomous road vehicles of the Universität der Bundeswehr at Munich.

A rearward-looking active camera set has been introduced for recognition of the traffic situation around the vehicle within 100 m range and for more extended mission performance capabilities like autonomous lane changes. Exploiting landmark navigation for mission control requires integral representations with maps and overall plans for vehicle guidance in addition to the differential ones in use for local recognition and control.

Besides the old van **VaMoRs** which is now being used for driving on nonplanar minor roads and for mission performance on road networks, the new sedan test vehicle **VaMoRs-P** has been developed for high-speed driving on highways. It has been tested on the French Autoroute A1 north of Paris at speeds up to 130 km/h in normal traffic for the final demonstrations of the project Prometheus.

1. INTRODUCTION

Visual autonomous road vehicle guidance has made considerable progress since the mid-1980s; a singular activity with technology abandoned meanwhile dates back to the late 1970s [33]. In the early 1980s this subject has been picked up independently in Europe [22] and the United States [18] exploiting the technology of digital microprocessors; in 1985/86 the first test vehicles became available on both sides of

375

the Atlantic Ocean [11, 32, 34, 39]. With the introduction of recursive estimation techniques into image sequence processing a breakthrough in the performance level and the price/performance ratio was achieved in 1986 [11].

In 1987 the German test vehicle for autonomous mobility and computer vision VaMoRs was able to perform road running at speeds up to 96 km/h over more than 20 km distance on a new stretch of Autobahn not yet turned over to public traffic [12]. At this stage of development the European EUREKA project Prometheus was launched and work started in 1988. The state of the art at that time was documented in the BBC video film "Self drive van" (Tomorrow's World, Summer 1988). Major performance items are listed in Table 1.

Table 1. Performance level of 1987 vision system BVV_2.

Video cameras	2 b/w, forward looking, wide-angle for road, tele for obstacle recognition
Pointing platform	large size with stepper motors, road fixation in preview distance (center of edge features)
Microprocessors	8 × 16-bit Intel 8086, 6 MHz, Multibus_I-system, plus Intel '286-based PC (about 30 MIPS total; peak performance)
Communication	two bus systems:
digital video bus	custom made, two 256 × 256 pixel images at 50 Hz
system bus	Intel Multibus_I, single bus controller for message passing, max. data rate of about 10 MB/s
Image evaluation	in at most 6 subareas (windows) of size 4KB pixels, one processor per window; communication of results via Multibus_I
Perceptual capabilities	sensors beside vision: odometer (incl. speed), steer angle, engine speed, throttle position, brake pressure
road recognition	on PC: planar road of constant width, horizontal curvature only, implicit model combined with relative ego-state; 10 Hz evaluation rate (100 ms)
obstacles	not available, under development for single object with separate data from tele-camera
Behavioral capability	lane following at speeds adjusted to road curvature

In the United States, using artificial intelligence methods and a variety of sensors, much more powerful computer systems have been in use; these activities concentrated on driving cross-country with an initial phase on minor roads at slow speeds.

Towards the end of the 1980s in the wake of Prometheus in Europe, and the US-DARPA project Autonomous Land Vehicle (ALV), activities were restarted again in Japan [25]; all major Japanese car manufacturing companies had their own activities afterwards [20, 21]. In Europe Prometheus had most of the car manufacturing companies working on projects including machine vision in one way or another;

monitoring and warning systems prevailed [21]. The number of groups working on this topic may be above two dozen at present worldwide.

Unrestricted automatic driving can still today only be performed by a few groups and in well-structured environments like on highways under favorable environmental conditions. The latter restriction is necessary because of the missing computing power for full region based image sequence processing. However, progress made over the last seven years both in base width and in depth has been impressive, and the generation of microprocessors performing 200 to 300 MIPS will change the picture dramatically.

Real-time vision system hardware can now be bought off the shelf, though to my judgment dynamic machine vision systems including well-blended hard- and software still have quite some distance to go until proven reliable and robust systems will be available.

This paper describes the state of the art reached at the Universität der Bundeswehr at Munich (UBM) in cooperation with the industrial partner Daimler-Benz AG.[1] From the two classes of approach to be observed in the literature, neural nets and recursive estimation, UBM as one of its pioneers, of course, emphasizes the latter one; it has demonstrated its efficiency and versatility in a wide range of applications [13, 26, 36, 37].

In Section 2 a survey on the state of development of the 4D approach to dynamic machine vision as the core of autonomous road vehicle guidance is given including the overall system architecture. Sections 3 and 4 then sketch the two lines of development for the future: VaMoRs-P, in short called **VaMP**, the new passenger-car companion of the 5-ton van VaMoRs, aims at high-speed driving on well structured roads (Section 3), and the proven test vehicle VaMoRs is being used for developing mission performance capabilities in less well structured environments (Section 4). In Section 5 some new experimental results will be discussed; conclusions and an outlook are given in Section 6.

2. STATE OF DEVELOPMENT OF THE 4D APPROACH

A survey on the first ten years of development has been given in [8]; the general background is explained in more detail in [5]. Only a short summary will be given here. Figure 1 shows the block diagram of the real-time core of the general vision system developed for dynamic scene understanding. To the left, the real world is shown by a block; control inputs to the own vehicle carrying the camera may lead to changes in the visual appearance of the world either by changing the viewing direction relative to the vehicle or through egomotion. The continuous changes of objects and their relative position in the world over time are sensed by CCD sensor arrays (shown as converging lines to the lower right, symbolizing the 3D to 2D data reduction). They record the incoming light intensity from a certain field of view at a fixed sampling rate. By this imaging process the information flow is discretized in several ways: There is a limited spatial resolution in the image plane (depending on

[1] Funding by BMFT and BMVg over about a decade is gratefully appreciated.

the focal length of the imaging objective) and a temporal discretization of 16 2/3 or 20 ms, usually including some averaging over time.

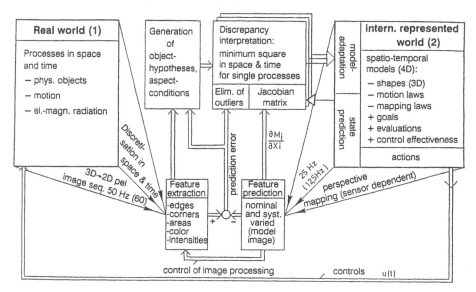

Figure 1. Servo-maintained internal representation of "the world" in 3D space and time by prediction error feedback.

Instead of trying to invert directly the image sequences for 3D-scene understanding, a different approach by analysis through synthesis using spatiotemporal models has been selected. From previous human experience, generic models of objects in the 3D world are assumed to be known in the interpretation process. This comprises both 3D shape, recognizable by certain feature aggregations given the aspect conditions, and motion behavior over time.

In an initialization phase, starting from a collection of features extracted by low-level pixel processing (lower center left in Figure 1), object hypotheses including aspect conditions and motion models in space (transition matrices) have to be generated (upper center left). They are installed in an internal "mental" world representation intended to duplicate the essential parts of the outside real world. According to the philosopher K. Popper this is sometimes called "world_2," as opposed to the real "world_1."

Once an aggregation of objects has been instantiated in world_2, exploiting the dynamical models the object states can be predicted for that point in time when the next measurements are going to be taken. By applying the *forward* perspective projection to those features which will be well visible, using the same mapping conditions as the TV sensors, model images can be generated which should duplicate the measured images if the situation has been understood properly. The situation is thus "imagined" (right and lower center right in Figure 1). The big advantage of this approach is that due to the internal 4D model not only the actual situation at the present time but also the sensitivity matrix of the feature positions with respect to state changes can be determined, the so-called Jacobian matrix (upper block in center right, lower right corner). This rich information is used for bypassing the direct perspective inversion via recursive least-squares filtering through feedback of the prediction errors of the features. This means that the perspective inversion can be achieved at no extra cost once the Jacobian has been computed. The spatial state is estimated in a least squares error sense including its spatial velocity components. Note that this signal to symbol transition from pixels via edge features to a high-level spatiotemporal object state is achieved in just two steps. However, both data-driven bottom-up and model-driven top-down components are traversed in each of the frequent (12.5 or 25 Hz in our system) cycles in this approach.

This approach has several very important practical advantages:

- no previous images need be stored and retrieved for computing optical flow or velocity components in the image plane as an intermediate step in the interpretation process;
- the transition from signals to symbols (spatiotemporal motion state of objects) is done in a very direct way, well based on scientific knowledge, with the 4D world model integrating spatial and temporal aspects;
- there is only one internal object representation for all sensors involved in perceiving this object; only the measurement models linking this single spatiotemporal object to special sensors are separate;
- intelligent nonuniform image analysis becomes possible, allowing one to concentrate limited computer resources to areas of interest known to carry meaningful information; this is valid both within a single image and between wide-angle and tele-image pairs;
- the position and orientation of well visible features can be predicted and the feature extraction algorithm can be provided with information for more efficiently finding the desired ones; outliers can easily be removed exploiting covariance information, thereby stabilizing the interpretation process;
- viewing direction control can be done directly in an object-oriented manner; known egomotion can be compensated for in order to achieve better fixation performance.

Processing a variable number of features measured from frame to frame is alleviated by using the sequential filtering version. For improving the numerical performance, the UD-factorized version of the square-root filter is used [6, 10, 29].

Special care has to be taken in the initialization phase when good object hypotheses are in demand. From feature aggregations which may have been collected in a systematic search covering extended regions of the image, the existence of objects has to be hypothesized; this will be discussed in connection with multiple object detection and tracking (see below).

The orientation towards physical objects in 3D space and time has led to the concept of a "4D object data base" comprising generic models for classes of objects as background knowledge for the visual recognition process. It contains parameterized model components with parameter ranges for special subclasses. The visual appearance is coded in parameterized feature distributions around the object center and the possible (and likely) aspect conditions. The temporal variation of the visual appearance is constrained by the parameterized dynamical model in which there are degrees of freedom for willfull (and likely) control decisions in certain situations.

Figure 2 gives the coarse structure of the perception and control system for road vehicle guidance with its likely classes of physical objects. The temporal expectations are hidden in the object processing groups "4D object recognition" (lower line of blocks, each block being called an "OPG") and in the viewing direction control (upper left block).

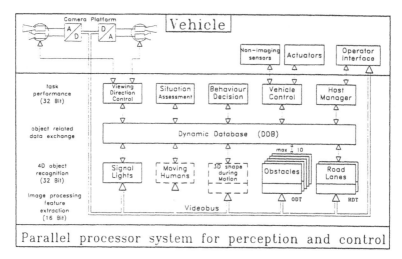

Figure 2. Overall object-oriented system architecture.

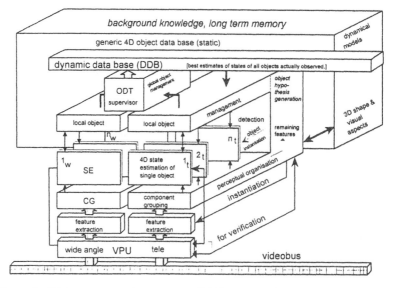

Figure 3. Object processing group ODT: Multiobject detection and tracking.

The video data of up to four cameras are A/D converted in the framegrabber stage of the transputer image processing system (TIP); two monochrome framegrabbers (MFG) and one color framegrabber are in use at present, each capable of handling several video signals in parallel. These digital data streams are then distributed to the "versatile processing units" (VPU) taking their needs for object-oriented data interpretation into account; for example, the "road detection and tracking" OPG (RDT) receives data from the wide-angle camera for road interpretation nearby and from the tele-camera for more distant road segments. Similarly, the "obstacle detection and tracking" OPG's receive both images and make use of them according to the actual situation. Blinking light recognition just takes the color image.

Each OPG (Figure 3), in general, consists of a VPU for data distribution according to the request of the "4D object recognition module" (see Figure 2, left column), the 16-bit integer processors T-222 for image feature extraction with the KRONOS software, and the upper level 32-bit T-805 object-processors (OP) which implement the recursive state estimation algorithms proper and the functions of process management for interpretation and object perception: the upper part of Figure 3 shows the common framework for perceptual organization and management (structure of a fork, open to the front end) and the slices in between, separate for each single object in each image (tele and wide-angle); this information is combined on the supervisor level on top. More details on the two OPG's for road and obstacle recognition and their functioning may be found in [1, 31].

The results of the OPG's are sent to the dynamic data base DDB (central horizontal bar in Figure 2) for further distribution. The DDB is the exchange platform defined as a standard for implementation-independent data communication. In the Daimler-Benz vehicle **VITA_II**, also equipped with the core of our transputer system, it is used for coupling other vision subsystems into the overall system; these other sytems may run on different hardware and with different software in a heterogeneous overall system.

On the higher levels in Figure 2 the block "vehicle control" (VC) is the important component in the autonomous system responsible for generating the correct control outputs. It closely cooperates with the modules for "behavior decision" (BD) and "situation assessment" (SA) developed for VaMP by our Computer Science partners at UBM [19]. This architecture has proven successful with the elder VaMoRs and VITA systems; it is becoming a stable standard.

Since angular perturbations of the vehicle body carrying the cameras may be both fast and unpredictable, and since data rate reduction is essential for a simultaneous wide angular range of visibility and high resolution at least in some image region, multifocal and saccadic vision has been set as a goal of our developments.

2.1. BIFOCAL AND SACCADIC VISION

In bifocal vision [6] two cameras with objectives of different focal lengths are mounted fixed relative to each other on a platform for viewing direction control. Inertial stabilization of the viewing direction at high frequencies (several hundred hertz) has been combined with event-triggered fast viewing direction changes for focussing attention with the tele-camera onto some area of special interest in the wide-angle image. In a special tracking mode the viewing direction may be locked onto an arrangement of well discernible features for fixation. This set of performance features of vertebrate vision in biological systems is considered to be the base for a new quality of vision systems. Though the functions are the same in our technical saccading "vertebrate eye," the implementation is quite different according to the different hardware base available.

The high angular agility of this type of eye requires special data processing features favored by the 4D approach with its explicit representation of temporal effects. The "eye" is a separate object with its own dynamics; because of its high bandwidth the normal vision processes need not take care of this fact except for special instants when a flag set by the control system of the "eye" tells them to disregard image data altogether because they are too blurred. The 4D interpretation processes then continue with just the prediction step based on the temporal model; when the flag disappears again the normal vision processes take the actual viewing direction of the "eye" as quasi-steady state, and scene interpretation is resumed with the correct transformation between viewing direction and body state. In [29] this saccadic viewing direction control onto a traffic sign is detailed (see Figure 4 from there); the corresponding video sequences of both the wide-angle camera for sign detection and the tele-camera for focussing and tracking of the traffic sign give a vivid impression of this behavior hard to convey in mere words.

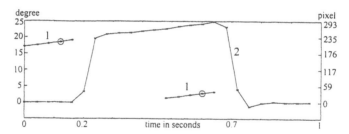

Figure 4. Saccade to traffic sign. 1: Traffic sign position in the image.
2: Camera angle at time of image acquisition.

This new subsystem yet has to be integrated into the overall vision systems normally in operation in the test vehicles.

2.2. KNOWLEDGE-BASED FEATURE EXTRACTION

Except for initialization and the detection of new objects (see below) the image processing paradigm resulting from the 4D approach is "model driven local object-oriented measurements" instead of "full image processing." From the spatiotemporal state estimate of the object, the position (and orientation) of edge features in the image are predicted. Because of model uncertainties and unknown perturbations these features are searched by the software system KRONOS in a local environment with oriented gradient masks adapted to the feature expected. The horizontal, diagonal, or vertical search paths are commanded as normal as possible to the feature direction. KRONOS has originally been written in OCCAM for 16-bit transputers T-222 with four links to other parallel processors, thereby allowing to form tightly connected "Object Processor Groups" (OPG, see also Figures 2, 3, and 17). In the meantime, C-versions have been derived for the new Power-PC becoming available in the transputer image processing system.

Scalable masks as shown in Figure 5 yield better measurement performance than standard Sobel operators by adapting size and orientation of the mask to the object image. Mask parameters are its length, half width, width of central zero area, and its angular orientation. The parameter "half width" allows for an area-based feature effect (average intensity value) and for contrast enhancement in larger homogeneous image areas with a single edge.

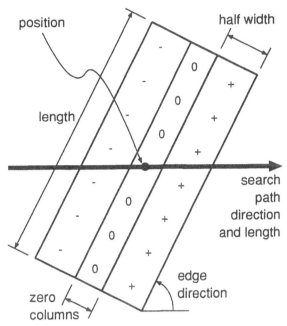

Figure 5. Parameters of scalable template (mask) for edge element matching.

Edges over the full range of 360° can be measured; for the largest masks currently implemented of 17 pixel length, the one out of the 64 mask directions closest to the predicted edge direction (and possibly the two neighboring ones) will be selected to selectively look for the edge of the object under scrutiny. This is important in the case of shadows from trees on the road or on other objects since the contrast of these shadows may be much more pronounced than the contrast of the object edge being looked for. However, in general the shadow edges will have different directions and will thus be eliminated from consideration right from the beginning, thereby deteriorating the feature correspondence problem only slightly.

A measurement command consists of the following arguments:

- position of the predicted edge,
- direction of predicted edge,
- search path direction (as normal to edge direction as possible, preferably horizontal or vertical),
- search path length (e.g., n times the variance),

- size parameters of mask,
- parameters determining the output format of the results,
- video display parameters determining the overlay marks on the video image.

Extrema in the mask response found along the search path are reported as edges found; for more details see [3, 4].

3. ROAD AND RELATIVE EGO-STATE RECOGNITION

The description of the road detection and tracking algorithm as given in [10] pretty much represents the basic method as it still stands today; the hardware base, however, has been changed to transputers [1] and feature extraction is performed with the software package KRONOS as described in the previous section. As may be seen from Figure 17 (below) an object processor group RDT including two versatile processing units (VPU), eight 16-bit processors T-222 for feature extraction, and three 32-bit floating point processors T-805 has been formed exploiting the tight interconnection capabilities provided by the transputer links; wide-angle (for nearby and number of lanes determination, see vertical center of Figure 6) and tele images (for larger distances) are evaluated in conjunction with adaptable feature extraction operators depending on the location in the image and the perspective mapping conditions (see sizes and orientations of masks in Figure 6). This intelligent control of feature extraction is one component of robust image sequence evaluation and dynamic scene interpretation.

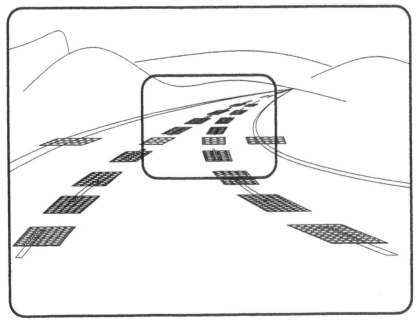

Figure 6. Intelligently controlled recognition of lane boundaries.

Options for lane width recognition, own-body pitching motion, and number of lanes recognition are available. The relative ego-state estimated 25 times per second includes heading direction and slip angle. Those image areas where other vehicles obscure the lane markings are indicated by message passing from ODT (see below); these areas are eliminated from road and lane recognition.

4. MULTIPLE-OBJECT DETECTION AND TRACKING (ODT)

With bifocal vision (forward and backward looking) up to five objects may be detected and tracked in parallel in each hemisphere at 12.5-Hz interpretation rate with the TIP system of VaMP. The objects may be distributed arbitrarily in the vehicle's own lane and each neighboring lane to the left and right. The corresponding OPG, the functioning of which has been coarsely shown in Figure 3, is realized in the transputer system as shown in Figure 17 (lower right); it consists of 2 VPU's, 8 feature extraction processors T-222, and 4 OP's.

The region below the horizon in the road area is steadily checked for aggregations of features indicative of obstacles on the road; the dark area beneath a vehicle is one such strong indicator. Figure 7 shows the search regions used for bottom-up obstacle detection and the features found (marked as black H).

Figure 7. Search regions for obstacle detection and features found in first step.

In its own lane, symmetry conditions help localize the vehicle which is being represented in minimal form just by an encasing rectangle, the upper closure of which may even be omitted. In neighboring lanes with oblique viewing conditions onto the 3D shape, symmetry is lost and only the innermost vertical object boundary is tracked (see Figure 8). Recursive estimation techniques are used to extract the following relative state vector of each vehicle by monocular vision exploiting a planarity assumption for the road: range, range rate and longitudinal acceleration, lateral position and speed relative to the lane occupied, and width of the object. These represent the minimal set of information considered to be necessary for decisions with respect to responsible vehicle guidance. Vehicles can be tracked up to distances of about 120 m with a focal length of 24 mm on a half-inch CCD camera.

Vehicles entering the field of view from the side will be recognized reliably when a major portion of their body has been visible for several cycles (of 80 ms duration). More details may be found in [31].

Computing power at present still is insufficient for robust obstacle detection and tracking under less favorable conditions like situations with many shadows from trees on the road; in these cases the system is saturated by the large numbers of candidate features delivered by KRONOS. It is expected that the new generation of processors will allow area-based image feature extraction like colors and textures in order to be able to resolve these limitations.

Figure 8. Object tracking in road scene.

The overall architecture of our saccadic vision system envisaged encompasses two subsystems for obstacle detection and tracking: the one discussed above, termed the "high temporal, low spatial frequency system" for overall situation assessment, and the "high spatial, low temporal frequency system" for more detailed object recognition under attention focussing including partial occlusions.

4.1. 3D OBSTACLE RECOGNITION AND OCCLUSIONS

Besides the low-level multiobject tracker it is considered necessary to have a more knowledge-based high-level subsystem available in the overall machine vision system which may allow for more detailed analysis of special aspects in some isolated image areas. This attention-focussed system needs to be available only once and will be directed by the higher system levels based on rough information derived from the wide-angle image (in general). By exploiting saccades and the fixation capabilities of the "vertebrate" eye design it keeps the object to be investigated centered in the tele-image, thereby reducing motion blur, and can work with an order of magnitude higher image resolution allowing many more details to be recognized and analyzed; this system does have more background knowledge on generic object classes at its disposal like 3D shapes, aspect graphs, 3D symmetry conditions, part hierarchies, and arrangement patterns which will allow it to find its way through much more complex feature arrangements and come up with reasonable object hypotheses.

Considerable effort went into developing this subsystem which is still waiting for more powerful microprocessors to become available in the TIP system before it can be integrated yielding real-time performance. The basic approach has been pioneered in [27]; a survey in the English language is given in [28]. In this study it has been proven by simulation results with artificially noise-corrupted "measurements" that, if the feature correspondence problem can be solved, simultaneous motion and object parameter estimation can be achieved. A vehicle driving on an oval track has been fixated, and all trajectory and vehicle shape parameters according to the polyhedral model of Figure 9 have been determined while the vehicle moved through all horizontal aspect conditions. Of course, when the viewing conditions did not allow for observation of certain parameters, these had to be frozen at their last value until observability was regained; observability can be judged by the entries of the Jacobian matrix depending on the aspect conditions. Here, the *spatial* invariance property of 3D shape is fully exploited; at the same time, the temporal invariance condition captured in the dynamical model is used by constraining dynamic scene understanding through the prediction error feedback mode of interpretation. Even steering wheel inputs for achieving the curved trajectory observed could be recovered.

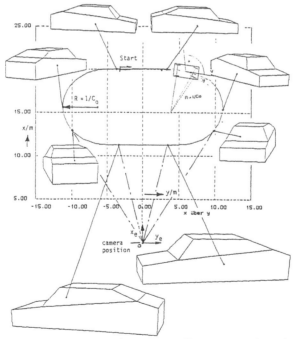

Figure 9. Oval track driven and corresponding perspective view of idealized passenger car (from [28]).

In [30] a first real-time implementation for special types of vehicles (trucks with predominantly box-like shapes) has been given; there a solution to the problem of instantiating a second vehicle after disocclusion from behind another vehicle has also been achieved. A more general attempt towards real-time implementation is discussed in [16]; in addition to the generic polyhedral shape approximation (see Figure 9), refinements with curved surfaces are under study [4].

4.2. MOVING HUMANS RECOGNITION

Since traffic is all about performing transportation tasks for humans in an environment with humans as participants in many different roles, the vision system of an autonomous vehicle should be capable of recognizing humans under a variety of conditions. First, humans walking, standing, running, bicycling, and waving hands for signalling information shall be recognized. In [17] an articulated generic 4D body model for humans has been derived and tested in off-line experiments both with systematically varied animated figures in simulation and with real-life video sequences; Figure 10 shows a simulation result for the recognition of a walking human (e.g., crossing a road). It is seen that after about two and one half seconds leg motion is reasonably well recognized. The initial hypothesis generation part still needs more processing power for real-time real-world implementation. 300-MIPS-class processors should be sufficient for achieving this; exploiting area-based and edge-based features in conjunction is a must for robust recognition performance.

4.3. CROSSROAD RECOGNITION AND TURN-OFFS

Navigation on freeway networks can easily be performed by proper lane changing and lane following activities in the right sequence. On normal roads, the capability of recognizing any type of crossroad is essential for autonomous mission performance. This ability has been developed over the past few years with the van VaMoRs [9, 23, 24] (see Figure 11).

A search process is commanded about 5 to 10 m to the side of the road driven upon in order to look for arrangements of features indicative of a crossroad in the further look-ahead range. Both edge- and area-based components in conjunction are utilized to detect crossroad candidates. If a candidate has been found it is tracked by several windows in the tele-image in parallel by shifting gaze control in order to keep this feature arrangement centered. At a certain distance from the crossroad the viewing range is no more decreased but the camera platform starts turning as if the centerpoint of observation on the crossroad would be the tip of a rigid pole pushed in front of the vehicle. This may be done with a feedforward component according to the dynamical model of the moving vehicle and the pointing platform in order not to induce too many time delay effects. The purpose of this viewing strategy is to improve observability conditions in order to be able to determine the parameters of the crossroad like width and intersection angle more precisely.

At a certain distance from the corner a structurally predefined steering action (a feedforward control time history with parameters adapted to the actual situation) is initiated such that the back wheels safely stay on the road not too far from the curb. At initiation of the turn, the camera heading (viewing) direction is almost perpendicular to the vehicle body axis (see Figure 11b at 15 s); it starts returning to normal straight ahead while the vehicle turns beneath the cameras fixating the crossroad at a certain look-ahead distance. After completion of the major part of the turn-off the lateral vehicle guidance feedback control loop is reactivated, taking care of the rest of the maneuver with its normal behavioral capability of guiding the vehicle in the rightmost lane.

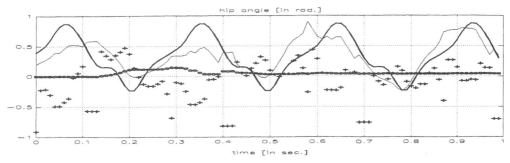

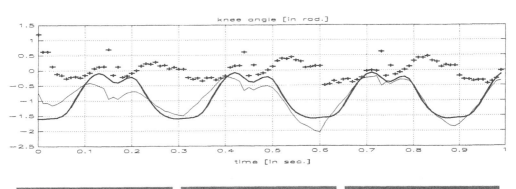

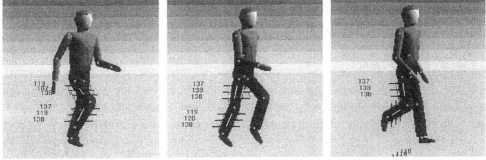

Figure 10. Results of a real-time simulator study with an animated articulated human body for temporal gait recognition: Angle between hip and upper leg (top), knee angle (center) when walking at a speed of 0.9 m/s normal to the line of sight; lower image line: limb positions at times 1.6, 1.7 and 1.8 seconds. Legend: - - (dashed line) real value to be recovered, — (solid line) value predicted with internal model, + prediction error.

This maneuver element symbolically named "turn-off," thus consists of a bunch of perceptual and behavioral capabilities representing the symbol grounding solution;

it is realized on a host of parallel processors set into proper action by invoking the
(parameterized) trigger symbol "perform turn-off onto next crossroad to the right."

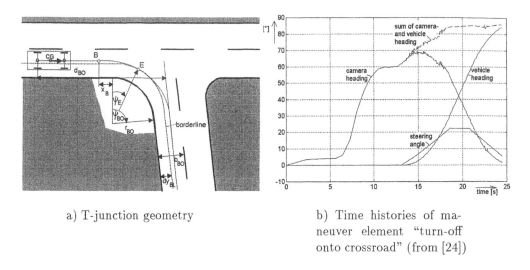

a) T-junction geometry

b) Time histories of ma-
neuver element "turn-off
onto crossroad" (from [24])

Figure 11. Turn-off maneuver with active vision.

4.4. LANDMARK RECOGNITION

In order to improve the capability of recognizing special crossroads for finding the
mission goal, global navigation abilities and capabilities for landmark recognition
are being added to the system at present. A GPS receiver has been installed which
allows position determination up to several tens of meters accuracy directly. It is
the goal of our approach to have the system determine its exact position based
on this rough estimate by using onboard instruments, map information, and vision
only. Both inertial sensors and odometry as well as information from predominantly
topological maps are being used. Only in so-called "islands" surrounding landmarks
used for navigation, precise geometrical information is required and exploited. This
approach minimizes dependency on either GPS and overall exact maps, yet allows
us to take advantage of these systems for flexible mission performance if they are
locally available.

The basic concept of landmark navigation (without GPS) has been developed
in [14, 15] first for indoor vehicle navigation (autonomously guided vehicles, AGV's)
and has then been carried over to road vehicles. Figure 12 shows a summary block
diagram of the hierarchical scheme developed; the distinct feature is that the perceptual competences (while driving) and the behavioral competences of road running
and local maneuvering (lower inverted-pyramid part) developed earlier [2, 23] are
fully exploited by the superimposed mission performance layer on top. The latter
one, shown in the upper box, combines static background knowledge on the environment (maps), on landmarks visual feature distribution, and on its own behavioral
capabilities into the mission plan. Right now this layer is implemented on a separate
PC and needs further development.

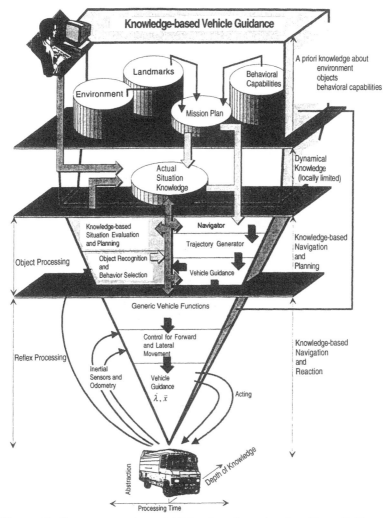

Figure 12. System overview of 4D landmark navigation (from [14]).

With powerful processors for image sequence evaluation in general natural environments not yet at hand, initially, landmarks have been confined to artificial rectangular signs, crossroads, and characteristic curvature patterns of the road section just driven. All these elements are modularly coded in generic form so that the system can be expanded easily when new perception modules become available.

In the initial off-line planning phase, the overall mission is broken down into mission elements according to the perceptual and behavioral capabilities of the underlying system layers. During mission performance the top layer just monitors and—at decision points—controls mission progress. It does not directly interact with the actuators; therefore, delay and run times on the highest level are not that critical in this layered approach since safe behavior should be provided by the lower levels on their own. Figure 13 shows yet another simplified block diagram of the three hierarchical layers with the nested control loops of object recognition and relative

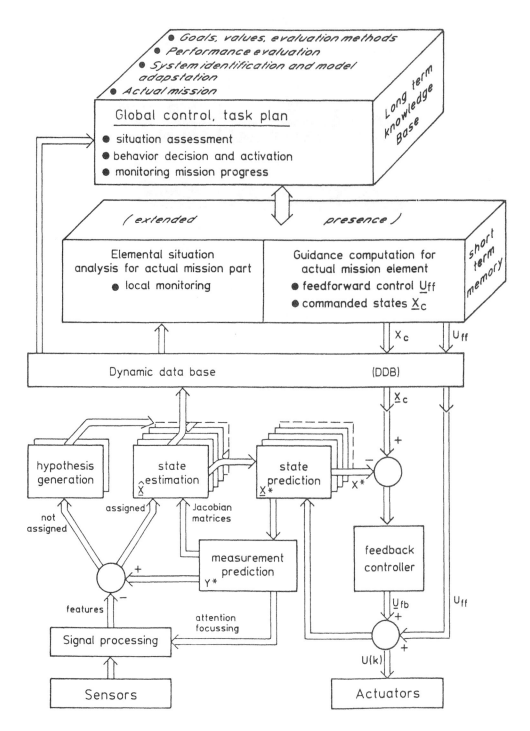

Figure 13. Hierarchical scheme of layered, behavior-based mission performance.

state stabilization (lower part), local guidance with short-term time horizon (middle part), and global mission control with navigation (upper part).

The overall system has become so complex that it is hard to display the many interactions in simple 2D figures and in the space available. The interested reader is referred to the many dissertations as the best source of detailed information. In the following section, the single most important methodical feature of representation will be detailed to some extent.

4.5. INTERNAL REPRESENTATIONS

The success of the 4D approach based on spatiotemporal models and recursive estimation rests to a large extent on the simultaneous use of differential and integral representations; although this feature has been there right from the beginning it has not been emphasized in the past since it has been considered to be quite normal in a control engineering framework. However, in order to better understand the power of the 4D approach, some implications will be detailed here; they may shed some more light on this efficient solution to intelligent autonomous systems.

The differential representations are minimal local descriptions of geometrical and physical properties of objects in the real 4D world. They do not contain the "integration constants" of, or the "time histories" underlying global descriptions. They are ideally suited for coding object-class-specific knowledge for local evolution both along some space curve (differential geometry) and along the time axis (differential equations for analog, or difference equations for time-discrete formulations).

When global aspects prevail or when extended elements in a global context have to be recognized, integral representations are required; the easiest example is road recognition in a certain lookahead range. Here, both geometrical and physical differential properties (and representations) interact: Curve steering is performed by turning the steering wheel directly, which results in a trajectory easily described by "curvature C over arc length" ($C = 1/R$, $R =$ radius of curvature; C is the heading change per arc length). At constant speed, constant steering wheel turn rates, therefore, lead to "clothoid" elements as trajectory arcs driven; high-speed roads are designed according to this fact. The road to be perceived by the vision system while driving, however, displays itself as the integral curve in space distorted by perspective projection. The "minimal description" differential geometry parameters for vehicle trajectory control, therefore, have to be recovered from an integral internal representation taking perspective mapping into account. This fact is at the core of the breakthrough achieved in visual autonomous road vehicle guidance in 1986 [11, 12].

The "lane changing" maneuver introduced in [2] gives another example of the usefulness of parallel differential and integral representations in mission element performance; it may serve as an example for solving the symbol grounding problem in this specific case. Figure 14 shows several alternative generic control time history for the steering angle which result in a parallel lateral offset at the end of the maneuver.

The two triangular pulses, at the beginning and at the end in Figure 13a, realized easily by constant steering wheel turn rate commands also shown (the real physical

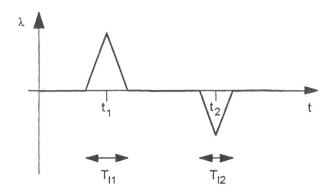

Figure 14. Generic steering control time histories for lateral offset.

control variable!), lead to a change in heading and driving direction with relatively little lateral offset during these control portions (second integral!); depending on the parameters chosen, the bulk of the lateral offset achieved over the entire maneuver may result mainly from the time span between the two pulses. By appropriate turn rates and their duration the magnitude of heading change (and of maximal lateral acceleration experienced) can be adjusted. Relatively simple dynamical models (e.g., single track or bicycle model) of low order allow us to approximately compute the trajectory resulting from this maneuver analytically (see [2]). The real, high-order system will perform a more complex maneuver involving slip angles, banking motion with load redistribution, etc., but the main part of the state change of all components of interest is correctly represented by simple analytical integrals, especially, if the maneuver is performed smoothly (as with control time histories shown in Figures 11b and c). Even the "ideal" trajectory corresponding to this feedforward control law can be determined easily; its components may be used as command functions for superimposed feedback control (see Figure 13, middle and lower levels), thereby reducing the effect of perturbations or of poor model match.

This parameterized feedforward maneuver element may be represented at higher system levels by the symbol "lane change" including the parameters of vehicle speed, steer rate, duration of single constant-turn-rate element, and delay time between the opposite pulses; for simplicity, some cumulative measure may be chosen as single maneuver parameter for fixed type and internal structure of the control sequence, e.g., total maneuver time. Through this dual representation on different levels— "differential" at the feedforward control actuation level, and "integral" at the upper planning level—the symbol "lane change" at the upper level has an exact meaning, and it will result in a trajectory known approximately beforehand; this yields an expectation on the higher levels. The trajectory really achieved will depend on the actual validity of the model underlying the integration. Since real-life systems have to be able to deal with perturbations anyway, the discrepancy between "intention" and the state actually achieved has to be corrected by feedback control "reflex-like" behavior without any need of the higher level to intervene.

These parallel representations of the same maneuver elements on different levels by different, but well-adapted means are considered to be an essential component of the 4D approach combining engineering type (procedural) and AI-type programming paradigms. Further developments of this approach will follow these lines and will include learning capabilities exploiting the explicitly given framework of 3D space and time and corresponding object models.

5. TWO LINES OF DEVELOPMENT

Different capabilities will be needed for the two different autonomous vehicles, VaMoRs and VaMP, in use at UBM and their respective fields of operation.

5.1. VaMP FOR HIGH-SPEED DRIVING ON HIGHLY STRUCTURED ROADS

Figure 15 shows this vehicle with the systems added for autonomous navigation.

a) VaMoRs-P (VaMP)

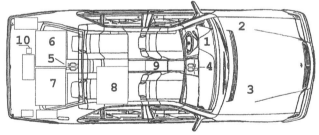

1 electrical steering motor	6,8 Transputer Image Processing system
2 electrical brake control	7 platform and vehicle controllers
3 electronic throttle	8 electronics rack, human interface
4 front pointing platform ⎱ for CCD-	9 accelerometers (3 orthogonal)
5 rear pointing platform ⎰ cameras	10 inertial rate sensors

b) Top view of VaMoRs-P, components for autonomous driving

Figure 15. VaMP with sensors and computers installed.

Most essential are the forward and backward looking bifocal vision systems hanging from the roof behind the front and rear windshield (labeled 4 and 5 in Figure 15). The focal lengths of the miniature 1/2-inch CCD cameras are 7.5 and 24 mm, respectively. Figure 16 shows the pointing platform with the two fingertip cameras of

17 mm diameter in relation to the rearward looking mirror. As a long-term development item for both a wide simultaneous field of view ($> 120°$) and high resolution
at several hundred meters distance we propose a quadrocular miniature camera set
with trinocular divergent stereo and trifocal lens arrangements for efficient saccadic
vision [7]. Viewing ranges of up to several hundred meters are considered to be
required for responsible high-speed driving. From an efficiency point of view this
necessitates focal staging for data rate reduction and active (saccadic) viewing direction control for flexibility in achieving high performance in a wide lateral field of
view (an entire hemisphere in azimuth).

Figure 16. Bifocal camera set of VaMP on pointing platform.

The goal of this vision system is to perform dynamic scene understanding in a
narrow channel above the road ranging up to several hundred meters in distance both
forward and backward. In this space about half a dozen objects shall be trackable
in parallel with full spatial relative state estimation at 25 Hz while, in addition,
one single object shall be foveated in the tele-image and analyzed in detail with
background knowledge about its 4D properties and visual appearance including
blinking of signal lights.

Classes of objects encompass the usual types of road vehicles including motor
bikes, humans, and traffic signs which are studied by industrial partners [38]. Emphasis will shift to situation assessment and handling of more complex traffic situations
off freeways but not in city traffic or more densely populated urban or rural areas.

The parallel processing system based on transputers realizing the part of Figure 2 drawn in solid lines is shown in Figure 17; for the overall system including
conventional data acquisition and platform control about 60 transputers (16-bit
T2's and 32-bit T8's) have been needed for realizing the functions described. Their
joint processing power is less than that of a single microprocessor chip available in
1995.

5.2. VaMoRs for mission performance in less highly structured environments

Work with this test vehicle concentrates on guidance in the nearby environment
at lower speeds (till about 60 km/h)—however, on roads and surfaces with much
less restricted properties and visual appearance. Roads in poor state, even unsealed

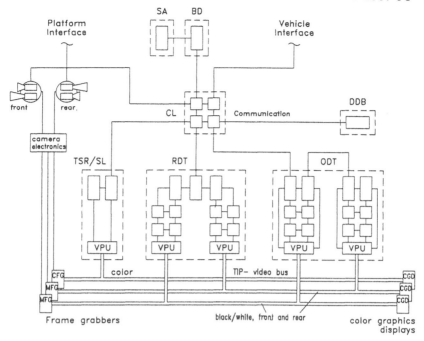

$\square$ = T-222, $\rule[0.1ex]{1em}{1.2ex}$ = T-805 ($\square$)

Figure 17. Parallel transputer realization of the VaMP visual perception and control system.

ones, shall be manageable due to the added capability of vertical surface profile recognition. For this purpose, binocular stereo is being added to motion stereo in the 4D approach, and the internal representation encompasses separate low- and high-frequency curvature components for better data fit [24]. These developments are feasible for real-time application with the 300 MIPS generation of microprocessors.

Natural landmarks will become manageable with these new processors when color and texture features are computable in real time. The steps envisaged proceed via more complex crossroad junctions and buildings or natural, very discernible objects not too far off the trajectory planned; active, multifocal vision will play an important role here, too. Especially from this line of development, further stimulations for improving the capabilities of this "vertebrate type" of machine vision with alternating phases of inertial stabilization, saccades, and fixations are expected. Vehicle motion induced by rough terrain calls for separate representations of all motion components and their relative phases of all objects involved, including the pointing platform. Dealing in parallel with different representations along the time axis over various durations will lead to more powerful schemes of handling temporal aspects than presently available. These multiple-scale temporal representations are considered essential for intelligent autonomous systems.

6. DISCUSSION OF EXPERIMENTAL RESULTS

As compared to what is required for really dynamic mission performance on rough ground, what has been achieved up to now is rather marginal; however, as compared to what was possible seven years ago, progress has been remarkable. Table 2 gives the corresponding reference for 1994 in similar terms as Table 1 did for 1987.

With VaMoRs, driving at speeds of up to 40 km/h on unpaved country roads with grass patches destroying a nice borderline between road and fields has been demonstrated in summer 1992; the system worked reasonably well with edge masks of large areas (e.g., 9 by 17 pixels). As could be expected, there were constellations when the edge-based algorithms were bound to fail. New algorithms for area-based road recognition in addition to the well-proven and newly improved edge-based ones will be put to test with the real vehicle after having shown their validity in laboratory tests with video sequences recorded.

Crossroad recognition and turning-off works well under favorable conditions [24]; here too, making system performance more robust against less favorable lighting conditions, e.g., with shadows from trees on the intersection, will need area-based image processing which requires orders of magnitude more computing power. An evolution over a longer period of time will be required to achieve a standard comparable to human driving performance. However, the feasibility with the approach developed has been shown.

Mission performance on a network of roadways has been demonstrated in 1993 on the taxiway system of the closed down military airport of Neubiberg with the help of artificial landmarks of rectangular shape [14]. Knowing the initial conditions only roughly (within several tens of meters), the system was able to localize its exact position after some distance driven exploiting only topological map information over wide areas, but precise landmark positions close to decision points.

The new seeing passenger car VaMoRs-P (in short VaMP) has demonstrated its capabilities at the final demonstrations of the EUREKA project Prometheus in October 1994 near Paris on the Autoroute A1 to Lille between the airport Charles-de-Gaulle and the city of Senlis in normal traffic. Together with its twin-vehicle VITA_II of Daimler-Benz it has been an official Common European Demonstrator Collision Avoidance (CED 301/302). During almost three weeks of preparations and demonstrations the vehicle has accumulated more than 1000 km of fully autonomous driving (both in the longitudinal and the lateral degrees of freedom) based on bifocal vision to the front and rear.

Lane keeping and convoy driving behind another vehicle are the basic modes of operation which have been demonstrated to guests at speeds up to 130 km/h. Passing vehicles cutting into its lane too early posed the most difficult problem with respect to keeping the "1.8 seconds distance" (see Table 2). Since they usually drive at higher speeds they do not pose a threat except when they have to stop suddenly; this case would have requested the safety driver to take over, but it did not occur. The recursive estimation procedure needs some time to stabilize the spatial interpretation, especially speed, which is rather noisy, initially. For a long-term practical solution it is felt that the lateral field of view should be much wider

Table 2. Performance level with 1994 transputer-based perception and control system (not all functions in single vehicle; some developed by academic and industrial partners~).

Video cameras	4 single chip miniature color cameras on 2 platforms (forward and backward), joint bifocal image evaluation
Pointing platform	fourth generation, brushless torquers; object fixation (center of edge features), inertially stabilized, saccades
Microprocessors	2 dozen 16-bit transputers T-222, 25 MHz; 3 dozen 32-bit transputer T-805 (with floating point unit on chip) plus '486 PC, total processing power about 1200 MIPS (theoret. peak; about 70 MFLOPS)
Communication	video bus plus transputer links:
digital video bus	transputer image processing system (TIP): 100 MB/s data rate between framegrabbers, versatile processing units and color graphics display
transputer links	4 links with bandwidth 20 Mbit/s each with each transputer; formation of closely coupled "object processor groups" and object-oriented "dynamic data base" for enhanced flexibility and easy modularity
Image evaluation	with T-222 in arbitrary subareas of arbitrary size per image, KRONOS software package; intelligently controlled edge extraction (tangents)
Perceptual capabilities	Sensors beside vision: odometer (incl. speed), steer angle, engine speed, throttle position, brake pressure, 3 linear accelerometers, 5 angular rates, GPS-position (VaMoRs only)
road recognition	on T-805's: horizontal and vertical curvature of lane driven, number of lanes, variable lane/road width; 25 Hz evaluation rate (40 ms); detection and tracking of arbitrary crossroads (VaMoRs only)
relative ego-state	vehicle acceleration, angular rates, estimation of actual pitch angle of vehicle, position in lane, lateral speed, slip angle, heading relative to road
object recognition	relative 4D-state of up to five objects on the road with data from wide-angle and tele-camera in parallel, both in front of and behind the vehicle (lower and lateral bounderies of vehicle as shape parameters only); 3D box-like convex hull of up to 2 truck bodies.
	Stoplights and blinking signal lights of 1 vehicle~; traffic signs~ (speed limit, passing prohibited), landmarks (artificial, very recognizable ones near the road)
Behavioral capabilities	lane following at speeds adjusted to road curvature, $V_{\max} = 130$ km/h; convoy driving at speed-dependent distance (e.g., "1.8-seconds rule," i.e., half the tachometer reading (km/h) in meters), "stop-and-go" driving; *autonomous lane* changes to left and right (VaMP only), stopping in front of an obstacle; turning-off onto crossroad (VaMoRs only).

than the approximately 40° actually available, in order to pick up and track passing vehicles earlier; this experience supports the proposal for two divergently looking wide-angle cameras in parallel [7].

The second reason for this proposal has also been substantiated by another driving experience with VaMP: when the vehicle approaches the vehicle in front too closely (e.g., in "stop and go" driving), the contact point of this vehicle to the ground is lost. This deteriorates the conditions for distance estimation by monocular vision considerably; in this case, however, binocular stereo even with a small stereo base would be sufficient for range determination exploiting just a single very visible and distinguishable feature. By having the field of view of each divergently looking wide-angle cameras overlap each other, in this region stereo computation can be performed; designing this overlapping region such that it falls in the field of view of the tele-camera, trinocular stereo with improved performance can be achieved. This is being investigated presently.

With respect to obstacle detection at large distances, reliable results have only been achieved up to about 100 m with the focal length of 25 mm and image discretization of 320×256 pixels; in the literature one can find claims of much better results achieved. Our results indicate that object size should be about 20 pixels in one dimension for robust detection under normal angular motion noise in a car driving on slightly uneven ground and in front of varying background intensities; this supports the design feature of a trifocal "vehicle eye" with at least 50 mm maximum focal length for a 1/2 inch CCD-camera and the resolution in digitization used [7]. Experience in multiobject tracking also indicates that the ratio of focal lengths should not exceed four in order to achieve easy transitions in evaluation between images of different resolution. This has led to the focal lengths proposed of 4 : 16 : 50 (better 64) mm for the trifocal camera set and allows the parallel availability of three pyramid stages two stages apart; saccadic vision allows us to direct the areas of higher resolution to where it is required and, thus, reduces the image data rate in the overall system by one and a half orders of magnitude as compared to full resolution everywhere (only about 2 to 3%!).

Image sequence evaluation of 25 Hz seems to be sufficient for tracking of moving objects, in general; however, estimation of fast-moving objects nearby and recognition of fast-blinking signal lights would gain from 50-Hz noninterlaced images.

A new level of competence has been shown with the forward and backward looking bifocal vision system of VaMP in October 1994; for the first time, a machine vision system has been able to demonstrate its capability of deriving autonomously the decision for lane changing and passing. Keeping "mentally" track over time of the vehicles that left the rearward field of view (that means making predictions over many cycles with a dynamical model and properly chosen, reasonable control inputs), and checking against the vehicles that entered the forward field of view, allowed it to conclude when the neighboring lane was empty to perform a lane change [35]. (In the Daimler-Benz vehicle VITA_II there was an additional set of 12 sideways looking cameras (6 to each side for stereo interpretation) which allowed checking the occupation of the neighboring lane directly [4]. A larger field of view sideways when looking forward with the tele-cameras will allow reduction of the prediction time required in our approach; with optional gaze shifts to the side for short periods of time the approach investigated with VaMP seems to be sufficient.

7. CONCLUSIONS AND OUTLOOK

The feasibility of all major components of a dynamic machine vision system for fully autonomous road vehicle guidance has been proven. Reliability and robustness have been improved over the last seven years but there is still room for further improvements. The new generation of several-hundred-MIPS microprocessors becoming available presently will allow us to further increase system capabilities over the next years while simultaneously shrinking both volume and power consumption of the system. The total computing power as indicated in Table 2 is available on a single chip at the end of 1994.

Both the perception subsystems and the overall system architecture are becoming more and more stable and powerful, which is a good indication of the systems becoming more mature. However, it should not be overlooked that in order to achieve robust performance approaching the level expected from human drivers there is still a long way to go. Region-based image feature extraction (color and textures) is becoming affordable in real time with current state-of-the-art processors. Experience will have to show under which circumstances which type of algorithm is superior; a knowledge base will have to be built up to improve robustness of recognition under various environmental conditions. Quite a bit of additional computing power has to be directed towards this goal in order to approach human capabilities.

Based on the experience gained with 4D object orientation, a general scheme for generic 4D object data bases is emerging which allows to solve the symbol grounding problem of AI by simultaneous differential and integral representations at different levels on multiple time scales with specific control time histories adapted to the problem to be solved.

"Subjects" as a special class of objects with the capability of willful locomotion based on decisions derived from internal "mental states" allows us to model a wide variety of situations efficiently. The internal mental states are derived from measurement data in combination with background knowledge about typical behaviors of objects and subjects (the dynamical models and their control inputs). This level of complexity is considered necessary for an autonomous system to become a sensible partner for humans in everyday traffic situations. Sensors, microprocessors, and software technology have reached a state of development now which allows realizing this type of autonomous system.

The decision for saccadic vision will affect the overall architecture of the visual perception system deeply; the advantage of a drastically reduced data stream from the vision sensors combined with the need for intelligent control of the perception system over time puts much more emphasis on temporal representations. However, this is not considered to be a disadvantage since intelligence per se needs powerful representations along the time axis. The engineering sciences have sufficiently flexible tools available for handling the problems encountered.

Our expectation is that the need for temporal smoothing and both inter- and extrapolation over saccadic periods will lead to further developments of dynamic machine vision considered unavoidable for achieving performance levels approaching the human one in the long run; however, there is a long way to go.

Figure 18 shows the fields of view with different functionalities considered desirable for a complex road vehicle eye [7]; this has been derived from experience of many thousands of kilometers of autonomous driving in a wide variety of real traffic situations.

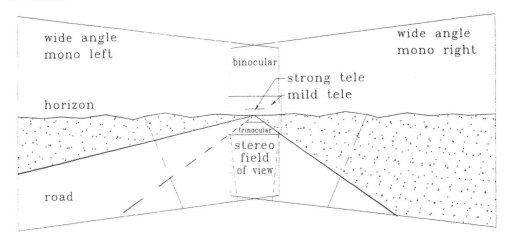

Figure 18. Fields of view of proposed complex road vehicle eye.

References

1. R. Behringer, "Road recognition from multifocal vision," *Proc. 'Intelligent Vehicles,'* Paris, October 1994.

2. C. Brüdigam, *Intelligente Fahrmanöver sehender autonomer Fahrzeuge in autobahnähnlicher Umgebung*, Dissertation, Universität der Bundeswehr München, Fakultät Luft- und Raumfahrttechnik (LRT), 1994.

3. D. Dickmanns, *KRONOS User's guide*, UniBwM/Inf./ 1992.

4. D. Dickmanns, "Knowledge based real-time vision," *Proc. IFAC Symposium on 'Intelligent Autonomous Vehicles '95,'* Helsinki, June 1995.

5. E.D. Dickmanns, "Machine perception exploiting high-level spatio-temporal models," AGARD LS-185, Machine Perception, Hampton, VA, Munich, and Madrid, 1992.

6. E.D. Dickmanns, "Active bifocal vision," in S. Impedovo (Ed.) *Progress in Image Analysis and Processing III*, World Scientific Publ. Co, Singapore, 1994, 481–496.

7. E.D. Dickmanns, "Road vehicle eyes for high precision navigation," *3rd International Workshop High Precision Navigation*, Stuttgart, April 1995.

8. E.D. Dickmanns and V. Graefe, "a) Dynamic monocular machine vision, b) Application of dynamic monocular machine vision," *J. Machine Vision & Application*, Springer-Int., 1988, 223–261.

9. E.D. Dickmanns and N. Müller, "Road scene recognition and landmark navigation for road vehicles," *Proc. IFAC Symposium on 'Intelligent Autonomous Vehicles '95,'* Helsinki, June 1995.

10. E.D. Dickmanns and B. Mysliwetz, "Recursive 3D road and relative ego-state recognition," *IEEE Transactions on Pattern Analysis and Machine Intelligence* **14** (2), Special Issue on 'Interpretation of 3D Scenes,' February 1992, 199–213.

11. E.D. Dickmanns and A. Zapp, "A curvature-based scheme for improving road vehicle guidance by computer vision," in *Proc. SPIE Mobile Robot Conference*, Cambridge, MA, October 1986, 161–168.

12. E.D. Dickmanns and A. Zapp, "Autonomous high speed road vehicle guidance by computer vision," *10th IFAC World Congress* Munich, Preprint 4, 1987, 232–237.

13. C. Fagerer, D. Dickmanns, and E.D. Dickmanns, "Visual grasping with long delay time of a free floating object in orbit," *J. Autonomous Robots* **1** (1), Kluwer Acad. Publ., Boston, 1994.

14. C. Hock, *Wissensbasierte Fahrzeugführung mit Landmarken für autonome Roboter*, Dissertation, Universität der Bundeswehr München, Fakultät LRT, 1994.

15. C. Hock, R. Behringer, and F. Thomanek, "Intelligent navigation for a seeing road vehicle using landmark recognition," in *Close Range Techniques and Machine Vision*, ISPRS, Melbourne, 1994.

16. V. von Holt, "Tracking and classification of overtaking vehicles on autobahnen," *Proc. 'Intelligent Vehicles,'* Paris, October 1994.

17. W. Kinzel, *PrΣattentive und attentive Bildverarbeitungsschritte zur visuellen Erkennung von Fußgängern*, Dissertation, Universität der Bundeswehr München, Fakultät LRT, 1994.

18. P.J. Klass, "DARPA envisions new generation of machine intelligence," *Aviation Week & Space Technology*, April 1985, 47–54.

19. C. Kujawski, "Deciding the behavior of an autonomous mobile road vehicle in complex traffic situations," *Proc. IFAC Symposium on 'Intelligent Autonomous Vehicles '95,'* Helsinki, June 1995.

20. I. Masaki, *Proc. Symposium on 'Intelligent Vehicles '93,'* Tokyo, 1993.

21. I. Masaki, *Proc. Symposium on 'Intelligent Vehicles '94,'* Paris, 1994.

22. H.G. Meissner, *Steuerung dynamischer Systeme aufgrund bildhafter Informationen*, Dissertation, Hochschule der Bundeswehr München, Fachbereich LRT, 1982.

23. N. Müller, "Feedforward control for curve steering for an autonomous road vehicle," *Proc. IEEE International Conference on Robotics and Automation*, Nice, 1992, 200–205.

24. N. Müller and S. Baten, "Image processing based navigation with an autonomous car," *Proc. Intelligent Autonomous Systems-4*, Karlsruhe, March 1995.

25. T. Ozaki, M. Ohzora, and K. Kurahashi, "An image processing system for an autonomous vehicle," *Proceedings of SPIE* **1195**, Mobile Robots IV, Philadelphia, PA, November 1989, 256–266.

26. R. Schell, *Bordautonomer automatischer Landeanflug aufgrund bildhafter und inertialer Meßdatenauswertung*, Dissertation, Universität der Bundeswehr München, Fakultät LRT, 1992.

27. J. Schick, *Gleichzeitige Erkennung von Form und Bewegung durch Rechnersehen*, Dissertation, Universität der Bundeswehr München, Fakultät LRT, 1992.

28. J. Schick and E.D. Dickmanns, "Simultaneous estimation of 3D shape and motion of objects by computer vision," *Proc. IEEE Workshop on Visual Motion*, Princeton, NJ, 1991.

29. J. Schiehlen and E.D. Dickmanns, "A camera platform for intelligent vehicles," *Proc. 'Intelligent Vehicles,'* Paris, October 1994.

30. M. Schmid, *3D-Erkennung von Fahrzeugen in Echtzeit aus monokularen Bildfolgen*, Dissertation, Universität der Bundeswehr München, Fakultät LRT, 1993.

31. F. Thomanek, E.D. Dickmanns, and D. Dickmanns, "Multiple object recognition and scene interpretation for autonomous road vehicle guidance," *Proc. 'Intelligent Vehicles,'* Paris, October 1994.

32. C. Thorpe, M. Hébert, T. Kanade, and S. Shafer, "Vision and navigation for the CMU Navlab," *Annual Review of Computer Science* **2**, 1987, 521–556.

33. S. Tsugawa, T. Yatabe, T. Hirose, and S. Matsumoto, "An automobile with artificial intelligence," *Proc. 6th International Joint Conference on Artificial Intelligence*, Tokyo, 1979, 893–895.

34. M.A. Turk, D.G. Morgenthaler, K.D. Gremban, and M. Marra, "Video road following for the autonomous land vehicle," *Proc. IEEE International Conference on Robotics and Automation*, Raleigh, South Carolina, U.S.A., 1987, 342–361.

35. B. Ulmer, "VITA II—Active collision avoidance in real traffic," *Proc. 'Intelligent Vehicles,'* Paris, October 1994.

36. S. Werner, A. Buchwieser, and E.D. Dickmanns, "Real-time simulation of visual machine perception for helicopter flight assistance," *International Conference on Aerospace/Defense Sensing and Dual-Use Photonics*, SPIE, Orlando, April 1995.

37. H.J. Wünsche, "Bewegungssteuerung durch Rechnersehen," *Fachberichte Messen, Steuern, Regeln*, Band 10, Springer-Verlag, Berlin, 1988.

38. Y.J. Zheng, W. Ritter, and R. Janssen, "An adaptive system for traffic sign recognition," *Proc. 'Intelligent Vehicles,'* Paris, October 1994.

39. W. Zimdahl, I. Rackow, and T. Wilm, "OPTOPILOT—ein Forschungsansatz zur Spurerkennung und Spurführung bei Straßenfahrzeugen," VDI Berichte 612, Elektronik im Kraftfahrzeugbau, 1986, 49–60.

SUBJECT INDEX

AUTHOR INDEX

A

Adiv, G., 61, 63, 64, 71, 344, 345, 348
Aggarwal, J.K., 179, 180
Ahuja, N., 61, 63, 71, 345
Aisbett, J., 71
Akilov, G.P., 187
Albus, J.S., 276, 277, 279
Aloimonos, Y., 2, 3, 6, 12, 16, 23, 61, 62, 71, 78, 79, 83, 84, 135, 137, 142, 143, 148, 152, 167, 174, 219, 236, 237, 275, 278, 299, 300, 313
Anandan, P., 63, 137, 344, 345, 348
Ando, H., 83
Ansari, N., 322
Arkin, R., 318
Atkeson, C.G., 272
Ayache, N., 180, 237, 322

B

Badal, S., 360
Baird, H.S., 322
Bajcsy, R., 237, 278
Baker, J., 9
Balasubramanyam, P., 344
Ballard, D.H., 6, 236, 278, 322
Baloh, R.W., 23
Bandopadhay, A., 6, 23, 62, 236, 278, 299
Barnes, W.J.P., 12
Barron, J.L., 62, 63, 82, 83, 311
Basri, R., 137, 237
Basu, A., 61, 83

Basye, K., 272
Baten, S., 388, 390, 397, 398
Beauchemin, S.S., 62, 82, 83, 311
Behringer, R., 381, 384, 390
Bellman, R., 261
Bergholm, F., 137
Bertsekas, D.P., 271
Beveridge, J.R., 317, 318, 326, 328, 329, 337, 351, 359, 360, 362
Beyrirch, K., 23
Bidwell, N.J., 35, 37
Bierman, G., 292, 302, 303
Binford, T.O., 180, 318, 322, 330
Blakemore, C., 9
Blanes, C., 18
Bleuler, S., 44
Bobick, A.F., 237
Boldt, M., 324, 345, 356
Bolle, R.M., 237
Bolles, R.C., 237, 322
Bostelman, R., 288, 294
Boutilier, C., 272
Bouzerdoum, A., 35
Bowyer, K.W., 339
Brady, J.M., 100
Braun, J., 48
Breiman, L., 184
Breuel, T.M., 323
Brodsky, T., 167, 174
Brolio, J., 279, 318, 362
Brooks, R.A., 236, 318, 360
Brown, C.M., 236, 237, 278
Brüdigam, C., 390, 393, 394
Brunelli, R., 237
Bruss, A., 71
Buchwieser, A., 377
Buffa, M., 127
Burns, J.B., 324, 345
Burrows, M., 53
Burt, P.J., 236

C

Cain, R.A., 237, 322
Caines, P.E., 272
Campani, M., 63
Cass, T.A., 323

For Product Safety Concerns and Information please contact our EU
representative GPSR@taylorandfrancis.com Taylor & Francis Verlag GmbH,
Kaufingerstraße 24, 80331 München, Germany

Printed and bound by CPI Group (UK) Ltd, Croydon, CR0 4YY

01/05/2025

01858327-0002